THE PSYCHOPHYSIOLOGY
OF SEX

THE KINSEY INSTITUTE SERIES

THE PSYCHOPHYSIOLOGY OF SEX

Edited by Erick Janssen

Indiana University Press
Bloomington • Indianapolis

This book is a publication of
Indiana University Press
601 North Morton Street
Bloomington, IN 47404-3797 USA

http://iupress.indiana.edu

Telephone orders	800-842-6796
Fax orders	812-855-7931
Orders by e-mail	iuporder @ indiana.edu

© 2007 by The Kinsey Institute for Research in Sex, Gender, and Reproduction, Inc.

The paper used in this publication meets the minimum requirements of American National Standard for Information Sciences—Permanence of Paper for Printed Library Materials, ANSI Z39.48-1984.

Manufactured in the United States of America

Library of Congress Cataloging-in-Publication Data

The psychophysiology of sex / edited by Erick Janssen.
     p. ; cm. — (Kinsey Institute series ; v. 8)
     "This book is the outcome of a conference, the first of its kind, on the psychophysiology of sex. The conference was held in Bloomington, Indiana, in July 2003."—Pref.
     Includes bibliographical references and index.
     ISBN-13: 978-0-253-34898-2 (cloth : alk. paper)
     1. Sexual disorders—Congresses. 2. Sex (Psychology)—Congresses. 3. Sex (Biology)—Congresses. I. Janssen, Erick. II. Series.
[DNLM: 1. Sexual Dysfunction, Physiological—psychology—Congresses. 2. Sexuality—physiology—Congresses. 3. Gender Identity—Congresses. 4. Sexual Behavior—physiology—Congresses. 5. Sexual Dysfunctions, Psychological—Congresses. WJ 700 P974 2007]
RC556.P7475 2007
616.6'9001—dc22

                                         2006038187

1 2 3 4 5 12 11 10 09 08 07

Contents

Acknowledgments

This book and the meeting on which it is based were made possible by grants from the National Institute of Child Health & Human Development (NICHD), the National Institute of Mental Health (NIMH), and the Social Science Research Council (SSRC). I would like to thank John Bancroft for his guidance in organizing this meeting; Nicole Prause for cohosting the preconference workshop; Jennifer Gentry of Indiana University Conferences; Sarah Hahn for her work on the index; and Michael Lundell, Elisabeth Marsh, Brian Herrmann, Rebecca Tolen, and Laura MacLeod of Indiana University Press for their help in finalizing the manuscript. Sandra Ham deserves my gratitude for helping me with everything from invitations, menus, and hotel arrangements, to the editing of the manuscript. This is the only part of the book that has not gone through her careful and competent hands. Last but not least, I thank Nadine Pinède for reminding me every day that following your dreams is not a luxury but essential to creating a meaningful life.

Introduction

ERICK JANSSEN

This book is the outcome of a conference, the first of its kind, on the psychophysiology of sex. The conference was held in Bloomington, Indiana, in July 2003, and brought together a selected group of researchers in the area of sexual psychophysiology. The goal of the meeting was to present up-to-date reviews, discuss commonalities and differences in conceptual and methodological approaches, and generate ideas and suggestions for future research. A secondary goal of the meeting was to work toward increased standardization and consensus in measurement and analysis procedures in psychophysiological sex research. The papers that were presented at the conference form the basis for the chapters in this book, most of which were updated in 2006.

Background

Although the field of sexual psychophysiology has made great strides over the past few decades, the progress made has not been accompanied by much effort to integrate research findings or to stimulate methodological and theoretical discussions among researchers. The last major review of the field was published almost 20 years ago (Rosen & Beck, 1988) and sexual psychophysiology, in contrast to many other subdisciplines in psychology and other social sciences, still does not have its own scientific organization, journal, or annual meeting.

But there were other reasons why we considered it to be important and timely to bring together researchers in this area. The development of psychopharmacological approaches to the treatment of sexual problems, for example, relies heavily on psychophysiological methods, and recent findings in this area raise important questions about the value and validity of conventional conceptual models of sexual function and the diagnostic classification systems (including the *Diagnostic and Statistical Manual of Mental Disorders,* American Psychiatric Association, 2000) that are based on them.

Also, while there is a growing body of literature on the role of mood and emotions in nonsexual decision making, the effects of mood and arousal, and individual differences in their relationship (i.e., how mood influences sexual function), on sexual decision making and behavior have only recently begun to be explored. This new research area has the potential to make substantial contributions to our understanding of a wide range of phenomena, including the spread of HIV and other sexually transmitted infections (STIs), sexual "addiction" or compulsivity, the use (or nonuse) of birth-control methods, sexual infidelity, and aggressive sexual behaviors. Psychophysiological methods can assist us in the exploration of the underlying psychological, physiological, and affective processes, and, perhaps more importantly, how they interact.

Another development, the increased availability of sexual stimuli and virtual venues (allowing for on- as well as offline sexual interactions) through the Internet, and the positive as well as negative effects this medium may have on people's sexual lives (e.g., through attitude formation or skill development, but also through its unknown potential for causing or reinforcing sexual "addictions," relationship problems, or risky forms of on- and offline sex), also underscores the need for a better understanding of the complex relationships among sexual desire, arousal, and behavior.

But even if we ignore recent pharmaceutical and technological developments, we believed the time was ripe for a scientific meeting, the first ever, to critically appraise the state of sexual psychophysiology. Psychophysiological methods are being applied to an increasingly broad array of questions, including the effects of aging, disease and disabilities, drugs, hormones, and mood on sexuality and sexual health. On a more applied level, psychophysiological methods are being used in the assessment of sex offenders, the diagnosis of sexual dysfunctions, and the evaluation of treatment efficacy. Although researchers in these various areas rely on the same instrumentation, work on the basis of related assumptions, and are confronted with similar conceptual and methodological issues, there has been little dialogue among them, limiting an integration and cross-fertilization of research efforts in the field of sexual psychophysiology.

Format

In order to maximize productivity and enhance dialog, the format of an invitational workshop was used. The Kinsey Institute has hosted a number of meetings before using a similar format (e.g., on sexual development and on the role of theory in sex research). The program of the psychophysiology meeting consisted of two parts. It started with a 1-day preconference workshop that specifically focused on measurement issues. Selected members of the workshop intend to work together, building on the discussions of that day, on the formulation of guidelines for the measurement of sexual response. The second part covered 3 days and involved the scientific meeting that resulted in this book. There were speakers, discussants, participant-observers, and a few observers present. Sessions were audio taped, and speakers were requested to provide drafts of their papers for circulation prior to the meeting so that all participants had the opportunity to read them before the meeting. The authors presented briefly (for about 15 minutes) on the topic of their paper, and each session had a designated discussant, who made a few comments on the presentations and topic in general, from their own professional expertise or disciplinary perspective, with the purpose to initiate and fuel general discussion, which included all the speakers, discussants, and participant-observers.

After the meeting, speakers and discussants were asked to finalize their manuscripts reflecting the interaction of the meeting and given the opportunity to update their papers in 2006. The transcripts of the general discussions were edited and circulated for review as well.

Themes

The program was organized around six themes. Although various topics were covered, general and recurring themes included the (neuro)physiology of sexual response; the relationship between subjective and physiological response; the relationship between sexual motivation and arousal; the relationship between motivation/arousal and behavior; and possible gender and individual differences in any and all of these relationships. The objective was to evaluate our current understanding of relevant mechanisms and processes (e.g., central and peripheral, cognitive and affective) and to assess the extent to which this understanding allows us to predict and explain sexual problems, preferences, and behavior. The order of chapters in this book follows the structure of the meeting.

The first session focused on the physiology and neurobiology of sexual response and included state-of-the-art overviews of basic (neuro)physiological processes and mechanisms involved in human sexual desire and response, based on research using neuroanatomical methods, animal models, and psychophysiological methods such as positron emission tomography (PET), functional magnetic resonance imaging (fMRI), and penile and vaginal photoplethysmography. The chapters by Stoléru and Mouras ("Brain Functional Imaging Studies of Sexual Desire and Arousal in Human Males") and Levin ("The Human Sexual Response—Similarities and Differences in the Anatomy and Function of the Male and Female Genitalia: Are They a Trivial Pursuit or a Treasure Trove?") fall in this category, as do the chapters by Meston and Bradford ("Autonomic Nervous System Influences: The Role of the Sympathetic Nervous System in Female Sexual Arousal"), Krüger, Schedlowski, and Exton ("Neuroendocrine Processes during Sexual Arousal and Orgasm"), and Heiman and Maravilla ("Female Sexual Arousal Response Using Serial Magnetic Resonance Imaging with Initial Comparisons to Vaginal Photoplethysmography: Overview and Evaluation"). John

Bancroft acted as discussant for the first two and Roy Levin for the latter three chapters.

The second theme involved theoretical perspectives and included reviews of some of the more influential cognitive/affective and psychophysiological models of and theoretical approaches to the study of sexual motivation, arousal, orgasm, and behavior. The chapters by Wiegel, Scepkowski, and Barlow ("Cognitive-Affective Processes in Sexual Arousal and Sexual Dysfunction"), Spiering and Everaerd ("The Sexual Unconscious"), Janssen and Bancroft ("The Dual Control Model: The Role of Sexual Inhibition and Excitation in Sexual Arousal and Behavior"), and Rowland, Tai, and Brummett ("Interactive Processes in Ejaculatory Disorders: Psychophysiological Considerations") belong to this category. James Geer, Serge Stoléru, and Donald Strassberg acted as discussants for these papers.

The third session focused on the role of basic learning processes, habituation, and (classical, operant, and evaluative) conditioning as well as on the determinants of genital responses and subjective sexual arousal, their variable and in many ways theoretically challenging relationships, and the role of situational and voluntary processes in their control and modification. To this theme belong Hoffmann's ("The Role of Classical Conditioning in Sexual Arousal"), Laan and Janssen's ("How Do Men and Women Feel? Determinants of Subjective Experience of Sexual Arousal"), and Strassberg's ("The Voluntary Control of Genital Response, Arousal, and Orgasm") chapters. Jim Pfaus and Walter Everaerd discussed these papers.

As a fourth theme, we discussed different theoretical views and experimental approaches to the relationships among sexual motivation, desire, sexual arousal, and behavior. One purpose of this session was to revisit the conventional notion that the relationship between sexual desire and sexual arousal is linear or unidirectional. The chapters of Both, Everaerd, and Laan ("Desire Emerges from Excitement: A Psychophysiological Perspective on Sexual Motivation") and Pfaus ("Models of Sexual Motivation") belong to this category. Erick Janssen acted as discussant for these two chapters.

The principal topic of the fifth session was the role of psychophysiological methods in research on sexual functioning and dysfunctioning, as well as the contribution of clinical research to our understanding of the relationships among and determinants of sexual motivation, arousal, orgasm, and sexual satisfaction and well-being. The chapters by Rosen, Wiegel, and Gendrano ("Sexual Dysfunction, Sexual Psychophysiology, and Psychopharmacology: Laboratory Studies in Men and Women") and Sipski ("Disabilities, Psychophysiology, and Sexual Functioning") make up this section and are followed by Julia Heiman's discussion of them.

The sixth and final session focused on gender, sexual orientation, and paraphilic sexual interests and explored the application of psychophysiological as well as cognitive psychological methods in research on gender differences in sexual response and on the study of paraphilias and the psycho-physiology of sexual orientation. The session included chapters by Geer and Hicks ("Cognitive Processes and Gender Differences in Sexuality"), Chivers and Bailey ("The Sexual Psychophysiology of Sexual Orientation"), and Seto ("Psychophysiological Assessment of Paraphilic Sexual Interests"). Ray Rosen and David Rowland were discussants for these final three papers.

References

Rosen, R. C., & Beck, J. G. (1988). *Patterns of sexual arousal.* New York: Guilford Press.

THE PSYCHOPHYSIOLOGY
OF SEX

Part 1.

Physiology and Neurobiology of Sexual Response

Brain Functional Imaging Studies of Sexual Desire and Arousal in Human Males

SERGE STOLÉRU AND HAROLD MOURAS

Why Use Brain Functional Imaging to Study Sexual Desire and Arousal?

Why Study the Brain to Understand Sexual Desire and Arousal?

The complex relationship between brain and mind has been the subject of philosophical and scientific debates for centuries. In the perspective presented in this paper, any mental operation—be it intellectual, emotional, or motivational—has two components that are not dissociable: the psychological and the cerebral. Furthermore, the brain should be viewed as a two-way interface between mental mechanisms and peripheral physiological processes. In this sense, the brain plays a pivotal role in psychophysiological phenomena. The idea that any mental operation involves two aspects, the psychological and the cerebral, does not imply any directional causality between brain and mind. Rather, what we see as psychological and cerebral can be conceived of as two correlated aspects of the same unified reality. This is consistent with the view about the body and the soul that Spinoza proposed in *Ethics*.

According to recent sociobiological developments (reviewed in Rolls, 1999), the pressure of natural selection has led to the emergence of brain systems in which reward is associated with those sexual behaviors that increase fitness. Fitness is understood here as the aptitude to transmit one's genes to the next generation. Evolutionary pressure thus selected the neurophysiologic implementation of brain reward systems associated not only with copulation per se, but also with sexual desire and sexual arousal (SDA) and with attraction to characteristics that reflect a potential partner's fitness.

The central nervous system (CNS) plays a role at all successive stages of sexual behavior (Meisel & Sachs, 1994). Regarding the initial stage of processing of external stimuli, it has been shown in various mammals, in particular in monkeys, that hormonally determined characteristics of females, such as odor (Baum, Everitt, Herbert, & Keverne, 1977) and visual signals (Bielert, 1982), promote sexual behavior in males. These characteristics are evaluated through the central processing of sensory information. In humans also, sexual attraction is based on various factors (Buss,

1989), and the significance of external stimuli as sexual incentives has to be assessed for the sexual response to develop. Although it has been hypothesized that the brain is involved in the assessment of such factors, and of their potential reward value (Rolls, 1999), the relevant brain mechanisms have not been systematically studied.

The cognitive aspects involved in later stages of SDA have been increasingly recognized in the literature. It has been proposed that human SDA cannot be defined adequately without highlighting the critical role of cognitive labeling and subjective experience in determining the response to a given stimulus as sexual (Rosen & Beck, 1988). Likewise, the concept of central arousal (Bancroft, 1989) refers to CNS activation and attentional factors that underlie the psychological processing of sexual stimuli. Finally, at least in humans, SDA is also characterized by emotional responses and by motivational processes. The conscious perception of sexual desire belongs to the latter processes. In recent years, intense research work has focused on the cerebral basis of various types of emotions and motivations and considerable advances have been made. In this sense, the study of the cerebral correlates of SDA is a specific aspect of the broader field of research on the neural correlates of emotion and motivation (Phan, Wager, Taylor, & Liberzon, 2002).

Why Use Functional Imaging to Study the Brain?

Functional imaging techniques are currently the method of choice in in vivo investigations of the cerebral physiological correlates of mental functions in human beings. Prior to the development of these techniques, studies of the cerebral basis of sexual motivation relied for a large part on animal models. In animals, the role played by subcortical structures in sexual behavior, in particular the septal nuclei, the amygdalas, and hypothalamic nuclei (medial anterior preoptic area, paraventricular nucleus, and ventromedial nucleus), has been well documented (Meisel & Sachs, 1994). Findings from animal research are relevant to our understanding of some aspects of human sexuality. Human sexual behavior, however, has unique characteristics that distinguish it from the homologous behavior in other species. For instance, cognitive aspects of sexuality—such as sexual imagery—are likely to be much more important in humans than in other species. Therefore, animal studies are notably inadequate to help understand these specifically human aspects of sexual behavior, and studies on humans are needed to characterize the regions of the brain involved in the species-specific aspects of human sexual behavior.

The other more traditional source of knowledge on the role of the brain in human SDA involves the study of neurological patients, for instance those suffering from epileptic seizures with sexual manifestations or those presenting sexual symptoms associated with focal lesions. However important, studies of pathological subjects are insufficient to describe the cerebral correlates of SDA in healthy individuals. A third group of studies has been based on postmortem examinations of the brains, for example, studies comparing specific hypothalamic nuclei in males with various sexual orientations.

The modern techniques of brain functional imaging have the great advantage of being minimally invasive, so that they may be performed in healthy volunteers. The most commonly utilized techniques are positron emission tomography (PET) and functional magnetic resonance imaging (fMRI). The very first study of sexual behavior using a neuroimaging technique was based on single photon emission tomography (SPECT), a technique with relatively low resolution (Tiihonen et al., 1994). By contrast, a more recently introduced technique is magnetoencephalography (MEG), but to our knowledge its use to investigate SDA is very preliminary. We shall focus here on PET and fMRI. Their spatial resolution, which is in the order of one millimeter, allows one to study brain areas at a macroscopic level. Their temporal resolution is different, PET having a temporal resolution of the order of 1 minute, while the temporal resolution of fMRI is 1–2 seconds. Very briefly, PET allows for the measurement of regional cerebral blood flow (rCBF). So-called "activation studies" are based on the administration of a small dose of a radioactive molecule—usually in the form of venous injection of ^{15}O-H_2O—that is carried to the brain by the bloodstream. The activity of brain areas is correlated to local blood flow, which itself is correlated to local radioactivity. Positrons from the radioactive tracer combine with electrons from the brain tissue to produce gamma rays (similar to x-rays). Special crystals, called photomultiplier-scintillator detectors, within the PET scanner detect the gamma rays. The camera records the millions of gamma rays being emitted, and a computer uses the information to generate 3-D pictures of the areas where radioactive substance has been present during the scan.

Functional MRI relies on the fact that the properties of the small bar magnets of water molecules in the brain change slightly between areas that are near blood with its oxygen exhausted relative to those near freshly oxygenated blood. The local increase in energy requirements arising as a consequence of neuronal firing is largely met through an increase in oxygen-based metabolism, with the increased demand for oxygen being delivered seconds later by an increase in the local blood flow (the *hemodynamic response*). Changes in the oxygenation level of the blood therefore occur as a consequence of neuronal activity, and so the magnitude of change in signal intensity can be used as an indirect measure of excitatory input to neurons, which is generally related closely to the cell firing rate. Thus, when there is a "blush" from increased activity, there is a small increase in signal intensity on the functional MRI scan (Parry & Matthews, 2002).

A first review article on the use of neuroimaging methods to investigate sexual arousal in healthy subjects has been published (Sumich, Kumari, & Sharma, 2003). Here, we provide a detailed and updated review of this area of research, including studies of patients with disorders of sexual arousal.

Studies Selected for This Review

In order to illuminate the patterns of activation and deactivation associated with SDA, we searched peer-reviewed journals indexed in MED-LINE for PET and fMRI studies focusing on sexual desire and/or arousal as the experimental condition of interest and published between January 1985 and June 2003. Papers focusing on monographic case studies were excluded. This search led to the following list of 10 studies of healthy men, presented in alphabetical order: Arnow et al., 2002; Beauregard, Levesque, & Bourgouin, 2001; Bocher et al., 2001; Holstege et al., 2003; Karama et al., 2002; Mouras et al., 2003; Park et al., 2001; Rauch et al., 1999; Redouté et al., 2000; Stoléru et al., 1999. In addition, the following studies focused on patients with disorders affecting SDA: Cohen et al., 2002; Hagemann et al., 2003; Hendricks et al., 1988; Montorsi et al., 2003a; Stoléru, Redouté, et al., 2003.

Review of Studies in Healthy Men

The methodological characteristics of the reviewed studies are presented in Table 1.

Samples

Sample sizes ranged from $n = 8$ to $n = 20$. Some studies have specified that subjects were heterosexual, while sexual orientation was left unspecified in others. No study so far has focused on homosexual men. Subjects were young, with mean ages ranging from 23 to 33 years. Very few studies used biological assays to verify that subjects were physically healthy. Not verifying this may be a problem. For example, we had to exclude a subject on the basis of an elevated prolactin plasma level. Also, subjects may self-select and participate in studies on the basis of doubts that they have about their sexual health. Such doubts may turn out to be grounded in real problems or disorders. For instance, we have been struck by the high proportion of volunteers reporting a history of childhood phimosis, a problem that may have represented a psychological difficulty when these subjects were children and that may, consciously or unconsciously, have driven some of those adults to volunteer for the study.

Techniques

Five studies have been based on fMRI and five on PET.

Table 1. *Methodological Characteristics of Reviewed Studies*

Study	Sample size, sex	Sexual orientation	Age (mean, range)	Reported assessment of health status: psychiatric/ psychological examination	Reported assessment of health status: biological assessments	Brain imaging technique	Sexual stimuli: type / warm-up period / length	Control stimuli	Paradigm	Measures of sexual arousal
Stoléru et al., 1999	8 M	Hetero	23 (23–25)	Y	N	PET	Films / 6-min stimulation, then PET scanning over 90 s of continued presentation	Neutral + Humor	Viewing	Self-report, phallometry, heart and respiratory rates, plasma T
Redouté et al., 2000	9 M	Hetero	31 (21–39)	Y	Y	PET	Films and photos / 1 min stimulation, then PET scanning over 60 s of continued presentation	Neutral + Humor	Viewing	Self-report, phallometry, plasma T, heart rate

Continued on the next page

Table 1. *(Continued)*

Study	Sample size, sex	Sexual orientation	Age (mean, range)	Reported assessment of health status: psychiatric/ psychological examination	Reported assessment of health status: biological assessments	Brain imaging technique	Sexual stimuli: type / warm-up period / length	Control stimuli	Paradigm	Measures of sexual arousal
Mouras et al., 2003	8 M	Hetero	26 (24–29)	Y	N	fMRI	Photos / 21-s long blocks	Neutral	Viewing	Self-report
Park et al., 2001	12 M	NR	23 (21–25)	Y	NR	fMRI	Films / 2 min	Documentary	Viewing	Self-report
Bocher et al., 2001	10M	Hetero	27 (24–32)	N	N	PET	Films / 30-min continuous watching, with scans at 10, 20, and 30 min	Neutral + Conversation	Viewing	Self-report
Rauch et al., 1999	8 M	NR	25 (21–32)	NR	NR	PET	Scripts of personal events, 30–40 s	Sport competition	Mental imagery	Self-report, heart rate, skin conductance, lateral frontalis EMG

Study	N	Orientation	Age		Method	Stimulus	Neutral	Task	Measures
Karama et al., 2002	20 M	Hetero	23 (21–29)	N	fMRI	Films / 179 s	Neutral	Viewing	Self-report
Arnow et al., 2002	14 M	Hetero	NR (18–30)	Y	fMRI	Films / 108–543 s	Relaxing scenes + sports	Viewing	Phallometry, heart rate, respiratory rate
Beauregard et al., 2001	10 M	NR	23.5 (20–42)	N	fMRI	Films / 39 s	Neutral	Viewing vs. inhibition of any emotional reaction	Self-report
Holstege et al., 2003	11 M	Hetero	33 (19–45)	N	PET	Ejaculation, manual stimulation by partner	Penile stimulation, manual stimulation by partner	Perceiving ejaculation/ stimulation	Visual control of ejaculation by experimenter

Hetero = heterosexual, NR = not reported, T = testosterone.

Paradigms

In the majority of studies, subjects were instructed to simply watch a series of stimuli. In one study, exploring the neural network associated with the ability to suppress SDA (Beauregard et al., 2001), subjects were asked, in one condition, to inhibit any emotional response. In another study, script-driven imagery was used (Rauch et al., 1999). Finally, in one study perception of manual stimulation of the penis by the subject's partner was used to induce sexual arousal and ejaculation (Holstege et al., 2003).

Stimuli

Six studies used films, one used films and photographs (Redouté et al., 2000), one used only photographs (Mouras et al., 2003), one study relied on mental imagery (Rauch et al., 1999), and one study involved manual stimulation of the penis by the subject's partner (Holstege et al., 2003). In functional imaging studies, what is measured is the increase—or the decrease—of regional brain activity in response to sexual stimuli as compared to a reference condition. The reference condition is based on the presentation of nonsexual stimuli. Almost all studies so far have used "emotionally neutral" stimuli. In addition, studies have used the presentation of visual stimuli representing nonsexual emotionally laden scenes and/or social interaction, such as humor scenes (Redouté et al., 2000) and sports highlights (Arnow et al., 2002). In the study by Holstege et al. (2003), brain activity during ejaculation was compared with activity during the phase of sexual stimulation preceding ejaculation.

Clearly, the expression "emotionally neutral" stimuli is a misnomer, as these stimuli are simply far less emotionally arousing than sexual stimuli. However, they must still catch the subject's attention to a sufficient degree so as not to be boring, as boredom would induce an unwanted emotional state. It should also be noted that efforts have been made to use nonsexual reference conditions in order to control the emotional aspects of SDA, but fewer attempts have been made to control for its motivational component. Progress remains to be made regarding the design and use of reference conditions that would induce nonsexual motivational states.

Length of exposure to visual sexual stimuli (VSS) is likely to be a major factor in the intensity of SDA experienced by subjects, and therefore is very likely to determine the pattern of recorded neural correlates. Here, two variables must be distinguished: the length of the period during which data acquisition is performed and the length of the period of VSS presentation that precedes data acquisition. The latter, which may be seen as a "warm-up period," has rarely been used in this type of study. In addition, in one study (Hagemann et al., 2003), data acquisition began immediately after the cessation of VSS. To illustrate the importance of these variables, the short length of stimulation used in one study (Mouras et al., 2003), consisting of 21-second blocks of VSS with no "warm-up period," was adapted to demonstrate the neural correlates of the early stage of SDA. By contrast, in another study (Stoléru et al., 1999), data acquisition started after 6 minutes of visual sexual stimulation and continued over 90 seconds. In the latter study, the paradigm was adequate to demonstrate the neural correlates of a full-blown state of SDA.

Results

Brain activations and deactivations recorded during the sexual arousal condition are presented in Tables 2 and 3.

THE OCCIPITOTEMPORAL CORTEX

Eight studies reported an activation in the associative visual areas that belong to the "ventral stream" of visual processing (Figure 1). Briefly, the ventral stream processes the information related to the content of the visual stimuli (the "what" aspect), while the dorsal stream, which involves parietal areas, processes the "where" aspect of visual stimuli. However, the activation of the occipitotemporal visual areas is probably not specific to the sexual nature of stimuli. As shown in a recent review (Phan et al., 2002), the majority of studies (60%) of visually induced emotional (non-sexual) states have reported an activation of the extrastriate occipital cortex, and the visual stimuli that activated these areas were diverse, including pleasant and aversive pictures. These results suggest that the activation of the middle and inferior occipital gyri is not specifically related to the sexual condition used in the papers reviewed here, but rather to the fact that VSS are emotionally laden stimuli. Reiman et al. (1997) have suggested that these visual association areas could be involved in the evaluation procedure of complex visual stimuli with emotional relevance. It has also been proposed that the visual association areas are under the control of top-down influences, so that higher attention to VSS may have resulted in higher activity in visual association areas (Corbetta, Miezin, Shulman, & Petersen, 1993).

THE ORBITOFRONTAL CORTEX

The orbitofrontal cortex (OFC; see Figure 2) is that part of the frontal cortex that lies above the orbit of the eye. It is commonly partitioned into the lateral and the medial OFCs. The OFC has been implicated as playing a major role in the assessment of the motivational relevance of stimuli (Rolls, 1999). This has been mainly established on the basis of studies in nonhuman primates and in human subjects. In our first study (Stoléru et al., 1999), we reported that the presentation of sexually stimulating film excerpts was associated with the activation of the right OFC. Importantly, it was the lateral part of the right OFC that was activated. Karama et al. (2002) also found an activation in the lateral part of both the right and the

Table 2. *Brain Activations Recorded in the Sexual Arousal Condition*

Study	IPL	SPL	ACG	PMv	Insula	Claustrum	Hypo-thalamus	Lateral orbito-frontal cortex	Caudate nucleus	Putamen	Thalamus	Occipito-temporal cortex	Inferior temporal cortex
Stoléru et al., 1999	NO	NO	YES, L	NO	YES	YES	NO	YES	YES	NO	NO	YES	NO
Redouté et al., 2000	YES	YES	YES, L & R	YES	NO	YES	YES	YES	YES	YES	YES	NO	NO
Mouras et al., 2003	YES	YES	NO	YES	NO	NO	NO	NO	NO	NO	NO	YES	YES
Park et al., 2001	NO	NO	YES	U	YES	NO	NO	U	YES	NO	YES	NO	YES
Bocher et al., 2001	YES	YES	NO	NO	NO	NO	NO	NO	NO	NO	NO	YES	YES
Rauch et al., 1999	NO	NO	YES, R	NO	NO	YES	NO	NO	NO	NO	NO	NO	NO
Karama et al., 2002	NO	NO	YES, R & L	NO	YES	NO	YES	YES	NO	NO	YES	YES	NO
Arnow et al., 2002	NO	NO	YES, L & R	YES	YES	YES	YES	NO	YES	YES	NO	YES	NO
Beauregard et al., 2001	NO	YES[a]	YES[a], R	NO	NO	NO	YES	NO	NO	NO	NO	YES	YES
Holstege et al., 2003	YES	NO	NO	NO	YES	YES	NO	YES	NO	YES	YES	NO	YES

ACG = anterior cingulate gyrus, IPL = inferior parietal lobule, L = left, PMv = premotor ventral area, R = right, SPL = superior parietal lobule, U = undeterminable from article. aIn this region, the fMRI signal increased in the attempted inhibition condition, not in the sexual arousal condition.

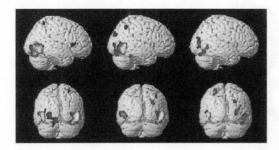

Figure 1. The occipitotemporal cortex. Clusters of voxels with higher regional cerebral blood flow in the sexual condition than in the baseline (white cross), neutral (documentary), and talk show conditions (columns 1, 2, and 3, respectively) (Bocher et al., 2001).

left OFC. In our second study (Redouté et al., 2000), we again found that the right OFC was activated, not only in response to films but also in response to sexually stimulating photographs. In this study, though the activation of the right OFC was not in the medial part of the OFC, its location was in a less lateral position than in our first study. While the distance from the sagittal plane was 52 mm in the first study, it was 20 mm in the second. Importantly, this second study also showed a unique pattern of rCBF response in the right OFC, characterized by a maximum rCBF in the condition where moderately sexually arousing photographs were presented, with lesser activation recorded in the conditions where highly arousing photographs or films were presented. This means that the activation of this area of the brain was not correlated to the level of SDA per se. Moreover, in this region, rCBF in response to stimuli representing women was much higher than in response to other stimuli, that is, documentary nature films and humor films where no women appeared. This was the case whatever the level of SDA that was induced by the pictures representing women. For instance, even photographs of the emotionally neutral category, reported by subjects as generating no SDA, induced a greater activation of the right OFC. To which aspect(s) of stimuli was the activation of the right OFC related? In our study, on debriefing after PET sessions it is only for moderately sexually arousing photographs—those that induced the highest response in the right OFC—that subjects commented on the beauty of the presented women. These comments reflected the evaluation processes induced by this kind of stimulus. The activation of the OFC may thus be related to these evaluation processes rather than to SDA per se. This interpretation was later corroborated by the findings of an fMRI study specifically targeted at the brain areas mediating the perception of facial attractiveness (Aharon et al., 2001), in which activation of the right OFC was related to perception of facial attractiveness. In another recent fMRI study on the neural correlates of facial attractiveness (O'Doherty et al., 2003), high attractiveness was again related to an activation in the OFC; however, the activation was located in the left medial OFC. In this study, the opposite contrast was also performed to detect areas with greater responses to low attractive faces relative to high attractive faces. Significant effects ($p <$

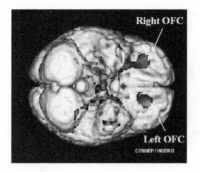

Figure 2. A view of the inferior surface of the brain showing the orbitofrontal cortex of both hemispheres (Redouté et al., 2000, unpublished figure). Clusters of voxels with higher regional cerebral blood flow in the sexual condition than in the humor condition. OFC = orbitofrontal cortex.

0.05, corrected for multiple comparisons) were evident in the right ventrolateral prefrontal cortex bordering right OFC.

Certain types of psychopathology may also raise questions on the functions of the OFC in sexual behavior. Burns and Swerdlow (2003) recently reported a case where a patient presented with acquired pedophilia and an inability to inhibit sexual urges despite preserved moral knowledge. The patient was found to have a right orbitofrontal tumor. The paper by Burns and Swerdlow raises questions regarding the role of the right OFC in the inhibition of sexual urges and in sexual orientation. It is important to note that this patient's tumor was very large, so that information regarding the roles of the various parts of the right OFC cannot be derived from this case. Dressing et al. (2001) reported a case study based on fMRI of a man presenting with pedophilia. In response to the presentation of VSS representing children in underwear, unlike healthy controls, this subject showed an activation of the right OFC.

THE SUPERIOR PARIETAL LOBULE

The superior parietal lobule (SPL) is known to be involved in attentional processes. Not surprisingly, it has been shown to be activated in five of the reviewed studies. Our group (Mouras et al., 2003) recently found a bilateral activation of the SPL in the S-N onset contrast (Figure 3). The analysis of the differential brain response to the onset of presentations of blocks of photographs belonging to sexually stimulating versus nonsexually stimulating photographs was performed to identify regions where the blood oxygenation level dependent (BOLD) signal would change within the first 500 milliseconds and last less than 5 seconds. We found that, in addition to the increased BOLD signal in the SPLs sustained during blocks of VSS, there was a transient initial increase of activity in response to the beginning of the first photograph of each VSS block. This suggests that the SPLs are involved in early sexual information processing. More specifically, this early activation of SPLs could mean that increased attention is part of the appraisal process of VSS, a process that also belongs to the cognitive com-

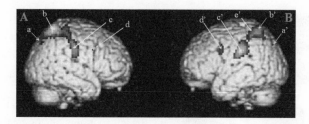

Figure 3. Brain areas showing a higher fMRI signal in response to sexual than to neutral photographic stimuli (Mouras et al., 2003). A. Right view of the brain: a = Parietooccipital sulcus; b = Superior parietal lobule; c = Postcentral gyrus; d = Precentral gyrus. B. Left view of the brain: a′ = Superior occipital gyrus; b′ = Superior parietal lobule; c′ = Inferior parietal lobule; d′ = Precentral gyrus; e′ = Intraparietal sulcus. For A and B, height threshold: $p < 0.05$, corrected for multiple comparisons.

ponent of our proposed model of SDA. The early neural response of SPLs fits well with the behavioral response times: In a categorization task involving sexual and neutral pictures, the mean reaction time ranged between 526 and 738 milliseconds (Spiering, Everaerd, & Elzinga, 2002), which documents the notion of early appraisal processes of VSS. In another domain of emotion, Pizzagalli et al. (2002) demonstrated a very early differential response (112–164 milliseconds) of parietal regions to affectively relevant information, that is, the presentation of liked versus disliked faces. Adolphs (2002) has suggested that a coarse categorization of faces as expressing an emotion or not could be mediated by a response of the occipital and temporal cortices occurring about 100 milliseconds after onset of stimulus exposure.

NEURAL NETWORK MEDIATING MOTOR IMAGERY AND MOTOR PREPARATION

As conceptualized by Decety and Grèzes (1999), from a cognitive neuroscience standpoint, motor imagery may be defined as a dynamic state during which the representation of a given motor act is internally rehearsed in working memory without any overt motor output. It has been proposed that such a simulation process corresponds to the conscious counterpart of many situations experienced in everyday life, such as watching somebody's action with the desire to imitate it, anticipating the effects of an action, preparing or intending to move, refraining from moving, and remembering an action. All of these tasks involve motor representations that recruit neural mechanisms specific to action planning. Planning of actions, preparing to move, simulating and observing actions can be regarded as having functional equivalence to the extent that they share these same motor representations and the same neural substrate. The motor representation consists of two parts: a representation of the body as a force generator, and a representation of the goal of the action encoded in a prag-

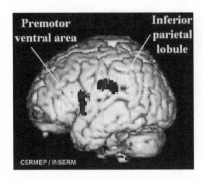

Figure 4. A left view of the brain showing the left ventral premotor area and the inferior parietal lobule activated in the sexual condition (Redouté et al., 2000, unpublished figure).

matic code. Many brain areas that we found to be activated in response to VSS belong to the neural network that mediates motor imagery. This is the case for the inferior parietal lobules, the left ventral premotor area, the anterior cingulate gyri, and the caudate nucleus.

The inferior parietal lobule (Figures 3 and 4) has been found to be activated in 4 out of 10 of the reviewed studies. The left inferior parietal lobule (Decety et al., 1994) or both inferior parietal lobules (Stephan et al., 1995) were activated by motor imagery tasks where subjects imagined they were performing movements with their right hand.

The left ventral premotor area (Figure 4) was reported being activated in only three studies. However, it is important to note that in patients with hypoactive sexual desire disorder (HSDD) this region did not respond to VSS (see below). As a result, when these patients were compared with healthy controls we found a statistically significant group by experimental condition interaction in this brain area (Stoléru et al., 2003). In interpreting this higher activation in healthy men, it is important to realize that motor imagery guided by an object in the visual field is associated with an activation in the ventral premotor area (Decety et al., 1994). This suggests that the actual presence of VSS in the environment may trigger the preparation of motor behavioral patterns in healthy men, but not in men with HSDD.

One or both anterior cingulate gyri (Figure 5) were reported as activated in seven of the reviewed studies. The anterior cingulate gyrus (ACG) is an extended complex region that mediates several functions, including a role in cognitive, emotional, motivational, and autonomic processes (Bush, Luu, & Posner, 2000). One of the areas within the ACG, the caudal part, is particularly interesting here, as its role in motor function is known to be similar to the role of premotor and supplementary motor area cortices (Dum, 1993). This has led us to propose that the activation of the caudal part of the anterior cingulate gyri in response to the presentation of VSS may be one of the neural correlates of the preparation of motor behavior associated with SDA (Redouté et al., 2000).

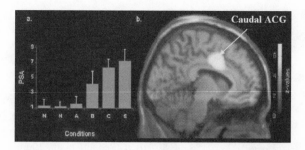

Figure 5. Perceived sexual arousal (PSA) and regional cerebral blood flow (rCBF) in left anterior cingulate gyrus. (a) Means and standard deviations of PSA in each condition; (b) Parasagittal section (4 mm left of midline) showing the positive correlation between rCBF in the left anterior cingulate gyrus (Brodmann area 24) and PSA. Height threshold: z = 3.71, p < 0.0001, uncorrected. Anterior is to the right (Redouté et al., 2000).

The caudate nuclei (Figure 6) have been reported as activated in four papers. In order to interpret the activation of the caudate nucleus, it is important to note that in the experimental paradigms used in these studies, no overt behavioral response was possible. Therefore, it is the premotor aspects of responses, as well as responses of regions concerned with withholding behavior, that were investigated. A recent model of basal ganglia function in motivated behavior (Rolls, 1999) is helpful to interpret the observed correlation between perceived sexual arousal and rCBF in the head of right caudate nucleus (Redouté et al., 2000). According to this model, once the neurons in the OFC have decoded the motivational significance of stimuli, it is essential that these reward-related signals should not be interfaced directly with motor behavior. Instead, what is required is that the signals enter an arbitration mechanism, which takes into account the cost of obtaining reward. It has been proposed that the basal ganglia participate in this function (Rolls). They receive input from numerous areas of the cerebral cortex, including the ACG, which is strongly connected with the caudate nucleus and with the putamen. Cortical inputs compete within the caudate nucleus for behavioral output, and this nucleus maps each particular type of input to the appropriate behavioral output, implemented via the return basal ganglia connections to premotor/prefrontal cortex. This model is consistent with evidence from neuroimaging studies, that is, (i) the activation of the putamen and/or the caudate nucleus in paradigms where the need for a motor response conflicts with the need to withhold it (Pardo, Pardo, Janer, & Raichle, 1990), and (ii) the activation of the head of the caudate nucleus upon volitional tic suppression in Tourette's syndrome (Peterson et al., 1998). Finally, the model is supported by clinical evidence, such as hypersexuality in patients with lesions circum-

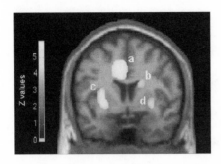

Figure 6. Coronal section demonstrating brain regions where rCBF was linearly correlated with levels of perceived sexual arousal. (a) Anterior cingulate gyrus; (b) head of caudate nucleus; (c) claustrum; and (d) putamen. Section is located 4 mm rostral to anterior commissure. Height threshold: z = 4.40, $p <$ 0.00001, uncorrected. Right is to the right (Redouté et al., 2000).

scribed to the head of the caudate nuclei (Richfield, Twyman, & Berent, 1987). The above development strongly suggests that the model of the neural correlates of SDA should include a component for the control of the motor expression of SDA. This would be consistent with the dual model of the control of sexual behavior (Bancroft, 1999; Bancroft & Janssen, 2000).

THE PUTAMEN

The putamen (Figure 6) was found bilaterally activated in three studies. Like the caudate nucleus, the putamen, which belongs to the basal ganglia and more precisely to the striatum, has been shown to play a similar function as the caudate in withholding motor output. However, a study has suggested a possible relationship of the putamen's ventral part with the hedonic properties of the expected reward (Schultz, Apicella, Scarnati, & Ljungberg, 1992). The putamen is also a region where electrical stimulation most often evoked an erection and/or genital manipulation in Macaca mulatta (Robinson & Mishkin, 1968). It is therefore interesting to point out that in the two studies that tested the correlation between penile tumescence and regional brain responses, a linear correlation was found between rCBF or the BOLD signal in the putamens and the magnitude of penile tumescence (Arnow et al., 2002; Redouté et al., 2000).

THE INSULA

The activation of the insula has been one of the most consistent findings in neuroimaging studies of SDA (n = five studies reporting insular activation). The activation of this region has been shown to be associated with various emotional states, such as sadness, happiness, anger, fear, and disgust (Damasio et al., 2000; Phillips et al., 1997). Therefore, one of the possible interpretations of the activation of the insula may be that this region mediates the emotional component of SDA.

However, another interpretation should be considered. In a recent study on hypogonadal patients, we have found that compared with healthy controls, the patients' right insula failed to be activated in response to VSS (Redouté et al., 2005). When patients were on hormonal replacement therapy, the response of the patients' right insula was no longer different from the response recorded in controls. Interestingly, two recent neuromorpho-logical studies (Gerendai, Tóth, Boldogkoi, Medveczky, & Halász, 2000; Lee, Miselis, & Rivier, 2002) have demonstrated the existence of a neural route between the central nervous system and the testes and identified neurons involved in the innervation, and presumably in the control, of testicular secretion. In these studies, neurotropic virus was injected into the testis and virus-infected neurons were visualized by immunocytochemistry. Virus-labeled neurons could be demonstrated in various regions, including the periaqueductal grey matter, the hypothalamic paraventricular nucleus, the lateral hypothalamus, and also in telencephalic structures including the preoptic area, the bed nucleus of the stria terminalis, the central nucleus of the amygdala, the insula, and the frontal cortex. In the insular cortex, intensive labeling was present and the infection was mainly restricted to pyramidal cells.

THE CLAUSTRUM

The claustrum (Figure 6) is a sheet of grey matter that lies beneath the insula, from which it is separated by white matter. It is one of the most mysterious structures of the brain and its embryologic origin remains controversial. Its activation in response to VSS has initially been a surprise. However, this finding was reported in three studies. The role of the claustrum in SDA is not clear. One proposed interpretation is that the claustrum mediates cross-modal transfer of visual input to imagined tactile stimulation (Arnow et al., 2002).

THE HYPOTHALAMUS

In four studies, an activation of the hypothalamus (Figure 7C) was found during SDA. Interestingly, in two studies there was a linear correlation between the magnitude of penile tumescence as measured by plethysmography and the magnitude of the hypothalamic response as measured in PET or fMRI (Arnow et al., 2002; Redouté et al., 2000).

THE AMYGDALA

It was surprising that only a few studies (Beauregard et al., 2001; Karama et al., 2002; Redouté et al., 2000) demonstrated a response of the amygdalas (Figures 7A and 7B), as results of studies in rodents had led to hypothesize a strong amygdalar activation.

DEACTIVATED TEMPORAL AREAS

Four studies have reported a deactivation of several areas belonging to the lateral or to the inferior temporal cortex (Figure 8). These areas were distinct from the areas of the temporooccipital cortex that were mentioned above as being activated in response to VSS. It is well known that in monkeys the removal of temporal lobes is followed by dramatic hypersexuality (Klüver & Bucy, 1939). In addition, in a study where subjects were re-

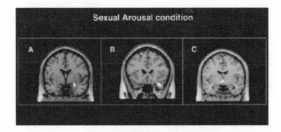

Figure 7. Images are coronal sections showing the right amygdala (*A*), right anterior temporal pole (*B*), and hypothalamus (*C*). The right hemisphere of the brain corresponds to the *right side* of the image (Beauregard et al., 2001).

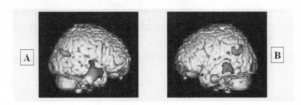

Figure 8. Left view (A) and right view (B) of the brain showing deactivated temporal regions and deactivated medial orbitofrontal cortex (Redouté et al., 2000, unpublished figure).

quested to actively attempt to inhibit the feeling of SDA in response to VSS, some temporal regions showed an activation (Beauregard et al., 2001). Together, these findings suggest that the alleviated inhibition from areas of the temporal lobes allows for the development of SDA. In other words, these temporal regions could exert a tonic, that is, continuous, inhibition on the development of SDA, while the role of the basal ganglia would be to withhold the behavioral expression of an already current state of SDA.

BRAIN CORRELATES OF EJACULATION

The first study based on a modern technique of brain functional imaging focused on the neural correlates of orgasm. This single photon emission computed tomography study (Tiihonen et al., 1994) indicated a decrease in blood flow in all cortical areas, except for a significant increase in the right prefrontal cortex. More recently, Holstege et al. (2003), using PET, studied the brain responses to ejaculation induced in healthy males by penile stimulation performed by their female partner. They compared brain activity at the time of ejaculation with the activity registered during sexual arousal preceding ejaculation. Activation was found in the mesodiencephalic transition zone, including the ventral tegmental area, which is involved in a wide variety of rewarding behaviors. Other reported activated mesodiencephalic structures were the midbrain lateral central tegmental field, zona incerta, subparafascicular nucleus, and the ventroposterior, midline, and intralaminar thalamic nuclei. Increased activation was also present in the lateral putamen and adjoining parts of the claustrum. Neocor-

Table 3. *Brain Deactivations Recorded in Sexual Arousal Condition*

Study	Posterior cingulate gyrus	Medial orbitofrontal gyrus	Occipito-temporal cortex	Inferior temporal cortex
Stoléru et al., 1999	Y	N	N	N
Redouté et al., 2000	Y	Y	Y	Y
Mouras et al., 2003	Y	N	Y	Y
Park et al., 2001	N	N	N	N
Bocher et al., 2001	Y	Y	Y	Y
Rauch et al., 1999	N	N	N	Y
Karama et al., 2002	N	N	N	N
Arnow et al., 2002	N	N	N	N
Beauregard et al., 2001	N	N	N[a]	N
Holstege et al., 2003	N	N	N	N

[a]In this region, fMRI signal increased in the attempted inhibition condition.

tical activity was only found in parietal (BA 7/40), occipital (BA 18), temporal (BA 21), posterior cingulate (BA 23), and lateral orbitofrontal areas (BA 47), exclusively on the right side. On the basis of studies in rodents, the medial preoptic area, bed nucleus of the stria terminalis, and amygdala were thought to be involved in ejaculation, but increased rCBF was not found in any of these regions. Conversely, in the amygdala and adjacent entorhinal cortex, a decrease in activation was observed. Finally, remarkably strong and extended rCBF increases were observed in the cerebellum.

Inconsistencies between Studies

Not all studies reported an activation of the inferior parietal lobules. Thus, the inferior parietal lobules were not found to be activated in a study of positively valenced high arousal states where script-driven imagery was used to induce experimental conditions, including sexual arousal and competitive arousal compared with a neutral emotional condition (Rauch et al., 1999). As the focus of this study was the valence of arousal, script-driven imagery was used in the same way for each condition, including the neutral condition, so that the lack of activation of inferior parietal lobules should not be taken as evidence against their role in mediating motor imagery. More surprising was the fact that in the right inferior parietal lobule (Brodmann area 40), regional blood flow was significantly lower during the sexual arousal condition than during the neutral condition.

Whereas Redouté et al. (2000) reported a significant correlation between penile tumescence and rCBF in the inferior parietal lobule, no such correlation was found in the Arnow et al. study (2002).

Similar discrepancies can be noted with regard to the activation of the SPLs, areas that mediate sustained attention. That these regions were not found to be activated in the study by Stoléru et al. (1999) was due to the limitations of the axial field of view (7.2 cm) of the PET scanner, which reduced the observed volume from Talairach z-coordinate = −28 mm below the bicommissural line (= line passing through anterior and posterior commissures of the brain) to Talairach z-coordinate = +40 mm above the bicommissural line (Talairach & Tournoux, 1988). Again, the *lower* activity of the SPL found in the sexual imagery condition, as compared to the neutral imagery condition, was surprising (Rauch et al., 1999).

The activation of the ACG seems to be a rather consistent finding. It may be dependent on the phase and extent of sexual arousal reached by subjects, as it was not found in the study by Mouras et al. (2003), where the initial response to VSS presentation was investigated. Bocher et al. (2001) did not find any activation of the ACG. Instead, they reported that rCBF was lower in the sexual condition than in the baseline condition, which was induced by presenting a white central cross. Such deactivation, however, was not found when the sexual condition was compared with the other control conditions used in this study, that is, the nature clip and the talk show clip featuring a conversation between two people. As Bocher et al. presented a sexually explicit film for 30 minutes continuously, with PET acquisitions at 10, 20, and 30 minutes, one intriguing possibility would be that rCBF in the ACG starts to decrease after a prolonged period of VSS presentation. If this is the case, and as Bocher et al. pooled data from the three scans performed during VSS, initial increases of rCBF could have been cancelled out by later decreases. Another possibility is that the right and left ACGs play contrasting roles, which is suggested by the report that the right ACG was found activated in a condition where subjects were instructed to voluntarily decrease the intensity of the sexual arousal felt in reaction to the erotic film excerpts (attempted inhibition condition; Beauregard et al., 2001).

The claustrum has been found to be activated in several studies, irrespective of the imaging technique used. The reason why some studies did not demonstrate a claustral activation is not readily apparent. Similarly, the demonstration of an activation of the hypothalamus has been inconsistent. Most of the demonstrations of a hypothalamic activation have relied on testing the correlation between hypothalamic response and penile tumescence (Arnow et al., 2002; Karama et al., 2002; Redouté et al., 2000). By contrast, analyses of the contrasts between experimental conditions have often failed to reveal hypothalamic response (Bocher et al., 2001; Mouras et al., 2003; Park et al., 2001; Rauch et al., 1999; Stoléru et al., 1999), with two exceptions (Beauregard et al., 2001; Karama et al., 2002).

Although studies of sexual function in rodents lead to the hypothesis of an increased activation of the amygdala, support for this finding has been very inconsistent, with only three studies reporting amygdalar activation (Beauregard et al., 2001; Karama et al., 2002; Redouté et al., 2000). Possible explanations for such inconsistency include rapid habituation of amygdala and lack of an adequate spatial resolution of current techniques. Another possibility would be that functions performed by the amygdala in rodents are partly taken up by other regions in man. A recent study supports the view that the claustrum and the basolateral complex of the amygdala have a common embryological origin (Swanson & Petrovich, 1998). The basolateral amygdala has been implicated in reward-related processes (Everitt, Morris, O'Brien, & Robbins, 1991). Specifically, the basolateral amygdala seems to interact with dopamine-dependent processes in the ventral striatum in mediating the control by conditioned incentives over instrumental behavior, while being of relative little importance in the control of unconditioned consummatory responses elicited by primary incentives cues (Everitt, 1990). Thus, it is possible that the human claustrum fulfills a function that in lower mammals is mediated by the basolateral amygdala.

Specificity of Neural Correlates of Sexual Arousal

This review supports the notion that SDA is a composite psychophysiological state correlated with the activation and deactivation of several brain regions. A majority of those regions have been associated with other emotional or motivational states. For instance, the ACG and the claustrum have been activated in several affective states, including negatively valenced emotions (Benkelfat et al., 1995; Dougherty et al., 1999). Then, what is specific of the neuroanatomical correlates of SDA? This specificity may be related to (i) a distinctive pattern of activated/deactivated areas, and/or (ii) the activation/deactivation of discrete areas within the broad regions demonstrated by PET, for example, the part of the rostral ACG reported to control erection in animals and the part of the somatosensory cortex related to the perception of penile tumescence, and/or (iii) small regions where activation cannot be recorded reliably with current neuro-imaging techniques.

Studies in Men Presenting Disorders Affecting Sexual Desire or Arousal

The application of brain functional imaging techniques to the investigation of disorders of SDA is still in the stage of infancy.

One of the first papers based on PET focused on pedophilia (Hendricks et al., 1988). Compared with controls, pedophiles showed a global decrease of cerebral blood flow in the grey matter of the brain. Moreover, decreased rCBF was demonstrated in each of the brain regions investigated in this study. In addition, Cohen et al. (2002) conducted a study on seven pedophiles based on the fluorodeoxyglucose PET technique, which provides a measure of regional brain metabolic activity. Compared with seven healthy controls, metabolic activity was higher in the right OFC of pedophiles when neutral stimuli were presented, but not when female pedophilic sexual cues or adult female nonpedophilic sexual cues were presented.

Two more recent studies have focused on patients with psychogenic erectile disorder and specifically on the effect of sublingually administered apomorphine on brain responses to erotic films. Apomorphine is a dopaminergic agonist used in the treatment of erectile dysfunction. In the study using fMRI (Montorsi et al., 2003a), 10 patients were studied before and after administration of apomorphine and compared with six sexually functional controls. In controls, viewing erotic versus neutral films induced bilateral activations in a network of occipito-parietal and temporal inferior regions, in dorsolateral and premotor frontal cortex, and in anterior temporal limbic areas and the thalamus, which were comparable to the activations in patients during erotic stimulation in the placebo condition. However, in comparison with sexually functional controls, a striking difference was found in patients receiving placebo, as only patients presented a significant and extended activation in the cingulate gyrus, frontal mesial, and OFC. These activated neural systems were modulated by apomorphine administration, which produced a picture that was similar to the one seen in sexually functional controls. Apomorphine caused a bilateral activation in parietal areas and premotor areas of the prefrontal cortex, plus additional activation foci in subcortical and deep structures, namely in the nucleus accumbens, hypothalamus, and mesencephalon: These activations were greater than those seen with placebo. Conversely, a decrease of the fMRI signal, reflecting a deactivation, was found in the frontal basal and temporal limbic cortex. However, the lack of specification of the coordinates of clusters of activated and deactivated brain regions makes it difficult to evaluate these results with precision.

The study by Montorsi et al. (2003b) appears to focus on a subset of subjects from the study discussed above, that is, on eight patients and four potent controls. It provides valuable information on the coordinates of activated clusters. In addition, it shows that only patients presented an activation of the medial OFC, a striking finding given the deactivation found in healthy volunteers in some studies (Table 2). Apomorphine administration reversed this activation of the medial OFC and induced a deactivation of this region. Other regions deactivated upon apomorphine administration were the left frontal polar region, the right frontal mesial cortex, the insulas, the caudate nuclei, the hippocampi, and the hypothalamus.

In the PET study (Hagemann et al., 2003), 12 patients were randomly assigned either to an apomorphine ($n = 6$) or a placebo ($n = 6$) group. No healthy control subjects were included in this study. PET scan acquisitions were performed right after the cessation of the presentation of VSS. Two PET scans were performed prior to administration of the study medication, the first immediately after a neutral audiovisual stimulus and the second following a sexually stimulating audiovisual presentation. After receiving the study medication, patients were subjected to two additional scans each preceded by a sexually stimulating stimulus. Penile rigidity was assessed with the RigiScan device. Cerebral activity increased significantly after the sexually stimulating video sequence compared to the neutral one in the inferior frontal cortex (Brodmann areas 47, 10, 11) and the rostral anterior cingulate (BA 32), and cerebral activity was observed to decrease in both inferior temporal cortices (BA 20). Four out of six patients showed significant penile rigidity after apomorphine compared to none of those receiving placebo. In these four patients, apomorphine was observed to increase cerebral activity in the right superior prefrontal area (BA 6), which was not seen with placebo, while neither apomorphine nor placebo produced decreased cerebral activity. No significant decreases in rCBF were detected after patients received apomorphine. In an analysis of the whole sample, that is, combining the two subgroups, penile rigidity correlated with increased cerebral activity in the right ACG and in the right prefrontal cortex and with decreased activity in the temporal cortex.

Although these two studies were discordant with respect to finding a decreased activity in frontal basal and temporal limbic cortex, they were concordant in demonstrating that apomorphine increases the response of premotor areas of the prefrontal cortex (Brodmann area 6) to the presentation of VSS. In our model of sexual arousal (see below), the activation of premotor areas belongs to the motivational component of sexual arousal. One possible interpretation of the effect of apomorphine on the activation of these regions would be that perception of increased penile erection reinforces the patient's desire to engage in sexual behavior and the correlated activation of premotor areas.

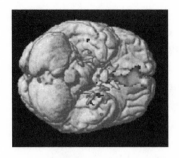

Figure 9. Patients with hypoactive sexual desire disorder: group by condition interaction resulting from maintained activity in the left gyrus rectus of patients in response to visual sexual stimuli, contrasting with a deactivation in controls. Inferior view of the brain (Stoléru et al., 2003; unpublished figure).

A third sexual dysfunction investigated with brain functional imaging is hypoactive sexual desire disorder. PET was used to compare seven male patients with eight healthy men on their rCBF responses to VSS of graded intensity (Stoléru et al., 2003). Whereas the medial OFC showed a deactivation in response to VSS in controls, there was an abnormally maintained activity of this region (Figure 9), which has been implicated in the inhibitory control of motivated behavior, in patients. By contrast, the opposite pattern—activation in controls, deactivation or unchanged activity in patients—was found in the secondary somatosensory cortex and inferior parietal lobules, regions mediating emotional and motor imagery processes, as well as in those areas of the ACG and of the frontal lobes that are involved in premotor processes.

Importantly, the medial OFC codes for the *lack* of reward expected in a given situation, as is the case in the extinction procedure, where the discharge of medial OFC neurons was recorded when reward was withheld (Rosenkilde, Bauer, & Fuster, 1981). Therefore, in animals, lesions of the medial OFC result in a marked tendency toward continued response during extinction paradigms (Butter, 1969). Similarly, a role has been demonstrated for neurons of the ventromedial prefrontal cortex in the memory for extinction (Quirk, Russo, Barron, & Lebron, 2000). Although the outcome of the extinction paradigm and low desire are clearly different situations, we suggest that they share an important common feature, that is, that in both cases the motivational significance of a stimulus has been devalued and that a motor response is no longer warranted. In low desire patients, the maintained activity of the medial OFC neurons might thus be coding for the learned suppression of reward in situations of sexual stimulation and/or for a higher restraint of downstream motivational processes.

We suggest that hypoactive sexual desire disorder and psychogenic erectile disorder may share an important pathophysiological anomaly, that is, a lack of deactivation of the medial OFC. Alternatively, this common feature may simply be related to the frequent comorbidity of these disorders. In a sample of 113 males with hypoactive sexual desire disorder, 53 (47%) had erectile impairment (Segraves & Segraves, 1991). Likewise, in our study (Stoléru et al., 2003) four of the seven patients presented also erectile disorder. In the studies by Montorsi and colleagues, the proportion of patients who also presented hypoactive sexual desire disorder is unknown. On the basis of currently available data, we cannot conclude as to whether the anomaly recorded in the medial OFC is related to low sexual desire or to erectile dysfunction.

We believe that in the long run, the progress made in research on the pathophysiology of SDA will allow for corresponding advancements in the treatment of SDA-related disorders.

A Proposed Model of SDA in Healthy Men

Redouté et al. (2000) have proposed a four-component neurobehavioral model of the brain processes involved in SDA, comprising cognitive, motivational, emotional, and autonomic components. In addition, each component is controlled by inhibitory processes. The cognitive component comprises (i) a process of appraisal through which stimuli are categorized as sexual incentives and quantitatively evaluated as such, (ii) increased attention to stimuli evaluated as sexual, and (iii) motor imagery in relation to sexual behavior. We have interpreted the activation of the right lateral OFC, of the right and the left inferior temporal cortices, of the SPLs, and of areas belonging to the neural network mediating motor imagery (inferior parietal lobules, left ventral premotor area) as the neural correlates of this cognitive component of the model (Stoléru et al., 2003). The process of appraisal is postulated as being the earliest one, with other downstream processes depending on it. Thus, cognitive appraisal of stimuli as sexual is not considered as preceding SDA, but as the first step of the whole process of unfolding SDA.

The emotional component includes the specific hedonic quality of SDA, that is, the pleasure associated with rising arousal and with the perception of specific bodily changes, such as penile tumescence. We have interpreted the activation of the right insula as one of the neural correlates of this emotional component.

The motivational component comprises the processes that direct behavior to a sexual goal, including the perceived urge to express overt sexual behavior. We have suggested that the activated *caudal part* of the left ACG, as well as the right and left claustrum, is a neural correlate of this motivational component.

The autonomic and endocrinological components include various responses (for example, cardiovascular, respiratory, genital) leading the subject to a state of physiological readiness for sexual behavior. We have proposed that the activation of the *rostral portion* of the ACG, of the anterior part of the right insula, and of the posterior hypothalamus participate in the mediation of the autonomic responses of SDA.

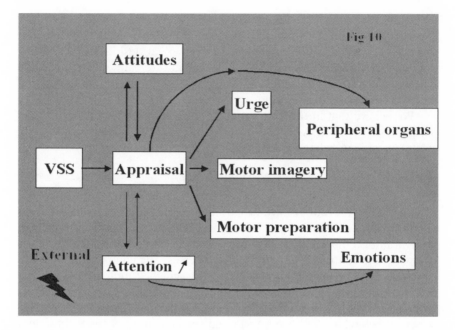

Figure 10. A diagram of the behavioral aspect of the proposed neurobehavioral model of sexual arousal.

These four components are conceived as closely interrelated and coordinated. For instance, the emotional component is partly based on the perception of bodily changes generated by the autonomic component.

Finally, inhibitory processes comprise (i) processes that are active between periods of SDA and that prevent its emergence; we have suggested that this type of inhibitory control is exerted by regions of the temporal lobes where activity decreases in response to VSS; (ii) cognitive processes that may—at least in patients with decreased sexual desire—"devalue" the sexual relevance of VSS; we have proposed that this type of control is mediated by the medial OFC (Stoléru et al., 2003); and (iii) processes that control the overt behavioral expression of SDA, once SDA has begun to develop; we have proposed that the head of the right caudate nucleus and the putamen bilaterally participate in this function.

The behavioral and the neural aspects of the model are tentatively and schematically represented in Figures 10 and 11.

Methodological Problems, Caveats, and Limitations

One of the problems encountered in using fMRI to image brain correlates of SDA is that the frequency of the block design should be chosen

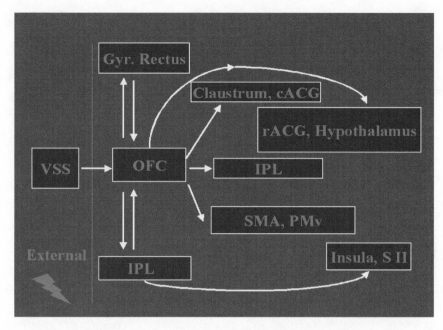

Figure 11. A diagram of the neural aspect of the proposed neurobehavioral model of sexual arousal. Abbreviations: cACG: caudal anterior cingulate gyrus; rACG: rostral anterior cingulate gyrus; IPL: inferior parietal lobule; OFC: orbitofrontal cortex; S II: secondary somatosensory area; SMA: supplementary motor area; PMv: premotor ventral area; VSS: visual sexual stimuli.

with an optimal block length around 14–20 seconds (Zarahn, Aguirre, & D'Esposito, 1997). This optimal length is determined by the intrinsic characteristics of the hemodynamic response function (HRF), which is the time course of the magnitude of the local blood flow response to the activation of the corresponding neuronal assembly. Thus, before it is recorded, the signal originating in neural activity has to pass a hemodynamic filter that smoothes and delays this signal. Blocks lasting 14–20 seconds are long enough to allow the variance of the stimulation, that is, the alternation of the different experimental conditions, to be passed by the HRF. Conversely, such lengths are short enough to avoid the elevated noise found at lower frequencies. Thus, block lengths around 14–20 seconds optimize the trade-off between statistical sensitivity and noise. Therefore, the long periods of blocks used in some of the reviewed fMRI studies are likely to have resulted in falsely negative findings due to the elevated noise found at lower frequencies of block alternation.

As noted by Canli and Amin (2002), it is important to keep in mind that when researchers identify a region as being active, they mean to say that the activation in that region during one condition (for example, seeing a sad face) is significantly greater than the activation of the same region during a control condition (for example, seeing a neutral face). What constitutes significantly greater activation is, in a way, in the eye of the beholder. Quantitatively, that decision will be made through statistical analysis: Activation in one condition will be called significantly greater than another if a certain threshold of statistical certainty is crossed. Thus, lowering the threshold will create more regions that are statistically significant, whereas raising the threshold will reduce the number of significant regions. The choice of the threshold is largely determined by convention amongst researchers, rather than by some absolute standard. Reporting a brain activation pattern is therefore primarily a statistical interpretation of a very complex dataset, which may be interpreted differently by different researchers.

Secondly, finding that certain brain regions respond when subjects are presented with VSS does not necessarily mean that these responses are the *cause* of sexual desire or of sexual arousal. Similarly, we cannot say that sexual desire or arousal are the causes of these responses. What can only be said is that these brain responses are associated or correlated with sexual desire or arousal induced by VSS. To demonstrate this point more clearly, it is at least theoretically possible that the activation of brain regions that are too small to be demonstrated by current techniques is the true cause of both sexual desire and arousal and of the other brain responses that can be shown by PET and fMRI.

A final point to keep in mind when clinical applications are considered is that, at least so far, brain functional imaging studies have shown to be valuable in increasing our understanding of the pathophysiology of neurological and psychiatric disorders, but not in diagnosing these disorders. Whereas results concerning the pathophysiology of disorders are based on groups of patients, diagnostic decisions concern individual patients. At present, these techniques should not be used to diagnose disorders in individual cases.

References

Adolphs, R. (2002). Neural systems for recognizing emotion. *Current Opinion in Neurobiology, 12*,169–177.

Aharon, I., Etcoff, N., Ariely, D., Chabris, C. F., O'Connor, E., & Breiter, H. C. (2001). Beautiful faces have variable reward value: fMRI and behavioral evidence. *Neuron, 32,* 537–551.

Arnow, B. A., Desmond, J. E., Banner, L. L., Glover, G. H., Solomon, A., Polan, M. L., et al. (2002). Brain activation and sexual arousal in healthy, heterosexual males. *Brain, 125,* 1014–1023.

Bancroft, J. (1989). *Human sexuality and its problems*. London: Churchill Livingstone.

Bancroft, J. (1999). Central inhibition of sexual response in the male: A theoretical perspective. *Neuroscience and Biobehavioral Reviews, 23*, 763–784.

Bancroft, J., & Janssen, E. (2000). The dual control model of male sexual response: A theoretical approach to centrally mediated erectile dysfunction. *Neuroscience and Biobehavioral Reviews, 24*, 571–579.

Baum, M. J., Everitt, B. J., Herbert, J., & Keverne, E. B. (1977). Hormonal basis of proceptivity and receptivity in female primates. *Archives of Sexual Behavior, 6*, 173–192.

Beauregard, M., Levesque, J., & Bourgouin, P. (2001). Neural correlates of conscious self-regulation of emotion. *Journal of Neuroscience, 21*, RC165.

Benkelfat, C., Bradwejn, J., Meyer, E., Ellenbogen, M., Milot, S., Gjedde, A., et al. (1995). Functional neuroanatomy of CCK4-induced anxiety in normal healthy volunteers. *American Journal of Psychiatry, 152*, 1180–1184.

Bielert, C. (1982). Experimental examinations of baboon (Papio ursinus) sex stimuli. In C. T. Snowdown, C. H. Brown, & M. R. Petersen (Eds.), *Primate communication* (pp. 373–395). London: Cambridge University Press.

Bocher, M., Chisin, R., Parag, Y., Freedman, N., Meir Weil, Y., Lester, H., et al. (2001). Cerebral activation associated with sexual arousal in response to a pornographic clip: A ^{15}O-H_2O PET study in heterosexual men. *NeuroImage, 14*, 105–117.

Burns, J. M., & Swerdlow, R. H. (2003). Right orbitofrontal tumor with pedophilia symptom and constructional apraxia sign. *Archives of Neurology, 60*, 437–440.

Bush, G., Luu, P., & Posner M. I. (2000). Cognitive and emotional influences in anterior cingulate cortex. *Trends in Cognitive Science, 4*, 215–222.

Buss, D. M. (1989). Sex differences in human mate preferences: Evolutionary hypotheses tested in 37 cultures. *Behavioral and Brain Sciences, 12*, 1–14.

Butter, C. (1969). Perseveration in extinction and in discrimination reversal tasks following selective frontal ablations in Macaca mulatta. *Physiology and Behavior, 4*, 163–171.

Canli, T., & Amin, Z. (2002). Neuroimaging of emotion and personality: Scientific evidence and ethical considerations. *Brain and Cognition, 50*, 414–431.

Cohen, L. J., Nikiforov, K., Gans, S., Poznansky, O., McGeoch, P., Weaver, C., et al. (2002). Heterosexual male perpetrators of childhood sexual abuse: A preliminary neuropsychiatric model. *Psychiatric Quarterly, 73*, 313–336.

Corbetta, M., Miezin, F. M., Shulman, G. L., & Petersen, S. E. (1993). A PET study of visuospatial attention. *Journal of Neuroscience, 13*, 1202–1226.

Damasio, A. R., Grabowski, T. J., Bechara, A., Damasio, H., Ponto, L. L., Parvizi, J., et al. (2000). Subcortical and cortical brain activity during the feeling of self-generated emotions. *Nature Neuroscience, 3*, 1049–1056.

Decety, J., & Grèzes, J. (1999). Neural mechanisms subserving the perception of human actions. *Trends in Cognitive Sciences, 3*, 172–178.

Decety, J., Perani, D., Jeannerod, M., Bettinardi, V., Tadary, B., Woods, R., et al. (1994). Mapping motor representations with positron emission tomography. *Nature, 371*, 600–602.

Dougherty, D. D., Shin, L. M., Alpert, N. M., Pitman, R. K., Orr, S. P., Lasko, M., et al. (1999). Anger in healthy men: A PET study using script-driven imagery. *Biological Psychiatry, 46*, 466–472.

Dressing, H., Obergriesser, T., Tost, H., Kaumeier, S., Ruf, M., & Braus, D. F. (2001). Homosexuelle Pädophilie und funktionelle Netzwerke—fMRI-Fallstudie [Homosexual pedophilia and functional networks—An fMRI case report and literature review]. *Fortschritte der Neurologie Psychiatrie, 69,* 539–544.

Dum, R. P. (1993). Cingulate motor areas. In B. A. Vogt & M. Gabriel (Eds.), *Neurobiology of the cingulate cortex and limbic thalamus* (pp. 415–441). Boston: Birkhäuser.

Everitt, B. J. (1990). Sexual motivation: A neural and behavioural analysis of the mechanisms underlying appetitive and copulatory responses of male rats. *Neuroscience and Biobehavioral Reviews, 14,* 217–232.

Everitt, B. J., Morris, K. A., O'Brien, A., & Robbins, T. W. (1991). The basolateral amygdala-ventral striatal system and conditioned place preference: Further evidence of limbic-striatal interactions underlying reward-related processes. *Neuroscience, 42,* 1–18.

Gerendai, I., Tóth, E., Boldogkoi, Z., Medveczky, I., & Halász, B. (2000). Central nervous system structures labeled from the testis using the transsynaptic viral tracing method. *Journal of Neuroendocrinology, 12,* 1087–1095.

Hagemann, J. H., Berding, G., Bergh, S., Sleep, D. J., Knapp, W. H., Jonas, U., et al. (2003). Effects of visual sexual stimuli and apomorphine SL on cerebral activity in men with erectile dysfunction. *European Urology, 43,* 412–420.

Hendricks, S. E., Fitzpatrick, D. F., Hartmann, K., Quaife, M. A., Stratbucker, R. A., & Graber, B. (1988). Brain structure and function in sexual molesters of children and adolescents. *Journal of Clinical Psychiatry, 49,* 108–112.

Holstege, G., Georgiadis, J. R., Paans, A. M., Meiners, L. C., van der Graaf, F. H., & Reinders, A. A. (2003). Brain activation during human male ejaculation. *Journal of Neuroscience, 23,* 9185–9193.

Karama, S., Lecours, A. R., Leroux, J. M., Bourgouin, P., Beaudoin, G., Joubert, S., et al. (2002). Areas of brain activation in males and females during viewing of erotic film excerpts. *Human Brain Mapping, 16,* 1–13.

Klüver, H., & Bucy, P. C. (1939). Preliminary analysis of functions of the temporal lobes in monkeys. *Archives of Neurology and Psychiatry, 42,* 979–1000.

Lee, S., Miselis, R., & Rivier, C. (2002). Anatomical and functional evidence for a neural hypothalamic-testicular pathway that is independent of the pituitary. *Endocrinology, 143,* 4447–4454.

Meisel, R. L., & Sachs, B. D. (1994). The physiology of male sexual behavior. In E. Knobil & J. D. Neill (Eds.), *The physiology of reproduction* (Vol. 2, pp. 3–105). New York: Raven Press.

Montorsi, F., Perani, D., Anchisi, D., Salonia, A., Scifo, P., Rigiroli, P., et al. (2003a). Brain activation patterns during video sexual stimulation following the administration of apomorphine: Results of a placebo-controlled study. *European Urology, 43,* 405–411.

Montorsi, F., Perani, D., Anchisi, D., Salonia, A., Scifo, P., Rigiroli, P., et al. (2003b). Apomorphine-induced brain modulation during sexual stimulation: A new look at central phenomena related to erectile dysfunction. *International Journal of Impotence Research, 15,* 203–209.

Mouras, H., Stoléru, S., Bittoun, J., Glutron, D., Pelegrini-Issac, M., Paradis, A-L., et al. (2003). Brain processing of visual sexual stimuli in healthy men: A functional magnetic resonance imaging study. *NeuroImage, 20,* 855–869.

O'Doherty, J., Winston, J., Critchley, H., Perrett, D., Burt, D. M., & Dolan, R. J. (2003). Beauty in a smile: The role of medial orbitofrontal cortex in facial attractiveness. *Neuropsychologia, 41,* 147–155.

Pardo, J. V., Pardo, P. J., Janer, K. W., & Raichle, M. E. (1990). The anterior cingulate cortex mediates processing selection in the Stroop attentional conflict paradigm. *Proceedings of the National Academy of Sciences, USA, 87,* 256–259.

Park, K., Seo, J. J., Kang, H. K., Ryu, S. B., Kim, H. J., & Jeong, G. W. (2001). A new potential of blood oxygenation level dependent (BOLD) functional MRI for evaluating cerebral centers of penile erection. *International Journal of Impotence Research, 13,* 73–81.

Parry, A., & Matthews, P. M. (2002). Functional magnetic resonance imaging: A window into the brain. Retrieved June 2003 from http://www.psy.vanderbilt.edu/faculty/blake/214_F2002/fMRI/fmri_intro.html.

Peterson, B. S., Skudlarski, P., Anderson, A. W., Zhang, H., Gatenby, J. C., Lacadie, C. M., et al. (1998). A functional magnetic resonance imaging study of tic suppression in Tourette syndrome. *Archives of General Psychiatry, 55,* 326–333.

Phan, K. L., Wager, T., Taylor, S. F., & Liberzon, I. (2002). Functional neuroanatomy of emotion: A meta-analysis of emotion activation studies in PET and fMRI. *NeuroImage, 16,* 331–348.

Phillips, M. L., Young, A. W., Senior, C., Brammer, M., Andrew, C., Calder, A. J., et al. (1997). A specific neural substrate for perceiving facial expressions of disgust. *Nature, 389,* 495–498.

Pizzagalli, D. A., Lehmann, D., Hendrick, A. M., Regard, M., Pascual-Marqui, R. D., & Davidson, R. J. (2002). Affective judgments of faces modulate early activity (approximately 160 ms) within the fusiform gyri. *NeuroImage, 16,* 663–677.

Quirk, G. J., Russo, G. K., Barron, J. L., & Lebron, K. (2000). The role of ventromedial prefrontal cortex in the recovery of extinguished fear. *Journal of Neuroscience, 20,* 6225–6231.

Rauch, S. L., Shin, L. M., Dougherty, D. D., Alpert, N. M., Orr, S. P., Lasko, M., et al. (1999). Neural activation during sexual and competitive arousal in healthy men. *Psychiatry Research, 91,* 1–10.

Redouté, J., Stoléru, S., Grégoire, M. C., Costes, N., Cinotti, L., Lavenne, F., et al. (2000). Brain processing of visual sexual stimuli in human males. *Human Brain Mapping, 11,* 162–177.

Redouté, J., Stoléru, S., Pugeat, M., Costes, N., Lavenne, F., Le Bars, D., Dechaud, H., Cinotti, L., and Pujol, J. F. (2005). Brain processing of visual sexual stimuli in treated and untreated hypogonadal patients. *Psychoneuroendocrinology, 30,* 461–482.

Reiman, E. M., Lane, R. D., Ahern, G. L., Schwartz, G. E., Davidson, R. J., Friston, K. J., et al. (1997). Neuroanatomical correlates of externally and internally generated human emotion. *American Journal of Psychiatry, 154,* 918–925.

Richfield, E. K., Twyman, R., & Berent, S. (1987). Neurological syndrome following bilateral damage to the head of the caudate nuclei. *Annals of Neurology, 22,* 768–771.

Robinson, B. W., & Mishkin, M. (1968). Penile erection evoked from forebrain structures in Macaca mulatta. *Archives of Neurology, 19,* 184–198.

Rolls, E. T. (1999). *The brain and emotion.* New York: Oxford University Press.

Rosen, R. C., & Beck, J. G. (1988). Patterns of sexual response. In R. C. Rosen &

J. G. Beck (Eds.), *Patterns of sexual arousal: Psychophysiological processes and clinical applications* (pp. 23–52). New York: Guilford.

Rosenkilde, C. E., Bauer, R. H., & Fuster, J. M. (1981). Single cell activity in ventral prefrontal cortex of behaving monkeys. *Brain Research, 209,* 375–394.

Schultz, W., Apicella, P., Scarnati, E., & Ljungberg, T. (1992). Neuronal activity in monkey ventral striatum related to the expectation of reward. *Journal of Neuroscience, 12,* 4595–4610.

Segraves, K., & Segraves, R. (1991). Hypoactive sexual desire disorder: Prevalence and comorbidity in 906 subjects. *Journal of Sex and Marital Therapy, 17,* 55–58.

Spiering, M., Everaerd, W., & Elzinga, B. (2002). Conscious processing of sexual information: Interference caused by sexual primes. *Archives of Sexual Behavior, 31,* 159–164.

Stephan, K. M., Fink, G. R., Passingham, R. E., Silbersweig, D., Ceballos-Baumann, A. O., Frith, C. D., et al. (1995). Functional anatomy of the mental representation of upper extremity movements in healthy subjects. *Journal of Neurophysiology, 73,* 373–386.

Stoléru, S., Grégoire, M. C., Gérard, D., Decety, J., Lafarge, E., Cinotti, L., et al. (1999). Neuroanatomical correlates of visually evoked sexual arousal in human males. *Archives of Sexual Behavior, 28,* 1–21.

Stoléru, S., Redouté, J., Costes, N., Lavenne, F., Le Bars, D., Dechaud, H., et al. (2003). Brain processing of visual sexual stimuli in men with hypoactive sexual desire disorder. *Psychiatry Research: Neuroimaging, 124,* 67–86.

Sumich, A. L., Kumari, V., & Sharma, T. (2003). Neuroimaging of sexual arousal: Research and clinical utility. *Hospital Medicine, 64,* 28–33.

Swanson, L. W., & Petrovich, G. D. (1998). What is the amygdala? *Trends in Neurosciences, 21,* 323–331.

Talairach, J., & Tournoux, P. (1988). *Co-planar stereotaxic atlas of the human brain.* Stuttgart: Thieme.

Tiihonen, J., Kuikka, J., Kupila, J., Partanen, K., Vainio, P., Airaksinen, J., et al. (1994). Increase in cerebral blood flow of right prefrontal cortex in man during orgasm. *Neuroscience Letters, 170,* 241–243.

Zarahn, E., Aguirre, G., & D'Esposito, M. (1997). A trial-based experimental design for fMRI. *NeuroImage, 6,* 122–138.

The Human Sexual Response— Similarities and Differences in the Anatomy and Function of the Male and Female Genitalia

Are They a Trivial Pursuit or a Treasure Trove?

ROY J. LEVIN

Historical Introduction

Fetal Sexual Differentiation

There has always been a fascination to compare and contrast the human male and female genitals that at first sight appear so very different. Despite the obvious external differences, an early anatomical portrayal of the female vagina was surprisingly drawn as being like the male's elongated penis but turned inside out. However, it was not until quite recent times, with the discoveries of the human X and Y chromosomes and the study of the development of the fertilized mammalian egg, that the mammalian male and female genitalia differentiation from the same primitive tissue (the genital anlagen) was shown to be driven differently by the Y chromosome. The Y chromosome encodes a gene referred to as TDF (testis determining factor), which initiates the conversion of the indifferent fetal gonad (the ovotestis) into a functional testis secreting locally the Anti-Mullerian Factor to prevent the development of the female Mullerian duct system and systemic testosterone to maintain and develop the male Wolffian duct system and the external genitalia (Jost, 1973; Wilson, 1978). In the absence of the Y chromosome, the testis-determining pathway is not initiated and the ovotestis develops as an ovary and the fetal differentiation takes the female route. Simplistically, female development can be regarded as the default model; it is the basic pattern onto which the male differentiation is impressed, and even the presence of estrogen is not thought of as necessary for the female genitalia to develop (Jost, 1973; Wilson, 1978).

External Fetal Genital Differentiation

Externally the structures of the urogenital tubercle formed the labia and clitoris. The fetal secretion of large amounts of testosterone (and its conversion in the prostate and penis to the active 5-dihydrotestosterone by the enzyme 5-alpha reductase), however, converts them into the scrotum and penis, respectively. The fact that a number of the underlying structures

35

of the genitals are developed from the same primitive anlagen may well be useful in understanding the functional control of the male and female genitals, so that rather than being merely an interesting academic exercise in comparing and contrasting, there may be a reward in their study.

Kinsey, Pomeroy, Martin, and Gebhard (1953) listed similarities and differences in the male and female anatomical structures involved in the sexual response. They summarized their discussion with, "In brief we conclude that the anatomic structures which are most essential to sexual response and orgasm are nearly identical in the human male and female. The differences are relatively few. They are associated with the different functions of the sexes in reproductive processes, but [my italics] they are *of no great significance on the origins and development of sexual response and orgasm.*"

The Hebrew word *chiddush* has one translation as "finding the new in the old"; this review is an attempt to do just that.

Innervation of the Male and Female Genitalia

In both sexes, genital innervation was essentially thought to be through the autonomic nervous system via the parasympathetic and sympathetic, supplying the former with its single neurotransmitter of acetylcholine (blocked by either atropine or tubocurare) and the latter with noradrenaline (blocked by alpha blockers viz phentolamine and beta blockers viz propranalol). It was simplistically thought that the two systems worked approximately in opposition, the excitatory parasympathetic being opposed by the inhibitory sympathetic. Such simplicity had to be abandoned with discovery of the nonadrenergic-noncholinergic (NANC) peptidergic and nitrergic neural systems and when it became apparent that nerves could contain and release more than one neurotransmitter at their endings. Many putative neurotransmitters were found to be quite large peptides (vasoactive intestinal peptide [VIP], Substance P, calcitonin gene related peptide [CGRP], endothelin). The full list would contain near 40 neuropeptides. An even greater revolution in the concept of peripheral innervation came from the discovery that the gas nitric oxide (NO) was a neurotransmitter. Another complexity that substantially altered our thinking about how the genitals were controlled came from the concept of neuromodulation—a substance released by the nerve endings that did not specifically activate a function but modulated the release or activity of another neurotransmitter.

The rapid application of some of these findings to the innervation of the genitalia has not been without its problems. Classical neurophysiology demanded a number of crucial pieces of evidence before the investigator was allowed to conclude that the candidate neurotransmitter under investigation was the true neurotransmitter of the organ's function.

These criteria are listed in Table 1. In the rush to characterize the neural control of the genitals, a number of these evidential steps have been

Table 1. *Classical Neurophysiological Evidence Needed to Conclude That a Candidate Neurotransmitter Was a True Neurotransmitter at the Site. Discovery of Gaseous Transmitters Has Made Some Criteria Obsolete (See Text)*

(i) presence at the site

(ii) synthesis at the site

(iii) physiological action when administered at the site

(iv) metabolizing enzyme(s) at the site

(v) blockade by specific antagonists at the site

bypassed and are probably now abandoned. A further problem with them is that gaseous neurotransmitters such as NO (and carbon monoxide [CO]) do not fulfill a number of the criteria viz they are not stored at the site (being manufactured as needed), they are not enzymatically catabolized, and there is no transmitter receptor site (neuromuscular junction) to block for anti-NO (CO) agents.

Penis—Erection and Flaccidity

The Ischiocavernosus and Bulbocavernosus Muscles

One of the earliest suggested anatomic mechanisms for erection was proposed by Varolius in 1573 and involved the contraction of the two striated muscles ischiocavernosus (ISC) and bulbospongiosus (BS) at the base of the penis (Gerstenberg, Levin, & Wagner, 1990). They were supposed to shut off the penile venous drainage and thus cause an erection due to the filling, without emptying, of the cavernosal chambers by the incoming arterial blood. Remarkably, this mechanism stayed quoted but unsupported by laboratory research in the literature for nearly 500 years. Numerous authors and textbooks repeated the mantra that the contractions of the two muscles were the basis for erection. However, when electromyogram recordings (EMG) of both muscles during erection to visual sex stimulation were actually monitored, it was clear that if no voluntary effort was made the muscles did not initiate or contract during the erection process (Gerstenberg, Levin, & Wagner, 1990). Shafik (1995a) stimulated separately each muscle electrically while recording the pressures in the urethra and corpora cavernosa. Contraction of the ISC created a rise in pressure in the corpora cavernosa, while BS contraction only caused pressure in the corpus spongiosum but not in the corpora cavernosa. This confirmed that the BS muscle plays no role in the erection process (but may play a part in ejaculation), while the ISC muscle can aid in increasing the corpora cavernosa pressure only when voluntarily contracted. Some men find that by voluntarily contracting the BS and ISC muscles they can facilitate their attainment of an erection and transiently increase its rigidity. In sleep, the BS and ISC muscles appear to become active for nocturnal erections, unlike conscious erections. The mechanism for the creation of the former is thus not identical to that for the latter, and some care has to be taken in using them as a model for normal, conscious erections.

The Neurotransmitter for Erection

The hunt for the mechanism that changes the flaccid urinary penis into the erect sexual one soon dismissed involving acetylcholine, as human erections are atropine insensitive. The finding of VIP in genitals led to testing VIP as the neurotransmitter, but in fact while VIP satisfied criteria (i) and (ii) in Table 1, it did not create a true erection when injected into the human corpora cavernosa; it caused a tumescent penis but not a rigid one (Adaikan, Kottegoda, & Ratnam, 1986; Wagner & Gerstenberg, 1987). Thus, it could not be the sole neurotransmitter. After much investigation and a good dose of serendipity, the remarkable discovery of the nitric oxidase (NOS)-arginine-NO-cyclic GMP pathway that caused the relaxation of the smooth muscles of the corpora cavernosa evolved (Burnett, Lowenstein, Bredt, Chang, & Snyder, 1992), and the complexity of penile tumescence and rigidity became apparent, especially aided by the action of sildenafil in inhibiting phosphodiesterase V, the enzyme that catabolized cyclic GMP. The cyclic GMP phosphorylates protein kinase G (PKG), which then phosphorylates numerous ion channels activating Ca^{2+} channels that hyperpolarize the arterial and cavernosal membranes, causing relaxation of the muscles. Most workers now agree that neurogenic NO is the principal agent for penile erection (Cartledge, Minhas, & Eardley, 2001). Subsequent investigation, however, has revealed a number of other vasoactive agents present in the cavernosal tissues, but their roles in creating the erectile and subsequently the flaccid penis are far from being fully understood (Hedlund, Ny, Alm, & Andersson, 2000). We do not know how the long-term mechanisms maintain a flaccid urinary penis. It is accepted wisdom that a high sympathetic (adrenergic) tone keeps the cavernosal smooth muscle contracted because of the n-adrenaline released at the nerve endings and acting on the alpha$_1$ adrenoreceptors. Part of the arousal/erection process is in reducing this tone, but this cannot be the whole answer because rare cases are known of males who cannot form n-adrenaline because of lack of the enzyme dopamine-betahydroxylase. These males have a delayed or absent ejaculation, and while they have erections, they do not suffer from priapism (Mathias et al., 1990). Clearly other vasoconstrictor mechanisms than n-adrenaline must be utilized in long-term flaccidity, possibly involving endothelin 1, angiotensin, thromboxane A_2, and some prostaglandins (PGF_2).

Vaginal and Clitoral Sexual Function

Vagina

There is no organ in the male comparable to the vagina; the penis is the homologous organ of the clitoris, yet, strangely, all the early studies on the blood flow of the female genitalia focused on the vagina and practically completely ignored the clitoris. This may have been due to the relative ease by which the vaginal blood flow could be studied once the photoplethysmograph had been redeveloped (Levin, 1997). It wasn't until the advent of Doppler ultrasound (measuring blood velocity as units of cm/sec rather than a true flow of ml/sec) that monitoring of the clitoral "blood flow" became facile. Indeed investigators are still publishing papers advocating the use of such techniques (Khalifé & Binik, 2003). Its major difficulty at the moment is that the probe has to be hand held at the right angle onto the clitoris, creating possible arousal.

The Neurotransmitter for Increasing Vaginal Blood Flow

The suggested role of acetylcholine as the major transmitter for the vasodilation of the vagina in sexual arousal was refuted when Wagner and Levin (1980) showed that atropine (the major antimuscarinic cholinergic antagonist) could not block the increased blood flow during arousal nor stop the orgasm from occurring. Early immuno-histological studies identified the presence of VIP in nerves innervating the smooth muscle and blood vessels of the vagina (Levin, 1991) (Table 1, criterion (i)). Subsequent functional studies in the conscious human female indicated that VIP increased the blood flow to the vagina and could induce the formation of a neurogenic vaginal transudate (lubrication), two features that operated in the vagina of a sexually aroused woman satisfying Table 1, criterion (iii). The strong inference was that VIP was the likely vaginal candidate neurotransmitter producing the genital arousal by increasing the arterial blood supply, creating conditions that would facilitate the formation of tissue fluid (increased arterial hydrostatic pressure) that would enter the interstitial space and ultimately trickle through the vaginal epithelium onto its luminal surface to become the vaginal lubricating transudate (Levin, 1999a). There have been no human (or even animal) studies to show that antagonists of VIP can alone blockade the increase in vaginal blood flow on arousal and only recently have there been investigations in rabbit vaginas of an inhibitor(s) of a neutral endopeptidase (NEP, EC 3.4.24.11) that catabolizes VIP (Wayman, Morren, Turner, Naylor, & van der Graaf, 2002). Its possible therapeutic use in humans to enhance vaginal blood flow is being investigated. Because, as described above, NO was found to be the key activator of the increased blood flow to the penis during sexual arousal, it was thought that an identical mechanism of similar importance would be found controlling the vaginal sexual blood flow response. This was proposed despite immuno-histological evidence in human vaginas that there was very little NOS in premenopausal vaginal tissues and practically none in postmenopausal (Hoyle, Stones, Robson, Whitley, & Burnstock, 1996), unlike the rich concentration in the clitoris (Burnett, Calvin, Silver, Peppas, & Docimo, 1997). Like the penis, the clitoris is an androgen-dependent tissue, while the vagina is basically estrogen-dependent.

The best controlled investigation on the possible influence of the NOS-arginine-NO-guanylate cyclase-cyclic GMP pathway in influencing vaginal blood flow is indirect from the study of Laan et al. (2002), who investigated the action of sildenafil (the inhibitor of PDE5 that catabolizes cyclic GMP) on vaginal blood flow measured by photoplethysmography in the basal and aroused states. Sildenafil treatment did not influence the basal flow and only gave rise to a modest 20% increase in the amplitude of the photoplethysmographic signal (vaginal pulse amplitude or VPA). In fact, as the VPA is a completely arbitrary index of vaginal blood volume changes, it cannot be assumed that a 20% increase in VPA means a 20% increase in blood flow per se. A more robust measure of vaginal blood flow is needed to quantify the change brought about by sildenafil (and thus indirectly by inference the NOS-NO-cyclic GMP mechanism). Clearly the more modest role of cyclic GMP (and by inference NO?) in influencing vaginal blood flow does not match its basic importance in influencing penile blood flow, but that is not unexpected because, as was stated at the beginning of this section, the vagina is not homologous with the penis—that honor rests with the clitoris.

One obvious fact that arises from reviewing the innervation of the vaginal peripheral circulation is the lack of follow-up functional studies. While Hoyle et al.'s (1996) excellent immunohistochemical study of a host of neuropeptides revealed their location amongst the various blood vessels of the organ, the surprising fact is that after 11 years we still do not know whether the exposed innervations are of motor nerves or of sensory nerves, nor what the various putative neurotransmitters actually do at their respective sites; function lags far behind location.

The Enigma of the Action of TRH in Women

One fascinating, and as yet unexplained, difference between men and women is their response to a central neurotransmitter, the tripeptide TRH (thyrotropin-releasing hormone), when it is injected intravenously. In both males and females it can give rise to transient side effects such as facial and body warmth, nausea, urinary urgency, and a metallic taste on the tongue. It had no effect on penile erection, the organ remaining completely flaccid and no activation of any sexual arousal feelings when injected i.v. (200 micrograms) into 6 men (Levin & Wagner, unpublished communication). However, when injected i.v. into women, the same side effects as in men can occur, but in 44% of women (7 out of 16 subjects), transient vaginal warmth, lubrication, and pressure similar to that of mild sexual arousal was induced (Blum & Pulini, 1980). Levin and Wagner (1986) examined the effects of an i.v. 200-microgram dose of TRH against a saline placebo injection in 9 female subjects, measuring their vaginal blood flow by both photoplethysmography and the heated oxygen electrode. Vaginal warmth was experienced in 7 of the 9 (78%), while 2 of the 9 (22%) had facial but not vaginal warmth. Small increases in power consumption of the heated electrode (an index of increased vaginal blood flow) were noted in 6 of 8 subjects (75%), while the saline i.v. either caused no effect or a decrease. Unfortunately movement artifacts made interpretation of the photoplethysmographic records difficult; 3 out of 9 (33%) showed clear-cut increases in VPA, while 4 out of 9 (44%) showed increases, but these were not significant. The conclusion was that 200 micrograms of i.v. TRH can induce small increases in both the blood flow and the feeling of its activation in the human vagina. Acute experiments in anaesthetized sheep also showed that close intraarterial injection of TRH to the vagina (via the femoral artery) increased vaginal blood flow before circulating around the systemic circulation, indicating a direct action at the vaginal level. Repeated injections rapidly caused tachyphylaxis. Thus, TRH has a unique action in causing a mild genital and central arousal in women but not in men. No other study of this action has yet been undertaken. Many fascinating questions arise. Is TRH another genital neurotransmitter in the female? Why has it no action in the male? Is the mild sexual arousal caused by the increased activation of vaginal blood flow or is it because it activates some area of the brain? Is TRH involved in normal sexual arousal in women? There is a harvest here yet to be reaped.

Clitoris

The clitoris has been known as a major focus for women's sexual enjoyment since antiquity (Levin, 2001). Despite this long history, it is only recently that serious scientific study of the organ has been undertaken; even its anatomy and histological structure has been poorly researched. Van Turnhout, Hage, and van Diest (1995) confirmed by dissection in fresh cadavers that the bilateral vestibular bulbs on either of the vagina terminated into the glans of the clitoris, while Toesca, Stolfi, and Cocchia (1996) reported that the corpora cavernosa of the clitoris are essentially similar to that of the penis except that there is no subalbugineal layer interposed between the tunica albuginea and the erectile tissue. In the penis, this tissue engorges with blood during sexual arousal and becomes compressed against the unyielding tunica, creating penile rigidity—a true erection. The lack of this plexus in the clitoris indicates that while the organ can become tumescent or engorged, it cannot, like the penis, become stiffly erect. The clitoris thus does not really become erect with sexual excitement, but engorged. Occasional papers are published describing clitoral priapism and claiming that the organ has a prolonged erection (Medina,

2002), but it would be more accurate to say a prolonged engorgement. Another difference between the clitoris and the penis is in the shape, extent, and orientation of the suspensory ligaments supporting the two structures (Rees, O'Connell, Plenter, & Hutson, 2000). O'Connell, Hutson, Anderson, and Plenter (1998) published a reevaluation of the gross clitoral structure based on cadaveric dissections of 10 females. They described it as a triplanar complex with a midline corpora (1–2 cm wide and 2–4 cm long) lying in the median sagittal plane that gave rise to the paired crura (5–9 cms long) lying parallel to the ischiopubic rami and separate bulbs (3–7 cm long, crescentric or triangular) sitting posterior to the corpora. This complex of erectile tissue surrounds the urethra. It was claimed that the so-called urethral bulbs did not form the core of the labia minora as usually portrayed, but are part of the clitoral tissue. The actual size of the clitoral tissue complex was also much larger than usually portrayed, but unfortunately the volume of the tissue was not quantified using modern stereological techniques. A more recent study of the clitoral anatomy using magnetic resonance imaging (MRI) in premenopausal women clearly showed that the urethral bulbs were on either side of the urethra and continued anteriorly to it meeting in the midline without merging. Their function either in the basal state or during sexual arousal was unclear (O'Connell & DeLancey, 2005).

The smooth muscle of the human penile corpora cavernosa is contracted during flaccidity under the influence of a high sympathetic tone. On sexual arousal, the tone is reduced and the muscle relaxes, allowing blood to flow into the erectile chambers. This change in the function of the smooth muscle (contraction to relaxation) can be monitored by measuring the electrical myographic activity of the smooth muscle inside the penis using a concentric electrode; contraction creates spontaneous electrical activity, relaxation produces none. Gerstenberg, Levin, and Wagner (1989) were the first to record these changes in the muscular electrical activity of the human cavernosal smooth muscle in situ, and since their publication a large literature has developed on the subject (Vardi, Gruenwald, & Sprecher, 2000). Just recently, Yilmaz, Soylu, Ozcan, and Caliskan (2002) have made similar electrical measurements in the clitoris and recorded spontaneous electrical myographic activity of similar sympathetic tonus as observed in the penis. It thus appears that both the penis and the clitoris are kept flaccid by a high sympathetic tone (Levin, 2005).

The Orgasm

Both sexes experience orgasms at the peak of their sexual arousal with similar changes in their respiratory, circulatory, and muscular systems, and as far as written descriptions with any gender references removed can be held to characterize the activity, male and female assessors cannot distinguish whether such descriptions are written by a male or a female (Vance & Wagner, 1976). This suggests that the mental experience of the orgasm is essentially similar for males and females. Typologies of orgasms only appear to have been created for females (Levin, 1981; Mah & Binik, 2002; Meston, Hull, Levin, & Sipski, 2004), perhaps because there are a number of separate sites that can produce orgasm in women, but in men most sexual attention is nearly always focused on the penis. No comparative descriptions of orgasm produced by stimulation of men's prostates (per rectum) compared to that produced by penile stimulation (like the previously mentioned study on male and female orgasms) have ever been published: are they longer, weaker, stronger, or of similar pleasure? It should always be remembered that absence of evidence for a men's orgasm typology is not evidence of an absence for a men's orgasm typology (see Levin, 2004).

There appear, however, to be significant differences in male and female orgastic activity, namely:

1. The female, unlike the male, can have repeated (multiple) orgasms separated by very short intervals (Masters & Johnson, 1966).
2. The female can have an extended orgasm (status orgasmus) lasting for a long time (Masters & Johnson, 1966).
3. With the recorded pattern of pelvic muscular contractions, males have a divided rhythmic pattern not seen in women (Bohlen, Held, Sanderson, & Ahlgren, 1982).
4. If the male orgasm is initiated, its expression continues automatically even if the sexual stimuli eliciting it is stopped; with females it is claimed that if the stimuli eliciting the orgasm is stopped, the orgasm ceases (Masters & Johnson, 1966; Sherfey, 1973).

What are the possible reasons/mechanisms for these differences?

In the case of the first, that women can have multiple orgasms while men do not, the explanation lies in the fact that men ejaculate while women normally do not (apart from the claims of those who have urethral discharges). Levin (2003b) has recently discussed critically and in some detail the proposed physiological mechanism of this behavior, which involves the hormone prolactin, claimed to be released only at orgasm and not by sexual arousal per se.

At present, there does not appear to be any obvious explanation for women having longer orgasms than men and there are no (as yet) known reasons for the differences in striated muscular activity between men and women in relation to their contractile activity at orgasm, but see below.

Pelvic Striated Muscular Contractions at Orgasm in Men and Women

Voluntary or striated muscles are found not only in limbs but also in the pelvic floor. The properties of the latter, however, are different from the former. Firstly, while they can be contracted voluntarily, they can also be contracted involuntarily, rhythmically during the clonic contractions at orgasm. Second, those of the female pelvis can contract spastically when the female is exposed to a threatening situation, giving rise to the so-called sexually dysfunctional condition called vaginismus, where spastic contraction of the muscles is so severe that it prevents entry of the penis and even of fingers into the vagina (Van der Velde, Laan, & Everaerd, 2001). These authors regard the involuntary pelvic muscle activity as part of a general defense mechanism that occurs during exposures to threatening situations, but strangely it does not appear to protect women from rape.

Shafik and El-Sibai (2002) studied the EMG activity of the levator ani, puborectalis, and bulbocavernosus muscles in normal controls and patients suffering from vaginismus. Even in the basal state the EMG activity of the patients was greater than the controls, and the induction of vaginismus by a vaginal dilator created even greater activity. The concept of a disordered sacral reflex arc was suggested, but the authors agreed that further studies are needed for verification.

Involuntary spasm of the pelvic muscles is not well recognized in men, although there are conditions of painful ejaculation (odynorgasmia; Donnellan, Breathnach, & Crown, 2001) and postejaculatory pain syndrome (Kaplan, 1993), which may involve spasm of certain muscles of the male genitalia. These conditions in men need as much workup as vaginismus has in women if we are to think of them as having the same etiology.

In both men and women, the pelvic striated musculature is normally activated at orgasm to give rhythmic contractions (Masters & Johnson, 1966). In men, these contractions (especially of the bulbocavernosus [BC] muscle; Shafik, 1995a) power the forceful ejaculatory spurts of semen (Gerstenberg, Levin, & Wagner, 1990) and are always present concomitant with the orgasm despite having separate mechanisms (Levin, 2003b). In the case of women, however, while many express pelvic contractions of their circumvaginal striated muscles (ISC and BC muscles) at orgasm, surveys and individual reports have revealed that a significant number do not experience (perceive?) or have these contractions, but yet claim to have orgasms (Bohlen, Held, Sanderson, & Ahlgren, 1982). Why there is this clear difference between the sexes has been ignored and remains unexplained. It may have something to do with the fact that women can have different types of smooth/striated muscular activity at orgasm, as shown in the record by John Perry published in Levin (2001). In this subject, when the anterior vaginal wall is the focus of the sexual stimulation, then the contractile activity is expressed in both uterine and pubococcygeus (PC) striated muscles; but if the clitoris is the focus, much greater activity was observed in the PC striated muscle with little activity from the uterine smooth muscle. Clearly much investigative work in this area needs to be undertaken.

Genital Smooth Muscle Contractions during Orgasm in Men and Women

At orgasm in males ejaculation usually takes place at the same time, although the mechanisms subserving both are different (see Levin, 2003b, for references). The ejaculatory muscular mechanism consists of adrenergic-activated contractions of the smooth muscle in the capsules of the genital accessory organs and peristalsis in the vas deferens and urethra. These are coordinated with the striated muscle contractions that force the ejaculate out under pressure; the smooth muscle contractions are to load up the urethra with the semen for the former. If the striated muscles are paralyzed, only a dribbling ejaculation occurs.

While there are no female ejaculatory phenomena directly comparable to that of the male (apart from the controversial urethral expulsions—see section on Skene's glands), some authors have suggested that the equivalent activity is the uterine contractions that occur at orgasm in women. Moreover, as it is known that the ejaculation mechanism is the cause of the refractory period in males (Masters & Johnson, 1966; Levin, 2003b), it has been proposed that when these uterine contractions occur in women they occur at their terminal orgasm, switching the female arousal off and preventing further orgasmic activity; they thus generate a female "refractory period."

It is interesting to note that Kinsey et al. (1953) and Masters and Johnson (1966) disagreed on the appearance of uterine contractions. According to the former authors, "the upper end of the uterus goes into rhythmic contractions of considerable frequency *whenever there is sexual arousal*" (my italics) but the latter claimed "that specific uterine patterns do not develop unless the individual subject *undergoes an orgasmic experience*" (my italics). Unfortunately, there are simply too few published recordings/data to allow a definitive answer to these interesting speculations and comments; only further study can resolve these anomalies or unanswered questions.

Genital Secretory Activities during Arousal

The genital secretions/fluids of the male involve those from the prostate, seminal vesicles, and glands of Littré and Cowper's or bulbourethral gland, while those of the female are from the uterine (endometrial) glands, the infolded cervical epithelial crypts (not true glandular tissue), the vaginal neurogenic transudate, and Skene's (paraurethral) and Bartholin's (paired vulvovaginal) glands.

Uterine (Endometrial) Glands

These glands are obviously unique to women. There is only one study that has investigated the possible effect of sexual arousal on the secretion of the uterine glands. This utilized the insertion into the uterus of a conscious subject of a radiotelemetering, pH-measuring capsule (Fox, Colson, & Watson, 1982). On 10 occasions of coitus there was a significant rise in the intraluminal pH of 0.5 to 0.95 with any form of sexual stimulation and increase to a peak some 2–3 minutes after orgasm, and it usually remained elevated for 30 minutes. Unfortunately, as Levin (1992) pointed out, while these changes may be highly relevant to reproductive processes influencing sperm function by changing the ionic makeup of the uterine fluid, the intrauterine capsule used was very large, had to be kept in place by an intrauterine device (IUD), and could well have created foreign body damage to the endometrial lining during motility, caused by the arousal allowing plasma to enter the uterus. Further studies with miniaturized and less damaging electrodes are essential.

Bartholin's Glands

Kinsey et al. (1953) claimed that "During sexual activity an increase in Bartholin secretions provide one of the best indications of erotic response. Of this fact many observant participants in sexual activities are aware." They quoted 16 references to support the statement. Yet, Masters and Johnson (1966), who can hardly be called poor observers of the arousal process, having studied some thousands of orgasms, reported on the changes in Bartholin's glands and all they could say was, "It is true that Bartholin's glands do respond to sexual stimulation by secretory activity. However this . . . develops only in the late excitement phase or early-plateau phase levels of sexual tension. The nulliparous study subjects rarely produce more than a drop of the mucoid material from each duct. The multiparous occasionally develops 2 or even 3 drops of the material. Under observation, however, there never has been sufficient secretory material produced to accomplish more than minimal lubrication of the vaginal introitus." The actual fluid that lubricates the vagina, the neurogenic transudate (Levin, 1999a, 1999b), is produced practically immediately when arousal is induced, while that produced by the glands is at the stage of arousal just before orgasm, which would hardly be of much use to lubricate the vagina for coitus. Masters and Johnson thus completely dismissed the importance of the secretion of the glands in relation to either lubrication or neutralization of vaginal acidity. So whose assessment of Bartholin's glandular function during arousal are we to accept?

Apart from a near 13-year-old French review by Chretien and Berthou (1994), there has been no published investigative study of Bartholin's glands in arousal since that of Masters and Johnson some 40 years ago. The only new interesting fact about the glands that has come to my attention was a personal report from an experimental investigation of sexual arousal in a female subject; no overt Bartholin's gland secretion was seen, but when the observer pressed into the glandular area a significant secretion was expressed. Could it be that Masters and Johnson missed the fact that the glandular secretion is normally expressed during coitus by the pressure of the thrusting penis at the introitus during coitus? We obviously need new observations and experimentation before we completely discount the introital lubricative function of these glands.

Skene's (Paraurethral) Glands

Kinsey et al. (1953) remarked that the prostate and seminal vesicles of the male have embryonic equivalents in the female embryo but that "they never develop in the adult female and do not produce any secretions equivalent to the male." This, unfortunately, is a piece of misinformation because about 90% of females do have some developed (vestigial) prostatic tissue that is known as Skene's glands (Tepper, Jagirdar, Heath, & Geller, 1984), found localized in the urethra, approximately 10% of the glandular tissue being around the area of the bladder sphincter but the main part of the tissue in the more distal urethra in 66% of women (Levin, 2003b). Masters and Johnson did not mention the glands or their activity in their studies of female sexual arousal, but in some women they can produce a small urethral discharge during sexual arousal and especially at orgasm, the so-called "female ejaculation." The glands have also been linked to the controversial G-spot (Levin, 2003b), an area of the anterior vaginal wall said to be highly sensitive to strong digital/penile stimulation (Grafenberg, 1950). Zaviacic (1999) has recently published a monograph on the glands and their possible function(s).

A fascinating pilot study by Santamaria (1997) investigated whether the vestigial paraurethral glands actually secreted in all women during orgasm, but found that the secretion of many (most?) back-fluxed retrogradely into the bladder and urine rather than becoming expressed through the urethra to the outside. Urine samples were estimated before and after orgasm with a microparticle enzyme immunoassay for the one of the gland's secretory product prostate specific antigen (PSA). It was found in the postorgasmic urine in 75% of women after orgasm, but not in their preorgasmic sample. If this result can be confirmed, it may be a possible forensic test/objective marker for orgasm in women. The study needs repeating with a more sensitive immunoradiometric test of the PSA and to see whether orgasm is essential to produce the PSA in the urine or whether just sexual arousal is the cause.

Corpus Spongiosum in Men and Women

In men, the softer erectile tissue of the corpus spongiosum surrounds the penile urethra, protecting it from being occluded by the hardness of the erect corpora cavernosa, and constitutes the erectile tissue of the glans, its softness preventing damage to the female genitalia. The corpus spongiosum system in the penis is a low-pressure erectile tissue being engorged with only one-third to one-half of that in the corpus cavernosum.

In women, the corpus spongiosum appears not to be as localized as in the male and has a controversial dispersed distribution. The erectile tissue invested around the urethra has been regarded as spongiosum; also the periurethral mucous membrane (the area surrounding the urethral meatus) as the equivalent of the penile glans (van Turnhout et al., 1995) and the vaginal bulbs that unite ventrally to the urethral meatus ending in the glans of the clitoris (van Turnhout et al.).

The penile glans (corpus cavernosum erectile tissue) is acknowledged as the most sensitive part of the human penis, while the clitoral glans (of similar erectile tissue makeup) is also thought of as the most sensitive part of the female's genitalia, but the "periurethral glans" has generally been ignored as an important part of the sensitive erotic tissue of the female. It has been suggested, from direct observations of erotic videos of coitus, that in-and-out coital penile thrusting stimulates the periurethral glans (Levin, 1991) and, moreover, this may be an important factor in the inducing of orgasm by coitus in some women. The erotic area has been ignored and no investigation, whether laboratory or questionnaire-based, has furthered our knowledge.

The Breasts

One obvious nongenital area that has strong sexual connotations is the breasts, with their attendant nipples and areola. According to Robinson and Short (1977), before puberty their sensitivity to pain and touch show no difference between the sexes, but after puberty the tactile sensitivity of a woman's breasts (all areas) becomes greater than that of the male's. Moreover, it varies with the menstrual cycle, having a maximal sensitivity at midcycle and at menstruation, both phases that have been proposed to be times when women have their greatest sexual desire (see Levin, 2001, for references). Stimulation of the nipple/areola leads to the release of prolactin in both men and nonlactating women (Kolodney, Jacobs, & Daughaday, 1972). It has been claimed that prolactin released at orgasm may be the biological "off switch" for human sexual arousal (see Levin, 2003c, for references). Whether its release by breast stimulation also reduces sexual arousal has not been studied, even though in the repertoire of most men's attempts at foreplay stimulation of the female breast is used in the belief that it arouses women sexually.

Kinsey et al. (1953) claimed that although female breasts are much larger than the male's, females are only moderately aroused by their tactile stimulation and that the handling of the female breast by males may well be more arousing to them than to the females. The stimulation of the male breast by females in order to arouse them is not so frequent an occurrence. Because these opinions were given over 50 years ago and sexual behaviors are known to change with time, Levin and Meston (2006) reinvestigated the use of breast/nipple stimulation during love making by young adult males and females (95% between the ages of 18 and 22) with a questionnaire. Unlike the opinion-based conclusions of Kinsey et al., they found that 82% of females and even 52% of males reported that breast/nipple stimulation caused or enhanced their sexual arousal. Of the women 59% had asked for their nipples to be stimulated during love making, while 17% of males also requested this activity. Only 7% of the males and females found that the stimulation decreased their sexual arousal. Exactly how breast/nipple stimulation induces or enhances sexual arousal is not known. No studies have yet been undertaken on brain imaging during such activity.

Genital Reflexes

Reflexes can be elicited from the male and female genitals. The vagina has often been thought of as a simple conduit for the passage of the menses, penis, semen, and fetus. Probably the first to reveal that female pelvic reflexes could be obtained was the study by Ringrose (1966). Unfortunately, the reflexes that he observed and described initially did not appear to have a significant physiological utility so the report was overlooked and ignored. In fact, in a fascinating short note some 11 years later, Ringrose (1977) reported that when he examined rape victims within 12 hours of the rape, 17 out of the 18 did not have these pelvic reflexes. When the examination occurred more than 12 hours after the alleged offense, 5 out of 7 had the reflexes present. These findings may be of great importance in forensic examinations of rape cases in that the inhibition of the reflexes may present objective evidence of the alleged rape. Obviously a lot more work needs to be undertaken. Since his studies, however, a number of workers have shown that reflexes can indeed be elicited from the vagina usually by increases/decreases in luminal pressure. These are listed in Table 2 in historical order with their name, method of activation by their respective stimuli, and their possible/suggested sexual role. They all involve either changes in pelvic or genital muscle activity or changes in genital blood flow. The stimuli used to activate most (but not all) of the reflexes to a very large extent mimic the activity of the thrusting penis during coitus. All of the reflexes, including those of the Ringrose (1966) study, have been described previously in some detail in a recent review by Levin (2003a). The rationale of that review was to examine whether women gained anything from coitus apart from pregnancy. The conclusion after the characterization of all the reflexes and their possible effects on the muscles and pelvic/genital blood flow was that the reflexes gained and maintained vaginal/clitoral and pelvic functionality.

It is surprising how our ideas about sperm transport in the female reproductive tract from coital ejaculation have changed. According to Dickinson (1949), in coitus, the canal of the penis and the canal of the uterus were frequently said to "become one continuous conduit, the two canals along an identical axis, the urinary meatus fast against the external os, and the semen being injected directly into the womb." This "interlocking"

Table 2. *Female Genital Reflexes (ISC = Ischiocavernosus Muscle, BC = Bulbocavernosus Muscle)*

Reflex	Stimulus/activation	Possible sexual role
Clitoro-pelvic Gillan & Brindley (1979)	clitoral vibration sustained tonic contraction of pelvic floor muscles	not specified
Vagino-cavernosus Shafik (1993)	vaginal balloon rapid distension—transient contraction of ISC and BC	increase in tumescence of clitoris "milking" penile urethra
Vagino-levator Shafik (1995b)	vaginal balloon rapid distension	aids in "vaginal tenting" lifts cervix away from posterior vaginal floor
Vagino-puborectalis Shafik (1995c)	vaginal balloon rapid distension contraction of puborectalis	not specified (prevents fecal leakage during coitus?)
Vagino-clitoral Lavoisier et al. (1995)	vaginal balloon rapid distension on insertion and withdrawal—increase in velocity clitoral blood flow	enhanced blood flow to clitoris
Vagino-vesicourethral Shafik & El-Sibai (2001)	vaginal balloon distension bladder relaxation and urethral sphincter contracts	prevents urine leakage during coitus protects sperm

mechanism was coupled with sterility on the basis that if the former didn't occur, it was the chief cause of the failure of conception. Dickinson, however, using a test tube as a phallus, observed that the glans and penile meatus usually overshot the downward pointing cervix and that the penile and cervical canals were usually at right angles to one another. He argued that as the penis delivers the ejaculate, the glans passing and repassing the cervical os rubs the semen against its slit and it is incorporated into any outhanging cervical mucous (a kind of inunction). In fact, most men when

Table 3. *Human Male Genital Reflexes (ISC = Ischiocavernosus Muscle, BC = Bulbocavernosus Muscle)*

Reflex	Stimulus/activation	Possible sexual role
Glans-ischiocavernosus Lavoisier, Proulx & Courtois (1988)	increase or decrease in pressure on glans (18–35mm Hg) contraction of ISC & BC	coital glans pressure changes promotes penile rigidity
Glans-perineal flow Lavoisier, Aloui, Schmidt, & Gally (1993)	pressure on glans (30, 150mm HG) increase (x 8) in perineal flow	coital glans pressure augments flow into corpus cavernosum
Peno-motor (glans-puborectalis & levator ani)	mechanical stimulation of glans	prevention of urine and fecal leakage during coitus
Shafik (1995d)	contraction levator ani & puborectalis (associated with contraction external urethral, prostatic, & anal sphincter)	squeezing prostate secretion into urethra
Glans-vasal Shafik (1998)	vibration glans ISC contracts	facilitates seminal emission
Urethromuscular Shafik (1998) Vodusek & Fowler (1999)	vibration glans contraction of BC and external urethral sphincter	facilitates seminal emission
Glans-external anal sphincter Shafik (1999)	stimulate glans contraction external anal sphincter	prevention of fecal expulsion during coitus

they ejaculate during coitus thrust the penis as high up into the vagina as possible and then remain relatively immobile as the sensitivity of the glans to frictional movement becomes transiently intolerable.

Levin (2002) has proposed a quite different model for coitus, ejaculation, and sperm transport. This involves the fundamental importance of "vaginal tenting" (see vagino-levator activity in Table 2), where the cervico-uterus complex is lifted well away from the posterior vaginal floor (and penis) and the back of the vagina balloons out, creating a seminal receptacle (Masters & Johnson, 1966). This delays any rapid sperm transport from the coital ejaculate deposited in it, facilitating seminal decoagulation and sperm capacitation priming and reducing the transport into the fallopian tubes of noncapacitated spermatozoa initially incompetent to fertilize. The fastest transport of spermatozoa from the cervix to the fallopian tubes occurs in the nonaroused female by uterine/subendometrial smooth muscle peristalsis, and there is some evidence that even this may be reduced for a time after coitus (see Levin, 2005, for references). It may also be a cause of the inhibition of pelvic reflexes observed by Ringrose (1977) after alleged rapes described in the section on genital reflexes.

What of genital reflexes in the male? A number have been described and can be elicited especially from the penile glans. They are suggested to be activated during coital thrusting and are claimed to be involved in enhancing erection stiffness and in emission and ejaculation. They are listed, as for the female, in Table 3.

Surprisingly, most textbook chapters of human reproductive physiology ignore both the female and male genital reflexes and do not bother to describe them. Such disregard does not give due acknowledgment to the complexities of genital function during coitus, regarding it merely as a simple piston moving in a cylinder. The range of the reflexes described shows the weakness of this approach.

Conclusion

Reviewing the human sexual response in relation to the anatomy and function of the male and female genitalia has revealed a number of significant differences that deserve study. Such study is not a trivial pursuit, as the knowledge gained will lead to a better understanding of normal genital function and hence of better treatment of sexual and reproductive dysfunction—the treasure trove, perhaps.

References

Adaikan, P. G., Kottegoda, S. R., & Ratnam, S. S. (1986). Is vasoactive intestinal polypeptide the principal transmitter involved in human penile erection? *Journal of Urology, 135,* 638–640.

Blum, M., & Pulini, M. (1980). Vaginal sensations after injection of thyrotropin releasing hormones. *Lancet, 2,* 43.

Bohlen, G., Held, J. P., & Sanderson, M. O. (1982). Response of the circumvaginal musculature during masturbation. In B. Graber (Ed.), *Circumvaginal musculature and sexual function* (pp. 43–60). Basel, Switzerland: Kager AG.

Bohlen, G., Held, J. P., Sanderson, M. O., & Ahlgren, A. (1982). The female orgasm: Pelvic contractions. *Archives of Sexual Behavior, 11,* 367–386.

Burnett, A. L., Calvin, D. C., Silver, R. I., Peppas, D. S., & Docimo, S. G. (1997). Immunohistochemical description of nitric oxide synthase isoforms in human clitoris. *Journal of Urology, 158,* 75–78.

Burnett, A. L., Lowenstein, C. J., Bredt, D. S., Chang, T. S., & Snyder, S. H. (1992). Nitric oxide: A physiologic mediator of penile erection. *Science, 257,* 401–403.

Cartledge, J., Minhas, S., & Eardley, I. (2001). The role of nitric oxide in penile erection. *Expert Opinion on Pharmacotherapy, 2,* 95–107.

Chretien, F. C., & Berthou, J. (1994). The major Bartholin vestibular glands and their secretion: Anatomy, physical properties, and physiological roles. *Contraception, Fertility, and Sexuality, 22,* 720–726.

Dickinson, R. L. (1949). *Human sex anatomy* (pp. 93–94). Baltimore: Williams & Wilkins Company.

Donnellan, P., Breathnach, O., & Crown, J. P. (2001). Odynorgasmia. *Scandinavian Journal of Urology and Nephrology, 35,* 158.

Fox, C. A., Colson, R. A., & Watson, B. W. (1982). Continuous measurement of vaginal and intra-uterine pH by radio-telemetry during human coitus. In Z. Hoch & H. L. Lief (Eds.), *Sexology* (pp. 110–113). Amsterdam: Excerpta Medica.

Gerstenberg, T. C., Levin, R. J., & Wagner, G. (1989). Electrical activity of corpus cavernosum during flaccidity and erection of the human penis: A new diagnostic method. *Journal of Urology, 142,* 723–725.

Gerstenberg, T. C., Levin, R. J., & Wagner, G. (1990). Erection and ejaculation in man. Assessment of the electromyographic activity of the bulbocavernosus and ischiocavernosus muscle. *British Journal of Urology, 63,* 395–402.

Gillan, P., & Brindley, G. S. (1979). Vaginal and pelvic floor responses to sexual stimulation. *Psychophysiology, 6,* 471–481.

Grafenberg, E. (1950). The role of the urethra in female orgasm. *International Journal of Sexology, 3,* 145–148.

Hedlund, P., Ny, L., Alm, P., & Andersson, K. E. (2000). Cholinergic nerves in human corpus cavernosum and spongiosum contain nitric oxide synthase and heme oxygenase. *Journal of Urology, 164,* 868–875.

Hoyle, C. H. V., Stones, R. W., Robson, I., Whitley, K., & Burnstock, G. (1996). Innervation of the vasculature and microcirculation of the human vagina by NOS and neuropeptide-containing nerves. *Journal of Anatomy, 188,* 633–644.

Jost, A. (1973). Becoming male. *Advances in Bioscience, 10,* 3–13.

Kaplan, H. S. (1993). Post-ejaculatory pain syndrome. *Journal of Sex & Marital Therapy, 19,* 91–103.

Khalifé, S., & Binik, Y. M. (2003). Clitoral blood flow as a measure of sexual arousal. *Ultrasound in Medicine & Biology, 29*(Suppl. 1), S150.

Kinsey, A. C., Pomeroy, W. B., Martin, C. E., & Gebhard, P. H. (1953). *Sexual behavior in the human female.* Philadelphia: W. B. Saunders.

Kolodney, R. C., Jacobs, L. S., & Daughaday, W. H. (1972). Mammary stimulation causes prolactin secretion in non-lactating women. *Nature, 238,* 284–286.

Laan, E., van Lunsen, R. H. W., Everaerd, W., Riley, A., Scott, E., & Boolell, M. (2002). The enhancement of vaginal vasocongestion by sildenafil in healthy premenopausal women. *Journal of Women's Health Gender-Gased Medicine, 11,* 357–365.

Lavoisier, P., Aloui, R., Schmidt, M., & Gally, M. (1993). Considerable increase in the perineal arterial flow secondary to stimulation of the glans penis. In French. *Annales d'urologie (Paris), 27,* 172–175.

Lavoisier, P., Aloui, R., Schmidt, M., & Watrelot, A. (1995). Clitoral blood flow increases following vaginal pressure stimulation. *Archives of Sexual Behavior, 24,* 37–45.

Lavoisier, P., Proulx, J., & Courtois, F. (1988). Reflex contractions of the ischiocavernosus muscles following electrical and pressure stimulations. *Journal of Urology, 139,* 396–399.

Levin, R. J. (1981). The female orgasm—a current appraisal. *Journal of Psychosomatic Research, 25,* 119–133.

Levin, R. J. (1991). VIP, vagina, clitoral and periurethral glans—an update on human female genital arousal. *Experimental & Clinical Endocrinology, 98,* 61–69.

Levin, R. J. (1992). The mechanisms of human female sexual arousal. *Annual Review of Sex Research, 3,* 1–48.

Levin, R. J. (1997). Assessing human female sexual arousal by vaginal photoplethysmography—a critical examination. *European Journal of Medical Sexology (Sexologies), 6,* 25–31.

Levin, R. J. (1999a). The impact of the menopause on the physiology of genital function. *Menopause Review, 1V,* 23–31.

Levin, R. J. (1999b). Measuring the menopause genital changes—a critical account of the laboratory procedures past and for the future. *Menopause Review, 1V,* 49–57.

Levin, R. J. (2001). Sexual desire and the deconstruction and reconstruction of the human female sexual response model of Masters and Johnson. In W. Everaerd, E. Laan, & S. Both (Eds.), *Sexual appetite, desire and motivation: Energetics of the sexual system* (pp. 63–93). Amsterdam: Royal Netherlands Academy of Arts.

Levin, R. J. (2002). The physiology of sexual arousal in the human female: A recreational and procreational synthesis. *Archives of Sexual Behavior, 31,* 404–411.

Levin, R. J. (2003a). Do women gain anything from coitus apart from pregnancy? Changes in the human female genital tract activated by coitus. *Journal of Sex & Marital Therapy, 29*(Supp.), 59–69.

Levin, R. J. (2003b). The G-spot—reality or illusion? *Sexual and Relationship Therapy, 18,* 117–119.

Levin, R. J. (2003c). Is prolactin the biological "off switch" for human sexual arousal? *Sexual and Relationship Therapy, 18,* 237–243.

Levin, R. J. (2004). An orgasm is . . . who defines what an orgasm is? *Sexual and Relationship Therapy, 19,* 101–106.

Levin, R. J. (2005). Sexual arousal—its physiological roles in human reproduction. *Annual Review of Sex Research, 16,* 154–189.

Levin, R. J., & Meston, C. (2006). Nipple/breast stimulation and sexual arousal in young men and women. *Journal of Sexual Medicine, 3,* 450–454.

Levin, R. J., & Wagner, G. (1986). TRH and vaginal blood flow—effects in conscious women and anaesthetized sheep. *Journal of Physiology (London), 378,* 83P.

Mah, K., & Binik, I. (2001). The nature of human orgasm: A critical review of major trends. *Clinical Psychology Review, 21,* 823–856.

Masters, W. H., & Johnson, V. E. (1966). *Human sexual response.* Boston: Little, Brown.

Mathias, C. J., Bannister, R. B., Cortelli, P., Helsop, K., Polak, J. M., Raimbach, S., et al. (1990). Clinical, autonomic and therapeutic observations of two siblings with postural hypotension and sympathetic failure due to an inability to synthesize nor-adrenaline from dopamine because of a deficiency of dopamine beta hydroxylase. *Quarterly Journal of Medicine, 75,* 617–633.

Medina, C. A. (2002). Clitoral priapism: A rare condition presenting as a cause of vulvar pain. *Obstetrics and Gynecology, 100,* 1089–1091.

Meston, C., Hull, E., Levin, R. J., & Sipski, M. (2004). Women's orgasm. In T. F. Lue, R. Basson, R. Rosen, F. Giuliano, S. Khoury, & F. Montorsi (Eds.), *Sexual medicine: Sexual dysfunctions in men and women* (pp. 783–850). Paris: Health Publications.

O'Connell, H. E., & DeLancey, J. O. L. (2005). Clitoral anatomy in nulliparous, healthy, premenopausal volunteers using unenhanced magnetic resonance imaging. *Journal of Urology, 173,* 2060–2063.

O'Connell, H. E., Hutson, J. M., Anderson, C. R., & Plenter, R. J. (1998). Anatomical relationship between urethra and clitoris. *Journal of Anatomy, 159,* 1892–1897.

Rees, M. A., O'Connell, H. E., Plenter, R. J., & Hutson, J. M. (2000). The suspensory ligaments of the clitoris: Connective tissue supports of the erectile tissues of the female urogenital region. *Clinical Anatomy, 13,* 397–403.

Ringrose, C. A.D. (1966). Pelvic reflex phenomena: Incidence and significance. *Journal of Reproduction and Fertility, 12,* 161–165.

Ringrose, C. A.D. (1977). Pelvic reflexes in rape complainants. *Canadian Journal of Public Health, 68,* 31.

Robinson, J. E., & Short, R. V. (1977). Changes in breast sensitivity at puberty, during menstrual cycle and at parturition. *British Medical Journal, i,* 1188–1191.

Santamaria, F. C. (1997). Female ejaculation, myth and reality. In *Proceedings of 13th World Congress of Sexology,* Valencia, Spain.

Shafik, A. (1993). Vaginocavernosus reflex—clinical significance and role in sexual act. *Gynecologic & Obstetric Investigation, 35,* 114–117.

Shafik, A. (1995a). Responses of the urethral and intracorporeal pressures to cavernosus muscle stimulation: Role of the muscles in erection and ejaculation. *Urology, 46,* 85–88.

Shafik, A. (1995b). Vagino-levator reflex: Description of a reflex and its role in sexual performance. *European Journal of Obstetrics, Gynecology, and Reproductive Biology, 60,* 161–164.

Shafik, A. (1995c). Vagino-puborectalis reflex. *International Journal of Gynaecology and Obstetrics, 51,* 61–62.

Shafik, A. (1995d). The peno-motor reflex: Study of the response of the puborectalis and levator ani muscles to glans penis stimulation. *International Journal of Impotence Research, 7,* 239–246.

Shafik, A. (1998). The mechanism of ejaculation: The glans-vasal and urethromuscular reflexes. *Archives of Andrology, 41,* 71–78.

Shafik, A. (1999). Physioanatomic entirety of external sphincter with bulbocavernosus muscle. *Archives of Andrology, 42,* 45–54.

Shafik, A., & El-Sibai, O. (2001). Effect of vaginal distention on vesicourethral function with identification of the vagino-vesicourethral reflex. *Journal of Urology, 165,* 887–889.

Shafik, A., & El-Sibai, O. (2002). Study of the pelvic floor muscles in vaginismus: A concept of pathogenesis. *European Journal of Obstetrics, Gynecology, and Reproductive Biology, 105,* 67–70.

Sherfey, M. J. (1973). *The nature and evolution of female sexuality.* New York: Vintage Books.

Tepper, S. L., Jagirdar, J., Heath, D., & Geller, S. A. (1984). Homology between the female paraurethral (Skene's) glands and the prostate. *Archives of Pathology and Laboratory Medicine, 108,* 423–425.

Toesca, A., Stolfi, V. M., & Cocchia, D. (1996). Immunohistochemical study of the corpora cavernosa of the human clitoris. *Journal of Anatomy, 188,* 513–520.

Van der Velde, J., Laan, E., & Everaerd, W. (2001). Vaginismus, a component of a general defensive reaction. An investigation of pelvic floor muscle activity during exposure to emotion-inducing film excerpts in women with and without vaginismus. *International Urogynecology Journal and Pelvic Floor Dysfunction, 12,* 328–331.

Van Turnhout, A. A. W. M., Hage, J. J., & van Diest, P. J. (1995). The female corpus spongiosum revisited. *Acta Obstetricia Scandinavica, 74,* 762–771.

Vance, E. B., & Wagner, N. N. (1976). Written descriptions of orgasm: A study of sex difference. *Archives of Sexual Behavior, 5,* 87–98.

Vardi, Y., Gruenwald, I., & Sprecher, E. (2000). The role of the corpus cavernosum electromyography. *Current Opinion in Urology, 10,* 635–638.

Vodusek, D. B., & Fowler, C. (1999). Clinical neurophysiology. In C. J. Fowler (Ed.), *Neurology of the bladder, bowel and sexual dysfunction* (pp. 109–143). Boston: Butterworth Heineman.

Wagner, G., & Gerstenberg, T. (1987). Intracavernosus injection of vasoactive intestinal polypeptide (VIP) does not induce erection in man *per se. World Journal of Urology, 5,* 171–177.

Wagner, G., & Levin, R. J. (1980). Effect of atropine and methyl atropine on human vagina blood flow, sexual arousal and climax. *Acta Pharmacologica et Toxicologica, 46,* 321–325.

Wayman, C., Morren, D., Turner, L., Naylor, A., & van der Graaf, P. (2002). Evidence that neutral endopeptidase is involved in the regulation of female genital blood flow. Abstract. In *Proceedings of Annual Meeting (Vancouver) International Society for the Study of Women's Sexual Health,* October 10–13.

Wilson, J. (1978). Sexual differentiation. *Annual Review Physiology, 140,* 279–308.

Yilmaz, U., Soylu, A., Ozcan, C., & Caliskan, O. (2002). Clitoral electromyography. *Journal of Urology, 167,* 616–620.

Zaviacic, M. (1999). *The human female prostate.* Bratislava: Slovak Academic Press.

Discussion Paper

JOHN BANCROFT

I feel privileged to be the discussant of these first two excellent papers, which are going to make a very substantial contribution to the book that will result from this meeting. There are many points raised by these papers that I would love to discuss, but I will restrict myself to just a few. Roy's comparison of the vagina and the clitoris raises an essential issue in our psychophysiological assessment of sexual response and indeed sexual arousal in women. Is the vagina telling us something different to the clitoris and, if so, what? As most of us are measuring changes in the vagina, how do they relate to the changes in the clitoris? We are aware of the limitations of the VPA assessment and Roy has his own methods of measuring genital response (Levin, 1992). But even with a better method the question of the comparison of the vagina and the clitoris remains, I think, of central importance. He's just been telling us that in the clitoris, nitrergic mediation is as important as in the penis, whereas in the vagina it is not. Are blood flow changes in the clitoris specific to sexual response, as they are in the penis? And to what extent are blood flow changes in the vagina part of a wider vascular arousal pattern than you would get with penile or clitoral tumescence? Julia Heiman is going to tell us later on that the VPA correlated better with subjective arousal than clitoral volume. That reminds me of an early study by Lennart Levi (1969), where he measured urinary catecholamines as physiological markers of general arousal and found that they correlated better with subjective ratings of sexual arousal in women than that in men, which I have always interpreted as meaning that men judge their arousal by how much erection they have and women by how aroused they feel in a more general arousal sense (Bancroft, 1978).

I also want to briefly return to another old study, which I did around 20 years ago with Chris Bell, a vascular physiologist from Australia (Bancroft & Bell, 1984), and which has been totally ignored since, like Roy's TRH study. We used exactly the same kind of photometer as used for VPA, to measure pulse amplitude on the dorsum of the penis, in parallel with penile circumference. Julia Heiman, I think, had done something similar before us, with John Hatch. Fixing the photometer to the dorsum of the penis was the first methodological challenge. If you fix it by strapping something around the penis, then, as the erection develops, pressure on the photometer increases, producing an artifactual reduction in the photometric signal. We ended up using a corn plaster to adhere the photometer to the dorsum of the penis, which did not result in increased pressure as tumescence developed. We also had a mercury-in-rubber strain gauge, proximal to the photometer. So we measured pulse amplitude and penile circumference in parallel. Typically we found an increase in pulse amplitude parallel with the development of tumescence. However, that wasn't always the case, and a pattern that we found in men with psychogenic erectile dysfunction showed a dissociation between the pulse amplitude and tumescence, with the pulse amplitude tending to go down with the onset of the stimulus, followed by some degree of tumescence and then an increase in pulse amplitude after the erotic stimulus was off, often remaining increased for some time (Bancroft et al., 1984). In some cases, there was quite a dramatic reduction in penile pulse amplitude with onset of erotic stimulus. We were measuring pulse amplitude in the ear in parallel, which didn't change. In men with diabetic autonomic neuropathy we found a further pattern where there was pulse amplitude increase but no tumescence. We assumed that the photocell was measuring what was happening in the dorsal artery. The dorsal artery is important because, unlike the deep penile artery within the corpora cavernosa, it is not affected by the increase in intracavernosal pressure as an erection develops. It seemed to us that whatever the pulse amplitude signal was measuring was under some sort of control independent of what was happening in the erectile tissues. It wasn't clearly related to finger or ear pulse amplitude, which we measured in parallel. This raises the question of whether, when we're looking at the vaginal pulse amplitude changing, we're looking at a vascular response pattern that may be distinct from that more specifically related to tumescence in the clitoris. I can't answer these questions. But I am suggesting that in our pursuit of vaginal pulse amplitude, however we're going to measure it, with whatever device, we should be looking closely at its relationship to other indices of arousal, such as blood pressure change, pulse pressure change, peripheral vasomotor tone, and so on.

Also, a few words about Serge Stoléru's paper. I have no doubts that the next chapter in human sex research, and I hope this is not too alarming for the animal researchers, is going to rely quite heavily on functional brain imaging. I found Serge's review very helpful. I particularly appreciated his layman's guide to how PET and fMRI work. Most of the papers on brain imaging that I've read have been in very technical journals, which for many of us are difficult to comprehend, and he gave very nice, simple, and friendly descriptions of these two methods. Early in the paper he makes a point that I think has significance for the whole of this meeting, and that is the issue of participation bias in psychophysiological research. What type of person is it who will go and sit in an fMRI scanner and be stimulated sexually? Erick will be touching on this in his presentation later on today, but we both feel there has been a curious neglect or even denial of individual differences and how they might impact on the results of psychophysiological research. Dysfunctional subjects may be compared to "normals," but how comparable so-called "normals" are, across studies, and how comparable the "normals" who participate are with the "normals" who don't participate are questions that have not been adequately addressed. I feel this field should be moving toward agreement on some basic trait measures that will allow comparability. Inevitably the *N*s are going to be small, very small, in these brain imaging studies. We should have some agreed way, some agreed measures that can allow comparability across studies as well as influence selection of subjects. Our Sexual Inhibition Scales/Sexual Excitation Scales (SIS/SES) offer one way of dealing with this.

I strongly suspect that as we progress in the use of brain imaging in this field, our basic concepts of sexual response and sexual arousal are going to be challenged. At the present, we may apply concepts of sexual desire and sexual arousal, although having said that, considerable confusion and disagreement prevails about which is which. As for sexual motivation—I have been struggling with the concept of motivation for some time. In any case, all these concepts assume the presence of a black box, which is the brain, and when we start to look into that black box we will probably have to start afresh with our conceptual analysis of what we're dealing with. Already brain imaging is restructuring how we conceptualize motivation. For example, a recent study by Breiter and his colleagues (Breiter, Aharon, Kahneman, Dale, & Shizgal, 2001) looking at dopaminergic mechanisms with brain imaging used a model of expectancy of gains and losses, the likelihood of winning and losing. There is animal work that is comparable, that might get us to think about motivation in a rather different way than we are used to thinking about it. We should not expect the complexities of brain activity to fit comfortably into our conceptual models. We don't want to make the same mistakes that the phrenologists did just over a hundred years ago. What we need are clear ideas of relevant processes that can be identified by brain imaging and how specific they are to situations and stimuli. And already, as we've been told, much of the activity being recorded in these brain imaging studies is not specific to sexual stimuli.

Serge, in his paper, gives us a very helpful review of the limited evidence so far. I've read some of the papers that he's reviewing and I think he's downplaying to some extent the variability in the results. He has to do this in order to give some sort of summary, but my impression is of incredible variability in which areas are activated and which are not, across subjects, with some "common ground" being apparent. Does it mean that when a person's brain is activated in area A and another one's in area B, they are doing different things? What do these differences mean? You could say this is in the nature of variance in scientific evidence, but we're going to have to deal with this noise and it's going to be very challenging in brain imaging research. In addition, apart from the imaging technology that is obviously going to be developing, this new field of brain imaging in sexual arousal has started with very varied methodologies in terms of stimulus patterns and the types of response one is trying to assess. In my view, it is essential that some methodological consistency become established. To begin with, I would propose that paradigms of stimulus and response are used that can be directly paralleled, using other psychophysiological techniques. So if you're using something in an fMRI scanner, what would happen if you used the same type of stimulus response paradigm in an ordinary psychophysiology lab where you can measure a lot of things that aren't measurable inside an fMRI scanner? You can't, I think I'm right in saying, measure genital response within an fMRI machine. We need rich, testable hypotheses, and we've got some good ones in Serge's paper. They need to be refutable, and they will need to be modified as evidence begins to collect, but I think a great start has been made.

References

Bancroft, J. (1978). Psychological and physiological responses to sexual stimuli in men and women. In L. Levi (Ed.), *Society, stress and disease: Vol. 3. The productive and reproductive age* (pp. 154–163). New York: Oxford University Press.

Bancroft, J., & Bell, C. (1984). Simultaneous recording of penile diameter and penile arterial pulse during laboratory-based erotic stimulation in normal subjects. *Journal of Psychosomatic Research, 29*, 303–313.

Bancroft, J., Bell, C., Ewing, D. J., McCulloch, D. K., Warner, P., & Clarke, B. F. (1984). Assessment of erectile function in diabetic and non-diabetic impotence by simultaneous recording of penile diameter and penile arterial pulse. *Journal of Psychosomatic Research, 29*, 315–324.

Breiter, H. C., Aharon, I., Kahneman, D., Dale, A., & Shizgal, P. (2001). Functional imaging of neural responses to expectancy and experience of monetary gains and losses. *Neuron, 20*, 619–639.

Levi, L. (1969). Sympatho-adrenomedullary activity, diuresis and emotional reactions during visual sexual stimulation in human females and males. *Psychosomatic Medicine, 31*, 251–268.

Levin, R. J. (1992). The mechanisms of human female sexual arousal. *Annual Review of Sex Research, 3*, 1–48.

General Discussion

Walter Everaerd: I have two questions, Serge. What I get from your paper and comparing it with imaging and studies about emotions is that it's quite similar and I'm curious about how you try to be specific in your task, the psychological task—the "activation" as they call it in imaging. Is the only thing you do show movies or do you also show pictures? How do you do that—the task specificity—to relate it to what you see in these imaging results?

Serge Stoléru: You're asking me about the nature of the stimuli we use?

Walter Everaerd: Yes, and I am asking about this because in most imaging studies about emotions, the stimuli are very well circumscribed and simple, and the stimuli we use in psychophysiological research—and maybe you use them too—are very complex. They are movies or complex pictures of people interacting and so on. My second question is about what you showed about the insulae. The insulae have become popular recently because they seem to represent, as a sensory area, the body, the integration of bodily and sensory information, and it might be a step up to knowing some things about consciousness and subjective experience. That's a speculation. You told us about activity in the insula as a manifestation of the low sexual desired people, and my question is whether you consider that to be a very specific sexual activation or a general emotional activation, because it's well known that when there's no arousal produced in the emotion, the insulae do not show any activation. There's my question: whether you consider what you saw in the insulae specific for sexual matters, or as a general emotional phenomenon. That is, there is no bodily autonomic or whatever activation, so no feedback from the body.

Serge Stoléru: In the first study, we used videos that were derived from commercially available films, which are complex stimuli. In the second study, we felt that if we used only films, there would be a problem because films trigger the activation of visual areas that mediate the analysis of body movements and we did not know whether these areas that we showed in the first study to be activated were analyzing body movements or were processing the sexual motivational significance of the targets, so we wanted to use still pictures. So in the second study we used both films and still pictures that were representing women and the analysis that we did—and that we have just shown in our presentation—is what is called *conjunction analysis* (Price & Friston, 1997). The purpose is to reveal the regions that respond both to films and to slides, but while less complex than films, such slides are also complex. I don't know how you could use simpler stimuli in this domain of investigation. You could imagine using very simple targets, if you will, maybe derived from Heather Hoffmann's talk about conditioning. If you condition a sexual response to a simple stimulus by previously pairing a complex sexual stimulus with a very simple one, maybe then you could show a very simple stimulus and record the brain response to this simple stimulus that would serve as a conditioned stimulus.

Regarding the insula, actually the HSDD patients did not differ from the healthy volunteers regarding the activation of the insula. The patients who differed were the untreated hypogonadal patients. What I tried to say is that the insula is a very, very large structure, and in the patients with hypogonadism, there is a special region of the insula that is located in the rostral and upper part of the insula and where activation in response to visual sexual stimuli was observed in healthy subjects but not in untreated hypogonadal patients.

Walter Everaerd: It is a sensory area, isn't it?

Serge Stoléru: The functional anatomy of the insula is not yet entirely known. However, recent evidence indicates that the anterior part of the insula mediates emotional functions and interoceptive, that is, visceral, awareness. On the other hand, the posterior part of the insula seems to be involved in processing painful sensory stimuli.

Walter Everaerd: I asked you that because Craig, in his *Nature Reviews Neuroscience* article (2002), has written an article titled "How Do You Feel?" and he shows the insula and the activation of the insula over a great number of emotional situations.

Serge Stoléru: Right, but this leads to the question of the specificity of the neural correlates of the sexual response, and, as I tried to discuss in the paper, the brain may code for the specificity of sexual emotion in one or more of several ways. Maybe it is not the insula as a whole but specific parts within the insula—which is an "ocean" of gray matter really—so it may be a specific part of the insula that is involved in mediating the emotional aspects of sexual arousal. To give an example of such topographic specificity, when we induced sexual arousal with visual sexual stimuli, we found that a very small part of the somatosensory cortex got activated, and this part corresponds somatotopically to the cortical representation of the penis, so it's a very small part at the top of each of the postcentral gyri, which are the primary somatosensory cortices. Maybe the situation is the same in the insula; it may be a very small part of the insula that is related to the emotional aspects of sexual arousal. Another way of thinking of the specificity would be to consider that it is not the activated or deactivated areas per se that are specific, but the pattern of activation/deactivation that is specific. And still another way to account for specificity is to admit that present state functional imaging techniques do not allow one to see very small structures, such as the bed nucleus of the stria terminalis (BNST) [2.49 ± 0.16 mm^3 in heterosexual men (Zhou, Hofman, Goren, & Swaab, 1995)], or maybe you see them but you cannot distinguish them from other structures, and it could be that at the present time the power of resolution of neuroimaging techniques is too low to really know the "sexual signature" of the activation/deactivation of brain regions.

Jim Pfaus: Just a couple of things. The insula and the claustrum are both steroid concentrating regions of the brain in rats, rabbits, and macaques, and, one would venture to guess, humans. This is another way in which animal research can inform human research, because we know that these regions bind androgens and estrogens. I do have a question regarding the hypogonadal men that you tested. When Julian Davidson did his original studies on hypogonadal individuals, he found a "theory of thirds," so to speak: that some individuals were perfectly normal with their sexual responses and motivation, another third that seemed to lose their responding intermittently, and then another third that were severely disrupted. I'm wondering, were the males in your study severely disrupted? What was their sexual activity like?

Serge Stoléru: I have looked at the means, the averages, and the standard deviations and actually I was surprised by the fact that even when they were untreated, they were not very dramatically different from the normal. They were significantly different, but they were not very, very different. In terms of sexual activity (intercourse, masturbation), they were impaired, though.

Jim Pfaus: So they had normal subjective and physiological arousal? Did they evidence normal sexual desire?

Serge Stoléru: No, there were clear differences; they were clearly different from the normals, with lesser arousability to visual sexual stimuli in untreated patients, but when I read the literature before doing the study I expected more clear-cut differences, and I think also that the treatment did not induce a complete clinical normalization. Also, when you look at the picture of brain responses, for example, in the insula of the treated subjects, there is no complete, but only partial, normalization. That was very interesting because I think that, as I said yesterday in the meeting, if the insula is really involved in mediating central stimulation of the testicular secretion, if you give hormonal replacement therapy, you do not replace the function of the insula—you are giving a dose of testosterone, but the normal process by which a visual or an auditory stimulus impacts the insula, and through which the insular signal is then transmitted by a purely neural route to the testes—this process is abolished. So there are reasons to think that you do not normalize the brain function.

Marca Sipski: I have a couple of questions; the first one is for Dr. Levin. I think measuring uterine contractions would be a nice thing to do. The question is, how would you do it? Because I've thought about it and I've never thought of a way that would be useful, noninvasive, and also something that the person could tolerate during sexual activity. And then a question for Dr. McKenna: In terms of the concept of the central pattern generator in persons with spinal cord injuries, now one of the topics is training the central pattern generator for ambulation, and my question is, what would you think about training the central pattern generator in terms of improving sexual responsiveness?

Roy Levin: One of the ways of measuring the pressures inside the uterus is to put a catheter in. You can get very small ones now, extremely small ones. One of the real problems about this, of course, is putting ascending infection up, but the standard technique that you can use is to put the catheter in a glove or something like this; you put the glove up and then you break through with the catheter and it goes in so you don't take the ascending infection in. I don't know whether you can still do that nowadays.

Marca Sipski: I guess I was thinking, what about ultrasound?

Roy Levin: Well, I really don't know if you could pick up the changes. There's a lot of ultrasound with endometrium so I see no reason why you couldn't use that. All the work now that's being done on sperm transport shows that sperm doesn't swim up, it's the endometrium underneath it. There's a thin layer of smooth muscle that takes the sperm up so you don't need swimming at all, so you can go down to about level. So I should think that you could use ultrasound very easily and there are handheld ones that you can use.

Marca Sipski: Is anyone aware of anyone who's done that?

Roy Levin: The sperm transport people have been doing it for years, but nobody has induced sexual arousal. I mean, they all back off that—obstetrics, gynecology, and all that—once you introduce the words *sexual arousal*. It's easy enough to do, though.

Kevin McKenna: I was in a spinal cord meeting recently and there was a discussion of central pattern generators because sexual climax is produced by central pattern generators in a manner very similar to fictive walking. I don't see any reason why you couldn't train this system, even in the spinal cord. There's a tremendous amount of plasticity that's possible and the idea, even in a completely transected spinal cord, that you could change over time the effectiveness of certain types of stimulations, I think, is entirely possible. No one's really worked at it. I heard a talk from a spinal cord injured man who described his use of the vibrator, and it has gotten better over time. At first it was very difficult to use and he was able to use it more effectively over time. Of course, pharmacological stimulation is also a possibility once we've mapped out all of the receptors that are on these generators and so on. I think that there'll be a lot of possibilities. I do think you can train it.

Marca Sipski: I'd be interested to see you do it in an animal model.

Tillmann Krüger: I have a question for Serge concerning the sexual stimulus used in the studies and the specificity of the reaction. What do you think: Is the reaction that you observed really sex-specific? Would it be helpful to have different modes of stimuli? For example, not only audio-visual stimuli but also auditive stimuli or imagery or even tactile stimulation, and then to examine which areas are activated during the different settings and then extract sex-specific neuronal activation from nonsexual reactions.

Serge Stoléru: I think it's very important to do that. There is one study that used sexual mental imagery and there is also one study that used odors. It was a very well-designed study performed in Scandinavia using sex hormone-like compounds, not pheromones but hormone-like products. This study found activated regions similar to regions that we found activated, but it is indeed necessary to do what you suggest, that is, to use other sensory routes to show that part of the system is independent from the modality of the sensory inputs, and that part is dependent.

References

Craig, A.D. (2002). How do you feel? Interoception: The sense of the physiological condition of the body. *Nature Reviews Neuroscience, 3,* 655–666.

Price, C. J., & Friston K. J. (1997). Cognitive conjunction: A new approach to brain activation experiments. *NeuroImage, 5,* 261–270.

Zhou, J.-N., Hofman, M. A., Gooren, L. J., & Swaab, D. F (1995). A sex difference in the human brain and its relation to transsexuality. *Nature, 378,* 68–70.

Autonomic Nervous System Influences

The Role of the Sympathetic Nervous System in Female Sexual Arousal

CINDY M. MESTON AND ANDREA BRADFORD

Anatomy of the Sympathetic Nervous System in the Female Genitalia

The autonomic nervous system provides most of the innervation to the internal genital organs and is essential to the sexual response. It has generally been presumed that parasympathetic activity is responsible for achieving sexual arousal through localized vasocongestion, resulting in genital swelling and lubrication, while orgasm is mediated through a sympathetic response. However, the interaction of these two systems is complex and remains poorly understood. Innervation of the genitalia in human females runs primarily through a common network of converging autonomic and sensory fibers known as the pelvic plexus. In some nonhuman mammals, it has been observed that sympathetic and parasympathetic fibers may dually innervate a few postsynaptic neurons in the pelvic plexus. In addition, sympathetic and parasympathetic neurons in the pelvic plexus may sometimes communicate laterally (Dail, 1996). However, the degree to which different nerve types in the plexus might interact with one another remains speculative. The significance of such interactions is likewise unknown.

Anatomical studies have indicated that the sympathetic nervous system's (SNS) contribution to the pelvic plexus originates from multiple sources. The superior hypogastric plexus gives rise to two sympathetic nerves that run bilaterally into the left and right pelvic plexuses (Donker, 1986; Maas, DeRuiter, Kenter, & Trimbos, 1999). Other inputs stem directly from sympathetic chain ganglia along the thoracolumbar spinal cord (Donker). In addition to these routes, genital tissues may receive innervation from so-called "short" adrenergic fibers that arise from localized ganglia. Ownman, Rosengren, and Sjoberg (1967) found that such ganglia were particularly abundant in the human vagina. Interestingly, estrogen and other sex steroids may significantly influence sympathetic innervation in the pelvic organs (e.g., Zoubina & Smith, 2001).

Consistent with histochemical studies of human genital tissues (e.g., Ownman, Rosengren, & Sjoberg, 1967), it is generally accepted that norepinephrine is the dominant neurotransmitter of the SNS. Adrenergic nerve fibers from the pelvic plexus target both vascular and nonvascular smooth muscle in most if not all female genital organs. The study of adrenoceptors in the genital tract is therefore extremely important to the understanding of the role of the SNS in physiological sexual arousal. However, this approach is not comprehensive. Studies of adrenoceptors alone cannot address the effects of nonadrenergic-noncholinergic (NANC) neurotransmitters, such as neuropeptide Y and galanin, which are often colocalized within sympathetic nerve fibers. The functional significance of these neuropeptides is only beginning to be understood (for review, see Argiolas, 1999).

Attempts have been made to characterize the distribution of adrenoceptors in genital tissue. Anatomical studies have suggested that mammalian vaginal, cervical, uterine, and clitoral tissues contain both $alpha_1$ and $alpha_2$ adrenoceptors. Beta adrenoceptors are also present in some genital tissues, particularly the uterus, although they have received considerably less attention in studies of sexual function. In humans, both $alpha_1$ and $alpha_2$ adrenoceptors appear to regulate smooth muscle tone in vaginal and clitoral tissue (Min et al., 2001; Traish, Moreland, Huang, Kim, & Goldstein, 2000). Traditionally, it has been thought that $alpha_1$ adrenoceptors are located postsynaptically and regulate smooth muscle contractility, while $alpha_2$ adrenoceptors are located presynaptically and serve an autoregulatory function to inhibit release of norepinephrine and other neurotransmitters (e.g., Iversen, Iversen, & Saper, 2000). However, it is known that the $alpha_2$ receptor subtype is found both pre- and postsynaptically. A recent study indicates that activation of postsynaptic $alpha_2$ adrenoceptors in male corpus cavernosum induces smooth muscle contraction (Gupta et al., 1998). Therefore, $alpha_2$ adrenoceptors appear to serve opposite ends, depending on their location within the synapse. This somewhat paradoxical conclusion must be approached with caution. Understanding how adrenergic mechanisms influence female sexual arousal is limited by current knowledge of the distribution of adrenergic receptors on the nerves serving the genitalia.

Animal Models of Sympathetic Nervous System Activity and Sexual Arousal

Pharmacological Manipulation of Sexual Behavior

Using pharmacological treatments, a number of studies have demonstrated the influence of adrenergic transmission in the regulation of sexual behavior in females. Most studies of this nature have used ovariectomized animals treated with standardized doses of estradiol and progesterone. This strategy serves two purposes: first, to elicit sexually receptive behavior from a sexually unreceptive baseline, and second, to control for the potential influence of unequal sex hormone levels on adrenergic transmission. Animal models of female sexual behavior may assess several different measures of sexual responding: receptivity (lordosis quotient), which is the ratio of the number of spinal reflexes in response to male attempts to mate; proceptivity, which is measured as the number of ear wiggles per minute; and rejection behaviors, which are measured as the number of kicking, boxing, running away, and squealing behaviors in response to a male's attempt to mate. Application of these behaviors to human sexual behavior is obviously limited. Although there is no human equivalent of lordosis, it is considered an analog of sexual arousal in other mammals.

Yanase (1977) found that epinephrine, but not norepinephrine, stimulated lordosis behavior in estradiol-treated, ovariectomized rats. However, other findings have supported the role of norepinephrine in stimulating lordosis. Vincent and Feder (1988) found that injection of either an alpha$_1$ or alpha$_2$ adrenergic agonist induced lordosis behavior in a small proportion of guinea pigs, but when used in combination, induced lordosis in 76% of the animals.

Studies examining the effects of adrenergic and antiadrenergic agents are complicated by the fact that some of the drugs used do not act exclusively on adrenergic systems. For example, yohimbine acts as both an alpha$_2$ adrenoceptor antagonist and a serotonin receptor antagonist (Broadley, 1996, p. 216). In such a case, the study must rule out the effects of different neurotransmitter systems on the phenomenon of interest. Nock and Feder (1979) observed that the dopamine beta-hydroxylase inhibitor U-14,624 abolished lordosis behavior in female guinea pigs. U-14,624 was believed to increase dopamine and serotonin availability while decreasing norepinephrine levels. After both dopamine and serotonin blockade failed to reverse the effects of U-14,624, the authors determined that only concurrent administration of the alpha$_2$ adrenergic agonist clonidine was able to restore lordosis behavior in animals treated with U-14,624. Thus, the inhibitory effects of U-14,624 on lordosis were concluded to be associated primarily with decreased availability of norepinephrine, rather than increased dopamine or serotonin levels.

Although central mechanisms have usually been implicated in the adrenergic control of lordosis, a peripheral mechanism cannot be ruled out. The facilitatory effect of norepinephrine on lordosis responses may indicate the involvement of the SNS. If so, one would expect drugs that decrease SNS activity might also decrease sexual arousal. To examine this possibility, Meston, Moe, and Gorzalka (1996) conducted a series of studies on sexual behavior in female rats treated with various drugs that inhibit SNS activity. The first study examined the influence of clonidine, an antihypertensive medication, on sexual responding. Clonidine acts centrally and peripherally as an alpha$_2$ adrenergic agonist, presumably with the effect of decreasing norepinephrine release. In the second and third studies, the effects of drugs guanethidine and naphazoline on sexual responding were examined. Naphazoline also acts as an alpha$_2$ adrenergic agonist, and guanethidine works by a distinct mechanism to directly block the release of norepinephrine from sympathetic neurons. These two drugs were chosen because they are believed to exert effects similar to those of clonidine, but they do not cross the blood-brain barrier. Each study included 15 ovariectomized female rats treated with estrogen and progesterone to induce heat, and each used a repeated measures design in which the animals received either saline or moderate or high doses of the drug.

Clonidine, guanethidine, and naphazoline all suppressed lordosis responses at both moderate and high doses. Clonidine and guanethidine significantly decreased proceptive behavior at both moderate and high doses, and naphazoline significantly decreased proceptivity at moderate doses. Clonidine significantly increased the number of rejection behaviors at both moderate and high doses; guanethidine and naphazoline also increased rejection behaviors, but the results did not reach statistical significance. Although these drugs have potential sedative effects and may have thus suppressed sexual behavior, this explanation alone is inconsistent with the observed increases in active rejection behaviors. Because guanethidine and naphazoline act to selectively inhibit peripheral sympathetic outflow without influencing adrenergic mechanisms at a central level, the results of this study suggest that inhibition of the SNS may inhibit sexual behavior in the female rat.

Effects of Direct Stimulation of Nerves and Tissues

In vivo studies of direct nerve stimulation can differentiate genital responses to parasympathetic and sympathetic outflow. Studies of this type have used electrical stimulation of dissected nerves in order to determine specific effects on target tissues. In rats, electrical stimulation of both the pelvic (parasympathetic) and hypogastric (sympathetic) nerves induced contractions of uterine and cervical smooth muscle, which were further enhanced by pretreatment with estrogen (Sato, Hayashi, & Garfield, 1989; Sato, Hotta, Nakayama, & Suzuki, 1996). Pelvic nerve stimulation increased uterine blood flow, while hypogastric nerve stimulation decreased blood flow. The decrease in uterine blood flow following hypogastric stimulation was eliminated with phenoxybenzamine, an alpha-adrenergic antagonist (Sato et al., 1996). Similarly, in guinea pigs, stimulation of the hypogastric nerve induced uterine contractions and increased uterine sensitivity to oxytocin; these effects could be blocked with the alpha-adrenergic antagonist phentolamine (Marshall & Russe, 1970). Stimulation of the pelvic plexus, which comprises both pelvic and hypogastric nerves, increased clitoral and vaginal blood flow in rats (Vachon, Simmerman, Zahran, & Carrier, 2000). However, another study found that direct stimulation of the sympathetic chain countered the increase in vaginal blood flow resulting from pelvic nerve stimulation (Giuliano et al., 2001).

A different strategy used to examine adrenergic influences on genital tissue function involves electrical stimulation of smooth muscle tissue dissected from genital organs. Subsequent treatment with antiadrenergics and other agents can be used to detect moderating influences of neurotransmitters on tissue responses. In a study of rabbit myometrium and cervical tissue, contractile responses to electrical field stimulation was attenuated by both guanethidine, an antiadrenergic agent, and atropine, an anticholinergic agent, but not by propalanol, a selective beta-adrenergic antagonist (Bulat, Kannan, & Garfield, 1989). Rabbit vaginal tissue contractile responses to electrical stimulation were attenuated by several alpha$_1$ and alpha$_2$ adrenergic antagonists (Kim, Min, Huang, Goldstein, & Traish, 2002).

The above studies suggest that stimulation of the sympathetic nerves supplying the genitalia results in contractions of both nonvascular and vascular smooth muscle, which may in turn limit blood flow to the uterus, vagina, and other tissues. Given that sexual arousal involves a vasocongestive response, the contention that arousal is mediated through activity of the SNS is apparently contradictory. To date, this discrepancy has been addressed infrequently in the literature. It has been suggested, however, that the vasoconstrictive effects of norepinephrine are superseded by the effects of other neurotransmitters that act as local vasodilators in the presence of sexual stimulation. If this is the case, then other peripheral effects of SNS activation, such as increased heart rate and blood pressure, may facilitate the vasocongestive response (Kim et al., 2002).

Human Models of SNS Activity and Sexual Arousal

Neuroendocrine Markers of Sympathetic Activity and Sexual Arousal

Indirect evidence for a facilitatory influence of SNS activation on female sexual arousal is provided by biochemical and physiological research that indicates that diffuse SNS discharge occurs during the later stages of sexual arousal (Jovanovic, 1971) with marked increases in heart rate and blood pressure occurring during orgasm (Fox & Fox, 1969). Significant increases in urinary (Levi, 1969) and plasma (Exton et al., 2000) norepinephrine concentrations have been found in women after viewing a sexually arousing film. Increases in plasma norepinephrine, a sensitive index of SNS activity, have also been shown to accompany increases in sexual arousal during intercourse and to decline rapidly following orgasm (Wiedeking, Ziegler, & Lake, 1979). Ende, Gertner, Hwang, and Kadi (1988) measured urinary vanillylmandelic acid (VMA) 1 hour before, within an hour after intercourse, and in a 23-hour pooled sample after intercourse in 11 females. Vanillylmandelic acid is the ultimate metabolic product of epinephrine and norepinephrine in the urine and thus one of the most accurate methods of studying total sympathetic activity. The authors found a significant increase in VMA 1 hour prior to intercourse and 1 hour postintercourse in comparison to preintercourse baseline levels. The pooled 23-hour sample showed levels of VMA higher than pre- but not postintercourse levels. These findings provide objective evidence for considerable involvement of the SNS during and in anticipation of intercourse.

Spinal Cord Injury Studies

The sexual impairments brought about by spinal cord injury (SCI) provide a novel model of sexual dysfunction with which to investigate the SNS contribution to sexual arousal. The origin of much of the sympathetic innervation to the genitalia can be localized to a discrete region of the thoracolumbar spinal cord. By observing sexual responses in women who have lesions to these areas, the effects of sympathetic disruption can be inferred to some degree. Research in this area has focused on specific arousal phase responses, notably vaginal vasocongestion, among women with varying types and degrees of SCIs. These studies have typically distinguished between "psychogenic" arousal, modeled by genital responses to erotic audiovisual stimuli, and "reflex" responses to tactile stimulation of the genitals.

Berard (1989) studied 15 women with complete and incomplete SCIs at the cervical, thoracic, and lumbar levels. According to their medical records, both reflex and psychogenic vaginal lubrication were absent among women with SCIs between T10 and T12, a region from which genital sympathetic nerves originate. In addition, these women reported an absence of sensations associated with sexual arousal. Only reflex lubrication was preserved in women with injuries above T10, whereas psychogenic lubrication was preserved in women with injuries below T12. The absence of vaginal lubrication and subjective sensation in women with injuries to the lower thoracic spinal cord suggests involvement of the sympathetic nervous system in these responses.

Using vaginal photoplethysmography, Sipski, Alexander, and Rosen (1997) studied vaginal pulse amplitude (VPA) responses to erotic stimulation in women with SCIs affecting sensation to the T11-L2 dermatomes. The authors reasoned that women with damage to sensory neurons at these levels would also have impaired SNS outflow from those regions, given the close proximity of the sympathetic and somatosensory neurons within the spinal cord. The authors compared women with SCI who had preserved some degree of pinprick sensation in the T11-L2 dermatomes to women who had lost all sensation in these areas. Each woman was examined under two conditions: audiovisual erotic stimulation alone and audiovisual erotic stimulation with manual clitoral stimulation. Both groups showed increases in subjective sexual arousal under the two conditions. Whereas women with some preserved dermatomal sensation showed increased VPA responses to audiovisual stimuli, women with absent sensation showed no vaginal response. When manual stimulation was added to the audiovisual stimulation, the groups showed similar increases in VPA responses. However, heart rate and respiration rate were significantly greater among women with preserved sensation during the combined stimulation condition..

A second study by Sipski, Alexander, & Rosen (2001) used a similar methodology to compare VPA responses of a control group of 21 able-bodied women to those of 68 SCI women under conditions of audiovisual stimulation alone and audiovisual plus manual stimulation. Consistent with previous findings, women with impaired sensation at the T11-L2 dermatomes showed decreased physiological sexual arousal compared to able-bodied women. Further, the degree of sensory impairment resulting from injury to the T11-L2 region was predictive of the intensity of the vasocongestive response, with less impaired women responding more like able-bodied women. When compared to women with injuries at different levels of the spinal cord, this pattern was unique to women with injuries between T11 and L2.

Effects of Physiologically Induced SNS Activation on Sexual Arousal

The above studies suggest an active role of the SNS during sexual arousal in women. Whether or not activation or inhibition of the SNS influences subsequent sexual arousal is a related but different question. Hoon, Wincze, and Hoon (1977) were the first to report that vaginal blood volume (VBV) responses were increased when women viewed an anxiety-evoking film prior to an erotic film versus a neutral travel film prior to an erotic film. Palace and Gorzalka (1990) replicated these findings in both sexually functional and dysfunctional women. To the extent that anxiety-evoking films increase SNS arousal, these findings support a facilitatory role of SNS activation on sexual arousal in women. However, it should be noted that heart rate, an indirect indicator of SNS activity, was either not measured or failed to increase significantly with exposure to the anxiety films. Hence, assumptions about SNS activation in these studies are highly speculative. Wolpe (1978) offered an alternative explanation for these findings. He described the finding as an "anxiety relief" phenomenon by which the anxiety films were so aversive that, by contrast, the erotic films were so much more appealing that they consequently facilitated sexual responding strictly via cognitive processes.

Meston and colleagues examined the effects of SNS activation on sexual arousal using intense, acute exercise as a means of eliciting SNS activity. Exercise was chosen based on numerous pharmacological and physiological studies that indicate that moderate to high intensities of exercise are accompanied by significant SNS activity (for review, see DiCarlo & Bishop, 1999). In the first of this series of studies (Meston & Gorzalka, 1995), 35 sexually functional women between the ages of 18 and 34 participated in two counterbalanced sessions during which they viewed a neutral film followed immediately by an erotic film. In one of the sessions, subjects engaged in 20 minutes of intense stationary cycling before viewing the films. Prior to engaging in the two experimental sessions, the women were given a submaximal bicycle ergometer fitness test in order to estimate their maximum volume of oxygen uptake (VO_2 max), an indicator of cardiovascular fitness. This allowed the workload and cycle speed to be set so that all participants exercised at a constant 70% of their VO_2 max. By having women exercise at relative workloads, differences in physiological responses resulting from variations in fitness levels are minimized (Grossman & Moretti, 1986). Sexual arousal was measured subjectively using a self-report questionnaire adapted from Heiman and Rowland (1983) and physiologically using a vaginal photoplethysmograph (Sintchak & Geer, 1975). Both VPA and VBV were used as indices of sexual arousal. Heart rate was used as an indirect indicator of SNS activation.

The results indicated a significant increase in both VPA and VBV responses to the erotic films after exercise. Heart rate significantly increased with exercise (70 bpm vs. 90 bpm); there were no significant changes in heart rate between the neutral and erotic films. There were no significant differences in self-report measures of sexual arousal, positive affect, or negative affect with exercise, and correlations between subjective and physiological indices were not significant.

Meston and Gorzalka (1996a) used the same methodology to examine the indirect effects of SNS activation in women with sexual difficulties. Twelve participants were sexually functional, 12 reported low sexual desire, and 12 were anorgasmic. There were no significant differences in VPA or VBV responses between the subject groups during the no-exercise condition. With exercise, however, there were significant increases in VPA and VBV among sexually functional women, a significant increase in VPA and VBV responses among women with low sexual desire, and a significant decrease in VPA and a nonsignificant decrease in VBV with exercise among anorgasmic subjects. Heart rate significantly increased with exercise among all subject groups. There were no significant effects of exercise on subjective ratings of sexual arousal, positive affect, negative affect, or anxiety, and no significant differences between groups on these measures.

A follow-up study conducted by Meston and Gorzalka (1995) examined whether the exercise-induced increases in VPA and VBV responses may have been the result of other potential "nonsexual" consequences of exercise or, alternatively, of the passage of time postexercise given that the presentation of the erotic films consistently followed that of the neutral films. Ten sexually functional women between the ages of 19 and 34 participated in a repeated-measures design study in which they engaged in two counterbalanced sessions where they viewed either a neutral film followed by an erotic film or two consecutive neutral films (Meston & Gorzalka, 1995). In both sessions, subjects engaged in 20 minutes of stationary cycling at 70% of their VO_2 max. Vaginal pulse amplitude and VBV were significantly increased with the presentation of an erotic film, but showed no change with the presentation of a second neutral film. The results of this experiment suggest that exercise per se does not simply increase VBV and VPA responses but, rather, exercise in the presence of an erotic stimulus enhances genital engorgement.

In the exercise studies noted above, approximately 15 minutes had passed from the cessation of exercise to the onset of the erotic stimulus. Although research indicates that SNS influences remain significantly elevated for approximately 30–40 minutes following intense exercise, at 15 minutes postexercise heart rate had declined considerably from levels during and immediately following exercise. This leads one to question whether exercise would have an even greater facilitatory influence on physiological sexual responses if measured immediately following exercise, and whether the level of SNS activation is in some way related to the level of physiological sexual arousal. Thirty-six sexually functional women between the ages of 18 and 45 participated in a study designed identically to the original exercise study with the following exception: Sexual arousal was measured at either 5 minutes, 15 minutes, or 30 minutes postexercise in an effort to examine the approximate influences of high, moderate, and low levels of SNS activation on sexual responding (Meston & Gorzalka, 1996b). Vaginal pulse amplitude responses were significantly decreased at 5 minutes, significantly increased at 15 minutes (a replication of the original study), and marginally increased at 30 minutes postexercise. Vaginal blood volume findings showed a similar pattern to the VPA results, but did not reach statistical significance. Heart rate significantly increased with exercise in each of the conditions (97, 87, 80 bpm at 5, 15, and 30 minutes postexercise, respectively), and there were no significant effects of exercise on subjective ratings of sexual arousal or positive or negative affect. One interpretation of these findings is that there may be an optimal level of SNS activation for physiological sexual arousal below and beyond which SNS activation may have less of a facilitatory influence or even an inhibitory influence on physiological sexual arousal.

Interpretation of the above studies that used exercise to increase SNS activity is confounded by the potential role of hormones. In addition to creating SNS dominance, exercise at the intensity used in the above studies has been shown to influence the secretion of hormones such as estrogen, testosterone, cortisol, and prolactin (e.g., Keizer, Kuipers, de Haan, Beckers, & Habets, 1987). To date, research has not adequately addressed whether short-term changes in these hormones influence sexual arousal in women.

Brotto and Gorzalka (2002) examined sexual responses in pre- and postmenopausal women using laboratory-induced hyperventilation as a means of increasing SNS activity. The authors did not measure heart rate or any other indicator of SNS activity, but cited research that this technique induces sympathetic dominance for approximately 7 minutes (Achenbach-

Ng, Siao, Mavroudakis, Chiappa, & Kiers, 1994). Twenty-five young pre-menopausal women, 25 postmenopausal women, and 25 premenopausal women age-matched to the menopausal group participated in two coun-terbalanced sessions in which VPA and subjective sexual arousal was meas-ured either during baseline or following the hyperventilation procedure. The authors found that SNS activation increased VPA responses compared to baseline only among the young premenopausal women. Using the same hyperventilation procedure to induce SNS activity, Brotto (unpublished manuscript) found that SNS activation significantly increased VPA responses among sexually healthy women, but significantly decreased VPA responses among women with sexual arousal difficulties that were psychological in nature. Women with sexual arousal difficulties that were physical in nature showed a marginal but nonsignificant increase in VPA with heightened SNS activity. In both studies, SNS activation using a hyperventilation tech-nique had no significant impact on subjective sexual arousal.

Effects of Adrenergic Agonists on Sexual Arousal

Meston and Heiman (1998) examined the effects of ephedrine, an alpha- and beta-adrenergic agonist, on VPA responses. Twenty sexually functional women participated in two counterbalanced conditions in which they re-ceived either placebo or ephedrine (50 mg) using a double-blind proto-col. Ephedrine significantly increased VPA responses to an erotic, but not neutral, film and had no significant effect on subjective ratings of sexual arousal or on measures of positive or negative affect. The finding that when subjects viewed a nonsexual travel film there were no significant dif-ferences in VPA responses between the ephedrine and placebo conditions parallels the finding that exercise significantly increased VPA responses to erotic but not neutral stimuli. As with exercise, this suggests that ephedrine did not simply facilitate physiological responses through a general increase in peripheral resistance but, rather, acted in some way that selectively pre-pared the body for genital response. While ephedrine substantially increases peripheral sympathetic outflow, interpretation of this study findings is lim-ited by the fact that ephedrine also has centrally acting properties that po-tentially could account for the results.

In a recent follow-up study, Meston (2004) examined whether ephed-rine would be effective in reversing sexual dysfunction induced by selec-tive serotonin reuptake inhibitors (SSRIs). Given that treatment for SSRI-induced sexual side effects using centrally acting serotonergic agents may diminish the antidepressant's therapeutic effectiveness (e.g., Gitlin, 1994), it was hypothesized that targeting peripheral rather than central mecha-nisms may be a more viable treatment approach. Presumably, this would circumvent the reversal of antidepressant's therapeutic effects on depres-sion that are presumably centrally mediated. Nineteen sexually dysfunc-tional women receiving either fluoxetine, sertraline, or paroxetine participated in an 8-week, double-blind, placebo-controlled, crossover study of the effects of ephedrine (50 mg) on self-report measures of sexual desire, arousal, orgasm, and sexual satisfaction. While there were significant improvements relative to baseline in sexual desire and orgasm intensity/ pleasure on 50-mg ephedrine 1 hour prior to sexual activity, significant improvements in these measures as well as in sexual arousal and orgasmic ability were also noted with placebo. Whether or not the women in this study experienced an increase in genital vasocongestion was not assessed, thus assertions regarding the indirect impact of SNS activation on physiological sexual arousal cannot be made. As was the case in the laboratory study noted above, ephedrine did not substantially impact the women's psychological experience of sexual arousal.

Two studies examined the effects of moderate doses of clonidine, a selective alpha$_2$ adrenergic agonist, on subjective and plethysmograph indices of sexual arousal (Meston, Gorzalka, & Wright, 1997). In the first study, 15 sexually functional women, ages 18–42, participated in two sessions in which they viewed a neutral film followed immediately by an erotic film. In one session the women received a placebo and in one session they received 0.2 mg clonidine 1 hour prior to viewing the films. The study was conducted using a double-blind, placebo-controlled, repeated-measures protocol. The second study followed the identical procedure with the exception of the following: In both sessions, subjects engaged in 20 minutes of intense stationary cycling 1 hour following either placebo or clonidine administration but prior to viewing the films.

In the first study, 9 out of 15 and 7 out of 15 subjects showed a decrease in VPA and VBV, respectively, with clonidine, but the results did not reach statistical significance. In the second study, which involved heightened SNS activation, there was a significant decrease in both VPA and VBV with clonidine administration during the erotic films. Heart rate was significantly decreased with clonidine during the second (heightened SNS) study only. Subjective ratings of sexual arousal were marginally decreased in the first study and significantly decreased in the second (heightened SNS) study. Because clonidine has both central and peripheral properties, it is unclear at which level clonidine acted to influence sexual responding. Centrally, clonidine may have suppressed sexual responses indirectly via changes in neurohypophyseal hormone release, or directly by activating central sites responsible for the inhibition of sexual reflexes (Riley, 1995). Peripherally, clonidine may have suppressed sexual arousal by decreasing norepinephrine release from sympathetic nerve terminals. Support for this latter notion is provided by the finding that clonidine inhibited sexual responding only when subjects were in a state of heightened SNS activity. The fact that clonidine has been reported to significantly inhibit SNS, but not hormonal, responses to exercise (Engelman et al., 1989) is consistent with the suggestion that clonidine acted to inhibit sexual responding via suppressed SNS activity. However, given that the role of the alpha$_2$ adrenoceptor in female sexual function has not been clearly elucidated, the presumption that clonidine inhibits SNS outflow to the genitalia is tentative.

Effects of Adrenergic Antagonists on Sexual Arousal

Several studies have examined adrenergic blocking drugs on sexual arousal in women. Rosen, Phillips, Gendrano, and Ferguson (1999) found a facilitatory effect of the nonselective alpha-adrenergic antagonist phentolamine mesylate (40 mg administered orally) on VPA and subjective sexual arousal responses in six postmenopausal women with female sexual arousal disorder (FSAD). A facilitatory influence of phentolamine mesylate on VPA responses was also noted in a larger sample of postmenopausal women with FSAD receiving hormone replacement therapy (HRT; Rubio-Aurioles et al., 2002). The study was conducted using a double-blind, placebo-controlled, randomized, four-way crossover design in which postmenopausal women either on ($n = 19$) or not on ($n = 22$) HRT received placebo (vaginal solution or oral tablet), 5-mg and 40-mg phentolamine vaginal solution, and 40-mg oral phentolamine. Physiological sexual responses were significantly greater than placebo with 40-mg phentolamine vaginal solution among the HRT, but not among the non-HRT women. Subjective sexual arousal was increased with 40-mg phentolamine oral tablet and to a lesser degree with 40-mg phentolamine vaginal solution only among the women receiving HRT. Because phentolamine crosses the blood-brain barrier, it is not known whether these effects are attributable to a central or peripheral mechanism, or both.

Meston and Worcel (2002) examined the effects of the alpha$_2$ adrenoceptor antagonist yohimbine, either alone or in combination with the nitric oxide precursor L-arginine, on subjective and physiological responses to erotic stimuli in postmenopausal women with FSAD. Twenty-four women participated in three treatment sessions in which subjective and VPA sexual responses to erotic stimuli were measured following administration of either L-arginine glutamate (6 g) plus yohimbine HCl (6 mg), yohimbine alone (6 mg), or placebo, using a randomized, double-blind, three-way crossover design. Sexual responses were measured at approximately 30, 60, and 90 minutes post-drug administration. The combined oral administration of L-arginine glutamate and yohimbine increased VPA responses at 60 minutes post-drug administration, compared with placebo. VPA responses at 30 and 90 minutes post-drug administration were increased compared to placebo, but did not reach significance. Yohimbine alone had no significant impact on VPA responses at any of the time periods. There were no significant increases in subjective measures of sexual arousal in any of the experimental conditions. These findings are limited by the fact that the study design was unable to control for potential central nervous system effects of yohimbine.

Conclusion

The traditional model of the female sexual response holds that the arousal phase is mediated by parasympathetic activity, with sympathetic impulses predominating at orgasm. However, several lines of evidence suggest that increased sympathetic nervous system activity is a prominent feature of sexual arousal. Lacking sufficient knowledge about the function and distribution of sympathetic nerves, as well as ethical and accurate means of directly manipulating SNS outflow, investigators have been limited to conclusions drawn from indirect observations of SNS activation and inhibition in humans. Studies of women before and after exposure to sexually arousing stimuli have shown that concentrations of norepinephrine and its metabolites are elevated immediately following sexual arousal. Research conducted on women with spinal cord injuries suggests that damage to the spinal cord at the level of sympathetic innervation significantly impairs the sexual response. Physical exercise at intensities that are thought to increase SNS outflow has been shown to enhance sexual arousal responses in women. Based on putative pharmacological manipulations of SNS outflow, several studies suggest that sexual arousal may be enhanced or inhibited by adrenergic potentiation or blockade, respectively. These findings are supported by observations in animal models suggesting that adrenergic agonists increase, and adrenergic antagonists decrease, sexual behavior. However, these findings do not positively establish SNS activation as a mediator of sexual arousal. At least one well-controlled pharmacological study has demonstrated that adrenergic blockade, an analog of SNS inhibition, enhances sexual arousal responses in some women.

Indirect studies of the effects of SNS stimulation have substantial limitations. Although experimental manipulations designed to increase sympathetic activity are informed by previous physiological research, their effectiveness cannot be verified directly. Further, the impact of these manipulations is generally not limited to the SNS, making it difficult to rule out effects due to hormonal or other nervous system changes. By using a more reductive animal model, several recent studies have been able to examine the effects of sympathetic and adrenergic stimulation on genital tissue with greater specificity. Using techniques to directly stimulate autonomic nerve branches in the pelvic region, these studies have supported the conclusion that sympathetic impulses cause genital vascular and nonvascular smooth muscle to contract, limiting blood flow and preventing a full vasocongestive response. However, it is not known to what degree the effects of experimentally induced nerve impulses in isolation resemble physiological processes in natural behavior.

In summary, studies of the role of the SNS in sexual arousal have reached seemingly contradictory conclusions. Although putative markers of increased SNS activity have been associated with enhanced sexual arousal, this is not in accord with physiological research suggesting that sympathetic outflow limits genital responses necessary for physiological sexual arousal. It is possible that indirect approaches to studying the SNS in sexual arousal are not measuring the effects of sympathetic activity, but rather the effects of some other physiological process. For example, pharmacological studies have not typically controlled for the central nervous system effects of the agents used, and exercise studies have not assessed the contribution of hormonal changes that accompany physical activity. On the other hand, it is possible that sympathetic activity may have a facilitatory effect on sexual arousal in the context of other processes. The localized effects of SNS activation on genital blood flow may be overridden by opposing activity of the parasympathetic nervous system, while the systemic effects of SNS activity, such as increased blood pressure, may facilitate genital engorgement (Kim et al., 2002). If this is the case, discrepancies among study findings may be attributable to the fact that some experiments, particularly in animal models, manipulate sympathetic outflow in relative isolation. However, these explanations are hypothetical, as the interaction of the parasympathetic and sympathetic systems during sexual arousal remains largely unknown. Better knowledge of the autonomic innervation to the genitalia and autonomic pharmacology is needed to facilitate the understanding of the processes involved in female sexual arousal.

References

Achenbach-Ng, J., Siao, T. C., Mavroudakis, N., Chiappa, K. H., & Kiers, L. (1994). Effects of routine hyperventilation on PCO2 and PO2 in normal subjects: Implications of EEG interpretations. *Journal of Clinical Neurophysiology, 11,* 220–225.

Argiolas, A. (1999). Neuropeptides and sexual behaviour. *Neuroscience & Biobehavioral Reviews, 23,* 1127–1142.

Berard, E. J. J. (1989). The sexuality of spinal cord injured women: Physiology and pathophysiology. A review. *Paraplegia, 27,* 99–112.

Broadley, K. J. (1996). *Autonomic pharmacology.* London: Taylor & Francis.

Brotto, L. A., & Gorzalka, B. B. (2002). Genital and subjective sexual arousal in postmenopausal women: Influence of laboratory-induced hyperventilation. *Journal of Sex and Marital Therapy, 28*(Suppl.), 39–53.

Bulat, R., Kannan, M. S., & Garfield, R. E. (1989). Studies of the innervation of rabbit myometrium and cervix. *Canadian Journal of Physiology and Pharmacology, 67,* 837–844.

Dail, W. G. (1996). The pelvic plexus: Innervation of pelvic and extrapelvic visceral tissues. *Microscopy Research & Technique, 35,* 95–106.

DiCarlo, S. E., & Bishop, V. S. (1999). Exercise and the autonomic nervous system. In O. Appenzeller (Ed.), *Handbook of clinical neurology, 74,* 245–272.

Donker, P. J. (1986). A study of the myelinated fibres in the branches of the pelvic plexus. *Neurourology and Urodynamics, 5,* 185–202.

Ende, N., Gertner, S. B., Hwang, S. G., & Kadi, R. S. (1988). Measurements of post-coital sympathetic activity in females by means of vanillylmandelic acid. *Hormones and Behavior, 23,* 150–156.

Engelman, E., Lipszyc, M., Gilbart, E., van der Linden, P., Bellens, B., Van Romphey, A., & de Rood, M. (1989). Effects of clonidine on anesthetic drug requirements and hemodynamic response during aortic surgery. *Anesthesiology, 71,* 178–187.

Exton, N. G., Truong, T. C., Exton, M. S., Wingenfeld, S. A., Leygraf, N., Saller, B., Hartmann, U., & Schedlowski, M. (2000). Neuroendocrine response to film-induced sexual arousal in men and women. *Psychoneuroendocrinology, 25,* 187–199.

Fox, C. A., & Fox, B. (1969). Blood pressure and respiratory patterns during human coitus. *Journal of Reproduction and Fertility, 19,* 405.

Gitlin, M. J. (1994). Psychotropic medications and their effects on sexual function: Diagnosis, biology, and treatment approaches. *Journal of Clinical Psychiatry, 55,* 406–413.

Giuliano, F., Allard, J., Compagnie, S., Alexandre, L., Droupy, S., & Bernabe, J. (2001). Vaginal physiological changes in a model of sexual arousal in anesthetized rats. *American Journal of Physiology: Regulatory, Integrative and Comparative Physiology, 281,* R140–R149.

Grossman, A., & Moretti, C. (1986). Opioid peptides and their relationship to hormonal changes during acute exercise. In G. Benzi, L. Packer, & N. Siliprandi (Eds.), *Biochemical aspects of physical exercise* (pp. 375–385). London: Elsevier Science Publishers B. V. (Biomedical Division).

Gupta, S., Moreland, R. B., Yang, S., Gallant, C. M., Goldstein, I., & Traish, A. M. (1998). The expression of functional postsynaptic alpha$_2$-adrenoceptors in the corpus cavernosum smooth muscle. *British Journal of Pharmacology, 123,* 1237–1245.

Heiman, J. R., & Rowland, D. L. (1983). Affective and physiological sexual response patterns: The effects of instructions on sexually functional and dysfunctional men. *Journal of Psychosomatic Research, 27,* 105–116.

Hoon, P. W., Wincze, J. P., & Hoon, E. F. (1977). A test of reciprocal inhibition: Are anxiety and sexual arousal in women mutually inhibitory? *Journal of Abnormal Psychology, 86,* 65–74.

Iversen, S., Iversen, L., & Saper, C. B. (2000). The autonomic nervous system and the hypothalamus. In E. R. Kandel, J. H. Schwartz, & T. M. Jessell (Eds.), *Principles of neural science* (4th ed.). New York: McGraw Hill (Health Professions Division).

Jovanovic, U. J. (1971). The recording of physiological evidence of genital arousal in human males and females. *Archives of Sexual Behavior, 1,* 309.

Keizer, H. A., Kuipers, H., de Haan, J., Beckers, E., & Habets, L. (1987). Multiple hormonal responses to physical exercise in eumenorrheic trained and untrained women. *International Journal of Sports Medicine, 8,* 139–150.

Kim, N. N., Min, K., Huang, Y., Goldstein, I., & Traish, A. M. (2002). Biochemical and functional characterization of alpha-adrenergic receptors in the rabbit vagina. *Life Sciences, 71,* 2909–2920.

Levi, L. (1969). Sympatho-adrenomedullary activity, diuresis, and emotional reactions during visual sexual stimulation in human females and males. *Psychosomatic Medicine, 31,* 251–268.

Maas, C. P., DeRuiter, M. C., Kenter, G. G., & Trimbos, J. B. (1999). The inferior hypogastric plexus in gynecologic surgery. *Journal of Gynecologic Techniques, 5,* 55–61.

Marshall, J. M., & Russe, M. W. (1970). Uterine responses to adrenergic nerve stimulation in the guinea-pig. *British Journal of Pharmacology, 39,* 187P–188P.

Meston, C. M. (2004). A randomized, placebo-controlled, cross-over study of ephedrine for SSIR-induced female sexual dysfunction. *Journal of Sex and Marital Therapy, 30,* 57–68.

Meston, C. M., & Gorzalka, B. B. (1995). The effects of sympathetic activation following acute exercise on physiological and subjective sexual arousal in women. *Behavior Research and Therapy, 33,* 651–664.

Meston, C. M., & Gorzalka, B. B. (1996a). The differential effects of sympathetic activation on sexual arousal in sexually functional and dysfunctional women. *Journal of Abnormal Psychology, 105,* 582–591.

Meston, C. M., & Gorzalka, B. B. (1996b). The effects of immediate, delayed, and residual sympathetic activation on physiological and subjective sexual arousal in women. *Behavior Research and Therapy, 34,* 143–148.

Meston, C. M., Gorzalka, B. B., & Wright, J. M. (1997). Inhibition of subjective and physiological sexual arousal in women by clonidine. *Psychosomatic Medicine, 59,* 399–407.

Meston, C. M., & Heiman, J. R. (1998). Ephedrine-activated physiological sexual arousal in women. *Archives of General Psychiatry, 55,* 652–656.

Meston, C. M., Moe, I. E., & Gorzalka, B. B. (1996). The effects of sympathetic inhibition on sexual behavior in the female rat. *Physiology and Behavior, 59,* 537–542.

Meston, C. M., & Worcel, M. (2002). The effects of yohimbine plus L-arginine glutamate on sexual arousal in postmenopausal women with sexual arousal disorder. *Archives of Sexual Behavior, 31,* 323–332.

Min, K., Munarriz, R., Berman, J., Kim, N. N., Goldstein, I., Traish, A., & Stankovic, M. R. (2001). Hemodynamic evaluation of the female sexual arousal response in an animal model. *Journal of Sex & Marital Therapy, 27,* 557–565.

Nock, B., & Feder, H. H. (1979). Noradrenergic transmission and female sexual behavior of guinea pigs. *Brain Research, 166,* 369–380.

Ownman, C., Rosengren, E., & Sjoberg, N. O. (1967). Adrenergic innervation of the human female reproductive organs: A histochemical and chemical investigation. *Obstetrics and Gynecology, 30,* 763–773.

Palace, E. M., & Gorzalka, B. B. (1990). The enhancing effects of anxiety on arousal in sexually dysfunctional and functional women. *Journal of Abnormal Psychology, 99,* 403–411.

Riley, A. J. (1995). Alpha adrenoceptors and human sexual function. In J. Bancroft (Ed.), *The pharmacology of sexual function and dysfunction* (pp. 307–325). New York: Elsevier.

Rosen, R. C., Phillips, N. A., Gendrano, N. C., & Ferguson, D. M. (1999). Oral phentolamine and female sexual arousal disorder: A pilot study. *Journal of Sex and Marital Therapy, 25,* 144–147.

Rubio-Aurioles, E., Lopez, M., Lipezker, M., Lara, C., Ramirez, A., Rampazzo, C.,

Hurtado, M. T., de Mendoza, H., Lowrey, F., Loehr, L. A., & Lammers, P. (2002). Phentolamine mesylate in postmenopausal women with Female Sexual Arousal Disorder: A psychophysiological study. *Journal of Sex and Marital Therapy, 28*(Suppl.), 205–215.

Sato, S., Hayashi, R. H., & Garfield, R. E. (1989). Mechanical responses of the rat uterus, cervix, and bladder to stimulation of hypogastric and pelvic nerves in vivo. *Biology of Reproduction, 40,* 209–219.

Sato, Y., Hotta, H., Nakayama, H., & Suzuki, H. (1996). Sympathetic and parasympathetic regulation of the uterine blood flow and contraction in the rat. *Journal of the Autonomic Nervous System, 59,* 151–158.

Sintchak, G., & Geer, J. H. (1975). A vaginal plethysmograph system. *Psychophysiology, 12,* 113–115.

Sipski, M. L., Alexander, C. J., & Rosen, R. C. (1997). Physiologic parameters associated with sexual arousal in women with incomplete spinal cord injuries. *Archives of Physical Medicine and Rehabilitation, 78,* 305–313.

Sipski, M. L., Alexander, C. J., & Rosen, R. (2001). Sexual arousal and orgasm in women: Effects of spinal cord injury. *Annals of Neurology, 49,* 35–44.

Traish, A., Moreland, R. B., Huang, Y-H., Kim, N. N., & Goldstein, I. (2000). Development of human and rabbit vaginal smooth muscle cell cultures: Effects of vasoactive agents on intracellular levels of cyclic nucleotides. *Molecular and Cellular Biology Research Community, 2,* 131–137.

Vachon, P., Simmerman, N., Zahran, A. R., & Carrier, S. (2000). Increases in clitoral and vaginal blood flow following clitoral and pelvic plexus nerve stimulations in the female rat. *International Journal of Impotence Research, 12,* 53–57.

Vincent, P. A., & Feder, H. H. (1988). Alpha$_1$- and alpha$_2$-noradrenergic receptors modulate lordosis behavior in female guinea pigs. *Neuroendocrinology, 48,* 477–481.

Wiedeking, C., Ziegler, M. G., & Lake, R. C. (1979). Plasma noradrenaline and dopamine-beta-hydroxylase during human sexual activity. *Journal of Psychiatric Research, 15,* 139–145.

Wolpe, J. (1978). Comments on "A test of reciprocal inhibition" by Hoon, Wincze, and Hoon. *Journal of Abnormal Psychology, 87,* 452–454.

Yanase, M. (1977). A possible involvement of adrenaline in the facilitation of lordosis behavior in the ovariectomized rat. *Endocrinologica Japonica, 24,* 507–512.

Zoubina, E. V., & Smith, P. G. (2001). Uterine sympathetic hyperinnervation in the estrogen receptor-alpha knock-out mouse. *Neuroscience, 103,* 237–244.

Neuroendocrine Processes during Sexual Arousal and Orgasm

TILLMANN H. C. KRÜGER, MANFRED
SCHEDLOWSKI, AND MICHAEL S. EXTON

Neuroendocrine Response to Acute Sexual Arousal

Despite investigation now spanning well over 30 years, little consensus has been reached regarding the endocrine control of sexual arousal in healthy humans. Historically, the approach to this question has been to measure the endocrine response to various modes of sexual stimulation. This undertaking allows an examination of hormones that may be involved in the up- or down-regulation of a sexual response, depending on the timing and magnitude of such changes. Numerous studies conducted during the past three decades have shown a high level of agreement in regard to cardiovascular responses to sexual activity (Carmichael, Warburton, Dixen, & Davidson, 1994; Littler, Honour, & Sleight, 1974; Nemec, Mansfield, & Kennedy, 1976; Whipple, Ogden, & Komisaruk, 1992). In contrast, studies that examined the responses of sympathetic, pituitary, and gonadal hormones have been notable for lack of consistency in their conclusions (Blaicher et al., 1999; Brown & Heninger, 1975; Carani et al., 1990; Carmichael et al., 1994, pp. 10–20; Fox, Ismail, Love, Kirkham, & Loraine, 1972; Heiman, Rowland, Hatch, & Gladue, 1991; La Ferla, Anderson, & Schalch, 1978; Lee, Jaffe, & Midgley, 1974; Levi, 1969; Lincoln, 1974; Pirke, Kockott, & Dittmar, 1974; Purvis, Landgren, Cekan, & Diczfalusy, 1976; Rowland et al., 1987; Stoléru, Ennaji, Counot, & Spira, 1993; Wiedeking, Lake, Ziegler, Kowarski, & Money, 1977). Nevertheless, we must be cognizant that technical advances, combined with the use of a number of very different methodological approaches, contribute significantly to the variance between or differences in the data from different experiments.

Inconsistent Methodology

Studies examining the neuroendocrine response to sexual arousal and orgasm have employed a number of different methodologies, thus making general interpretations difficult. One potential confound involves the differences in the methods employed for the induction of sexual arousal. Researchers have employed the viewing of stimulating films, imagery of fantasies, masturbation, and coitus. These methods clearly demonstrate different characteristics of sexual stimulation, with differences in duration and intensity of exposure, as well as the amount of physical contact. Additionally, differences between such studies are further compounded by some studies requesting participants to achieve orgasm, while others did not. Together, such factors have contributed to the inability to directly compare data generated from different laboratories.

Additionally, a primary concern limiting the evaluation of results from these studies is the method of blood collection. Blood has often been sampled at single discrete time points, sometimes with the experimenter entering the experimental room. Such a methodology has a number of potential deficits. Firstly, short-term alterations of certain neuroendocrine variables may be missed by using this technique. Secondly, entering the experimental room may cause the participant undue concern, which may potentially contribute to any observed endocrine alterations. Thirdly, punctual blood sampling may induce physical discomfort that also may impact hormonal status.

Therefore, we designed a method for the examination of the neuroendocrine response to sexual arousal and orgasm in healthy males and females (Exton et al., 1999; Exton, Krüger, Bursch, et al., 2001; Exton, Krüger, Koch, et al., 2001; Exton et al., 2000; Krüger et al., 1998). We established this paradigm so as to eliminate difficulties due to punctual blood sampling, as well as the influence of the presence of the experimenter. By keeping these factors constant, we are able to compare factors that are incomparable in the existing literature—namely the effect of different modes of stimulation, as well as the influence of orgasm on endocrine alterations following sexual arousal.

Improved Methodology

For the examination of the endocrine response to sexual arousal and orgasm, we developed a laboratory model of continuous blood sampling that we formerly established in experimental field studies. Most experiments were conducted in 10 healthy male or female volunteers. Each experiment was conducted in participants naive to the experimental conditions. All subjects were exclusively heterosexual and reported a relaxed attitude toward masturbation and pornography. All volunteers underwent an intensive nonstructured clinical interview to exclude men and women with confounding physical or mental health problems (e.g., drug or alcohol abuse, medication intake, or sexual dysfunctions). Volunteers were requested to refrain from any kind of sexual activity and to avoid alcoholic beverages or other drugs 24 hours prior to the laboratory investigation. The study paradigm is displayed in Figure 1. A balanced crossover design was implemented, involving two sessions on consecutive days, with each session commencing in the afternoon (at 3 P.M.). Subjects lay down on a comfortable bed in front of a video screen, with their head propped by pillows to allow viewing of the video. In the control session, volunteers viewed a video of a neutral documentary, while the experimental session was composed of three video sequences, each lasting 20 minutes. The first and last sections of this video consisted of the same documentary film. The middle 20 minutes of the experimental video was a sexually explicit film depicting different heterosexual couples having sexual intercourse.

To ensure accuracy of measurements and privacy of the participants, our method of continuous blood withdrawal was achieved through the use of a small portable pump. An intravenous cannula was inserted into a brachial vein and then connected to heparinised silicon tubing that passed through the test room wall into the adjoining room. The use of the mini-pump allowed adjustment of blood flow, which was typically 1–2 ml/min. Blood was collected into EDTA tubes, which allows variation of the time period of each collection, simply via replacing the tubes. For the current series of experiments, we changed tubes every 10 minutes to allow a time kinetic of endocrine variables. Samples were centrifuged at 4°C and plasma stored at −70°C until assayed.

By using our specific method of blood collection, we established an accurate paradigm for the measurement of hormone concentrations over a period of sexual arousal. This allowed a comparison of various methods for inducing sexual arousal on hormone concentrations, and furthermore, the impact of orgasm on these responses. Thus, we completed three sets of experiments in both males and females, altering the stimulation paradigm:

1. Following 10 minutes' viewing of the pornographic video (anticipatory phase), subjects in the experimental session were asked to masturbate until orgasm.
2. Following 10 minutes' viewing of the pornographic video, subjects in the experimental session were asked to have coitus until orgasm. Heterosexual couples participated in this experiment. In this paradigm, subjects who were being examined for endocrine changes lay comfortably on the bed, while all the movement was conducted by their partner. This reduced any possible changes in hormone concentrations due to movement, allowing direct examination of the specific neuroendocrine response to sexual arousal and orgasm.
3. Subjects in the experimental session watched the sexually explicit film for 20 minutes, but did not masturbate to orgasm.

Endocrine Response to Orgasm: Prolactin May Be a Regulator of Postorgasmic Sexual Drive

In our laboratory, sexual stimulation consistently produces high levels of subjective sexual arousal, as assessed by visual-analogue scale. Furthermore, this finding has been corroborated by objective measurements of sexual arousal in females, using vaginal photoplethysmography. These data

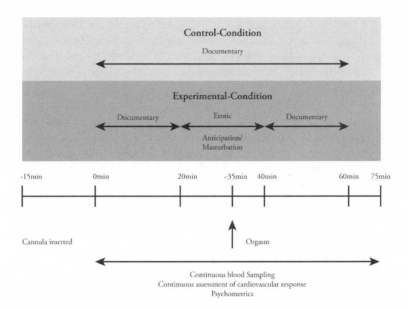

Figure 1. Experimental design for examination of sexual arousal and orgasm-induced prolactin secretion. Each subject participates in a control and an experimental condition. Both control and experimental conditions involve viewing of an emotionally neutral documentary film. However, subjects view a pornographic film in the middle 20 minutes of the experimental condition. Additionally, in some experiments, following 10 minutes viewing of the pornographic film participants are required to achieve orgasm via masturbation or coitus.

give face validity to our endocrine measurements, as they reflect hormonal changes that would occur in "real world" sexual situations.

Measurement of cardiovascular responses and sympathetic hormones also demonstrate a consistent response to sexual arousal and orgasm, increasing heart rate, blood pressure, adrenaline, and noradrenaline, which return rapidly to control levels after orgasm. Further consistent responses were observed in cortisol, follicle-stimulating hormone (FSH), luteinizing hormone (LH), testosterone, b-endorphin, progesterone, and estradiol: Orgasm produced no reliable alteration of these hormones.

In contrast, prolactin (PRL) was shown to be consistently and specifically altered by orgasm in both men and women. Figure 2 demonstrates the PRL response to various forms of sexual arousal in both genders. Across all experiments, no changes in PRL were observed during the first 20 minutes of documentary film. Furthermore, no changes of any significance were observed following the first 10 minutes of pornographic film viewing. However, the generation of orgasm, via either self-masturbation or coitus, produced pronounced increases in PRL concentrations in peripheral circulation of both males and females. Additionally, these alterations remained

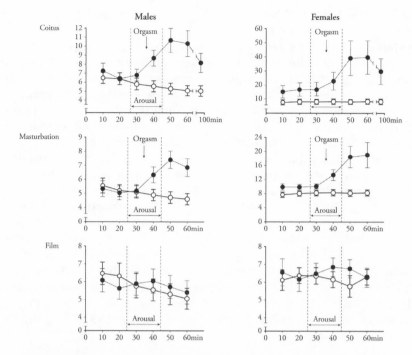

Figure 2. Effect of coitus-induced orgasm (a), masturbation-induced orgasm (b), and sexual arousal without orgasm (c) on peripheral prolactin concentrations in males and females. Experimental sessions are depicted by filled circles, control conditions by hollow circles.

significantly elevated 60 minutes following orgasm. Furthermore, the PRL response is clearly specific to orgasm, as sexual arousal alone (both film and masturbation without orgasm) induced no changes of PRL in either males or females. This was confirmed in a recent study where we employed a 2-minute blood sampling interval (Krüger, Haake, Chereath, et al., 2003). Interestingly, in this study, we observed for the first time in our laboratory an orgasm-induced increase in oxytocin, although this was small and nonsignificant. As this hormone has been considered responsive to sexual arousal and orgasm, these data support the significance of the pronounced and long-lasting impact of orgasm on PRL. Indeed, together the data suggest that PRL may play a role in the acute regulation of sexual arousal and/or reproductive functions following orgasm.

Does Prolactin Regulate Sexual Function and Behavior?

Support from Physiology

The physiological role of the pituitary peptide hormone PRL contributes to the feasibility that it may be involved in the acute regulation of sexual drive. Indeed, although PRL was considered initially to be a mechanism of lactation (Stricker & Grueter, 1928), it has broad physiological importance, being ascribed over 300 biological functions (Bole-Feysot, Goffin, Edery, Binart, & Kelly, 1998). Unlike most pituitary hormones whose release is triggered by specific releasing hormones from the hypothalamus, PRL is under tonic inhibitory control by the hypothalamus. Of particular importance to PRL control of sexual function is that the primary inhibitory input is dopamine (Maruyama et al., 1999), a neurotransmitter that is intimately involved in the regulation of sexual drive and behavior.

The possibility that PRL may be involved in regulation of sexual drive is underscored by the expression of the PRL receptor within central nervous system (CNS) structures that are known to regulate sexual behavior. Specifically, PRL receptors are located in the hippocampus, cortex, amygdala, and various hypothalamic nuclei (Pi & Grattan, 1999a, 1999b; Roky et al., 1996). In addition, PRL receptors have been characterized within both male and female reproductive organs. In addition to the mammary gland, PRL receptors are located in females in the ovary and uterus and in males in the testis, epididymis, and prostate (Howell Skalla, Bunick, Bleck, Nelson, & Bahr, 2000; Pérez-Villamil, Bordiu, & Puente-Cueva, 1980; Prigent-Tessier et al., 1996; Reddy, Reddy, & Govindappa, 1985; Yoshimura et al., 1992).

Clinical Support

Key to the theory that acute PRL may regulate acute sexual drive is an extrapolation from extensive animal and clinical evidence of the impact of chronic elevations of PRL (hyperprolactinemia) on sexual behavior and function. Animal data consistently demonstrate that hyperprolactinemia impairs sexual function on both motivational and physiological levels in both the male (increased latency to mounting and ejaculation, decreased frequency of mounts, intromissions, and ejaculations) and female rat (lordosis behavior; Doherty, Bartke, Smith, & Davis, 1985; Doherty, Baum, & Todd, 1986; Doherty et al., 1989; Doherty, Wu, & Matt, 1990; Kooy, Weber, Ooms, & Vreeburg, 1988).

This animal evidence is well supported clinically. Hyperprolactinemia commonly occurs during pregnancy and lactation. Additionally, hyperprolactinemia may be produced by pathological mechanisms, such as prolactinoma, para- and suprasellar tumors affecting hypothalamic PRL regulatory factors, "empty sella"-syndrome, severe primary hypothyreosis, and chronic renal failure. The development of a prolactinoma, an adenoma of pituitary lactotrophs, is one of the most common reasons for hyperprolactinemia.

Hyperprolactinemia is associated with pronounced reductions of both sexual motivation and function. Elevated levels of PRL inhibit gonadotropin-releasing hormone (GnRH) pulsatility (Sauder, Frager, Case, Kelch, & Marshal, 1984) and thus can cause low gonadotropin production, amenorrhoea, gynaecomastia, and galactorrhoea in some women. In men, hyperprolactinemia is commonly associated with low testosterone levels and oligospermia (Buvat et al., 1985; Sobrinho, 1993; Walsh & Pullan, 1997). Although some experimental evidence suggests that hyperprolactinemia suppresses physiological reproductive functions while maintaining sexual drive (Carani, Granata, Faustini Fustini, Marrama, 1996), other studies clearly indicate that chronic PRL elevation also negatively impacts sexual libido (Koppelman, Parry, Hamilton, Alagna, & Loriaux, 1987). This has in particular been observed in clinical psychopharmacology.

For example, newer generations of antidepressants such as selective serotonin reuptake inhibitors (SSRIs) produce hyperprolactinemia (Rosen, Lane, & Menza, 1999). The increased PRL secretion induced by this type of medication is associated with dramatically reduced sexual appetence and delayed ejaculation in men (Rosen et al.; Waldinger & Olivier, 1998). In women symptoms range from decreased sexual drive to orgasmic disturbances such as anorgasmia and delayed orgasm (Montejo-Gonzalez et al., 1997; Shen & Hsu, 1995). Further, typical neuroleptics, and some atypicals, used to treat schizophrenia produce a strong elevation of plasma PRL. Hyperprolactinemia is associated with loss of libido, erectile dysfunction, and anorgasmia, with this effect not observed with atypical neuroleptics that do not elevate PRL (e.g., olanzapine).

Underscoring the importance of PRL in regulating sexual function, dopaminergic agonists have become a common approach to the treatment of hyperprolactinemia. Recently, the first commonly utilized dopaminergic agonist, bromocriptine, has been replaced by cabergoline, which produces striking normalization of hyperprolactinemia (Verhelst et al., 1999). Indeed, carbergoline has recently been shown in a number of large studies to normalize PRL levels and thereby restore libido and gonadal function in hyperprolactinemic patients (De Rosa et al., 1998).

Together, these data suggest a strong association between chronic elevations of PRL and marked suppression of both sexual drive and gonadal functions. This raises the possibility that acute elevations of PRL following orgasm may play a role in the regulation of sexual arousal and function. Indeed, some evidence suggests that this hormone may play an integral role in acute regulation of sexual behavior.

Comparing Apples with Apples: Implications of Hyperprolactinemia for PRL Release Following Orgasm

While the effects of chronic elevations of PRL on sexual drive and reproductive function are well described, the relevance of acute changes in PRL to sexual activity is equivocal. This raises the question of whether it is feasible to extrapolate the well-known effects of chronic prolactin elevation to acute changes. Indeed, animal models have demonstrated that acute increases in peripheral PRL, particularly at levels that are in the normal physiological range (e.g., 50 ng/ml), stimulate the sexual behavior of male rats (Drago & Lissandrello, 2000). In contrast, other reports have demonstrated that acute increases of peripheral PRL increase, decrease, or have no effect on rat sexual behavior (Cruz-Cassalas, Nasello, Hucke, & Felicio, 1999; Nasello, Vanzeler, Madurieira, & Felicio, 1997).

Thus, the biological effects of acute increases in PRL on sexual behavior are unclear. Nevertheless, some evidence suggests that orgasm-induced PRL secretion may contribute to the acute regulation of sexual arousal and reproductive function. Indeed, acute elevations of this peptide may have both peripheral and central consequences for sexual function and arousal.

Peripheral Actions

In addition to the well-characterized impact of PRL in regulating reproductive functions such as spermatocyte-spermatid conversion in germ cells, enhanced energy metabolism in spermatozoa, transport of ejaculated and epididymal spermatozoa, formation and destruction of the corpus luteum, uterine endometrial development, and blastocyst implantation (Bole-Feysot et al., 1998; Outhit, Morel, & Kelly, 1993), some evidence suggests that acute PRL may impact sexual functions. Specifically, in males, the acute release of PRL following orgasm may impact sexual behavior via direct action on the penile tissue. Although not extensively examined, some data clearly demonstrate that acute increases in PRL inhibit erectile function via inhibition of smooth muscle relaxation of the corpus cavernosum (Aoki et al., 1995; Ra et al., 1996). This suggests that an acute increase in PRL levels may participate in penile detumescence. However, our findings showing that acute increases in PRL remain over 60 minutes following orgasm suggest a complex interaction of this hormone with the neural regulation of erection. It is plausible that initial PRL increases may contribute to penile detumescence, which is then reversed by other central and local factors. This would concur with the known physiological regulation of erection, which represents a balance between different neural and endocrine inputs at multiple levels (Andersson & Wagner, 1995). Indeed, the effects of PRL are likely to interact both with other neuroendocrine factors as well as with behavioral variables, as drugs inhibiting basal PRL have been shown not to alter erectile functions in impotent males (Cooper, 1977; March, 1979). However, it must be noted that the expression of PRL receptors in the corpus cavernosum has yet to be demonstrated.

Thus, these data show that in contrast to the negative impact of hyperprolactinemia on fertility, the acute increase in PRL following orgasm in males and females may contribute to an environment that ensures successful conception. However, the acute increase of PRL may also provide a feedback signal to nuclei in the CNS controlling both peripheral reproductive functions as well as centers involved in the regulation of sexual drive.

Central Actions

The three major dopaminergic networks in the CNS may form the primary targets for peripheral PRL feedback. These networks are, firstly, the neuroendocrine hypothalamic and incerto-hypothalamic neurons (diencephalic; DC), secondly, the mesolimbocortical (MLC) dopaminergic neurons, and finally, the nigrostriatal dopamine system (NS). Together, these systems are recognized as playing a major role in modulating sexual motivation, behavior, and function, with both sensory stimulation and copulation producing dopaminergic activity in all three systems (Hull et al., 1999; Mas, 1995). The central role of dopamine in regulating sexual activity is underscored by the pronounced impact of dopaminergic drugs on both animal and human sexual function (Bancroft, 1999; Meston & Frohlich, 2000). Thus, these systems present as primary targets for PRL feedback to the CNS, and some evidence indeed suggests that the activity of each system is modified by PRL.

The most established pathway of PRL feedback to the CNS involves hypothalamic neuroendocrine neurons. Three populations of hypothalamic dopaminergic neurons regulate PRL release (DeMaria, Lerant, & Freeman, 1999; DeMaria, Livingstone, & Freeman, 1998; DeMaria, Zelena, Vecsernyés, Nagy, & Freeman, 1998): tuberoinfundibular dopaminergic neurons (TIDA) originating in the arcuate nucleus (ARN) and terminating in the median eminence (ME) (Fuxe, 1964); tuberohypophyseal dopaminergic neurons (THDA) extending from the rostral ARN and terminating in the intermediate (IL) and neural (NL) lobes of the pituitary gland (Bjorklund, Moore, Nobin, & Stenevi, 1973); and periventricular-hypophyseal dopaminergic neurons arising in the hypothalamic periventricular nucleus (PeVN) and terminating exclusively in the IL (Goudreau, Lindley, Lookingland, & Moore, 1992). These neurons express PRL receptors (Freeman, Kanyicska, Lerant, & Nagy, 2000), thus providing the prerequisites for a feedback loop by peripheral PRL. Although PRL is not able to pass the blood-brain barrier it can be secreted by the choroids plexus into the cerebrospinal fluid, or pass the area postrema and subsequently reach the brain tissue (Sobrinho, 1993). The capacity of PRL to reach the CNS is shown by a series of studies demonstrating that subcutaneously administered ovine PRL activates all three populations of hypothalamic dopaminergic neurons. Importantly, this effect occurred within 1 hour, thus contradicting the notion that peripheral PRL requires up to 5 days to reach optimal brain concentrations through active transport mechanisms (Walsh, Slaby, & Posner, 1987). Thus, PRL forms a negative feedback loop to control its own release, similar to pathways observed for many other pituitary hormones.

In addition to feedback on neurons controlling its own secretion, PRL may also feed back to dopaminergic systems that have been implicated in controlling sexual arousal. Specifically, animal studies have revealed three (main) integrative dopaminergic systems primarily responsible for the control and modulation of sexual behavior. First, the incerto-hypothalamic dopaminergic system that projects to the medial preoptic area (MPOA) is identified as one of the most important areas for the control of motivational and consummatory aspects of sexual behavior. Specifically, the generation of genital reflexes required for erection and ejaculation, the focusing of male attention on sexually relevant stimuli, and the increase of species-specific motor patterns during copulation are controlled by the MPOA. Importantly, the PRL receptor is strongly expressed in the MPOA (Pi & Grattan, 1998), with increased PRL decreasing the dopaminergic activity of the MPOA (Lookingland & Moore, 1984). Although no data exist showing that the PRL-induced inhibition of MPOA activity reduces sexual drive, PRL has been demonstrated to inhibit maternal behaviors also driven by dopaminergic MPOA activity (Bridges, Rigero, Byrnes, Yang, & Walker, 2001). Thus, peripheral PRL is clearly capable of modifying the dopaminergic activity of the MPOA, and indeed appears to act as a negative feedback mechanism.

The MLC dopaminergic system, which originates in the ventral tegmental area and projects to the mesial components of the limbic system (e.g., nucleus accumbens, amygdala, mesial frontal cortex), is the second potential target of PRL feedback. Similar to its role in reward processes, the dopaminergic output of the MLC is primarily responsible for appetitive/motivational regulation of sexual activity. This is evidenced by stimulation of MLC dopamine in response to sexually related sensory stimuli (Bradley & Meisel, 2001; Fiorino, Coury, & Phillips, 1997). Similar to the MPOA, dopaminergic activity of the nucleus accumbens and limbic forebrain is antagonized by acute peripheral or central PRL administration (Chen & Ramirez, 1988a; Gonzales-Mora, Guadalupe, & Mas, 1990). In contrast, other reports have demonstrated increased MLC dopaminergic activity following direct PRL infusion in the nucleus accumbens (Hernandez et al., 1994). These contrasting data are likely to be attributable to differences in PRL concentrations, resulting from the route of administration. Nevertheless, these data clearly demonstrate a mechanism whereby peripherally secreted PRL may feed back to modify MLC dopaminergic control of sexual motivation.

In addition, the NS, which originates in the substantia nigra and projects primarily to the putamen and caudate nucleus, is a candidate for a feedback mechanism of PRL. The NS is proposed to integrate both sensory and motor aspects of sexual behavior, with NS dopamine enabling a state of "preparedness." Dopaminergic activity of the NS thus contributes to generation of consummatory motor functions, such as the pursuit of a sexual partner before copulation (Robbins & Everitt, 1992). PRL is clearly capable of modifying dopaminergic activity within the NS. Acute central and peripheral administration of PRL modifies the activity of dopaminergic neurons in the striatum, with both excitatory and inhibitory effects noted (Cebeira et al., 1991; Chen & Ramirez, 1988b). Furthermore, dopamine production by superfused slices of striatum in vitro is stimulated by PRL (Chen & Ramirez, 1988b). Indeed, stimulation of striatal dopamine output by acute PRL administration has been demonstrated to be associated with facilitation of sexual behavior in the male rat (Cruz-Casallas et al., 1999). Thus, dopaminergic activity of NS is clearly influenced by peripheral PRL and associated with altered sexual behavior.

A Model of PRL Regulation of Sexual Function Following Orgasm

We have argued that the weight of data suggests that PRL may be an endocrine regulator of human sexual behavior, which is integrated with neural control of sexual function. The pathways whereby PRL may fill this role are schematically displayed in Figure 3. PRL may impact upon peripheral reproductive organs to either facilitate physiological mechanisms essential for successful conception and/or inhibit further reproductive activity. Alternatively, PRL may form a feedback mechanism to the CNS, modifying the activity of DC, MLC, and NS dopaminergic neurons.

As no direct experimental evidence exists demonstrating a feedback role of PRL in modulating sexual arousal and function, extrapolations have clearly been made in proposing the current model. First, although chronic hyperprolactinemia is related to the suppression of both reproductive function and sexual arousal, this is commonly characterized by PRL levels > 200 ng/ml, which are experienced over a number of months. In contrast, PRL levels are increased following orgasm to levels between 15 and 25 ng/ml for at least an hour, although the exact duration of this effect is unknown. Thus, the marked inhibitory effect of hyperprolactinemia cannot be directly inferred to occur following acute PRL increases. Nevertheless, data from animal experiments suggest that acute PRL administration, in levels that we observe following orgasm, may produce meaningful modification of sexual behavior as well as alterations of central and peripheral systems responsible for sexual drive and reproductive function. Yet the only way to confirm this position experimentally is to manipulate PRL levels acutely in healthy humans and examine the impact of this on sexual arousal and behavior. We have recently completed the first experiment of this kind in our laboratory, with data indicating that pharmacological manipulation of comparatively small changes in PRL is sufficient to produce significant changes in sexual drive (Krüger et al., 2003). Although the different pharmacological sites of action of prolactin-altering drugs (Cabergoline and/or Protirelin) have to be considered, this study demonstrates that acute changes in PRL plasma levels may be one factor modulating sexual drive and function

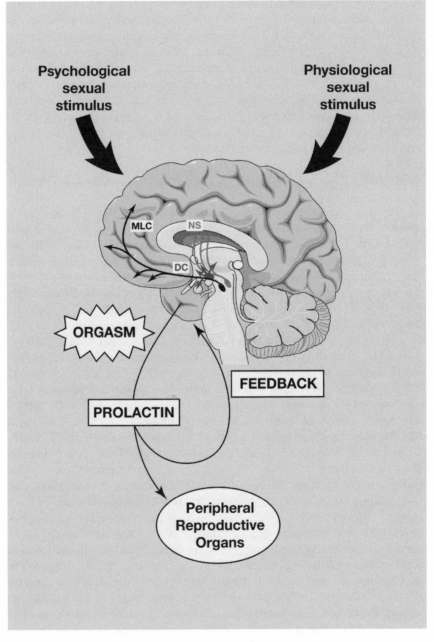

Figure 3. Theoretical model of the impact of PRL secretion following orgasm. PRL may influence peripheral reproductive organs and/or may feed back to dopaminergic systems in the CNS (DC, MLC, NS) recognized to play an important role in regulation of sexual behavior.

in males. Furthermore, a recent statistical reanalysis, incorporating data from studies in males, females, and couples, revealed that the postorgasmic PRL increase is greater following intercourse than following masturbation, suggesting greater satiety and further supporting the hypothesized role for PRL (Brody & Krüger, 2006). Another study, in ecstasy (methylenedioxymethampethamine [MDMA]) users, revealed that the phenomenological features of the psychological state induced by MDMA show similarities with characteristics of the postorgasmic state. In contrast to the induced emotions of affection and sensual enhancement, MDMA usually impairs sexual drive and functioning (Passie, Hartmann, Schneider, Emrich, & Krüger, 2005). In parallel with these psychotropic and physiological effects, MDMA induces a prominent increase in PRL with a time kinetic similar to the postorgasmic prolactin increase. Clearly, however, further investigation is required to elucidate the effect of acute increases in PRL on human sexual arousal.

An important assumption in the current model is PRL access to the CNS. Certainly, although the size of PRL does not allow it to cross the blood-brain barrier (Walsh, Posner, Kopriwa, & Brawer, 1978), it can directly pass into the brain via the highly permeable circumventricular organs such as the area postrema, subfornical organ, and medien eminence (Ganong, 2000), all of which express PRL receptors (Mangurian, Jurjus, & Walsh, 1999). Additionally, PRL may be indirectly transported into the brain via cerebrospinal fluid (Sobrinho, 1993). Thus, acute PRL is able to access brain tissue via mechanisms that enable rapid transport. This suggests that rather than time-consuming transport across the blood-brain barrier by active transport, peripheral PRL can rapidly access the CNS, supporting the role of this peptide in feedback to sites regulating sexual drive and function. It is important, however, that we continue to examine the accessibility of PRL to the CNS; ongoing studies in our laboratory are specifically examining CNS involvement in PRL and functional changes following orgasm.

The model also assumes that PRL plays a role in regulating sexual drive and function in both males and females, although the genders display distinct differences in sexuality, such as the characteristics of the refractory period (Masters & Johnson, 1966). Nevertheless, although the PRL response to orgasm is similar in both genders, it must be recognized that the effect of this response is dependent upon a number of other factors, such as receptor expression and sensitivity (Bole-Feysot et al., 1998). Accordingly, the PRL response may differ between the genders according to impact upon peripheral and central regulation of sexual arousal and function, thus potentially differentially regulating physical and psychological components of the refractory period. Clearly, the specific consequences of acute PRL increases for both genders warrant further investigation.

A final assumption of the model is that the secretion of PRL is biologically relevant. In contrast to this position, as PRL secretion is dopaminergically controlled, it is possible that it instead represents a downstream effect of the well-known dopaminergic involvement in the regulation of sexual behavior. Although possible, this position is counteracted by the specificity of the dopaminergic control of sexual behavior. The discrete secretion of PRL following orgasm suggests a directed response that is not initiated during both sensory and motor phases of sexual arousal. Thus, it is unlikely that the PRL response represents generalized dopaminergic activity during sexual encounters. Rather, the data suggest that the PRL response represents a directed, biologically relevant response that is initiated by inhibition of neuroendocrine dopaminergic neurons.

In summary, we have hypothesized that the pituitary hormone PRL may represent an important endocrine regulator of sexual drive and behavior. As we proceed with examining the role of PRL in postorgasmic sexual drive, it is becoming clear that, while this hormone plays a role, it is likely one among a constellation of neuroendocrine factors. An understanding of the multiple physiological levels of human sexual behavior represents a worthy challenge, with the promise of an understanding of normal, pathological, and psychopathological sexual behavior (Haake et al., 2003).

References

Andersson, K-E., & Wagner, G. (1995). Physiology of penile erection. *Physiological Reviews, 75*, 191–236.

Aoki, H., Fujioka, T., Matsuzaka, J., Kubo, T., Nakamura, K., & Yasuda, N. (1995). Suppression by prolactin of the electrically induced erectile response through its direct effect on the corpus cavernosum penis in the dog. *Journal of Urology, 154*, 595–600.

Bancroft, J. (1999). Central inhibition of sexual response in the male: A theoretical perspective. *Neuroscience and Biobehavioral Reviews, 23*, 763–784.

Bjorklund, A., Moore, R. Y., Nobin, A., & Stenevi, U. (1973). The organization of tubero-hypophyseal and reticulo-infundibular catecholamine neuron systems in the rat brain. *Brain Research, 51*, 171–191.

Blaicher, W., Gruber, D., Bieglmayer, C., Blaicher, A. M., Knogler, W., & Huber, J. C. (1999). The role of oxytocin in relation to female sexual arousal. *Gynecologic and Obstetric Investigation, 47*, 125–126.

Bole-Feysot, C., Goffin, V., Edery, M., Binart, N., Kelly, P. A. (1998). Prolactine (PRL) and its receptor: Actions, signal transduction pathways and phenotypes observed in PRL receptor knockout mice. *Endocrine Reviews, 19*, 225–268.

Bradley, K. C., & Meisel, R. L. (2001). Sexual behavior induction of c-Fos in the nucleus accumbens and amphetamine-stimulated locomotor activity are sensitized by previous sexual experience in female Syrian hamsters. *Journal of Neuroscience, 21*, 2123–2130.

Bridges, R., Rigero, B., Byrnes, E., Yang, L., & Walker, A. (2001). Central infusions of the recombinant human prolactin receptor antagonist, S179D-PRL, delay the onset of maternal behavior in steroid-primed, nulliparous female rats. *Endocrinology, 142*, 730–739.

Brody, S., & Krüger, T. H. (2006). The post-orgasmic prolactin increase following intercourse is greater than following maturbation and suggests greater satiety. *Biological Psychology, 71*, 312–315.

Brown, W. A., & Heninger, G. (1975) Cortisol, growth hormone, free fatty acids, and experimentally evoked affective arousal. *American Journal of Psychology, 132*, 1172–1176.

Buvat, J., Lemaire, A., Buvat-Herbaut, M., Fourlinnie, J. C., Racadot, A., & Fossati, P. (1985). Hyperprolactinemia and sexual function in men. *Hormone Research, 22*, 196–203.

Carani, C., Bancroft, J., Del Rio, G., Granata, A. R. M., Facchinetti, F., & Marrama, P. (1990). The endocrine effects of visual erotic stimuli in normal men. *Psychoneuroendocrinology, 15*, 207–216.

Carani, C., Granata, A. R. M., Faustini Fustini, M., Marrama, P. (1996). Prolactin and testosterone: Their role in male sexual function. *International Journal of Andrology, 19*, 48–54.

Carmichael, M. S., Warburton, V. L., Dixen, J., & Davidson, J. M. (1994). Relationships among cardiovascular, muscular, and oxytocin responses during human sexual activity. *Archives of Sexual Behavior, 23*, 59–79.

Cebeira, M., Hernandez, M. L., Rodriguez de Fonsesca, F., de Miguel, R., Fernandez-Ruiz, J. J., & Ramos, J. A. (1991). Lack of effect of prolactin on the dopaminergic receptor sensitivity of striatal and limbic areas after experimentally-induced alterations in peripheral levels. *Life Sciences, 48*, 531–541.

Chen, J. C, & Ramirez, V. D. (1988a). Comparison of the effect of prolactin on dopamine release from the dorsal and ventral striatum and from the mediobasal hypothalamus superfused in vitro. *European Journal of Pharmacology, 149*, 1–8.

Chen, J. C, & Ramirez, V. D. (1988b). In vivo dopaminergic activity from the nucleus accumbens, substantia niagra and ventral tegmental area in the freely moving rat: Basal neurochemical output and prolactin effect. *Neuroendocrinology, 48*, 329–335.

Chen, J. C, & Ramirez, V. D. (1989). Effects of prolactin on tyrosine hydroxylase activity of central dopaminergic neurons of male rats. *European Journal of Pharmacology, 166*, 473–479.

Cooper, A. J. (1977). Bromocriptine in impotence. *Lancet, 2*, 567.

Cruz-Casallas, P. E., Nasello, A. G., Hucke, E. E., & Felicio, L. F. (1999). Dual modulation of male sexual behavior in rats by central prolactin: Relationship with in vivo striatal dopaminergic activity. *Psychoneuroendocrinology, 24*, 681–693.

De Rosa, M., Colao, A., Di Sarno, A., Ferone, D., Landi, M. L., Zarilli, S., et al. (1998). Cabergoline treatment rapidly improves gonadal function in hyperprolactinemic males: A comparison with bromocriptine. *European Journal of Endocrinology, 138*, 286–293.

DeMaria, J. E., Lerant, A. A., & Freeman, M. E. (1999). Prolactin activates all three populations of hypothalamic neuroendocrine dopaminergic neurons in ovariectomized rats. *Brain Research, 837*, 236–241.

DeMaria, J. E., Livingstone, J. D., & Freeman, M. E. (1998). Characterization of the dopaminergic input of the pituitary gland throughout the estrous cycle of the rat. *Neuroendocrinology, 67*, 377–383.

DeMaria, J. E., Zelena, D., Vecsernyés, M., Nagy, G. M., & Freeman, M. E. (1998). The effect of neurointermediate lobe denervation on hypothalamic neuroendocrine dopaminergic neurons, *Brain Research, 806,* 89–94.

Doherty, P. C., Bartke, A., Smith, M. S., & Davis, S. L. (1985). Increased serum prolactin levels mediate the suppressive effects of ectopic pituitary grafts on copulatory behavior in male rats. *Hormones and Behavior, 19,* 111–121.

Doherty, P. C., Baum, M. J., & Todd, R. B. (1986). Effects of chronic hyperprolactinemia on sexual arousal and erectile function in male rats. *Neuroendocrinology, 42,* 368–375.

Doherty, P. C., Lane, S. J., Pfeil, K. A., Morgan, W. W., Bartke, A., & Smith, M. S. (1989). Extra-hypothalamic dopamine is not involved in the effects of hyperprolactinemia on male copulatory behavior. *Physiology and Behavior, 45,* 1101–1105.

Doherty, P. C., Wu, D. E., & Matt, K. S. (1990). Hyperprolactinemia preferentially inhibits erectile function in adrenalectomized male rats. *Life Sciences, 47,* 141–148.

Drago, F., & Lissandrello, C. O. (2000). The "low dose" concept and the paradoxical effects of prolactin on grooming and sexual behavior. *European Journal of Pharmacology, 405,* 131–137.

Exton, M. S., Bindert, A., Krüger, T., Scheller, F., Hartmann, U., & Schedlowski, M. (1999). Cardiovascular and endocrine alterations after masturbation-induced orgasm in women. *Psychosomatic Medicine, 61,* 280–289.

Exton, M. S., Krüger, T. H. C., Bursch, N., Knapp, W., Schedlowski, M., & Hartmann, U. (2001). Neuroendocrine response to masturbation-induced orgasm following a 3-week sexual abstinence. *World Journal of Urology, 19,* 377–382.

Exton, M. S., Krüger, T. H. C., Koch, M., Paulson, E., Knapp, W., Hartmann, U., et al. (2001). Coitus-induced orgasm stimulated prolactin secretion in healthy subjects. *Psychoneuroendocrinology, 26,* 287–294.

Exton, N. G., Truong, T. C., Exton, M. S., Wingenfeld, S. A., Leygraf, N., Saller, B., et al. (2000). Neuroendocrine response to film-induced sexual arousal in men and women. *Psychoneuroendocrinology, 25,* 189–199.

Fiorino, D. F., Coury, A., & Phillips, A. G. (1997). Dynamic changes in nucleus accumbens dopamine efflux during the Coolidge effect in male rats. *Journal of Neuroscience, 17,* 4849–4855.

Fox, C. A., Ismail, A. A. A., Love, D. N., Kirkham, K. E., & Loraine, J. A. (1972). Study on the relationship between plasma testosterone levels and human sexual activity. *Journal of Endocrinology, 52,* 51–58.

Freeman, M. E., Kanyicska, B., Lerant, A., & Nagy, G. (2000). Prolactin: Structure, function, and regulation of secretion. *Physiological Reviews, 80,* 1523–1631.

Fuxe, K. (1964). Cellular localization of monoamines in the median eminence and in the infundibular stem of some mammals. *Acta Physiologica Scandinavica, 58,* 383–384.

Ganong, W. F. (2000). Circumventricular organs: Definition and role in the regulation of endocrine and anatomic function. *Clinical and Experimental Pharmacology and Physiology, 27,* 422–427.

Gonzales-Mora, J. L., Guadalupe, T., & Mas, M. (1990). In vivo voltammetry study of the modulatory action of prolactin on mesolimbic dopaminergic system. *Brain Research Bulletin, 25,* 729–733.

Goudreau, J. L., Lindley, S. E., Lookingland, K. J., & Moore, K. E. (1992). Evidence that hypothalamic periventricular dopamine neurons innervate the intermediate lobe of the rat pituitary. *Neuroendocrinology, 56,* 100–105.

Haake, P., Krüger, T. H. C., Exton, M. S., Giepen, C., Hartmann, U., Osterheider, M., et al. (2003). Acute neuroendocrine response to sexual stimulation in sexual offenders. *Canadian Journal of Psychiatry, 48,* 265–271.

Heiman, J. R., Rowland, D. L., Hatch, J. P., & Gladue, B. A. (1991). Psychophysiological and endocrine responses to sexual arousal in women. *Archives of Sexual Behavior, 20,* 171–186.

Hernandez, M. L., Fernandez-Ruiz, J. J., Navarro, M., de Miguel, R., Cebeira, M., Vatic, S., et al. (1994). Modifications of mesolimbic and nigrostriataldopaminergic activity after intracerebroventricular administration of prolactin. *Journal of Neural Transmission General Section, 96,* 63–79.

Howell Skalla, L., Bunick, D., Bleck, G., Nelson, R. A., & Bahr, J. M. (2000). Cloning and sequence analysis of the extracellular region of the polar bear (Ursus maritimus) luteinizing hormone receptor (LHr), follicle stimulating hormone receptor (FSHr), and prolactin receptor (PRLr) genes and their expression in the testis of the black bear (Ursus americanus). *Molecular Reproduction and Development, 55,* 136–145.

Hull, E. M., Lorraine, D. S., Du, J., Matuszewich, L., Lumley, L. A., Putnam, S. K., et al. (1999). Hormone-neurotransmitter interactions in the control of sexual behavior. *Behavioral Brain Research, 105,* 105–116.

Kooy, A., Weber, R. F., Ooms, M. P., & Vreeburg, J. T. (1988). Deterioration of male sexual behavior in rats by the new prolactin-secreting tumor 7315b. *Hormones and Behavior, 22,* 351–361.

Koppelman, M. C. S., Parry, B. L., Hamilton, J. A., Alagna, S. W., & Loriaux, D. L. (1987). Effect of bromocriptine on affect and libido in hyperprolactinemia. *American Journal of Psychiatry, 144,* 1037–1041.

Krüger, T., Exton, M. S., Pawlak, C., von zur Mühlen, A., Hartmann, U., & Schedlowski, M. (1998). Neuroendocrine and cardiovascular response to sexual arousal and orgasm in men. *Psychoneuroendocrinology, 23,* 401–411.

Krüger, T. H. C., Haake, P., Chereath, D., Knapp, W., Janssen, O. E., Exton, M. S., et al. (2003). Specificity of the neuroendocrine response to orgasm during sexual arousal in men. *Journal of Endocrinology, 177,* 57–64.

Krüger, T. H. C., Haake, P., Haverkamp, J., Krämer, M., Exton, M. S., Saller, B., et al. (2003). Effects of acute prolactin manipulation on sexual drive and function in males. *Journal of Endocrinology, 179,* 357–365.

La Ferla, J., Anderson, D., & Schalch, D. (1978). Psychoendocrine response to sexual arousal in human males. *Psychosomatic Medicine, 40,* 166–172.

Lee, R., Jaffe, R., & Midgley, A. (1974). Lack of alteration of serum gonadotropins in men and women following sexual intercourse. *American Journal of Obstetrics and Gynecology, 120,* 985–987.

Levi, L. (1969). Sympatho-adrenomedullary activity, diuresis, and emotional reactions during visual sexual stimulation in human females and males. *Psychosomatic Medicine, 31,* 251–268.

Lincoln, G. (1974). Luteinising hormone and testosterone in man. *Nature, 252,* 232–233.

Littler, W. A., Honour, A. J., & Sleight, P. (1974). Direct arterial pressure, heart rate and electrocardiogram during human coitus. *Journal of Reproductive Fertility, 40,* 321–331.

Lookingland, K. J., & Moore, K. E. (1984). Effects of estradiol and prolactin on incertohypothalamic dopaminergic neurons in the male rat. *Brain Research, 313,* 83–91.

Mangurian, L. P., Jurjus, A. R., & Walsh, R. J. (1999). Prolactin receptor localization to the area postrema. *Brain Research, 836,* 218–220.

March, C. M. (1979). Bromocriptine in the treatment of hypogonadism and male impotence. *Drugs, 17,* 49–58.

Maruyama, M., Matsumoto, H., Fujiwara, K., Noguchi, J., Kitada, C., Hinuma, S., Onda, H., Nishimura, O., Fujino, M., Higuchi, T., & Inoue, K. (1999). Central administration of prolactin-releasing peptide stimulates oxytocin release in rats. *Neuroscience Letters, 276,* 193–196.

Mas, M. (1995). Neurobiological correlates of masculine sexual behavior. *Neuroscience and Biobehavioral Reviews, 19,* 261–277.

Masters, W. H., & Johnson, V. E. (1966). *Human sexual response.* Boston: Little, Brown.

Meston, C. M., & Frohlich, P. F. (2000). The neurobiology of sexual function. *Archives of General Psychiatry, 57,* 1012–1030.

Montejo-Gonzalez, A. L., Llorca, G., Izquierdo, J. A., Ledesma, A., Bousono, M., Calcedo, A., et al. (1997). SSRI-induced sexual dysfunction: Fluoxetine, paroxetine, sertraline, and fluvoxamine in a prospective, multicenter, and descriptive clinical study of 344 patients. *Journal of Sex and Marital Therapy, 23,* 176–194.

Nasello, A. G., Vanzeler, M. L., Madurieira, E. H., & Felicio, L. F. (1997). Effects of acute and long term domperidone treatment on prolactin and gonadal hormone levels and sexual behavior of male and female rats. *Pharmacology, Biochemistry, & Behavior, 58,* 1089–1094.

Nemec, E. D., Mansfield, L., & Kennedy, J. W. (1976). Heart rate and blood pressure during sexual activity in normal males. *American Heart Journal, 92,* 274–277.

Outhit, A., Morel, G., & Kelly, P. A. (1993). Visualization of gene expression of short and long forms of prolactin receptor in the rat reproductive tissues. *Biol Reprod., 49,* 528–536.

Passie, T., Hartmann, U., Schneider, U., Emrich, H. M., & Krüger, T. H. (2005). Ecstasy (MDMA) mimics the post-orgasmic state: Impairment of sexual drive and function during acute MDMA-effects may be due to increased prolactin secretion. *Medical Hypotheses, 64,* 899–903.

Pérez-Villamil, B., Bordiu, E., & Puente-Cueva, M. (1980). Involvement of physiological prolactin levels in growth and prolactin receptor content of prostate-glands and testes in developing male rats. *Journal of Endocrinology, 132,* 449–459.

Pi, X. J., & Grattan, D. R. (1998). Differential expression of the two forms of prolactin receptor mRNA within microdissected hypothalamic nuclei of the rat. *Brain Research. Molecular Brain Research, 59,* 1–12.

Pi, X. J., & Grattan, D. R. (1999a). Increased expression of both short and long term forms of prolactin receptor mRNA in hypothalamic nuclei of lactating rats. *Journal of Molecular Endocrinology, 23,* 13–22.

Pi, X. J., & Grattan, D. R. (1999b). Increased prolactin receptor immunoreactivity in the hypothalamus of lactating rats. *Journal of Neuroendocrinology, 11,* 693–705.

Pirke, K., Kockott, G., & Dittmar, F. (1974). Psychosexual stimulation and plasma testosterone in man. *Archives of Sexual Behavior, 3,* 577–584.

Prigent-Tessier, A., Pageaux, J. F., Fayard, J. M., Lagarde, M., Laugier, C., & Cohen, H. (1996). Prolactin up-regulates prostaglandin E2 production through increased expression of pancreatic-type phospholipase A2 (type 1) and prostaglandin G/H synthase 2 in uterine cells. *Molecular and Cellular Endocrinology, 122,* 101–108.

Purvis, K., Landgren, B., Cekan, Z., & Diczfalusy, E. (1976). Endocrine effects of masturbation in men. *Journal of Endocrinology, 70,* 439–444.

Ra, S., Aoki, H., Fujioka, T., Sato, F., Kubo, T., & Yasuda, N. (1996). In vitro contraction of the canine corpus cavernosum penis by direct perfusion with prolactin or growth hormone. *Journal of Urology, 156,* 522–525.

Reddy, Y. D., Reddy, K. V., & Govindappa, S. (1985). Effect of prolactin and bromocriptine administration on epididymal function: A biochemical study in rats. *Indian Journal of Physiology and Pharmacology, 29,* 234–238.

Robbins, T. W., & Everitt, B. J. (1992). Functions of dopamine in the dorsal and ventral striatum. *Seminars in Neuroscience, 4,* 119–128.

Roky, R., Paut-PaganTo, L., Goffin, V., Kitahama, K., Valatx, J. L., Kelly, P. A., et al. (1996). Distribution of prolactin receptors in the forebrain: Immunohistochemical study. *Neuroendocrinology, 63,* 422–429.

Rosen, R. C., Lane, R. M., & Menza, M. (1999). Effects of SSRIs on sexual function: A critical review. *Journal of Clinical Psychopharmacology, 19,* 67–85.

Rowland, D. L., Heiman, J. R., Gladue, B. A., Hatch, J. P., Doering, C. H., & Weiler, S. J. (1987). Endocrine, psychological, and genital response to sexual arousal in men. *Psychoneuroendocrinology, 12,* 149–158.

Sauder, S. E., Frager, M., Case, G. D., Kelch, R. P., & Marshall, J. C. (1984). Abnormal patterns of pulsatile luteinizing hormone secretion in women with hyperprolactinemia and amenorrhea: Responses to bromocriptine. *Journal of Clinical Endocrinology and Metabolism, 59,* 941–948.

Shen, W. W., & Hsu, J. H. (1995). Female sexual side effects associated with selective serotonin reuptake inhibitors: A descriptive clinical study of 33 patients. *International Journal of Psychiatric Medicine, 25,* 239–248.

Sobrinho, L. G. (1993). The psychogenic effects of prolactin. *Acta Endocrinology, 129,* S38–40.

Stoléru, S. G., Ennaji, A., Counot, A., & Spira, A. (1993). LH pulsatile secretion and testosterone blood levels are influenced by sexual arousal in human males. *Psychoneuroendocrinology, 18,* 205–218.

Stricker, P., & Grueter, R. (1928). Action du lobe antérieur de l'hypophyse sur la montée laiteuse. *Comptes Rendus Soc Biologies, 99,* 1978–1980.

Verhelst, J., Abs, R., Maiter, D., van den Bruel, A., Vandeweghe, M., Velkeniers, B., et al. (1999). Cabergoline in the treatment of hyperprolactinaemia: A study in 455 patients. *Journal of Endocrinology and Metabolism, 84,* 2518–2522.

Waldinger, M. D., & Olivier, B. (1998). Selective serotonin reuptake inhibitor-induced sexual dysfunction: Clinical and research considerations. *International Clinical Psychopharmacology, 13,* S27–33.

Walsh, J. P., & Pullan, P. T. (1997). Hyperprolactinaemia in males: A heterogeneous disorder. *Australian & New Zealand Journal of Medicine, 27,* 385–390.

Walsh, R. J., Posner, B. I., Kopriwa, B. M., & Brawer, J. R. (1978). Prolactin binding sites in the rat brain. *Science, 201,* 1041–1043.

Walsh, R. J., Slaby, F. J., & Posner, B. I. (1987). A receptor-mediated mechanism for the transport of prolactin from blood to cerebrospinal fluid. *Endocrinology, 120,* 1864–1850.

Whipple, B., Ogden, G., & Komisaruk, B. R. (1992). Physiological correlates of imagery-induced orgasm in women. *Archives of Sexual Behavior, 21,* 121–133.

Wiedeking, C., Lake, C. R., Ziegler, M., Kowarski, A., & Money, J. (1977). Plasma noradrenaline and dopamine-beta-hydroxylase during sexual activity. *Psychosomatic Medicine, 39,* 143–148.

Yoshimura, Y., Nakamura, Y., Oda, T., Ando, M., Ubukata, Y., Kayama, N., et al. (1992). Effects of prolactin on ovarian plasmin generation in the process of ovulation. *Biology of Reproduction, 46,* 322–327.

Female Sexual Arousal Response Using Serial Magnetic Resonance Imaging with Initial Comparisons to Vaginal Photoplethysmography

Overview and Evaluation

JULIA R. HEIMAN AND KENNETH R. MARAVILLA

Introduction

Although the sexual arousal and response of women has been empirically studied over the past 4 decades, measurement methods have been minimally available. This is particularly the case in understanding the physiology and psychophysiology of female sexual dysfunction (FSD), even though problems of sexual functioning may be as prevalent as 25–40% (Bancroft, Loftus, & Long, 2003; Laumann, Paik, & Rosen, 1999). Attempts to test and validate differences between functional and dysfunctional sexual response, as well as treatments for FSD subtypes, have been difficult due in part to the limited availability of physiological measures that are reliable, reproducible, and relatively noninvasive. Since 1999, we have tested and presented a new method for objectively monitoring female sexual arousal response using serial magnetic resonance imaging (MRI). Initially this was performed in conjunction with MS-325 (EPIX Medical, Inc.), an investigational new gadolinium-based blood pool agent (Deliganis et al., 2002; Maravilla et al., 2003; Suh et al., 2004), and, more recently, employing a modified MRI technique without contrast agent (Maravilla et al., 2005).

The most commonly used female sexual arousal measurement method, vaginal photoplethysmography (VPP), has been used as a relative arousal measurement method for over 3 decades (Heiman, 1977, 1998; Laan, Everaerd, & Evers, 1995; Morokoff & Heiman, 1980). VPP has been shown to be a sensitive and reliable indicator of female sexual arousal, but it remains limited due to its lack of absolute scaling and thus must be used in within-subject or crossover designs.

We have conducted initial studies to develop the MRI method and technique for female genital measurement. Pelvic MRI to examine genital response is an emerging method and thus it is likely to be modified with greater and wider use. The present paper is intended to critically review results to date, to evaluate the advantages and disadvantages of the MS-325 enhanced and nonenhanced serial MRI technique, and to provide comments on the comparison of MRI to VPP. Both techniques also included subjective measures of arousal.

Materials and Methods Used

In order to give specifics on the use of MRI and comparison to VPP, we will detail the methods used.

Participants

This work will summarize our experience with 25 healthy, sexually functional women. Premenopausal women between the ages of 23 and 38 together with postmenopausal women between the ages of 53 and 66 were enrolled into the combined research studies. The university institutional review board approved the protocol and consent form, and subjects signed a written consent prior to study entry. Subjects were recruited by the use of advertising in local newspapers and flyers placed on the university campus. Potential subjects were initially screened by telephone. Subjects were invited to the study site if they were healthy and had no sexual disorders.

All subjects underwent a complete physical examination, including a pelvic examination and a Papanicolaou (Pap) smear. Blood samples were drawn to assess baseline chemistry, hematology, coagulation, iron, and endocrinology values; and a urine sample was obtained for microscopic urinalysis in all subjects. All results showed no significant abnormalities. Pregnancy was excluded in the premenopausal group at both the screening visit and on the day of the MR visit. Premenopausal females were scanned (and for those women in the comparison study, run in the VPP procedure within 8 days of that window) between day 7 and day 21 inclusive of their menstrual cycle. The postmenopausal subjects had additional hormonal testing performed including estradiol, serum luteinizing hormone, and follicle-stimulating hormone levels, which had to be within a specified laboratory range typical for postmenopausal women. Subjects with a history of previous vaginal surgery, hysterectomy, abnormal menstrual cycles, and/or having taken hormone replacement therapy or birth-control pills within the preceding 6 months were excluded from the study.

There were some weight restrictions due to limitations of the MRI procedure and equipment. Weights ranged between 47 and 90 kg and height from 157 cm to 180 cm.

Safety assessments, including vital signs, 12-lead electrocardiograms (ECGs), blood samples, urine tests, and physical examination were documented at specified intervals up to 96 hours postinjection of MS-325. These are detailed in the first report on MRI results (Deliganis et al., 2002).

Measures

MRI MEASURES

Contrast dosing. MS-325 is a small (MW 957) gadolinium chelate that binds reversibly to albumin. While bound to albumin, the agent increases its relaxivity 4- to 10-fold, depending on field strength. The agent shows a bi-exponential clearance, with a terminal clearance phase half-life of 10 to 14 hours. MS-325 is currently in phase III clinical trials for use in MR angiography. MS-325 is formulated at a concentration of 0.25 mmol/mL. After initial piloting with 4 women on dosage and imaging protocols (see Deliganis et al., 2002), 12 women received a dose of MS-325 calculated at 0.05 mmol/kg of body weight. Contrast MS-325 was injected intravenously at a maximum rate of 1.5 mL/second, followed by a 30 mL normal saline flush.

Videotaped material. The videotapes (the same videotapes as were used in the VPP when we compared the two methods) contained segments of neutral and erotic (sexually explicit) material. The neutral materials were nature or geographic scenes and the erotic materials were commercially available, sexually explicit heterosexual videos, selected and piloted as being more women-focused. The videotape format included a 21-minute neutral section, a 15-minute erotic section, and another 9-minute neutral section. Magnetic resonance imaging was performed during the entire 45-minute videotape presentation. Subjects were able to see and hear the video material through a fiber-optic audiovisual display system (Avotec, Inc., Stuart, Florida) while in the magnet bore. Two subjects, one pre- and one postmenopausal woman, served as controls. They were injected with MS-325 but saw only neutral video material.

Subjective measurements. Subjective (self-report) sexual and affective response were measured using a 30-item Film Evaluation Scale (FES), a shortened 7-item version of which was used after the neutral video, that has been found to be a reliable and sensitive measure of sexual response and affect in women and men (e.g., Hackbert & Heiman, 2002; Heiman, 1977; Heiman & Rowland, 1983; Meston & Heiman, 1998). The scale, also referred to as the Subjective Experience Scale, consists of questions that begin with, "During the tape/film (or in the case of the baseline condition, "During the past 5 minutes), I felt" followed by a list of words that tap subjective sexual arousal, perceived genital and other bodily changes, and, in the full-length version, positive and negative affective states. A version of that measure (some items vary depending upon the goals of the study) is in Table 1.

All subjects were asked to complete the FES at three time points: immediately prior to entering the magnet and viewing the neutral video material, just prior to viewing the erotic video material while in the magnet, and immediately after the MRI was completed (to document responses during the erotic videotape). The shortened 7-point questionnaire was employed for use in the magnet to record arousal/nonarousal level at the end of the neutral video and just prior to the subject viewing the erotic stimulus video. Using a PowerPoint computer display, the abbreviated questionnaire was displayed through the video presentation system for the subject in the magnet. The subject gave the numerical score for each of the 7 questions by calling verbally over an intercom to an investigator outside the magnet who recorded the questionnaire responses.

Magnetic resonance imaging. Magnetic resonance images were obtained on a GE Signa 1.5 Tesla system (General Electric Medical Systems, Waukesha, Wisconsin). Images of the perineum were acquired using specially designed phased-array (PA) coils built by scientists at the University of Washington. Subjects were imaged using a T1 weighted fast, 3-D spoiled gradient recalled echo (SPGR), acquired in an axial orientation (TR/TE/flip angle = $11/1.7/35°$, 256×256, FOV = 24 cm, 2.0-mm slice thickness, 1 NEX). Voxel size was very small, measuring approximately $0.9 \times 0.9 \times 2$ mm for a total voxel volume of 1.6 mm^3. This small voxel size was felt to be necessary since the clitoral structures are small and require fine detail imaging for accurate measurement. The use of local PA coils boosted the signal-to-noise ratio to enable detailed imaging of the external genitalia and to provide both reliable anatomical structure outlines and measures of signal intensity (SI) within small regions of interest (ROIs). Shim values, transmitter gain, and receiver gain settings were kept constant for the entire 45-minute imaging session to provide accurate time versus signal intensity plots for calculation of regional blood volume changes.

One 3-D volume series was obtained prior to contrast administration. Intravenous contrast injection was followed by a 3-minute delay for contrast level equilibration. Postcontrast images were then acquired every 3 minutes while subjects simultaneously viewed the video material.

VPP MEASURES

A vaginal photoplethysmograph (Behavioral Technology Instruments, Salt Lake City, Utah) was used to measure vaginal pulse amplitude (VPA) and vaginal blood volume (VBV) responses. The vaginal photoplethysmograph has been shown to be a valid and reliable measure of sexual arousal in women. The software program AcqKnowledge III, version 3.3 (BIOPAC Systems, Inc., Santa Barbara, California) and data acquisition unit (model MP100WS, BIOPAC Systems, Inc.) were used with a personal computer (Power Macintosh 6100/70, Apple, Cupertino, California) to collect, convert (from analog to digital), and transform data.

Subjective measurements. Subjective (self-report) sexual responses were measured using the same 30-item FES that was described for use with the MRI study. To be comparable in methods to the MRI procedure, a short-

Table 1 *Tape/Film Scale also known as the Film Evaluation Scale and the Subjective Experiences Scale (Hackbert & Heiman, 2002; Heiman, 1977; Heiman & Rowland, 1983; Meston & Heiman, 1998)*

TAPE/FILM SCALE

Instructions: Please use the following scale to evaluate how you felt during the last tape/film. Please answer honestly and carefully. On the scale, circle any of the numbers from 1 (not at all) to 7 (intensely).

During the tape/film, I felt:

		Not at all						Intensely
1.	Sexually aroused	1	2	3	4	5	6	7
2.	Mentally sexually aroused	1	2	3	4	5	6	7
3.	Physically sexually aroused	1	2	3	4	5	6	7
4.	Anxious	1	2	3	4	5	6	7
5.	Worried	1	2	3	4	5	6	7
6.	Angry	1	2	3	4	5	6	7
7.	Disgusted	1	2	3	4	5	6	7
8.	Embarrassed	1	2	3	4	5	6	7
9.	Guilty	1	2	3	4	5	6	7
10.	Sensuous	1	2	3	4	5	6	7
11.	A desire to be close to someone	1	2	3	4	5	6	7
12.	Any physical reaction at all	1	2	3	4	5	6	7
13.	Any genital feelings	1	2	3	4	5	6	7
14.	Feelings of warmth	1	2	3	4	5	6	7
15.	Genital pulsing or throbbing	1	2	3	4	5	6	7
16.	Warmth in genitals	1	2	3	4	5	6	7
17.	Genital wetness or lubrication	1	2	3	4	5	6	7
18.	Perspiration	1	2	3	4	5	6	7

Continued on the next page

Table 1. *(Continued)*

	Not at all						Intensely
19. Breast sensations	1	2	3	4	5	6	7
20. Faster heartbeat	1	2	3	4	5	6	7
21. Faster breathing	1	2	3	4	5	6	7
22. Pleasant	1	2	3	4	5	6	7
23. Interested	1	2	3	4	5	6	7
24. Attracted	1	2	3	4	5	6	7
25. Excited	1	2	3	4	5	6	7
26. Sexy	1	2	3	4	5	6	7
27. Feminine	1	2	3	4	5	6	7
28. Dirty	1	2	3	4	5	6	7
29. Loving	1	2	3	4	5	6	7
30. Sexually attractive	1	2	3	4	5	6	7
31. Inhibited	1	2	3	4	5	6	7
32. Easy to arouse	1	2	3	4	5	6	7
33. Incompetent	1	2	3	4	5	6	7
34. Sexually turned off	1	2	3	4	5	6	7
35. Aggressive	1	2	3	4	5	6	7
36. Relaxed	1	2	3	4	5	6	7
37. Masculine	1	2	3	4	5	6	7
38. Sexual desire	1	2	3	4	5	6	7
39. Pleasure	1	2	3	4	5	6	7

Julia R Heiman 1977/1998 ©

ened 7-item version of the FES was given immediately after the presentation of the neutral (and prior to the erotic) videotaped material. The full-length FES was completed immediately after the termination of erotic segment (before removal of the photoplethysmograph).

VAGINAL PHOTOPLETHYSMOGRAPHY DATA SAMPLING AND REDUCTION

Vaginal responses to neutral and erotic stimuli were measured during the initial adaptation period and throughout the presentation of the videotaped material. Physiological responses were sampled at a rate of 60 samples per second throughout the adaptation (baseline phase), the entire 10 minutes of neutral film, and 14 minutes of erotic film. The BIOPAC software allowed for an automated transformation of raw data into VPA and VBV scores that were converted to an Excel spreadsheet and then transferred for statistical analysis.

Procedures

Protocols were carried out at two separate locations at the University of Washington Medical Center, depending on the method used: (i) MRI at the MR Research Laboratory of the Department of Radiology, and (ii) VPP at the Reproductive and Sexual Medicine Clinic of the outpatient clinics. The same neutral and erotic videos were used at both sites, but were presented in counterbalanced order. A familiarization visit conducted at each site prior to the experimental session ensured that women were comfortable with the procedures. The same FES was used at both sites to measure sexual arousal and affect.

MRI

During the MRI session, the participant viewed the audio and video presentation through fiber optic coupled goggles and headphones while lying quietly in the magnet. Subjects viewed 20 minutes of neutral documentary video followed by a 15-minute segment of sexually stimulating video and then a final 9 minutes of neutral video. Serial MRI was continuously acquired at 3-minute intervals during the entire video presentation. Following completion of the MR study, the image data was transferred to an offline computer workstation for processing and analysis.

VPP

During the VPP experimental session, the participant was given instructions about the VPP probe and she inserted the vaginal probe in the privacy of the experimental room. She then watched a 10-minute neutral and 14-minute erotic film segment and completed the FES. The VPP data were collected on a computer located in a separate room and an intercom allowed for communication between the subject and experimenter. Subjective data were collected before presentation of neutral video material but after the subject had inserted the photoplethysmograph, immediately after the presentation of the neutral videotaped material, and after the termination of the erotic segment, but before removal of the photoplethysmograph.

Data Analysis

The MRI images were subjectively evaluated for pre- and postcontrast image quality and for visualization of the anatomy of the genital tract by two experienced radiologists. Signal intensities were measured by selection of ROIs positioned within the vaginal wall, vaginal mucosa, common femoral vein, muscle, clitoris, and in the air outside the subject to provide a measure of background noise. The size of the ROI varied depending on the size of the structure being analyzed. For example, across all subjects the measurements of the vaginal wall ROI ranged in size between 4 mm^2 and 22 mm^2, while the clitoral body ROI was between 7 mm^2 and 70 mm^2. Within each subject, the size of the ROI was kept consistent at each time point throughout the neutral and erotic segments. Image volumes for each time point within a given subject were analyzed in random order to attempt to reduce bias. However, all volumes with a given subject were analyzed together.

MRI CHANGES IN REGIONAL BLOOD VOLUME

Relative regional blood volume was estimated from signal intensity versus time curves derived from ROI measurements of the vaginal wall and clitoris using the following equation:

$$rRBV_{structure} = \frac{SI_{structure}(t) - SI_{structure}(t_0)}{SI_{femoral}(t) - SI_{femoral}(t_0)}$$

where rRBV is the relative regional blood volume, SI(t) refers to the signal intensity measurements from the ROI taken at the various time points, and t_0 refers to the precontrast scan. The denominator compensates for the slow clearance of MS-325 over the time of the study. In order to smooth statistical fluctuations in SI measurements of the femoral vein, the femoral signal intensity data was fit to a bi-exponential clearance, and then the fit values were used in Equation 1. ROI measurements were taken separately over the body and glans of the clitoris. From these signal intensity measurements, SI versus time curves were generated and rRBV measurements over time were calculated using femoral vein SIs corrected for the bi-exponential decay of MS-325 over time.

To determine whether erotic video material differentially changed estimated rRBV, the estimated rRBV changes were fit as a function of time to the following three-parameter model (A, B, and C) to account for these changes:

$$rRBV(t) = A + B(t) + C\ video(t)$$

where (t) is the time, video(t) equals 1 during erotic video and 0 during neutral video corresponding to the last 11 image data sets acquired. Typically, this represents 18 minutes of neutral video material, followed by 15 minutes of erotic video material and 6 minutes of neutral video material. The "A" coefficient depends on the initial blood volume and "B" reflects both slow extravasation of the agent over time as well as potential incomplete return of blood volume to a baseline state after the erotic video. "C" reflects the video-dependent changes in rRBV. The presence of a significant influence of the C term in Equation 2 was tested using the *t* statistic in the regression, and the relative change in rRBV associated with the video segments was estimated and tabulated as C/A on a subject-by-subject basis for clitoral body and glans clitoris measurements.

MRI CHANGES IN CLITORAL ANATOMICAL VOLUME

The various structures comprising the clitoris, including the crura, body, and glans, were identified and outlined from each slice containing clitoral tissue. These areas were summed and the total volume was measured at each time point using a planimetric method, with volumes reported in cubic centimeters (cc). If there was difficulty defining the precise boundary between the clitoris and adjacent mucosal or glandular tissue, all of the enhancing tissues were included. This was often the case in the area of the clitoral body, but this was not felt to cause a problem with comparative measurements within a given subject since the same anatomical areas were outlined at each time point. However, this method may have resulted in a slight overestimation of the true clitoral volume in some subjects. Data analysis and graphic presentation were done using a two-tailed *t* test with commercially available spreadsheet and graphing programs.

VPP

Baseline was the mean of the first 3 minutes of data; the erotic mean was the mean of all observations taken during the erotic video; the erotic maximum was the maximum of all 30-second observations taken during the erotic video; the mean change was the difference between the baseline and the erotic mean; percentage change was converted from the mean change score; and the maximum change was the difference between the baseline and the erotic maximum. Given the small sample used in the comparison study, the analyses were limited to nonparametric Wilcoxon, paired *t,* and Pearson correlations.

Findings across Studies

The initial studies have been designed to explore the best method of study design and measurement to evaluate whether the method was valid, reliable, and feasible. To summarize that information, the following presents some key questions that the studies have attempted to answer.
1. Can a woman's genitals be clearly visualized during neutral and erotic stimulation? If so, how do the relative regional blood volume and clitoral anatomical volume measures compare?

In Deliganis et al. (2002), both of these questions were addressed. Using the contrast agent MS-325, each woman's genitals were well visualized under neutral and erotic conditions. However, important differences were noted depending on which genital structure was examined. Overall, there was an increase in both degree of enhancement (rRBV) and overall size of the *clitoris* during the erotic video segment as compared to the first neutral segment. However, when ROI measurements of the *vaginal wall* were analyzed, there was very low contrast enhancement and no significant trends were observed in the vaginal wall blood volume curves. Vaginal mucosa was not well visualized as a separate structure and attempts to generate measurements of this very thin structure proved unfeasible. Thus the focus in this study (and later ones) was on the clitoral area for measurement.

rRBV. For the glans clitoris, rRBV changed 40% + 10% (SEM) in the subjects viewing the erotic video versus −3% + 5% for the control subjects. In the clitoral body, rRBV increased 24% + 8% in the group shown erotic videos versus 3% + 8% for the neutral only control group. No significant differences were observed for the pre- and postmenopausal groups, although average rRBV increases were slightly greater in the postmenopausal group in the clitoral body (premenopausal, 9% + 4%, postmenopausal, 39% + 12%).

Clitoral volume. Quantitative changes in clitoral volume over time proved more robust than rRBV measures. The average clitoral volume increased from 10.74 cc at baseline (during the first neutral segment) to 21.17 cc while viewing the erotic material and then decreased to 15.42 cc while viewing the second neutral segment. Thus, there was a mean volume change of 118% + 73% (range 51–280%). There was no significant difference in clitoral volume changes between premenopausal subjects and postmenopausal subjects. Clitoral volume measurements compared between the first neutral and erotic segments in the premenopausal group showed an average increase of 107% + 26% (range of 51–181%), while the postmenopausal group averaged 129% + 43% (range of 55–280%). No significant change in clitoral volume was measured in the control subjects that viewed only neutral material. Figures 1 and 2 illustrate a sample of the transverse T1 weighted MR clitoral volume images.

More recently, Suh et al. (2004) retrospectively analyzed a subset of data from 19 subjects (11 pre- and 8 postmenopausal women) that overlapped with the present group. Using 2-D instead of 3-D analysis measurements, there were significant changes during sexual arousal seen only in the labia minora and vestibular bulbs. No significant changes were detectable in clitoral body width. They did find clitoral contrast enhancement of 62.6% in premenopausal and 39.8% in postmenopausal women. (Labia minora, vestibular bulb, contrast enhancement changes also were significant, though more modest.) Signal intensity change was used in place of rRBV because it did not require baseline acquisitions (which were not available in all subjects) or extra calculations to account for fluctuation in femoral vein signal intensity. The differences between the Deliganis et al. (2002) and Suh et al. findings help to illustrate that changes in measurement ap-

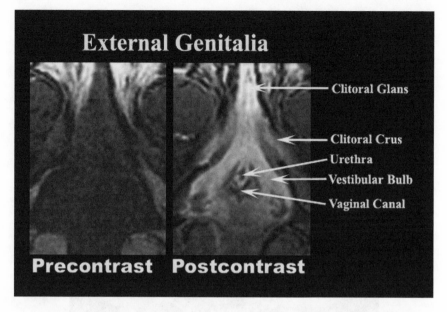

External Genitalia

Clitoral Glans

Clitoral Crus

Urethra

Vestibular Bulb

Vaginal Canal

Precontrast **Postcontrast**

Figure 1. Transverse T1 weighted MR images of the external genitals of one woman before and after MS-325. The postcontrast image was obtained 3 minutes after contrast agent injection while the subject watched a neutral video segment (Deliganis et al., 2002).

proach may greatly impact results, even when the same study site, imaging protocols, and equipment are used. In this case, 3-D measurements proved critical for detecting changes in clitoral engorgement with arousal. Thus, careful attention to data selection and analysis methods is obviously important.

2. Can actual genital organ dimensions be calculated?

This can be done using serial postcontrast images and making structural measurements in either two dimensions or three dimensions (Suh, Yang, Cao, Garland, & Maravilla, 2003; Suh et al., 2004). To date, actual measurements for some structures have only been done in 2-D, which may not be adequate to capture all of the changes occurring during arousal (Suh et al., 2004; Table 2). Suh et al. (2004) noted that volumetric measurement of the vagina, urethra, bulbs, labia minor, and labia majora is difficult due to indistinct borders and boundary uncertainties of these structures. Structural measurement during arousal remains important for further exploration as we few data little available since Dickenson (1949), Masters and Johnson (1966), and these recent MRI studies (Suh et al., 2003, 2004).

3. Do women report subjective sexual arousal to visual stimuli in the MRI setting?

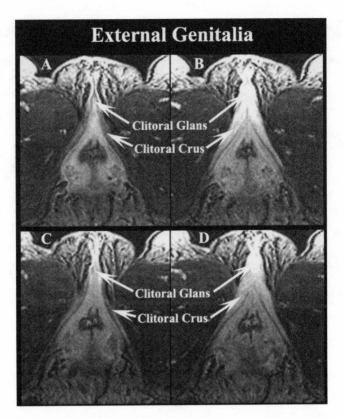

Figure 2. Genital images in one subject demonstrating visual increase in clitoral signal intensity and volume between neutral and erotic video segments in two different sessions. (Key: a = neutral session 1, b = erotic session 1, c = neutral session 2, d = erotic session 2; Maravilla et al., 2003.)

They report a range from little to intense arousal. For example, in Deliganis et al.(2002), all 12 study subjects reported no feelings of sexual arousal on the first two assessments prior to viewing the initial neutral and again prior to viewing the erotic videotape segments (average score = 1.0). After viewing the erotic material, all subjects reported sexual arousal with an average score for all subjects of 3.87 (range of 2–6 on the 7-point scale).
4. What is the evidence for the reliability and stability of MRI and subjective arousal findings?

We only have two studies so far, on a small sample of 10 premenopausal and 7 postmenopausal women, which have examined intrasubject reproducibility of findings (Maravilla et al., 2003, 2005). Using a similar protocol design involving 15 minutes of neutral, followed by 15 minutes of sexually explicit and 15 minutes of neutral video material, two separate

Table 2. *Mean Structural Measurements in Pre- and Postmenopausal Subjects: Significant Results (Suh et al., 2004)*[a,b]

	neutral	arousal	difference	*p* value
labia minora width				
premenopausal	11 ± 2 (9–15)	13 ± 2 (10–15)	1 ± 1 (1–4)	p < 0.01
postmenopausal	9 ± 2 (7–13)	10 ± 2 (7–14)	1 ± 1 (0–2)	p < 0.01
bulb width				
premenopausal	8 ± 1 (6–10)	9 ± 2 (7–14)	1 ± 1 (0–4)	p < 0.01
postmenopausal	5 ± 2 (3–8)	6 ± 2 (5–10)	1 ± 1 (0–2)	p < 0.01

[a] All measurements were made using T1 postcontrast images. Average + std dev (in mm), range expressed in parentheses.
[b] Only significant measures listed here. See Suh et al. (2004) for data on labia majora, clitoral body, urethral diameter, vagina, and cervix.

MRI sessions were conducted for each subject approximately 45 minutes apart for the MS-325 study, during which time the subject exited from the MRI lab and took a rest break. The reason for the rather brief intertrial interval was to complete both imaging sessions with only a single injection of contrast to avoid reexposing subjects to the MS-325, since it is still an investigational agent. Subsequently, the research team developed a noncontrast MRI method to do the trial without the need for a contrast agent. It was important to validate that the measurements could be replicated at different time points within a given subject, as that may be useful for application of this technique to some types of future genital studies.

Signal intensity measures from baseline to arousal increased approximately 90% in session 1 and 32% in session 2, with a range between 13% and 177% over the two sessions. The decrease in session 2 was due to the residual engorgement from the arousal experience of session 1, as shown in Figure 3. Since MR tuning changes were required before session 2, baseline signal intensity values could not be reliably extrapolated from session 1 to session 2 to normalize signal intensity. Thus the SI_δ data were considered less reliable than the anatomic clitoral volume analysis. By comparison the clitoral volume measures performed well. There was a 107% mean increase in session 1 and a 110% mean increase in session 2, resulting in an excellent correlation of $r^2 = 0.95$ between sessions. Figures 3a and 3b illustrate these effects in one subject.

Also interesting, the overall sexual arousal levels were similar to earlier trials, with mean subjective arousal levels at 4.2 (range 2.33–5.33) in session 1 and 4.3 (range 2.0–6.33) in session 2 and the resulting correlation at $r^2 = 0.52$ between sessions. Thus the reliability of findings was excellent

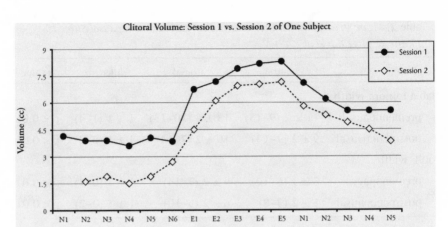

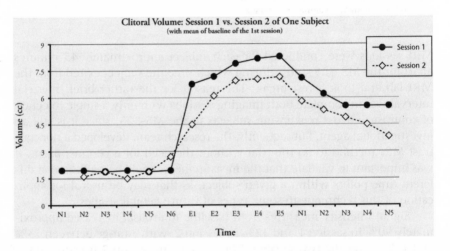

Figure 3a, b. Clitoral volume change in one subject with the neutral and erotic video segments. Figure 3a: actual neutral volumes, Figure 3b: normalized neutral volumes across sessions 1 and 2. The percent change is > 250% in both sessions 1 and 2 (Maravilla et al., 2003).

for clitoral volume, good for subjective report, and inconclusive for signal intensity changes (Maravilla et al., 2003). Although very encouraging, the reliability data would benefit from replication on larger samples, with anatomical 2-D and 3-D measures recorded on clitoral as well as the other genital area structures, as well as another look at analyzing the signal intensity change measure.

5. What can be said about differences, if any, in sexual arousal patterns between premenopausal and postmenopausal women?

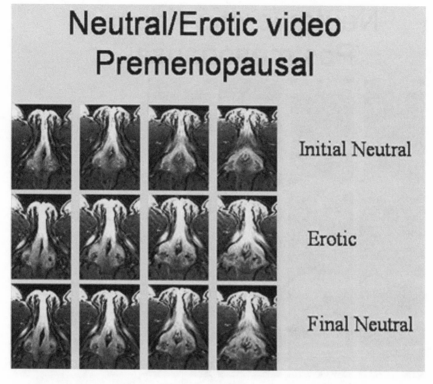

Figure 4. Samples of genital volume changes during neutral-erotic-neutral video segments for four different premenopausal women.

Sample sizes are small and generalizations not warranted beyond these study participants. Also, the postmenopausal women were not on any hormone replacement therapies (HRT). Data from the prior studies summarize a total of 17 (11 new subjects, 6 crossovers) postmenopausal women and 23 (17 new subjects, 6 crossovers) premenopausal women. The postmenopausal sample is particularly limited as Deliganis et al. (2002), Suh et al. (2004), and Maravilla et al. (2003) used different data analysis measures, and thus we really have a sample of 5 (who were exposed to VSS), 9, and 3 postmenopausal subjects, respectively. With these cautions in mind, a pattern is beginning to emerge suggesting that there are may be some differences in genital volume and enhancement measures, depending on menopausal (without HRT) status. Although Deliganis et al. found no differences, there appears to have been some movement artifact in three of the premenopausal subjects that produced artificially low rRBV values. On the clitoral volume measure there was also 1 subject who was a possible outlier in the postmenopausal group whose response was 70% higher than the next highest postmenopausal subject. Figures 4, 5, and 6 illustrate

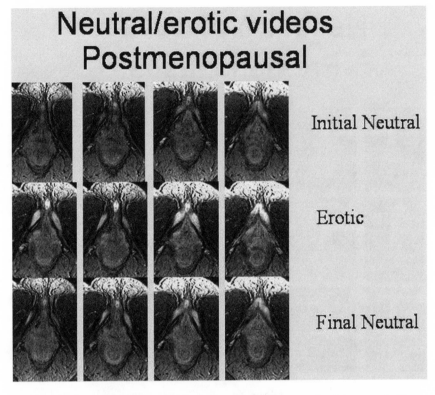

Figure 5. Samples of genital volume changes during neutral-erotic-neutral video segments for four different postmenopausal women.

sample genital images of pre- and postmenopausal women during different points in the procedure.

In Suh et al. (2004), vaginal wall enhancement increased significantly only in premenopausal subjects. However an earlier analysis of Suh et al. (2003), using these same subjects, measured only the time points 9 minutes after contrast medium injection and before any sexually explicit video materials were presented. Anatomic structures were measured and Suh et al. (2003) found there were significant differences between pre- and postmenopausal women on several anatomical structures. Postmenopausal women showed significantly less labia minora width, less vestibular bulb width, less vaginal width, less vaginal wall thickness, and less cervical diameter. These changes are in agreement with expected changes in a decreasing estrogenic environment. However, what the Suh et al. (2004) study shows is that, in spite of these decreases, postmenopausal women showed significant volumetric increases during VSS in the same genital structures as premenopausal women (labia minora width and bulb width).

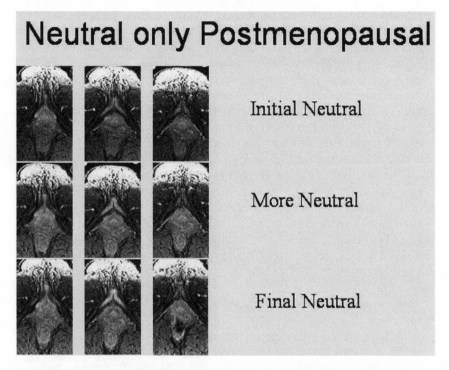

Neutral only Postmenopausal

Initial Neutral

More Neutral

Final Neutral

Figure 6. Samples of genital volume changes during neutral only conditions for three postmenopausal women.

In the reproducibility study that confirmed the value of the clitoral volume measure, there were no direct tests of pre- and postmenopausal differences, as there were only 3 postmenopausal women. Still if one looks at Table 2 in Maravilla et al. (2003), it suggests there may be differences in the percent of change in clitoral volume (% D CV). Premenopausal women increased on average 118% in session 1 and 125% in session 2, while the figures for postmenopausal women were 85% and 80%, respectively. The indications thus far are, though tentative, that non-HRT postmenopausal women in these studies showed comparatively smaller sizing of some genital structures but significant increases during VSS arousal in the same genital structures.

Two pelvic MRI studies have reported arousal scores separately by menopausal status. As noted, Maravilla et al. (2005) is based on only 3 postmenopausal and 6 premenopausal women, so no statistical analyses were performed. Premenopausal women rated their sexual arousal during VSS (mean values calculated from Table 2 of the article) as 3.66 during session 1 and 3.6 during session 2, while postmenopausal women rated their levels at 5.1 for session 1 and 5.86 for session 2. The other study is the noncontrast study of Maravilla et al. (2005) that included 4 premenopausal and 4 postmenopausal women. However, 7 of these women had been in the Maravilla et al. (2003) study, thus they are not an independent sample. However, their subjective data are worth attending to briefly as the stimuli used in the present study were different and these presentations were the third and fourth exposures to experimental visual sexual stimulation. Thus, one might expect their arousal levels to be a bit lower than the first exposures, although the evidence from VSS studies is that this habituation does not predictably occur in laboratory investigations (Laan & Everaerd, 1995). Although the data are not analyzed in the Maravilla et al. (2005) study, several figures can be derived from Table 1 of the article. Premenopausal participants' Subjective Experience Questionnaire (SEQ), which is identical to the FES, mean scores were 3.65 (range 3.3–4.3) and 3.025 (range 2–3.7) in sessions 1 and 2, respectively. Postmenopausal participants' SEQ mean scores were 5.0 (range 4–6) and 5.025 (range 3.7–6) in sessions 1 and 2, respectively. In this sample then, the postmenopausal women reported considerably more subjective sexual arousal in terms of means and range of scores.

6. How do the MRI results compare with those of vaginal photoplethysmography?

We have some initial data on this question. Twelve (only 10 of whom could be included in the MRI data here as the others used a different dose and were in the pilot phase of the Deliganis et al. study) of the 16 women, 6 premenopausal and 6 postmenopausal, who participated in the Deliganis et al. (2002) MRI study also volunteered for a VPP trial, using the same design, video materials (counterbalanced across VPP and MRI sites), and subjective measurements (Heiman, Maravilla, et al., 2005). The main methodological differences were necessitated by the differences in the genital measurement requirements, including the presentation of stimuli though a monitor and headphones versus a fiber-optic audiovisual display system, body position of partial reclining versus lying flat, a greater requirement to remain immobile with the MRI, injection of the contrast agent for the MRI procedure, and the presentation of the subjective FES varying slightly between the two methods.

The genital measures used were based on the difference between the responses during baseline/neutral stimulus and the erotic video. A definite response to erotic content was demonstrated in both measurement settings. Looking at mean values across the entire stimulus condition, VPA showed a 61–70% change between the neutral and erotic stimuli, while VBV showed a 9–26% change. MRI measurements showed anatomical changes in the glans (113–133%) and whole clitoris (105–126%) and relative regional blood volume changes in the glans (68–88%), body (51–70%), and whole clitoris (83–86%). Because the MRI measures more clearly capture the "maximum response" to the erotic stimulus, VPP maximum response

Table 3. *Correlations between Subjective and MRI and VPP Measures (Heiman, Maravilla, et al., 2006)*

	Change VPA	Change VBV	Change AV	Change BV
During the tape, I felt				
(1) Sexually aroused	0.65*	0.47	0.50	0.51
(2) Any genital feeling	0.73*	0.54	0.45	0.42
(3) Genital pulse throb	0.59	0.47	0.54	0.55
(4) Warmth in genitals	0.63*	0.42	0.62	0.60
(5) Genital wetness/lubrication	0.10	0.09	0.43	0.34

*$p < .05$; $n = 10$ subjects; VPP measures: VPA = vaginal pulse amplitude, VBV = vaginal blood volume; MRI measures: AV = anatomical volume, BV = relative blood volume.

figures were also reported. The maximum percentage change during the erotic stimulus compared to baseline was 69–97% for VPA and 11–26% for VBV.

Baseline values were correlated with erotic values on all measures: VPA ($r = 0.89$), VBV ($r = 0.98$), MRI anatomical volume ($r = 0.84$), and rRBV ($r = 0.72$). There were no significant correlations or trends in the relationship between any of the VPP and MRI measures including baselines, erotic means, and changes from baseline. This may either be explained by the differences in the measurement methods themselves, or the possibility that at these levels of arousal (moderate and during visual erotic stimuli without additional kinesthetic stimuli), the two clitoral and vaginal systems are overlapping and partially independent. Although this may seem a peculiar idea at first glance, one can imagine a staged process of arousal to the genital area and that the vaginal probe detects a set of changes to vaginal tissue that does not correspond directly to anatomical or regional blood volume changes in the external genital structures.

There were similar levels of subjective sexual arousal reported during the MRI and VPP erotic stimulus conditions, averaging between 4.1 and 4.6 (on the 7-point scale) for either mental or sexual arousal. In addition, there were correlations between the SEQ questions asking about sexual arousal and perceived genital feelings and each of the measures, as shown in Table 3.

If we use a cutoff of $r = 0.60$ as indication of a notable association, then VPA showed the stronger associations between subjective and physiological measures, with "sexually aroused," "any genital feelings," "warmth in geni-

tals," and the positive affect cluster of items showing the strongest correlations with VPA. The item asking about the level of "warmth in genitals"
was correlated above 0.60 in three of the four genital measures. Overall
these data confirmed the value of each measure and suggest that a larger
study correcting some of the issues and testing across the two methods is
warranted and worth doing in women with and without well-described
sexual dysfunctions. In addition, these data support the decision by most
prior work that VPA is a better, more reliable measure of arousal than VBV
(Heiman, 1977; Heiman, Guess, et al., 2004; Laan, Everaerd, van der
Velde, & Geer, 1995).

7. What are the advantages and disadvantages of using MRI with MS-325
for research of female sexual response, and is it possible to perform good
pelvic imaging for this purpose without a contrast agent?

MS-325 is a gadolinium-based chelate that reversibly binds to serum
albumin and has a half-life estimated to be as high as 10–14 hours when
injected in humans intravenously (Parmalee, Walovitch, Oullet, & Lauffer,
1997). The long half-life of MS-325 allowed for a relatively constant blood
signal through the time course of the experiment. Furthermore, although
some of the contrast does extravasate, the agent creates a much larger enhancement effect when it is bound to albumin. Since the extracellular albumin concentration is typically ¼ that of the plasma, it tends to create
blood pool contrast even in the presence of this extravasation (Worsley &
Friston, 1995). In addition, the female genitals had not been clearly visualized before, and it was helpful to have a method for identifying structures
and changes that we could use as a reference. Indeed, MS-325 has permitted the capturing of quite clear images of female genitals and further work
with it, especially related to how it might be explored in other types of
vascular processes, remains to be explored.

The main disadvantages to using any contrast agent are that it is physically invasive and runs a small risk of a contrast reaction and that, if one
wanted to test a medication or other therapy for sexual problems, there
could be an interaction between the contrast agent and the medication. In
the Deliganis et al. (2002) study, the contrast agent and procedure were
well tolerated and there were no serious adverse events reported. A total of
40 adverse events of mild to moderate severity were noted. Of the adverse
events reported, 17 were considered unlikely related to study drug, while
5 were considered possibly and 18 were considered probably related to the
use of the study drug, MS-325. All of the 23 adverse events considered possibly or probably related to study drug resolved spontaneously without
medical intervention. A breakdown of those adverse events revealed 14 reports of groin itching, burning, or tingling in the perineum. There were
also 2 reports of nausea, 2 reports of general malaise or fatigue, and 1 report each of metallic taste, scalp itch, lightheadedness, and a thick, tingling
tongue. One subject demonstrated a transient increase in urine white blood

cells. No other clinically significant laboratory changes were reported. There were no clinically significant changes seen in the electrocardiograms, vital signs, or physical examination findings.

To address some of the advantages of not using a contrast agent, Maravilla et al. (2005) tested a new high-resolution, noncontrast MRI technique of the pelvic genital structures of women to determine if it could be used to reliably visualize and quantify clitoral changes associated with sexual arousal. Thus for this study on clitoral volume changes, neither rRBV nor enhancement intensity measures were used. This was felt to be justified since these latter measures had been shown thus far to be less promising for sexual arousal studies. Nine healthy women took part, including 8 who had been in a previous MS-325 study so that image quality could be compared. Inclusion and exclusion criteria were similar to other studies and the design involved 15-minute neutral, followed by 15-minute erotic, and a last 15-minute neutral videotape sequence.

A 3-D fast spin echo (FSE) sequence acquired in an axial plane was used for the dynamic imaging sequences. Imaging time for this sequence was approximately 2 minutes and 50 seconds and it was repeated at 3-minute intervals while subjects viewed the 45-minute video presentation to obtain serial MR images displaying changes in genital engorgement over time.

Data analysis measurements were made by a single experienced imager knowledgeable about the MR appearance of female genital anatomy. Volume measurements were determined using a planimetric technique from each 3-D imaging volume. These calculated clitoral volumes were then plotted on a graph of clitoral volume versus time. The level of subjective sexual arousal was determined by the SEQ used in prior research on VSS. The questions of interest were three that rated the degree of mental sexual arousal, physical sexual arousal, and the overall feelings of sexual arousal by the subject. Answers to the three questions were averaged to yield an overall arousal score.

Subjective assessments of the noncontrast MR studies indicated that they compared favorably with the contrast-enhanced MR and that anatomic visualization was excellent. With regard to clitoral volume measures over time, there was excellent agreement over the two sessions. Percent change in clitoral volume was correlated with an $r = 0.99$ (0.997 for the postmenopausal women and 0.88 for the 4 premenopausal women). The average clitoral volume change for the 8 subjects was 120%. Overall, one can say that the results were stable and reliable.

The patterns of the 7 women who participated in both contrast and noncontrast protocols were compared. The percentage change in clitoral volume for each of the studies was plotted on a correlation curve and the r value was 0.89.

Subjective sexual arousal was correlated between session 1 (mean 4.3, range 3.3–6) and 2 (mean 4.0, range 2.7–6) of the noncontrast study, $r = 0.73$.

Concluding Discussion

The purpose of this paper was to review and critique pelvic MRI methods used to date in women and to compare it to VPP methods where possible. We have detailed the small number of studies done to date, expecting and looking forward to a growth in the area of pelvic imaging to basic and applied questions in women's genital response. Certainly the samples to date are too small to make broad generalizations. We can say what appear to be the strengths and weaknesses in hopes they can be further tested and compared to methods such as VPP or other genital measures as research moves forward.

First of all both methods can track genital and subjective response experiences in a controlled setting and a relatively brief period of time. They each have at least some documented reliability and validity. The procedures are acceptable to those who participate and few—we estimate based on our last six laboratory studies about 10–12% of those responding to a generic advertisement for female sexuality research—who call decide not to participate. Both methods involve little physical risk and invasiveness. The sensitive topic requires a carefully trained research team to attend to the subjects' concerns and allow them to stop at any point should they wish to for any reason. Both methods focus on visual stimulation rather than kinesthetic and, though some studies have been published involving a couple in the magnet (Faix, Lapray, Callede, Maubon, & Lanfrey, 2002; Schultz, van Andel, Sabelis, & Mooyaart, 1999), the most likely use is for individual sexual arousal rather than couple sexual response. How these laboratory methods compare to real world sexual experiences, either solo or couple, has not been well researched—not at all in the case of MRI and with contradictory results in VPP work (Heiman, 1980; Hackbert & Heiman, 2002; Heiman & Rowland, 1983; Laan, Everaerd, van der Velde, & Geer, 1995; Meston, 2004; Morokoff & Heiman, 1980; Tuiten et al., 1996).

The *advantages of the pelvic MRI* include the enabling of anatomical imaging with the ability to quantify anatomical and volumetric changes on an absolute scale. In particular, the clitoral anatomy under aroused and nonaroused conditions can be quantified and the detailed process of anatomical changes can be specified. These are significant advantages, allowing for the documentation of normative anatomy as well as changes that might accompany lifespan reproductive changes (e.g., pregnancy, childbirth), as well as medical conditions such as diseases or procedures. Although not as robust a measure, the signal intensity, from which is estimated the rRBV, could be further investigated as it is an estimate of true blood volume in a specific area and may offer complementary information to some clinical conditions. Because of the rather impressive responses to the clitoral anatomical measure, we have so far selectively focused on it, but further exploration of the parameters of the rRBV measure are warranted.

The *disadvantages of the pelvic MRI measurement* include the fact that the subject must remain very still for accurate anatomical measures; even small movements are a problem. Not all important areas can be equally well visualized and thus may inadvertently put the emphasis on certain genital areas as being the more important. For example, the vaginal wall thickness can be measured and the vaginal lumen (which includes mucosa) can be imaged (Suh et al., 2003). However, the vaginal mucosa itself was poorly visualized, and it is an important area to consider in genital health and sexual functioning. Another limitation of the MRI method is that protocols must be time limited in terms of time in the magnet due to subject comfort and expense. In addition, the measurement, particularly the anatomical measurement, requires sampling over a 3-minute period, which is fairly long as genital response begins within seconds of the sexually explicit content. Thus, this measure may be less appropriate for continuous measures of the arousal process.

The *advantages of VPP* include its ease of use, relatively modest expense, and history of use since the 1970s. It can be used in greater privacy than the MRI measure, though this is often an unimportant point for many physiological studies but can be quite essential for studies of psychological variables. In fact, the VPP method has been used to examine psychological variables such as anxiety and guilt, which play moderating roles in the arousal process (Laan, Everaerd, van der Velde, & Geer, 1995; Morokoff, 1985; Palace & Gorzalka, 1990). VPP responds quickly, within seconds, and provides a continuous signal across the arousal experience. Overall, the AC signal is used more often as it has been found to be the more reliable and understandable (Heiman, Guess, et al., 2004).

The *disadvantages of VPP* are that it is a relative measure with no absolute baseline and thus restricted to within-subject designs. This is inconvenient for studies where one wants a direct comparison, say between pre- and postmenopausal women, or for parallel arm trials. Thus the typical design is a repeated measure crossover, which also helps control for the known and unknown wide intersubject variability in responses, even for psychologically based experimental conditions. The largest objection to the VPP measure has been the fact that it is unknown what the exact physiological process being measured is. We use it as an indicator variable for vaginal blood flow, but physiologists are quite dissatisfied with this (Levin, 1992). Thus the VPP is a sound measure of arousal but to date it is not helpful in identifying and understanding the physiological mechanisms of the blood vessels. Like MRI, VPP is subject to movement artifact interfering with the signal, though several attempts have been made to study orgasm, with statements that a recovered signal is possible.

So as we move into the future, we will need to continue to explore the value of MRI with different designs and samples, in particular sexually dysfunctional samples, to see how genital changes are related to diagnosis and treatment. Subjective measures would benefit from more development to address the factors important to these settings and to women themselves, keeping in mind that there may be differences between studying the process of sexual arousal and measuring the outcome of treatments to change sexual response. In addition, recognizing that the vascular (and subjective) changes occur in the context of neuroendocrine and psychosocial variables will broaden our questions and measurement. And finally, external validity of these measures is crucial to clarify the extent as well as the limitations of their usefulness.

Notes

The authors acknowledge the support of Pfizer, Inc., Groton, Connecticut, and EPIX Medical, Inc., Cambridge, Massachusetts, who provided funding for the methodological pelvic imaging research.

References

Bancroft, J., Loftus, J., & Long, J. S. (2003). Distress about sex: A national survey of women in heterosexual relationships. *Archives of Sexual Behavior, 32*, 193–208.

Deliganis, A., Maravilla, K., Heiman, J., Carter, W, Garland, P., Peterson, B., et al. (2002). Dynamic MR imaging of the female genitalia using MS-325: Initial experience evaluating the female sexual response. *Radiology, 225*, 791–799.

Dickenson, R. L (1949). *Atlas of human sexual anatomy.* Baltimore: Williams & Wilkins.

Faix, A., Lapray, J. F., Callede, O., Maubon, A., & Lanfrey, K. (2002). Magnetic resonance imaging (MRI) of sexual intercourse: Second experience in missionary position and initial experience in posterior position. *Journal of Sex and Marital Therapy, 28*(Suppl. 1), 63–76.

Hackbert, L., & Heiman, J. R. (2002). Acute dehydroepiandrosterone (DHEA) effects on sexual arousal in postmenopausal women. *Journal of Women's Health & Gender-Based Medicine, 11*, 155–162.

Heiman, J. R. (1977). A psychophysiological exploration of sexual arousal patterns in females and males. *Psychophysiology, 14*, 266–274.

Heiman, J. R. (1980). Female sexual response patterns: Interactions of physiological, affective, and contextual cues. *Archives of General Psychiatry, 37*, 1311–1316.

Heiman, J. R. (1998). Psychophysiological models of female sexual response. *International Journal of Impotence, 10*, S84–S97.

Heiman, J. R., Guess, M. K., Connell, K., Melman, A., Hyde, J. S., Segraves, T., et al. (2004). Standards for clinical trials in sexual dysfunctions of women: Research designs and outcomes assessment. In R. Basson, S. Khouri, F. Giuliano, R. Rosen, & T. Lue (Eds.), *The second international consultation on sexual medicine: Men's and women's sexual dysfunction.* Paris: Health Publications Ltd.

Heiman, J. R., Maravilla, K. R., Hackbert, L., Garland, P. A., Peterson, B. T., Carter, W. O., et al. (2006). Evaluating female sexual arousal response with two measures: Serial MR Imaging with MS-325 and vaginal photoplethysmography. Manuscript submitted for publication.

Heiman, J. R., & Rowland, D. (1983). Affective and physiological sexual response patterns: The effects of instruction on sexually functional and dysfunctional men. *Journal of Psychosomatic Research, 27,* 105–116.

Laan, E., & Everaerd, W. (1995). Habituation of female sexual arousal to slides and film. *Archives of Sexual Behavior, 24,* 517–541.

Laan, E., Everaerd, W., & Evers, A. (1995). Assessment of female sexual arousal: Response specificity and construct validity. *Psychophysiology, 32,* 476–485.

Laan, E., Everaerd, W., van der Velde, J., & Geer, J. H. (1995). Determinants of subjective experience of sexual arousal in women: Feedback from genital arousal and erotic stimulus content. *Psychophysiology, 32,* 444–451.

Laumann, E. O., Paik, A., Rosen, R. C. (1999). Sexual dysfunction in the United States: Prevalence and predictors. *Journal of the American Medical Association, 281,* 537–544.

Levin, R. L. (1992). The mechanisms of human female sexual arousal. *Annual Review of Sex Research,* 3, 1–48.

Maravilla, K. R., Cao, Y., Heiman, J. R., Garland, P. A., Peterson, B. T., Carter, W. O., et al. (2003). Serial MR imaging with MS-325 for evaluating female sexual arousal response: Determination of intrasubject reproducibility. *Journal of Magnetic Resonance Imaging, 18,* 216–224.

Maravilla, K. R., Cao, Y., Heiman, J. R., Yang, C., Garland, P. A., Peterson, B. T., et al. (2005). Noncontrast dynamic MRI for quantitative assessment of female sexual arousal. *Journal of Urology, 173,* 162–166.

Masters, W., & Johnson, V. E. (1966). *Human sexual response.* Boston: Little, Brown.

Meston, C. M. (2004). The effects of hysterectomy on sexual arousal in women with a history of benign uterine fibroids. *Archives of Sexual Behavior, 33,* 31–42.

Meston, C. M., & Heiman, J. R. (1998). Ephedrine-activated physiological sexual arousal in women. *Archives of General Psychiatry, 55,* 652–656.

Morokoff, P. J. (1985). Effects of sex guilt, repression, sexual "arousability," and sexual experience on female sexual arousal during erotica and fantasy. *Journal of Personality and Social Psychology, 49,* 177–187.

Morokoff, P., & Heiman, J. (1980). Effects of erotic stimuli on sexually functional and dysfunctional women: Multiple measures before and after sex therapy. *Behaviour Research and Therapy, 18,* 127–137.

Palace, E. M., & Gorzalka, B. B. (1990). The enhancing effects of anxiety on arousal in sexually dysfunctional and functional women. *Journal of Abnormal Psychology, 99,* 403–411.

Parmalee, D. J., Walovitch, R. C., Oullet, H. S., & Lauffer, R. B. (1997). Preclinical evaluation of the pharmacokinetics, biodistribution, and elimination of MS-325, a blood pool agent for magnetic resonance imaging. *Investigative Radiology, 32,* 741–747.

Read, S., & Watson, J. (1997). Sexual dysfunction in primary medical care: Prevalence, characteristics and detection by the general practitioner. *Journal of Public Health Medicine, 19,* 387–391.

Rosen, R. C., Taylor, J. F., Leiblum, S. R., & Bachmann G. A. (1993). Prevalence of sexual dysfunction in women: Results of a survey study of 329 women in an outpatient gynecological clinic. *Journal of Sex and Marital Therapy, 19,* 171–188.

Schultz, W. W., van Andel, P., Sabelis, I., & Mooyaart, E. (1999). Magnetic resonance imaging of male and female genitals during coitus and female sexual arousal. *British Medical Journal, 319,* 1596–1600.

Suh, D. D., Yang, C. C., Cao, Y., Garland, P. A., & Maravilla, K. R. (2003). Magnetic resonance imaging of the female genitalia in premenopausal and postmenopausal women. *Journal of Urology, 170,* 138–144.

Suh, D. D., Yang, C. C., Cao, Y., Heiman, J. R., Garland, P. A., & Maravilla, K. R. (2004). MRI of female genital and pelvic organs during sexual arousal: Initial experience. *Journal of Psychosomatic Obstetrics and Gynecology, 25,* 153–162.

Tuiten, A., Laan, E., Panhuysen, G., Everaerd, W., de Haan, E., Koppeschaar, H., et al. (1996). Discrepancies between genital responses and subjective sexual function during testosterone substitution in women with hypothalamic amenorrhea. *Psychosomatic Medicine, 58,* 234–241.

Worsley, K., & Friston, K. (1995). Analysis of fMRI time-series revisited again. *NeuroImage, 2,* 173–181.

Discussion Paper

ROY J. LEVIN

A problem I have with the study that Cindy has done, and she's known this for a long time, is that she relies on vaginal pulse amplitude (VPA) as an interpretive method of saying what happens to the genital physiology. The trouble with VPA is that we really don't know when it increases or exactly where the increase in terms of the peripheral circulation takes place (see also appendix). VPA is the measure of the total peripheral microcirculation; the signal is obtained from a light shining in and reflected back from a set of blood vessels; the more blood in the vessels or the more vessels open and filled with blood the bigger the amplitude of the signal. These vessels are arteries, arterioles, met-arterioles, capillaries, venules, and veins. Many are innervated so when you get to the SNS, you don't really know where the focus of the innervation is that's creating the changes. On the one hand, it could be a straightforward increase in the flow, but on the other hand, it could be causing contractions of the venules or the veins, which may itself create an increase in VPA. Now there is a sympathetic innervation of the veins and the venules, and certainly in the vagina we have no idea at all about the innervation of the venous circulation. I don't know of any work that's ever looked at this even in animals where you can restrict the veins and see the effect on VPA. The amazing thing is that there is so little work on VPA in animals. It's absolutely staggering, especially as there are a large number of "uncontrolled" studies in humans. In fact, I used VPA when I was teaching our honors physiology degree students at Sheffield University. We used to do it in the anaesthetized dog. We inserted a photoplethysmograph in the dog's vagina and injected intraarterially a variety of bioactive agents because we could do close arterial injections through the femoral artery so that the drug went first to the vagina. When either noradrenaline or adrenaline was injected, the amplitude of the AC signal or VPA (an index of the "blood flow") always decreased (see experiment in Figure 1). There's no question that it goes down. You can do a similar experiment in humans, which Gorm Wagner and I did in Copenhagen. If you inject noradrenaline or adrenaline subepithelial underneath a heated oxygen electrode (used to monitor vaginal blood flow), you find that the electrode gives a decrease in power consumption and shows a dramatic fall to zero of the surface pO_2; in other words, the blood flow is greatly decreased (see experiment in Figure 2). So, in both dogs and in humans that I've had experience of (although a relatively limited number), in these conditions you get a constriction of the blood vessels in the vagina to the neurotransmitters of the sympathetic system. I thus find it very difficult to say that the SNS is going to give you an increase of the blood flow from interpreting the changes in VPA. The amplitude of the VPA under these changed circulatory circumstances is not an artifact, but it is very sensitive to changes in the peripheral circulation. You only have to do a very simple experiment to see effects of changes in the peripheral circulation on the VPA; I've talked about this many times. Hold a photoplethysmograph in the palm of your closed hand and then just lift it high above your head; you will see when you do that an increase in the amplitude occurs. Then hold it below the heart and you get a decrease in the amplitude. All you've done by these maneuvers is elevate and decrease the hydrostatic pressure on the venous side of the arterioles because the arterial pressure doesn't change when you lift the arm up. So you can get very big changes in the photoplethysmographic signal (and presumably the VPA) simply by altering the pressure on the venous side of the microcirculation. As a physiologist, that's my real concern.

I think the studies are fine, but I would like to see another independent measure of changes in the hemodynamics as opposed to just using the VPA. So that's my biggest criticism of the work.

I noticed that even Cindy is tending to say, well, there might be other things going on, so there is awareness that this is a possibility. There are, however, some things that don't fit quite with even veins contracting. As regards the VBV (vaginal blood volume), I think, and Julia thinks the same as me, it is simply an unreliable measure. It is so variable and prone to artifacts. Women, if they hold their breath, if they breathe faster, if they just move, it can change the characteristics of the trace (see Levin, 1992, for examples). I really don't think you can use VBV to interpret any significant physiological change. The other thing that is interesting of course is if you compare some of the penis work with some of the vagina work. Rosen, Phillips, Gendrano, and Ferguson (1999) used an oral dose of the alpha-adrenergic blocker phentolamine (in postmenopausal women) and got an increase in VPA, which suggests that there is a vaginal sympathetic tone. Unfortunately, the study doesn't tell us whether the tone is generated centrally or peripherally (or both), but it suggests that there is a sympathetic tone just like there is in the penis contracting the vessels and reducing the blood flow. If you measure the oxygen tension, for example, in the basal or sexually unexcited vagina, it is extremely low—hypoxic practically—something in the region of 5–10 millimeters of mercury (Wagner & Levin, 1978). As soon as the person gets sexually aroused, it increases in the blood flow and up goes the oxygen tension into the 40–80 millimeters. So I would think that the vaginal peripheral circulation is normally under a

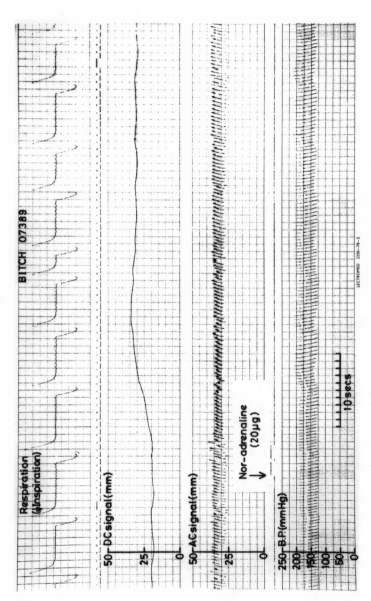

Figure 1. Traces monitoring various physiological changes in an anaesthetized dog (bitch 07389). The upper trace records respiration (inspiration is the down curve), the DC signal (mm) is the vaginal blood volume (VBV) from the vaginal photoplethysmograph; note that the signal is reversed—an increase in signal indicates a decrease in blood volume (the scale is a negative one), the AC signal (mm) is the VPA from the photoplethysmograph, and the last trace is the arterial blood pressure measured at the carotid artery by a Statham gauge. The time base is shown as a 10-second scale. The close-arterial injection of noradrenaline (20 micrograms) was into the femoral artery so that the dose was washed directly into the arterial supply to the vagina within 5 seconds. The decreases in both the VPA (transient lasting approximately 30 seconds) and the VBV (of much longer duration) can easily be seen (R. J. Levin, unpublished observations).

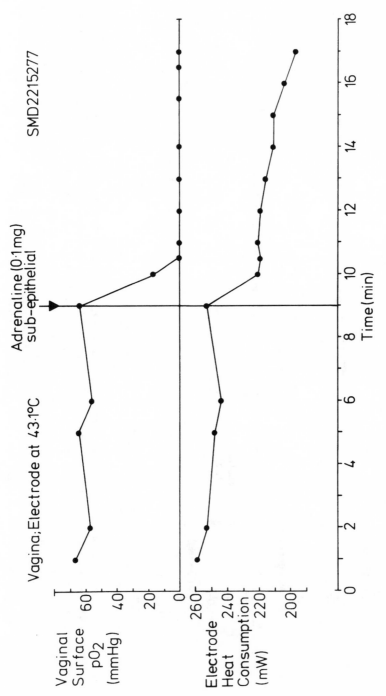

SMD2215277

Figure 2. Heated oxygen electrode attached by suction to the vaginal wall of a human female. The electrode was set to run at 43.1°C. The surface pO2 is approximately 60 mmHg while the power consumption needed to maintain the electrode at the set temperature was some 25 milliwatts. On sub-epithelial injection of a small volume containing 0.1 mg adrenaline under the electrode, the surface pO2 fell to zero within a minute and a half, while the electrode's power consumption fell to 200 milliwatts in approximately 8 minutes. Both show clear-cut evidence of a reduced vaginal blood flow (Levin & Wagner, unpublished observations).

sympathetic tone; in other words, constricted as in the penis. It would make sense. If I had been on God's celestial "making-a-female" committee, I wouldn't have wasted a lot of energy in trying to create a high basal blood flow to an organ that's only going to be used intermittently—in some cases very intermittently!

I think there's something happening in the SNS supply to the vagina that doesn't seem to me to be sensible in terms of the circulatory physiology that I know, but I'm always prepared to acknowledge that I could be wrong. That ends my comments on that study.

Julia's paper, well, it is lovely work. I mean who could, when you see wonderful pictures like that, even criticize it, but as I'm here to criticize, so criticize I must! One of the things that I didn't like about the study was that the VPA and the MRI were done separately, well apart in time, and that worries me just a little bit. There might be nothing in that, but they were done, as far as I can remember, up to 2 weeks apart and they also crossed the menstrual cycle phases. You used day 7 to day 21. That seems to me a possibly dangerous thing to do. I'm far from certain that there is any difference between vaginal blood flow or VPA from the pre- and postovulatory parts of the cycle. There have been studies that say yes there is and others that say no there is not. I'm not convinced about the studies at all, but as you have spanned the two menstrual phases there is always the possibility. Moreover, I don't know from the study how many people were in different parts of the cycle. It might pay just to have a look; maybe there's nothing there at all, but I think you should say who's in the various groups (viz follicular and luteal phases).

The areas that you image are extremely small in the vagina and you could get different results in different areas because of heterogeneity. I think it was 4 mm to 22 mm square, so how homogenous is it in the vagina at this level? I personally don't know. I wonder whether you have to be a little bit careful, especially if we're doing drug and dysfunctional studies. You could get effects, as you do with the measurement of vaginal pH. One area responds very well to sexual arousal but another area hardly responds at all. In the one you can get a positive change of one whole pH unit, while in the other the change is actually negative; you can get quite big changes in different parts of the vagina (Wagner & Levin, 1984).

You talked about genital wetness. What I thought was so nice is that when you matched it with the MRI you got such good correlations; you suddenly shot up from 0.09, which you could hardly calculate, to 0.43 and 0.35. We had a long discussion about vaginal wetness yesterday and how women estimate it and even whether they could estimate it with any confidence if they had no tactile feedback. Hardly any work has been done in this area and no one has validated women's subjective judgments by assessing the lubrication objectively at the same time.

It's a disappointment that you weren't able to image the vagina; it would really be nice to see whether such images correlated with VBV, for example. If you could image the vaginal wall, I would think that that is where the correlation should be, because VBV is supposed to be a measure of the total blood volume. The other thing is that your MRI does not seem very fast. I did some coital studies using an open configuration MRI in Germany recently and they were able to sample every 3 seconds so you could actually see penile movement going in and out of the vagina. I think you can certainly get much faster imaging than you were getting. The other thing is that in your manuscript you actually mentioned that it is a better, I think it was, nonintrusive technique. It, however, is an invasive procedure, not intrusive. Intrusive means that you go into body cavities. Invasive means you have to go underneath the skin into a blood vessel. With the contrast medium you are doing an invasive technique; you can't call it intrusive. I would think that because of the expense and the cost of injecting contrast medium into people, it's not going to diffuse across the world until you get rid of the contrast medium. I don't think a lot of people would countenance injecting contrast material with possible side effects in normals.

Finally we come to the last paper I am commenting on. I'm afraid that the last one always gets the rush, doesn't it? This particular group's work I found fascinating and I've actually written a review on this proposal that prolactin is the "off switch" in humans for sexual arousal, but with special reference to the differences between men and women (Levin, 2003). In their previous review (Krüger, Haake, Hartman, Schedlowski, & Exton, 2002), they actually made out that prolactin was the off switch for sexual arousal without stating gender, but didn't focus on the fact that it doesn't fit too well for women. I notice that in this present review that you're actually backtracking just a little saying, well, it could be the one in men but possibly not in women. I'm happy to agree with you there!

We know that women don't have refractory periods; they can go on having orgasms until they get fed up with them, yet prolactin is released in women at orgasm. So I think that it is in men that prolactin may be at least part of the off switch. However, there are problems that you have with the data because when you look at hyperprolactinemia and inhibition of sexual arousal, you're talking about greater than 200 nanograms/ml in the plasma, but you're looking at the small increase in prolactin during and after orgasm, which is only 15–25 nanograms/ml. You were trying, I noticed, to get small increases in the experiments to see what it did with sexual arousal/drive. The other thing, of course, with both women and also with men, is that you didn't quote the early work of Kolodney, Jacobs, and Daughaday (1972), where they had stimulated the nipples and the areolae, and prolactin is secreted. The release of prolactin is thus not specific for orgasm alone. Even in coitus when a man is on top and moving backward and forward, he could be stimulating the nipples and you could get prolactin release. In fact, Jacobs and Daughaday (1974) found increased prolactin secretion after coitus. You completely ignored that area. The other interesting thing in men and nipples is that if you twiddle your own nipples, prolactin isn't secreted. If, however, you get a woman to twiddle your nipples, then prolactin is secreted, but if you ask the men were they sexually aroused by the twiddling they report "no." Thus you can get prolactin release from nipple stimulation without actually having sexual arousal. I think there are some areas of prolactin secretion that you missed. Prolactin secretion also does increase in work and exercise. I don't know how much "work" these people did in coitus (about equal to climbing a good flight of stairs?), but you should also take that into cognizance. I didn't think your literature research was as thorough as it could have been, frankly, but I think the work is brave and I know how difficult it is to conduct orgasm research in academia. What I would like to know is whether we could monitor pro-lactin in fluids other than having to sample the blood. For example, if we could find it in saliva (or in cervical fluid in females), then it would be a really easy test for orgasm in males and females, rather than have to take blood out, which is always difficult even in laboratories.

My final points are about oxytocin. Oxytocin is secreted at orgasm with prolactin (oxytocin also causes the release of prolactin). You actually said that you got small increases in oxytocin, which was not significant, but a lot of people have shown quite significant increases in oxytocin (see Levin, 2003, for references). Vernon Pickles, in my old department years ago, showed that if a woman was sexually aroused when she was lactating and she had an orgasm, milk spurted out of her breasts because of the milk letdown reflex and the oxytocin secreted; the milk letdown reflex is a very sensitive indicator in vivo of oxytocin release (Harris & Pickles, 1953). I think you have to look at your method of estimating oxytocin and its sensitivity, as I'm not quite sure how you did it. Moreover there is a now a modern concept of oxytocin that it possibly is a switch-off mechanism just like prolactin. There's a review about how oxytocin can actually switch off cells rather than switch cells on (Caldwell, 2002). You have to relook at oxytocin release in the context of your prolactin release because it might well be that oxytocin is doing part of the switch off.

References

Caldwell, J. D. (2002). A sexual arousability model involving steroid effects at the plasma membrane. *Neuroscience and Biobehavioral Reviews, 26,* 13–20.

Harris, G. W., & Pickles, V. J. (1953). Reflex stimulation of the neurohypophysis (posterior pituitary gland) and the nature of the posterior hormone(s). *Nature, 172,* 1049.

Jacobs, L. S., & Daughaday, W. (1974). In J. B. Josimovich, M. Reynolds, & E. Cobo

(Eds.), *Lactogenic hormones, fetal nutrition and lactation* (pp. 351–378). New York: Wiley.

Kolodney, R. C., Jacobs, L. S., & Daughaday, W. H. (1972). Mammary stimulation causes prolactin secretion in non-lactating women. *Nature, 238,* 284.

Krüger, T. H. C., Haake, R., Hartman, U., Schedlowski, M., & Exton, M. S. (2002). Orgasm-induced prolactin secretion: Feedback control of sexual drive. *Neuroscience and Biobehavioral Reviews, 26,* 31–44.

Levin, R. J. (1992). The mechanisms of human female sexual arousal. *Annual Review of Sex Research, 3,* 1–46.

Levin, R. J. (2003). Is prolactin the biological "off switch" for human sexual arousal? *Sexual and Relationship Therapy, 18,* 237–243.

Rosen, R. C., Phillips, N. A., Gendrano, N. C., & Ferguson, D. M. (1999). Oral phentolamine and female sexual arousal disorder: A pilot study. *Journal of Sex and Marital Therapy, 25,* 137–144.

Wagner, G., & Levin, R. J. (1978). Oxygen tension of the vaginal surface during sexual stimulation in the human. *Fertility and Sterility, 30,* 50–53.

Wagner, G., & Levin, R. J. (1984). Human vaginal pH and sexual arousal. *Fertility and Sterility, 41,* 389–394.

General Discussion

Jim Pfaus: Just a couple of comments. If there's one thing about prolactin and sex, it's that it is released after copulation in females. This is certainly true in rats and other primates, although its release is pulsatile. So you may actually not see it if you're taking lengthy blood samples in females, because it is not released in a continuous manner. One of its functions is to stimulate a continuous release of progesterone by the corpora lutea, which in turn facilitates and maintains pregnancy. In fact, it's one of the first inducers of pseudopregnancy in animals who show pseudopregnancy responses, like the rat. So you do get it, but its neuroendocrine effect is obviously different in the female than it might be in the male. I mean, here we may, in fact, have a neuroendocrine reflex plus a brain reflex that are doing two different things. The neuroendocrine response may actually be shutting down the ability to get an erection, and the brain effects, which are anyone's guess in the human, may, in fact, be to counteract a dopaminergic response, not only in the hypothalamus but elsewhere in the brain to reduce mental sensitivity, or as Whalen used to call it, arousability to sexual stimuli.

Kevin McKenna: I just have a couple of comments about the autonomic nervous system and blood flow and so on. There's a danger of talking about sympathetic activation as if it's a unified thing. In fact, in the male if you stimulate the hypothalamus and increase penile erection, you see a decrease of sympathetic tone to the penis, an increase in parasympathetic tone, but there's actually an increase in sympathetic tone outside the penis in the pelvis. It pushes the blood toward the penis so that the responses can be very sensitively tuned. The other thing is, especially when you're giving vasoactive drugs and you're measuring some vascular response, I think it's really important to in some way control for general systemic variables. It's typical in penile erection studies to always normalize ICP (intracavernous pressure) measurements over systemic blood pressure because you can have effects of giving a drug that have nothing to do with the penis at all, but just a general human dynamics. So it might be worth looking at some of these controversies in vaginal blood flow in the context of an overall change in the general arousal rather than something specific in the vagina.

Roy Levin: Could I just come back on that? I mean, if you do the cold-pressure test with females and you put the hand in cold water, your measure of vaginal blood flow goes up. So there are these sorts of responses that have been done and they go back a long time actually. They began getting ignored because they're back in the 1970s and 1960s and people never look back more than 5 years.

John Bancroft: I think the work of the Hanover group is great and methodologically very sound, but I have a problem with the idea that prolactin is being used as the "switch off" during the refractory period. There has been a problem for many years in understanding prolactin's physiological role. Jim Pfaus has talked about some peripheral functions of prolactin in the female. But, in many respects, it is still something of a mystery hormone. It is, however, very closely related to dopaminergic activity and controlled by "prolactin inhibiting factor," which is principally dopamine. Most of the effects that you are seeing with increase in prolactin could equally well be explained by a reduction in dopaminergic activity. So the prolactin increase after orgasm could be an epiphenomenon associated with reduced dopaminergic activity, rather than a cause of the refractory period. Research on the neuroendocrinology of the refractory period in nonhumans has been limited, but in the last few years there has been interesting work done on the "sexually satiated" animal by Rodriguez-Manzo and Fernandez-Guasti (1994, 1995a, 1995b), which suggests that there is a fairly complex neuroendocrine picture underlying the sexual satiation, which involves dopamine among other things, and which relies on the integrity of the norepinephric system of the brain. More research needs to be done before we have a clear understanding of the refractory period in humans.

Ray Rosen: I agree with you about the dopamine and prolactin, but maybe rather than viewing it as an epiphenomenon, one might think more in terms of a feedback loop. An increase in dopamine may be associated with a decrease in prolactin, and vice versa.

John Bancroft: If prolactin decreased dopamine, then prolactin would never go down, because the lowering of dopamine would increase the prolactin. What happens with a prolactinoma is not adequately understood. Sometimes you have a relatively independent change in the prolactin-producing cells, and you have a genuinely independent prolactin-secreting tumor. But sometimes it seems to be related to some malfunction in the hypothalamus. We also need to distinguish between central changes in prolactin and changes in the peripheral circulation. The prolactin secreted by the pituitary is primarily released into the circulation, and because it does not cross the blood-brain barrier, it has limited access to the brain. It is very difficult to work out what is going on in feedback terms.

Jim Pfaus: It may be related to sexual satiety. For example, pituitary adenomas, which of course cause hyperprolactinemia, also cause hypersecretion of endogenous opioids and other pituitary peptides that can act as hormones. These feed back in the brain, and if you look at the sexual satiety literature, noradrenergic and opioid neurotransmitter systems seem to be playing a role in that. Treatment of a sexually exhausted male rat with the opioid antagonist naloxone can release copulation from inhibition. Noradrenergic agonists can do the same thing. So there's a very interesting interplay between events that stimulate sympathetic arousal but also stimulate the brain's ability to be responsive to sexual stimuli. In this regard, noradrenaline may be very much like dopamine, although it is a very understudied neurotransmitter with regard to stimuli that increase sexual arousal, sexual arousability, and responses to sexual incentives.

Walter Everaerd: I have a question about another topic. It's for Julia, about your correlations. There were few subjects, and before people go away with the correlation between the VPA and subjective experience, I'm curious whether you looked at the scattergrams of the various variables you had and what was the reason for the lower correlations. Were there outliers and with the other measures, more outliers?

Julia Heiman: Well, yes, there were a lot of correlations so I can't answer exactly. I think it's a good point. I do not recall anything notable about the scatterplots.

Walter Everaerd: But that suggests only that you have less variation than in your other measures. Is that true?

Julia Heiman: I think so but I would want to recheck it. The only other point, Walter, to emphasize is though some things were not significant in the MRI (versus VPP), the degree of association was quite high in both settings. So I think as soon as more subjects are included, we are likely to have significance in the MRI as well. So far, the degree of association between VPA and reported sexual arousal and genital response was greater than the subjective-MRI relationship, which I wouldn't have predicted. But we'll see. We need larger subject samples and replication in other labs to have more clarity about these findings.

Erick Janssen: Tillmann, I wonder if you could you say a little bit more about your experimental procedures? You had women masturbate while you measured their VPA, and you asked men and women to have sexual intercourse, at least during some of the conditions, correct?

Tillmann Krüger: In the "couple" experiments, there was one "active" and one "inactive" person, and we examined only the "inactive" person who lay on the bed to avoid movement artifacts on endocrine parameters. However, both of them watched the videos so that they knew when the experimental part started. After 10 minutes they started to have sexual intercourse. Within these 10 minutes, the "inactive" partner usually reached orgasm. However, the endocrine response pattern during coitus is nearly the same to that which we detected during masturbation-induced orgasm, at least with this paradigm. There are, of course, sex-specific differences in the processing of sexual arousal, but we cannot find differences in the peripheral neuroendocrine response pattern.

References

Rodriguez-Manzo, G., & Fernandez-Guasti, A. (1994). Reversal of sexual exhaustion by serotonergic and noradrenergic agents. *Behavioral Brain Research, 62,* 127–134.

Rodriguez-Manzo, G., & Fernandez-Guasti, A. (1995a). Opioid antagonists and the sexual satiation phenomenon. *Psychopharmacology, 122,* 131–136.

Rodriguez-Manzo, G., & Fernandez-Guasti, A. (1995b). Participation of the central noradrenergic system in the reestablishment of copulatory behavior of sexually exhausted rats by yohimbine, naloxone, and 8-OH-DPAT. *Brain Research Bulletin, 38,* 399–404.

Part 2.

Theoretical Perspectives and Models

Cognitive-Affective Processes in Sexual Arousal and Sexual Dysfunction

MARKUS WIEGEL, LISA A. SCEPKOWSKI,
AND DAVID H. BARLOW

In 1986, Barlow published his model of sexual dysfunction. Cranston-Cuebas and Barlow (1990) summarized the early empirical work supporting this model. The present paper briefly reviews the original model and details the empirical and theoretical work since 1990, after which an updated version of the model is presented based on the reviewed studies as well as advances in anxiety research (see Barlow, 2002, for a detailed review of anxiety research). Barlow's model can be conceptualized as concerning itself with three broad areas of cognitive and emotional processes in which individuals with and without sexual dysfunction differ: (i) cognitive schemata and affective associations with which an individual enters a sexual situation, (ii) differences in cognitive processing of sexual stimuli including the person's own arousal, and (iii) cognitive, affective, and behavioral responses to their sexual performance and the experience of sexual arousal.

Review of the Original Model of Sexual Dysfunction

Barlow (1986) conceptualized early efforts aimed at understanding and treating sexual dysfunction in his model of cognitive and affective contributions to sexual functioning (Figure 1). In this model, dysfunctional sexual performance is seen as being maintained by means of a negative feedback loop (Barlow, 1986; Cranston-Cuebas & Barlow, 1990; van den Hout & Barlow, 2000). Individuals with and without sexual dysfunction approach sexual situations differently. In response to implicit or explicit (i.e., implied or expressed) demands for sexual performance, men and women without sexual dysfunction experience positive affect, success expectancies, and perceptions of control. In contrast, in individuals with sexual dysfunction, implicit or explicit demands for sexual performance evoke a state of anxious apprehension that is characterized by heightened tension and arousal, negative affect, and failure expectancies. In essence, from experience of prior sexual difficulties, sexual stimuli elicit anxiety and expectancies of poor performance in the individual with sexual dysfunction.

In all individuals, heightened autonomic arousal is associated with

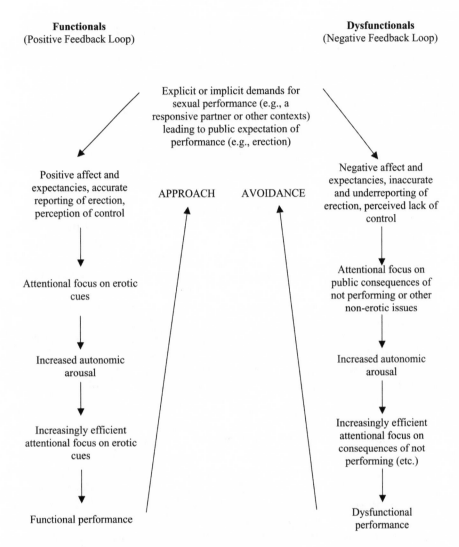

Figure 1. Barlow's 1986 model of sexual dysfunction.

a narrowing of the attentional focus (for a discussion of this process in anxiety disorders see Barlow, 2002). However, differences in the emotional and cognitive aspects of how individuals with and without sexual dysfunction enter the sexual situation result in the two groups responding differently. Since individuals with sexual dysfunction expect failure and negative consequences, their focus of attention narrows to sources of threat, setting the stage for additional distortions in the processing of information, either through attentional or interpretive biases (reflecting preexisting hypervalent cognitive schemata).

A variety of *cues* or *propositions,* to use the terms of Lang (1985, 1994a, 1994b), would be sufficient to evoke anxious apprehension. These cues may be broad based or very narrow, such as a highly responsive partner (Abrahamson, Barlow, Sakheim, Beck, & Kelly, 1985). Importantly, this process could occur without the necessity of a conscious, rational appraisal. For example, one might experience anxiety without awareness of the specific trigger or cue, such as an object or situation that represents a past sexual failure experience, or an internal somatic sensation, as is seen in patients with panic disorder. Janssen, Everaerd, Spiering, and Janssen (2000), using a preattentive priming paradigm, demonstrated that such automatic (preattentive) processing of sexual stimuli influenced both genital (erectile tumescence) and behavioral (decision time) measures.

At sufficient intensity, the shift to nonerotic cues in conjunction with the narrowing of the attentional focus results in disruption of performance (e.g., sexual arousal). Thus, at low levels of autonomic arousal an individual may still be able to attend to sexual cues while attention is focused on sexual performance concerns; however, as autonomic arousal increases, whether resulting from sexual arousal or anxious arousal, the focus of attention narrows, increasing the salience of the attended to stimuli. In individuals with sexual dysfunction, this process increases the salience of nonerotic cues and results in further decreases in sexual arousal (e.g., erectile tumescence). In contrast, for individuals without sexual dysfunction, increased arousal amplifies the salience of erotic cues and results in greater sexual arousal. This focus on nonerotic, task-irrelevant stimuli and the resulting disruption in performance is analogous to cognitive interference models of test anxiety in which preoccupation with task-irrelevant thoughts concerning inadequacy, helplessness, failure, and its consequences diminish performance in test-anxious students (e.g., Arkin, Detchon, & Maruyama, 1982; Arkin, Kolditz, & Kolditz, 1983).

The repeated experiencing of disrupted sexual response and the associated negative affect may result in several cognitive, affective, and behavioral consequences. First, the individual may become hypervigilant for cues or stimuli associated with sources of anxious apprehension (e.g., implicit or explicit demands for sexual performance, cues that could indicate sexual failure). Secondly, sexual situations and stimuli may be associated with increased negative affect and further confirmation of failure expectancies. Thirdly, in an attempt to cope the individual may subsequently avoid sexual activity and stimuli. As a result, individuals with repeated experiences of sexual dysfunction approach sexual situations differently than individuals without sexual dysfunction, or begin avoiding such situations entirely.

Prior to further interpreting past work and reviewing more recent empirical findings, several important distinctions need to be clarified. First, anxiety is frequently (and mistakenly) used as a general term loosely referring to a number of affective states that include fear, panic, and worry. However, these various "anxiety" states have unique characteristics. Anxiety defined more specifically refers to a state of "anxious apprehension" that incorporates a sense of uncontrollability focused largely on future negative events, a strong physiological or somatic component (sympathetic nervous system), a vigilance (or hypervigilance) for threat-related cues, and a shift in attention to a self-focus (self-preoccupation) in which the evaluation of one's (inadequate) capabilities to cope with the threat is prominent (Barlow, 2002).

Secondly, sexual arousal is likewise composed of a complex triad involving physiological, cognitive, affective, and behavioral components. These components frequently correspond, but are also discordant. Janssen et al. (2000) note that there seems to be a strong link between sexual stimuli and the activation of genital responses, while subjective sexual arousal seems to be more variable and more strongly influenced by situational factors. Janssen et al. (2000) and Bancroft (1989) conclude that, at least to some degree, the components of sexual arousal and response are under the control of different mechanisms.

Thirdly, different components of "anxious apprehension" as well as various related states of negative affect (worry or fear) influence the various components of sexual arousal differentially, and not always in the same direction (i.e., facilitate or inhibit sexual arousal). For example, research by Meston and her colleagues (Meston & Gorzalka, 1995, 1996a, 1996b; Meston, Gorzalka, & Wright, 1997; Meston & Heiman, 1998) has attempted to separate the effects of increased sympathetic nervous system (SNS) arousal on sexual response from the effect of cognitive and affective components of anxiety on sexual response. In general, these studies found that in women without sexual dysfunction and women with hypoactive sexual desire disorder, increased SNS activation prior to watching an erotic film increases genital sexual response, as measured by vaginal photoplethysmography. Subjective reports of sexual arousal, on the other hand, do not seem to be influenced by SNS activation. The implication of this line of research is that the somatic component of anxious apprehension may facilitate genital response, while the negative affective component may concurrently decrease physiological and/or subjective arousal. The cognitive component (selective attentional focus) may facilitate or interfere with physiological sexual arousal depending on whether or not the individual has a sexual dysfunction. Furthermore all of these processes interact with one another and themselves through feedback loops, creating a truly complex web of influences that determines sexual arousal. We will now review the influence of some of these variables in more detail.

Cognitive Schemata

Men with sexual dysfunction evidence a "sexually dysfunctional mentality" that includes perceived lack of control over sexual arousal, sexual failure expectancies, maladaptive causal attributions, and cognitive bias (hypervigilance). For example, an earlier study indicated that men with erectile disorder in the laboratory reported feeling that they have less control over their arousal (Mitchell, Marten, Williams, & Barlow, 1990). In contrast, sexually functional men, much like individuals without anxiety disorders, engage in cognitive and attentional processes that allow them to maintain an "illusion of control," which serves as a protection against developing a "dysfunctional mentality." In studies of sexual arousal in the laboratory, it has been shown that sexually functional participants overlooked small changes in their performance and failed to report decreases in their physiological arousal (Abrahamson, Barlow, Sakheim, Beck, & Athanasiou, 1985; Abrahamson, Barlow, Beck, et al., 1985). This finding was recently replicated (Mitchell, DiBartolo, Brown, & Barlow, 1998). A growing body of research by Barlow and his colleagues provides evidence (reviewed below) for the different mentalities of men with and without sexual dysfunction. However, it is important to note that it is not possible to determine whether this "sexually dysfunctional mentality" is a cause of sexual dysfunction or the result of experiencing sexual difficulties based on the research studies conducted to date, since these have been cross-sectional in design. Longitudinal studies are required in order to determine whether individuals evidence a dysfunctional mentality prior to or as a result of experiencing sexual difficulties.

One aspect of the sexual cognitive schema evidenced by men with erectile disorder is feelings of lack of control over their erectile response. Studies have found that the use of fantasy, or the ability to form vivid mental representations, is important for the voluntary control of sexual arousal (e.g., Stock & Geer, 1982). Since sexually dysfunctional patients report less use of fantasy in sexual situations (Marten & Barlow, 1991), the relationship between imagery ability, fantasy content, and voluntary arousal was explored (Weisberg, Sbrocco, & Barlow, 1994). Sexually functional participants were asked to engage in either a fantasy in which they would not be able to attain and maintain an erection, or a fantasy in which their performance was satisfactory. Contrary to expectations, differences in arousal between fantasy groups were not found. Fantasies in which participants imagined sexual scenarios during which they either did or did not experience sexual difficulties evoked equivalent levels of penile tumescence and subjective arousal. Upon examination of the fantasies written by participants in the "sexual dysfunction" fantasy condition, it was found that while participants included accounts of sexual problems as instructed, these problems were not the focus of the fantasies. In other words, these participants created arousing fantasies in which problems occurred (such as detumescence), but were not specifically focused on, or the participants fantasized the problems as being only temporary. These findings support the notion that sexually functional men may demonstrate a "resistance to a sexually dysfunctional mentality" (Abrahamson, Barlow, Beck, et al., 1985; Abrahamson, Barlow, Sakheim, et al., 1985).

More recent research performed by our group has examined the portion of Barlow's (1986) model of sexual functioning that suggests that functional and dysfunctional men enter sexual situations with different expectancies for their performance. Individuals with sexual dysfunction expect to perform poorly, while individuals without sexual difficulties expect to perform well. Results from misattribution experiments (Cranston-Cuebas & Barlow, 1995; Cranston-Cuebas, Barlow, Mitchell, & Athanasiou, 1993; see Barlow, Chorpita, & Turovsky, 1996) revealed that men with erectile disorder evidenced a direct placebo effect in response to ingesting what they thought were "arousal enhancing" and "arousal detracting" pills (all pills were placebo) prior to watching an erotic film. The detraction manipulation ("This pill will interfere with erectile response") may be viewed as creating a context in which one might predict that subjects would form negative expectancies regarding their sexual performance. Men with erectile disorder evidenced significantly decreased levels of tumescence in the detraction condition and their highest level of erectile response in the enhancement condition. It could be suggested that these men experienced less interference with arousal in this manipulation because they believed that their arousal was going to be influenced by something other than themselves, thereby allowing them to rely on external attributions for their performance. In a related study, Palace (1995) was able to induce increases in positive expectancies for sexual arousal in female participants with various sexual dysfunctions by giving them positive false feedback about their level of arousal after viewing an erotic film segment. Not only were positive expectancies found to increase after positive false feedback, but physiological sexual arousal during a subsequent film was found to increase significantly as well. This study corroborates findings regarding the relevance of expectancies in sexual arousal for women with sexual dysfunction.

In contrast to the direct placebo effect in men with erectile disorder, Cranston-Cuebas et al. (1993) found that sexually functional men evidenced a reverse placebo effect. These men evidenced significantly enhanced tumescence after the "arousal detraction" pill condition, despite the fact that preerotic film questionnaires revealed that participants' expectations were in line with the manipulation (i.e., functional subjects expected to have less arousal in the detraction pill condition). These findings mirror the results of similar misattribution studies conducted with individuals suffering from insomnia (Brockner & Swap, 1983; Storms & Nisbett, 1970).

In a more recent false feedback experiment (Bach, Brown, & Barlow, 1999), the effects of low efficacy expectancies for obtaining adequate erectile responses on subsequent sexual arousal in sexually functionally men were examined. Twenty-six males were randomly assigned to either a false negative feedback group or a no feedback group. After viewing several erotic film segments, the participants in the negative false feedback group were told that their responses were less than that of the average participant in the laboratory. The control group received no such feedback. Efficacy expectancies were found to be considerably lower when the negative false feedback group viewed a subsequent erotic film, as were physiological responses measured by the penile strain gauge. Despite these effects on physiological arousal, and counter to predictions of Barlow's (1986) model, the negative false feedback led to neither a decline in reports of subjective arousal nor an increase in negative affect. Thus, consistent with the model, a self-focus on potential inadequate responding *did* lower physiological sexual arousal. However, this physiological effect was *not* associated with changes in subjective arousal, self-estimates of arousal, or negative affect.

A follow-up study that extended the findings of Bach et al. (1999) utilizing a similar paradigm found similar results when attributions for perceived erectile failure were manipulated following a similar bogus feedback condition (Weisberg, Brown, Wincze, & Barlow, 2001). Specifically, 52 young men with normal sexual functioning viewed similar sexually explicit films while wearing a penile strain gauge and were told that they did not become as aroused as did the typical study participant. However, in this procedure, participants received an attributional manipulation in which they were then given either an external-unstable attribution (i.e., the films must have been very poor quality) or an internal-stable attribution (i.e., it seems from questionnaires you filled out that you may have a type of belief about sex that sometimes makes it difficult to get aroused here in our lab) to explain the cause of their poor erectile performance. All participants then viewed an additional film to examine responding under the different attributions.

A manipulation check indicated that the participants in each of the two groups did in fact attribute the supposed erectile difficulty to internal or external causes according to the feedback given by the experimenter. The results indicated that participants in the external-unstable attribution group showed greater physiological and subjective sexual arousal during a third film than did participants with the internal causal attribution. Interestingly, the attributional manipulation did not significantly affect levels of negative affect, perceived erectile control, or expected degree of erection. Thus, the results of this study demonstrated that physiological responding could be influenced in sexually functional men independent of negative affect, perceived lack of control, or negative expectancies. Weisberg et al. (2001) suggest that the lack of cognitive and affective response to the negative false feedback could be related to the relative importance imparted upon a perceived sexual failure in a laboratory setting. It is possible that for participants, a poor sexual performance in the lab is not important because they may not generalize it to real-life sexual situations (where they may be judged negatively by a partner), thereby constituting resilience against developing negative cognitions and affect from the feedback. This study is currently being replicated in female participants without sexual dysfunction. Overall, the results of this line of research suggest that the attribution for a perceived "sexual failure" is more important than expectancies alone. The degree to which men attribute sexual difficulties to internal causes may explain the maintenance of erectile dysfunction in some men.

Recent work undertaken to develop a measure of sexual attributional style, the Sexual Attributional Style Questionnaire (SASQ; Scepkowski et al., 2004; Weisberg et al., 1998), is beginning to shed light on the differences in explanatory styles possessed by sexually functional and dysfunctional men. As indicated by this self-report measure, and as predicted by earlier research (Fichten, Spector, & Libman, 1988; Loos, Bridges, & Critelli, 1987; Quadland, 1980), men with erectile disorder made more internal, stable, and global causal attributions for negative sexual events than men without sexual dysfunction. This is consistent with results from Weisberg et al. (1998), who found that scores on the negative sexual event subscale of the SASQ could differentiate between men with and without erectile disorder. Also as predicted by previously discussed research supporting the contention that functional men maintain positive expectancies for their sexual performance despite experimental manipulation, sexually functional men rated the stability of negative sexual events significantly lower than men with erectile disorder. Sexually functional men rated the importance of negative sexual events lower than did men with erectile disorder. Dysfunctional men did not differ from functional men in their causal attributions for positive sexual events, and unexpectedly, both groups ascribed more external, unstable, and specific attributions to positive sexual events than positive nonsexual events. This finding indicates than even functional men approach sexual activities with less "self-serving" attributional bias than is typically shown in their attributions for nonsexual positive events.

Positive and Negative Affect

Barlow's model (1986) also theorizes that individuals with sexual dysfunctions react to erotic stimuli with greater negative affect. The link between depression and reductions in sexual function has been well established and studied in men (e.g., Nofzinger et al., 1993) and women (Frohlich & Meston, 2002). In addition, past studies have found that individuals with sexual dysfunction report significantly less positive affect during erotic exposure (Beck & Barlow, 1986b; Heiman & Rowland, 1983). Similarly, several studies have found a strong association between positive affect and subjective sexual arousal in men with and without sexual dysfunction (Koukounas & McCabe, 2001; Rowland, Cooper, & Heiman, 1995; Rowland, Cooper, & Slob, 1996) and in women (Heiman, 1980; Laan, Everaerd, van Bellen, & Hanewald, 1994).

Several studies have manipulated affect during laboratory studies of sexual arousal. Meisler and Carey (1991), using Velten Mood Induction Procedure (Velten, 1968), found that participants had a longer latency to maximum subjective sexual arousal following the depression affect induction as compared to the elation affect induction. However, erectile tumescence did not differ significantly as a result of the affect inductions. Laan, Everaerd, van Berlo, and Rijs (1995) used musical selections to induce a "positive sexual mood" in 51 women and examined its effects on subjective and genital measures of sexual arousal during both fantasy and in response to erotic films. Results indicated no significant effect of the mood induction on post-film/fantasy measures of subjective or genital sexual arousal. There was a marginally significant reduction in negative emotions in response to the erotic film in the mood induction group compared to the no-induction group. Although pre- versus postinduction measures of affect and subjective sexual arousal differed significantly, the postinduction (pre-film/fantasy) between groups comparison (induction group vs. no-induction group) was not significant. Perhaps the research setting (e.g., participants' expectations of watching erotic films) may have created a "positive mood for sex" that confounded the results. The Laan et al. study did not attempt to induce positive affect, per se, but rather a positive sexual mood (i.e., the authors used music to attempt to get the participants "in a mood"). Thus, conclusions regarding positive affect's role in sexual arousal are unclear from this study.

Mitchell et al. (1998) also used musical selections to induce positive (elated) and negative (depressed) affect in 24 men without sexual difficulties. The Positive and Negative Affect Schedule–State version (PANAS–state; Watson, Clark, & Tellegen, 1988) was used to measure affect pre- and postinduction, as well as post–erotic film. In contrast to Laan et al. (1995), this study used a repeated measures design, thus controlling for individual differences in sexual desire, sexual arousability, and susceptibility to the mood induction. The manipulation check indicated that the positive affect induction significantly increased positive affect compared to both the preinduction scores and the neutral control condition. The negative affect induction resulted in significantly decreased positive affect and increased negative affect, compared to the preinduction scores and the control condition. During an erotic film, participants evidenced greater subjective and genital (erectile) response following the positive affect induction and significantly lower genital response following the negative affect induction, as compared to a neutral control condition. Interestingly, these sexually functional participants did not report less subjective arousal following the negative affect induction, despite the successful affect manipulation and reductions in their erectile tumescence during the erotic film. These findings further support the notion of individuals without sexual dysfunction employing a cognitive bias in order to maintain an "illusion of control." The Mitchell et al. (1998) study is currently being replicated in men with erectile disorder. The findings of Meisler and Carey (1991) and Mitchell et al. demonstrate that positive and negative affect can influence genital and subjective sexual arousal. These studies also support the notion that positive affect is especially relevant for subjective sexual arousal.

Focus of Attention, Self-Focused Attention, and Interoceptive Awareness

A number of past studies have examined differences in focus of attention during exposure to erotic stimuli between men with and without erectile dysfunction (e.g. Abrahamson, Barlow, Beck, et al., 1985; Abrahamson, Barlow, Sakheim, et al., 1985; Beck & Barlow, 1986a, 1986b; Beck, Barlow, & Sakheim, 1983). The findings from this body of research indicate that men with erectile disorder are focused on nonerotic cues during exposure to sexual stimuli. Research in both men (Geer & Fuhr, 1976) and women (Elliott & O'Donohue, 1997) has demonstrated that distraction, operationalized as a dichotomous listening task, has detrimental effects on sexual arousal in sexually functional individuals. However, such distracting laboratory tasks do not seem to decrease the erectile tumescence of men with erectile disorder (Abrahamson, Barlow, Beck, et al., 1985; Abrahamson, Barlow, Sakheim, et al., 1985). The best explanation for these results is that men with erectile disorder are already distracted from the erotic stimulus by sexual performance-related concerns, which are the focus of their attention. In fact, distracting them from these performance concerns may have a disinhibiting effect on their sexual arousal.

While a person concerned with a sexual performance failure might be thought to be hypervigilant for signs of lack of arousal, thereby focusing intensely on his/her own sexual response rather than on the erotic cues, a second and more impairing shift of attention occurs. Analogous to what occurs in individuals with social phobia, when an individual with sexual dysfunction is confronted with implicit or explicit (i.e., implied or expressed) demands for sexual performance, a critical shift of attention occurs from an external focus (on erotic cues) to an internal, predominantly self-evaluative, focus (Barlow, 2002). Mansell, Clark, and Ehlers (2003) used an imaginative paradigm to simultaneously monitor attentional focus to external and internal events. Individuals high and low in speech anxiety were randomly assigned to a social-threat condition (anticipation of giving a speech) or a no-threat condition and asked to perform a computer-based attention task. The computer task involved looking at either pictures of faces or objects, while monitoring two types of stimuli. One was an internal stimulus that consisted of a light vibration to the fingertip, which participants were led to believe reflected changes in their heart rate and sweating. The other stimulus was an external one that involved detecting the letter "E" superimposed on the picture on a computer screen. The researchers used the relative latency to detect the external stimulus versus the internal stimulus to determine the balance of the internal/external attentional bias. The results indicated that high speech-anxious individuals selectively attended internally in the social-threat condition, but not in the no-threat condition.

Flexible self-focused attention may be part of adaptive process when it motivates behavioral change by highlighting discrepancies between one's current state and desired internal standards of performance (Carver & Scheier, 1981, 1998). However, excessive and/or rigid self-focused attention may have several dysfunctional consequences. During sexual situations, this shift to self-evaluative concerns clearly distracts an individual's attention away from the sexually arousing cues in the situation; however, the most important consequence of this self-focus concerns its effect on emotions. Self-directed focus and the resulting sensitivity to physiological or proprioceptive sensations (interoceptive awareness) are likely to result in greater subjective intensity of the emotional experience after the emotion has been elicited. Evidence suggests that this shift to a self-evaluative focused attentional state further increases arousal and negative affect, thus forming its own small negative feedback loop. Individuals with a greater disposition to self-focus were found to experience experimental provocation of various emotions as more intense than individuals with a greater disposition to external focus (Ingram, 1990; Wells & Matthews, 1994).

When individuals with sexual dysfunction are confronted with situations where they feel they should become aroused, two consequences occur as a result of the shift in attention. First, their attention becomes focused on the discrepancy between their current state of sexual performance and their internal a priori standards of sexual performance. This results in a negative evaluation of themselves, increases in negative affect, and predictions of not being able to cope, which further increase anxious arousal. Secondly, their increased internal focus and sensitivity to physiological sensations intensifies their experience of the negative affect. Thus, a small negative feedback loop within the larger negative loop is created by the intensification of arousal and negative affect that follows the shift of attention to an internal and self-evaluative focus. A further important consequence of self-focused attention is a failure to habituate to external stimuli while in the attentional mode. This selective internal attentional focus also functions as avoidance of the anxiety-producing stimuli; in the case of sexual dysfunction, this is the lack of arousal or latency to orgasm (either too short or too long). Paradoxically, individuals with sexual dysfunction may be more interoceptively aware of the somatic consequences of negative affect, while at the same time being less aware of their degree of sexual arousal. Numerous studies have found that men with erectile dysfunction underestimate their level of arousal (see van den Hout & Barlow, 2000, for a review). A similar process is posited to occur in sexually functional individuals, except via a feedback loop that increases the experience of sexual arousal. Dekker and Everaerd (1988) found that for sexually functional males and females, subjective experiences of sexual arousal were stronger when participants attended to both sexual stimuli and the associated sexual feelings rather than just focusing on the sexual stimuli.

Results from a recent study (Nobre et al., 2004) exemplify the relationship between interoceptive awareness, sexual arousal, and affect. Nobre et al. assessed the ability of 60 sexually functional males to estimate their degree of erection. During the procedures, a table was placed over participants' laps, blocking visual feedback and forcing them to rely on interoceptive awareness to estimate their level of erection. Contrary to expectations, over half of the sample (56.8%) consistently (in three out of four erotic films) underestimated their degree of erection. Despite there being no differences in physiological erection (as measured by penile plethysmography) from the group that estimated accurately, the group that underestimated reported significantly lower levels of positive affect and significantly lower levels of subjective sexual arousal. The participants in this study were sexually functional undergraduate males, and therefore they may have been able to attain erections despite the lower levels of positive affect and subjective arousal. However, will these young men, as they get older, be the men that develop erectile dysfunction? To answer such questions, longitudinal studies with large sample sizes that focus on identifying the bio-psycho-social vulnerabilities for developing sexual dysfunction are required.

For men, the ability to adequately attain and maintain a rigid erection is intimately tied to their self-esteem and self-evaluation (see Zilbergeld, 1992, 1999, for a review of clinical cases). However, for women, where the signs of sexual arousal are less publicly evident, arousal interfering concerns may have a different but equally self-esteem relevant focus. Wiederman (2000) found that one-third of college women indicated experiencing body image self-consciousness during physical intimacy at least some of the time. Dove and Wiederman (2000) found that in a sample of women a measure of cognitive distraction during sexual activity (assessing performance-based and appearance-based concerns) was positively associated with lower sexual esteem, less sexual satisfaction, less consistent orgasm, and a higher incidence of pretending orgasm, even after other relevant variables such as sexual desire and sexual attitudes were statistically controlled. Interestingly, the measure of cognitive distraction remained a significant predictor of sexual outcomes (sexual esteem, sexual satisfaction, and orgasm consistency) when trait self-focus was controlled statistically. This finding is consistent with an additional finding by Nobre et al. (2004), in that individuals who underestimated their arousal did not differ on dispositional measures of self-focused attention (private self-consciousness) or interoceptive awareness from those who accurately estimated their level of erection. Trapnell, Meston, and Gorzalka (1997) also did not find support for the role of dispositional measures of chronic self-focus in women. The lack of significant differences in dispositional measures of self-focused attention and/or interoceptive awareness may imply that impairment in self-monitoring in individuals with sexual dysfunction is characterized by situation-specific and avoidance-motivated shifts of attention away from anxiety-provoking stimuli (e.g., one's own lack of sexual arousal). In support of this hypothesis, Trapnell et al. found a significant association in women between poorer body image, higher social anxiety, and lower trait self-focus scores.

Worry

According to Barlow's (1986) model, the result of the negative feedback loop comprising the cognitive-affective process in individuals with sexual dysfunction is eventual avoidance of sexual activity. Avoidance of situations that provoke anxiety only further increases anxiety in those situations, thus potentiating the negative impact on future sexual function in these individuals. However, it is important to realize that attempts at coping and/or avoiding can take other forms than behavioral avoidance, namely worry. Worry is distinct from but related to the phenomenon of "apprehensive anticipation." The process of nonpathological worry is a natural and often-adaptive response to coping with and problem solving anticipated negative events. However, in the case of sexual dysfunction, this normal coping attempt can have implications for sexual functioning. Barlow (2002) characterizes the normal process of worry as potentially successful problem-solving activity, but only if *not* accompanied by significant anxiety. Unfortunately, individuals with sexual dysfunction frequently do experience significant anxiety. Several of the characteristics of worry make it a prime candidate for interfering in sexual functioning. Research by Borkovec and his colleagues (e.g., Borkovec, 1994) indicates that worry is a principally verbal or semantic activity that actually serves to prevent full experience of anxiety or fear-provoking stimuli. That is, the arousal driven, attention occupying, verbal/linguistic process of worry effectively suppresses the full experience of the negative state of anxiety. A related characteristic of worry is that negative worrisome cognitions result in intrusive negative thoughts that are particularly difficult to dismiss (Wells & Morrison, 1994). This effect tends to be greatest during short periods of worry. Borkovec, Robinson, Pruzinsky, and DePree (1983) found that a priming period of 15 minutes of worry, compared to 30 minutes or zero minutes, produced the greatest number of negative intrusive thoughts. Thus, worry as a coping response (in particular for sexual dysfunction) results in attentional avoidance of the anxiety-producing stimuli (e.g., the sexual situation), increases in negative intrusive thoughts (distraction), and an increase in negative affect—all of which have been shown to interfere with sexual functioning. To date, the exact role of worry in contributing to and maintaining sexual dysfunction awaits empirical elucidation and represents one of the areas of future research for the field of sexual dysfunction.

Update of the Model of Sexual Dysfunction

Barlow's 1986 model of sexual dysfunction needs to be updated to incorporate the above detailed findings and advances in the conceptualization of anxious apprehension (Barlow, 2002). Specifically, the recent empirical work on cognitive schemata, negative and positive affect, self-focused attention, and worry warrant inclusion in the model. The updated model of sexual dysfunction has largely been based on a revised model of anxious apprehension that is detailed in *Anxiety and Its Disorders: The Nature and Treatment of Anxiety and Panic* (Barlow, 2002) and the original model of sexual dysfunction (Barlow, 1986). The updated sexual dysfunction model continues to posit a negative feedback loop in individuals with sexual dysfunction and a positive feedback loop in individuals without sexual dysfunction (see Figure 2).

A more detailed version of feedback loop that characterizes individuals with sexual dysfunctions is represented by Figure 3. A bio-psycho-social perspective has been added to the model in recognition of factors that predispose individuals to develop sexual dysfunctions. These include relationship factors, physiological factors, and cognitive/emotional factors. The relationship factors and major physiological factors have not been extensively reviewed in this paper, since the focus is on the cognitive and emotional process in sexual arousal. Wincze and Carey (2001) provide a review of relationship and medical factors. In addition, Janssen, Vorst, Finn, and Bancroft (2002a, 2002b) provide an excellent explanation of their dual control model and the individual differences in proclivity for sexual inhibition or sexual excitation. Within this dual control model, sexual inhibition is conceptualized as having essential and adaptive functions; however, individuals with maladaptive levels may be predisposed to developing sexual dysfunctions (or sexual disorders in the case of too little inhibition). The cognitive schemata theorized to predispose individuals to experiences of sexual dysfunction are based on the cognitive differences in how individuals with and without sexual dysfunction approach sexual situations and

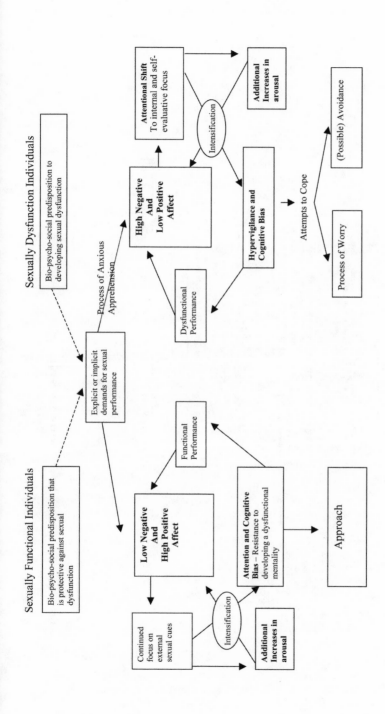

Adapted from Barlow (2002), The Nature of Anxious Apprehension, p. 65 and Barlow, 1986.

Figure 2. Model of cognitive affective sexual processes in sexual functioning.

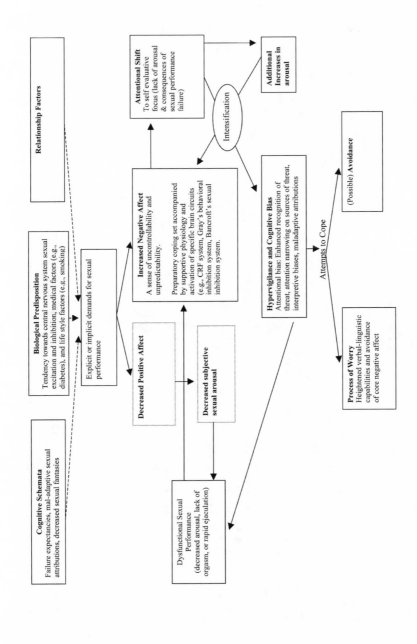

Adapted from Barlow (2002), The Nature of Anxious Apprehension, p. 65 and Barlow, 1986.

Figure 3. Detail of model of sexual dysfunction.

may be the result of learning history and personality factors (Barlow, 2000). Sexually dysfunctional cognitive schemata are characterized by negative expectancies (Bach, Brown, & Barlow, 1999; Cranston-Cuebas et al., 1993) and may include predictions of erectile failure or rapid ejaculation for men and negative evaluations by a partner of her physical attributes or performance for women. In addition, these negative expectancies are maintained and reinforced by situation-specific sexual attributional styles that attribute stable causes to negative sexual function events (Scepkowski et al., 2004; Weisberg et al., 2001).

The major revision of the model has to do with the shifts in attentional focus. In the original model (Figure 1), the negative feedback loop characteristic of individuals with sexual dysfunctions included a shift of attention to nonerotic cues and a further increase in the salience of those nonerotic cues due to narrowing of the attentional focus. However, research on self-focused attention has demonstrated that during anxious apprehension attention rapidly shifts to a self-evaluative internal focus. This shift to self-focused attention, as well as increases in autonomic arousal, actually intensifies the experience of negative affect. In addition, this shift to a self-evaluative perspective focused on lack of coping ability contributes to the maintenance of hypervigilance and cognitive biases. This negative feedback loop nested within the overall feedback loop has been incorporated into the model (Figure 3).

The separation of affect into decreased positive and increased negative affect represents a further change in the model. The association between positive affect and subjective sexual arousal has been found in multiple studies (e.g., Meisler & Carey, 1991; Nobre et al., 2004). However, other studies (e.g., Mitchell et al., 1998) have failed to find an effect of manipulating affect on subjective sexual arousal, and therefore this portion of the model is in need of further empirical research.

Lastly, worry as an attempt at coping as well as a maintaining factor in sexual dysfunction has been added as an additional avoidance response. Worry as a coping response (in particular for sexual dysfunction) results in attentional avoidance of the anxiety-producing stimuli (e.g., the sexual situation), increases in negative intrusive thoughts (distraction), and an increase in negative affect—all of which can potentially interfere with further sexual arousal. A more detailed analysis of the impact of worry on aspects of sexual arousal also awaits empirical study.

Conclusion

In summary, it may be that an affect-laden attentional process focusing on erectile function (for men), body image (for women), sexual performance, and other self-evaluative concerns, combined with a tendency to exhibit biased observation of one's functioning (lack of accurate interoceptive awareness or interoceptive focus), may characterize the cognitive-affective processes in sexual dysfunction. In other words, self-focused attention, as reflected in pathological and affect-laden worry processes turned inward, may be fundamentally an avoidance technique (Borkovec, 1994; Brown, Barlow, & Liebowitz, 1994; Roemer & Borkovec, 1993) that is orthogonal to accurate interoceptive awareness and focus. Specifically, in the case of sexual dysfunction, this process would be situationally bound, since the research discussed has shown that sexual concerns are only relevant in the context of implicit or explicit demands for performance (or in the case of women, being physically on display and judged on attractiveness by a partner).

Finally, the relationship between objective measures of arousal in a sexual context and subjective arousal seem to differ considerably among dysfunctional and functional populations, with functional populations showing the well-established "illusion of control" in which subjective estimates of arousal do not decrease in a correlated fashion with more objective measures of arousal. This also implies a lack of awareness of performance insufficiency, and yet the above research demonstrates that objective arousal is directly impacted by cognitive and affective manipulations. This "low road to the amygdala" (LeDoux, 1996) may provide a key to understanding vulnerabilities to anxiety-driven deficits in performance when it is investigated more rigorously.

A bio-psycho-social perspective on the etiology of sexual dysfunction is crucial for developing a comprehensive understanding of cognitive processes involved in these disorders. Predisposing factors that can lead one to develop the cognitive schemata seen in individuals with recurrent sexual difficulties can be conceptualized similarly to the triple vulnerability theory of the etiology of anxiety disorders (see Barlow, 2002). In this model, individuals will vary in generalized biological vulnerability factors (e.g., temperament, androgen levels), generalized psychological vulnerability factors (e.g., perceived uncontrollability of life events as a result of experience, depression, anxiety), and specific psychological vulnerabilities (e.g., sexual attitudes, sexual inhibition as described in the dual control model [Janssen et al., 2002a, 2002b], sexual self-concept). Factors in each category of vulnerabilities can influence approaches to sexual situations, cognitive processing of sexual stimuli in terms of bias and affective valence, expectancies for successful or unsuccessful sexual outcomes, and coping styles for dealing with occasions of sexual difficulty.

For now, it seems clear that further research on cognitive and affective aspects of sexual functioning and, by inference, other areas of performance, may further strengthen models of anxiety-related deficient functioning, particularly when considered in interaction with neurobiological factors. In fact, it is unlikely that either neurobiological etiological accounts or pharmacological interventions for performance deficits such as sexual dysfunction will provide anything near a comprehensive account of the genesis or treatment of performance deficits without a full explication of the impact of cognitive and affective factors.

References

Abrahamson, D. J., Barlow, D. H., Beck, J. G., Sakheim, D. K., & Kelly, J. P. (1985). The effects of attentional focus and partner responsiveness on sexual responding: Replication and extension. *Archives of Sexual Behavior, 14,* 361–371.

Abrahamson, D. J., Barlow, D. H., Sakheim, D. K., Beck, J. G., & Athanasiou, R. (1985). Effects of distraction on sexual responding in functional and dysfunctional men. *Behavior Therapy, 16,* 503–515.

Arkin, R. M., Detchon, C. S., & Maruyama, G. M. (1982). Roles of attribution, affect, and cognitive interference in test anxiety. *Journal of Personality and Social Psychology, 43,* 1111–1124.

Arkin, R. M., Kolditz, T. A., & Kolditz, K. K. (1983). Attributions of the test-anxious student: Self-assessments in the classroom. *Personality and Social Psychology Bulletin, 9,* 271–280.

Bach, A. K., Brown, T. A., & Barlow, D. H. (1999). The effects of false negative feedback on efficacy expectancies and sexual arousal in sexually functional males. *Behavior Therapy, 30,* 79–95.

Bancroft, J. (1989). *Human sexuality and its problems* (2nd ed.). New York: Churchill Livingstone.

Barlow, D. H. (1986). The causes of sexual dysfunction: The role of anxiety and cognitive interference. *Journal of Consulting and Clinical Psychology, 54,* 140–148.

Barlow, D. H. (2000). Unraveling the mysteries of anxiety and its disorders from the perspective of emotion theory. *American Psychologist, 55,* 1245–1263.

Barlow, D. H. (2002). The nature of anxious apprehension. In *Anxiety and its disorders: The nature and treatment of anxiety and panic* (2nd ed., pp. 64–104). New York: Guilford Press.

Barlow, D. H., Chorpita, B. F., & Turovsky, J. (1996). Fear, panic, anxiety, and disorders of emotion. In D. A. Hope (Ed.), *Perspectives on anxiety, panic, and fear* (Vol. 43, pp. 251–328). Lincoln, Nebraska: University of Nebraska Press.

Beck, J. G., & Barlow, D. H. (1986a). The effects of anxiety and attentional focus on sexual responding: I. Physiological patterns in erectile dysfunction. *Behaviour Research and Therapy, 24,* 9–17.

Beck, J. G., & Barlow, D. H. (1986b). The effects of anxiety and attentional focus on sexual responding: II. Cognitive and affective patterns in erectile dysfunction. *Behaviour Research and Therapy, 24,* 19–26.

Beck, J. G., Barlow, D. H., & Sakheim, D. K. (1983). The effects of attentional focus and partner arousal on sexual responding in functional and dysfunctional men. *Behaviour Research and Therapy, 21,* 1–8.

Borkovec, T. D. (1994). The nature, functions, and origins of worry. In G. C. L. Davey & F. Tallis (Eds.), *Worrying: Perspectives on theory, assessment, and treatment* (pp. 5–53). New York: Wiley.

Borkovec, T. D., Robinson, E., Pruzinsky, T., & DePree, J. A. (1983). Preliminary exploration of worry: Some characteristics and processes. *Behaviour Research and Therapy, 21,* 9–16.

Brockner, J., & Swap, W. C. (1983). Resolving the relationships between placebos, misattribution, and insomnia: An individual-differences perspective. *Journal of Personality and Social Psychology, 45,* 32–42.

Brown, T. A., Barlow, D. H., & Liebowitz, M. R. (1994). The empirical basis of generalized anxiety disorder. *American Journal of Psychiatry, 151,* 1272–1280.

Carver, C. S., & Scheier, M. F. (1981). *Attention and self-regulation: A control-therapy approach to human behavior.* Berlin: Springer-Verlag.

Carver, C. S., & Scheier, M. F. (1998). *On the self-regulation of behaviour.* Cambridge, UK: Cambridge University Press.

Cranston-Cuebas, M. A., & Barlow, D. H. (1990). Cognitive and affective contributions to sexual functioning. In J. Bancroft (Ed.), *Annual review of sex research* (pp. 119–161). Philadelphia: Society for the Scientific Study of Sex.

Cranston-Cuebas, M. A., & Barlow, D. H. (1995). *Attentional focus and the misattribution of male sexual arousal.* Unpublished manuscript.

Cranston-Cuebas, M. A., Barlow, D. H., Mitchell, W. B., & Athanasiou, R. (1993). Differential effects of a misattribution manipulation on sexually functional and dysfunctional males. *Journal of Abnormal Psychology, 102,* 525–533.

Dekker, J., & Everaerd, W. (1988). Attentional effects on sexual arousal. *Psychophysiology, 25,* 45–54.

Dove, N. L., & Wiederman, M. W. (2000). Cognitive distraction and women's sexual functioning. *Journal of Sex and Marital Therapy, 26,* 67–78.

Elliott, A. N., & O'Donohue, W. T. (1997). The effects of anxiety and distraction on sexual arousal in a nonclinical sample of heterosexual women. *Archives of Sexual Behavior, 26,* 607–624.

Fichten, C. S., Spector, I., & Libman, E. (1988). Client attributions for sexual dysfunction. *Journal of Sex and Marital Therapy, 14,* 208–224.

Frohlich, P. F., & Meston, C. M. (2002). Sexual functioning and self-reported depressive symptoms among college women. *Journal of Sex Research, 39,* 321–325.

Geer, J. H., & Fuhr, R. (1976). Cognitive factors in sexual arousal: The role of distraction. *Journal of Consulting and Clinical Psychology, 44,* 238–243.

Heiman, J. R. (1980). Female sexual response patterns: Interactions of physiological, affective, and contextual cues. *Archives of General Psychiatry, 37,* 1311–1316.

Heiman, J. R., & Rowland, D. L. (1983). Affective and physiological sexual response patterns: The effects of instructions on sexually functional and dysfunctional men. *Journal of Psychosomatic Research, 27,* 105–116.

Ingram, R. E. (1990). Self-focused attention in clinical disorders: Review and conceptual model. *Psychological Bulletin, 107,* 156–176.

Janssen, E., Everaerd, W., Spiering, M., & Janssen, J. (2000). Automatic processes and the appraisal of sexual stimuli: Toward an information processing model of sexual arousal. *Journal of Sex Research, 37,* 8–23.

Janssen, E., Vorst, H., Finn, P., & Bancroft, J. (2002a). The Sexual Inhibition (SIS) and Sexual Excitation (SES) scales: I. Measuring sexual inhibition and excitation proneness in men. *Journal of Sex Research, 39*(2), 114–126.

Janssen, E., Vorst, H., Finn, P., & Bancroft, J. (2002b). The Sexual Inhibition (SIS) and Sexual Excitation (SES) scales: II. Predicting psychophysiological response patterns. *Journal of Sex Research, 39*(2), 127–132.

Koukounas, E., & McCabe, M. P. (2001). Sexual and emotional variables influencing sexual response to erotica: A psychophysiological investigation. *Archives of Sexual Behavior, 30,* 393–408.

Laan, E., Everaerd, W., van Bellen, G., & Hanewald, G. (1994). Women's sexual and emotional responses to male- and female-produced erotica. *Archives of Sexual Behavior, 23,* 153–169.

Laan, E., Everaerd, W., van Berlo, R., & Rijs, R. (1995). Mood and sexual arousal in women. *Behavior Research and Therapy, 33,* 441–443.

Lang, P. J. (1985). The cognitive psychophysiology of emotion: Fear and anxiety. In A. H. Tuma & J. D. Maser (Eds.), *Anxiety and the anxiety disorders* (pp. 131–170). Hillsdale, N.J.: Erlbaum.

Lang, P. J. (1994a). The motivational organization of emotion: Affect-reflex connections. In S. H. M. Van Goozen, N. E. Van de Poll, & J. A. Sergeant (Eds.), *Emotions: Essays on emotion theory* (pp. 61–93). Hillsdale, N.J.: Erlbaum.

Lang, P. J. (1994b). The varieties of emotional experience: A meditation on James-Lange theory. *Psychological Review, 101,* 211–221.

Loos, V. E., Bridges, C. F., & Critelli, J. W. (1987). Weiner's attribution theory and female orgasmic consistency. *Journal of Sex Research, 23,* 348–361.

Mansell, W., Clark, D. M., & Ehlers, A. (2003). Internal versus external attention in social anxiety: an investigation using a novel paradigm. *Behaviour Research and Therapy, 41,* 555–572.

Marten, P. A., & Barlow, D. H. (1991, November). *Differences in dimensions of fantasy between sexually functional and dysfunctional males: Preliminary results and treatment implications.* Paper presented at the annual meeting of the Association for Advancement of Behavior Therapy, New York, New York.

Meisler, A. W., & Carey, M. P. (1991). Depressed affect and male sexual arousal. *Archives of Sexual Behavior, 20,* 541–554.

Meston, C. M., & Gorzalka, B. B. (1995). The effects of sympathetic activation on physiological and subjective sexual arousal in women. *Behaviour Research and Therapy, 33,* 651–664.

Meston, C. M., & Gorzalka, B. B. (1996a). Differential effects of sympathetic activation on sexual arousal in sexually dysfunctional and functional women. *Journal of Abnormal Psychology, 105,* 582–591.

Meston, C. M., & Gorzalka, B. B. (1996b). The effects of immediate, delayed, and residual sympathetic activation on sexual arousal in women. *Behaviour Research and Therapy, 34,* 143–148.

Meston, C. M., Gorzalka, B. B., & Wright, J. M. (1997). Inhibition of psychological and subjective sexual arousal in women by clonidine. *Journal of Psychosomatic Medicine, 59,* 399–407.

Meston, C. M., & Heiman, J. R. (1998). Ephedrine-activated physiological sexual arousal in women. *Archives of General Psychiatry, 55,* 652–656.

Mitchell, W. B., DiBartolo, P. M., Brown, T. A., & Barlow, D. H. (1998). Effects of positive and negative mood on sexual arousal in sexually functional males. *Archives of Sexual Behavior, 27,* 197–207.

Mitchell, W. B., Marten, P. A., Williams, D. M., & Barlow, D. H. (1990, November). *Control of sexual arousal in sexual dysfunctional males.* Paper presented at the annual meeting of the Association for Advancement of Behavior Therapy, San Francisco, California.

Nobre, P., Wiegel, M., Bach, A. K., Weisberg, R. B., Brown, T. A., Wincze, J. P., & Barlow, D. H. (2004). Determinants of sexual arousal and the accuracy of its self-estimation in sexually functional males. *Journal of Sex Research, 41,* 363–371.

Nofzinger, E. A., Schwartz, R. M., Reynolds, C. F. 3rd, Thase, M. E., Jennings, J. R., Frank, E., et al. (1993). Correlation of nocturnal penile tumescence and day-time affect intensity in depressed men. *Psychiatry Research, 49,* 139–150.

Palace, E. M. (1995). Modification of dysfunctional patterns of sexual response through autonomic arousal and false physiological feedback. *Journal of Consulting and Clinical Psychology, 63,* 604–615.

Quadland, M. C. (1980). Private self-consciousness, attribution of responsibility, and perfectionistic thinking in secondary erectile dysfunction. *Journal of Sex and Marital Therapy, 6,* 47–55.

Roemer, L., & Borkovec, T. D. (1993). Worry: Unwanted cognitive experience that controls unwanted somatic experience. In D. M. Wegner & J. Pennebaker (Eds.), *Handbook of mental control* (pp. 229–238.). Englewood Cliffs, N.J.: Prentice-Hall.

Rowland, D. L., Cooper, S. E., & Heiman, J. R. (1995). A preliminary investigation of affective and cognitive response to erotic stimulation in men before and after sex therapy. *Journal of Sex and Marital Therapy, 21,* 3–20.

Rowland, D. L., Cooper, S. E., & Slob, A. K. (1996). Genital and psychoaffective response to erotic stimulation in sexually functional and dysfunctional men. *Journal of Abnormal Psychology, 105,* 194–203.

Scepkowski, L. A., Wiegel, M., Bach, A. K., Weisberg, R. B., Brown, T. A., & Barlow, D. H. (2004). Attributions for sexual situations in men with and without erectile disorder: Evidence from a sex-specific attributional style measure. *Archives of Sexual Behavior, 33,* 559–569.

Stock, W., & Geer, J. (1982). A study of fantasy-based sexual arousal in women. *Archives of Sexual Behavior, 11,* 33–47.

Storms, M. D., & Nisbett, R. E. (1970). Insomnia and the attribution process. *Journal of Personality and Social Psychology, 16,* 319–328.

Trapnell, P. D., Meston, C. M., & Gorzalka, B. B. (1997). Spectatoring and the relationship between body image and sexual experience: Self-focus or self-valence? *Journal of Sex Research, 34,* 267–278.

van den Hout, M., & Barlow, D. H. (2000). Attention, arousal, and expectancies in anxiety and sexual disorders. *Journal of Affective Disorders, 61,* 241–256.

Velten, E. (1968). A laboratory task for induction of mood states. *Behaviour Research and Therapy, 6,* 473–482.

Watson, D., Clark, L. A., & Tellegen, A. (1988). Development and validation of brief measures of positive and negative affect: The PANAS scales. *Journal of Personality and Social Psychology, 54,* 1063–1070.

Weisberg, R. B., Bach, A. K., Wiegel, M., Brown, T. A., Wincze, J. P., & Barlow, D. H. (1998, November). *Attributional style specific to sexual events: A comparison of men with and without erectile disorder.* Paper presented at the meeting of the Association for Advancement of Behavior Therapy, Washington, D.C.

Weisberg, R. B., Brown, T. A., Wincze, J. P., & Barlow, D. H. (2001). Causal attributions and male sexual arousal: The impact of attributions for a bogus erectile difficulty on sexual arousal, cognitions, and affect. *Journal of Abnormal Psychology, 110,* 324–334.

Weisberg, R. B., Sbrocco, T., & Barlow, D. H. (1994, November). *A comparison of sexual fantasy use between men with situational erectile disorder, generalized erectile disorder, and sexually functional males: Preliminary results.* Paper presented at the annual meeting of the Association for Advancement of Behavior Therapy, San Diego, California.

Wells, A., & Matthews, G. (1994). *Attention and emotion.* Hove, UK: Lawrence Erlbaum.

Wells, A., & Morrison, A. (1994). Qualitative dimensions of normal worry and normal obsessions: A comparative study. *Behaviour Research and Therapy, 32,* 867–870.

Wiederman, M. W. (2000). Women's body image self-consciousness during physical intimacy with a partner. *Journal of Sex Research, 37*(1), 60–68.

Wincze, J. P., & Carey, M. P. (2001). *Sexual dysfunction: A guide for assessment and treatment* (2nd ed.). New York: Guilford Press.

Zilbergeld, B. (1992). *The new male sexuality.* New York: Bantam Books.

Zilbergeld, B. (1999). *The new male sexuality* (Rev. ed.). New York: Bantam.

The Sexual Unconscious

MARK SPIERING AND WALTER EVERAERD

Introduction

Unconscious processes set up sexual responding. To acquire knowledge about the activation of a sexual response, one has to focus on unconscious mechanisms. We propose that (i) sexual features are preattentively processed, (ii) sexually competent stimuli elicit physiological arousal before and independent of conscious evaluation, and (iii) the subjective experience of a sexual emotion is constructed by attentional amplification of unconscious cognitions. We will describe models of the generation of emotion (Damasio, 2003; LeDoux, 1996) and extrapolate them to the sexual emotions as was earlier done by Janssen, Everaerd, Spiering, and Janssen (2000). Empirical studies that we recently conducted will be discussed.

The title of this paper is derived from papers by Kihlstrom (1987) and Kihlstrom, Mulvaney, Tobias, and Tobis (2000), "The Cognitive Unconscious" and "The Emotional Unconscious," respectively. In these papers, the importance of implicit processes in cognitive and emotional responding is highlighted. Percepts, memories, and other mental states, which are inaccessible to phenomenal awareness and are somehow independent of voluntary control, influence conscious experience, thought, and action.

The Cognitive Sexual System

Sex can be viewed to be among the emotions. Sexual excitement has a specific pattern of activity and there is coherence in expression and physiology linked to prototypical situational events (Everaerd, 1988). For a full-blown sexual emotion, specific components have to be activated (e.g., genital arousal, a subjective experience of sexual arousal) as well as nonspecific components (e.g., heart rate changes, a subjective experience of tension). When writing about the "sexual system," we mean sexually specific as well as nonspecific modules within the brain, which interact to produce a sexual response.

What are the requirements for the sexual system to operate? Sexuality is prepared at birth. During development and growth there is interaction with the environment, which builds up experience and potentiation of

166

"sexual" stimuli (Everaerd, Laan, & Spiering, 2000). The most probable development is that, in the beginning, pleasurable sensations from tactile stimulation and later from visual, auditory, or olfactory stimulation were pleasurable and not sexual, like many other sensations for which labels and meanings have to be learned after the first experience. It is implied that stimuli are cognitively transformed into messages that eventually result in a sexual response, subjective sexual experience in particular. Thus, a stimulus is not intrinsically sexual; it becomes sexual by its transformation (Everaerd, Laan, & Spiering).

Sensitivity of the sexual system is dependent on biological and psychological factors. On the side of biological factors, the androgen hormones as well as the neurotransmitters norepinephrine and dopamine are considered as most influential (Bancroft, 2002). The focus of this paper is on psychological factors. Emotional reactions depend on appraisal of the stimulus, which includes memory and attentional processes interacting with each other.

Long-term memory is not a unitary entity, but can be subdivided into explicit (or declarative) and implicit (or procedural) memory (Squire, 1992; Tulving & Schacter, 1990). Explicit memory is consciously accessible; implicit memory is not. Regarding "sexual memory," that is, memory associated with sexual responding, explicit memory refers to, for instance, recollections of sexual encounters, attitudes toward sex, sexual fantasies, and knowledge about sexual rewards or costs. Implicit sexual memory refers to, for instance, innate sexual reflexes, learned (automatized) sexual scripts, and classically conditioned sensations. A stimulus may convey several meanings depending on the circumstances or the individual's history. Different messages, in the same or in different individuals, may thus be accessed by the same stimulus. Sexual meaning and other meanings relevant for different emotions, such as anxiety, anger, or elation, may be present at the same time. The different meanings will be processed as different messages that, by further processing, may develop divergent physiological and behavioral responses and experiences (Everaerd, Laan, & Spiering, 2000).

What happens when a person is confronted with a sexually competent stimulus? How is stimulus information transformed into particular sorts of actions? When confronted with a sexual stimulus, arousal will be generated, which subsequently signals reward. At the same time, motor preparation is activated for eventual approach to the rewarding stimulus (Both, Everaerd, & Laan, 2003). The emotional experience of sexual arousal is the subjective awareness of autonomic arousal, of the reward expectancy, and of the felt tendency to act (Everaerd, 1988; Frijda, 1986). Arousal alone is not sufficient to produce subjective sexual experience; this experience ultimately depends on the individual's awareness and definition of the response as sexual.

Central regulation of emotional responses is essential for adaptive functioning. When a stimulus has been identified as sexual, regulation of information processing is needed. Although sexual excitement can be enhanced by intentionally bringing (explicit) sexual memories into awareness, probably most of the time regulation actually consists of inhibition. Since sexual behavior goes together with important concerns (e.g., reproduction, intimacy), attentional mechanisms are triggered and activational stages are accompanied by conscious inhibitory control (Baars, 1998a; Fuster, 1997; Gross, 1998).

Unconscious versus Conscious Processes

Information processing in the brain can be divided into unconscious and conscious. For every conscious state, there is an associated neural state; a change of conscious state is impossible without a corresponding change in neural state. However, not all neural activities have corresponding conscious representations (Frith, Perry, & Lumer, 1999). Unconscious processes have two essential features: they are inaccessible for phenomenal awareness and independent of voluntary control.

Kihlstrom et al. (2000) distinguish between the "cognitive unconscious" and the "emotional unconscious." The cognitive unconscious constitutes four categories of phenomena: implicit memory, implicit learning, implicit perception, and implicit thought. Implicit or nondeclarative memory can be defined as an unconscious influence of past experience on current performance of behavior (Schacter & Buckner, 1998). Implicit learning refers to one's acquisition of new patterns of behavior without being aware of the patterns themselves (Kihlstrom et al., 2000). Automatization is a relevant concept in this. Implicit perception includes preattentive or preconscious processing. It is defined as the effects of a current event on one's performance, in the absence of conscious perception of that event. Finally, implicit thought, for example the correct solution to a problem, influences experience, thought, or action even though one is unaware of the thought itself (Kihlstrom et al., 2000).

How does the emotional unconscious relate to this? If emotion is defined as a conscious feeling state, an emotional unconscious is precluded. But when the subjective component of an emotion (i.e., the conscious feeling state) is absent, while the behavioral and physiological components persist outside of phenomenal awareness, why can't we say that there is an unconscious emotion or at least an unconscious emotional response (Kihlstrom et al., 2000)? From an information-processing perspective, subjective components of an emotion, just as physiological and behavioral components, are the products of processing, which is inaccessible for phenomenal awareness and independent of voluntary control, that is, emotional unconscious processes.

We will now look at unconscious processes from the other side, by describing conscious processes. The essential feature of consciousness is awareness; to be conscious is to be aware of things. Attention is a prerequisite of consciousness. Consciousness refers to those thoughts, memories, sensations, and actions of which one is aware, whereas attention refers to those processes that modulate neuronal activity (Tassi & Muzet, 2001). The results of selection are always conscious, whereas the processes of selecting, deselecting, and maintaining selection may or may not be. "Attention involves the selection of targets for the searchlight to shine on, while consciousness results from illumination of the target" (Baars, 1998b, p. 59). Phenomenally, we experience conscious visual scenes, but we are not necessarily conscious of visual selection processes that can reasonably be called attentional. Attention can be subdivided in three systems with different functions: orienting to sensory stimuli, activation of ideas from memory, and maintaining the alert state (Posner, 1994). Consciousness is a form of output associated with focal attentive processing that does not enter into cerebral processing (Velmans, 1991).

Dehaene and Naccache's (2001) global neural workspace hypothesis describes the relation between unconscious processes and a conscious state. At any given time, many modular cerebral networks are active in parallel and process information in an unconscious manner. Information becomes conscious if the neural population that represents it is mobilized by top-down attentional amplification into a brain-scale state of coherent activity that involves many neurons distributed throughout the brain. The long-distance connectivity of these "workspace neurons" can make the information available to a variety of processes including perceptual categorization, long-term memorization, and intentional action. It is postulated that this global availability of information through the workspace is what we subjectively experience as a conscious state (Dehaene & Naccache).

Top down should not be taken too literally. Since there is no single organizational summit to the brain, it means only that such attentional amplification is not just modulated bottom up by features internal to the processing stream in which it rides, but also by sideways influences, from competitive, cooperative, collateral activities (Dennet, 2001). It is "not that this global availability causes some further effect or a different sort altogether—igniting the glow of conscious qualia, gaining entrance to the Cartesian Theatre, or something like that—but that it is, all by itself, a conscious state" (Dennet, p. 223).

In the next three sections, we will review our three hypotheses that were mentioned at the start of this paper. Theoretical and empirical arguments are presented in a temporal structure: Unconsciously, sexual features attract attention, produce motor output, and enable a conscious experience.

Preattentive Selection of Sexual Features

Taken literally, the term *preattentive* means before attention operates. So-called preattentive search is really a search in which attention is distributed widely over the whole display rather than narrowly focused and is directed serially to one subgroup at a time (Treisman & Gormican, 1988; Treisman & Souther, 1985). Preattentive search can be construed as a filtering of information so that some features or aspects of an array are "passed through" and others are "filtered out." A feature passed through is more likely to come to focal attention than one filtered out (Öhman, Flykt, Esteves, 2001). It would seem to the (attentive) individual as if the feature commanded attention; it would appear to "pop out" from the array (Treisman & Gormican). Preattentive visual search is defined as fast, automatic, and parallel, and works on low-level stimulus features with the primary objective of delineating objects in the spatial surroundings. Focal attention is slow, deliberate, and serial, and is concerned with more complex inferential and interpretative processes in identifying the located objects in perceptual awareness (Posner & Snyder, 1975; Schneider & Shiffrin, 1977; Shiffrin & Schneider, 1977). When unexpectedly encountered, peripheral significant events may interrupt ongoing processing and call for prioritized focal attentive processing (Öhman et al.).

We propose that sexual features are preattentively processed. We derive this from emotion research in which threat features preattentively elicit focal attention: the face-in-the-crowd paradigm. No direct empirical support for this proposal regarding sexual features is present yet; however, some indirect support is discussed later in this section.

Hansen and Hansen (1988) introduced the face-in-the-crowd effect. In experiments, participants were presented with arrays of faces in which one facial expression differs from the others in emotional valence. Participants were asked to detect the "odd face out" as quickly as possible. Angry faces were found more efficiently in happy crowds than were happy faces in angry crowds. Also, the latency to discover an angry face in a happy crowd was not influenced by the number of happy face distractors in the crowd, whereas the number of angry face distractors dramatically influenced the latency to discovery of a discrepant happy face. It was surmised that the face-in-the-crowd effect was due to a stimulus confound (Purcell, Stewart, & Skov, 1996). However, recently Öhman, Lundqvist, and Esteves (2001) successfully replicated the findings with schematic facial stimuli.

Facial threats command attention. An angry face in a happy crowd is found quite readily, whereas a happy face in a crowd of attention-grabbing angry faces is easily overlooked. Arrays are preattentively searched in parallel for features of facial threat; an angry face in a happy crowd pops out and does not require an extensive, time-consuming, serial attentive search to discover its presence. However, a happy face in an angry crowd is not preattentively distinctive; it does not pop out, and discovering its presence requires a serial search of the faces.

Detection and location of a feature can be accomplished preattentively, whereas discrimination requires attentional processing. An angry face could

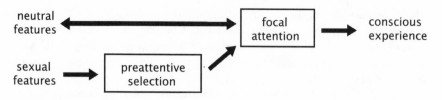

Figure 1. Unlike neutral stimuli, sexual features may be preattentively selected to trigger focal attention.

be detected and located in a happy crowd, but its content (i.e., that it was, in fact, an angry face) could not be discriminated preattentively. The consequence of preattentive face processing from which the face-in-the-crowd effect was derived, then, would be a shift of attention to a preattentive located point in the crowd. Given time to complete an attentional shift to that point, the target could be seen as an angry face (Hansen & Hansen, 1988).

Öhman, Flykt, et al. (2001) examined another class of evolutionary fear-relevant stimuli within the same paradigm: snakes and spiders. Stimuli related to recurrent survival threats in the environment of evolutionary adaptedness may have been selected to become more or less automatic triggers of attention. The reproductive potential of individuals was predicated on the ability to efficiently locate critically important events in the surroundings. To detect threatening events outside the spotlight of focused, conscious attention, there must be perceptual processes that automatically scan and analyze the perceptual field.

Participants were faster in finding snakes and spiders against backgrounds of flowers and mushrooms (neutral stimuli) than the other way around (Öhman, Flykt, et al., 2001). Furthermore, whereas it took longer to locate fear-irrelevant targets with more distractors, finding fear-relevant targets was independent of matrix size. The effect of fear relevance was enhanced in fearful participants. Similar to controls, fearful participants were faster to find a fear-relevant target that they did not fear (e.g., a spider for a snake-fearful participant) than fear-irrelevant targets, but they were even faster to find a fear-relevant stimulus (e.g., a snake for a snake-fearful participant). Threatening stimuli were located in a preattentive, parallel-processing perceptual stage, whereas nonthreatening targets had to be searched for with a more laborious postattentive strategy.

The data suggest that snake- and spider-fearful participants were sensitized specifically to have their attention captured by the feared stimulus. Gilboa-Schechtman, Foa, and Amir (1999) tested social phobics and found greater attentional bias after angry faces in this paradigm. There might be attention control settings that tune the likelihood to capture attention in accordance with their relevance for the current goals of the individual

(Folk, Remington, & Johnston, 1992). If emotions are action sets (Frijda, 1986), which imply a set of goals, it could be suggested that the generation of emotions involves attention control settings that make goal-relevant stimuli salient. As a result, these stimuli may then automatically capture attention (Folk et al., 1992).

Junghöfer, Bradley, Elbert, and Lang (2001) provide converging empirical data, with negative as well as positive (including sexual) pictures. They introduced a new experimental paradigm: rapid serial visual presentation. It allows investigation of rapid detection and perceptual processing of emotionally salient stimuli after a single scan, as stimuli occur fleetingly, or as the eye flicks rapidly through a scene. Participants viewed 700 complex pictures, varying in affective arousal, at high-speed presentation (3 or 5 per second). Event-related potentials (ERPs) are assessed to determine attention capture. ERPs were more negative for high than low arousal pictures, suggesting that the brain is specially tuned to detect and process motivationally relevant stimuli (Lang et al., 1998). Affect discrimination of pictures was independent of formal visual properties of the stimuli, including color, brightness, spatial frequency, and complexity (Junghöfer et al., 2001).

We propose that sexual features also can be preattentively processed (see Figure 1). Which arguments do we have for this? In daily life, one may recognize the attention-grabbing capacity of sexual features by its use in advertisement and video clips. Theoretically, the fact that the pop-out effect was not found for happy faces does not imply that all approach stimuli are excluded from being preattentively processed. Both sexually appetitive and anxiety inducing stimuli generate action tendencies, although the direction of eventual behavior is presumed to be different, that is, approach versus avoidance (Both et al., 2003). Regarding the criteria of goal relevance and reward value, sexual stimuli may have a higher valence than happy faces.

A straightforward test for preattentive selection of sexual features would be to include them in the face-in-the-crowd paradigm. This has not been done. There is some indirect support for our hypothesis. The findings described before fit into a voluminous literature showing attentional bias for threat in anxiety patients, for example, the dot-probe paradigm or the emotional Stroop task (Mogg & Bradley, 1998; Williams, Mathews, & MacLeod, 1996). The general tendency, even among nonanxious individuals, to attend to threatening stimulus content may reflect the same type of preattentive process as displayed in the face-in-the-crowd paradigm.

Geer and colleagues discovered a delay in information processing caused by sexual words (Geer & Bellard, 1996; Geer & Melton, 1997). This could very well be compared to the attentional bias phenomenon caused by threatening information (Mogg & Bradley, 1998; Williams et al., 1996). Recently, we conducted an experiment in which both sexual and threatening pictures, which had to be ignored, decelerated categorical decisions (Spiering,

Everaerd, & Elzinga, 2002). This deceleration effect replicates Geer's findings and extends it to threatening information, resembling the emotional Stroop effect. Sexual information, just like threatening information, interferes with information processing by automatic activation of focal attention. This could indicate the preattentive processing of sexual features.

Unconscious Activation of the Sexual System

Emotional responses are consequences of affective computations outside conscious awareness. In this section, we will review evidence of unconscious activation of sexual response. We propose that sexual features activate implicit memory and bodily responses before conscious appraisal. First, LeDoux's (1996) work on the role of the amygdala is presented because of its great influence on thinking about unconscious activation of emotions. Next, relevant studies from emotion and sex research are discussed.

The amygdala is the core of the network that computes the affective value of the stimuli an organism encounters (LeDoux, 1993). Empirical support for this was found in negative as well as positive emotions, including the sexual (Zald, 2003). LeDoux discovered parallel transmission to the amygdala from (i) the thalamus and (ii) the cortex (1996, 2000). The thalamo-amygdala projections appear to be involved in the processing of the affective significance of relatively simple sensory features. These subcortical pathways provide a crude image of the external world. The thalamo-cortico-amygdala projections are necessary when more complex aspects of stimuli are processed. More detailed and accurate representations become available from the cortex. While the pathway from the thalamus to amygdala only involves one link, at least two links are required to activate the amygdala by way of the cortex. Since each link adds time, the thalamus pathway is faster. This direct route, initiated by the amygdala, can preattentively initiate bodily responses. Low-level stimulus features can trigger emotional functions by the rapid arrival of crude stimulus information from the thalamus to the amygdala (LeDoux, 1996).

Data from recent experiments using functional magnetic resonance imaging (fMRI) and positron emission tomography (PET) scans corroborate the pivotal role of the amygdala in unconscious emotional activation. Subliminally presented angry faces lead to neural activity in the amygdala along with heightened skin conductance responses (SCRs) (Morris, Öhman, & Dolan, 1998). In an experiment of Whalen and colleagues (Whalen et al., 1998), signal intensity within the amygdala changed following subliminally presented angry faces as well as happy faces. Although LeDoux (1996) offers a specific neurobiological model by which stimulus features activate emotional responses, the temporal resolution of the designs of Morris et al. and Whalen et al. does not directly address the issue that the amygdala receives stimulus information directly from the thalamus. However, it supports the main thesis of LeDoux that affective computations are made without the need and before focal attention or awareness. Stimulus features automatically activate bodily responses, and conscious appraisal of the stimulus occurs against a background of physiological activation.

Besides these neurocognitive studies, others have stressed which features are capable of unconsciously activating responses and which bodily responses can be elicited unconsciously. Öhman and Soares (1994) subliminally presented pictures of snake and spiders to snake-fearful and spider-fearful participants. Snake-fearful participants showed enhanced SCRs to snake stimuli and spider-fearful participants to spider stimuli. Merely a preattentive analysis of emotionally relevant features is sufficient to elicit a fear response, and very brief presentations of emotional slides thus do not seem to prevent a relatively specific analysis of content.

Reactions in facial muscles were successfully elicited in participants unconsciously exposed to pictures of angry and happy faces. Just as in full-awareness conditions (Cacioppo, Petty, Losch, & Kim, 1986), increased zygomatic muscle ("smile-muscle") activity was found after subliminally presented pictures of angry faces and increased corrugator muscle activity ("frown-muscle") after subliminally presented pictures of happy faces (Dimberg, Thunberg, & Elmehed, 2000; Rotteveel, De Groot, Geutskens, & Phaf, 2001). It was suggested that unconscious facial reactions are even larger compared to conscious ones, because they are unaffected by conscious regulation (Rotteveel et al., 2001).

To what extent has unconscious activation of the sexual system been studied? Janssen et al. (2000) tested the hypothesis of genital activation without awareness. Consciously perceived sexual slides were subliminally primed with sexual versus neutral slides. In Figure 2, LeDoux's model (1996) is depicted with a sexually competent stimulus; by presenting slides subliminally, the pathway from explicit memory to attention was blocked. Genital blood flow of the first 5 seconds after presentation of the target was measured by penile circumference differences (only men were tested). Contrary to prediction, penile responses on sexually primed slides were smaller than responses on neutrally primed slides. However, in early stages of arousal, the penis may primarily grow in length, which is associated with a simultaneous decrease in circumference (Earls & Marshall, 1982; Kuban, 1997; McConaghy, 1974). Instead of circumference measures, future studies might profit from volumetric measures or from registration of corpus cavernosum smooth muscle action potentials to pick up small priming effects (Geer & Janssen, 2000; Jiang, Speel, Wagner, Meuleman, & Wijkstra, 2003; Wagner, Gerstenberg, & Levin, 1989). Still, initial support for preattentive genital activation seems present.

In a sequel study (Spiering, Everaerd, & Janssen, 2003), the activation process was tapped in an earlier phase. The way explicit memory mediates between stimulus and subjective experience, implicit memory can be seen as the mediator between stimulus and bodily response. It was found that

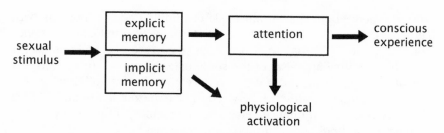

Figure 2. A sexual stimulus activates bodily responses implicitly and explicitly. The implicit pathway is independent of conscious experience.

subliminally presented sexual pictures facilitate the identification of following sexual pictures without an effect on subjective sexual arousal. It can be concluded that sexual features activated implicit sexual memory, bypassing products of explicit memory.

Also, in this study only men were tested. A replication in women succeeded, but showed weaker effects (Spiering, Everaerd, Karsdorp, Both, & Brauer, 2003). Several hypotheses can be formulated for this. Emotional responses to sexual stimuli are more blended in women than in men (Everaerd, Laan, Both, & van der Velde, 2000), which can make implicit activation more diffuse. Another hypothesis is that men and women do differ on a primary level of responding. Dissimilarities between prehistoric gender roles might have influenced preattentive processing of sexual features nowadays (Bjorklund & Kipp, 1996). Men have been selected to maximize their mating opportunities; women do not benefit by increasing the number of sexual partners and would risk producing offspring of low quality if they mated indiscriminately (Bailey, Gaulin, Agyei, & Gladue, 1994). Furthermore, ontogenetic and cultural factors differentially influence men and women.

Finally, preattentive activation of sexual representations was found in relation to sexual harassment (Bargh, & Raymond, 1995; Bargh, Raymond, Pryor, & Strack, 1995). In an analogue study, an unconscious unidirectional link was shown between the concept of power and sex. Participants were male students who indicated on a self-report measure that they were attracted to sexual aggression. Using a subliminal priming paradigm, the activation of representations related to sex was established through the activation of other representations (i.e., power), outside of the individual's awareness.

The Making of Subjective Experience

In this section, the final stage of activation is discussed, in which a subjective experience of sexual arousal is added to physiological activation. A feeling is defined as "the perception of a certain state of the body along with the perception of a certain mode of thinking and of thoughts with certain themes" (Damasio, 2003, p. 86). A complete emotional experience consists of awareness of bodily responses (e.g., "I feel sexually aroused") plus the cognitive appraisal of the stimulus as emotional (e.g., "this is a sexual arousing stimulus"). We introduce the concepts of "hot" versus "cold" cognition to distinguish between these two experiences and will see that they originate in implicit versus explicit memory, respectively. At the end, empirical findings on this topic are presented.

In the previous sections, we stated that in the first stage of activation a sexually competent stimulus activates bodily responses by a match with implicit memory. Conscious appraisal of the stimulus is not necessary for this. Two different pathways can now lead to a subjective experience: (i) Attentional focus results in conscious appraisal. The appraisal process is contingent on the match between stimulus characteristics and explicit memory. The individual defines the stimulus as sexual. (ii) Feedback representations of peripheral arousal provide input to conscious awareness (Critchley, Mathias, & Dolan, 2002). Body-sensing brain regions produce a map of what is occurring in the body (Damasio, 2003), and the perception of this map can result in a conscious sexual feeling.

The concepts of "hot" versus "cold" cognition were introduced in social psychology to contrast between affectively laden and motivationally driven versus anhedonic and purely informational processes (Lepper, 1994). We incorporated these concepts in our model (see Figure 3). Cold cognitions are defined as representations activated in explicit memory; hot cognitions are defined as bodily feedback representations that originally result from implicit activation. The focus of attention in emotion can switch between hot and cold cognitions and yield awareness of bodily phenomenology or emotion thoughts (Lambie & Marcel, 2002).

We will now describe both pathways more precisely and describe the main brain structures involved. Explicit memory is situated in the neocortex and is mediated by the hippocampus (LeDoux, 1996; Squire, 1992). The amygdala is the central brain structure for implicit memory. LeDoux describes the parallel functioning if stimuli that were present during a trauma reactivate both structures. "Through the hippocampal system you will remember who you were with and what you were doing during the trauma, and will also remember, as a cold fact, that the situation was awful. Through the amygdala system the stimuli will cause your muscles to tense up, your blood pressure and heart rate to change, and hormones to be released, among other bodily and brain responses" (LeDoux, 1996, p. 202).

The insula might be a crucial brain structure in the way bodily feedback provides input to awareness (Craig, 2002; Damasio, 2003; Sumich, Kumari, & Sharma, 2003). The hot cognition—the feeling—is an interoceptive sensation, based on an image of the state of the body. The insula is

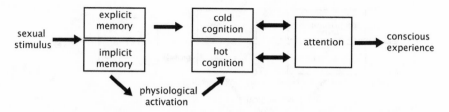

Figure 3. The conscious experience is constructed by attentional amplification of unconscious hot and cold cognitions. These cognitions can be seen as the products of implicit and explicit activation.

engaged in the transfer of bodily responses and subjective feelings (Morris, 2002).

How does a conscious state appear from an unconscious cognition? Information becomes conscious if the neural population that represents it is mobilized by top-down attentional amplification (Dehaene & Naccache, 2001). The prefrontal cortex and anterior cingulate are presumed to represent this attentional amplifier (Fuster, 1997; Posner, 1994). In Figure 4, the psychological concepts of Figure 3 are replaced by its main neurological structures.

Disagreement between sexual response components was explained by independent contributions from explicit and implicit memory. For instance, low self-reported emotional ratings and a relatively high physiological response were found when women were exposed to male-centered erotic film excerpts (Laan, Everaerd, van Bellen, & Hanewald, 1994). The stimulus matched with implicit sexual memory and led to physiological sexual arousal. Meanwhile, the stimulus activated nonsexual meanings (e.g., awful, coarse, obscene) in explicit memory. When focus of attention is directed to these activated cold cognitions, a genital response is present, while the subjective experience of sexual arousal is absent (Everaerd, Laan, Both, & van der Velde, 2000; Geer, Lapour, & Jackson, 1993; Janssen et al., 2000).

In a recent study (Spiering, Everaerd, & Laan, 2002), we manipulated focus of attention in other to create different access to memory (Robinson & Clore, 2002). Men and women were asked to rate sexual pictures that were primed by male- versus female-oriented sexual pictures (i.e., explicit vs. romantic). Two ratings were collected. First, participants were asked for a hot cognition: "To what degree do you feel sexually aroused at this moment?" Second, they were asked for a cold cognition: "To what degree do you find the last slide sexually arousing?" In this way, we may distinguish between implicit versus explicit contributions to emotional self-report.

A gender difference was not present in hot cognitions (first question) and was present in cold cognitions (second question). Women rated targets

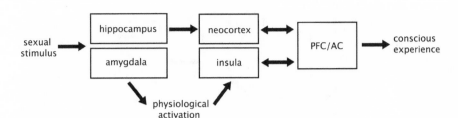

Figure 4. The main brain structures that underlie the psychological concepts of Figure 3. PFC/AC = prefrontal cortex and anterior cingulate.

as less arousing when they had been preceded by explicit primes than did men. Correlations between the two questions were higher for men than for women. Especially after the male-oriented explicit primes, the correlation for women was low. Explicit primes match with implicit sexual memory and activate physiological arousal. When asked for an introspective assessment (i.e., first question), physiological feedback might result in subjective sexual arousal. However, conscious evaluation of the stimulus (i.e., second question) is more dependent on explicit memory, and explicit sexual primes were evaluated as not arousing by women. This pattern could be a manifestation of response disagreement, as was found in the Laan et al. study (1994); however, considering the lack of a physiological measure of sexual arousal in the Spiering, Everaerd, and Laan (2002) study, this explanation remains somewhat speculative.

An Evolved Sex Module within the Brain?

We proposed that different unconscious mechanisms are involved in activation of sexual response. Sexual features are the subject of a preattentive search. It would seem to the attentive individual as if the feature commanded attention (Figure 1). Sexually competent stimuli activate motor output by a match with implicit memory. Activation of representations in explicit memory and subsequent conscious evaluation is not necessary for this (Figure 2). Hot and cold cognitions were postulated as unconscious products of bodily feedback and explicit memories. Attentional amplification of these cognitions results in a conscious experience of sexual feelings and sexual thoughts (Figure 3). Empirical support for these hypotheses mainly stems from emotion research in general; for instance, imaging studies in which these psychological pathways are representations of underlying neurological structures (Figure 4).

Öhman and Mineka (2001, 2003) recently proposed a fear module in the brain that represents an evolved adaptation. This concept is presumed to integrate diverse findings on fear from many domains and to set an agenda for research on fear. Is there also a sex module inside? For this, we should abandon the assumption of function generality. Decision rules have coevolved with search engines and memory systems, and what kind of information they will retrieve will depend on what adaptive problem they were designed to solve (Klein, Cosmides, Tooby, & Chance, 2002). The brain can be seen as a set of computational machines that are adaptive specializations: systems equipped with design features that are organized such that they solve an ancestral problem reliably, economically, and efficiently. A host of specialized systems may exist, including ones related to sexual motivation (Duchaine, Cosmides, & Tooby, 2001).

The sex module could be seen as a device for activating sexual physiological responses and sexual feelings to sexual stimuli. According to Öhman and Mineka (2001), a module has four characteristics: selectivity, automaticity, encapsulation, and a specific neural circuitry. The sex module could meet these criteria.

Selectivity. There is selectivity with regard to the input to which the module responds. Rather than being open to any stimulus, the sex module is assumed to be particularly sensitive to stimuli that have been correlated with successful sexual encounters in the evolutionary past, for example, cues indicating genetic quality.

Automaticity. Automaticity refers to identification of sexual stimuli after a minimum of neural computations to immediately give them priority, for example, in terms of efficient attention capture. Features trigger responses in the absence of conscious awareness of the stimulus event. The sex module is not under voluntary control and has a stimulus-driven onset.

Encapsulation. Whereas automaticity is primarily related to the initiating of activity, encapsulation refers to the maintaining of activity over time. Once activated, the sex module tends to run its course with a few possibilities for other processes to interfere or stop it.

Specific neural circuitry. The sex module is to be controlled by a specific neural circuit that has been shaped by evolution because it mediates the functional relationship between ecological events and behavior. The brain circuits are likely to be located in subcortical or even brainstem areas. Its subcortical location suggests that it has an ancient evolutionary origin.

The scientific utility of the concept of a sex module still has to be shown. Our model of activation also remains speculative. It mainly is an extrapolation of models of Damasio (2003) and LeDoux (1996) that are still more theoretical than empirical and, besides, these models are not about sex. In our view, it is fruitful to implement these cognitive-emotional concepts in sex research. Hypotheses can be specified and tested in paradigms that allow the study of unconscious mechanisms (e.g., the face-in-the-crowd paradigm, priming). Neuroimaging studies could reveal the specific neural circuitry involved in sex (Sumich et al., 2003).

Much can be done with little or no conscious attention. Circumstances that mobilize attention tend to involve novel challenges or unpredictable events to which we need to devote a substantial part our psychological resources. From a functionalistic perspective, consciousness plays an important role in directing our waking behavior (Zeman, 2001). For sustained response, attention to internal or external sexual cues is needed. Without attention, the sexual response will fade away. Also, regulation of the response merely functions through conscious evaluation, for which attention is a prerequisite. However, activation of sexual response is largely unconscious. To increase knowledge about activational mechanisms, one has to focus on the "sexual unconscious," the different processes, inaccessible for phenomenal awareness and independent of voluntary control, which set up sexual responding.

References

Baars, B. J. (1998a). The function of consciousness [Reply to a letter of O. G. Cameron]. *Trends in Neurosciences, 21,* 201.

Baars, B. J. (1998b). Metaphors of consciousness and attention in the brain. *Trends in Neurosciences, 21,* 58–62.

Bailey, J. M., Gaulin, S., Agyei, Y., & Gladue, B. A. (1994). Effects of gender and sexual orientation on evolutionarily relevant aspects of human mating psychology. *Journal of Personality and Social Psychology, 66,* 1081–1093.

Bancroft, J. (2002). Sexual arousal. In L. Nadel (Ed.), *Encyclopedia of cognitive science* (pp. 1165–1168). London: Wiley.

Bargh, J., & Raymond, P. (1995). The naive misuse of power: Nonconscious sources of sexual harassment. *Journal of Social Issues, 51,* 85–96.

Bargh, J. A., Raymond, P., Pryor, J., & Strack, F. (1995). Attractiveness of the underling: An automatic power-sex association and its consequences for sexual harassment and aggression. *Journal of Personality and Social Psychology, 68,* 768–781.

Bjorklund, D. F., & Kipp, K. (1996). Parental investment theory and gender differences in the evolution of inhibition mechanisms. *Psychological Bulletin, 120,* 163–188.

Both, S., Everaerd, W., & Laan, E. (2003). Modulation of spinal reflexes by aversive and sexually appetitive stimuli. *Psychophysiology, 40,* 174–183.

Cacioppo, J. T., Petty, R. E., Losch, M. E., & Kim, H. S. (1986). Electromyographic activity over facial muscle regions can differentiate the valence and intensity of affective reactions. *Journal of Personality and Social Psychology, 50,* 260–268.

Craig, A.D. (2002). How do you feel? Interoception: The sense of the physiological condition of the body. *Nature Reviews, 3,* 655–666.

Critchley, H. D., Mathias, C. J., & Dolan, R. J. (2002). Fear conditioning in humans: The influence of awareness and autonomic arousal on functional neuroanatomy. *Neuron, 33,* 653–663.

Damasio, A. (2003). *Looking for Spinoza: Joy, sorrow, and the feeling brain.* Orlando: Harcourt.

Dehaene, S., & Naccache, L. (2001). Towards a cognitive neuroscience of consciousness: Basic evidence and a workspace framework. *Cognition, 79,* 1–37.

Dennet, D. (2001). Are we explaining consciousness yet? *Cognition, 79,* 221–237.

Dimberg, U., Thunberg, M., & Elmehed, K. (2000). Unconscious facial reactions to emotional facial expressions. *Psychological Science, 11,* 86–89.

Duchaine, B, Cosmides, L., & Tooby, J. (2001). Evolutionary psychology and the brain. *Current Opinion in Neurobiology, 11,* 225–230.

Earls, C. M., & Marshall, W. L. (1982). The simultaneous and independent measurement of penile circumference and length. *Behavior Research Methods and Instrumentation, 14,* 447–450.

Everaerd, W. (1988). Commentary on sex research: Sex as an emotion. *Journal of Psychology and Human Sexuality, 1,* 3–15.

Everaerd, W., Laan, E., Both, S., & van der Velde, J. (2000). Female sexuality. In L. T. Szuchman & F. Muscarella (Eds.), *The psychological science of human sexuality* (pp. 101–146). New York: Wiley.

Everaerd, W., Laan, E., & Spiering, M. (2000). Male sexuality. In L. T. Szuchman & F. Muscarella (Eds.), *The psychological science of human sexuality* (pp. 60–100). New York: Wiley.

Folk, C. L., Remington, R. W., & Johnston, J. C. (1992). Involuntary covert orienting is contingent on attentional control settings. *Journal of Experimental Psychology: Human Perception and Performance, 18,* 1030–1044.

Frijda, N. H. (1986). *The emotions.* Cambridge: Cambridge University Press.

Frith, C., Perry, R., & Lumer E. (1999). The neural correlates of conscious experience: An experimental framework. *Trends in Cognitive Sciences, 3,* 105–114.

Fuster, J. M. (1997). *The prefrontal cortex: Anatomy, physiology, and neuropsychology of the frontal lobe* (3rd ed.). New York: Lippincott Raven.

Geer, J. H., & Bellard, H. S. (1996). Sexual content induced delays in unprimed lexical decisions: Gender and context effects. *Archives of Sexual Behavior, 25,* 379–395.

Geer, J. H., & Janssen, E. (2000). The sexual response system. In J. Cacioppo, L. Tassinari, & G. Bernston (Eds.), *Handbook of psychophysiology* (pp. 315–341). New York: Cambridge University Press.

Geer, J. H., Lapour, K. J., & Jackson, S. R. (1993). The information processing approach to human sexuality. In N. Birbaumer & A. Öhman (Eds.), *The structure of emotion: Psychophysiological, cognitive, and clinical aspects* (pp. 139–155). Toronto: Hogrefe-Huber.

Geer, J. H., & Melton, J. S. (1997). Sexual content-induced delay with double-entendre words. *Archives of Sexual Behavior, 26,* 295–316.

Gilboa-Schechtman, E., Foa, E. B., & Amir, N. (1999). Attentional biases for facial expressions in social phobia: The face-in-the-crowd paradigm. *Cognition and Emotion, 13,* 305–318.

Gross, J. J. (1998). Antecedent- and response-focused emotion regulation: Divergent consequences for experience, expression, and physiology. *Journal of Personality and Social Psychology, 74,* 224–237.

Hansen, C. H., & Hansen, R. D. (1988). Finding the face in the crowd: An anger superiority effect. *Journal of Personality and Social Psychology, 54,* 917–924.

Janssen, E., Everaerd, W., Spiering, M., & Janssen, J. (2000). Automatic cognitive processes and the appraisal of sexual stimuli: Towards an information processing model of sexual arousal. *Journal of Sex Research, 37,* 8–23.

Jiang, X. G., Speel, T. G. W., Wagner, G., Meuleman, E. J. H., & Wijkstra, H. (2003). The value of corpus cavernosum electromyography in erectile dysfunction: Current status and future prospect. *European Urology, 43,* 211–218.

Junghöfer, M., Bradley, M. M., Elbert, T. R., & Lang, P. J. (2001). Fleeting images: A new look at early emotion discrimination. *Psychophysiology, 38,* 175–178.

Kihlstrom, J. F. (1987). The cognitive unconscious. *Science, 237,* 1445–1452.

Kihlstrom, J. F., Mulvaney, S., Tobias, B. A., & Tobis, I. P. (2000). The emotional unconscious. In E. Eich, G. H. Bower, J. P. Forgas, & P. M. Niedenthal (Eds.), *Cognition and emotion* (pp. 30–86). London: Oxford University Press.

Klein, S. B., Cosmides, L., Tooby, J., & Chance, S. (2002). Decisions and the evolution of memory: Multiple systems, multiple functions. *Psychological Review, 109,* 306–329.

Kuban, M. (1997). *A comparison of volumetric and circumferential penile plethysmographic methods: The effect of response magnitude on method agreement.* Unpublished master's thesis, University of Toronto, Canada.

Laan, E., Everaerd, W., van Bellen, G., & Hanewald, G. (1994). Women's sexual and emotional responses to male- and female-produced erotica. *Archives of Sexual Behavior, 23,* 153–169.

Lambie, J. A., & Marcel, A. J. (2002). Consciousness and the varieties of emotion experience: A theoretical framework. *Psychological Review, 109,* 219–259.

Lang, P. J., Bradley, M. M., Fitzsimmons, J. R., Cuthbert, B. N., Scott, J. D., Moulder, B., & Nangia, V. (1998). Emotional arousal and activation of the visual cortex: An fMRI analysis. *Psychophysiology, 35,* 199–210.

LeDoux, J. (1993). Cognition versus emotion, again—this time in the brain: A response to Parott and Schulkin. *Cognition and Emotion, 7,* 61–64.

LeDoux, J. (1996). *The emotional brain.* New York: Touchstone.

LeDoux, J. (2000). Emotion circuits in the brain. *Annual Reviews of Neuroscience, 23,* 155–184.

Lepper, M. R. (1994). "Hot" versus "cold" cognition: An Abelsonian voyage. In R. C. Schank & E. Langer (Eds.), Beliefs, reasoning, and decision making: Psychologic in honor of Bob Abelson (pp. 237–275). Hillsdale, N.J.: Lawrence Erlbaum Associates.

McConaghy, N. (1974). Measurements of change in penile dimensions. *Archives of Sexual Behavior, 3,* 381–388.

Mogg, K., & Bradley, B. P. (1998). A cognitive-motivational analysis of anxiety. *Behaviour Research and Therapy, 36,* 809–848.

Morris, J. S. (2002). How do you feel? *Trends in Cognitive Sciences, 6,* 317–319.

Morris, J. S., Öhman, A., & Dolan, R. J. (1998). Conscious and unconscious emotional learning in the human amygdala. *Nature, 393,* 467–470.

Öhman, A., Flykt, A., & Esteves, F. (2001). Emotion drives attention: Detecting the snake in the grass. *Journal of Experimental Psychology: General, 130,* 466–478.

Öhman, A., Lundqvist, D., & Esteves, F. (2001). The face in the crowd revisited: A threat advantage with schematic stimuli. *Journal of Personality and Social Psychology, 80,* 381–396.

Öhman, A., & Mineka, S. (2001). Fears, phobias, and preparedness: Towards an evolved fear module of fear and fear learning. *Psychological Review, 108,* 483–522.

Öhman, A., & Mineka, S. (2003). The malicious serpent: Snakes as a prototypical stimulus for an evolved module of fear. *Current Directions in Psychological Science, 12,* 5–9.

Öhman, A., & Soares, J. J. F. (1994). "Unconscious anxiety": Phobic responses to masked stimuli. *Journal of Abnormal Psychology, 103,* 231–240.

Posner, M. I. (1994). Attention: The mechanisms of consciousness. *Proceedings of the National Academy of Sciences of the United States of America, 91,* 7398–7403.

Posner, M. I., & Snyder, C. R. R. (1975). Attention and cognitive control. In R. L. Solso (Ed.), *Information processing and cognition: The Loyola symposium* (pp. 55–85). Hillsdale, N.J.: Erlbaum.

Purcell, D. G., Stewart, A. L., & Skov, R. B. (1996). It takes a confounded face to pop out of a crowd. *Perception, 25,* 1091–1108.

Robinson, M. D., & Clore, G. L. (2002). Belief and feeling: Evidence for an accessibility model of emotional self-report. *Psychological Bulletin, 128,* 934–960.

Rotteveel, M., De Groot, P., Geutskens, A., & Phaf, R. H. (2001). Stronger suboptimal than optimal priming. *Emotion, 1,* 348–364.

Schacter, D., & Buckner, R. L. (1998). Priming and the brain. *Neuron, 20,* 185–195.

Schneider, W., & Shiffrin, R. M. (1977). Controlled and automatic human information processing: I. Detection, search, and attention. *Psychological Review, 84,* 1–66.

Shiffrin, R. M., & Schneider, W. (1977). Controlled and automatic human information processing: II. Perceptual learning, automatic attending, and a general theory. *Psychological Review, 84,* 127–190.

Spiering, M., Everaerd, W., & Elzinga, E. (2002). Conscious processing of sexual information: Interference caused by sexual primes. *Archives of Sexual Behavior, 31,* 159–164.

Spiering, M., Everaerd, W., & Janssen, E. (2003). Priming the sexual system: Implicit versus explicit activation. *Journal of Sex Research, 40,* 134–145.

Spiering, M., Everaerd, W., Karsdorp, P., Both, S., & Brauer, M. (2003). *Unconscious processing of sexual information: A generalization to women.* Manuscript in preparation.

Spiering, M., Everaerd, W., & Laan, E. (2002). *Conscious processing of sexual information: Mechanisms of appraisal.* Manuscript submitted for publication.

Squire, L. R. (1992). Memory and the hippocampus: A synthesis from findings with rats, monkeys, and humans. *Psychological Review, 99,* 195–231.

Sumich, A. L., Kumari, V., & Sharma, T. (2003). Neuroimaging of sexual arousal: Research and clinical utility. *Hospital Medicine, 64,* 28–33.

Tassi, P., & Muzet, A. (2001). Defining the states of consciousness. *Neuroscience and Biobehavioral Reviews, 25,* 175–191.

Treisman, A., & Gormican, S. (1988). Feature analysis in early vision: Evidence from search asymmetries. *Psychological Review, 95,* 15–48.

Treisman, A., & Souther, J. (1985). Search asymmetry: A diagnostic for preattentive processing of separable features. *Journal of Experimental Psychology: General, 114,* 285–310.

Tulving, E., & Schacter, D. L. (1990). Priming and human memory systems. *Science, 247,* 301–306.

Velmans, M. (1991). Is human information processing conscious? *Behavioral and Brain Sciences, 14,* 651–726.

Wagner, G., Gerstenberg, T., & Levin, R. J. (1989). Electrical activity of corpus cavernosum during flaccidity and erection of the human penis: A new diagnostic method. *Journal of Urology, 142,* 723–725.

Whalen, P. J., Raunch, S. L., Etcoff, N. L., McInerney, S. C., Lee, M. B., & Jenike, M. A. (1998). Masked presentations of emotional facial expressions modulate amygdala activity without explicit knowledge. *Journal of Neuroscience, 18,* 411–418.

Williams, J. M. G., Mathews, A., & MacLeod, C. (1996). The emotional Stroop task and psychopathology. *Psychological Bulletin, 120,* 3–24.

Zald, D. H. (2003). The human amygdala and the emotional evaluation of sensory stimuli. *Brain Research Reviews, 41,* 88–123.

Zeman, A. (2001). Consciousness. *Brain, 124,* 1263–1289.

Discussion Paper

JAMES H. GEER

I want to thank our presenters for sharing their interesting models with us. There's no question, I think, that any field will progress to the extent that good theory is available to work with, and both of the presenters have taken important steps in terms of trying to develop theory and to make us think about some of the issues involved. I was very pleased to see them using very broad concepts from a number of different disciplines, not just relying upon their own work but gathering work from social psychology, from experimental cognitive psychology, from physiology, from all of these areas. These are major strengths in any attempt to deal with the complex issues that we have. To Dave Barlow and his colleagues, the willingness to look at new data and be able to modify and explore and change their models is, I think, a strength. As you know, far too often people develop a theory and that's the way it is. They live with it and they fight anybody trying to change it. Not only do Wiegel et al. change their model, but they make significant changes. To Walter, his courage to talk about the unconscious: Think about how that would have been viewed by a group like this 10 years ago or 15 years ago. I applaud that and indeed I am working in areas that are somewhat similar to his.

I do have some general concerns, and then I have some suggestions as to some literature that might be useful to explore. One concern is that I saw very little in terms of how we could test and therefore discard these models. That's what Karl Popper (1959) said we needed to be able to do. Science progresses by testing. There were notions of some hypotheses, but they didn't sound very specific to me, nor did I see what would be the crucial test in any of these models that would allow us to throw out chunks of the model. I have to say chunks because, for example, the model that Dave Barlow and his colleagues have put forward is very complex and obviously I don't think one can test it at one fell swoop, unless one got into some of these complex models via path analyses or LISREL analyses. I only vaguely understand their analytic strategies and don't know how one would even begin. However, I think testing is truly important.

I would like to offer some suggestions to our presenters about some areas they might look at that I think overlap their work. These are areas from experimental cognitive psychology, which I think will inform the models. They may not change a lot, but perhaps they'll give some suggestions as to how one might look at things. I have picked the brain of my colleague Jason Hicks, who is indeed a memory expert and researcher on some of these things, so I don't want to make it sound as though I know this area as deeply as I would like. In terms of the Barlow model, I would suggest that they look very carefully at the work on source monitoring in experimental cognitive psychology. When you speak of shifting to self-focus, the source monitoring literature would talk about these sorts of things. The source monitoring literature looks at all sorts of fascinating kinds of things and one of the topics I have seen is the heading "Focus of attention, self-focus attribution and interoceptive awareness." Those concepts are clearly different sources of information input and indeed the source monitoring things look at those sorts of variables. When you talk about internal stable and external fluctuating and so forth, the notion of source monitoring becomes relevant.

Jason reminded me of some fascinating literature on what is called *intention superiority effects.* That is the effect of intending to do something upon what you perceive later on. We'll return to this in just a minute. The source monitoring literature looks at memory. It examines what is encoded and finds that what gets encoded into memory differs as a function of the source that it's attributed to, and I think that literature can be useful. Perceived loss of control certainly talks about a source that's internal; we're talking about things that are ongoing. Maladaptive sexual causal attributions—again the attribution literature overlaps considerably with the source monitoring literature and I would think it would be most useful to look at it. I remember Marsha Johnson a number of years ago began work on what seemed to be silly question that I realized was a terribly complicated question: How do we tell the difference between imagining something and actually doing it? We all think we know the answer as to how we tell the difference, but in reality, there is no simple answer. We talk about fantasy and that's part of what the experimental cognitive psychologists are talking about and I think we would be well served by looking at that literature.

Both papers talk about something that I'm concerned about and that is the concept of inhibition. What I'm concerned about is that the term *inhibition* is used so many different ways and in so many different settings. The physiologist clearly has a different meaning of inhibition or a specific meaning of inhibition. John and Erick and their work on inhibitory processes may be talking about the output of those physiological systems, but it also may be something entirely different. The cognitive literature is looking a lot at inhibition at this point. There's an interesting phenomenon, which perhaps all of you know, but I'll describe it, as perhaps some of you are not familiar with the notion. The phenomenon is called *retrieval based forgetting.* You take a list of 10 words and you ask a subject to read those 10 words because they're important to the study. Then what you do after they've read their 10 words is to say, okay, now we have selected 5 of those for you to really study in detail, so you do. The participants study each of those 5 words. They repeat them and they learn them. Then after a break you then ask them unexpectedly, "We changed our mind, we want you to recall all those 10 at which you first looked." They'll recall the practiced 5 perfectly, but of those that they didn't study, they will actually recall fewer than would be the case for an appropriate control condition. There is some automatic inhibition there, a blocking of memory. Is that the same inhibition that we're talking about when John and Erick are talking about inhibitory processes? Walter, for example, talks about inhibition a lot, about how it's a control kind of function. So, I think we ought to look at these things. I am concerned about the broad use of the term inhibition because it probably is talking about entirely different mechanisms in many different settings. I don't have a resolution to this problem. I don't know of a literature that's going to clarify the nomenclature, but I think we have to be careful not to use that same term in what looks to me to be dramatically different phenomena.

A concern I do have about Walter's paper is a suggestion that implicit and explicit processes are really different things. Jacoby, who is a prominent cognitive researcher, argues that no given process is truly independently either explicit or implicit, that indeed the concepts are mixed together (Jacoby, 1991). They are coexistent processes and they don't exist truly independent of each other. They can influence each other, sometimes they facilitate each other, and sometimes they inhibit each other. I think Walter needs to be a little careful in making it sound like they are really two different things that never speak to each other, whereas in reality they, of course, speak to each other quite a bit.

I'm also a little concerned about the concept of schema as used in Barlow's work because schema as used in the experimental cognitive literature refers to very specific, often small units of memory. I don't know how much information one can get from examining the experimental cognitive literature on schema, but I think we need to look at it.

Another thing I'd like to speak to and I didn't hear from either of those papers, was how did we get this way? That is, what are the variables and processes that lead people to the end result of different processing systems? There's no hint of how they developed. We can say, "Well, they learned it," but when we start talking about some of these processes, that doesn't clarify the question.

When Walter suggests notions about implicit demands—I don't know what an implicit demand is. *Implicit* in most of the experimental cognitive literature refers to internal states of the individual. An implicit demand is, as I understand Walter's use of the term, something in the environment. However, I don't think he means subliminal stimuli, but I'm not exactly sure what it means.

As I noted earlier, I think it would be useful to explore in greater detail the intentional superiority effect, which may explain some of the phenomena we study. What the cognitive psychologists have shown, and I know that Jason has literature on this, is if you have an intention to do something—they use uninteresting things like mail a letter, we use the example of expecting to have sex—what you can find is that the perceptual processing of material related to that concept is greatly facilitated by having that intention. That is, the person who intends to mail a letter, when he walks down the street sees more mailboxes than somebody who doesn't intend to mail a letter. The person who expects to have sex, intends to have sex, when they see an appropriate or what they deem appropriate object, is going to see it quicker and react more to it. I think that literature on intentional processes would be very helpful in terms of trying to understand some of these processes.

So what I wanted to try to say is that I think there are important sets of literature out there in experimental cognitive psychology. I noted the source monitoring literature, the literature on the explicit/implicit values, and work on intentional processes. There are many other kinds of concepts that could be very useful in trying to both strengthen our work and suggest research paradigms. In collecting some data having to do with implicit attitudes, we have shown that at an implicit level, women have negative attitudes toward sexual material more than males do at an "unconscious level." If we're using Walter's model, I think these data are fascinating. They demonstrate the value of exploring the experimental cognitive literature to evaluate its relevance to our own work in sexuality. I want to commend the authors for their papers because I think they are very helpful for beginning to develop useful theoretical models.

References

Jacoby, L. L. (1991). A process dissociation framework: Separating automatic from intentional uses of memory. *Journal of Memory and Language, 30,* 513–541.
Popper, K. (1959). *The logic of scientific discovery.* London: Hutchinson.

General Discussion

Julia Heiman: I just wanted to pick up on something. I think, at least for most of us, until the last decade, we weren't talking at all about implicit memories in sex research. Just before I left Seattle, Tony Greenwald, who is a well-known cognitive psychologist, published a study on implicit attitudes toward race. I think implicit attitude measurement may be especially important in areas like sex and race/ethnicity, where one may be swayed by socially desirable responding. Mark and Walter's paper suggests important and interesting directions for future research.

Ray Rosen: I agree with Jim that these were both excellent papers. Walter and David have made significant contributions in formalizing many of these ideas into elegant, well-articulated models. Having said that, I'd like to bring up two potentially troubling issues. The first is that if you look at Barlow's work in the area of anxiety, and Markus correctly drew a number of parallels between the sexual function model that he presented and Barlow's anxiety model, I'm struck by the difference in clinical impact. Whereas Barlow's anxiety model has had enormous impact on the management of anxiety disorders and the development of cognitive behavioral therapy, I'm struck by the overall lack of impact of Barlow's model on the management of sexual disorders. I see a similar issue with the work of the Amsterdam group, which has been very intellectually stimulating, yet seems to have little influence on clinical practice in this area. Regarding possible explanations for this, two or three thoughts come to mind. Could it be availability of prosexual drugs? I don't think that's a sufficient explanation since Viagra has only been available since 1998. The drugs may complicate this situation, but of course there are also drugs for anxiety disorders and that hasn't impeded the development of cognitive behavioral therapy for anxiety disorders. Could it be a difference in the importance of organic factors? Could it be that sexual problems intrinsically involve a more physiological component than anxiety disorders? Certainly with erectile dysfunction (ED) there's a focus now on the physiological aspect, but again anxiety disorders have a strong physiologic component and it doesn't make the cognitive model any less applicable. And this is certainly not the case in women's sexual dysfunction, where drugs have been much less important in treatment. There may be other factors. It may be that these models are harder to apply clinically in the area of sexuality than they are in the area of anxiety disorders, but again this may not be an adequate explanation.

A second comment is that throughout my own involvement in this field, there's been a sense of sexual psychophysiological theories as largely borrowed or adapted from other areas of psychology. Many of the key elements in the Barlow model, in Walter's model, and I think also in John and Erick's model, are in one sense or another adaptations of models that were developed originally in other areas of psychology or neuroscience. Models in one area of science are often adapted from other areas, but I wonder whether there is a need for more "sex-specific models" in this area? These are all borrowed or adapted models, and I think Jim was encouraging us to go even further in that direction. The question I'm bringing up for consideration, and a potential criticism of each of the models presented in this section, is the models' lack of independence as "sex-specific" models. Certainly, it is evident that none of these models have significantly impacted on clinical practice to date and this issue warrants further consideration.

Markus Wiegel: I will comment on both points. First, Dr. Barlow's original model of sexual dysfunction in 1986 was sex-specific, and his model of anxiety disorders actually grew out of the sexual dysfunction model. He used the erectile response as a way of quantifying performance to empirically study the impact of manipulating anxiety. Now we're pulling in other research also. Secondly, in terms of the lack of impact on clinical practice, I think that's an excellent question and I've actually wondered about that myself. I wonder whether in sex therapy we haven't moved very far beyond Masters and Johnson, and that their model and thinking still dominate the clinical practice of sex therapy. I don't know if their therapy approach would actually contradict Dr. Barlow's model; I think they fit together pretty well.

John Bancroft: I don't want to anticipate too much what Erick's going to be saying, but this might pave the way for his presentation. Jim Pfaus talked about the different ways in which the concept of inhibition is used and that, of course, is very true. We are fairly specific about our use of inhibition. I think there's a consensus here amongst the more physiologically oriented people at this meeting, and elsewhere, that there are clearly inhibitory mechanisms from the brain down the spinal cord, which restrict our sexual responsiveness, and there are excitatory pathways down the spinal cord also. Our model is focusing on those inhibitory and excitatory pathways, and what influenced them and, in particular, the idea that people varied in their propensity for their activation of these two pathways. In the first paper that I wrote as a theoretical background to this model (Bancroft, 1999), I described four situations in which inhibition of sexual response was likely to be adaptive across species, with evidence in other species of these inhibitory mechanisms being relevant. One of them we talked about this morning, and that is the refractory period after orgasm, at least in the male; you might argue about the ways in which this adaptive. That is a direct physiological mechanism, which doesn't require any cognitive mediation for the postejaculatory inhibition to occur. Secondly there's the inhibition of reproductive and sexual behavior that is associated with what you might call *chronic stress*; in the animal kingdom this is most clearly associated with overcrowding. We can speculate about the neurophysiology and neuroendocrinology of this chronic stress effect, but there are likely to be hormonal mechanisms that again are not dependent on any information processing. I think there is an interesting parallel between chronic stress in this respect and chronic depression in the human situation, which has not yet been fully explored. The other two situations where inhibition is likely to be invoked or increased do require some sort of information processing. One of them is the perception of a threat in an otherwise sexual situation, and the other one is recognition of a threat that is not sexual but which requires us to avoid distractions by other things such as sex so we can focus on that particular threat. Both of those obviously involve some sort of information processing. To come back to Ray's point, although we certainly acknowledged Jeffrey Gray's model and very much made use of his idea of a "conceptual nervous system" approach, and we looked carefully at the extent to which our concepts overlapped with his concept of behavior inhibition and behavior activation, we were focusing on specific neurophysiological inhibition of sexual response and the various factors that could invoke it.

Kim Payne: Could I just make a small point regarding what Dr. Geer said? I agree that we need more direct measurement of these models and that it is now possible to directly measure these things from paradigms borrowed from cognitive psychology. I've been doing some work, particularly with hypervigilance to pain in women with dyspareunia, and there are lovely paradigms out there—Stroop paradigms, dot detection paradigms—where we can measure the allocation of attention. Working with attention, it's difficult to control the direction of attention and the content of attention and we really have to be careful with the type of stimuli we use in the paradigm, but it is out there and it is not impossible to test the various components of these models. In my own work, what I've found is there are also differences with respect to the levels of processing that come out in using these models. So it was interesting to see the distinction between preattention and conscious attention, because what these paradigms allow you to do is indeed get at the preattentive level, the automatic processing. You can also use self-report to assess conscious allocation of attention and measures of affective distress to look at the mediation of attention that way, and then again use paradigms such as memory recall to look at the processing and the encoding of the threatening information and the effects of affect on that. So I do think we now have the technology, the methods, and the paradigms to look at these models empirically and start to develop a larger body of evidence.

Markus Wiegel: I wanted to just get back to one comment Dr. Geer made, which also relates to Dr. Bancroft's comment. I think in contrast to Drs. Bancroft and Janssen's model, Dr. Barlow's model probably doesn't relate to inhibition of sexual arousal, but instead involves a mechanism of interference with arousal.

Walter Everaerd: I think your point about clinical application is well taken. It's true that since the 1980s, I think, there have been almost no studies about the effectiveness of psychological therapies. In fact, I felt dismayed about psychological interventions and therefore started our psychophysiological work. Your second point was, whether we should work in the infrastructure of general science or have a sexological science? Well, I think I cannot agree because what you told about drug therapies, like sildenafil, it came from a very general principle about vascular smooth muscle that's not specifically sexual the finding there. And I think that the work that's done currently on sexual motivation is very illuminating about what we should do. Since we worked within the general motivational theory framework, it became clear that the ideas that we have from Freud about sexual motivation are typically empirically unfounded. It's an idea that's more culturally than scientifically based, I think. So I believe that we should adhere to the general discipline we come from, or the disciplines we can adhere to; I have no need to look for a very specific sexual theory. I'm looking for a specific theory about sexual phenomena, and that's something else.

Ray Rosen: This is obviously a discussion we'll have to continue over dinner tonight, but, Walter, I agree and disagree. I certainly agree with you that we should be cognizant of the larger world scientifically. Your analogy about sildenafil is a particularly interesting one because in one way you're right; it came out of work on nitric oxide, cyclic GMP, and so forth. But, the PDE-5 enzyme that's concentrated in the corpus cavernosum and is responsible for the drug's effectiveness had to do with a very sex-specific biological element. Sexuality is something that is, I think we would all agree, such a unique part of our lives. The question I would ask is, are our theories capturing adequately what is unique or different, or in the effort to try to embed it in this larger cognitive science or larger theoretical perspective, are we somehow losing the essence of it and in that sense maybe the theories are not having the fullest impact? In a way, I would argue that it was sildenafil's specific effect of the PDE-5 enzyme and that enzyme's specific role in penile erection that really made it important, as opposed to some general vasodilator or other kind of vasoactive substance.

Nicole Prause: I had a question regarding both of your models. You talk about attention and it makes sense to embed your theories in the existing attention literature. As Kim was talking about, we have these new paradigms now where you can look at several types of attention. You're talking more about the unconscious, preconscious, attention, and how people might select stimuli out of their environment. Barlow suggests you could look at it as the sexual demand if that's just the attention, but there's also, subsequent to that, an additional level of attention that we might examine. When I was trying to develop a test of some of the ways that sexual dysfunctions might work, it was hard to operationalize Barlow's model. I wasn't really sure what you're trying to say about attention and sexual functioning: that the preconscious has an effect downstream and so we should be focusing preconsciously, or that sexual functioning is so socially mediated that preconscious attention is going to be less important, other than just for understanding stimulus processing. I don't know if that makes sense, but what level of attention should we be using our psychophysiological methods to investigate?

Markus Wiegel: It depends on the research question. When you're looking at maintaining factors of sexual dysfunction, you're going to focus on different things than if you're interested in basic processes in terms of preattentive cognitive processes. Hopefully, at some point, we can integrate all of those levels.

Kim Payne: I definitely would suggest from my work looking at all levels; I found differential mediation effects of affect depending on the level of attention that was being measured.

Walter Everaerd: I would like to react to Jim's remark about implicit and explicit, the concepts. I think it's important to see that what we did was using implicit and explicit as operations, accessibility of memory, and so on. When you refer to explicit and implicit memory to materials, contents of memory, the situation is totally different. Take, for example, sexual pictures that we all use. Sexual pictures can be used in explicit paradigms and implicit paradigms, but the content associated with the pictures is easily accessible to explicit memory. So what we did is using the operational terms and we did not refer to content. You understand what I'm saying? What Larry Jacoby says is about content, not about operations.

Jim Geer: You have to talk more about it—I'm not exactly sure what you mean by the distinction you are suggesting.

Erick Janssen: One comment about paradigms and the issue of working in a broader scientific framework. When it comes to the treatment of sexual dysfunctions we seem fine applying everything that is known within the medical sciences, and we borrow paradigms and methods, for example, to develop drug treatments. I think the same applies here. We use and adopt paradigms—paradigms that have proven useful in other research areas. And I think the same even applies to theories and models. As long as they have predictive value and add to our understanding of aspects of sexual response and behavior, we should explore them, regardless of their disciplinary origin. Emotion research, I think, is a great example of how one can examine what phenomena may have in common, while leaving room for their uniqueness. We study anxiety. We study happiness. What do they have in common? What makes them different? They are both emotions, require the appraisal of stimuli, involve arousal and valence, stir body and soul. Yet they are different. The same applies to the specificity of sexual excitation and inhibition. Maybe most of it can be explained using a more general theory, like the one Jeffrey Gray proposed years ago. Perhaps they are relatively specific to sex. That is exactly the question we are interested in: To what degree are neurophysiological mechanisms involved in the activation and regulation of sexual response specific to sex? So, I don't see anything wrong with applying and exploring the value of paradigms and models from other disciplines.

I would like to raise another issue. I am interested in how we might be able to use the kinds of models we have been talking about to help us understand discordance between response systems. I am fascinated, and increasingly so, by the pattern of findings that seems to be emerging from psychophysiological studies in men. A growing number of studies, including those on negative feedback, distraction, and misattribution, show effects of experimental manipulations on men's genital response, while they do not appear to change their subjective arousal. So, while we indeed tend to see higher correlations (especially between-subject ones) in men, at the same time we see, in a growing number of studies, a lack of concordance in terms of men's response *patterns*. What does that mean? Remember, we are talking about men. Men, whose subjective experience of sexual arousal, we believe, should be largely determined (although I do not think there is much empirical support for this belief) by what happens in their penis. But when we introduce manipulations that change erection levels, we don't see these changes being translated in differences in subjective arousal. Why is that? To take this a step further, a puzzling incongruity is emerging from psychophysiological research, where most of our experimental manipulations appear to influence genital responses in men and subjective responses in women. To what degree do our models help? Most of them, including Barlow and colleagues', treat sexual arousal as some uniform construct. In our 2000 *JSR* article (Janssen Janssen, Everaerd, Spiering, & Janssen, 2000), we made an attempt to explain discordance between genital and subjective responses. We talk about the weighing of different "meanings," or the possibility that some weighing of nonsexual and sexual meanings may determine levels of subjective arousal. But still, it does not seem sufficient to help me understand why genital responses would vary with the instructions we give, with the films we show, and why, especially in men, we would not see those changes in genital response being translated into different levels of subjective sexual arousal.

Markus Wiegel: Erick, I think you're making a very important point that we're not careful enough in how we define constructs in our research. Dr. Geer pointed some of that out. I think it's an extremely complex interaction. In the updated model, we attempted to separate the effect of reductions in positive affect from the effect of increases in negative affect on subjective arousal. However, I think we really need to be more specific by what we mean with "negative affect." For example, anxious apprehension tends to increase sympathetic arousal, including increased heart rate. In contrast, psychophysiological research indicates that embarrassment seems to activate the parasympathetic system associated with decreases in heart rate. Yet, both anxious apprehension and embarrassment could be considered negative affect. I think as we learn more, we can make more specific distinctions. I don't think all of the components of affect and attention impact the subjective and the physiological processes in the same direction. For example, whereas increases in sympathetic arousal, as a result of anxious apprehension, increase physiological responding (e.g., erectile tumescence), the associated narrowing of attentional focus on nonerotic cues decreases arousal, that is, has an effect in the opposite direction. It's a very complex picture and we just don't know enough.

Ellen Laan: Can I comment on your very important question, Erick? These are issues that I'm obviously struggling with as well. Two quick responses come to mind and maybe we can talk about this some more tomorrow. One is that we actually have much more knowledge about men's genital response than we have on men's subjective response. Interestingly, many researchers only seem interested in male genital response. Maybe if we would have as much data on subjective sexual response in men, as we do on women, we would be able to see more variation in subjective arousal as well. Second, I think you're right in concluding that, thus far, most of the manipulations in studies with men seem to affect genital and not subjective response. Perhaps the manipulations have been too weak to be noticed subjectively. Possibly subjective sexual response in men is not affected by the psychological manipulations you mention as long as these are done in the context of strong sexual stimuli such as explicit erotic film clips.

Jim Pfaus: I hope we don't let history repeat itself and go down the path that the animal literature went for approximately 40 years in which sexual behavior was regarded as something distinct from normal motivation. Normal motivations like feeding or drinking were considered hydraulic processes. For example, what you eat you've got to expend in terms of calories or energy production or else you get fat. Conversely, if you don't eat or drink, you'll die. Sex wasn't that simple because nobody ever died from not having sex, as Frank Beach once said, so we didn't need to have sex individually, even if we needed it as a species. Because it didn't follow normal rules of motivation, sex was rarely contained within the more general study of motivation. Recently, however, sex has found its way back into general motivational theory. This was aided by the finding that sex releases dopamine. Of course so does feeding, drinking, and listening to music, so we have begun to ask what neural properties of these incentives and rewards are common and how an animal knows when to use particular responses, even conditioned responses, to get what it wants or needs. I don't think we should go back down the path of arguing that, because a rat will bar press for food or other reinforcers, bar pressing for a sexual stimulus isn't a "real" sexual response. Sex has to be more than an erect penis, vagina, or clitoris. It is more than copulation. Sexual desire resides in the brain. It is a cognitive response. We need to study it in a variety of circumstances and perhaps using cognitive processing models, such as distraction tasks. From a scientific and funding standpoint, we can't afford to limit sexuality to the genitalia.

References

Bancroft, J. (1999). Central inhibition of sexual response in the male: A theoretical perspective. *Neuroscience and Biobehavioral Reviews, 23,* 763–784.

Janssen, E., Everaerd, W., Spiering, M., & Janssen, J. (2000). Automatic cognitive processes and the appraisal of sexual stimuli: Towards an information processing model of sexual arousal. *Journal of Sex Research, 37,* 8–23.

The Dual Control Model

The Role of Sexual Inhibition and Excitation in Sexual Arousal and Behavior

ERICK JANSSEN AND JOHN BANCROFT

Psychophysiological studies of sexuality have largely, if not completely, ignored issues of individual variability in responsiveness. Most of the research published in this area involves the comparison of subject groups, experimental conditions, or treatments. The few attempts to evaluate individual variability have been largely restricted to the measurement of sexual attitudes and behavioral tendencies. Erotophobia-erotophilia is a well-known example (Fisher, Byrne, White, & Kelley, 1988). This construct is measured with the Sexual Opinion Survey (SOS), a questionnaire that assesses affective and evaluative responses to different types of sexual activity or stimuli. Until recently, no models or measures existed that focus specifically on individual differences in sexual response.

The dual control model of sexual response postulates that sexual arousal and associated behaviors depend on the balance between sexual excitation and inhibition. It is an example of a state-trait model, although most research so far has focused on the trait dimension of the model. The model proposes that the weighing of excitatory and inhibitory processes determines whether or not a sexual response occurs within an individual in a given situation, and at the same time it assumes individual variability in the propensity for these processes. The model was developed in an attempt to synthesize existing research findings in the area of male sexual dysfunction, to contribute to this research by underscoring the relevance of exploring individual differences, and to stimulate new research, in this and other areas of sexual response and behavior. In this paper, we will present the model's background, discuss findings from several lines of research, reflect on the model's strengths and weaknesses, and consider directions for future research.

Background

From the late 1970s on, psychophysiological research on the mechanisms of sexual arousal—and the models in which this research culminated—has had a strong focus on the exploration of cognitive processes, in particular the role of attention. For example, Barlow's model, published in

1986 and integrating most of the then available research, proposes that the activation of sexual response is dependent upon "task-relevant" cognitive processing of a sexual stimulus (Barlow, 1986). Problems with sexual functioning would result from "task-irrelevant" processing, or distraction. Barlow's model was based on findings from a series of studies exploring differences between men with and without erectile problems in how they process and respond to sexual stimuli. In men with psychogenic[1] erectile dysfunction, fear of failure or sexual worries were believed to interfere with the sexual response because they distract from attending to sexual cues (Barlow, 1986). Janssen and Everaerd (1993) proposed, consistent with Barlow's model, that men with psychogenic erectile problems fail to respond due to a predominantly nonsexual processing of relevant stimuli, a process indeed dependent on attentional processes (i.e., distraction), but initiated at an unconscious or "automatic" cognitive level in response to psychological threats or performance-related worries (see also Janssen, Everaerd, Spiering, & Janssen, 2000). Through a cognitive window, the interface between psychological processes and genital response thus seems to depend heavily on two factors: the presence of a sexual stimulus and the absence of processes interfering with the activation of a response to a sexual stimulus.

Bancroft (1995) questioned the strong reliance on the role of attention in these theoretical approaches and suggested that a third component, involving direct neurophysiological inhibition of erectile response, was missing. Bancroft (1995, 1999) reviewed findings from, among others, pharmacological studies and research on erections during sleep (NPT) and made a convincing case for the idea that more direct forms of inhibition should be considered. To give just one example, erections induced by the intracavernosal injection of smooth muscle relaxants are considered a peripheral, target organ effect, or an effect not mediated by psychological mechanisms. However, a substantial proportion of men with psychogenic erectile dysfunction have been found to respond poorly to such injections (e.g., Bancroft & Malone, 1995), indicating that inhibition can occur to stimuli (in this case pharmacological) that rule out explanations in terms of "task-irrelevant" processing.

It could be argued that most research on the role of cognitive processes in sexual dysfunction has not dealt with inhibitory but excitatory mechanisms (Janssen & Bancroft, 1996). That is, "distraction models" are perhaps more accurately described as models that treat inhibition as a "lack of excitation." They thus conceptualize sexual arousal one-dimensionally, as something that is activated or not. The dual control model emphasizes the role of inhibition, where responses are suppressed or not, as well as excitation, implying that in studying sexual arousal we have to discern both excitatory and inhibitory influences.

Broader Context and Assumptions

When contemplating the many ways the control of sexual response can be conceptualized, the notion of "level of analysis" comes to mind. At a lower, or "molecular," level, sexual responses are most likely controlled by multiple inhibitory and excitatory neurophysiological processes (e.g., Stoléru & Mouras, this volume). Even at some intermediate level, the evidence points to highly complex interactions, involving, for example, the norepinephric activation of arousal, the disinhibition of dopaminergic systems, the involvement of testosterone-dependent systems, neuropeptidergic as well as serotonergic processes, and peripheral mechanisms (Bancroft, 1999). The dual control model represents a higher, or "molar," level of analysis. The model postulates the involvement of two neurophysiological systems, one relevant to activation and the other to suppression of sexual response, much like the "conceptual nervous system" proposed by Gray (1982). Gray's theory, and related work by researchers like Eysenck (1967) and Depue (e.g., Depue & Collins, 1999), concerns more general mechanisms of activation and inhibition and can be described as a theory of approach and avoidance and the associated concepts of reward and punishment.

The idea of regulation by forces and counterforces, or by the interaction between activation and suppression, is not uncommon in other areas of psychological inquiry, such as psychophysiology, memory and cognition, and emotions and affect. As is true for the dual control model of sexual response, this typically includes assumptions (or questions) about independence or orthogonality. For example, the sympathetic and parasympathetic branches of the autonomic nervous system have traditionally been viewed to have reciprocal or counteractive effects. Therefore, their functional outcomes were reducible to a single dimension. More recent research, however, shows that the two autonomic systems can be activated at the same time and act independently from each other (e.g., Berntson, Cacioppo, & Quigley, 1991). Similarly, in research on "affect," there is an increased recognition of the possibility that positivity and negativity are outcomes of independent processes and can co-occur (e.g., Cacioppo, Gardner, & Berntson, 1999). In other words, more traditional views of affect, involving one-dimensional, bipolar constructs (where positive and negative activation are reciprocal), are being challenged and proposed to be replaced with (at least) two-dimensional, or bivariate, approaches. As a final example, in cognitive psychology, in particular in memory research, interference and inhibition are considered independent processes. Inhibition involves active suppression (for example of memory intrusions), whereas interference is usually defined as the result of competition among multiple stimuli, processes, or responses (Harnishfeger, 1995). This is not unlike the distinction between the effects of distraction (sexual worries competing with sexual cues, interfering with excitation) and those of active neurophysiological inhibition on sexual response.

Clearly, the above examples in themselves do not directly support the notion that the regulation of sexual response would involve two independent mechanisms. From a conceptual point of view, the more parsimonious approach would be to focus not on two but on one mechanism of control. Considering that a review of the literature leads us to conclude that excitation, or the lack of excitation, fails to explain response outcomes in all relevant situations, perhaps the study of inhibition would suffice. However, research on the behavioral tendencies of approach and avoidance (e.g., Gray, 1982), the workings of the autonomic nervous system, and on affect, although just examples, underscore the importance of considering the existence of multiple control systems. In the case of sexual response, we believe that there indeed is a role for excitation, both at a state and a trait level, as it may help in explaining the responsivity or sensitivity of the sexual response system in the absence of inhibition.

The dual control model is first of all a conceptual device, a way to structure and formulate research questions. Reality is without question more complex. For example, even distraction, or the activation of interference, might be the result of inhibitory processes (cf. Gray, 1982). And, inhibition will need to be activated or require some type of excitatory activity (Bancroft, 1999). Also, although we assume that inhibitory and excitatory processes, at a trait level, are orthogonal or independent, at a state level they may not be as disconnected and could possibly modify each other's output levels or "set points." Perhaps we should think of it in similar ways as research shows the autonomic nervous system works, where there can be coactivation, uncoupled activation, and reciprocal activation (Berntson et al., 1991). Again, many levels of analysis are possible, and we approach the dual control model as a starting point for new research as much as we believe it integrates existing findings. Many if not most questions concerning the value or appropriateness of the model are empirical in nature and thus open to examination.

A number of other assumptions are associated with the dual control model. First, it is assumed that our putative sexual inhibition and excitation systems reflect specifically sexual rather than general mechanisms of activation and inhibition (cf. Gray, 1982). Secondly, we assume that sexual inhibition and excitation are both adaptive, and that they serve, across species, a number of biological functions. Whereas the relevance of sexual excitation is relatively straightforward, functions of sexual inhibition could include the refractory period, the suppressing effects of chronic stress on reproductive behavior, and the detection of threat, either sexual or nonsexual, when inhibition of sexual response facilitates avoidance of that threat (see Bancroft, 1999, for a more extensive discussion). Thirdly, although learning may play a role in determining individual variabilities in response tendencies, it is assumed that individual variation in sexual inhibition and excitation is a stable trait and may be, at least in part, genetically determined. Finally, we embarked on our research program with the idea that a high propensity for sexual inhibition (and a low one for sexual excitation) would be associated with a vulnerability to sexual dysfunction (see Bancroft & Janssen, 2000, 2001, for fuller discussion) and a low propensity for sexual inhibition (and a high one for excitation) with an increased likelihood of sexual risk taking (see also Bancroft, 2000; Bancroft et al., 2003b; Bancroft et al., 2004).

The SIS/SES Questionnaire

We started our research on the dual control model with the development of a paper-and-pencil measure of propensities for sexual inhibition and excitation, the Sexual Inhibition Scales/Sexual Excitation Scales, or the SIS/SES questionnaire (Janssen, Vorst, Finn, & Bancroft, 2002a, 2002b). Although the concepts of excitation and inhibition are probably just as relevant (if not more; cf. Bjorkland & Kipp, 1996) to women's sexual responses, and although the SIS/SES questionnaire has demonstrated its value in research in women (Carpenter, Graham, Janssen, Vorst, & Wicherts, 2007), the measure was originally developed for use in men because the available research underlying the dual control model was largely restricted to the neurophysiology and psychophysiology of male sexual response. In designing the questionnaire, we followed a "facet design" approach, although not in its most comprehensive form. Facet design is a conceptual method that integrates aspects of instrument construction, construct development, and data analysis (e.g., Shye & Elizur, 1994). The majority of questions for the SIS/SES questionnaire were written in an "if-then" form. For items relevant to excitation, the "if" statement described a potential sexual stimulus and the "then" statement, the occurrence of a sexual response. We attempted to include a variety of "facets," including the type of stimulus (e.g., fantasy, visual, auditory, and olfactory stimuli, and social interactions) and type of response (sexual arousal and/or genital response). For inhibition, we started from the premise that it would play a specific role in modifying sexual responses in the avoidance or reduction of "threat." Threats were conceptualized as being either intrapersonal or interpersonal in nature, and items were constructed to cover inhibition due to negative consequences of sex, performance anxiety, norms and values, and physical or psychological harm.

Factor analysis on the data of a sample of 408 sexually functional, heterosexual men (with a mean age of 23 years) identified 10 factors, involving 45 items. A further factor analysis, carried out on the subscale scores, identified a single excitation factor (SES), but differentiated sexual inhibition into two factors, which we have called "Inhibition due to threat of performance failure" (SIS1) and "Inhibition due to the threat of performance consequences" (SIS2). Confirmatory factor analysis on the data from two additional samples of 459 (mean age of 21 years) and 313 (mean age of 46 years) heterosexual men showed the 10-factor model to be best, but only marginally better that the nested 3-in-10 model, and supported our continued use of the higher-level factor structure. The three scales showed close to normal distributions in all three samples and respectable levels of internal consistency and test-retest reliability. SES and SIS1, but not SIS2, were related to age (negatively and positively, respectively). In addition, correlations between the excitation and the two inhibition factors were low, showing excitation and inhibition to be relatively independent, and a significant but low correlation revealed little overlap between the two inhibition scales.

In evaluating the scales' discriminant and convergent validity, we found a small degree of overlap with measures of global traits of behavioral inhibition, neuroticism, harm avoidance, and reward responsivity, suggesting that the SES scale taps aspects of reward responsivity and the SIS scales (especially SIS2) aspects of global behavioral inhibition. However, the modest degree of overlap supports the idea that the SIS/SES questionnaire predominantly measures propensities that are specific to sexual responsivity.

Two Types of Sexual Inhibition?

We had not anticipated the identification of two inhibition scales. The questions making up the two scales were conceptually different, however, and it became apparent that the items of the SIS1 scale mainly assess situations where the most obvious threat is the anticipated failure of sexual response, whereas in the items of the SIS2 scale, the threat is in the anticipated consequence of sexual response. Hence our descriptive title "Inhibition due to threat of performance *failure*" for SIS1 and "Inhibition due to threat of performance *consequences*" for SIS2.

It is possible that the two scales reflect two distinct inhibitory systems. Our lack of understanding of the nature and specificity of central inhibition of sexual response should leave us open to this possibility (Bancroft, 1999). However, in more detailed discussions of this issue (Bancroft & Janssen, 2000, 2001), we postulated that as SIS1 appears relevant to the anticipation of failure of response, the threat is more intrinsic. While this could be a consequence of learning, it nevertheless implies some inbuilt tendency for response failure. We proposed that this could be a consequence of a basically high inhibitory tone. By contrast, SIS2 seemed to involve inhibition that is activated or triggered by external threats. We will return to this distinction later.

Application of the Model in Nonlaboratory Research

Sexual Dysfunction

As the dual control model evolved from research on sexual dysfunction, a logical first application of the model involved the exploration of its relevance to sexual function. Starting with a somewhat older, nonclinical male heterosexual sample ($N = 313$, mean age = 46 years; Janssen et al., 2002a), we asked men whether they had (i) *ever* had difficulties in obtaining or keeping an erection, and (ii) whether they had such difficulties in the past 3 months. We explored the relationships between our scales and these two questions using multiple regression, with the three SIS/SES scales and age as the independent variables. In predicting answers to the "ever had difficulties" question, SIS1, SIS2, and age were significant. SES did not figure in the equation. For erectile difficulties in "the past 3 months," SIS1 and age were both strong predictors, SES predicted weakly and negatively, but SIS2 did not enter the equation. We thus found SIS1 strongly predictive of erectile problems in this nonclinical sample, for both time periods, whereas SIS2 was only relevant on the "ever had difficulties" basis. The findings are consistent with the SIS1 measure reflecting some trait vulnerability that would persist and, as the previously found correlation with age suggests, may be amplified by the effects of aging. In contrast, SIS2 indeed appears to measure a tendency to respond with inhibited erection when a threat is present, a situation that is likely to occur with lower probability over a 3-month period than for "ever." We found a similar association between SIS1 (and age) and erectile problems in a study comparing a convenience sample of homosexual men ($N = 1,379$) with an age-matched sample of heterosexual men ($N = 1,558$; Bancroft, Carnes, Janssen, Goodrich, & Long, 2005). In this study we also asked about problems with rapid ejaculation. Erectile problems were reported more frequently by homosexual men and rapid ejaculation more frequently by heterosexual men. Homosexual men scored higher on SIS1 whether or not they reported erectile problems. Interestingly, in a related study in which we compared HIV+ and HIV− homosexual men (Bancroft, Carnes, & Janssen, 2005), we found that HIV+ men were both more likely to report erectile problems and to have higher SIS1 scores. These combined findings, considering that they involve convenience samples, suggest that there may be differences in the propensity for sexual inhibition as measured by SIS1 between homosexual and heterosexual men, differences that seem consistent with Sandfort and de Keizer's (2001) speculation that homosexual men are more prone to performance anxiety, which may, possibly, be associated with higher risk taking (e.g., related to a reluctance to use condoms). Trait anxiety—but not sexual excitation and inhibition scores—was predictive of rapid ejaculation, but only in the heterosexual men. If replicated, the differences we found between homosexual and heterosexual men may reflect a greater importance of erectile function in the sexual lives of homosexual men and greater importance of ejaculatory control in heterosexual relationships.

We have started collecting relevant data from clinical subjects. In comparing a small sample of men seeking help for erectile problems with a nonclinical male sample, we found that the men with erectile problems had the lowest SES as well as highest SIS1 and SIS2 scores (Bancroft & Janssen, 2000). In another study (Bancroft, Herbenick, et al., 2005), we compared 171 men attending sexual problem clinics for a variety of problems (e.g., erectile problems, rapid ejaculation) with an age-matched nonclinical sample of 446 men. We found similarly low SES and high SIS1 scores for men in the two samples who reported having erectile problems. Again, our SIS/SES scales were not related to rapid ejaculation. In the clinical group, SIS/SES scores were related to some features of the sexual history of potential etiological relevance. For example, SES was higher in men with normal waking erections and with erections better during masturbation than during sexual intercourse. However, SIS1 was not as clearly associated with clinical features and sexual history variables in this sample.

Although this research is at an early stage, we have made an attempt to formulate a number of predictions relevant to prognosis and treatment (Bancroft & Janssen, 2000, 2001). For example, we predicted that men presenting with erectile dysfunction who have normal or low SIS1 scores, but normal or raised SIS2 scores, may benefit from psychological treatment that focuses on the presence of psychological or interpersonal threat (e.g., certain types of partner response patterns). Men with erectile dysfunction who have a high SIS1 score may, we suggested, be more resistant to psychological treatment, at least if it is used on its own. In such cases, the use of pharmacological treatment in combination may be successful. We also predicted that when the problem exists with a low SES and a normal or low SIS1 and SIS2, an excitation facilitator (e.g., Viagra) or focus on more effective methods of stimulation might prove to be effective. In a small pilot study in men with mild to moderate erectile problems (Rosen et al., 2006), we found that performance anxiety and negative expectations regarding treatment at baseline were negatively related to effects of Viagra. In contrast, SIS/SES scores were not a significant predictor of treatment efficacy. However, because effects of SIS/SES may have been obscured by the small number of subjects who completed the study ($N = 34$) and by the predominant effects of pharmacotherapy in this sample, further research on the relevance of propensity of sexual inhibition and excitation to prognosis and treatment is clearly warranted.

Mood and Sexuality

Although negative mood is generally believed to be associated with a loss of sexual interest and impairment of sexual arousability, recent research shows that the relationship is more variable, with *increased* sexual interest occurring in association with negative mood in a proportion of individuals. We have explored the extent to which individual variability in the relation between mood and sexuality can be explained using our dual control model in two studies, one involving straight men ($N = 919$, mean age = 28 years; Bancroft et al., 2003a), the other involving gay men ($N = 662$, mean age = 36 years; Bancroft, Janssen, Strong, & Vukadinovic, 2003). We proposed that, for the majority of individuals, negative mood would be associated with a reduction in sexual responsiveness. However, in an individual who has a low propensity for sexual inhibition, and/or a high propensity for sexual excitation, the coexistence of negative mood and sexual arousal would be a possibility.

Using a simple, newly developed measure, the Mood and Sexuality Questionnaire (MSQ), we found that while a majority of the heterosexual subjects experienced a decrease in sexual interest when depressed, 9% reported an increase. For anxiety, 21% reported an increase. In a regression analysis on the MSQ's total score, age, SIS2, SIS1, ZDPR (a measure of depression proneness; Zemore, Fischer, Garratt, & Miller, 1990), and SES entered the model, in that order. Using ordinal logistic regression we examined the same variables for the individual MSQ scales, which resulted, overall, in a similar pattern. Qualitative data from in-depth interviews demonstrated that the picture is more complex with depression than with anxiety and revealed that sexual behavior may be more likely with depression because of a need for intimacy, for self-validation, or simply for sexual pleasure. The motivation to engage in sexual activity when anxious seemed more simply related to the postorgasmic calming effect.

Quantitative and qualitative results from the study in gay men showed that they, like the heterosexual sample, vary in how their sexual interest and response is affected by negative mood. Of those who had been depressed or anxious enough to recognize a predictable pattern, a substantial minority reported increased sexual interest when depressed (16%) or anxious (24%). The qualitative data from interviews revealed, as with the heterosexual men, that the relationship with anxiety/stress was relatively straightforward; either the individual found that anxiety or stress increased attention to sexual cues, with sexual activity, particularly masturbation, providing some temporary reduction in anxiety, or the individual's attention was focused on the cause of the anxiety and not on sex. However, with depression, the relationship was more complex, even more so than we found with heterosexual men; a number of gay men described how negative mood made them more likely to take sexual risks, because in such a mood they "didn't care" about consequences.

Of the similarities between gay and straight men, SIS2 played a similar role in the regression analyses for both groups; the higher the SIS2 score the less likelihood of experiencing a positive mood-sexuality relationship.

SES played a role in both the gay and straight sample, although in the analysis for the gay men it showed an increased likelihood of a positive relationship between mood-sexuality with anxiety, but not depression.

We are in the process of testing a new, more sophisticated version of the MSQ. The original version does not take differences in the effects of depression on masturbation and on interactions with a partner into account, nor does it assess the intensity of experienced mood states, the co-occurrence of mood states (e.g., anxiety and depression), the effects of sexual activity on mood, or the relationship between mood and behavior. With the new version, which assesses a wider range of emotional states (including happiness), we try to evaluate the complexities in the relationships between mood and sexual desire, response, and behavior in more depth.

We believe this is a new and promising area of research, where sexual excitation and inhibition may not only help explain paradoxical patterns in the relationship between mood and sexuality, but where interactions between all these elements may prove of relevance to our understanding of a variety of topics, including "risky" and "compulsive" sex. For example, Bancroft and Vukadinovic (2004) found, in a small sample of self-designated "sex addicts," increased sexual interest in states of both depression and anxiety to be typical for these subjects. Overall, "sex addicts" scored higher on SES than a control group, but they did not differ in SIS2. There was an interesting exception to this finding: the "sex addicts" who did not use masturbation as their principal form of "acting out" had lower SIS2 than both "compulsive masturbators" and controls, as well as relatively high SES. These preliminary findings suggest that in striving to understand "compulsive" sexual behavior, we should be expecting a range of etiological mechanisms associated with different behavioral patterns. Our dual control model may be relevant to only some of those patterns.

Sexual Risk Taking

Although the past few years have demonstrated an increased awareness of the relevance of studying the role of sexual arousal and other emotional states in sexual risk taking, this has not yet been translated in much systematic research. In one of our research projects, we examined the relevance of the dual control model, and the role of mood and its effects on sexual interest and response, to sexual risk taking in samples of gay (N = 589, mean age = 36 years; Bancroft et al., 2003b) and straight men (N = 879, mean age = 25 years; Bancroft et al., 2004). Although we looked at the relevance of a number of other variables (e.g., sensation seeking, trait anxiety, and depression), we will focus here only on findings related to the SIS/SES and MSQ.

In the gay sample, we found low SIS2 scores to be predictive of sexual risk taking in terms of unprotected anal intercourse (cf. Bancroft, Carnes,

& Janssen, 2005) and oral sex, but not of number of casual partners or cruising behavior. Similarly, in the straight sample, SIS2 scores were strongly and negatively predictive of number of partners with whom no condoms were used in the past 3 years. SES scores, although strongly predictive of number of sexual partners in gay men, were not related to any of the other "risk behavior" variables and not related to any of the measures in the straight sample. The fact that SIS2 but not SES was involved in risk taking suggests that the relevant mediation of the effects of sexual arousal on risk taking is not simply a matter of arousability but of the likelihood of inhibiting arousal, and hence behavior, in certain situations.

Interestingly, although SIS1 was not predictive of any of our risk measures in the (younger) straight sample, we found that *high* SIS1 was predictive of unprotected anal intercourse and the number of casual partners in the gay sample. This suggests that high inhibitory "tone," or a lowered ability to reliably achieve an erection, may reduce an individual's likelihood of using a condom and at the same time increases the likelihood of having more "one-time" partners.

In both samples, we found evidence that men who report an increased interest in sex when depressed, as measured by our MSQ, also reported a greater number of sexual partners and, in the gay sample, a higher frequency of cruising behavior. Thus, the tendency to experience more interest in sex when in a negative mood appears to increase the likelihood of looking for sexual partners, as reflected in casual sex and cruising, but was not predictive of how risk is managed once the partner is found (i.e., whether condoms are used). As predicted, SIS2 proved more relevant to the latter.

Studies in Women

We now also have a substantial amount of data from women on the role of sexual excitation and inhibition and of the relationship between mood and sexuality. In a study involving a sample of heterosexual women ($N = 1,067$), and a comparison group of heterosexual men ($N = 978$), we examined the factor structure, reliability, and validity of SIS/SES scores in women (Carpenter et al., 2007). Confirmatory factor analyses of women's SIS/SES scores provided moderate support for the higher-level model found in men. As we had previously found in men, correlations in women between the sexual excitation (SES) factor and the two sexual inhibition factors (SIS1 and SIS2) were low, while the SIS1 and SIS2 factors exhibited a modest positive correlation. Gender differences were found, with women scoring higher on the two original inhibition factors and lower on the sexual excitation factor in comparison with men. The test-retest reliability and convergent and discriminant validity of women's SIS/SES scores, using the original factor structure, were similar to those we found for men. In this study we also developed and tested a short version of the

SIS/SES questionnaire (SIS/SES—Short Form), which features items with similar psychometric properties in women and men. The 14-item version of the SIS/SES showed to be associated with test-retest reliability and convergent/discriminant validity that closely resemble the longer, 45-item measure.

While these preliminary findings suggest that the SIS/SES questionnaire may also be of value in research on sexual response, functioning, and behavior in women, substantial progress has been made in work on the development of a new measure, designed specifically for use in women (Graham, Sanders, Milhausen, & McBride, 2004; Graham, Sanders, & Milhausen, 2006). One of the starting points of this project is that the SIS/SES questionnaire may not tap all relevant sources of sexual excitation and inhibition in women, including effects of body self-consciousness, concerns related to reputation, and relationship variables. Comparison of women's (and men's) responses on the old and new questionnaires should increase our understanding of the processes involved in sexual response.

In another recent study, we examined the relationship between mood and sexuality in heterosexual women (N = 663; Lykins, Janssen, & Graham, 2006). The female sample was compared with a sample of heterosexual men (N = 399). Men and women differed in their responses to the questions about the effects of anxiety and depression on sexual interest and response. Women reported more of the negative effects of these mood states on their sexual interest and response than did men. The distributions within the male and female groups, however, were comparable. Although scores on SIS2, as we had found before, were the best predictor of the relationship between mood and sexuality in men, the picture was more complex for women, where SES turned out to be the best predictor of this relationship.

Psychophysiological Studies on Sexual Inhibition and Excitation

Psychophysiological Validation of the SIS/SES Questionnaire

In a first laboratory study, we explored the SIS/SES questionnaire's value in predicting actual psychophysiological responses in a group of male heterosexual college students and compared and contrasted participants by grouping them in three ways, by high and low SES, SIS1, and SIS2 scores (Janssen et al., 2002b). We expected high SES individuals to show greater genital response than low SES individuals to erotic stimuli in general. Regarding SIS1, we predicted that a distracting task during the presentation of sexual film clips would reduce genital response in low SIS1 scorers, while having no effect or a positive effect on the high SIS1 group. In addition, we expected high SIS1 subjects to show a reduced genital response under high performance demand (operationalized by emphasizing in some conditions that we were particularly interested in their erectile response).

To explore the predictive value of SIS2, we decided to use erotic stimuli that vary in their potential to invoke inhibition. Two types of erotic film were used, one nonthreatening (involving consensual sex) and the other threatening (involving coercive sex; cf. Laan, Everaerd, & Evers, 1995; van der Velde, Laan, & Everaerd, 2001). We predicted that low and high scorers on the SIS2 factor would differ in their sexual responses to the coercive films, with genital responses in the low inhibition group being less influenced by the content of these films. We did not expect to find differences in their emotional responses, with both groups responding negatively to the coercive films, which would support the assumption that both groups processed the threatening content of these films. Emotional responses were measured by means of self-ratings and startle responses (e.g., Graham, Janssen, & Sanders, 2000). Startle response is typically enhanced during negative emotions and diminished during positive emotions.

The findings of our study provided clear validation of the SES scale. The high SES group showed generally higher genital and subjective sexual arousal responses regardless of erotic stimulus type. We did not succeed in providing validation of our SIS1 scale, which may partly be attributable to the fact that the subjects were young, sexually functional men. Analyses of variance revealed no interactions between the high and low SIS groups and either "performance demand" or "distraction" conditions. There was, however, good validation of the SIS2 scale. High and low SIS2 groups did not differ in their genital response to the consensual sexual stimuli, but the low SIS2 group showed significantly greater genital response to the sexually threatening stimuli. This pattern was not apparent with the subjective reports of sexual arousal, and of particular interest, both groups showed evidence of negative affect during the threatening stimuli, both in subjective reporting and objectively with the startle response. Thus, in spite of a negative affective response, the low inhibition participants showed more genital response.

Shock-Threat: A Laboratory Analogue of Risky Sex?

In a second experiment, a pilot study (Janssen, 1998), we made an attempt to evaluate the relevance of the dual control model to both sexual response *and* behavior. In this study, we presented a group of sexually functional men with three erotic films. As a measure of sexual risk taking, the men were given control over the duration of the erotic film—they could press a button to terminate its presentation—under variable (incremental) levels of shock-threat. To explore the interaction between sexual arousal and risk taking, the men were exposed to two shock-threat conditions: one where they were at risk of receiving a shock from the beginning of the film and one where the threat of shock was started after a delay of 1.5 minutes. For both conditions, the risk of receiving a shock increased the longer the subject watched the film. Feedback about the level of risk (i.e., the probability of receiving an electric shock) was provided by a bar that appeared on the left side of the screen and that increased in height over time. In contrast to earlier studies using shock-threat (e.g., Barlow, Sakheim, & Beck, 1983; Beck, Barlow, Sakheim, & Abrahamson, 1987), participants were at risk of receiving actual shocks, which were applied, beginning when risk levels reached 80%, to the inside of the elbow of their nondominant arm. The two film conditions were presented in counterbalanced order and were followed by an erotic film excerpt that was not combined with shock-threat (after shock electrodes had been removed).

Initially, we established shock levels for each individual participant at the beginning of the session. Subjects were given shocks of variable intensity and asked to rate them on how painful (1 = not painful to 10 = extremely painful) and unbearable (1 = doesn't bother me to 10 = completely unbearable) they found them to be. The final shock level was selected as the one where the sum of the subjects' scores on the two scales was 15 or 16. Of the first 20 subjects, only 3 ended at least one film presentation. Although all participants indicated that the electric shocks were unpleasant (the experimenter, located in an adjacent room, could at times hear subjects verbally express their anguish), the majority watched all three erotic film clips for the full duration. Only after several modifications were made to the procedure (e.g., using preset instead of individually determined shock levels, shifting the emphasis in the study description from our interest in *whether* to *when* participants would end film presentations), 7 of an additional 10 participants pressed the button at least once. Some preliminary analyses showed that the termination of shock threat was negatively correlated with sexual sensation seeking and erotophilia and positively correlated with harm avoidance and one lower level SIS2 factor (i.e., sexual inhibition related to "getting caught," or being observed by others during sexual activity). This latter finding, combined with an absence of correlation with other sexual inhibition factors, suggests that risk taking in the laboratory, at least in terms of terminating the sexual films, may have been influenced more by the laboratory situation than by the experience of pain (Scepkowski & Janssen, 2006).

Regarding viewing time and sexual arousal, we had predicted that both would be inversely related to SIS2 scores. However, the low number of subjects that actually ended a film presentation prohibited the statistical evaluation of the first prediction. Genital response data were missing in 5 subjects. Multiple regression analyses, with genital response during shock-threat conditions as dependent, and the three SIS/SES scales and state anxiety (STAI; Spielberger, Gorsuch, & Lushene, 1970) as independent variables, showed only SIS1 to be of relevance (correlations for penile rigidity during the two shock-threat films and SIS1 were +.44 and +.41). SES, like SIS2, did not figure as a predictor of genital response, although it proved relevant to the degree of sexual desire subjects experienced during the various conditions. None of the four independent variables predicted the level of subjective sexual arousal for any of the film presentations.

Thus, SIS1, and not SIS2, proved to be predictive of genital responses in this study. Did we, using shock-threat, unintentionally implement a more effective manipulation of SIS1-relevant processes than we had tried to create in our earlier study (in which we tested the effects of distraction and performance demand)? In our discussion of the findings of that study, we suggested that either clinical subjects or stronger manipulations were needed to reveal the impact of SIS1. So perhaps we managed to do the latter, unintentionally, in the current study. For example, it is possible that the shock-threat (in combination with a bar on the screen, changing in size and representing the level of threat), functioned as a distractor. But why did we fail to demonstrate a role for SIS2? Did the fact that subjects could end the film presentation at any time reduce the amount of ("external" or SIS2-relevant) threat? We expected low SIS2 to be important as it would allow for "excitation transfer," or at least for the co-occurrence of sexual arousal and anxiety (induced by shock-threat). However, it seems that this mechanism was not of relevance in this study, as state anxiety levels (measured by STAI) were not related to genital response levels. It should be noted that while the participants in this study had nonexceptional SES scores (mean = 58.3), in comparison to our earlier questionnaire studies (e.g., Janssen et al., 2002a), they exhibited relatively low SIS1 (mean = 24.5) and SIS2 (mean = 25.2) scores. It thus appears that there was a volunteer bias, with high sexual inhibition individuals (both SIS1 and SIS2) avoiding participation.

Response Patterns in High and Low Sexual Risk Takers

As part of our research on sexual risk taking, presented earlier in this paper, we invited our questionnaire and interview subjects to also participate in a psychophysiological study (Janssen, Goodrich, Petrocelli, & Bancroft, 2006). In view of the complexity of the preliminary findings of the shock-threat study, we instead decided to use the design of our first laboratory study on the dual control model (Janssen et al., 2002b). When we applied this design (with the two types of sexual film, distraction and performance demand) to this new sample, however, we encountered another unanticipated, yet intriguing, phenomenon. Twelve men, or almost 50% of the first 25 subjects (mean age = 29 years), did not respond to the sexual stimuli (i.e., penile rigidity of less than 5% to the noncoercive film clips; 8 men had 0% rigidity). This is, to our knowledge, one of the few psychophysiological studies in which men participated who were recruited from the community—in our case, from bath houses, STD clinics, bars, and so on. In some of these venues, sexual stimuli (including video screens) are omnipresent, and this, in combination with comments from participants about the lack of more interesting, specialized ("niche"), or more extreme

Table 1. *Differences between Low and High Sexual Responders*

Variable	Low Responder [a] M	SD	High Responder [b] M	SD	F(1, 74)
Physiological arousal					
Self-selected short film[c]	2.0	4.8	61.2	24.2	151.5***
Self-selected long film[c]	7.0	12.4	75.9	10.8	632.0***
Researcher-selected film 1[c]	4.8	14.4	41.3	33.0	28.8***
Researcher-selected film 2[c]	2.9	7.0	51.5	30.3	64.6***
Threat film 1	3.3	13.3	8.7	21.0	1.4
Threat film 2	1.5	6.5	16.9	26.7	8.5**
Subjective arousal					
Self-selected short film	5.8	3.0	6.5	2.2	1.5
Self-selected long film	6.7	2.6	7.6	2.0	2.8
Researcher-selected film 1	5.2	3.2	5.6	2.8	.3
Researcher-selected film 2	5.6	2.8	6.5	2.4	2.1
Threat film 1	3.1	2.8	2.8	2.5	.2
Threat film 2	2.8	3.0	2.5	2.4	.2
Age	34.2	10.5	29.5	9.5	3.8*
SES	56.6	10.4	58.7	8.2	.9
SIS1	28.6	6.4	27.0	5.2	1.4
SIS2	28.2	6.1	27.4	5.3	.4
Erotic films seen (past year)	2.7	.9	2.5	.7	2.4
Erectile difficulties (past 3 months)	1.5	.8	1.4	.6	.3
Sexual risk taking (past 3 years)	1.9	1.9	3.0	3.1	2.7†

[a](n = 26); [b](n = 50); [c]Used in the formation of the clusters. SES = Sexual Excitation, SIS1 = Sexual Inhibition-1, SIS2 = Sexual Inhibition-2, Sexual risk taking = Number of sexual partners without using a condom. *p = .05. **p < .01. ***p < .001. †p < .10. Physiological arousal = penile rigidity (0–100%).

stimuli, made us consider the possibility that the unusually high rate of nonresponders could be related to high levels of exposure to and experience with sexually explicit materials. Conversations with the subjects reinforced our idea that in some of them a high exposure to erotica seemed to have resulted in a lower responsivity to mainstream erotica and an increased need for novelty and variation, in some cases combined with a need for very specific types of stimuli in order to get aroused.

We redesigned the study and decided to eliminate the distraction and performance demand manipulations and to include newer, more varied clips, as well as some longer film clips. Also, instead of presenting subjects with a set of preselected ("researcher-selected") videos only, we let them choose two clips themselves from a set of 10, of which 10-second previews were shown and that included a wider range of sexual behaviors (e.g., group sex, interracial sex, S & M, etc.). We recruited an additional 51 subjects and found that with the improved design still 20 men, or approximately 25%, did not respond well to the sexual video clips (penile rigidity of less than 10% in response to the long self-selected film).

We employed a Ward's (Ward, 1963) hierarchical cluster analysis using the means of the four nonthreatening sexual films and found evidence for two distinct clusters, a low and a high response cluster. The clusters differed in genital responses to all four of the film clips, as well as to the second threatening film (see Table 1). Interestingly, the clusters did not differ with respect to genital responses to the first of the two threatening sexual films nor to subjective sexual arousal to *any* of the six films.

We conducted a logistic regression analysis to determine if high responders could be differentiated from low responders using age, sexual orientation, SES, SIS1, SIS2, experience with erotic videos, self-reported erectile difficulties, and sexual risk taking as predictor variables. The regression model significantly discriminated between the two groups ($\chi^2(8) = 22.26$, $p < .01$; see Table 2), explaining 39% of the variance. In total 78% of the participants were correctly classified ($z = 4.61$, $p < .001$), with hit rates of 82% for high and 59% for low responders ($ps < .01$). The results indicate that a participant was more likely to be classified as a high responder as his age decreased and his SES and sexual risk taking scores increased. Homosexual participants were more likely to be classified as low responders than heterosexual participants. Finally, the analyses suggested that as the number of erotic films seen within the past year increased a participant was more likely to be classified as a low responder.

In addition to genital and subjective sexual arousal, we measured electrodermal, startle eye-blink, and cardiovascular responses in this study. Following from our questionnaire studies (Bancroft et al., 2003b, 2004; which revealed a negative relationship between sexual risk taking and SIS2) and our study in college students (Janssen et al., 2002b; showing SIS2 to be associated with genital responses to threatening, but not nonthreaten-

Table 2. *Predictors of Low and High Responders*

Predictor	B	SEB	EXP(B)	Wald
Age	−.09	.04	−.91	5.47*
Sexual orientation	1.29	.78	3.62	2.74†
SES	.10	.04	1.10	5.08*
SIS1	−.07	.07	−.94	.92
SIS2	.04	.07	1.04	.36
Erotic films seen (past year)	−.86	.46	−.42	3.46†
Erectile difficulties (past 3 months)	.39	.55	1.47	.49
Partners w/o condoms (past 3 years)	.33	.17	1.40	3.82*
Constant	−.52	3.99	−.59	.02

EXP(B) = Exponentiated *B* (odds ratio). Low responders were coded as 0 and high responders as 1. Sexual orientation was dummy coded as heterosexual = 0 and homosexual = 1. SES = Sexual Excitation, SIS1 = Sexual Inhibition-1, SIS2 = Sexual Inhibition-2. The Wald statistic is a measure of the significance of *B*. *$p < .05$, †$p < .10$.

ing, sexual stimuli), we predicted that sexual risk taking would be associated with stronger sexual arousal to threatening sexual stimuli. With regard to the other response measures, we included those to allow us to explore whether sexual risk taking would be associated with stronger responses (or decreased inhibition) of specifically *sexual* responses to threatening sexual stimuli or (also) with other, nonsexual psychophysiological response patterns, and in particular ones that could reflect a hyporeactive autonomic or (e.g., when it comes to startle responses) defensive response to such stimuli and that, thus, could imply a role for more general inhibitory mechanisms (cf. Iacono, Carlson, & Malone, 2000).

We found differences between our low and high risk groups in genital response to the second threatening sexual film (T2) only. In addition, the groups also differed in their responses to the two researcher-selected films (RS1 and RS2). Subjective sexual arousal was highest in the high risk group as well, but in contrast to our findings on genital response, this effect was not restricted to some subset of films. With respect to the other psychophysiological variables, we did not find any clear effects related to sexual risk taking for the electrodermal and cardiovascular responses. We did, however find an effect for startle responses: Regardless of film type, eyeblink responses were smaller for the high than for the low sexual risk taking groups.

We also examined, in an exploratory fashion, the relationship between

Table 3. *Predictors of Sexual Risk Taking (SOI3)*

Predictor	b	SEB	B	t
Age	.06	.03	.22	1.90†
Sexual orientation	−1.92	.68	−.35	−2.84**
Number of sexual partners	.16	.04	.45	4.10**
SSS	.06	.06	.13	1.08
SIS2	−.02	.05	−.05	−.44
Skin conductance TA (T2)	−.01	.01	−.13	−1.21
Systolic BP (T2)	.03	.04	.09	.08
Startle eye-blink (T2)	−1.00	.35	−.29	−2.82**
Genital response (T2)	.03	.01	.26	2.52**

Unstandardized (b) and standardized (B) regression coefficients are given with standard errors (SEB). Sexual orientation was dummy coded as heterosexual = 0 and homosexual = 1. T2 = The second threatening sexual film, SSS=Sensation Seeking Scale, SIS2 = Sexual Inhibition-2, TA = total amplitude, BP = blood pressure. †$p < .10$. *$p < .05$, **$p < .02$.

sexual risk taking, personality-related variables, and psychophysiological responses to the threatening sexual films in a multiple regression analysis. We decided on the basis of our findings from the cluster analysis to focus on the second threat film (T2). Thus, we explored the possibility that sexual risk taking (using the number of sexual partners in past 3 years without using condoms as our primary dependent measure) could be predicted by relevant personality and behavioral variables and that responses to the threatening sexual film would contribute to the prediction of sexual risk taking above and beyond the other variables. We performed the regression analysis with age, sexual orientation, number of sexual partners in the past year, sensation seeking, SIS2, and eye-blink and genital responses to the second threatening sexual film (T2) as independent variables. Although our findings on the cardiovascular and electrodermal response measures were less clear and consistent (Janssen et al., 2006), we included change in systolic blood pressure and total skin conductance during the second threatening sexual film (T2) as additional independent variables. Of the electrodermal measures, we selected change in total amplitude as it was the variable with the highest, and in fact significant, correlation with our measure of sexual risk taking ($r = −.23$, $p < .05$). The model explained 38% of the variance in risky sexual behavior (see Table 3). The number of partners the participants reported having had sex with in the past year was a significant predictor, as was sexual orientation, with higher risk levels being associated with a heterosexual sexual orientation. Age played a role as well but was not significant ($p < .07$). Our personality measures of sensation seeking and sexual inhibition (SIS2) did not predict sexual risk taking. Neither did systolic blood pressure and skin conductance. However, sexual risk taking was associated with smaller eye-blink responses and stronger genital responses to the sexually threatening film.

A second regression analysis was run to explore to what degree the findings of the first analysis were specific to responses to the sexually threatening film (T2). For this purpose, we replaced the last four predictors (systolic blood pressure, skin conductance, eye-blink, and genital responses to the second threatening sexual film) with the average systolic blood pressure, skin conductance, eye-blink, and genital responses to the four non-threatening sexual films. This analysis showed that eye-blink responses to the nonthreatening sexual films were not a significant predictor ($p > .8$) of sexual risk taking, and although average genital response to the four non-threatening films significantly contributed to the model ($p < .03$), its effect was slightly less strong than that of genital responses to specifically the second threatening sexual film ($p < .02$). Also, this model explained a somewhat smaller proportion of the variance (30%). A final exploratory regression analysis, combining the two genital response variables, revealed that they largely nullified each other's influence. However, while the effect of genital responses to nonthreatening sexual stimuli was now nonsignificant ($p > .2$), genital responses to the threatening film still contributed, although only marginally ($p < .10$), to the model.

Overall, these results suggest, consistent with the findings from our questionnaire studies (Bancroft et al., 2003b, 2004), that sexual risk behavior, at least to some degree, is associated with differences in (the regulation of) sexual response. Whereas we had predicted that such differences would be relatively specific to stimuli relevant to sexual inhibition (cf. Janssen et al., 2002b), and although the findings on the second threatening sexual film do suggest that differences in inhibitory control of sexual response may be involved, on the whole the findings also imply a role for other, more general sexual response mechanisms. In addition, our findings suggest a role for psychophysiological mechanisms that reflect not sexual but more general approach/avoidance response mechanisms (or, in the case of startle eye-blink, defensive motivation; Benning, Patrick, & Iacono, 2005).

Our measure of sexual inhibition did not predict sexual risk taking. In our study with college students (Janssen et al., 2002b), SIS2 predicted genital responses to threatening sexual films. That study, however, did not focus on or incorporate any measures of sexual risk taking. In our questionnaire studies on sexual risk taking (Bancroft et al., 2003b, 2004), we found evidence for a relationship between sexual inhibition/excitation proneness (and also sensation seeking) and sexual risk taking. Those two studies, however, did not involve any psychophysiological measures. The findings of these studies combined with those of the one discussed here clearly suggest that the relationships among (self-report) measures of risky sexual behavior and sexual excitation/inhibition proneness on the one hand, and psychophysiological responses, as measured in the laboratory, on the other, are more complex than we assumed. Obviously, differences in samples, designs, and procedures all contribute to variability in research findings. However, other possible explanations need to be considered as well, including ones that involve limitations of or problems with the use of self-report measures to assess individual differences in the not readily observable activity and reactivity of putative neurophysiological systems or mechanisms (cf. Brenner, Beauchaine, & Sylvers, 2005). Thus, this involves questions about the validity and reliability, and their interaction, of such measures. More specifically, the use of SIS/SES in a relatively small experimental study may be more problematic than its use in survey studies, which typically involve larger samples. Our earlier psychophysiological study may not have been affected by this as much, as participants in that study were recruited on the basis of their SIS/SES scores, allowing for a comparison of more extreme groups.

Conclusions and Future Directions

The Kinsey Institute's dual control model and its spin-off, the SIS/SES questionnaire, were developed in the hope that they would contribute to our understanding of individual differences in sexual response, function, and behavior. Although with this review we hope to have demonstrated their potential for research on various aspects of male and female sexual response and behavior, we acknowledge that we still have a long way to go in improving our grasp on the complex roles of inhibitory and excitatory processes in human sexual response and behavior. For one, our model emphasizes the importance of interactions between, or the weighing of, sexual inhibition and excitation, and more advanced statistical analyses, allowing for a more rigorous assessment of their relative contribution (e.g., through the inclusion of interaction factors), would be required to explore this further. But other issues, concerns with, and limitations to the use of the SIS/SES questionnaire warrant discussion. Our model postulates a conceptual nervous system involving central mechanisms that are relevant to sexual inhibition and excitation; yet our research strongly relies on the use of a self-report measure, the SIS/SES questionnaire, to establish the sensitivity of these putative neurophysiological systems. Although we believe this instrument has shown to be of value, a number of factors could limit its applicability. People vary not only in their sexual responsiveness but also in their sexual experiences, and the two are related in intricate ways, potentially confounding the inferences we make on the basis of people's

SIS/SES scores. That is, we don't know if a person's lack of experience with certain sexual stimuli or situations is a result of external circumstances (e.g., related to demographic factors, "opportunity") or of exactly those traits that we are trying to measure—their proneness for sexual inhibition and excitation. In our questionnaire, we ask people, in case they have no experience with certain stimuli or situations (and this may be of particular relevance to SIS2), to *imagine* how they would respond. This means that in some cases, we will use a person's own predictions as a basis for our own predictions regarding his or her responses or behavior in our research studies. In addition to other factors that threaten the validity of self-report measures (e.g., social desirability, response biases), this may be an inherent problem of factor-analytically derived measures, where multiple questions are needed to reliably assess a trait.

A related issue involves the failure to capture a person's full range of experiences, and the associated levels, or intensity, of their inhibitory and excitatory responses, using a questionnaire of this kind. For example, although it is not unlikely that a person with a highly sensitive inhibitory "system" will respond with inhibition to a wide variety of relevant cues, it is also possible that in some people inhibition is triggered only by very specific stimuli (just like for some, only certain stimuli may lead to sexual excitation). This information is not conveyed by our SIS/SES questionnaire, as the person indicating high responsiveness to one or two specific inhibitory cues could end up receiving a low overall SIS2 score (because the scales are based on sum scores involving larger numbers of questions).

Then, of course, there is the issue of how well the questionnaire captures the multi-dimensional nature of sexual response (e.g., distinguishes between genital response and subjective sexual arousal) and the stability of individual propensities of sexual inhibition and excitation over the life span. To start with the latter, we assume that people vary in the sensitivity of our putative neurophysiological response systems and that this variability could be established in individuals from an early age on. At the same time, however, it would be naive to assume that such traits, while stable to some degree, could not be shaped and modified through experience. Longitudinal studies, behavioral genetics studies, and studies measuring SIS/SES before and after treatments of various kinds could shed more light on this.

As for the various components of sexual response, it is true that although the SIS/SES questionnaire strongly focuses on genital response, it does not consistently do so. Considering that we combined questions about "sexual arousal" with questions about erectile responses, it could be argued that our questionnaire implicitly treats sexual arousal as some uniform construct. The SIS/SES factors indeed make no distinction between subjective sexual arousal (and its motivational aspects) and genital response. This is a limitation that has been considered more carefully in the development of the new questionnaire measure for women (Graham, Sanders, & Milhausen, 2006).

The introduction of the notion of "conceptual nervous systems" in personality research has been attributed to Pavlov (Pickering, 1997; Strelau, 1997). In his research on conditioning in dogs, Pavlov observed individual differences in the speed of conditioning and the stability of conditioned reflexes. On the basis of his observations, he proposed a typology of central nervous system properties, which included a role for excitation and inhibition, as well as for the balance between the two. Both Eysenck's (1967) and Gray's (1982) theories on personality were influenced by Pavlov's ideas (Strelau, 1997). Pavlov used his conditioning paradigm as an experimental and psychophysiological method to study "temperament." That is, he used experimental manipulations and related individual differences in their effects to aspects of personality. We believe that, in our research on the role of sexual excitation and inhibition, we should also consider alternative ways of studying their relevance to sexual response and behavior. While the SIS/SES questionnaire has already proven to be of value, future research on the dual control model should probably give greater emphasis to the fact that it, in essence, is a state-trait model, and we thus should attempt to incorporate ways of manipulating sexual excitation and inhibition at a state level as well.

Some of the research presented in this paper was made possible by NIMH Grant R01-MH60519-02 and an unrestricted grant from Pfizer, Inc. We wish to thank John Petrocelli for his help with the cluster and regression analyses presented in the section on response patterns in high and low sexual risk takers.

Note

1. The term *psychogenic* is considered to be of diminishing clinical value. Here, as in the research by Barlow and others, it refers to erectile problems that are not attributable to peripheral (vascular, hormonal, or neurological) factors.

References

Bancroft, J. (1995). Effects of alpha-2 antagonists on male erectile response. In J. Bancroft (Ed.), *The pharmacology of sexual function and dysfunction* (pp. 215–224). Amsterdam: Excerpta Medica.

Bancroft, J. (1999). Central inhibition of sexual response in the male: A theoretical perspective. *Neuroscience and Biobehavioral Reviews, 23,* 763–784.

Bancroft, J. (2000). Individual differences in sexual risk taking by men—a psycho-socio-biological approach. In J Bancroft (Ed.), *The role of theory in sex* research (pp. 177–212). Bloomington: Indiana University Press.

Bancroft, J., Carnes, L., & Janssen, E. (2005). Unprotected anal intercourse in HIV-positive and HIV-negative gay men: The relevance of sexual arousability, mood, sensation seeking, and erectile problems. *Archives of Sexual Behavior, 34,* 299–305.

Bancroft, J, Carnes, L., Janssen, E., Goodrich, D., & Long, J. S. (2005). Erectile and ejaculatory problems in gay and heterosexual men. *Archives of Sexual Behavior, 34,* 285–297.

Bancroft, J., Herbenick, D., Barnes, T., Hallam-Jones, R., Wylie, K., Janssen, E., & members of BASRT. (2005). The relevance of the dual control model to male sexual dysfunction: The Kinsey Institute/BASRT collaborative project. *Sexual & Relationship Therapy, 20,* 13–30.

Bancroft, J., & Janssen, E. (2000). The dual control model of male sexual response: A theoretical approach to centrally mediated erectile dysfunction. *Neuroscience and Biobehavioral Review, 24*(5), 571–579.

Bancroft, J., & Janssen, E. (2001). Psychogenic erectile dysfunction in the era of pharmacotherapy: A theoretical approach. In J. Mulcahy (Ed.), *Male sexual function: A guide to clinical management* (pp. 79–89). Totowa, N.J.: Humana Press.

Bancroft, J., Janssen, E., Carnes, L., Goodrich, D., Strong, D., & Long, J. S. (2004). Sexual risk taking in young heterosexual men: The relevance of sexual arousability, mood, and sensation seeking. *Journal of Sex Research, 41,* 181–192.

Bancroft, J., Janssen, E., Strong, D., Carnes, L., Vukadinovic, Z., & Long, J. S. (2003a). The relation between mood and sexuality in heterosexual men. *Archives of Sexual Behavior, 32,* 217–230.

Bancroft, J., Janssen, E., Strong, D., Carnes, L., Vukadinovic, Z., & Long. J. S. (2003b). Sexual risk taking in gay men: The relevance of sexual arousability, mood and sensation seeking. *Archives of Sexual Behavior, 32,* 555–572.

Bancroft, J., Janssen, E., Strong, D., & Vukadinovic, Z. (2003). The relation between mood and sexuality in gay men. *Archives of Sexual Behavior, 32,* 231–242.

Bancroft, J., & Malone, N. (1995). The clinical assessment of erectile dysfunction: A comparison of nocturnal penile tumescence monitoring and intracavernosal injections. *International Journal of Impotence Research, 7,* 123–130.

Bancroft, J., & Vukadinovic, Z. (2004). Sexual addiction, sexual compulsivity, sexual impulse disorder or what? Towards a theoretical model. *Journal of Sex Research, 41,* 225–234.

Barlow, D. H. (1986). Causes of sexual dysfunction: The role of anxiety and cognitive interference. *Journal of Consulting and Clinical Psychology, 54,* 140–157.

Barlow, D. H., Sakheim, D. K., & Beck, J. G. (1983). Anxiety increases sexual arousal. *Journal of Abnormal Psychology, 92,* 49–54.

Beck, J. G., Barlow, D. H., Sakheim, D. K., & Abrahamson, D. J. (1987). Shock treatment and sexual arousal: The role of selective attention, thought content, and affective states. *Psychophysiology, 24,* 165–172.

Benning, S., Patrick, C. J., & Iacono, W. G. (2005). Psychopathy, startle blink modulation, and electrodermal reactivity in twin men. *Psychophysiology, 6,* 753–762.

Berntson, G. G., Cacioppo, J. T., & Quigley, K. S. (1991). Autonomic determinism.

The modes of autonomic control, the doctrine of autonomic space and the laws of autonomic constraint. *Psychological Review, 98*(4), 459–487.

Bjorkland, D. F., & Kipp, K. (1996). Parental investment theory and gender differences in the evolution of inhibition mechanisms. *Psychological Bulletin, 120,* 163–188.

Brenner, S. L., Beauchaine, T. P., & Sylvers, P. D. (2005). A comparison of psychophysiological and self-report measures of BAS and BIS activation. *Psychophysiology, 42*(1), 108–115.

Cacioppo, J. T., Gardner, W. L., & Berntson, G. G. (1999). The affect system has parallel and integrative processing components: Form follows function. *Journal of Personality and Social Psychology, 76,* 839–855.

Carpenter, D., Janssen, E., Graham, C., Vorst, H, & Wicherts, J. (2007). *Women's scores on the Sexual Excitation/Sexual Inhibition Scales (SIS/SES): Gender similarities and differences.* Manuscript submitted for publication.

Depue, R. A., & Collins, P. F. (1999). Neurobiology of the structure of personality: Dopamine, facilitation of incentive motivation, and extraversion. *Behavioral and Brain Sciences, 22,* 491–569.

Eysenck, H. J. (1967). *The biological basis of personality.* Springfield, Illinois: Charles C. Thomas.

Fisher, W. A., Byrne, D., White, L. A., & Kelley, K. (1988). Erotophobia-erotophilia as a dimension of personality. *Journal of Sex Research, 25,* 123–151.

Graham, C., Janssen, E., & Sanders, S. A. (2000). Effects of fragrance on female sexual arousal and mood across the menstrual cycle. *Psychophysiology, 37,* 76–84.

Graham, C., Sanders, S., & Milhausen, R. (2006). The Sexual Excitation/Sexual Inhibition Inventory for Women: Psychometric properties. *Archives of Sexual Behavior, 35,* 1–13.

Graham, C., Sanders, S., Milhausen, R., & McBride, K. (2004). Turning on and turning off: A focus group study of the factors that affect women's sexual arousal. *Archives of Sexual Behavior, 33,* 527–538.

Gray, J. A. (1982). *The neurophysiology of anxiety: An enquiry into the functions of the septo-hippocampal system.* Oxford: Oxford University Press.

Harnishfeger, K. K. (1995). The development of cognitive inhibition: Theories, definitions, and research evidence. In F. N. Dempster & C. J. Brainerd (Eds.), *Interference and inhibition in cognition* (pp. 175–204). San Diego, California: Academic Press.

Iacono, W. G., Carlson, S. R., & Malone, S. M. (2000). Identifying a multivariate endophenotype for substance use disorders using psychophysiological measures. *International Journal of Psychophysiology, 38,* 81–96.

Janssen, E. (1998). [Shock threat and viewing time: A laboratory analogue of risky sex?]. Unpublished raw data.

Janssen, E., & Bancroft, J. (1996). Dual control of sexual response: The relevance of central inhibition. In R. C. Schiavi (symposium chair), *New research on male sexual dysfunction.* Presented at 22nd Conference of the International Academy of Sex Research (IASR), Rotterdam, the Netherlands.

Janssen, E., & Everaerd, W. (1993). Determinants of male sexual arousal. *Annual Review of Sex Research, 4,* 211–245.

Janssen, E., Everaerd, W., Spiering, M., & Janssen, J. (2000). Automatic processes and the appraisal of sexual stimuli: Toward an information processing model of sexual arousal. *Journal of Sex Research, 37*(2), 8–23.

Janssen, E., Goodrich, D., Petrocelli, J., & Bancroft, J. (2006). *Psychophysiological response patterns and risky sexual behavior.* Manuscript submitted for publication.

Janssen, E., Vorst, H., Finn, P., & Bancroft, J. (2002a). The Sexual Inhibition (SIS) and Sexual Excitation (SES) Scales: I. Measuring sexual inhibition and excitation proneness in men. *Journal of Sex Research, 39,* 114–126.

Janssen, E., Vorst, H., Finn, P., & Bancroft, J. (2002b). The Sexual Inhibition (SIS) and Sexual Excitation (SES) Scales: II. Predicting psychophysiological response patterns. *Journal of Sex Research, 39,* 127–132.

Laan, E., Everaerd, W., & Evers, A. (1995). Assessment of female sexual arousal: Response specificity and construct validity. *Psychophysiology, 32*(5), 476–485.

Lykins, A., Janssen, E., & Graham, C. A. (2006). The relationship between negative mood and sexuality in heterosexual college women and men. *Journal of Sex Research, 43,* 136–143.

Pickering, A.D. (1997). The conceptual nervous system and personality: From Pavlov to neural networks. *European Psychologist, 2,* 139–163.

Rosen, R., Janssen, E., Wiegel, M., Bancroft, J., Althof, A., Wincze, J., Segraves, R. T., & Barlow, D. (2006). Psychological and interpersonal correlates in men with erectile dysfunction and their partners: Predictors of pharmacotherapy outcome. *Journal of Sex and Marital Therapy, 32,* 215–234.

Sandfort, T. G. M., & de Keizer, M. (2001). Sexual problems in gay men: An overview of empirical research. *Annual Review of Sex Research, 12,* 93–120.

Scepkowski, L., & Janssen, E. (2006). *Shocking null-effects in a shock-threat paradigm.* Poster presented at the 32nd annual meeting of the International Academy of Sex Research (IASR), Amsterdam, the Netherlands.

Shye, S., & Elizur, D. (1994). *Introduction to facet theory: Content design and intrinsic data analysis in behavioral research.* Thousand Oaks, California: Sage.

Spielberger, C. D., Gorsuch, R. L., & Lushene, R. E. (1970). *STAI manual for the State Trait Anxiety Inventory.* Palo Alto, California: Consulting Psychologists Press.

Strelau, J. (1997). The contribution of Pavlov's typology of CNS properties to personality research. *European Psychologist, 2,* 125–138.

van der Velde, J., Laan, E., & Everaerd, W. (2001). Vaginismus, a component of a general defensive reaction: An investigation of pelvic floor muscle activity during exposure to emotion-inducing film excerpts in women with and without vaginismus. *International Urogynecology Journal, 5,* 328–331.

Ward, J. H. (1963). Hierarchical grouping to optimize an objective function. *Journal of the American Statistical Association, 58,* 236–244.

Zemore, R., Fischer, D. G., Garratt, L. S., & Miller, C. (1990). The Depression Proneness Rating Scale: Reliability, validity, and factor structure. *Current Psychology: Research & Reviews, 9,* 255–263.

Discussion Paper

SERGE STOLÉRU

The starting point of the dual control model, the DCM, is the proposition that in studying sexual arousal we may have to discern both excitatory and inhibitory influences. This proposition really sets the stage for research on the regulation of sexual arousal. I think it's a heuristic proposition within which research can be conducted with a clear starting point. It gives to sexual arousal the same status as other motivational entities such as hunger or thirst, in that it suggests we should try to understand not only the mechanisms that give rise to these motivational states, but also those mechanisms that regulate their level of intensity and that lead to a state of restraint or satiety.

In this brief discussion, I shall mainly use the insights we have gained through studies of sexual arousal based on brain functional imaging. The sequence of my comments will follow the order of issues presented in the paper that we have just listened to. In the paper's introduction, the authors write that "no models or measures existed that focus specifically on individual differences in sexual response." The development by the authors of the Sexual Inhibition Scales/Sexual Excitation Scales or SIS/SES questionnaire has purported to provide measures that would reveal and quantify individual variability in sexual responsiveness. However, isn't it the case that previous measures of arousal or of desire, such as the Sexual Arousal Inventory (Hoon, Hoon, & Wincze, 1976), were designed to assess such individual variability? Thus, it seems to me that the originality, the real importance of the SIS/SES questionnaire and its specific contribution, is that it provides an assessment of inhibitory psychological influences.

The DCM "postulates the involvement of two neurophysiological systems, one relevant to the activation, the other to the suppression of sexual response." Brain functional imaging studies suggest that the neurophysiological system relevant to the suppression of the sexual response is comprised of several components that operate at different stages of the sexual response. Therefore, based on findings from brain functional imaging studies, it would seem useful to explore and measure the various psychological inhibitory factors that correspond to the different inhibitory neurophysiological systems. First, neuroimaging studies suggest the existence of permanent tonic inhibitory control that prevents the unfolding of sexual arousal. When a potential sexual stimulus is presented to the subject, this tonic inhibitory control may be alleviated. If, instead of laboratory conditions, we consider everyday situations; for example, if a person is reading a book in a library and an attractive person walks nearby, the person may stop reading and start to have sexual fantasies. The previous state of sexual quiescence is terminated. We suspect that this first kind of inhibitory system, which accounts for sexual quiescence, is neurally mediated by temporal areas. This would mean that sexual quiescence is not simply a "default mode," but an actively maintained state. In various samples to which we presented visual sexual stimuli, we obtained a response in temporal areas that was not activation, but deactivation. What this means is that the blood flow in these regions decreased. In monkeys, the experimental bilateral removal of the temporal cortex, including the medial aspects of the temporal cortex, is followed by dramatic hypersexuality and frantic sexual activity, called the Klüver and Bucy syndrome. However, the idea that temporal areas mediate sexual quiescence is only an interpretation and the decrease of regional blood flow in temporal areas may be explained by other interpretations. At least in humans, one could argue, for instance, that deactivation of temporal areas reflects the fact that in response to visual sexual stimulation, a person is ceasing to have intellectual thoughts. Thus, deactivation of temporal areas doesn't necessarily mean that those areas are exerting inhibitory control, but the Klüver and Bucy syndrome adds support to this interpretation.

A second neurophysiological system is what I refer to as a devaluation system: at least in patients with hypoactive sexual desire disorder (HSDD), but possibly in milder forms in healthy subjects, it is a system that will mediate a critical evaluation of the object of desire and will disconnect the perception of this object from the regions implicated in motor imagery and sexual motivation. This is the way we have interpreted the lack of deactivation of the medial orbitofrontal cortex in patients with HSDD. This is what I showed you this morning, of course. There has been recent support for this interpretation in two papers that demonstrated that the medial orbitofrontal cortex is involved in extinction of conditioning of responses to unconditioned stimuli. These are papers reporting experiments conducted in rats by the group of Quirk (Milad & Quirk, 2002; Quirk, Russo, Barron, & Lebron, 2000).

Brain functional imaging studies suggest the existence of a third inhibitory system that comes into play once sexual arousal has begun. When a person is sexually aroused, he or she must, in most circumstances, refrain from acting out his or her motor imagery or motivation. This function is probably mediated by the caudate nucleus and the putamen, regions of the brain that belong to the basal ganglia.

The reason why I'm saying all this is that it may be useful to incorporate into questionnaires, such as the SIS/SES, questions derived from insights gained from neuroimaging studies. For instance, I was fortunate enough to get the SIS/SES questionnaire from Erick and I think that most of the questions that are asked probably belong to the first inhibitory system, the tonic one, but it could be interesting to devise questions relating to the two other inhibitory systems. For instance, a question could be, "Do you often generate devaluating critical comments on persons that you first find attractive?" Actually, the concept of devaluation of actual or potential sexual partners was originally generated by Kaplan and she found that patients with HSDD had this type of cognitive dysfunction (Kaplan, 1995). So, it was really fascinating to use her clinical insights to interpret the findings of our study of patients with HSDD. The process of exploring in a questionnaire the various inhibitory systems could also be mirrored in a process of exploring the various excitatory systems. For instance, it could be useful to specify and detail some of the terms that are often used in the questions, such as "I get sexually aroused," and use also, in other items, questions about perceived desire to engage in sexual activity (that would be corresponding to what I call the motivational component of sexual arousal, the urge to act), or questions about the perceived pleasure of watching erotic photographs (emotional component), or increased attention or perceived attractiveness (that would be exploring the cognitive components).

Regarding methodological aspects, I was wondering, but I'm not wondering now, whether the assessment of rigidity was the best measurement in situations where subjects respond with low levels of erection, such as was the case in the study of subjects from the community that was reported previously. But, you showed that even tumescence was not rising. However, I think that in certain circumstances volumetric phallometry would be more sensitive to low levels of responses. More generally speaking, I am wondering whether rigidity and volume increases are mediated by partly different physiological systems that may be differentially altered in various disorders. Thus, it may be useful to implement different assessments of the genital response to answer different research questions. For instance, people can get "soft erections," erections with tumescence but without rigidity, and that may be a signature of anxiety and it would be more interesting in these circumstances to use a rigidity assessment than volumetric assessment.

Finally, it seems to me that the suggestion of the paper as to the importance of developing a state measure of sexual arousal is crucial. The Film Evaluation Scale (FES) (Heiman, personal communication) is probably one such instrument. In developing a state measure of sexual arousal, it seems to me that it would be essential to include specific descriptors of sexual arousal, such as increased heartbeat, increased feelings of heat—especially for women, feeling of genital changes—and specify what those feelings are because in this sense, subjective reports would be less subjective if we asked the subject to assess really specific events that they are perceiving. Now, subjective reports would remain subjective, but not with the meaning of individual bias associated with the word *subjectivity*. Before I started working in sexuality research, I used to work with infants, and there was a very interesting assessment of the neonate that was called the Brazelton Neonatal Behavioral Assessment Scale. For all the items there are nine descriptors, which specify nine levels of response, and for each level the examiner is supposed to rate on a scale ranging from 1 to 9, based on very objective criteria. For example, we assess the degree of visual orientation, the capacity of the neonate to turn its head and follow an object, and the child is rated 9 if he can turn left, on the right, when he follows a ball, he turns his head upward, downward, in a circle, and there are really objective and specific descriptors for each level. I wonder whether this approach could be used when we are trying to assess the subjective experience of arousal. I know sexual arousal is qualitatively variable among various individuals, but it may be at least informative to try to specify descriptors that are subjectively perceived.

References

Hoon, E. F., Hoon, P. W., & Wincze, J. P. (1976). An inventory for the measurement of female sexual arousability. *Archives of Sexual Behavior, 5,* 291–300.

Kaplan, H. S. (1995). *The sexual desire disorders: Dysfunctional regulation of sexual motivation.* New York: Brunner/Mazel.

Milad, M. R., & Quirk, G. J. (2002). Neurons in medial prefrontal cortex signal memory for fear extinction. *Nature, 420,* 70–74.

Quirk, G. J., Russo, G. K., Barron, J. L., & Lebron, K. (2000). The role of ventromedial prefrontal cortex in the recovery of extinguished fear. *Journal of Neuroscience, 20,* 6225–6231.

Interactive Processes in Ejaculatory Disorders

Psychophysiological Considerations

DAVID L. ROWLAND, WENDI TAI, AND
KLYNT BRUMMETT

Defining Ejaculatory Disorders

Ejaculatory response is the efferent (motor) component of a spinal reflex that typically begins with sensory stimulation to the glans penis (Kedia, 1983; McKenna, 1999). This reflex actually consists of two distinct efferent phases: an emission phase involving sympathetically controlled bladder neck closure and seminal emission from the prostate; and an expulsion phase involving somatically controlled (pudendal nerve) contractions of striate bulbocavernosal muscle and subsequent semen expulsion. Because this reflex is modulated by central processes, it is not surprising that most men report some degree of control over its timing (Rowland, Houtsmuller, Slob, & Cooper, 1997; Rowland, deGouvea Brazao, Strassberg, & Slob, 2000). Men show substantial variation in ejaculatory thresholds and, therefore, along the latency-to-ejaculation continuum, with most men reporting latencies between about 2 and 10 minutes. However, some men ejaculate uncontrollably before or shortly after vaginal intromission and consequently may be classified as having premature ejaculation (PE). Others have difficulty reaching ejaculation and may be classified as having retarded or inhibited ejaculation (IE). These men either do not reach orgasm during intercourse or do so only after prolonged stimulation.

Although a number of measures have been suggested to define ejaculatory disorders, those that seem to have the most efficacy (and are most likely to show change following therapy) include latency to ejaculation and a sense of self-control over the timing of ejaculation (Rowland, 2003; Rowland, Cooper, & Schneider, 2001). Men who indicate no ejaculatory problems typically report fairly high control over the timing of ejaculation (e.g., 5 or higher on a 7-point scale, where 1 = none at all). In contrast, men with PE report short latencies of less than 1 or 2 minutes, as well as a lack of control over ejaculatory timing (e.g., 4 or lower). Men with IE typically report very long latencies or an absence of ejaculation, although no specific criteria have yet been proposed for men with this understudied dysfunction.

The context in which the rapid or delayed ejaculation occurs is also relevant to a diagnostic classification. For example, some men classified as

PE or IE report difficulty controlling the timing of their ejaculatory response only during coitus and not during masturbation; that is, the problem is most likely to surface during coital activity. Even then, mitigating factors such as the novelty of the partner or situation need to be considered when making an ejaculatory dysfunction diagnosis (American Psychiatric Association, *Diagnostic and Statistical Manual of Mental Disorders*, 2000). Other factors such as time since the last ejaculation (and, more generally, the frequency of orgasm; Grenier & Byers, 2001), use of medication, and the persistence of the problem are important to the diagnosis of an ejaculatory disorder. In all instances, the lack of efficacy regarding the problem is presumed to cause sufficient distress for the man and/or his partner to interfere with normal healthy sexual interaction. In some instances, the couple may eventually avoid sexual activity altogether because of the problem.

Purported Causes of Ejaculatory Disorders in Men

Various somatic pathologies are known to disrupt normal ejaculatory function in men. For example, various medications and surgical procedures (radical prostatectomy) have been associated with PE. Spinal cord injury, multiple sclerosis, pelvic-region surgery, severe diabetes, selective serotonin reuptake inhibitor (SSRI) antidepressants, and medications that inhibit a-adrenergic innervation of the ejaculatory system have been associated with inhibited or retarded ejaculation in men (Master & Turek, 2001; Vale, 1999; Witt & Grantmyre, 1993). In the absence of obvious pathologies, however, no single etiology can clearly account for the majority of cases of PE or IE. Rather, as with most components of sexual response, ejaculation appears to be under the influence of both psychological-behavioral and biological processes. Therefore, it is not surprising that causes for ejaculatory disorders have been attributed to one domain or the other, or both (see Waldinger, 2002).

Premature Ejaculation

Cognitive-behavioral explanations of PE have typically focused on centrally mediated processes, and more specifically, on the interactions among levels of sexual arousal, awareness of arousal, and ejaculatory control. For example, such explanations posit that PE men may be less accurate in their ability to anticipate the moment of ejaculation, perhaps because they are less attuned to their level of arousal and therefore tend to underestimate it. Alternatively, these men may ejaculate rapidly because they reach high levels of sexual arousal very quickly, the result of a lack of control over their rapidly rising levels of sexual arousal (Kaplan, 1974; Masters & Johnson, 1970). Although recent studies are mixed regarding the idea that PE men may be less attuned to their arousal than functional counterparts, PE men may nevertheless ejaculate prior to their anticipated maximal arousal. That is, instead of ejaculating when they have reached maximum sexual excitement, they do so well before that moment, thus climaxing unexpectedly or prematurely. Due to the repeated experience of sexual failure, such cognitive inaccuracy and lack of control may be coupled with negative affect or anxiety, which itself may lower the sympathetically mediated threshold to ejaculation.

Physiologically based explanations of PE emphasize the spinal reflexive processes involved in the ejaculatory process. A number of studies have examined the latency and strength of event-related potentials (ERPs) measured along afferent or efferent pathways of the spinal reflex, or within specific areas of somatosensory cortex. Although the evidence does not uniformly support differences between PE men and others (Rowland, Haensel, Bloom, & Slob, 1993; Xin, Chung, Choi, Seong, & Choi, 1996), several studies report that PE men show greater penile sensitivity and stronger cortical ERPs to stimulation of the pudendal afferent nerves and shorter latencies in the efferent processes involved in bulbocavernosal contractions eliciting seminal expulsion (Colpi, Fanciullacci, Beretta, Negri, & Zanollo, 1986; Fanciullacci, Colpi, Beretta, & Zanollo, 1988). Furthermore, because many antidepressants that affect central monoaminergic functioning also inhibit ejaculation, a role for centrally acting serotonin and/or norepinephrine has been postulated. While animal studies strongly argue for a role for serotonergic (5-HT$_1$a) receptors in ejaculatory latency (e.g., Ahlenius, Larsson, Svensson, Hjorth, & Carlsson, 1981; Haensel, Mos, Olivier, & Slob, 1991), no direct neurophysiological evidence yet exists to support a role for this system in the etiology of rapid ejaculation in men. Indeed, due to the efficacy of pharmacological and/or biomedical treatments in countering rapid ejaculation, the cause of PE may sometimes be misattributed to physiological factors. Since all psychological and/or psychosocial factors are ultimately mediated through biological systems, any ejaculatory problem, whether the cause is biological or psychological, may be ameliorated by alterations in the functioning of biological pathways. With the investigative tools currently available, it is difficult to distinguish psychological-arousal processes related to ejaculation from the neural pathways and systems that mediate these processes.

Until more evidence becomes available, a clear understanding of the etiology of PE is unlikely. However, two ideas are worth reiterating: (i) As with most sexual disorders, there is probably no single cause for PE; rather this behavioral endpoint may result from a number of different causes. And (ii), in the absence of either an obvious somatic or psychological etiology, premature ejaculation probably represents a mix of psychogenic and organogenic factors and, therefore, might best be viewed in terms of a psychophysiological model (Strassberg, Kelly, Carroll, & Kircher, 1987). Such a model postulates that the disorder represents a combination of physiological vulnerabilities (e.g., hyperresponsivity or low threshold within the spinal reflex) and psychological conditions that interact to establish and maintain the dysfunction.

Given the lack of consensus (and supporting data) regarding possible etiologies of PE, it is not surprising that identification of clear subtypes of PE based upon *cause* has not been successful. Nevertheless, classification of PE into various subtypes based upon *developmental histories* and *response characteristics* has sometimes proved useful. For example, most clinicians and researchers distinguish between lifelong and acquired PE, and between PE that is limited to specific situations or partners and that which is more global. Thus, knowing that the patient has had a lifelong history of PE not specific to one partner may argue toward a biological and/or cognitive etiology. As such, the need to address interpersonal and relationship issues may be less important in these men. In contrast, knowing that the PE developed recently in specific situations and in conjunction with erectile dysfunction may suggest the need to address relationship issues and attend less to a biological etiology.

Inhibited Ejaculation

Many men with inhibited or retarded ejaculation have no clear somatic factors that account for the disorder. As the result of their inability to ejaculate, these men also do not experience orgasm. Such men have been characterized as lacking awareness of their bodies, being inhibited psychologically due to guilt or wanting to maintain control, having inadequate sexual arousal and performance anxiety, being overly focused on pleasing the partner, or exhibiting negative affect (e.g., resentment or hostility) toward their partner (Frank, Anderson, & Kupfer, 1976; Geboes, Steeno, & De-Moor, 1975; Kaplan, 1974; Masters & Johnson, 1970; Muntjack & Kanno, 1979; Perelman, 2001). Largely due to the dearth of men with this dysfunction, empirical evidence supporting such assumptions has been based primarily on a handful of individual case studies rather than a systematic investigation of populations of men with this disorder. In fact, so little is known about this group that until recently there have been no normative data on general aspects of these men's sexual response; for example, whether they demonstrate normal erectile response or levels of arousal in response to psychosexual stimulation. It is, therefore, not surprising that in the absence of any commonly delineated biological, psychological, or behavioral etiology, standardized treatment procedures for this disorder have not been fully developed (Perelman, 2001).

Psychophysiological Exploration of Ejaculatory Disorders

One of the advantages of the psychophysiological approach is that it enables the exploration of interacting psychological and physiological factors in the study of sexual response in a controlled laboratory environment.

Not only is it possible to control the stimulus conditions, but both outcome and predictor variables can be assessed with substantial precision and reliability. Psychophysiological analysis, then, allows investigation of genital response measures such as erection and ejaculation as a function of variables of presumed salience to these outcomes. With respect to PE, such covariates may include the kinds of stimuli that are most likely to elicit the dysfunctional response, the patient's self-reported levels of sexual arousal, the mitigating effects of anxiety and negative affect, various dyadic relationship factors, and so on. Although the generalizability of laboratory findings to nonlaboratory situations has been raised as a concern, psychophysiological studies appear to generate findings consistent with sexual response under more natural conditions; for example, with one's partner (see Rowland, 1999; Rowland et al., 2000).

Psychophysiology of Premature Ejaculation

Stimulus Relevance

Early psychophysiological research on men with PE was unable to differentiate their response from that of sexually functional counterparts. For example, contrary to the expectation of hyperarousal in PE men (defined by shorter latencies to maximum arousal), several researchers (Kockott, Feil, Ferstl, Aldenhoff, & Besinger, 1980; Speiss, Geer, & O'Donohue, 1984) reported no differences between PE men and controls on erectile response to erotic visual stimuli. More recent research, however, suggests that in order to simulate conditions most likely to evoke the dysfunctional response of rapid ejaculation in PE men, the inclusion of direct penile stimulation (e.g., vibrotactile) is important (Rowland et al., 1997).

Interestingly, self-selected intensity of penile vibrotactile stimulation (based on the criterion of "most pleasant") does not seem to differ between controls and PE men. Nevertheless, when vibrotactile stimulation (VIB) is applied to the penis in conjunction with visual sexual stimulation (VSS), PE men's responses clearly diverge from those of functional counterparts in several ways. First, regarding *maximum* penile response, penile stimulation has greater impact on men with PE than functional controls. Specifically, comparing across stimulus conditions (VSS vs. VSS + VIB), functional controls respond with equivalent maximum penile response, whether or not penile stimulation is included. In contrast, PE men's maximum erectile responses increase by 15–20% when penile stimulation is included. Second, comparing across PE and functional groups, under VSS alone, PE men show lower maximum erectile response than functional counterparts, but equivalent erectile response under the stronger stimulus condition of both VSS + VIB. In other words, compared with controls, PE men do not show stronger maximum penile response to VSS + VIB, but rather weaker maximum penile response to just VSS.

Actual ejaculation as well as self-assessed measures of impending ejaculation also differ across PE and control groups. In the presence of VSS only, ejaculatory rates between PE men and controls are about the same. However, with the inclusion of penile stimulation, about 50–60% of PE men ejaculate compared with only about 0–8% of controls. In addition, those PE men who do not ejaculate during the session consistently report greater proximity to the ejaculatory threshold than functional counterparts. Furthermore, when subjects are asked about the *control* they felt over their ejaculation, functional subjects indicate no change between VSS alone versus VSS + VIB, whereas PE men report a significant decrease in control during the combined visual and penile stimulation. Exactly what factors contribute to this sense of decreasing control in men with PE continues to be the subject of ongoing investigation and is discussed later in this review. Interestingly, when men with just PE are compared with those with coexisting ED, the latter group reports *greater* loss of control over ejaculation. This finding calls into question the assumption that men with coexisting PE and ED may ejaculate rapidly primarily because they fear losing their erection (e.g., Buvat, Buvat-Herbaut, Lemaire, Marcolin, & Quittelier, 1990; Kaplan, 1974).

While these findings suggest that maximal erotic pleasure is derived from about the same penile stimulation intensity for both groups, they also verify the long-standing supposition regarding the particular relevance of penile stimulation to overall genital arousal and dysfunctional sexual response in PE men. Furthermore, this pattern appears consistent with the findings of Fanciullacci et al. (1988), who report that sensory stimulation of the penis has greater cortical representation (electrophysiologically), and thus perhaps subjective significance, in PE men than controls.

Self-Reported Sexual Arousal

Conceptualizations of PE have often included the idea that men with this dysfunction become hyperaroused during sexual activity. For example, Kaplan (1974) has suggested that perhaps due to their anxiety, PE men are less cognizant of their sexual arousal, and in underestimating their state of high arousal, they ejaculate prior to expectation. Furthermore, the finding of a positive correlation between ejaculatory latency and frequency of sexual activity (Grenier & Byers, 2001; Spiess et al., 1984) has further implicated level of sexual arousal as a factor in PE. This correlation has been interpreted in two ways. The first is based on the fact that sexual arousal habituates to repeated stimulation (O'Donohue & Geer, 1985; Over & Koukounas, 1995). Specifically, habituation of arousal to sexual stimulation and/or ejaculatory inhibition due to the impact of refractory periods is less likely to occur in PE men because of their lower overall frequency of activity (LoPiccolo & Stock, 1986). The second is that because of their lower sexual activity along with their short ejaculatory latency, PE men may have had fewer opportunities to learn adequate control over their level of arousal and therefore the ejaculatory process (Kaplan, 1974). To date, however, such relationships are primarily correlational.

The issue of arousal is actually twofold. First, whether PE men report higher levels of sexual arousal to psychosexual stimulation than functional controls. And second, whether PE men are less aware of their level of sexual arousal than others. Regarding the former, overall levels of self-reported sexual arousal to erotic visual stimulation appear to be no greater in PE men than controls (Kockott et al., 1980; Speiss et al., 1984). More recent analysis of self-reported sexual arousal to sexual stimuli that includes penile stimulation seems to confirm this pattern—PE men report neither higher levels of arousal nor greater ease of becoming aroused to psychosexual stimulation than controls (Rowland et al., 2000).

Regarding the second issue—whether PE men are less cognizant of their level of arousal—again there is no clear distinction between PE men and controls. Strassberg et al. (1987), for example, have demonstrated that self-assessments of level of sexual arousal were not less accurate for PE men than controls. Furthermore, Rowland et al. (2000) reported no differences in the correlation between erectile response and self-reported arousal, or between erectile response and estimated erectile response, for PE men versus controls. Such findings tend to negate the idea that PE men are less attuned to their level of sexual excitation.

However, one puzzling finding has emerged. Given their closer (self-reported) proximity to ejaculation than controls under VSS + VIB, the fact that PE men do *not* report higher levels of arousal (Rowland et al., 2000) is surprising. Perhaps simple correlations between genital and subjective arousal do not capture all the relevant parameters regarding such psychophysiological relationships. For example, it is plausible that PE men show strong correlations between genital and subjective response, while at the same time consistently underestimating their genital response.

Anxiety and Affective Response of PE Men

Relevant to the understanding of PE is whether affective states play a critical role in the etiology of the disorder. The affective component of sexual response—particularly anxiety—has long been theorized to play an underlying role in causing or sustaining sexual dysfunctions in men (Barlow, 1986; Kaplan, 1974; Masters & Johnson, 1970; Strassberg, Mahoney, Schaugaard, & Hale, 1990). However, even when specific affective states have been related to dysfunctional sexual response, it often remains unclear whether these states are part of the original etiology of the dysfunction, or whether they represent a reaction to failed genital response that then serves to exacerbate the problem (Bancroft, 1989).

Psychophysiological laboratory studies have provided some insight into the role of affect in dysfunctional response in men. Compared with sexually functional groups, men with PE exhibit higher negative and lower positive affect in response to erotic stimulation (Rowland, Cooper, & Heiman, 1995; Rowland, Cooper, & Slob, 1996), although this pattern has not always been demonstrated consistently (Strassberg et al., 1990).

Recently we (Rowland, Tai, & Slob, 2003) attempted to identify ways in which men with PE differ from functional counterparts on specific positive and negative emotional dimensions, as well as to identify patterns of emotional responding that undergo change as the result of pharmacotherapy. Consistent with previous findings, PE men reported higher levels of negative emotions such as embarrassment/guilt, tense/worry, and anger/annoyed during baseline—prior to any psychosexual stimulation—than controls. Although specific negative affects diminished somewhat in PE men who responded positively to the ejaculatory-retarding effects of clomipramine, levels of both guilt/embarrassed and anger/annoyed were still elevated in comparison with controls.

Positive affect was also different between PE men and controls. Both at baseline and throughout the treatment phases, global positive affect was lower in PE men who did not experience beneficial effects from clomipramine than in either PE men who did or controls. Specific positive affects showed different patterns of variation. For example, arousal/sensual increased during erotic stimulation (relative to baseline), but decreased under clomipramine (relative to placebo). In contrast, pleasant/enjoyable decreased for PE "nonresponders" during erotic stimulation (relative to baseline) under clomipramine, whereas under these same conditions it increased for PE "responders." The decrease in arousal/sensual during erotic stimulation under clomipramine in these presumably "strongly aroused" PE men may help explain why pleasant/enjoyable increased in PE responders during treatment—attenuated arousal due to clomipramine might have been one of several factors that counteracted the dysfunctional response of rapid ejaculation. However, PE men who did not respond positively to clomipramine also showed a decrease in arousal/sensual during pharmacotherapy, indicating that the ejaculatory-inhibiting effects of clomipramine involve more than merely a blunting of sexual arousal.

The fact that successful pharmacotherapeutic treatment of rapid ejaculation imparts beneficial effects with respect to the overall enjoyment of sex suggests that the initial lower positive affect in PE men emanates from their dysfunctional response. Because positive affect increased spontaneously with successful treatment—perhaps due to a greater sense of efficacy and control over ejaculation—such emotions appear to be tied directly to the man's level of functionality. The greater the level of sexual functioning, the greater the positive affect. In contrast, the finding that two of three negative emotions continued at higher levels in PE men relative to functional counterparts, even among PE men who were benefiting from the pharmacotherapy, suggests that elevated negative affect may play a role in the etiology of dysfunctional response in PE men. Further study is needed to determine whether specific negative affects associated with sexual dysfunction might generally be resistant to the beneficial effects of drugs that delay ejaculation in PE men. It may be, for example, that particular negative affects are more dispositional than response related in PE men, an idea that has received some support from various psychometric analyses of men with this disorder (Cooper, Cernovsky, & Colussi, 1993; Tondo et al., 1991). Alternatively, had alleviation of the dysfunctional response been sustained through clomipramine treatment over a longer period of time, specific negative affects may have eventually decreased to levels comparable to controls. In either case, the implications of these findings are clear. PE men undergoing treatment with ejaculatory-retarding agents might well benefit from psychological intervention emphasizing open communication and relaxation with the partner to ease embarrassment and tension and to assist in overcoming negative dispositions associated with sexual contexts.

Detailed Analysis of Penile and Heart Rate Responses in PE Men

Assuming that rapidly induced high levels of arousal in PE men lead to their short ejaculatory latencies, we might then also expect PE men to show strong erectile responses and short latencies to maximum tumescence. Yet existing evidence does not support this expectation—the two psychophysiological studies investigating this possibility have found no differences between PE and control groups on various erectile parameters, including latency to maximum erection (Kockott et al., 1980; Strassberg et al., 1987). Perhaps the stimulus parameters in these studies were not adequate to reveal such differences, as they were limited to VSS or manual self-stimulation. In contrast, controlled penile VIB enables simulation of conditions leading to rapid ejaculation in PE men (Rowland et al., 1997, 2000), yet minimizes variation in erectile and ejaculatory response due to individual differences in penile stroke pressure, duration, and rate, as might occur with self-stimulation.

Perhaps somewhat counterintuitive, even though PE men ejaculate rapidly, there is reason to believe that they might actually exhibit weaker erectile responses compared with functional counterparts. As mentioned previously, men with PE report higher negative affect—a condition generally considered antierectile—in response to erotic stimuli than functional counterparts (Rowland, et al., 1996, 2003). In addition, in response to psychosexual stimulation, PE men report greater difficulty getting an erection and weaker overall erections than functional counterparts, despite greater self-reported proximity to ejaculation (Rowland et al., 2000). Such affective states and self-perceptions of erectile response might suggest disruption of the typical autonomic processes involved in erection and ejaculation in these men. Specifically, parasympathetic dominance early in the sexual response cycle is normally necessary to initiate and sustain erection, with later sympathetic dominance responsible in part for mediating ejaculation. In men with PE, this typical progression from parasympathetic to sympathetic control may be disrupted, such that sympathetic activation dominates earlier in the sexual response cycle (e.g., from anxiety or negative affect), which in turn could interfere with parasympathetically controlled erectile tumescence. At the same time, this sympathetic dominance may trigger ejaculation prematurely, perhaps even before the man reaches maximum sexual arousal. That is, even though PE men ejaculate rapidly following intromission and/or once coital or manual stimulation has begun, they might have greater difficulty and take longer to achieve an erection sufficient for intromission than functional counterparts. Although direct evidence supporting this hypothesis has yet to be garnered, circumstantial evidence is provided in a study by Ertekin, Colakoglu, and Altay (1995), who reported that during papaverine-induced erections, PE men showed less suppression of sympathetically mediated skin potentials than controls. Such findings suggest greater sympathetic activation than usual in PE men during the earlier phases of sexual response.

To determine whether the physiological response of PE men differs from that of sexually functional counterparts, we undertook a detailed minute-by-minute analysis of penile response and heart rate in groups of PE and functional men during visual sexual stimulation and penile vibrotactile stimulation. Interestingly, 4 of 25 PE men (16%) did not show any erectile response (< 5 mm increase) during one or more of these sessions (VSS or VSS + VIB), whereas only 1 of 13 (8%) of controls showed no response. Under VSS, PE men showed lower average penile response than controls (Figure 1). Under VSS + VIB (Figure 2), PE men who did not ejaculate during the session continued to show lower average penile response than controls. PE men ejaculating prior to or after 3 minutes during the session did not differ from controls in their average penile response (although sample sizes were small).

Patterns of heart rate appear to distinguish PE men even more clearly from functional counterparts (Figures 3 and 4). PE men exhibited higher heart rate throughout most of the VSS and VSS + VIB sessions. During VSS by itself, functional men showed a pattern of slightly decreasing heart rate as sexual arousal increased, whereas PE men showed an initial decrease followed by significant elevation (relative to controls) toward the end of the session. Differences between the groups were more pronounced when penile stimulation—the stimulus condition more likely to evoke the dysfunctional response—was introduced. Under VSS + VIB, functional men continued to exhibit a pattern of decreasing heart rate, just as they did under VSS alone. However, 3 PE men who ejaculated within the first 3 minutes of VSS + VIB showed immediate acceleration of heart rate. Nine PE men who ejaculated sometime after 3 minutes during the session showed an

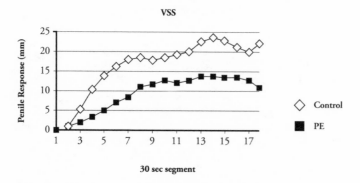

Figure 1. Penile circumference (mm change from baseline) during VSS for sexually functional controls (*n* =13) and PE men (*n* = 25).

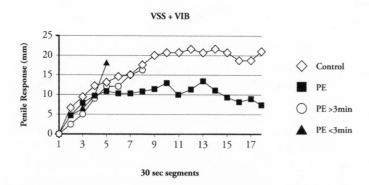

Figure 2. Penile circumference (mm change from baseline) during VSS + VIB for sexually functional controls (*n* = 13), PE men who did not ejaculate during the session (PE: *n* = 12), PE men who ejaculated within the first 3 minutes of the session (PE < 3 min: *n* = 4), and PE men who ejaculated after 3 minutes (PE > 3 min: *n* = 9).

initial deceleration followed by an increase. And 12 PE men who did not ejaculate showed gradually increasing heart rates. Indeed, rapidly rising heart rate appears to be a reliable precursor to ejaculation in PE men. Maximum heart rates, maximum heart rate change from baseline (positive or negative), and heart rates at the end of each man's recordings (this was variable, due to differing ejaculation times for these men) were all higher in PE men than controls.

Such patterns suggest that the physiological responses of PE men and controls may serve as distinguishing characteristics. Assuming both penile tumescence and heart rate adequately reflect sympathetic-parasympathetic control, these patterns suggest that sympathetic dominance may appear

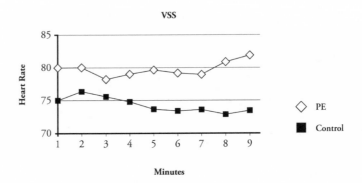

Figure 3. Heart rate during VSS for sexually functional controls (*n* = 13) and PE men (*n* = 25).

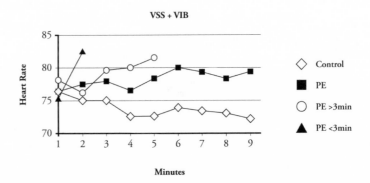

Figure 4. Heart rate during VSS + VIB for sexually functional controls (*n* = 13), PE men who did not ejaculate during the session (PE: *n* = 12), PE men who ejaculated within the first 3 minutes of the session (PE < 3 min: *n* = 4), and PE men who ejaculated after 3 minutes (PE > 3 min: *n* = 9).

earlier in the session in PE men than controls. Alternatively, erection in PE men may be under greater sympathetic influence than in functional counterparts, an idea consistent with recent data suggesting that psychogenic genital vasocongestion in women depends strongly on sympathetic innervation (Sipski, Alexander, & Rosen, 2001). In either case, because ejaculation is a sympathetically mediated reflex, such early or strong sympathetic dominance may partially explain the rapid ejaculation typical of PE men. These findings do not, however, clarify why sympathetic control might dominate earlier during psychosexual stimulation in PE men than controls. For example, might higher negative affect or some other psychobiological process shift control from the parasympathetic system, normally dominant during the erectile phase, to the sympathetic system, normally dominant during the ejaculatory phase? Or is the rapid sympathetic activation merely the manifestation of close proximity to ejaculation because of low ejaculatory thresholds?

Psychophysiology of Inhibited Ejaculation

To our knowledge, the sexual response of men with inhibited ejaculation has not been studied in the psychophysiological laboratory until recently. In a retrospective study using data from psychophysiological testing, we (Rowland, Keeney, & Slob, 2004) recently reported on the sexual response of men having retarded or inhibited ejaculation with no overt somatic etiology. We were interested in whether IE men show inhibited erectile response or self-reported sexual arousal to psychosexual stimulation relative to sexually functional men and other sexually dysfunctional groups studied in our psychophysiological laboratory. We also attempted to identify dyadic relationship variables that might explain variation in erectile response and self-reported sexual arousal in men with this dysfunction. The exploration of this latter group of variables (dyadic relationship factors) was predicated upon prior theorizing that such factors may play a key role in this dysfunction.

Perhaps the most notable finding of this study was the relevance of self-reported sexual arousal in differentiating IE men from the other groups. Specifically, during psychosexual stimulation in the lab, IE men showed low self-reported sexual arousal relative to other groups of sexually dysfunctional and functional men. This factor, more than actual erectile response, appeared to characterize men with this particular dysfunction. In fact, IE men had fairly robust erectile responses, comparable to PE men, suggesting that although their erectile response may have been adequate for achieving vaginal intromission, their level of subjective sexual arousal may not have been sufficient for the onset of the ejaculatory reflex. A similar pattern of adequate genital response in the absence of comparable subjective arousal has been described in women (Morokoff & Heiman, 1980).

Several dyadic relationship variables were correlated with self-reported arousal in IE men. Higher arousal value of the partner was significantly related to higher self-reported sexual arousal during psychosexual stimulation, whereas lower self-reported fear of sexual failure was related to higher sexual arousal. The fact that the few dyadic relationship variables investigated in this study could help explain variation in arousal among IE men reinforces the need to address potential dyadic interactions as part of an effective treatment strategy for this disorder. Procedures that reduce sexual anxiety and fear of failure through conflict resolution and trust building, that reduce inhibition of arousal resulting from the need to control the sexual encounter, or that increase partner communication and stimulation may serve to effectively increase subjective levels of sexual arousal in IE men.

Summary and Conclusions

The psychophysiological exploration of ejaculatory disorders both confirms and questions long-standing hypothetical assumptions about the causes and mechanisms of PE and IE. Through such analyses, a number of patterns have been uncovered:

- Rapid ejaculation in PE men occurs mainly in response to genital stimulation, not to erotic stimulation in general.
- The intensity of penile vibrotactile stimulation preferred by PE men is not different from that of sexually functional counterparts, as might have been anticipated.
- Self-reported sexual arousal is not greater in PE men than in sexually functional counterparts, suggesting that such men are not "hyper-aroused."
- PE men exhibit equally strong correlations between subjective arousal and penile response as controls, indicating either that they are adequately tuned to their levels of arousal or that this measure does not provide an adequate assessment of such attunement. The latter interpretation is made more likely by the fact that PE men, even though reporting closer proximity to ejaculation, do not report higher levels of sexual arousal than controls.
- PE men show lower positive affect to psychosexual stimulation than controls. Effective treatment of the disorder eliminates this difference, suggesting that low positive affect is primarily an outcome to the dysfunctional response rather than part of its cause.
- PE men are characterized by higher negative affect than controls, some of which does not diminish even with effective treatment. Negative affect may be more resistant to the beneficial effects of pharmacotherapy, supporting the idea that it may be more dispositional than situational in PE men.
- Penile response parameters in PE men may be weaker than in non-PE men. In addition, heart rate tends to accelerate in PE men, but decelerate in sexually functional controls during sexual stimulation in the lab. These differences suggest variation in autonomic control across groups during sexual arousal.
- Inhibited or retarded ejaculation may result from low arousal, as IE men show erectile responses comparable to PE men and, in some instances, controls. Relationship factors may play a mitigating role in levels of arousal in these men.

In conclusion, the psychophysiological model continues to afford heuristic value to the understanding of disorders of ejaculatory function in men. Despite the increasing availability of effective pharmacological agents for altering ejaculatory latencies, the causes of these disorders are yet largely unknown. Further delineation of the interaction between psychological and physiological covariates of ejaculatory dysfunction is likely to improve the application of integrated treatment approaches that take into consideration the psychological and dyadic relationship concerns that mediate and/or mitigate physiological response in men with PE or IE.

Note

The authors are grateful for the assistance of A. Koos Slob, Donald Strassberg, and Carlos deGouvea Brazao.

References

Ahlenius, S., Larsson, K., Svensson, L., Hjorth, S., & Carlsson, A. (1981). Effects of a new type of 5-HT receptor agonist on male rat sexual behavior. *Pharmacology, Biochemistry, & Behavior, 15*, 785–792.

American Psychiatric Association. (2000). *Diagnostic and statistical manual of mental disorders* (text revision). Washington, D.C.: Author.

Bancroft, J. (1989). *Human sexuality and its problems* (2nd ed.). Edinburgh: Churchill Livingstone.

Barlow, D. H. (1986). Causes of sexual dysfunctions: The role of anxiety and cognitive interference. *Journal of Consulting and Clinical Psychology, 54*, 140–148.

Buvat, J., Buvat-Herbaut, M., Lemaire, A., Marcolin, G., & Quittelier, E. (1990). Recent developments in the clinical assessment and diagnosis of erectile dysfunction. *Annual Review of Sex Research, 1*, 265–308.

Colpi, G. M., Fanciullacci, G., Beretta, G., Negri, L., & Zanollo, A. (1986). Evoked sacral potentials in subjects with true premature ejaculation. *Andrologia, 18*, 583–586.

Cooper, A. J., Cernovsky, Z. Z., & Colussi, K. (1993). Some clinical and psychometric characteristics of primary and secondary premature ejaculators. *Journal of Sex & Marital Therapy, 19*, 277–288.

Ertekin, C., Colakoglu, Z., & Altay, B. (1995). Hand and genital sympathetic skin potentials in flaccid and erectile penile states in normal potent men and patients with premature ejaculation. *Journal of Urology, 153*, 76–79.

Fanciullacci, F., Colpi, G. M., Beretta, G., & Zanollo, A. (1988). Cortical evoked potentials in subjects with true premature ejaculation. *Andrologia, 20*, 326–330.

Frank, E., Anderson, C., & Kupfer, S. J. (1976). Profiles of couples seeking sex therapy and marital therapy. *American Journal of Psychiatry, 133*, 559–562.

Geboes, K., Steeno, O., & DeMoor, P. (1975). Primary anejaculaton: Diagnosis and therapy. *Fertility and Sterility, 26*, 1018–1020.

Grenier, G., & Byers, S. (2001). Operationalizing premature or rapid ejaculation. *Journal of Sex Research, 38,* 369–378.

Haensel, S., Mos, J., Olivier, B., & Slob, A. K. (1991). Sex behavior of male and female Wistar rats affected by the serotonin agonist 8-OH-DPAT. *Pharmacology, Biochemistry, & Behavior, 40,* 221–228.

Kaplan, H. S. (1974). *The new sex therapy* (pp. 86–123). New York: Brunner/Mazel.

Kedia, K. (1983). Ejaculation and emission: Normal physiology, dysfunction, and therapy. In R. Krane, M. Siroky, & I. Goldstein (Eds.), *Male sexual dysfunction* (pp. 37–54). Boston: Little, Brown.

Kockott, G., Feil, W., Ferstl, R., Aldenhoff, J., & Besinger, U. (1980). Psychophysiological aspects of male sexual inadequacy: Results of an experimental study. *Archives of Sexual Behavior, 9,* 477–493.

LoPiccolo, J., & Stock, W. (1986). Treatment of sexual dysfunction. *Journal of Consulting and Clinical Psychology, 54,* 158–167.

Master, V. A., & Turek, P. J. (2001). Ejaculatory physiology and dysfunctions. *Urologic Clinics of North America, 28,* 363–375.

Masters, W. H., & Johnson, V. E. (1970). *Human sexual inadequacy* (pp. 116–136). Boston: Little, Brown.

McKenna, K. E. (1999). Central nervous system pathways in the control of penile erection. *Annual Review of Sex Research, 10,* 157–183.

Morokoff, P. J., & Heiman, J. R. (1980). Effects of erotic stimuli on sexually functional and dysfunctional women: Multiple measures before and after treatment therapy. *Behavioral Research and Therapy, 18,* 127–137.

Muntjack, D. J., & Kanno, P. H. (1979). Retarded ejaculation: A review. *Archives of Sexual Behavior, 8,* 138–151.

O'Donohue, W. T., & Geer, J. H. (1985). The habituation of sexual arousal. *Archives of Sexual Behavior, 14,* 233–246.

Over, R., & Koukounas, E. (1995). Habituation of sexual arousal: Product and process. *Annual Review of Sex Research, 6,* 187–223.

Perelman, M. A. (2001). Integrating sildenafil and sex therapy: Unconsummated marriage secondary to erectile dysfunction and retarded ejaculation. *Journal of Sex Education & Therapy, 26,* 1–11.

Rowland, D. L. (1999). Issues in the laboratory study of human sexual response: An overview for the non-technical sexologist. *Journal of Sex Research, 36,* 1–29.

Rowland, D. L. (2003). Treatment of premature ejaculation: Selecting outcomes to determine efficacy. *Bulletin of the International Society for Sexual and Impotence Research, 10,* 26–28.

Rowland, D. L., Cooper, S. E., & Heiman, J. R. (1995). A preliminary investigation of affective and cognitive response to erotic stimulation in men before and after sex therapy. *Journal of Sex and Marital Therapy, 21,* 3–20.

Rowland, D. L., Cooper, S. E., & Schneider, M. (2001). Defining premature ejaculation for experimental and clinical investigations. *Archives of Sexual Behavior, 30,* 235–253.

Rowland, D. L., Cooper, S. E., & Slob, A. K. (1996). Genital and psychoaffective response to erotic stimulation in sexually functional and dysfunctional men. *Journal of Abnormal Psychology, 105,* 194–203.

Rowland, D. L, deGouvea Brazao, C., Strassberg, D. A., & Slob, A. K. (2000). Ejaculatory latency and control in men with premature ejaculation: A detailed analysis across sexual activities using multiple sources of information. *Journal of Psychosomatic Research, 48,* 69–77.

Rowland, D. L., Haensel, S. M., Bloom, J. H. M., & Slob, A. K. (1993). Penile sensitivity in men with premature ejaculation and erectile dysfunction. *Journal of Sex & Marital Therapy, 19,* 189–197.

Rowland, D. L., Houtsmuller, E. J., Slob, A. K., & Cooper, S. E. (1997). The study of ejaculatory response in the psychophysiological laboratory. *Journal of Sex Research, 34,* 161–166.

Rowland, D. L., Keeney, C., Slob, A. K. (2004). Sexual response in men with inhibited or retarded ejaculation. *Journal of Sexual Medicine, 16,* 270–274.

Rowland, D. L., Tai, W., & Slob, A. K. (2003). An exploration of emotional response to erotic stimulation in men with premature ejaculation: Effects of treatment with clomipramine. *Archives of Sexual Behavior, 32,* 145–154.

Sipski, M. L., Alexander, C. J., & Rosen, R. (2001). Sexual arousal and orgasm in women: Effects of spinal cord injury. *Annals of Neurology, 49,* 35–44.

Spiess, W. F., Geer, J. H., & O'Donohue (1984). Premature ejaculation: Investigation of factors in ejaculatory latency. *Journal of Abnormal Psychology, 93,* 242–245.

Strassberg, D. S., Kelly, M. P., Carroll, C., & Kircher, J. C. (1987). The psychophysiological nature of premature ejaculation. *Archives of Sexual Behavior, 16,* 327–336.

Strassberg, D. S., Mahoney, J. M., Schaugaard, M., & Hale, V. E. (1990). The role of anxiety in premature ejaculation. *Archives of Sexual Behavior, 19,* 251–257.

Tondo, L., Cantone, M., Carta, M., Laddomada, A., Mosticoni, R., & Rudas, N. (1991). An MMPI evaluation of male sexual dysfunction. *Journal of Clinical Psychology, 47,* 391–396.

Vale, J. (1999). Ejaculatory dysfunction. *BJU International, 83,* 557–563.

Waldinger, M. D. (2002). The neurobiological approach to premature ejaculation. *Journal of Urology, 168,* 2359–2367.

Witt, M. A., & Grantmyre, J. E. (1993). Ejaculatory failure. *World Journal of Urology, 11,* 89–95.

Xin, Z., Chung, W., Choi, Y., Seong, D., & Choi, H. (1996). Penile sensitivity in patients with primary premature ejaculation. *Journal of Urology, 156,* 979–981.

Discussion Paper

DONALD S. STRASSBERG

When David and I were talking last night, he suggested that I could limit my comments to simply saying, "This work represents the gold standard in the area, we really don't need much, if any, discussion." As much as I'd like to do that . . . Much of the data that David talks about in his full paper comes from work that he's done with Koos Slob and work that the three of us have done together. And you know, after a good deal of research in this area, both by others and by us, there really still are a great many unanswered questions concerning premature ejaculation. In particular, there have been a number of theories offered over the years as to the etiology of this condition. Masters and Johnson early on argued that premature ejaculation was the result of early sexual experiences in which there was a value in the male coming quickly in order to avoid detection, such as the couple making love downstairs while parents were asleep upstairs or having sex in the backseat of a car. It always seemed to me that if this were a major etiological factor in premature ejaculation, virtually every guy would be a premature ejaculator simply because relatively few guys in their early partner-related sexual experiences have the luxury of all the time in the world. For example, few 16-year-olds are able to take their girlfriends away for lazy weekends of lovemaking. So, the Masters and Johnson explanation never was very persuasive for me.

Some years ago, I spent a year as a postdoctoral Fellow with Helen Kaplan. Helen believed that premature ejaculation was the result of anxiety—anxiety that interferes with the man's ability to recognize how close to orgasm he really is and as a result prevents him from instituting the normal kind of slowdown mechanisms that most men are able to employ in order to prolong stimulation without reaching orgasm. But if you've had a chance clinically to talk to a lot of men with premature ejaculation, what you find, especially with the more extreme cases, is that their orgasm occurs within seconds after penetration, or even at the point of intromission. It's hard to imagine that such a low threshold represents an inability to recognize (i) how close to orgasm one is, or (ii) the need to institute some kind of stimulus-reducing technique. Also, some of the work that others and I have done indicates that premature ejaculators are no better or worse than nonpremature ejaculators in assessing their level of arousal. So,

Kaplan's hypothesis, while interesting, doesn't seem to fit either the data or clinical experience.

All of the above, as David pointed out, has allowed us to rule out a number of hypothesized etiologies for premature ejaculation, but we have yet to arrive at an agreed-upon explanation for the disorder. In anticipation of my presentation tomorrow, I'd like to share my belief about this sexual dysfunction. I've long argued that premature ejaculation, for most men with the disorder, simply represents a physiologically based low threshold for a reflex. For most human reflexes, such as the gag or patella reflex, we find a distribution of sensitivities. That is, our thresholds for the triggering of that reflex vary, forming something like a normal distribution. Why not assume that the amount of physical stimulation required in order to trigger orgasm, that is the orgasmic threshold, is also normally distributed, or at least distributed? That is, a range of thresholds exists. Men who fall on the low end of the distribution, the men who reach orgasm in less than a minute or 2, we call premature ejaculators. Men who take 10–15 minutes or longer and still may not reach orgasm regularly are the ones we've defined as having delayed or inhibited orgasm. While this is a fairly simplistic model, it's one that, as well as, if not better than any other, fits the data that we have available to us, including the data that David described.

David's data on affect is very interesting. He found that when you help premature ejaculators to last longer (via clomipramine), their anxiety seems to quickly reduce. This is consistent with the model that Erick and John have been talking about and some of my own data. Some years ago, I showed that anxiety in general (that is, trait anxiety) did not distinguish premature ejaculators from nonpremature ejaculators; they are not *generally* more anxious folks. However, at the moment they are anticipating being sexual, their state anxiety may very well be higher than that of nonpremature ejaculators. When you effectively treat their prematurity (as we did in the study David described), this state anxiety appears to reduce rather quickly. However, David's data also suggests that other negative affect, depression, didn't seem to go away, or at least not as much, even after successful control of the rapid ejaculation. Unlike David, I don't believe that this means that depression (or something like it) is etiologically critical in rapid ejaculation. Rather, I think it likely that the unhappiness and self-esteem implications of lifelong premature ejaculation may take longer than a few days or even weeks to dissipate. Give these guys 6 months of having better control and you'd probably find that the negative affect (i.e., depression) would go away, as did the anxiety. The data reported by David may simply have been too short term to evidence the reduction in depression. I could, of course, be wrong about this.

I don't quite know what to make of the heart rate differences David reported. I like one of the ideas that David offered at the end of his paper: that the heart rates of some of these premature ejaculators may go up and stay up simply because of how quickly they are approaching and reaching orgasm. That is, the entire sexual response cycle, from arousal through orgasm, is so brief for these men that there's virtually no time for their heart rate to go down. As soon as the sexual stimulation starts, the autonomic nervous system quickly kicks in; everything (heart rate, blood pressure, galvanic skin response) is right up there until only a minute or 2 later when they've reached orgasm. There may simply not be sufficient time for any of these indices to go down, at least for some of these men (i.e., those with the shortest latencies).

In summary, I think that the kind of work that David described is terribly important because only through work that looks at both a variety of physiological indices as well as self-reports will we be able to fully understand a psychophysiological phenomenon such as premature ejaculation. I hope it's not the case that, as with erectile dysfunction, now that we have such effective medical treatments for rapid ejaculation, we pay less attention to learning its etiology or to continuing to evaluate nonmedical approaches to treatment.

Premature ejaculation is, by far, the most common male sexual dysfunction, yet it has received far less research attention than some less common sexual problems. The kind of empirical and theoretical work described by David is critical to our ultimate understanding of this prevalent disorder.

General Discussion

John Bancroft: David Rowland raised the question of the erectile responsiveness of men with premature ejaculation (PE). We now have fairly large nonclinical samples of men where we've used our Sexual Inhibition Scales/Sexual Excitation Scales (SIS/SES) questionnaire, and asked them whether they have problems with erections and whether they have problems with rapid ejaculation. The men complaining of problems with rapid ejaculation do not have raised SIS1 or SIS2 scores. In contrast, men who report problems with erection have clearly raised SIS1 scores (and to some extent raised SIS2). In the clinical context, of course, we do see, not infrequently, men who've had long-standing PE who subsequently develop erectile problems. Clearly there's an overlap and a man could be susceptible to both PE and erectile problems, but our nonclinical data would suggest that the underlying mechanisms for the two types of problem are fundamentally different. Your recent study of men with PE, 28 men I think—it would be good to have some measures that would allow comparability across such studies, as I suggested in my discussion of the first session. It's possible, for example, that your PE men in that study may have scored relatively high on SIS1, which would be reflected in the difference in erectile responsiveness that you observed. Another sample of PE men might differ, with normal SIS1 scores.

I wanted to comment on Serge's reaction to our paper, which I found absolutely fascinating. I think it was an excellent example of research feeding research—the idea that we should be getting ideas for questions in questionnaires from brain imaging studies. Erick and I have been struggling with some conceptual issues around the SIS/SES in the last few months, some situations where it works and others where it doesn't seem to work. We're probably getting to the point of considering version 2 of this assessment instrument, in which we may have some additional or different questions.

Serge also talked about tumescence and rigidity as possibly being differentially controlled. I'm not sure about that, but I will comment on some research that I've been involved in. For a number of years we did a series of studies on hypogonadal men, comparing them when they were on and when they were not on testosterone replacement (for review, see Bancroft,

2003). And for quite a long time we found no difference in the erectile response to visual erotic stimuli in the hypogonadal and the eugonadal state, and that was using maximum penile circumference increase as the measure of response. And then somewhat later, when I was working with Cesare Carani in Italy, the Rigiscan was available, so we also measured rigidity and, in addition, the duration of the response (Carani, Granata, Bancroft, & Marrama, 1995). Once again, we didn't find any difference in terms of maximum circumference, but we did find that with testosterone replacement, rigidity was higher. Also the duration of the response was longer with T replacement, and this was mainly due to a continuation of the response beyond the duration of the stimulus. These findings were consistent with the idea that testosterone was enhancing the central arousability of these men. They weren't just responding to a stimulus on and then a stimulus off, but they were getting aroused in a way that persisted longer than the stimulus presentation. So to some extent this was consistent with what you were saying; for some time we have postulated that there is a testosterone-dependent and a testosterone-independent system involved in sexual response. The testosterone component is mainly associated with central arousal; the nontestosterone component probably involves the more minimal erectile responses that you were suggesting we should use a volumetric measure to detect.

Kevin McKenna: I have a couple of comments. I thought both papers were fascinating. The idea that premature ejaculation is simply the tail of the distribution is an interesting one, but that really requires that we actually know what that distribution looks like. Using a standardized stimulus, where do men fall? I have a little bit of a problem with the intravaginal ejaculation latency, because it's a question of doing *what* intravaginally and after doing what and so on. There's a lot of variability there and with a defined stimulus, what is the range? That information just doesn't seem to exist.

David Rowland: I know of at least one study that did this with a fairly sizeable sample. It was, I believe, a Japanese or Korean study and the latency was actually quite low, 2 or 3 minutes was the average for that particular sample. I don't know if this short latency represents a cultural phenomenon or if this can be considered a more universal standard. I have periodically looked at all of the control subjects that we have run through our laboratory—about 70 or 80 men—and calculated medians and ranges of ejaculatory latencies for this group. I have used these statistics as a reference for my own understanding of latencies in functional controls; typically we find a range of about 2–10 minutes and a median of about 6. These are self-estimations of ejaculatory latencies, so if you believe in stopwatch measures, then you're not going to find these data very satisfactory.

Don Strassberg: One very relevant but complicated question is just how long the man is actually lasting during intercourse. While the answer a man gives regarding how long he lasts is obviously relevant information, it's often a very imperfect piece of information. If you've ever done any clinical work, just ask the husband and the wife how often they have sex or how long he lasts in intercourse and you'll find how variable their estimates can be. This relates to why it's been so difficult to define the disorder both in research and clinical work. Some have said we should use the time from penetration to orgasm as our index. However, if you're not thrusting very quickly, how long you last is maybe irrelevant. So, others have argued that number of thrusts should be the criteria, but some people can get in 20 thrusts in the same time it takes someone else to get in 5, so this too is an imperfect index. Finally, some have argued that the degree of perceived control over the occurrence of the orgasm should be the basis for making the diagnosis. While this seems reasonable, it creates its own problem because you'll find lots of nonpremature ejaculators telling you that they experience relatively little control, basically saying that, yes, I may last longer than some other guys, but I still don't feel like I can last long enough.

Kevin McKenna: That's why I thought it might be useful to study this in the laboratory with a range of men, using standardized stimuli.

Don Strassberg: Well, what we need is a kind of device that we don't really have, something that could provide a measured level of stimulation that would result in most men reaching orgasm, although the device that Koos developed comes close, at least with premature ejaculators. As David said, with Koos's vibrator and the explicit film, about 60% of our PEs reached orgasm, but less than 5% of the normal men did. I've brought men into the lab and had them masturbate and, without their knowing it, timed them. Very interestingly, the premature ejaculators reached orgasm substantially more quickly than the nonpremature ejaculators, which for me got around a lot of these dyadic explanations for the condition, like that these guys are really passive-aggressive, for example. And the time that they reached orgasm in masturbation seemed to be reasonably close to the times that David was describing, at least for our normal guys. That is, a range from about 3–10 with about 6 minutes being average. Now again that's masturbation, that's not intercourse, but it is laboratory determined and not just self-report.

Jim Pfaus: That's interesting, because you're getting people who are already set in their ways. To some extent, we all have expectations of what normal behavior is. If normal for one person is abnormal to another or to society, then their expectancy probably gives rise to some degree of anxiety. In that regard, it is interesting to find an individual who ejaculates prematurely during sexual intercourse and also does so in the lab by his own hand. I think expectancy exists in habitual patterns of sexual behavior. I think hormones and arousal set the stage, but experience and expectancy determine the characters, if you will. It is nice to take snapshots of these individuals when they come for therapy, or after the intervention is over, but to really understand how the process gets set into a habitual pattern, we need to understand their early sexual experiences. Unfortunately, I don't know how to study adolescent sexuality in a meaningful way that ethical review boards will allow.

Ray Rosen: Those were very interesting and thought-provoking papers. I think the bulk of the evidence supports Don's point of view, although I have difficulty with the small group of men who ejaculate before intromission. These men are so far to one side of the continuum that it's tempting to believe in a pathological mechanism. Aside from the men in that group, overall I think the data does support what Don is suggesting.

Regarding the heart rate data that David presented, it could be interpreted in several ways. For example, it could be increased heart rate due to the growing apprehension that they're about to climax (and lose control). Increased heart rate and sympathetic activation could be interpreted in several ways. It's not consistent, for example, with the pharmacologic data, where we know that selective serotonin reuptake inhibitors (SSRIs) are very effective drugs for premature ejaculation and yet have little effect on sympathetic arousal. If sympathetic arousal was the key, beta blockers would be an effective treatment for premature ejaculation, although beta blockers and other sympatholytics, to my knowledge, don't have much effect.

David Rowland: Pharmacologically it may not, but empirically it, in fact, does, because when we give clomipramine and measure the heart rate of PE men whose ejaculation latency was extended because of the clomipramine, they show a pattern of decreasing heart rate similar to controls, with the exception of a small subsample that continues to ejaculate to the visual sexual stimulation (VSS) plus vibrotactile stimulation. Whether that's a pharmacological effect or some other effect, I don't know. The point is that under clomipramine, the pattern in PE men begins to coincide with what you see in functional men.

Don Strassberg: No, they may be just closer to orgasm and if the heart rate is a measure of how close they are.

David Rowland: This is the point that I made previously. I didn't interpret the elevated heart rate as necessarily being either the cause or the effect of the PE; that's what I don't know.

Marca Sipski: Well, I guess one comment I would make is that, as I put this all together, I see this all in a very different way. You made the comment that erection is thought of as parasympathetic, but if we look at studies of spinal cord injured men, some of those men, who do not have parasympathetic nerves intact, still have erections. So there's some sympathetic component to erection. So as I look at this, the way I interpret it, and I'm not a psychologist and I'm looking from a very different set of eyes, what I see in it potentially is that the sympathetic nervous system has some regulatory effect on sexual arousal and perhaps the men that are premature ejaculators tend to have a higher level of sympathetic response as they go into erection. And then if you take Kevin's theory of the reflex responsiveness and how the orgasm occurs or climax occurs, maybe that higher level of tone there is bringing them to orgasm more quickly than others. It's just a different viewpoint.

Kim Payne: I wonder whether genital sensory testing could help clarify some of this situation because we mentioned maybe there's simply a difference in their threshold or the amount of physical stimulation required to trigger this reflex. Or, perhaps it's that the same physical stimuli are perceived very differently in these men.

David Rowland: That has been done with mixed results. My data show no difference in vibrotactile thresholds between premature ejaculators and controls. Others have reported differences, and that's been a source of anxiety for me because I like to think my data are consistent with what others are finding. But I did recently talk with John Mulhal, who has used vibrotactile sensitivity on hundreds of PE men in his practice. He has never seen increased sensitivity in this group, so that comment made me more confident about these findings. But let me add, even if there were a difference between PE men and controls, I don't know whether penile surface receptors—the ones assessed in these kinds of procedures—are really relevant to the ejaculatory process.

Roy Levin: We talked about the problem of vibrotactile sensitivity because it doesn't match up, does it, when you look at the things like hypogonadal men with vibrotactile stimulation—it's they're more sensitive than people with testosterone. It doesn't seem to be right, that that sort of thing goes along and I'm really suspect about vibrotactile sensitivity as a measure of the sensitivity of the penis because when you're erect you get less vibrotactile sensitivity than when you're flaccid.

David Rowland: That may be, and if you used a different kind of stimulus it might be different. But from what others and I have found, it's pretty clear that sensitivity decreases with erection. There are some other anomalies as well, for example with hypogonadal conditions there is an increase in sensitivity. I've also heard—but I've never found this report—that postmenopausal women who lack estrogen sometimes complain about clitoral hypersensitivity, and so there may be some consistency there. Also, I don't know what it would be about vibrotactile sensitivity that would make it so anomalous.

Roy Levin: The thing that always interested me is the free nerve endings in the penis. I mean, it's always thought of as pain, but I guarantee you that it's not pain that the free nerve endings are picking up on, and that probably isn't sensitive to vibrotactile sensitivity, and they're probably the ones that give us the great thing when we push it into the vagina.

David Rowland: Well it's an empirical question, and all it takes is some Von Frey hairs, some penises, and some time.

Kevin McKenna: I actually have some questions for Erick. I thought your talk was very interesting and it raised a million issues there. You talked about the possibility of genetic components to excitation and inhibition proneness and so on. But there was an implication in one of the slides of an age effect. In your horny students, you get a very different response than in other people and that seems to be, again, one of these selection bias things. You might get different results if you study students who are young versus these other people. The other question I wondered about was when you were looking at risky behavior and you looked for people from bathhouses and so on, did you separate out the amount of recent sexual activity? I mean, these guys are getting a lot of sex and maybe your students aren't. So you start showing them dirty movies, and they're responding off the chart. So how do you control for that kind of issue?

Erick Janssen: Those are excellent points. Age definitely plays a role. But even if, in general, you find a negative effect of age on sexual responsiveness, differences between individuals probably exist that themselves could be relatively stable. To paraphrase a cliché, the best predictor of current sexual responsiveness may be past responsiveness. With respect to genetics, we definitely are open to the possibility that learning processes could influence the sensitivities of our putative inhibitory and excitatory systems—it would be strange if there was no room for that. I would love to hear John's opinion on that as well. When it comes to responsiveness, and comparing student and other samples, we are still looking at those data and examining the effects of sexual experience, sexual activity, and so on. We are intrigued by these issues and are using a questionnaire, which we did not discuss in our chapter, in which we ask men questions about how easily they can become turned on by the same type of stimulus, whether their preference for a certain type of sexual stimulus is stable or changes over time, how strong their need is for novel stimuli in order to become and stay aroused, and so on. Those questions were partly based on our interest in exploring the use of the Internet for sexual purposes. We're intrigued by the fact that so many websites seem to target very specific groups of people, or very specific preferences. You cannot think of a website or it seems to exist and we are trying to figure out what that means. In our postexperimental interviews, we have heard a lot of men who did not respond to the films say "this simply doesn't do it for me." From several of our gay subjects we would hear that they can only get aroused from very specific stimuli (for example, "bears," or hairy men) and I don't think we understand much about how that works. The Internet is right there, in our face, telling us that there is so much more variability than we perhaps realized. Some people seem to respond to anything. Some may respond only to very specific stimuli (women who smoke, hairy men). Some respond to only a very specific type of stimulus, but have a higher need for novelty within their preferred stimulus category. We know very little about what we sometimes like to call "the new fetishes." How they come about, or develop, and how, and when, they might fade out again.

John Bancroft: This issue of specificity versus novelty is, in my opinion, one of the big unresearched issues in the field of sexuality and indeed maybe in psychology. As yet, I haven't been able to find any relevant paradigm in psychology that enables us to get at this issue. I have come across people who throughout their lives have required very specific types of sexual stimuli in order to be aroused, whereas many other people require novelty. What is the difference between those two types of people? I don't begin to understand, and I think this is a question that needs to be researched.

Jim Geer: One observation goes data way back to 1976 and raises an interesting question. When we were working with the vaginal probe, we had women masturbate to orgasm, and it turned out that, I don't remember the exact data, but over 60% reached orgasm within 2 and a half minutes. Are they premature to orgasm? I just want to raise that question. I don't have an answer. The other question that I would ask is that one of the things that I find complicated about sex is that people experience both positive and negative affect about sex. Can you tell me or do you have any feelings about what is the overlap between that observation and excitation and inhibition processes?

Erick Janssen: I think there still is a lot of work to do when it comes to the relationship between sexual arousal and positive and negative affect. I found David's findings about decreased positive affect in his premature ejaculation sample very interesting. And Marcus, in one of your studies, it also mainly was positive, not negative, affect that turned out to be related to subjective sexual arousal, if I am not mistaken. At least in men. I don't know exactly what to make of that, but that is one thought I had. When it comes to inhibition, excitation, and mood, as I suggested earlier, it may depend on what it is we are talking about, subjective sexual arousal or genital response? When it comes to mood and genital response, we have been exploring that in questionnaires and we discussed some of that in our chapter. We will be looking in more depth at the relationship between mood, genital as well as subjective sexual arousal, and our measures of sexual inhibition and excitation in a series of experimental studies. This definitely is another topic we could talk about more. A lot more. Do you have specific ideas about this?

Jim Geer: I don't know; I don't have any specific ideas about it, but it's always struck me as important. I recall asking undergraduates, when you walk into a room crowded with people and you see an attractive person and you both find you're attracted, why don't you immediately have sex? And the answer was not an inhibitory process, rather the answer dealt with morals. "I would be wrong to do that." I'm wondering, how much are morals just an epiphenomenon, reacting to inhibitory processes? Or are morals just a label for an inhibitory process? I have no idea.

Michael Seto: That question is very interesting to me because it made me think of research that some people have been doing for the last little while. They're interested in the relationship between mood and sexual offending and, for what it's worth because this is based on offender report, they asked men who were in clinical settings about their moods prior to their sexual offenses and distinguished between two subgroups. One group was honest and admitted that their sexual offenses were associated with positive affect; they were feeling good at the time they committed their offenses. In the case of pedophiles, they find children attractive; they want to have sex with children and they did it. Another group claimed that their sexual behavior was motivated by negative affect, that they were feeling down, or they were feeling anxious because they might be losing their job or they had an argument with their wife or something like that, and that was what led them down this sequence of events to sexual offending. I wonder if that kind of dual-pathway model might be useful in thinking about normal sexual behavior as well.

John Bancroft: We just published two papers in the *Archives of Sexual Behavior* on straight and gay men, looking at the relationship between mood and sexuality (Bancroft, Janssen, Strong, & Vukadinovic, 2003; Bancroft, Janssen, Strong, Vukadinovic, & Long, 2003). For those particular samples, Michael, we didn't have any particular reason to disbelieve them. But this is another crucial source of individual variability and there was a substantial minority of men, both straight and gay, who described being more involved sexually when they are in a negative mood state. And at least in straight men, we accounted for something like 19% of the variance, not a huge amount, using our SIS/SES questionnaire.

David Rowland: Just briefly, we often refer to negative and positive affect, or mood, and one thing we have found is that talking about these affects in global terms is okay, but—and I think that this is the point that you made before, Marcus—you really have to look at the components of these global affects. That is, you see a lot of variation in certain kinds of negative affects that are associated with sexual situations. Ones we have seen variation in have been ones related to embarrassed/guilt, anger/annoyed, and worry/tense. But when you look at some of the other specific negative affects—sadness or pain, for example—you get zero variance. When you look at some of the positive affects you find the same pattern. Some positive affects vary a lot with sexual arousal or sexual situations, while others don't vary at all. My point is that it is important to analyze global positive and negative affects into their components. I'm not saying that we have been highly successful at this, but this might be worth considering as you look at excitation and inhibition processes in the model.

Roy Levin: Can I just come back—one interesting thing is why a fantasy keeps working for a certain period of time and gets you aroused, then all of a sudden that fantasy doesn't arouse you anymore and in terms of novel things and things like that. I never understand why a fantasy goes on fine and then all of a sudden you find it's not arousing and you need a new one.

Julia Heiman: That's not true if you have very specific sexual interests.

Roy Levin: No, I was just saying that he was interested in the sort of saying why did you need novel stimuli. That would be an interesting area to us.

Don Strassberg: I'm not sure if it even necessarily relates to negative affect and dyadic sex, but I know clinically the men that I've worked with over the years who come in with what I'll call "compulsive masturbation"— I've never had a female come in with that complaint—that in most of these cases it turns out to be actually a way of dealing with dysphoric mood. Anxious or depressed, they simply find that the orgasm from masturbating helps them to simply feel better. Again, I don't know if that dynamic or how often that dynamic operates in dyadic sex, but I suspect it does.

John Bancroft: In a group of self-defined "sex addicts" we have recently studied (Bancroft & Vukadinovic, 2004), increased sexuality in both depression and anxiety were extremely relevant to these "out of control" patterns of behavior. In our larger nonclinical samples, we found this effect for anxiety to be most likely manifested as increased masturbation. In contrast, those who report the sexual increase in relation to depression are more likely to go out and seek a partner; so in a sense that is dyadic (Bancroft, Janssen, Strong, & Vukadinovic, 2003; Bancroft, Janssen, Strong, Vukadinovic, & Long, 2003).

Julia Heiman: These talks have been very much about male sexuality; these last two, really focused on men. You're working on those scales I presume, for women?

Erick Janssen: Yes, we have collected data in women using a modified version of the SIS/SES questionnaire, which was originally developed for men. Stephanie, would you like to elaborate on this?

Stephanie Sanders: Cindy Graham and I have done a study with focus groups of women looking at factors that would lead to excitation or inhibition of arousal. We came up with some categories that we think weren't addressed very well on the questionnaire that was developed for men and then modified for women. We just have our data in from over 600 women on the initial items and just from quickly looking at it, women put a lot more emphasis on relationship issues than men seem to—at least that's the preliminary finding. There are some interesting age differences as well. We saw that even with the qualitative data, older women tended to have a little more sense of what it took to get themselves aroused, while younger women often focused on partner variables and how arousing that was to them.

Erick Janssen: Just an observation. It often comes up when we discuss the development of the SIS/SES questionnaire at the institute and it involves, as I see it, the culture of science. Or the influence of gender, and that would include our more or less implicit assumptions about gender, in science. We sat down together and developed this measure for men because we, of course, understood men. So we, the experts, did not need qualitative research or conversations with men about what might turn them on or off. That involved a bit of sarcasm, in case you missed it, because I do not think we understand men that well at all. But when Stephanie and Cindy decided to work toward a new questionnaire for women, the first thing they decided to do was to talk with women about what might be potentially relevant stimuli, and I think that is very interesting—how we went about doing this and what we potentially may have missed in the male questionnaire due to our approach and our preconceptions about men.

Julia Heiman: I brought up the issue of women to really reinforce the suggestion that Serge made with regard to his work. Walter, I wonder if you care to make a comment with regards to this very conscious cognitive measure (the SIS/SES) and how it might be included in a study that you were doing on more implicit measures and whether you would combine these measures in any way.

Walter Everaerd: From my point of view, what people report is what they are conscious about, what is accessible to them, and there are lots of things that are not accessible. So we try to do both things at the same time. And the difficult thing is that we have no notion at this moment of what exactly is the relationship between what you get when you ask people about their experience and what happens, because the ideas, the conceptual idea that an emotion is a very general reaction of our system and that what becomes conscious is only a very small part of it, so it's very difficult to get a good relationship between the two things.

Julia Heiman: It's an interesting and important problem.

Walter Everaerd: I think in physiology it's a common idea that most things that happen to us, occur in our system, we are not conscious of. And that's also true for emotions, of course. The thing we have done up to now is using the accessibility, what we know about what's happening, and I think that that's a disadvantage of many psychological approaches that go for that part of our functioning. And it's only a very small part, of course, so it will not explain too many things, I guess.

References

Bancroft, J. (2003). Androgens and sexual function in men and women. In W. Bremner & C. Bagatell (Eds.), *Androgens in health and disease* (pp. 259–290). Totowa, N.J.: Humana Press.

Bancroft, J., Janssen, E., Strong, D., & Vukadinovic, Z. (2003). The relation between mood and sexuality in gay men. *Archives of Sexual Behavior, 32,* 231–242.

Bancroft, J., Janssen, E., Strong, D., Vukadinovic, Z., & Long, J. S. (2003). The relation between mood and sexuality in heterosexual men. *Archives of Sexual Behavior, 32,* 217–230.

Bancroft, J., & Vukadinovic, Z. (2004). Sexual addiction, sexual compulsivity, sexual impulse disorder or what? Towards a theoretical model. *Journal of Sex Research,* 41, 225–234.

Carani, C., Granata, A. R. M., Bancroft, J., & Marrama, P. (1995). The effects of testosterone replacement on nocturnal penile tumescence and rigidity and erectile response to visual erotic stimuli in hypogonadal men. *Psychoneuroendocrinology, 20*(7), 743–753.

Part 3.

Learning Processes, Subjective
Experience, and Genital Response

The Role of Classical Conditioning in Sexual Arousal

HEATHER HOFFMANN

Conditioning models hold intuitive appeal for explaining the etiology of atypical sexual arousal. The majority of treatments for sexual disorders are based on such models (Plaud & Martini, 1999), and numerous case studies attest to the effectiveness of behavior or response modification techniques in dealing with paraphilias (Gaither, Rosenkranz, & Plaud, 1998). It is also a common theoretical assumption that learning plays an important role in the development of normative sexual arousal patterns (e.g., Ågmo, 1999; Hardy, 1964; McConaghy, 1987; Pfaus, Kippin, & Centeno, 2001; Roche & Barnes, 1998; Woodson, 2002). Yet there are limited laboratory data, at least in humans, showing the effects of learning on sexual arousal, and precisely how conditioning processes affect what we find erotic remains unclear.

Classical conditioning would appear to most directly contribute to how stimuli acquire sexually arousing properties; however, operant conditioning is probably also involved. Classical (a.k.a. Pavlovian or respondent) conditioning consists of learning about the relationship between an initially "ineffective" cue (the CS) and a behaviorally significant stimulus (the US) and typically results in a conditioned emotional or motivational state (the CR). Operant (a.k.a. Skinnerian or instrumental) conditioning typically creates changes in the frequency of (goal-directed) behavior (R) resulting from its association with reinforcing or punishing consequences (S^R). Pavlovian and instrumental conditioning can be distinguished at a conceptual and procedural level, but in practice it has been difficult to separate their effects (Schwartz, 1989). For example, it was once thought that the different types of conditioning were applicable to different classes of behavior (i.e., classical to autonomic responses and operant to skeletal ones). However, operant procedures have been shown to affect reflexive behavior and voluntary responding can be classically conditioned. Procedures exist for separating the roles of classical and operant contingencies in the control of behavior, and a recent study suggests a mechanistic distinction at the cellular level (Lorenzetti, Mozzachiodi, Baxter, & Byrne, 2006), but the interactions between these types of conditioning are complex and both processes appear to simultaneously affect any given learning situation. For example, in sexual learning situations, stimuli that have acquired arousing properties through Pavlovian procedures can also contribute to the approach of those stimuli. Such an explanation has been used to describe the development of paraphilias (Junginger, 1997; McGuire, Carlisle, & Young, 1965). An accidental pairing of a neutral object (CS) with arousal or orgasm (US) gives the stimulus erotic value. Sexual arousal to the object (CR) elicits approach and/or masturbation (R) that is positively reinforced by an increase in sexual arousal and orgasm (S^R). The majority of both animal and human studies aimed at examining the role of learning in sexual arousal have employed Pavlovian procedures.

The Laboratory Evidence

Nonhumans

Pfaus, Kippin, and Centeno (2001) and Akins (2004) provide the most recent review of the influence of learning on sexual and reproductive behaviors in a variety of species, including humans. They concluded that classical and operant conditioning produce both temporary and lasting changes in appetitive, precopulatory, and consummatory sexual behavior. Although Sachs and Garinello (1978) found conditioned decreases in the time to display penile erection in rats, sexual arousal in nonhumans is usually measured indirectly through changes in latencies to engage in other sexual behaviors. For example, Domjan and colleagues found conditioned approach, conditioned courtship, and conditioned copulatory behaviors in male quail in the presence of CSs (e.g., colored lights, orange feathers, bird models, and contextual cues) that were previously paired with either visual exposure to a female or the opportunity to copulate with a female (for review, see Domjan & Holloway, 1998). In male rats, Zamble, Hadad, Mitchell, and Cutmore (1985) found conditioned decreases in ejaculatory latency in the presence of a CS (plastic tub) that had previously been paired with exposure to a female without consummation. Kippin, Talianakis, and Pfaus (1997) found conditioned ejaculatory preference to females scented with an odor that was previously associated with the ability to copulate. Studies on conditioning of female sexual arousal are less common. Gutiérrez and Domjan (1997) found increases in squatting behavior (an index of sexual receptivity) in female quail following the paired presentation of a particular compartment (CS) and copulatory opportunity. Coria-Avila, Ouimet, Pachero, Manzo, and Pfaus (2005) showed a conditioned partner preference in female rats for males scented with an odor that had been paired with the ability to pace copulation, which is rewarding for female rats (Paredes & Alonso, 1997).

Humans

O'Donohue and Plaud (1994) and Akins (2004) have provided the most recent reviews of the conditioning of human sexual arousal. O'Donohue and Plaud concluded that while there is some evidence for classically conditioned sexual arousal in men as measured by changes in penile circumference or volume (e.g., Kantorowitz, 1978; Langevin & Martin, 1975; Rachman, 1966; Rachman & Hodgson, 1968), interpretation of the results is complicated by methodological problems. They reported no studies showing that conditioning can affect sexual arousal in women. Since the O'Donohue and Plaud review was published, two well-controlled studies using nonclinical samples have shown convincing evidence for respondent conditioning of male sexual arousal. Lalumière and Quinsey (1998) found enhanced genital responding to slides of partially nude females after they had been paired with sexually explicit videotapes of heterosexual interactions, and Plaud and Martini (1999) found increases in penile circumference to a penny jar after it was paired with slides of nude or partially nude females. Letourneau and O'Donohue (1997) examined the role of classical conditioning in women's sexual responses, but they failed to show conditioned genital or subjective responses to a CS (an amber light) that had been repeatedly paired with an erotic film. In contrast, Hoffmann, Janssen, and Turner (2004) found conditioned genital arousal in women. Procedural differences may account for the discrepancy. Like Letourneau and O'Donohue, we used a visual stimulus as the CS and erotic film clips as USs, yet our stimulus and interval parameters were more succinct (paralleling those used in studies finding conditioned genital arousal in men) and our USs were more effective in inducing genital arousal.

Our study was aimed at more than showing that women's sexual arousal could be influenced by conditioning. We used the same experimental paradigm to examine the conditioning of genital arousal in both women and men. Photographs presented on videotape served as CSs and erotic film clips that had been rated as arousing by both men and women (Janssen, Carpenter, & Graham, 2003) served as the USs. Domjan and Hollis (1988) proposed that males might show conditioned sexual arousal more readily, and to a wider range of cues, than females. It has also been suggested that women's sexual arousal may not be as readily conditionable as men's (Bancroft, 1989; Kinsey, Pomeroy, Martin, & Gebhard, 1953). However, Baumeister's (2000) proposal that women are more erotically plastic suggests that they could be more sensitive to conditioning than men. Further, potential differences in the propensity for sexual conditioning may involve gender differences in the effectiveness of various CSs and USs in the conditioning of arousal. In addition to examining gender differences in conditionability, we also explored the notion of biological preparedness (e.g., Dellarosa Cummins & Cummins, 1999; Mineka & Öhman, 2002; Seligman, 1970) in sexual conditioning, proposing that a sexually relevant CS (photograph of an abdomen of the opposite sex) would be more effective than a sexually irrelevant CS (photograph of a gun). Finally, assuming that subjects would be less likely to alter their expression of arousal if they did not realize they were being conditioned, we also varied the subjects' awareness of CS presentation and in doing so their awareness of the CS-US contingency. CSs were presented either "subliminally" (i.e., for 30 m/sec followed immediately and hence backward masked by the film US) or "consciously" (i.e., for 10 sec).

When stimuli were presented outside the subjects' awareness, both women and men showed conditioned genital arousal to the abdomen CS but not to the gun CS. These results are similar to those found by Öhman, Esteves, and Soares (1995) using a fear conditioning paradigm; that is, they found conditioned increases in skin conductance to fear relevant, but not fear irrelevant, stimuli that were presented outside the subject awareness and paired with a mild shock to the fingers. Even though our manipulation and measurement of awareness were rather crude, our results suggest a prepared link between sexually relevant stimuli and genital responses and support an independent role for automatic processing in sexual responding consistent with some models of sexual arousal (Janssen, Everaerd, Spiering, & Janssen, 2000).

When consciously perceived CSs were used, however, men again showed conditioned increases in penile tumescence to the abdomen but not the gun CS, whereas women showed the opposite effect, that is, conditioning to the gun but not the abdomen stimulus. The latter result was unexpected. Perhaps the gun-arousal associations in women may have been facilitated by increased attention (Beylin & Shors, 1998; Shors & Matzel, 1997) or excitation transfer (Hoon, Wincze, & Hoon, 1977; Meston & Gorzalka, 1995, 1996; Meston & Heiman, 1998) as women (but not men) showed increased skin conductance responses to the gun (but not the abdomen) CS. Small sample size in the target group prevented appropriate assessment of this hypothesis, but we intend to examine this issue in the future.

A more recent study conducted in my lab by Stefanie Turner and Nate Ewigman found that if the subjects were explicitly told that they were being conditioned they were more likely to show learning. In particular, men showed conditioned genital arousal to a cartoon sketch of a mason jar after it was paired with erotic films clips, but only when they were aware of being conditioned, although there was trend for learning in unaware subjects. The effects appeared weaker in women, with only aware subjects showing a trend for learning. Taken together, our studies suggest that awareness of the contingency may facilitate conditioning to sexually irrelevant CSs, but learning about sexually relevant stimuli may occur without such knowledge. It has been suggested that in order for classical conditioning to occur in humans they need to be aware of CS-US contingencies (e.g., Lovibond & Shanks, 2002), but this may not be the case for learning about prepared stimuli (e.g., Esteves, Parra, Dimberg, & Öhman, 1994). The observation that women showed conditioned arousal to the "conscious" gun (but not the conscious abdomen) does not fit neatly within this hypothesis. However, as mentioned previously, excitation transfer could have facilitated such learning. Further, approximately half of the women conditioned with the conscious gun guessed the hypotheses for the study in a postconditioning interview. Even though there was not a direct relationship between awareness of the contingency and the strength of the CR in this group, the relationship could have been obscured by a low sample size and/or an imprecise measure of awareness.

Our studies hinted at gender differences in the conditions under which sexual learning occurs, at least when consciously perceived CSs were employed. However, the lack of a common physiological measure of arousal prevents a direct gender comparison. We have also begun to examine individual differences in conditionability, as well as to use CSs from other sensory modalities.

Individual differences. There are most likely various individual differences in classical conditionability (e.g., Martin, 1997). Kvale, Psychol, and Hugdahl (1994) found that autonomic (cardiovascular) reactivity is positively correlated with the susceptibility to learning a tone-noise association and to acquiring anticipatory nausea and/or vomiting in people receiving chemotherapy. Kantorowitz (1978) showed a significant correlation between extraversion and conditioning of preorgasmic sexual arousal and a significant correlation between introversion and postorgasmic sexual arousal. In our study, we found that conditionability did not appear to be related to the amount of experience subjects had with erotic film; however, there was not much variation among our participants on this measure. We also collected survey data from some of our subjects and correlated it with the strength of the CR. Specifically, we measured introversion/extraversion and we administered the Sexual Experience Scales (SES) subscale for Psychosexual Stimulation (Frenken, 1981) and the Sexual Inhibition Scales/Sexual Excitation Scales (SIS/SES) (Janssen, Vorst, Finn, & Bancroft, 2002). The former scale measures the extent that someone seeks sexual stimuli of an auditory-visual or imaginary kind and the latter measures sexual excitation (SE) or the propensity for sexual arousal and two forms of sexual inhibition (SIS-1 and SIS-2). SIS-1 is inhibition related to performance failure and SIS-2 is inhibition related to negative consequences. For women the strength of the CR was inversely related to their scores on both inhibition scales, but the correlations were not significant ($p = .12$, $p = .13$, respectively). This suggests that women who are low in sexual inhibition may be more likely to show conditioned sexual arousal. However, what sexual inhibition means for women is unclear, as the SIS/SES-female version that was used was adapted from research with men. For men there was a nonsignificant trend for the strength of the CR to be inversely related to Frenken scores. Similarly, in a more recent study using an olfactory CS (described below), CR strength was inversely related ($p = .007$) to sexual sensation seeking (SSS; Kalichman, 1994). These results seem to contradict

Kantorowitz (1978) if you assume that extraversion is positively correlated with sensation seeking. However, Eysenck (1967) suggested that the strength of the US may moderate the relationship between personality and conditionability. With a strong US such as masturbation to orgasm (which Kantorowitz used), extraverts condition better, but with weak US such as the brief erotic film clips used in our study, extraverts may become bored and inattentive and hence show weaker learning.

Olfactory CSs. Olfactory cues play a large role in sexual arousal in animals, and odors have been used as effective CSs in the conditioning of sexual arousal in a variety of nonhuman species (Domjan & Holloway, 1998; Pfaus et al., 2001). While noxious odor stimuli have been used as USs to decrease sexual arousal in clinical settings (e.g., Colson, 1972; Earls & Castonguay, 1989; Junginger, 1997), olfactory stimuli have not been used as CSs in the conditioning of human sexual arousal. Studies indicate that smell plays a significant role in human sexual attraction. Herz and Cahill (1997) found that odor is an important guide for mate selection in women and men, and that women value odor more so than men. Herz and Inzlicht (2002) showed that, for women, body odor was more important than looks (the reverse was true for men), and that, for women, smell was more valuable than all but one social factor (i.e., pleasantness). Because people report that smell is important in attraction and since the majority of fetishes are related to olfactory or tactile stimuli (Money, 1988), humans, and in particular women, may be likely to associate sexual arousal with odor cues.

In a recent study we used discrete odor cues as CSs and 30-second erotic film clips as USs (Hoffmann & Janssen, 2006). Subjects received, over a 2-day period, 28 pairings of either lemon or strawberry odor, which were delivered via an olfactometer, with different film clips. Genital and subjective arousal to the CS, as well as preference for the odor that served as the CS, were assessed before and after training. Men showed convincing learning: Although genital conditioned responses (CRs) were not robust, they were comparable to those obtained with visual CSs (e.g., Hoffmann et al., 2004; Lalumière & Quinsey, 1998). There was some suggestion that women also showed learning, but the effect on their genital response was much less clear. The measure of subjective arousal did not yield evidence of learning in either men or women. However, there was a trend for men to prefer the odor CS more after conditioning. In addition, we are currently conducting a study in which we pair olfactory cues with a vibrotactile US in women. In this study we are finding some initial evidence of learning using measures of genital responding and odor preference.

The Specifics of What Is Learned

Classical conditioning has the potential to form multiple types of psychological or neural representations. A CS can become directly associated with preparatory and/or consummatory URs elicited by the US, it can come to evoke an affective state associated with the US, and/or it can become associated with specific sensory properties of the US (Cardinal, Parkinson, Hall, & Everitt, 2002; Konorski, 1967; Wagner & Brandon, 1989). For example, a flavor cue that has been paired with a nausea-inducing agent not only comes to signal impending negative consequences but also itself becomes distasteful. Taste cues that predict the onset of shock or other cutaneous phenomenon result in avoidance but not acquired distaste (Pelchat, Grill, Rozin, & Jacobs, 1983; Pelchat & Rozin, 1982). If a person becomes ill after eating something, he or she may become disgusted by the taste or smell of that food, whereas if one experiences an allergic reaction (e.g., breaking out in hives) after consuming that food, it typically does not become unpalatable. Conditioned taste aversion (CTA) learning appears to involve shifts in the hedonic value of the CS. Perhaps this also occurs in some instances in the conditioning of sexual arousal. Rozin, Wrzesniewski, and Byrnes (1998) proposed that the acquisition of fetishes (as well as taste aversions and phobias) may involve aspects of what is known in the human conditioning literature as evaluative conditioning (EC). A common paradigm used in EC is pairing a picture of a "neutrally rated" face (CS) with attractive or unattractive faces (USs), which results in a positive or negative shift in the evaluation or "liking" of the CS. Levey and Martin (1975) coined the term and described EC as an associative transfer of valence as a result of exposure to Pavlovian procedures. Sexually conditioned cues may come to signal sexual opportunity and/or they may themselves acquire erotic value.

Similarly, in reviving Razran's (1971) levels of learning idea as a means of integrating animal and human work on the acquisition of phobias, Öhman and Mineka (2001) propose that an emotional response as well as a cognitive contingency can develop from exposure to Pavlovian procedures. They suggest that fear learning is mediated by an amygdala-based system or fear module. Learning that a cue predicts danger without the involvement of significant emotionality, on the other hand, potentially occurs in a different, hippocampus-based, neural system that mediates explicit memories. Likewise, Spiering and Everaerd (this volume) postulate the existence of a sex module, a specialized neural system responsible for activating physiological responses and sexual feelings to sexually relevant stimuli. Such a system that preattentively processes sexual stimuli would function independently from the cognitive sexual system. Sexual conditioning may involve one or both of these systems yielding expectancy and/or emotional learning.

Evidence for a sex module is preliminary and if and how it may mediate conditioned arousal is not yet known, but the concept may help account for adaptive specializations seen in sexual learning. To explain the unique features of conditioned taste aversion learning compared with other types of avoidance learning (e.g., long-delay learning, palatability shifts, and selective associations), Garcia, Lasiter, Bermudez-Rattoni, and Deems (1985) proposed the existence of gut and skin defense systems. Each system had a specific anatomical pathway and potentially functioned using different principles for establishing relationships. More recently, however, Field (2005) suggested that the mechanisms of response generation rather than of association may differ between expectancy and evaluative conditioning. The sex module may contribute to the eroticization of stimuli by employing somewhat different rules of association and/or response generation than those used during expectancy learning about sexual cues. Animal research has shown that sexual conditioning shares many features with other types of Pavlovian learning (e.g., acquisition, extinction, discrimination learning, second-order conditioning) (Crawford, Holloway, & Domjan, 1993; Zamble, Mitchell, & Findlay, 1986), but some instances of conditioned sexual arousal do not fit neatly within conventional expectancy learning. For example, in male quail, sexual conditioning, like CTA learning, has been shown to occur in a single trial (Hilliard, Nguyen, & Domjan, 1997). Further, if species-typical CSs (e.g., head and neck cues) are used, sexual conditioning occurs with a significant delay between the CS and US (Akins, 2000) and such learning appears more resistant to extinction (Cusato & Domjan, 2003; Domjan & Hall, 1986), blocking (Köksal, Domjan, & Weisman, 1994), and CS preexposure effects (Cusato & Domjan, 1998). In rats, Pfaus, Theberge, and Kippin (2003) found that an initially aversive odor can become appetitive after copulation with females scented with this odor, which suggests a hedonic shift in CS valence. Additionally, Villarreal and Domjan (1998) found that male gerbils showed conditioned approach to an odor CS even though it was inconsistently paired with copulation, suggesting that learning in this situation may not have been particularly sensitive to contingency. In humans, the acquisition of a fetish appears to involve affective change. Also, Langevin and Martin (1975) found some evidence that the strength of conditioned arousal in men did not vary as a function of US intensity, which is an effect seen in EC research as well (Rozin et al., 1998). Further, as mentioned above, Hoffmann and Janssen (2006) measured changes in olfactory preference on a visual analogue scale before and after classical conditioning with an olfactory CS and found increased odor preference after conditioning, at least for some subjects.

Different types of associations may develop during classical conditioning of sexual arousal. Öhman and Mineka (2001) believe that typical human fear conditioning experiments most likely yield predictive but not emotional learning. Similarly, most human sexual conditioning in the laboratory may only engage the cognitive system since, as with fear conditioning, it also involves artificial settings, relatively weak (nonconsummatory) USs, and in some instances arbitrary CSs. The most common measure of human conditioned sexual arousal is changes in genital responding.

Since an increase in genital blood flow may be expected in anticipation of a sexual stimulus as well as in the presence of a cue with erotic value, additional measures of learning are needed to better assess the nature of the CR. Letourneau and O'Donohue (1997) assessed but did not find a change in subjective arousal ratings of the CS in classical conditioning of sexual arousal in women. However, this is not necessarily informative since their procedures did not produce conditioned genital arousal. Indirect measures of CS valence (e.g., an affective priming task) may be more appropriate as they avoid the influence of demand characteristics (De Houwer, Thomas, & Baeyens, 2001).

Conclusion

Establishing reliable procedures for obtaining conditioned arousal in humans (particularly women), employing different measures of learning, and examining more variations in conditioning phenomenon will allow for a more sophisticated analysis of gender and other individual differences in conditioned arousal. These data will also assist in answering more general questions about the nature of associations established during sexual conditioning. Such information may be helpful in refining models of sexual arousal as well as in improving therapeutic techniques based on conditioning models.

References

Ågmo, A. (1999). Sexual motivation—an inquiry into events determining the occurrence of sexual behavior. *Behavioral Brain Research, 105,* 129–150.

Akins, C. (2000). Effects of species specific cues and the CS-US interval on the topography of the sexually conditioned response. *Learning and Motivation, 31,* 211–235.

Akins, C. (2004). The role of Pavlovian conditioning in sexual behavior: A comparative analysis of human and nonhuman animals. *International Journal of Comparative Psychology, 17,* 241–262.

Bancroft, J. (1989). *Human sexuality and its problems.* Edinburgh, UK: Churchill Livingstone.

Baumeister, R. (2000). Gender differences in erotic plasticity: The female sex drive as socially flexible and responsive. *Psychological Bulletin, 126,* 347–374.

Beylin, A. V., & Shors, T. J. (1998). Stress enhances excitatory trace eyeblink conditioning and opposes acquisition of inhibitory conditioning. *Behavioral Neuroscience, 112,* 1327–1338.

Cardinal, R. N., Parkinson, J. A., Hall, J., & Everitt, B. J. (2002). Emotion and motivation: The role of the amygdala, ventral striatum, and prefrontal cortex. *Neuroscience and Biobehavioral Reviews, 26,* 321–352.

Colson, C. E. (1972). Olfactory aversion therapy for homosexual behavior. *Journal of Behavior Therapy & Experimental Psychiatry, 3,* 185–187.

Coria-Avila, G. A., Ouimet, A. J., Pachero, P., Manzo, J., & Pfaus, J. G. (2005). Olfactory conditioned partner preference in the female rat. *Behavioral Neuroscience, 119,* 716–725.

Crawford, L. L., Holloway, K. S., & Domjan, M. (1993). The nature of sexual reinforcement. *Journal of the Experimental Analysis of Behavior, 60,* 55–66.

Cusato, B., & Domjan, M. (1998). Special efficacy of sexual conditioned stimuli that include species typical cues: Tests with a conditioned stimuli preexposure design. *Learning and Motivation, 29,* 152–167.

Cusato, B., & Domjan, M. (2003). Extinction of conditioned sexual responding in male Japanese quail (Coturnix japonica): Role of species typical cues. *Journal of Comparative Psychology, 117,* 76–86.

De Houwer, J., Thomas, S., & Baeyens, F. (2001). Associative learning of likes and dislikes: A review of 25 years of research on human evaluative conditioning. *Psychological Bulletin, 127,* 853–869.

Dellarosa Cummins, D., & Cummins, R. (1999). Biological preparedness and evolutionary explanation. *Cognition, 73,* B37–B53.

Domjan, M., & Hall, S. (1986). Determinants of social proximity in Japanese quail (Coturnix japonica): Male behavior. *Journal of Comparative Psychology, 100,* 59–67.

Domjan, M., & Hollis, K. L. (1988). Reproductive behavior: A potential model system for adaptive specializations in learning. In R. C. Bolles & M. D. Beecher (Eds.), *Evolution and learning* (pp. 213–232). Hillsdale, N.J.: Erlbaum.

Domjan, M., & Holloway, K. S. (1998). Sexual learning. In G. Greenberg and M. M. Haraway (Eds.), *Encyclopedia of comparative psychology* (pp. 602–613). New York: Garland.

Earls, C. M., & Castonguay, L. G. (1989). The evaluation of olfactory aversion for a bisexual pedophile with a single-case multiple baseline design. *Behavior Therapy, 20,* 137–146.

Esteves, F., Parra, C., Dimberg, U., & Öhman, A. (1994). Nonconscious associative learning: Pavlovian conditioning of skin conductance responses to masked fear-relevance facial stimuli. *Psychophysiology, 31,* 375–385.

Eysenck, H. J. (1967). *The biological basis of personality.* Springfield, Ill.: Charles Thomas.

Field, A. P. (2005). Learning to like (or dislike): Associative learning of preferences. In A. J. Wills (Ed.), *New directions in human associative learning* (pp. 221–252). Hillsdale, N.J.: Erlbaum.

Frenken, J. (1981). *SES (Sexual Experience Scales) manual.* Netherlands Institute for Social Sexological Research (NISSO). Zeist, the Netherlands: Swets and Zeitlinger B. V.

Gaither, G. A., Rosenkranz, R. R., & Plaud, J. J. (1998). Sexual disorders. In J. J. Plaud & G. H. Eifert (Eds.), *From behavior theory to behavior therapy* (pp. 152–177). Needham Heights, Massachusetts: Allyn & Bacon.

Garcia, J., Lasiter, P. S., Bermudez-Rattoni, F., & Deems, D. A. (1985). A general theory of aversion learning. In N. S. Braveman & P. Bronstein (Vol. Eds.), *Experimental assessments and clinical applications of conditioned food aversions. Annals of the New York Academy of Sciences, 443,* 8–21.

Gutiérrez, G., & Domjan, M. (1997). Differences in the sexual conditioned behavior of male and female Japanese quail. *Journal of Comparative Psychology, 111,* 135–142.

Hardy, K. R. (1964). An appetitional theory of sexual motivation. *Psychological Review, 71,* 1–18.

Herz, R. S., & Cahill, E. D. (1997). Differential use of sensory information in sexual behavior as a function of gender. *Human Nature, 8*(3), 275–286.

Herz, R. S., & Inzlicht, M. (2002). Sex differences in response to physical and social factors involved in human mate selection: The importance of smell for women. *Evolution and Human Behavior, 23,* 259–364.

Hilliard, S., Nguyen, M., & Domjan, M. (1997). One-trial appetitive conditioning in the sexual behavior system. *Psychonomic Bulletin & Review, 4,* 237–241.

Hoffmann, H., & Janssen, E. (2006, July). *Classical conditioning of sexual arousal to an olfactory cue in women and men: Who learns and what is learned.* Paper presented at the 32nd annual meeting of the International Academy of Sex Research (IASR), Amsterdam, the Netherlands.

Hoffmann, H., Janssen, E., & Turner, S. L. (2004). Classical conditioning of sexual arousal in women and men: Effects of varying awareness and biological relevance of the conditioned stimulus. *Archives of Sexual Behavior, 33*(1), 1–11.

Hoon, P. W., Wincze, J. P., & Hoon, E. F. (1977). A test of reciprocal inhibition: Are anxiety and sexual arousal in women mutually inhibitory? *Journal of Abnormal Psychology, 86,* 65–74.

Janssen, E., Carpenter, D., & Graham, C. A. (2003). Selecting films for sex research: Gender differences in erotic film preference. *Archives of Sexual Behavior, 32,* 243–251.

Janssen, E., Everaerd, W., Spiering, M., & Janssen, J. (2000). Automatic processes and the appraisal of sexual stimuli: Towards an information processing model of sexual arousal. *Journal of Sex Research, 37,* 8–23.

Janssen, E., Vorst, H., Finn, P., & Bancroft, J. (2002). The Sexual Inhibition (SIS) and Sexual Excitation (SES) Scales: Measuring sexual inhibition and excitation proneness in men. *Journal of Sex Research, 39,* 114–126.

Junginger, J. (1997). Fetishism: Assessment and treatment. In D. R. Laws & W. O'Donohue (Eds.), *Sexual deviance: Theory, assessment and treatment* (pp. 92–110). New York: Guilford.

Kalichman, S. C. (1994). Sexual attention seeking: Scale development and predicting AIDS-risk behavior among homosexually active men. *Journal of Personality Assessment, 62,* 385–397.

Kantorowitz, D. A. (1978). Personality and conditioning of tumescence and detumescence. *Behavioural Research and Therapy, 6,* 117–123.

Kinsey, A., Pomeroy, W. B., Martin, C. E., & Gebhard, P. (1953). *Sexual behavior in the human female.* Philadelphia and London: W. B. Saunders.

Kippin, T. E., Talianakis, S., & Pfaus, J. G. (1997). The role of ejaculation in the development of conditioned sexual behaviors in the male rat. *Social Behavioral Neuroendocrinology Abstracts, 1,* 38.

Köksal, F., Domjan, M., & Weisman, G. (1994). Blocking of sexual conditioning of differentially effective conditioned stimulus objects. *Animal Learning & Behavior, 20,* 163–181.

Konorski, J. (1967). *Integrative activity of the brain.* Chicago: University of Chicago Press.

Kvale, G., Psychol, C., & Hugdahl, K. (1994). Cardiovascular conditioning and anticipatory nausea and vomiting in cancer patients. *Behavioral Medicine, 20,* 78–85.

Lalumière, M. L., & Quinsey, V. L. (1998). Pavlovian conditioning of sexual interests in human males. *Archives of Sexual Behavior, 27,* 241–252.

Langevin, R., & Martin, M. (1975). Can erotic response be classically conditioned? *Behavioral Therapy, 6,* 350–355.

Letourneau, E. J., & O'Donohue, W. (1997). Classical conditioning of female sexual arousal. *Archives of Sexual Behavior, 26,* 63–78.

Levey, A. B., & Martin, I. (1975). Classical conditioning of human "evaluative" responses. *Behaviour Research and Therapy, 4,* 205–207.

Lorenzetti, F. D., Mozzachiodi, R., Baxter, D. A., & Byrne, J. H. (2006). Classical and operant conditioning differentially modify the intrinsic properties of an identified neuron. *Nature Neuroscience, 9,* 17–19.

Lovibond, P. F., & Shanks, D. R. (2002). The role of awareness in Pavlovian conditioning: Empirical evidence and theoretical implications. *Journal of Experimental Psychology: Animal Behavior Processes, 28,* 3–26.

Martin, I. (1997). Classical conditioning and the role of personality. In H. Nyborg (Ed.), *The scientific study of human nature: Tribute to Hans J. Eysenck at eighty* (pp. 339–363). Amsterdam: Pergamon/Elsevier Sciences.

McConaghy, N. (1987). A learning approach. In J. Geer & W. O'Donohue (Eds.), *Theories of human sexuality* (pp. 287–334). New York: Plenum.

McGuire, R. J., Carlisle, J. M., & Young, B. G. (1965). Sexual deviations as conditioned behaviour: A hypothesis. *Behavioral Research & Therapy, 2,* 185–190.

Meston, C. M., & Gorzalka, B. B. (1995). The effect of sympathetic activation on physiological and subjective sexual arousal in women. *Behaviour Research and Therapy, 33,* 651–664.

Meston, C. M., & Gorzalka, B. B. (1996). The effects of immediate, delayed, and residual sympathetic activation on sexual arousal in women. *Behaviour Research and Therapy, 34,* 143–148.

Meston, C. M., & Heiman, J. R. (1998). Ephedrine-activated physiological arousal in women. *Archives of General Psychiatry, 55,* 652–656.

Mineka, S., & Öhman, A. (2002). Phobias and preparedness: The selective, automatic, and encapsulated nature of fear. *Biological Psychiatry, 51,* 927–937.

Money, J. (1988). *Gay, straight and in-between.* New York: Oxford University Press.

O'Donohue, W., & Plaud, J. J. (1994). The conditioning of human sexual arousal. *Archives of Sexual Behavior, 23,* 321–344.

Öhman, A., Esteves, F., & Soares, J. J. F. (1995). Preparedness and preattentive associative learning: Electrodermal conditioning to masked stimuli. *Journal of Psychophysiology, 9,* 99–108.

Öhman, A., & Mineka, S. (2001). Fears, phobias, and preparedness: Toward an evolved module of fear and fear learning. *Psychological Review, 108,* 483–522.

Paredes, R. G., & Alonso, A. (1997). Sexual behavior regulated (paced) by the female induces conditioned place preference. *Behavioral Neuroscience, 111,*123–128.

Pelchat, M. L., Grill, H. J., Rozin, P., & Jacobs, J. (1983). Quality of acquired responses to tastes by Rattus norvegicus depends on type of associated discomfort. *Journal of Comparative Psychology, 97,* 140–153.

Pelchat, M. L., & Rozin, P. (1982). The special role of nausea in the acquisition of food dislikes by humans. *Appetite, 3,* 341–352.

Pfaus, J. G., Kippin, T. T., & Centeno, S. (2001). Conditioning and sexual behavior: A review. *Hormones and Behavior, 40,* 291–321.

Pfaus, J. G., Theberge, S., & Kippin, T. E. (2003). *Changing an aversive UCS into an appetitive CS with sexual reinforcement.* Manuscript submitted for publication.

Plaud, J. J., & Martini, R. (1999). The respondent conditioning of male sexual arousal. *Behavior Modification, 23,* 254–268.

Rachman, S. (1966). Sexual fetishism: An experimental analogue. *Psychological Record, 16,* 293–296.

Rachman, S., & Hodgson, R. J. (1968). Experimentally induced sexual fetishism: Replication and development. *Psychological Record, 18,* 25–27.

Razran, G. (1971). *Mind in evolution: An East-West synthesis of learned behavior and cognition.* New York: Houghton Mifflin.

Roche, B., & Barnes, D. (1998). The experimental analysis of human sexual arousal: Some recent developments. *Behavior Analyst, 21,* 37–52.

Rozin, P., Wrzesniewski, A., & Byrnes, D. (1998). The elusiveness of evaluative conditioning. *Learning and Motivation, 29,* 397–415.

Sachs, B. D., & Garinello, L. D. (1978). Interaction between penile reflexes and copulation in male rats. *Journal of Comparative and Physiological Psychology, 92,* 759–767.

Schwartz, B. (1989). *Psychology of learning and behavior.* New York: W. W. Norton.

Seligman, M. E. P. (1970). On the generality of the laws of learning. *Psychological Review, 77,* 406–418.

Shors, T. J., & Matzel, L. D. (1997). Long-term potentiation: What's learning got to do with it? *Brain & Behavioral Sciences, 20,* 597–655.

Villareal, R., & Domjan, M. (1998). Pavlovian conditioning of social-affiliative behavior in the Mongolian gerbil (Meriones unguiculatus). *Journal of Comparative Psychology, 112,* 26–35.

Wagner, A. R., & Brandon, S. E. (1989). Evolution of a structured connectivist model of Pavlovian conditioning (AESOP). In S. B. Klein & R. R. Mowrer (Eds.), *Contemporary leaning theories: Pavlovian conditioning and the status of traditional learning theory* (p. 14). Hillsdale, N.J.: Erlbaum.

Woodson, J. C. (2002). Including "learned sexuality" in the organization of sexual behavior. *Neuroscience and Biobehavioral Reviews, 26,* 69–80.

Zamble, E., Hadad, G. M., Mitchell, J. B., & Cutmore, T. R. H. (1985). Pavlovian conditioning of sexual arousal: First and second-order effects. *Journal of Experimental Psychology: Animal Behavior Processes, 11,* 598–610.

Zamble, E., Mitchell, J. B., & Findlay, H. (1986). Pavlovian conditioning of sexual arousal: Parametric and background manipulations. *Journal of Experimental Psychology: Animal Behavior Processes, 12,* 403–411.

Discussion Paper

JAMES G. PFAUS

I'd like to commend Heather for putting the human literature into a very interesting perspective. I think it offers some very important insights to things that were hinted at yesterday with regard to cognitive models and individual differences. I was impressed with how brave it is to actually start doing sexual conditioning studies in humans. I think that these are under-represented in the sex behavior literature, if not the entire human conditioning literature. They're very difficult to do and it warms my heart that CRs can actually be generated to things like subliminal pairing of an abdomen or a gun. That's very interesting and also I find very reassuring that you can get changes in vaginal pulse amplitude (VPA) to these stimuli. I think that also speaks to some research we discussed yesterday about the nature of sympathetic and parasympathetic arousal and how the two interact to produce the end product, a subjective awareness of engorgement. I think that the fact that you can get this kind of conditioning, albeit not strong, means that we're going in the right direction. I think we need to do more of these studies. Particularly interesting in the paper is your discussion of individual differences in conditionability. This harkens back to Richard Whalen's 1966 paper on sexual motivation where he talks about arousability and individual differences in arousability (Whalen, 1966). The fact that you have gender differences that are superimposed orthogonally over those, I think, is very important to consider. The evaluative conditioning and the associative transfer valence is something that was particularly sticky in the animal literature because, of course, we don't know if it's an epiphenomenon or something inherent to second-order conditioning. So, for example, you pair a neutral or even unattractive face with one that is very attractive and you get a small degree of transfer to the unattractive or neutral face. Could this explain why it is in some little high school subcultures that homely people sometimes hang out with attractive people? So that they can look more attractive? It's hard to know what that means, but I find it very interesting because it is essentially a sexual strategy. Second-order conditioning occurs all the time, right? So my major concern with the human literature is that we can't do the studies we really want to do. We can't pair a green-haired individual with a subject's first orgasm to see whether the subject will start finding people with green hair attractive.

274

That might very well happen, and might be a large conditioned response, but it just can't be done. There was a study by Jack Rachman in 1966, where he paired a picture of a boot with an audiotape of a couple having sex (Rachman, 1966). Some of the men who viewed this got aroused, subjectively and physiologically. The only problem is that other researchers couldn't replicate the finding. But we have to ask, did they use the same audiotape? A different audiotape? They may have had a ridiculous audiotape. It's hard to know. It's hard to know exactly what to use as a stimulus. It's hard to know how to standardize our stimuli across different experiments. This is where we need more inspired intuitions from researchers brave enough to start doing these kinds of studies in humans. We really need to understand what those cognitive processes are that were defined in theoretical terms in yesterday's talks.

Now the animal literature, I think, is something that could be mined fruitfully. You'll notice here that there have been many studies on Pavlovian conditioning of appetitive sexual behavior—some of them recently from my lab, some of them from Mike Domjan's lab a few years ago, and some of them by researchers a long, long time ago who have been almost forgotten in the literature. Of course, in animals we can control events like their first sexual experience. For example, we can give male rats their first sexual experience with an almond-scented female and subsequently examine their copulatory place and mate preferences. You can discover many things so long as you ask the proper questions in rat language. We can specify what the CS is. Of course, we can do that in the human literature as well, but we can also specify what the UCS is because we can vary that. We can determine whether it is ejaculation or feedback from penile intromission because we can study that explicitly. This is something we cannot do ethically in humans. The results have a huge bearing on the social and perhaps even evolution history of the animal. You have phenomena like conditioned partner preference in male rats. They should just be going after novel partners, as would be predicted by the Coolidge effect. But they don't. Conditioning seems to be in a balance with their putatively innate preference novelty. Susceptibility to conditioning is just as instinctual as following a reproductive law like the Coolidge effect that may have been laid down to begin with: all things being equal, go after the novel partner. But it's very easy to condition male rats to show a preference for a set of familiar cues like the presence of almond odor. But why should they do that? Where in their evolutionary history have they ever had to do that? Perhaps this speaks to the fact that conditioning is what goes on as soon as you are out of the womb and open your eyes. Everything we learn in our culture is conditioned, including things that we think are immutable, like the kinds of stimuli we are attracted to sexually. Copulation itself comes under conditioned control. For example, we have conditioned male rats to associate wearing a rodent jacket with having sex. We train one group with the jacket and another without. On the final test day, half the animals in each group get the jacket or don't. The males trained without the jacket are now wearing it, and their copulatory behavior is normal. The males trained with the jacket for their first few sexual experiences and wearing it are fine too. The males trained with the jacket but that are not wearing it are not fine. They take a very long time to start copulating and the females often have to display supersolicitational behaviors. Why do they have to turn up the incentive gain? Because the male's arousal is lessened. But why is the arousal lessened? Are they fetish rats to begin with? No. Their primary sexual experiences have generated an expectancy. And that's what conditioning does—it creates expectancies. We can generate conditioned external place cues, for example, using a light as Domjan has done with noncopulatory exposure to a sexually receptive partner. The light becomes an arousing stimulus, and male birds respond to the light with elements of courtship behavior. And it goes the other way as well: We can produce Pavlovian aversive sexual conditioning, for example, by pairing odors with gastrointestinal distress. A taste aversion to sex, if you will. Under such conditions, we observe decreases in arousal and in the proportion of rats that initiate copulatory behavior. We can pair a neutral odor with thwarted copulation. This can be done by simply pulling the male out after five intromissions or perhaps putting the odor on a nonreceptive female who fights rather than copulates. The male learns that anything that smells of that odor is going to beat him up and he's not going to have sex, so what does he do? Well, we observe inhibited arousal and a conditioned partner preference against the odor, meaning that the male will actively reject copulating with a scented but now sexually receptive partner. Another form of conditioning accrues to place cues associated with sexual reward. For this, we use a conditioned place preference paradigm, in which we pair one of two distinctive sides of a place preference box with a postcopulatory condition or state. One state can be induced by copulation but no ejaculation, whereas another state can be produced by copulation to ejaculation. Previous researchers, like Mike Baum and Anders Ågmo, have found that ejaculation, but not stimuli from penile intromissions alone, induces a conditioned place preference. Now, we can vary the type of copulation too, for example, by forcing males in one group to work harder to obtain intromissions from females. We do this simply by restricting access to females using a pacing chamber with two kinds of divider—one hole or four hole— which the females, but not the male, can pass freely. Males in the four-hole condition have very short interintromission intervals compared to males in the one-hole condition, because in the latter case, the male tends to block the hole trying to get to the other side. He has to learn to back off to let the female through, but that takes time. Well, it turns out that males get more aroused under those circumstances. They ejaculate with roughly half the number of intromissions, indicating a kind of "enforced interval effect" that increases their arousal. If ejaculation rides on top of increased arousal, the kind we've forced them to have by giving them a situation in which access to females is restricted, then males show a robust conditioned place preference for the place associated with that state. So, in other words, if you restrict access to females, the arousal goes up. If the arousal increases, then the males ejaculate with less stimulation and they find it more rewarding than "normal" copulation. This speaks to the role of sexual excitement in arousal and reward, and how sympathetic arousal in particular impacts on an unconditional sexual stimulus. I think arousal is probably one of the most important UCSs for us to study in the animal literature, along with sexual reward. It's obviously important for us to study in the human literature, so we really have to start generating it in our studies and perhaps have more cross talk between the animal and human literature. Again, there are many things we can do with animals that simply cannot be done experimentally with human subjects. This is why the animal literature will continue to be instructive for the human literature, and I recommend that it be mined highly for paradigms and models.

References

Rachman, S. (1966). Sexual fetishism: An experimental analogue. *Psychological Record, 16,* 293–296.
Whalen, R. E. (1966). Sexual motivation. *Psychological Review, 73,* 151–163.

How Do Men and Women Feel?

Determinants of Subjective Experience of Sexual Arousal

ELLEN LAAN AND ERICK JANSSEN

According to one of the founding fathers of psychology, William James, bodily responses and emotional experience are two sides of the same coin (James, 1884). In James's theory, bodily (visceral) changes follow directly the perception of the emotional stimulus, and "our feeling of the same changes as they occur IS the emotion" (p. 190). James's position implies that, in order for bodily changes to take this central role, they need to be consciously perceived and processed. What is more, without these bodily changes, "a cold and neutral state of intellectual perception is all that remains" (p. 193). Recent cognitive neuroscience perspectives acknowledge that bodily changes are an apparent aspect of emotional response. According to Damasio (2003), feelings consist, among other things, of "the perception of a certain state of the body" (p. 86).

The question is, however, to what extent bodily changes contribute to emotional experience and whether this contribution is similar in men and women. James's theory appears less appropriate for women than for men with respect to the experience of sexual emotions. A review of the literature on female sexual arousal reveals that there is little agreement between reported genital sensations and changes in genital vasocongestion (Laan & Everaerd, 1995a). Across studies, between- and within-subjects correlations between changes in genital vasocongestion and subjective sexual arousal range from significantly negative, to nonsignificant, to significantly positive. In contrast, correlations between genital and subjective sexual arousal in men are usually significantly positive, despite differences in methodology and procedures. Studies designed to compare female and male sexual arousal patterns in one experimental design, thus precluding methodological variation, consistently report higher correlations in men than in women (cf. Dekker & Everaerd, 1988; Heiman, 1977; Steinman, Wincze, Sakheim, Barlow, & Mavissakalian, 1981; Wincze, Venditti, Barlow, & Mavissakalian, 1980). A very recent study found that the association between genital and subjective sexual arousal was lower for women than for men and postoperative male-to-female transsexuals (Chivers, Rieger, Latty, & Bailey, 2004).

Anecdotal evidence suggests that discrepancies between genital response and sexual feelings are not limited to laboratory situations. According to reports of subjects, therapists, and patients, women may notice that they have increased vaginal lubrication, but in such instances often do not experience any feelings of sexual arousal, nor any inclination to engage in sexual activity. Other anecdotal evidence suggests that during rape or other types of sexual abuse women may notice increased vaginal lubrication even though they find the situation highly aversive. There have even been reports of women having had an orgasm during such situations (Levin & van Berlo, 2004).

This paper reviews possible explanations for the observed gender differences in agreement between genital response and sexual feelings and offers some tentative answers to the question of what, if not genital response, determines the experience of sexual arousal in women.

Measurement Artifacts

A number of explanations have been forwarded to explain the low correlations between genital response and sexual feelings in women. The most obvious one is measurement error of instruments designed to assess vaginal vasocongestion. However, low correlations between genital response and sexual feelings are not restricted to a single measure of genital response (e.g., Slob, Bax, Hop, Rowland, & van der Werff ten Bosch, 1996). Heiman and colleagues compared the most often used instrument to assess vaginal vasocongestion, the vaginal photoplethysmograph, with pelvic MRI during erotic film (Heiman et al., 2001). They found that correlations with MRI were even lower than with the vaginal photoplethysmograph.

The discrepancy between genital arousal and sexual feelings in women is not affected by the way in which sexual feelings are assessed (by Likert scales to be filled out directly after exposure to an erotic stimulus, or by continuous measures with which the intensity of feelings can be assessed concurrent with erotic stimulus exposure) or which sexual feelings are measured (from a single item about sexual or genital sensations to extensive emotion questionnaires with a wide range of possible sexual feelings).

Anatomy or Sensitivity?

Many men seem to infer their sexual feelings from changes that take place in their genitals (Sakheim, Barlow, Beck, & Abrahamson, 1984), which is what William James suggested we all do. When it comes to sexual arousal, men are likely to have more cues they can use to detect genital response than women do. Think, for instance, of visual feedback, or tactile feedback when an erect penis is pressing against clothing. It is therefore possible that women can detect their genital responses less easily than men can, for reasons related to the anatomy of the genitals. Even though such cues can aid in making inferences about feelings, the data from Chivers,

Rieger, Latty, and Bailey (2004) suggest that they are not strictly necessary. Postoperative male-to-female transsexuals, who lack visual and tactile genital feedback from a penis, showed associations between genital arousal and sexual feelings that were as high as in men. While processes relevant to memory and learning may need to be considered, these findings indicate that direct feedback from the genitalia may not be sufficient in explaining gender differences.

According to Damasio's "somatic marker" hypothesis, feelings require the participation of brain regions that are involved in the mapping and/or regulation of our continuously changing internal states (Damasio et al., 2000). Perhaps the gender differences in associations between genital arousal and sexual feelings can be explained by gender differences in the somato-sensing regions of the brain, that is, the insula and the anterior cingulate, reflecting stronger proprioceptive genital feedback to the brain, or a greater sensitivity of the brain to genital feedback, in men than in women. One of the most robust findings from imaging studies of sexual arousal is bilateral activation of the insula (Sumich, Kumari, & Sharma, 2003). One of the few studies comparing brain activity between genders during erotic stimulus exposure using functional magnetic resonance imaging found significant increases in the insula and anterior cingulate, indicating that the mapping of body states had been significantly modified during the process of feeling (Damasio, 2003), but no gender differences in activity in these regions were found (Karama et al., 2002).

The study by Karama et al. (2002) also showed that in male subjects only, processing of the erotic cues was associated with significant activation in the hypothalamus and thalamus. The authors assert that the greater hypothalamic activation found in male subjects implies that they were more physiologically aroused than the female subjects, and that the greater thalamic activation, mirroring the higher reports of sexual arousal in men, suggests that this region is implicated in the cognitive dimension of sexual arousal. There was a positive correlation between the intensity of sexual feelings and the magnitude of hypothalamic activation in men, but not in women. These findings may suggest that women are less sensitive to sexual stimuli than men are and that women would need stronger stimuli to reach a comparable level of genital arousal. There is evidence that still pictures evoke genital response in most men (O'Donohue & Geer, 1985) but hardly any in women (Laan & Everaerd, 1995b). On the other hand, the erotic stimuli that were shown in the Karama et al. study may not have been sufficiently sexually arousing for the women. These stimuli had been pre-selected so as to evoke lowest disgust ratings in women, but they were not selected based on their sexually arousing qualities for women. It can therefore not be ruled out that the erotic film excerpts used in this study were less effective in generating sexual arousal in the female subjects, which may have explained the differences in thalamic and hypothalamic activity.

Indeed, the female subjects reported lower levels of sexual arousal than the male subjects. When controlling for these gender differences in arousal, the gender differences in brain activity disappeared.

In a recent functional magnetic resonance imaging (fMRI) study (Hamann, Herman, Nolan, & Wallen, 2004) sexually explicit pictures were used that had been preselected for generating equal sexual attractiveness ratings in both sexes. The pictures had been preselected for self-reported physical arousal as well. Unfortunately, this was a measure of general physical arousal, not of genital arousal. Subjects were screened to verify that they found visual erotica sexually arousing. This study showed greater amygdala activation to the sexually explicit pictures in men than in women. Because we cannot directly compare genital responses in men and women it is as yet impossible to say which of the two explanations, the anatomy explanation or the sensitivity (of brain or genitals) explanation, is more likely.

Learning and Attention

Perhaps women have learned less well than men to become aware of their sexual responses. Women and men undergo quite different learning experiences in understanding their bodies' signals. Girls are generally discouraged to attend to their lower body parts. Steiner-Adair (1990) for instance, has argued that society's insistence on the shamefulness of menstrual events is a powerful socialization that encourages young women to turn away from and even mistrust their bodies' physiological cues. With regard to sexual arousal, women are more socialized to restrict knowledge of their genitalia (Gartrell & Mosbacher, 1984). They may not have had the learning experiences that men have to become accurate perceivers of bodily signs of sexual arousal. For instance, in western cultures, more men than women masturbate and the women that masturbate do so less frequently than men (Oliver & Hyde, 1993). Perhaps, masturbatory behavior is the learning experience par excellence in making an individual an accurate perceiver of bodily signs of sexual arousal. Laan, Everaerd, van Aanhold, and Rebel (1993) indeed found that women who masturbate often had higher correlations between both measures of sexual arousal than women who do not or only rarely masturbate.

If learning experiences are a key component in the discrepancy between genital and subjective sexual arousal in women, one would predict that instructing women to attend to bodily cues would improve response concordance. Merrit, Graham, and Janssen (2001) found that correlations between genital arousal and sexual feelings remained low even when women were asked to estimate their genital response during erotic stimulation. Cerny (1978) found that even when women received feedback concerning their level of vaginal engorement, correlations were low and statistically nonsignificant. Conscious efforts of women to monitor their genital response do not seem to enhance response concordance. A recent study however suggests that some type of learning may be involved. Laan and van Lunsen (2002) found that women who were sexually stimulated to orgasm by watching an erotic video combined with clitoral vibration, evidenced low correlations between genital and subjective sexual arousal, even though vibrotactile stimulation of the clitoris combined with visual sexual stimulation is significantly more genitally and subjectively sexually arousing than visual stimulation alone (Laan, Sonderman, & Janssen, 1995). That study required women to return to the lab two more times, with a few days between sessions, in which they underwent the exact same procedure, including the use of the same visual stimuli. In the second and third session, correlations between genital and subjective sexual arousal were substantially higher. A different focus of attention in the second and third session could account for these findings as well. With the visual stimulus and the laboratory environment being familiar, women may have shifted their attention towards feelings in their genitals, aided by the clitoral stimulation. Their subjective report may thus have been less influenced by their evaluation of the visual stimulus (cf. Laan & Everaerd, 1995a, Laan, Everaerd, van Bellen, & Hanewald, 1994).

Social Desirability

Now we consider the possibility that women are generally aware of their genital arousal response, but that they, as a result of socialization pressures, tend to downplay their subjective reports of sexual arousal. Studies into the characteristics of people who are and people who are not willing to participate in sexuality research convincingly show that participants hold more liberal attitudes toward sexuality, experience less sex guilt, are less sexually inhibited, evaluate explicit sexual stimulus materials more positively, and are more sexually active than nonparticipants (e.g., Catania, Gibson, Chitwood, & Coates, 1990; Morokoff, 1986). Given that for participants the expression of sexuality is less restricted than for nonparticipants, it seems unlikely that underreporting of sexual feelings is a significant factor. But there are other indications that consciously underreporting of sexual feelings, or plain lying, cannot be an important explanation for disagreement between genital and subjective response.

Firstly, the phenomenon of response disagreement occurs quite systematically. Unless one wants to assume that all these women are lying, other mechanisms should be at work. Secondly, in a study in which we showed women erotic film clips, but also a clip in which the beginning of rape was shown, most women reported having experienced feelings of anger and resentment during the rape scene but also feelings of sexual arousal (Laan, Everaerd, & Evers, 1995). The fact that women report sexual feelings during a scene depicting nonconsensual sex makes it unlikely that women would not report sexual feelings during consensual sex scenes. In addition, in a study in which we compared sexual responses of lesbian and heterosexual women, we found that women with less liberal sexual attitudes regarding sexuality do not report lower levels of sexual arousal to heterosexual and lesbian film clips (Laan, Sonderman, & Janssen, 1995). And finally, women who scored high on a questionnaire measuring social desirability did not show lower correlations between genital arousal and sexual feelings than women who had low scores on that same questionnaire (Brody, Laan, & van Lunsen, 2003).

To summarize, women seem to be less able to detect genital responses, for reasons related to genital anatomy, sensitivity, or attentional focus. A more important reason for disagreement between sexual response components may be that genital responses can be activated without conscious cognitive control.

Automatic Activation of Genital Response

A surprising finding from our studies was the ease with which healthy women become genitally aroused in response to erotic film stimuli (Laan & Everaerd, 1995a). When watching an erotic film depicting explicit sexual activity, most women respond with increased vaginal vasocongestion. This increase occurs within seconds after the onset of the stimulus, which suggests a relatively automatized response mechanism for which conscious cognitive processes are not necessary. Even when these explicit sexual stimuli are negatively evaluated, or induce little or no feelings of sexual arousal, genital responses are elicited. Genital arousal intensity was found to covary consistently with stimulus explicitness, defined as the extent to which sexual organs and sexual behaviors are exposed (Laan, Everaerd, van der Velde, & Geer, 1995). This automatized response occurs in young women without sexual problems, but also in women with a testosterone deficiency (Tuiten et al., 1994), in postmenopausal women (Laan & van Lunsen, 1997; Laan, van Lunsen, & Everaerd, 2001), and also in women with sexual arousal disorder (Laan, van Driel, & van Lunsen, 2003).

Such a highly automatized mechanism is adaptive from a strictly evolutionary perspective. If genital responding to sexual stimuli did not occur, our species would not survive. For women, an increase in vasocongestion produces vaginal lubrication, which obviously facilitates sexual interaction. One might be tempted to assume that, for adaptive reasons, the explicit sexual stimuli used in our studies represent a class of unlearned stimuli, to which we are innately prepared to respond.

Emotional stimuli can evoke emotional responses without the involvement of conscious cognitive processes (Spiering & Everaerd, 2005). For instance, subliminal presentation of slides with phobic objects results in fear responses in phobic subjects (Öhman & Soares, 1994). Before stimuli are recognized and processed, they are evaluated, for instance as being good or bad, attractive or dangerous. According to Öhman (1993) the evolutionary relevance of stimuli is the most important prerequisite for such a quick, preattentive analysis. As was argued earlier, perhaps sexual stimuli fall within this category and they can be unconsciously evaluated and processed. A number of experiments in which sexual stimuli were presented subliminally to male subjects showed that this is indeed possible (see Spiering & Everaerd, this volume, for a review). Preattentive processing of sexual stimuli occurs in women as well, but appears to be dependent upon the type of prime. Explicit sexual primes do not lead to priming-effects, but romantic sexual primes do (Spiering, Everaerd, Karsdorp, Both, & Brauer, in press). That seems to contradict Öhman's (1993) notion that evolutionary relevant primes can be unconsciously processed. On the other hand, romantic sexual stimuli might be more evolutionary relevant for women than explicit sexual stimuli. Preattentive processing might not be entirely governed by evolution, but could partly be the result of overlearning or conditioning.

Automatic Activation and Regulation

A prerequisite of automatic processing seems to be that sexual meaning resulting from visual sexual stimuli is easily accessible in memory. Based on a series of priming experiments Janssen, Everaerd, Spiering, and Janssen (2000) presented an information processing model of sexual response. Two information processing pathways are distinguished (cf. LeDoux, 1996). The first pathway is about appraisal of sexual stimuli and response generation. This pathway is thought to depend largely on automatic or unconscious processes. The second pathway concerns attention and regulation. In this model sexual arousal is assumed to begin with the activation of sexual meanings in memory. This in turn activates physiological responses. It directs attention to the stimulus and ensures that attention remains focused on the sexual meaning of the stimulus. This harmonic cooperation between the automatic pathway and attentional processes eventually results in genital responses and sexual feelings. Disagreement between sexual response components would occur, according to this model, when the sexual stimulus elicits sexual meanings but also nonsexual and, more specifically, negative emotional meanings. The sexual meanings activate genital response, but the balancing of sexual and nonsexual meanings determines to what extent sexual feelings are experienced.

Thus, this model allows for an alternative view on discordance; one that gives less emphasis to peripheral feedback. If sexual arousal starts with the appraisal of a sexual stimulus, coactivation of genital and subjective sexual arousal can be expected in situations where only sexual meaning is activated. If multiple meanings, including nonsexual or even negative meanings, are present, discordance may occur. There indeed is some evidence that sexual stimuli generate negative sexual meanings in women more often than in men (Dekker, 1988; Everaerd, 1993). Sexual stimuli evoke mostly sexual emotions in men, but a host of other nonsexual meanings, both positive and negative, in women.

Thus, we hypothesize that the experience of sexual arousal is the result of an amalgam of stimulus characteristics (content and intensity), unconditioned and conditioned autonomic nervous system (ANS) responses, and conscious assessment of the response as "sexual." Experience of sexual arousal, which by definition involves awareness, is hypothesized to depend on what is retrieved from explicit (declarative) memory. The conscious balancing of sexual and nonsexual meanings evoked by the sexual stimulus eventually determines the intensity of our sexual feelings. We have recently started a series of studies aimed at establishing that genital sexual arousal is possible without awareness of the sexual stimulus, but that sustained sexual response (both genital arousal and sexual feelings) requires awareness of the stimulus and hence the involvement of explicit memory.

"Male" and "Female" Regulation?

We presume that this information processing model of sexual response applies to both men and women. Sexual meanings of the stimulus will automatically generate a genital response, granted that the genital response system is intact. The difference between men and women in experienced sexual feelings has to do with the relative contribution of two sources (see Figure 1). The first source is the awareness of this automatic genital response (peripheral feedback), which, as was argued above, will be a more important source for men's sexual feelings as for women's sexual feelings. For women a stronger contribution to sexual feelings will come from a second source, the meanings generated by the sexual stimulus. In other words, women's sexual feelings will be determined to a greater extent by all kinds of (positive and negative) meanings of the sexual stimulus, meanings that are stored in explicit memory.

Canli, Desmond, Zhao, and Gabrieli (2002) found support for the idea that emotional stimuli activate memory more readily in women than in men. They asked 12 women and 12 men during fMRI to rate the intensity of their emotional arousal to 96 neutral to negative pictures. After three weeks they were given an unexpected memory task. It was found that women rated more pictures as highly negatively arousing than did men. The memory task revealed that women had better memory for the most intensely negative pictures. Exposure to the emotional stimuli resulted in left amygdala activation in both sexes, the central brain structure for implicit memory (LeDoux, 1996). In women only, the left amygdala and right hippocampus were activated during the most emotionally arousing stimuli

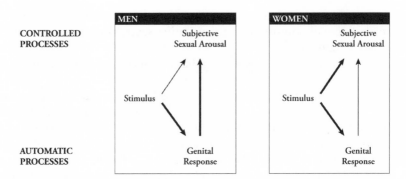

Figure 1. A simplified representation of the determinants of subjective sexual arousal in men and women. The size of the arrows represents the relative contribution of different sources to subjective sexual arousal.

that were also recognized three weeks later. Explicit memory is situated in the neocortex and is mediated by the hippocampus (Squire, 1992). These findings may suggest that in processing emotional stimuli, explicit memory is more readily accessible in women. If these findings would hold for sexual stimuli, we may have a neural basis for our suggestion that sexual stimuli activate explicit memory in women, and that the different meanings sexual stimuli may have influence sexual feelings.

Our hypothesis is that in women other (stimulus or situational) information beyond stimulus explicitness determines sexual feelings, whereas for men peripheral feedback from genital arousal (and thus stimulus explicitness) is a more important determinant of experience of sexual arousal. This hypothesis fits well with the observed gender difference in response concordance. It coincides with Baumeister's (2000) assertion that women evidence greater erotic plasticity than men. After reviewing the available evidence on sexual behavior and attitudinal data of men and women he concluded that women's sexual responses and sexual behaviors are shaped by cultural, social, and situational factors to a greater extent than men's. This view, however, is not incompatible with the possibility that women's stronger responsivity to situational cues in sexual situations itself has a biological basis.

Both women's and men's sexuality are likely to be driven by an interaction of biological and sociocultural factors. Evolutionary arguments often invoke differential reproductive goals for men and women (e.g., Buss & Schmidt, 1993). The minimal reproductive investment for females is higher than for males. Given these reproductive differences, it would have been particularly adaptive for the female, who has a substantial reproductive investment and a clearer relationship to her offspring, to manifest strong attachments to her infants but also to be selective in choosing mates who can provide needed resources. This selectivity mandates a complex, careful decision process that attends to subtle cues and contextual factors. Consistent with men's and women's reproductive differences, Bjorklund and Kipp (1996) proposed that cognitive inhibition mechanisms evolved from a necessity to control social and emotional responses.

Social and Situational Cues and Sexual Feelings

Concurrent with our hypothesis we predict that variations in gender-relevant social and situational factors accompanying explicit sexual stimuli will affect women's experience of sexual arousal more than men's. Genital arousal in both women and men, however, will be a function of stimulus explicitness and will be less sensitive to social and situational manipulations. In a first experiment to test this hypothesis, situational factors were manipulated by varying the characteristics of the sexual stimuli used. We showed 33 men and 36 women a female-initiated and female-centered erotic film and a male-initiated and male-centered erotic film (Laan, 2006). Both film types were matched for explicitness and sexual activity. As predicted, both men and women's genital responses to the two film types were equal. In women, subjective sexual arousal to the female-initiated film was higher than to the male-initiated film, despite the absence of differences in genital arousal. Sexual feelings of men did not differ between films.

Other social and situational cues that could be studied include whether the context in which a sexual stimulus is presented is safe or unsafe, whether it involves a long-term relationship or a one-night-stand, and whether or not other, nonsexual stimuli are present that require attention. For each of these examples we predict that women's feelings will be affected more strongly than the men's by situational factors.

In conclusion, men's sexual feelings appear to be more strongly determined by what happens in their body than women's sexual feelings. This does not mean that women's bodies do not play an important role in women's sexual lives; it means that more conditions need to be met before women experience bodily sensations as pleasurable and exciting.

References

Baumeister, R. F. (2000). Gender differences in erotic plasticity: The female sex drive as socially flexible and responsive. *Psychological Bulletin, 126,* 347–374.

Bjorklund, D. F., & Kipp, K. (1996). Parental investment theory and gender differences in the evolution of inhibition mechanisms. *Psychological Bulletin, 120,* 163–188.

Brody, S., Laan, E., & van Lunsen, R. H. W. (2003). Concordance between women's physiological and subjective sexual arousal is associated with consistency of orgasm during intercourse but not other sexual behavior. *Journal of Sex and Marital Therapy, 29,* 15–23.

Buss, D. M., & Schmidt, D. P. (1993). Sexual strategies theory: An evolutionary perspective on human mating. *Psychological Review, 100,* 204–232.

Canli, T., Desmond, J. E., Zhao, Z., & Gabrieli, J. D. E. (2002). Sex differences in the neural basis of emotional memories. *Proceedings of the National Academy of Sciences, 99,* 10789–10794.

Catania, J. A., Gibson, D. R., Chitwood, D. D., & Coates, T. J. (1990). Methodological problems in AIDS behavioral research: Influences on measurement error and participation bias in studies of sexual behavior. *Psychological Bulletin, 108,* 339–362.

Cerny, J. A. (1978). Biofeedback and the voluntary control of sexual arousal in women. *Behavior Therapy, 9,* 847–855.

Chivers, M. L., Rieger, G., Latty, E., & Bailey, J. M. (2004). A sex difference in the specificity of sexual arousal. *Psychological Science, 15,* 736–744.

Damasio A. (2003). *Looking for Spinoza: Joy, sorrow, and the feeling brain.* Orlando: Harcourt.

Damasio, A. R., Grabowski, T. J., Bechara, A., Damasio, H., Ponto, L. L. B., Parvizi, J., & Hichwa, R. D. (2000). Subcortical and cortical brain activity during the feeling of self-generated emotions. *Nature Neuroscience, 3,* 1049–1056.

Dekker, J. (1988). *Voluntary control of sexual arousal.* Academisch proefschrift, Universiteit Utrecht.

Dekker, J., & Everaerd, W. (1988). Attentional effects on sexual arousal. *Psychophysiology, 25,* 45–54.

Everaerd, W. (1988). Commentary on sex research: Sex as an emotion. *Journal of Psychology & Human Sexuality, 1,* 3–15.

Gartrell, N., & Mosbacher, D. (1984). Sex differences in the naming of children's genitalia. *Sex Roles, 10,* 867–876.

Hamann, S., Herman, R. A., Nolan, C. L., & Wallen, K. (2004). Men and women differ in amygdala response to visual sexual stimuli. *Nature Neuroscience, 7,* 411–416.

Heiman, J. R. (1977). A psychophysiological exploration of sexual arousal patterns in females and males. *Psychophysiology, 14,* 226–274.

Heiman, J. R., Maravilla, K. R., Hackbert, L., Delinganis, A. V., Heard, A., Garland, P., Carter, W., Weisskoff, R. M., & Peterson, B. (2001, July). *Vaginal photoplethysmography and pelvic imaging: A comparison of measures.* Poster presented at 27th annual meeting of the International Academy of Sex Research, Montreal, Canada (see also http://www.iasr.org/conferences/2001abstracts.html).

James, W. (1884). What is an emotion? *Mind, 9,* 188–205.

Janssen, E., & Everaerd, W. (1993). Determinants of male sexual arousal. *Annual Review of Sex Research, 4,* 211–245.

Janssen, E., Everaerd, W., Spiering, M., & Janssen, J. (2000). Automatic processes and the appraisal of sexual stimuli: Toward an information processing model of sexual arousal. *Journal of Sex Research, 37,* 8–23.

Karama, S., Lecours, A. R., Leroux, J-M., Bourgouin, P., Beaudoin, G., Joubert, S., & Beauregard, M. (2002). Areas of brain activation in males and females during viewing of erotic film excerpts. *Human Brain Mapping, 16,* 1–13.

Laan, E. (2006). *Sexual and emotional responses of men and women to male- and female-*

produced erotica: A replication and extension of earlier findings. Manuscript in preparation.

Laan, E., & Everaerd, W. (1995a). Determinants of female sexual arousal: Psychophysiological theory and data. *Annual Review of Sex Research, 6,* 32–76.

Laan, E., & Everaerd, W. (1995b). Habituation of female sexual arousal to slides and film. *Archives of Sexual Behavior, 24,* 517–541.

Laan, E., Everaerd, W., & Evers, A. (1995). Assessment of female sexual arousal: Response specificity and construct validity. *Psychophysiology, 32,* 476–485.

Laan, E., Everaerd, W., van Aanhold, M., & Rebel, M. (1993). Performance demand and sexual arousal in women. *Behavior Research and Therapy, 31,* 25–35.

Laan, E., Everaerd, W., van Bellen, G., & Hanewald, G. (1994). Women's sexual and emotional responses to male- and female-produced erotica. *Archives of Sexual Behavior, 23,* 153–170.

Laan, E., Everaerd, W., van der Velde, J., & Geer, J. H. (1995). Determinants of subjective experience of sexual arousal in women: Feedback from genital arousal and erotic stimulus content. *Psychophysiology, 32,* 444–451.

Laan, E., Sonderman, J., & Janssen, E. (1995, September). *Straight and lesbian women's sexual responses to straight and lesbian erotica: No sexual orientation effects.* Poster presented at 21st annual meeting of the International Academy of Sex Research, Provincetown, Massachusetts.

Laan, E., van Driel, E., & van Lunsen, R. H. W. (2003). Seksuele reacties van vrouwen met een seksuele opwindingsstoornis op visuele seksuele stimuli [Sexual responses of women with sexual arousal disorder to visual sexual stimuli]. *Tijdschrift voor Seksuologie, 27,* 1–13.

Laan, E., & van Lunsen, R. H. W. (1997). Hormones and sexuality in postmenopausal women: A psychophysiological study. *Journal of Psychosomatic Obstetrics and Gynaecology, 18,* 126–133.

Laan, E., & van Lunsen, R. H. W. (2002). *Orgasm latency, duration and quality in women: Validation of a laboratory sexual stimulation technique.* Poster presented at 28th annual meeting of the International Academy of Sex Research, Hamburg, Germany (see also http://www.iasr.org/meeting/2002/abstracts_2002.html).

Laan, E., van Lunsen, R. H. W., & Everaerd, W. (2001). The effects of tibolone on vaginal blood flow, sexual desire and arousability in postmenopausal women. *Climacteric, 4,* 28–41.

LeDoux, J. (1996). *The emotional brain.* New York: Simon and Schuster.

Levin, R. J., & van Berlo, W. (2004). Sexual arousal and orgasm in subjects who experience forced or non-consensual sexual stimulation—a review. *Journal of Clinical Forensic Medicine, 11,* 82–88.

Merrit, N., Graham, C., & Janssen, E. (2001). *Effects of different instructions on within- and between-subject correlations of physiological and subjective sexual arousal in women.* Poster presented at 27th annual meeting of the International Academy of Sex Research (IASR), Montreal, Canada (see also http://www.iasr.org/meeting/2001/abstracts_2001.html).

Morokoff, P. J. (1986). Volunteer bias in the psychophysiological study of female sexuality. *Journal of Sex Research, 22,* 35–51.

O'Donohue, W. T. & Geer, J. H. (1985). The habituation of sexual arousal. *Archives of Sexual Behavior, 14,* 233–246.

Oliver, M. B., & Hyde, J. S. (1993). Gender differences in sexuality: A meta-analysis. *Psychological Bulletin, 114,* 29–51.

Öhman, A. (1993). Fear and anxiety as emotional phenomena: Clinical phenomenology, evolutionary perspectives, and information-processing mechanisms. In M. Lewis & J. M. Haviland (Eds.), *Handbook of emotions* (pp. 511–526). New York: Guilford Press.

Öhman, A., & Soares, J. J. F. (1994). "Unconscious anxiety": Phobic responses to masked stimuli. *Journal of Abnormal Psychology, 103,* 231–240.

Sakheim, D. K., Barlow, D. H., Beck, J. G., & Abrahamson, D. J. (1984). The effect of an increased awareness of erectile cues on sexual arousal. *Behavior Research and Therapy, 22,* 151–158.

Slob, A. K., Bax, C. M., Hop, W. C. J., Rowland, D. L., & van der Werff ten Bosch, J. J. (1996). Sexual arousability and the menstrual cycle. *Psychoneuroendocrinology, 21,* 545–558.

Spiering, M., Everaerd, W., Karsdorp, P., Both, S., & Brauer, M. (in press). Unconscious processing of sexual information: A generalization to women. *Journal of Sex Research.*

Steiner-Adair, C. (1990). The body politic: Normal female adolescent development and the development of eating disorders. In C. Gilligan, N. P. Lyons, & T. J. Hammer (Eds.), *Making connections: The relational worlds of adolescent girls at Emma Willard School* (pp. 162–182). Cambridge: Harvard University Press.

Steinman, D. L., Wincze, J. P., Sakheim, B. A., Barlow, D. H., & Mavissakalian, M. (1981). A comparison of male and female patterns of sexual arousal. *Archives of Sexual Behavior, 10,* 529–547.

Squire, L. R. (1992). Memory and the hippocampus: A synthesis from findings with rats, monkeys, and humans. *Psychological Review, 99,* 195–231.

Sumich, A. L., Kumari, V., & Sharma, T. (2003). Neuroimaging of sexual arousal: Research and clinical utility. *Hospital Medicine, 64,* 28–33.

Tuiten, A., Laan, E., Everaerd, W., Panhuysen, G., de Haan, E., Koppeschaar, H., & Vroon, P. (1996). Discrepancies between genital responses and subjective sexual function during testosterone substitution in women with hypothalamic amenorrhea. *Psychosomatic Medicine, 58,* 234–241.

Wincze, J. P., Venditti, E., Barlow, D., & Mavissakalian, M. (1980). The effects of a subjective monitoring task in the physiological measure of genital response to erotic stimulation. *Archives of Sexual Behavior, 9,* 533–545.

The Voluntary Control of Genital Response, Arousal, and Orgasm

DONALD S. STRASSBERG

It is unlikely that the issue of control of sexual arousal represents much of a problem for any organism other than humans. Getting aroused too quickly or to the "wrong" targets probably does not represent a common challenge for most other species. For most organisms, sexual arousal (including the physiological correlates of this arousal) and ejaculation/orgasm occur largely without conscious attempts to exert any control over these processes. Among humans, however, the story is often rather different. Experience, both direct and indirect, along with our cognitive capacities allow for the enhancement as well as the interference with otherwise innate sexual responsivity. Thus, the targets of our arousal are more varied than in other species, as well as our capacities consciously (or without awareness) to enrich or detract from our sexual pleasure via a variety of cognitive and behavioral mechanisms.

While assessing this capacity for voluntary control of our sexual arousal has both theoretical and clinical value, it also represents significant methodological challenges. Our usual methods of assessment, involving questioning our research participants or clients, still have substantial value, but they are complicated by the nature of sexual arousal. What exactly are the best questions to ask? How accurate are men and women in assessing their current and past sexual arousal? When might they be inclined to misrepresent such evaluations, either to us or to themselves? Can genital plethysmography help to avoid the methodological complications of relying on self-reports? If so, how shall we handle the frequently reported lack of consistency between self-reports and plethysmographic assessment of arousal, particularly among women and under some conditions more than others? How much do we need to worry about someone's ability to misrepresent his or her plethysmographically assessed sexual arousal, for example, during the assessment of a sex offender (Golde, Strassberg, & Turner, 2000)? Such questions represent more than just methodological challenges. More importantly, they speak to the very essence of what we mean by sexual arousal, including attempts to control it.

As a clinical science, human sexology has included the study and treatment of a variety of conditions in which our capacity to exert some degree of voluntary control over our sexual arousal has been the focus. The study of, and attempts to treat, these "conditions" has added to the applied value of our discipline, increased our understanding of the psychophysiology of sexual arousal, and identified how much we still need to learn in this area. Among the clinical areas in which control of sexual arousal has been studied, rapid (or premature) ejaculation and so-called "inappropriate" targets of arousal (e.g., same-sex adults, prepubescent children) are particularly often described and discussed. Those of us who have studied these clinical phenomenon have come to appreciate (i) how difficult it can be to conduct methodologically sound, ecologically valid research in these areas, as well as (ii) how much we have yet to learn about the psychosocial and physiological mechanisms that underlie the "normal" processes of sexual arousal and orgasm. Simply put, assessment of change in sexual arousal as a function of voluntary control strategies includes all the problems associated with measuring arousal, and then some.

The vast majority of research on attempts to control the sexual arousal process (herein taken to mean arousal and orgasm) has been conducted on men. This is primarily a function of the fact that the clinical phenomena at issue (i.e., rapid ejaculation/orgasm and "inappropriate" targets of arousal) are assumed to be more often male than female problems. One could argue that there are, in fact, clinical phenomena associated with arousal control that impact women as (or more) often than they do men. For example, one might take the position that female hypoactive sexual desire or female orgasmic dysfunction represents disorders that are associated with the "control" of sexual arousal. That is, some have argued that many of the instances of these female sexual disorders are a consequence of involuntary (or otherwise unconscious) cognitive "control" mechanisms (e.g., Kaplan, 1974).

While this argument is a reasonable one, this paper will focus primarily on those instances in which sexological scientists and clinicians have looked specifically at circumstances where individuals (primarily males) have attempted to use cognitive and behavioral techniques in order to control either the timing or direction of the sexual arousal process.

The Nature and Treatment of Rapid ("Premature") Ejaculation

Rapid ejaculation, while often described as the most common male dysfunction (e.g., Spector, 1990), impacting as many as a third of men, has proven to be more difficult to assess and define than one might expect. Most operational definitions described in the research literature rely on self-reports of such phenomenon as (i) time from penetration to orgasm, (ii) degree of satisfaction with time to orgasm, (iii) number of penile thrusts till orgasm, and (iv) sense of control over the occurrence of orgasm during sexual stimulation. These measures involve a great deal of subjectivity, or even guesswork, yet they form the basis of most of our evidence regarding the nature of the dysfunction and the efficacy of various treatment approaches. Some researchers have gone beyond such self-reports and included partner evaluations (e.g., Strassberg, deGouveia Brazao, Rowland, Tan, & Slob, 1999), objective timing of orgasmic latency (e.g., Strassberg, Mahoney, Schaugaard, & Hale, 1990), or penile plethysmography (e.g., Strassberg, et al., 1999).

Among the various self-report indices of orgasmic latency, many researchers seem to agree that, while all of these features of the condition are defensible (although not always highly correlated), the self-perceived *sense of control* over the occurrence of orgasm during sex is a particularly important element. There is evidence, for example, that perceived sense of control is the feature most closely associated with sexual satisfaction (Grenier & Byers, 1997).

There are many reasons why a man would prefer to have substantial control over the timing of his orgasm. Perhaps the most important of such reasons is the desire (for both his partner's sake and his own) to be able to engage in intercourse long enough so that his female partner has the greatest opportunity to reach her orgasm during the act. Yet, because intercourse appears to be a generally more efficient technique for men to reach orgasm than for women, many men (including many nonrapid ejaculators) will have difficulty engaging in intercourse long enough for their partner to climax at or before the time that they do. For rapid ejaculators, this can be a particular challenge since their average time to orgasm during intercourse can be two or three minutes, or less!

Many men, therefore, have learned a variety of cognitive and behavioral techniques by which to prolong their sexual arousal without reaching orgasm. The cognitive techniques usually involve some sort of distraction, attempting to focus their attention on something other than the psychological state or physical sensations associated with their current sexual interaction. While there is little direct empirical evidence of the effectiveness of distraction during intercourse, the virtual universality of the use of the technique, and extensive anecdotal data, suggest that it probably is of some value to at least a significant number of men, both rapid ejaculators and otherwise. But even when effective, its use may come at a price. In effect, distraction allows men to delay orgasm during intercourse by interfering with their attention to the sensations that make the act so pleasurable. Imagining one's partner as unattractive or STD-infected, doing math problems, or thinking about one's hated boss or financial woes might well help to prolong the sexual act, but it does so at the cost of the pleasure of the act itself. Just what is it that one has now managed to prolong?

Cognitive distraction is not the only way men have learned to control their sexual arousal prior to orgasm. Simply slowing or stopping thrusting, penile withdrawal, changing intercourse positions, thrusting in a "circular motion," ejaculating prior to intercourse, and the use of one or more condoms are all self-reported to prolong intercourse (e.g., Grenier & Byers, 1997).

Masters and Johnson (1970), Kaplan (1974), and others have popularized the squeeze (Semens, 1956) and stop-start techniques as treatments for clinical levels of rapid ejaculation. In most cases, this includes men who report reaching orgasm either while attempting vaginal penetration or within 2 minutes (or so) of beginning thrusting. There is substantial clinical and research data attesting to the efficacy of these techniques, at least in the short term. These therapy-related techniques are essentially systematically applied variants of some of the procedures, described above, followed by so many "normal" men in trying to prolong their sexual arousal prior to orgasm (e.g., Grenier & Byers, 1997).

Whether stop-start, squeeze, and related procedures lengthen intercourse simply because of the delays they introduce (i.e., by slowing down or stopping intercourse), or whether they actually change the orgasmic threshold (i.e., the absolute amount of physical stimulation someone can sustain without reaching orgasm) remains unclear. While this distinction may be important for scientists, it is probably less critical to men (and their partners) who are trying to lengthen the period of intercourse. As long as they continue to stop active thrusting, or at least slow it down, the reduction in stimulation experienced by the man will allow them to lengthen the time during which they engage in coitus.

Other clinical procedures for treating serious rapid ejaculation also rely on reducing the level of physical stimulation experienced by the man during intercourse and are identical (or similar) to techniques many men seem to learn on their own. These include (i) experimenting with different intercourse positions toward finding one that may produce less stimulation (e.g., female superior or side-by-side positions), (ii) using one (or more) condoms, or (iii) using a desensitizing cream. As mentioned above, one must weigh the relative costs and benefits associated with the lengthening of intercourse while reducing arousal during the process. This is especially true for the last two of these three techniques.

The newest, and most controversial, of the techniques used clinically in the treatment of serious rapid ejaculation is the use of medication. For many years, psychiatrists and others prescribing psychoactive medications noted that, in many instances, the drug interfered with some aspect of the patient's sexual functioning, usually reducing the ability to obtain or maintain an erection, or to achieve orgasm. In particular, the selective serotonin reuptake inhibitor (SSRI) class of antidepressants (e.g., Prozac) were notorious for lengthening the time it took a man to reach orgasm, in many cases preventing him from doing so (e.g., Rowland, Cooper, Slob, & Houtsmuller, 1997; Strassberg et al., 1999).

A number of clinical reports began to appear in which a clinician described success in using an antidepressant medication to treat rapid ejaculation, using one man's unwanted drug side effect as another's very much desired therapeutic effect. These case reports were eventually followed by sophisticated, double-blind, placebo-controlled studies in which the efficacy of antidepressants (e.g., clomipramine) in treating rapid ejaculation was clearly demonstrated (e.g., Strassberg et al., 1999).

What makes the use of psychoactive drugs in the treatment of rapid ejaculation controversial is not the issue of efficacy. These drugs clearly allow rapid ejaculators to last longer during intercourse and to feel more in control of their arousal in the process (Strassberg et al., 1999). The controversy centers around the use of any medication in treating sexual dysfunctions, that is, the medicalizing of sexual functioning (Tiefer, 1994). The debate (Strassberg, 1994) over the validity of such concerns is beyond the scope of this paper.

Other controversies in this area concern the very nature of rapid (premature) ejaculation. There seems little doubt that there is a subgroup of men who are less able to tolerate significant levels of physical genital stimulation than most other men and who also tend to report less control over the onset of their orgasm and less sexual satisfaction (Strassberg, Kelly, Carroll, & Kircher, 1987). How many such men there are depends on one's definitions of normal and premature ejaculation. What remains unclear and debated is (i) whether rapid (premature) ejaculators actually experience less control over their orgasm than other men, and (ii) the etiology of rapid ejaculation.

There is little doubt that rapid ejaculators report lower levels of control over the onset of their orgasms than other men (e.g., Rowland et al., 1997; Strassberg et al., 1999). What remains unclear is if this is simply a perceptive side effect of reaching orgasm so quickly—that is, many men (perhaps most men) report that they wish they could last longer during intercourse (e.g., Grenier & Byers, 1997). If these men have substantially more genuine control over their level of arousal than rapid ejaculators, why aren't they able to prolong intercourse as long as they'd like, or at least longer than they currently can? The higher (relative to rapid ejaculators) levels of control these men report may not represent greater (than rapid ejaculators) control, but just the *perception of greater control* owing to their higher arousal threshold and therefore their ability to last longer during intercourse.

Yet one more debate associated with premature ejaculation and the presumed arousal control deficiency it represents concerns the etiology of the condition. Masters and Johnson (1970) believed that the condition was the result of early ejaculatory experiences in which reaching a quick orgasm was of value (e.g., to avoid being interrupted by an adult while masturbating or during early attempts at intercourse). The primary flaw in this argument is that concerns about interruption during early sexual experiences are so ubiquitous that it is unlikely that such experiences would be far more characteristic of any one group than others. In contrast, Kaplan (1974) argued that premature ejaculators were, for psychological reasons, less able than others to recognize the physical sensations that indicated one was dangerously close to reaching orgasm. As a result, these men could not work to control their level of arousal (e.g., through slowing down thrusting) until it was too late. However, there is compelling evidence that rapid ejaculators are no less able than others to assess their level of sexual arousal (Strassberg et al., 1987).

A number of other theories have been put forth over the years explaining rapid ejaculation as the consequence of a variety of intra- and interpersonal psychological problems, including unresolved oedipal conflicts, anger, passive-aggressiveness, performance anxiety, and too little sex. However, there is little (if any) empirical support for any of these hypotheses. In contrast, it has long been my position that, for most men, the amount of physical genital stimulation they can tolerate before they reach orgasm is primarily a physiologically determined threshold, one that they have exhibited since puberty across virtually all types of genital stimulation (Strassberg, 1994). Why not assume that the orgasmic reflex, like most other human reflexes (e.g., the gag reflex or the patella reflex) is normally distributed in terms of the amount of stimulation required to trigger it. Men on the low side of this distribution would represent those we refer to as rapid or premature ejaculators, while men at the other end of the distribution would represent those currently diagnosed as having an orgasm phase disorder (previously termed retarded ejaculation). Consistent with this hypothesis is the fact that in most clinically significant cases of rapid ejaculation, men report that they've always had the problem, across both time and partners. Further, these men have been demonstrated to reach orgasm more quickly than normal controls even in masturbation (Strassberg et al., 1990).

Irrespective of the etiology of rapid ejaculation, it is clear that men who obviously fit the diagnosis reach orgasm with very little physical stimulation (I once treated a man for whom the act of removing his underwear was sufficient) and (perhaps as a result) experience little control over their level of arousal during sexual acts (e.g., Rowland, Strassberg, deGouveia Brazao, & Slob, 2000). As mentioned above, even men whose orgasmic latency during intercourse is average (or even above) often express the desire to have greater control of their arousal so as to last longer. One of the reasons reported (anecdotally) by some men without erectile dysfunction for using Viagra is that the drug allows them to maintain an erection for at least a short time following orgasm/ejaculation. Clearly, the issue of control of arousal is a significant one for many men, not just those who orgasm so quickly as to meet diagnostic criteria for rapid ejaculation.

Control of Sexual Arousal: Other Populations

In addition to rapid ejaculators, there are several other groups of (predominantly) men for whom the issue of control of sexual arousal is of significant clinical relevance and has also been the target of substantial research. Specifically, there are several groups of men, and some women, who are so bothered by (or have been made to feel so uncomfortable about) the primary target of their sexual interest that they have searched for (or been otherwise subjected to) interventions designed to help (or make) them control their arousal by (i) decreasing their arousal to their current target, and (ii) increasing it toward some other target. The two most common examples of such efforts involve those with a same-sex orientation (or variations thereof) and pedophiles. Readers should understand that the inclusion of these two categories in the same part of this paper is, in no way, meant to equate these phenomena.

Sexual Orientation

Much attention has been paid to the issue of the flexibility (or malleability) of sexual orientation. Some men and women (the numbers of which are unknown, but estimated to be much higher for men) seek help, or are *strongly encouraged* by others to seek help, to change the adult target of their sexual/romantic interest. These are virtually always same-sex oriented individuals. Among sexual scientists and clinicians, there is a substantial range of opinions regarding how likely, or even possible, such changes are. These opinions are often closely tied with theories regarding the origins, development, and clinical normalcy of same-sex orientation. There is not sufficient room in this paper to consider the many etiological theories that have been offered in this area or to review the research evidence that has been offered for each. Rather, we will focus on the anecdotal and research evidence that speaks to the issue of control of arousal: specifically, the degree of success achieved by those who have tried to become less aroused to same-sex targets and more aroused to opposite-sex targets.

Unfortunately, the nature of this issue and a variety of methodological factors (e.g., even the definition of sexual orientation, e.g., Diamond, 2003a; Veniegas & Conley, 2000) have resulted in there being virtually no well-designed and controlled experimental study of change in sexual orientation (Strassberg, 2003; Zucker, 2003). There are certainly reports of individuals who say they have changed orientation (e.g., Diamond, 2003b; Kinnish, Strassberg, & Turner, 2005; Spitzer, 2003), and many others where attempts at change have met with little, if any, success (e.g., Shidlo & Schroeder, 2002).

The evaluation of successful change in orientation is complicated by the very nature of sexual orientation. What should we be measuring: sexual behavior, romantic attraction, sexual fantasy, all three, or something else? A recent study by Kinnish, Strassberg, and Turner (2005) demonstrated that change, when it occurs, along any one of these dimensions is often unrelated to change along the others. Must change occur across *all* such dimensions to be considered successful? Irrespective of which or *how many* of these dimensions must reflect change is the issue of *how much* change must occur to consider it meaningful (e.g., is 1 point on a 7-point Kinsey scale sufficient)? Further, *how long* must any change be evidenced before we consider it stable? Some say that self-reports of change are insufficient, arguing that genital plethysmography is necessary for "true change" in orientation to be demonstrated.

With methodological complexities such as this, it is not surprising that there is far from a consensus among researchers and clinicians regarding how common significant change in sexual orientation really is. It seems fair to say that even those most convinced of the possibility of change in sexual orientation and the data they use in support of this belief suggest that such change, especially for men who early in life recognize a strong and exclusive same-sex attraction, is, at best, very difficult (e.g., Haldeman, 1994). Over the years, gay men have been lectured to, preached to, electrically shocked, and made to feel guilty, sick, or doomed. Still, exerting sufficient control over the target of their sexual arousal has frequently proven illusive. While some report having changed their behavior (e.g., Spitzer, 2003), most have found it very difficult (bordering on impossible) to substantially change the sex of those who fill their fantasies and are the objects of their sexual desires (e.g., Shidlo & Schroeder, 2002). One suspects that such a change would be no less difficult for exclusively heterosexual individuals. At this point, it seems fair to conclude that control of arousal, at least when it concerns the sex of the target of that arousal, is generally very difficult to achieve. How difficult and for whom remain open questions that will, among other things, require that a greater agreement is reached regarding the empirical evidence needed to demonstrate such change (see the entire Volume 32(5) of *Archives of Sexual Behavior* for a detailed discussion of this issue).

Pedophilia

The issue of control of sexual arousal becomes highly relevant in the assessment and treatment of men who sexually offend against children. For example, evidence of deviant sexual interest (e.g., toward prepubescent children) is one of the most reliable predictors of sexual reoffending (e.g., Serin, Mailloux, & Malcolm, 2001).

Despite the importance of accurately assessing the target of sexual interest among child molesters, it is often difficult to obtain owing to the frequent efforts of many offenders to misrepresent (both to themselves and others) their deviant response patterns. The introduction of penile plethysmography provided the first objective measure of sexual arousal (Simon & Schouten, 1991), one that was not dependent on the honest self-report of the offender. However, even this "objective" measure of arousal is not without its limitations (e.g., Barker & Howell, 1992). Because male erectile structures are enervated by the autonomic nervous system, the prevailing view for many years was that the penile erection was a totally involuntary response. However, the presence of neural pathways leading to and from higher brain centers suggests that, like some other autonomically mediated responses (e.g., eye-blinking), penile tumescence may also be under some degree of voluntary control.

In general, the research results suggest that, when used with cooperative adult males who have no motive for misrepresenting the targets of their sexual arousal, penile plethysmography (PPG) can yield reasonably accurate assessments that correlate substantially and significantly with self-reports and external behavior (Strassberg et al., 1987). However, some data also suggests that (i) many men (perhaps one-third or more) are able to inhibit (by as much as 50%) their plethysmographically assessed sexual arousal in a laboratory setting, even while attending to the stimuli (Mahoney & Strassberg, 1991), and (ii) some (but substantially fewer) men are able to generate, to a very modest degree, partial arousal in the absence of any external erotic stimulus (e.g., Hatch, 1981; Mahoney & Strassberg, 1991; Quinsey & Carrigan, 1978). Perhaps these are some of the reasons why the plethysmograph has yielded mixed results in distinguishing pedophiles from nonpedophiles (e.g., Barbaree & Marshall, 1989; Rice, Quinsey, & Harris, 1991; Simon & Schouten, 1991; Wormith, 1986).

While the degree of incentive one has to dissimulate (i.e., control) his PPG-assessed arousal seems unrelated to the ability to do so (Mahoney & Strassberg, 1991; McAnulty & Adams, 1991), several other variables have been found to impact such dissimulation efforts. For example, experience with the procedure (Freund, Watson, & Rienzo, 1988) and the type of stimulus material used (e.g., audio vs. visual stimuli) has, in some instances, been shown to impact a man's ability to control his arousal (primarily through suppression of arousal toward preferred stimuli) so as to misrepresent the true nature of what "turns him on" (e.g., Card & Farrall, 1990; Golde, Strassberg, & Turner, 2000; Malcolm, Davidson, & Marshall, 1985). Further, many men find it increasingly difficult to suppress arousal the longer they are attempting to do so, resulting in PPG traces that often start low but then increase over time (Mahoney & Strassberg, 1991).

When experimental participants have been questioned about the techniques they used when attempting to suppress their arousal (i.e., their penile response), most describe either trying to avoid perceiving the target stimulus (e.g., looking away whenever possible) or employing competing imagery or cognitions (Mahoney & Strassberg, 1991). These strategies are similar to those reported by "normal" men who are attempting to exert greater voluntary control over their arousal so as to lengthen intercourse (Grenier & Byers, 1997). It becomes important, therefore, that researchers and clinicians assessing someone via the plethysmograph attempt to ensure that the individual is attending to the stimuli throughout the procedure, although this does not ensure an accurate assessment (Mahoney & Strassberg, 1991).

Even when men are successful in suppressing their PPG-assessed arousal to "undesirable" targets (e.g., children), the meaning of this "success" remains unclear. That is, does their success in getting less erect when exposed to "undesirable" targets in any way reflect their ability to control the sexual desirability or arousability of such targets outside of the assessment setting, or their likelihood of acting on such feelings? Are they really controlling their arousal or just their erections . . . or are these the same thing? These are just a few of the important questions that remain to be answered concerning the plethysmographic assessment of sexual arousal among sexual offenders.

A second way in which the issue of control of sexual arousal impacts the clinical population of pedophiles is in the area of therapeutic efforts at changing the targets of their sexual arousal. That is, most sex offender treatment programs attempt to encourage, motivate, threaten, or otherwise convince pedophiles to become less sexually interested in children and more sexually interested in adults. Among the behavioral techniques that have been used in the service of such change are orgasmic reconditioning, aversion therapy, covert sensitization, and masturbatory satiation.

While there is substantial anecdotal evidence of at least the sporadic effectiveness of each of these approaches (e.g., Foote & Laws, 1981), there is little persuasive empirical support for any. These are the same techniques that have been used over the years in an attempt to change homosexuals into heterosexuals, again with little empirical support of their effectiveness.

The interventions with perhaps the most reliably (albeit, still imperfectly) demonstrated effectiveness in reducing a pedophile's sexual interest in prepubescent children are chemical and surgical castration (Prentky, 1997). Reducing the availability of testosterone to a pedophile frequently, but hardly always, appears to significantly reduce his experience of sexual interest in children. Of course, it does nothing to increase his sexual interest in more appropriate targets; rather, it essentially renders him asexual or hyposexual. This hormone-induced "control" of his deviant sexual arousal, of course, lasts only as long as his testosterone remains lowered.

Summary

Sex researchers and clinicians have long recognized the value of accurately assessing the direction and strength of one's sexual arousal. We've learned, however, that as simple and straightforward as the construct of arousal might first appear, its evaluation is actually quite complicated and frequently very difficult. This is certainly the case where the object of the assessment is to evaluate the degree to which an individual is able to control some aspect of his or her sexual arousal.

Several examples have been offered here of relatively common clinical circumstances in which people's (usually men's) ability to control the level or target of their sexual arousal has been studied. Many of the evaluative complications associated with such assessment are described. It seems clear that, in part because of the complications associated with arousal assessment, many basic questions regarding the control of sexual arousal are far from answered. It is equally clear that the difficulties associated with assessing the effectiveness of arousal control are much the same as those impacting virtually all other areas of research and practice where accurate assessment of sexual arousal is important.

References

Barbaree, H. E., & Marshall, W. L. (1989). Erectile responses among heterosexual child molesters, father-daughter incest offenders, and matched non-offenders: Five distinct age preference profiles. *Canadian Journal of Behavioural Science, 21,* 70–82.

Barker, J. G., & Howell, R. J. (1992). The plethysmograph: A review of recent literature. *Bulletin of the American Academy of Psychiatry and the Law, 20,* 13–25.

Card, R. D., & Farrall, W. (1990). Detecting faked penile responses to erotic stimuli: A comparison of stimulus conditions and response measures. *Annals of Sex Research, 3,* 381–396.

Diamond, L. M. (2003a). Reconsidering "sexual desire" in the context of reparative therapy. *Archives of Sexual Behavior, 32,* 429–431.

Diamond, L. M. (2003b). Was it a phase? Young women's relinquishment of lesbian/bisexual identities over a 5-year period. *Journal of Personality and Social Psychology, 84,* 352–364.

Foote, W. E., & Laws, D. R. (1981). A daily alternation procedure for orgasmic reconditioning with a pedophile. *Journal of Behavior Therapy and Experimental Psychiatry, 12,* 267–273.

Freund, K., Watson, R., & Rienzo, D. (1988). Signs of feigning in the phallometric test. *Behavior Research and Therapy, 26,* 105–112.

Golde, J. A., Strassberg, D. S., & Turner, C. M. (2000). Psychophysiologic assessment of erectile response and its suppression as a function of stimulus media and previous experience with plethysmography. *Journal of Sex Research, 37,* 53–59.

Grenier, G., & Byers, E. S. (1997). The relationships among ejaculatory control, ejaculatory latency, and attempts to prolong heterosexual intercourse. *Archives of Sexual Behavior, 26,* 27–47.

Haldeman, D. C. (1994). The practice and ethics of sexual orientation conversion therapy. *Journal of Consulting & Clinical Psychology, 62,* 221–227.

Hatch, J. P. (1981). Voluntary control of sexual responding in men and women: Implications for the etiology and treatment of sexual dysfunctions. *Biofeedback and Self-Regulation, 6,* 191–205.

Kaplan, H. S. (1974). *The new sex therapy: Brief treatment of sexual dysfunctions.* New York: Brunner/Mazel.

Kinnish, K. K., Strassberg, D. S., & Turner, C. M. (2005). Sex differences in the flexibility of sexual orientation: A multidimensional retrospective assessment. *Archives of Sexual Behavior, 35,* 173–183.

Mahoney, J. M., & Strassberg, D. S. (1991). Voluntary control of male sexual arousal. *Archives of Sexual Behavior, 20*(1), 1–16.

Malcolm, P. B., Davidson, P. R., & Marshall, W. L. (1985). Control of penile tumescence: The effects of arousal level and stimulus content. *Behaviour Research and Therapy, 23,* 273–280.

Masters, W. H., & Johnson, V. E. (1970). *Human sexual inadequacy.* Boston: Little, Brown.

McAnulty, R. D., & Adams, H. E. (1991). Voluntary control of penile tumescence: Effects of an incentive and signal detection task. *Journal of Sex Research, 28,* 557–577.

Prentky, R. A. (1997). Arousal reduction in sexual offenders: A review of anti-androgen interventions. *Sexual Abuse: Journal of Research & Treatment, 9,* 335–347.

Quinsey, V. L., & Carrigan, W. F. (1978). Penile responses to visual stimuli: Instructional control with and without auditory sexual fantasy correlates. *Criminal Justice & Behavior, 5,* 333–342.

Rice, M. E., Quinsey, V. L., & Harris, G. T. (1991). Sexual recidivism among child molesters released from a maximum security psychiatric institution. *Journal of Consulting and Clinical Psychology, 59,* 381–386.

Rowland, D. L., Cooper, S. E., Slob, A. K., & Houtsmuller, E. J. (1997). Dissimulation in phallometric testing of rapists' sexual preferences. *Archives of Sexual Behavior, 28,* 223–232.

Rowland, D. L., Strassberg, D. S., deGouveia Brazao, C. A., & Slob, A. K. (2000). Ejaculatory latency and control in men with premature ejaculation: An analysis across sexual activities using multiple sources of information. *Journal of Psychosomatic Research, 48,* 68–77.

Semens, J. M. (1956). Premature ejaculation: A new approach. *Southern Medical Journal, 49,* 453–457.

Serin, R. C., Mailloux, D. L., & Malcolm, P. B. (2001). Psychopathy, deviant sexual arousal and recidivism among sexual offenders: A psycho-culturally determined group defense. *Journal of Interpersonal Violence, 16,* 234–246.

Shidlo, A., & Schroeder, M. (2002). Changing sexual orientation: A consumers' report. *Professional Psychology, 33,* 249–259.

Simon, W., & Schouten, P. (1991). Plethysmography in the assessment and treatment of sexual deviance: An overview. *Archives of Sexual Behavior, 20,* 75–91.

Spector, I. P. (1990). Incidence and prevalence of the sexual dysfunctions: A critical review of the empirical literature. *Archives of Sexual Behavior, 19,* 389–408.

Spitzer, R. L. (2003). Can some gay men and lesbians change their sexual orientation? 200 participants reporting a change from homosexual to heterosexual orientation. *Archives of Sexual Behavior, 32,* 403–417.

Strassberg, D. S., (1994). A physiologically based model of early ejaculation: A solution or a problem? *Journal of Sex Education and Therapy, 20,* 215–217.

Strassberg, D. S. (2003). A candle in the wind: Spitzer's study of reparative therapy. *Archives of Sexual Behavior, 32,* 451–452.

Strassberg, D. S., deGouveia Brazao, C. A., Rowland, D. L., Tan, P., & Slob, A. K.

(1999). Clomipramine in the treatment of rapid (premature) ejaculation. *Journal of Sex & Marital Therapy, 25,* 89–102.

Strassberg, D. S., Kelly, M. P. Carroll, C., & Kircher, J. C. (1987). The psychophysiological nature of premature ejaculation. *Archives of Sexual Behavior, 16,* 327–336.

Strassberg, D. S., Mahoney, J. M., Schaugaard, M., & Hale, V. E. (1990). The role of anxiety in premature ejaculation: A psychophysiological model. *Archives of Sexual Behavior, 19*(3), 251–257.

Tiefer, L. (1994). Might premature ejaculation be organic? The perfect penis takes a giant step forward. *Journal of Sex Education and Therapy, 20,* 7–8.

Veniegas, R. C., & Conley, T. D. (2000). Biological research on women's sexual orientations: Evaluating the scientific evidence. *Journal of Social Issues, 56,* 267–282.

Wormith, J. S. (1986). Assessing deviant sexual arousal: Physiological and cognitive aspects. *Advances in Behavior Research and Therapy: An International Review Journal, 8,* 101–137.

Zucker, K. J. (2003). The politics and science of "reparative therapy." *Archives of Sexual Behavior, 32,* 399–402.

Discussion Paper

WALTER EVERAERD

First, I have a few remarks about your paper, Don, because it's a beautiful paper, and it poses problems in connection with your work too, Dave. I wondered what you know about the processing aspects? In one of your slides there is a very steep increase in heart rate in some of your subjects and the others showed a normal lowering after the acceleration of heart rate when presented with a new stimulus, and I don't know whether you have data about what they are doing exactly at that moment, because before the steep increase they must have been ruminating about sex or they did something else at that moment. But that's an important point, I think—the processing aspect. And there's a more general topic that pertains to your paper that I find interesting. In many problems we have with men, there is a lack of control of emotions and regulation of emotions, and it seems to me that a function of emotional intensity is this disinhibition of certain behaviors. Frank Beach has told us that sexual arousal elicits reflexes: the erection reflex and the orgasm reflex. The idea is that emotion intensity has something to do with releasing the actions that should follow from the emotion and the point is that we didn't give much attention to how that may work. What are the triggers for arousal going over into action? That may be relevant to your problem; it may also be relevant just for people with paraphilias. It is a very general problem. In aggression, for example, it's very clear that some people act very quickly on their emotion and some can postpone it for a very long time. Ellen referred to Bjorklund and Kipp's review (1996) about the differences between men and women and their ability to control emotional reactions, and women seem to be very good in restraining their emotional output at an early stage. They're much better in controlling and regulating their emotions. And Bjorklund and Kipp's idea is that it is an evolutionary thing—that women are evolved to control, because their task is to acquiesce to the group they live in, while men are evolved to do things outward and that the function of the behavior, the expression of emotion into action, is an evolved thing in men. But I'm not sure about that. Thinking about regulation and control of emotions is important. It may be that we are most helpless in relation to aggression; it is very difficult to treat.

Then I come to Ellen and Erick's paper and I have some general remarks about it that may help them think about feelings and objective measures connected with it, and so forth. The disagreement between physiological arousal and what people tell you about what they are feeling or experiencing has been a puzzle for a long time and the situation has changed a bit in recent years. John Morris (2002) has given us some clues as to what might have changed. The original idea was, as Ellen told you, William James's idea that what we feel is a direct feedback of peripheral arousal, although William James didn't have any idea how that may work in the brain. Ellen told you that feeling as a direct reflection of peripheral arousal is not a good model for women's experience of sexual arousal. This may be true because it stresses the contribution of the peripheral physiological arousal too much maybe. The new conceptualization from Morris, among others, is that the situation is a bit more complicated. He proposes, and there are lots of imaging studies to support it, that the sensory information or the information from peripheral arousal feeds back into the insula and there creates an integrated representation of what's going on in the body, which interacts with all kinds of contributions from memory to arrive at an integrated representation of what's going on. It's unclear how that becomes conscious, but it may be a step before it becomes conscious. So the important idea is that the experience of a situation is a construction of many data available to the brain and the clue now is that the insula may have a very crucial role in bringing those things together. Now we have to make another step. In cognitive science, it's clear that experience, whether it's a construction or not, is something that has to sustain for some time in the brain to be able to attend to it and we think that this happens in working memory, which is a construct of something that may happen in the frontal cortex. The idea is that several kinds of information contribute to the experience, such as the stimulus, the attention you have for the stimulus, the somatic and autonomic reactions generated through the activation of the amygdala.

So there are several contributions and it's clear from this point of view that differences in experience may be generated because there may be different contributions from these different sources. The hippocampus-dependent contribution is something where progress has been made that may help us understand why there are so many differences. In our original approach we used psychophysics, and in the psychophysics approach you have a sensory event and you vary that sensory event and look at how and when the subject is perceiving that event. When you do that, you have several difficulties in doing your studies. The first is that there may be technical difficulties in specifying the sensory event and varying that event; that is also true with sex, of course. Then another point is that when you do those studies, it's very dependent on contextual factors, how good people are in discriminating these sensations, which is well known, for example, from heart rate studies on the perception of heart rate. When you study heart rate perception in the lab, men are normally better than women, but when you do heart rate studies in a significant context, then women perform as good as men do. So there are different contributions to the perception. That's a first point. For a long time we had the suspicion that the contribution of memories about emotional events must be very important to explain those differences. We are currently doing studies to see whether or how the memory of emotional events, the encoding and retrieval of emotional events, differs and is lateralized in men and women. And to show you a little bit of those data I will explain to you the experiment of Canli, Desmond, Zhao, and Gabrieli (2002). We have known for a long time that visual, spatial characteristics and verbal characteristics are differently organized in the brains of men and women, and women are normally good in verbal tasks and men in spatial tasks and so on. But now it becomes clear that this also has some influence on how we go about remembering emotional events, and that's very important. I will show you some data to give an idea of how that might work. An important thing, when you look at imaging data, is to be aware of the fact that what they show you is always relative. When Ellen told you that in Karama et al.'s studies (2002) lateral hypothalamus is active in men, that it remains relatively more active than in women, that doesn't mean that there's no activity in women, of course. That's true here too. But it's fascinating when you see these data. What Canli et al. (2002) did was the following: They had 96 pictures out of a standardized picture series of Peter Lang in Gainesville, Florida. The valence of these pictures, positive or negative, to elicit positive or negative emotions, is demonstrated and their emotion intensities are also well known. So you can select from the set of, I think it is 700 pictures now, according to valence and intensity. These pictures were shown to people and Canli et al. had arranged the pictures to have differences in valence and what he wanted to see is whether people scored differently on valence. That is in the table of his article. Emotional intensity is also indicated. He scanned his subjects with a functional magnetic resonance imaging (fMRI) machine after viewing those pictures or while they saw those pictures. And what he wanted to do was see, when retrieving those pictures, which differences appeared between men and women and, of course, he expected the emotional pictures to do better than the nonemotional pictures. It's a well-known fact in memory studies about emotional events that it is easier to remember emotional events than nonemotional events, so in week 4—that's 4 weeks after the scan was done—he did a retrieval session, for which a recognition test was used. He had the 96 old and scanned pictures and 48 new pictures and he simply asked in the recognition test, did you see the picture before, and the scoring was done by the subjects in a (meta-memory) way so they could say, I've forgotten that picture, I'm familiar with it, or I remember it. A feeling of knowing and remembering is a typical difference. Canli et al. (2002) compared the recognition score of people and scanning data about the pictures. The emotional manipulation succeeded. And then, in the lower panel [Figures 2 and 3 from the article were shown], you see the memory performance and you see slight differences between men and women and when you look at the data in general, women do a little bit better in remembering the events. That suggests, from a naïve point of view, that women have encoded better, have encoded these pictures in a more elaborated way, and what Canli et al. demonstrated is that possibly in coding, different brain areas are involved in men and women and that this may explain this difference. Here (in the figures) you see the emotional arousal in men. This is the amygdala mainly or activated and in emotional memory you see a difference that in men, the right amygdala are more activated and in the women the left amygdala and it's well known that there are quite a lot of connections between the amygdala, the left amygdala, and the language areas in the brain. You see different structures that are revealed and here you see from the relative differences that the amygdala is more activated in women. When you look at the hippocampus and the cortex, you see more activation in women, which suggests that during the encoding of pictures, women use their declarative memory to form or construct a representation of the content of the picture at encoding and that may explain why they remember better, because they create cues in this way about those pictures. So a possible difference in between men and women in explaining their subjective experience may be that they have encoded and remember their experiences in a different way. And, when confronted with a sexual stimulus, they retrieve very different things and construct in a very different way their experience.

References

Bjorklund, D. F., & Kipp, K. (1996). Parental investment theory and gender differences in the evolution of inhibition mechanisms. *Psychological Bulletin, 120,* 163–188.

Canli, T., Desmond, J. E., Zhao, Z., & Gabrieli, J. D. E. (2002). Sex differences in the neural basis of emotional memories. *Proceedings of the National Academy of Sciences, 99,* 10789–10794.

Karama, S., Lecours, A. R., Leroux, J-M., Bourgouin, P., Beaudoin, G., Joubert, S., & Beauregard, M. (2002). Areas of brain activation in males and females during viewing of erotic film excerpts. *Human Brain Mapping, 16,* 1–13.

Morris, J. S. (2002). How do you feel? *Trends in Cognitive Sciences, 6*(8), 317–319.

General Discussion

John Bancroft: It's been a fascinating morning as far as I'm concerned. What has always fascinated me about sexual development are some old data that I don't think have ever been replicated because it's difficult to do so. Glen Ramsey was a teacher who interviewed boys about their sexual development, around puberty (Ramsey, 1943a, 1943b); he showed how difficult it was to do because he lost his job over it—he apparently didn't get parental consent! He collaborated closely with Kinsey, who included his data in his final male sample. Ramsey described a phase of relatively unspecific responsivity when boys were getting erections in a variety of different situations, which were not sexual. This implied that there was a period of development when genital responsiveness was fairly nonspecific, but after a while, became more specifically linked to sexual stimuli. This needs to be looked at again. Clearly it focuses on the role of conditioning, the relationship between conditioning and the developmentally emerging genital responsiveness, and as such can be considered a fundamental part of sexual development.

I also want to make a strong recommendation, following on from Heather's paper. Unquestionably, having an erection can be an arousing experience for a man, but a man can have an erection without being aroused and I would strongly suggest that we stop using the term *arousal* to describe a genital response and that we talk about "genital response" instead. We should use "arousal" when we talk about the activation of the norepinephric system in the brain, which is related to sexual arousal as well as to other times of arousal (Bancroft, 2002). So that is my recommendation.

Heather Hoffmann: Regarding your first point, this is part of the critical period issue that I was talking about. The conditioning could potentially be much stronger if we were working with younger subjects.

Jim Pfaus: I think the literature in male rats certainly suggests that whatever gets there first, wins. It doesn't mean that plasticity is over, but it means that your primary experiences are profoundly important. In rats, of course, we're talking about copulation to ejaculation, but in humans we have no idea what that might mean. It could be a primary experience with sexual arousal as it emerges when you are 10 and not really understanding what it is; it can be your first sexual experience with masturbation, especially if you link the pleasure you receive with some external stimulus, a picture or an image. It can also be the first experience with sexual intercourse, and we certainly make a great deal out of the loss of "innocence." I think it is the case that puberty starts long before GnRH is released into the pituitary, long before the first ovulation or the first evidence of pubic hair or swimming sperm. It may very well be the case that it's on a continuum. As we become aware of genital sensations we link them to reward. That reward becomes more sexual in nature as you get older and get a bit more familiar with it, and we link the induction of those sensations to external incentives. That entire process becomes the sum total of your earlier experiences and starts to dictate the gender of the individual that is the object of your desire, the facial features of that individual, whether they have black hair, brown hair, blonde hair, whatever is salient from an individual standpoint. That experience also comes to determine the type of sexual response that you like. These are all individually defined. We all don't necessarily like the missionary position. We all have preferences and we don't necessarily agree on them, nor should we, because we are all individuals. Our experiences are individually defined, even in a culture that tries to constrain us to common experience and practices.

John Bancroft: Kinsey would be proud of you.

Heather Hoffmann: I'd like to add that, on a more limited level, I did look at the relationship between experiences, at least with erotic stimuli, and the strength of the CR, and there wasn't one, for men or for women. Most of my subjects had some experience, men more than women, but there wasn't a relationship.

Ray Rosen: Can I raise one element that I felt was missing from the discussion previously, and that's the role of consummatory responses either as part of the UCS or UCR in the conditioning model. There is a longstanding literature including early research by McGuire, Carlyle, and Youngand others that in males, in particular, reinforcement via masturbation occurs in which consummatory responses in the sense of orgasm and ejaculation are essential to the conditioning process. The conditioning paradigms that you're looking at in your model, Heather, and some of the animal work, do involve consummatory aspects. Sexual stimuli that are followed by consummatory behaviors may be especially strongly conditioned and it's that repetition of consummatory behaviors that may be crucial to the conditioning process, and I wonder if that's the reason you're getting relatively weak CRs. One might wonder whether in the absence of consummatory responses, are you always going to get weak CRs.

Heather Hoffmann: Again, that was my question about the intensity of the US. There was that one Kantorowitz paper, I believe, in which he used a consummatory response as the US and his conditioning; again, it's hard to compare relative strength across studies, but at least I know in turns of duration he was still able to see a CR after 2–3 months, which is amazing. I don't think I'd see that. So yes, I agree.

Jim Pfaus: I think it is much easier to determine what that might be in animals. In our conditioning studies in males, my former graduate student Tod Kippin went through a series of controls to determine exactly what the UCS was. It turned out not to be intromissions but rather ejaculation and postejaculatory exposure to the female. In fact, if you let the males intromit with females that smelled of almond, but not ejaculate, they displayed a subsequent aversion to females that smelled of almond, probably because they didn't ejaculate. So, the postejaculatory period is a state that links sexual reward to the environmental circumstances that induced it. It's the state that Stendhal talked about in the 18th century. If lovers remain close facially next to each other in that postorgasmic bliss, they will form a preference, a preference that he refers to as bonding. They'll bond to the features of one another, such that similar features will become preferred in other individuals. Now, whether it's due to oxytocin and/or endorphin release, it is a critical period, a critical UCS. And it is a consummatory UCS because you can't get there any other way. Sexual reward for females, on the other hand, is their ability to control the initiation and rate of copulation. The work of Raul Paredes has been particularly important in this regard (Paredes & Alonso, 1997; Paredes & Martinez, 2001; Paredes & Vazquez, 1999). If you don't allow females to do that, they'll certainly copulate and get pregnant, but they won't show any place or partner preference. I'll talk more about this phenomenon this afternoon. But briefly, if you place an almond odor on a male rat in a situation where the female can pace copulation, relative to no odor on a male rat in a situation in which the female cannot pace effectively, she will display a subsequent preference for males that bear the odor. It is critical in studies of conditioned sexual behavior to know what the UCS is. We can do that in animal research. We can't do that at all in humans.

Michael Seto: I wonder if Heather and Jim could comment on the notion of preparedness in terms of learning of sexual responses. In terms of my interest in paraphilias, you look at the types of paraphilias, not just those that are criminal but those that are commonly identified, and they're neither randomly nor uniformly distributed. I just wondered, based on your understanding of the conditioning literature, what you think of that notion—that there might be a preparedness for particular types of paraphilic sexual interests?

Heather Hoffman: I would answer based on Garcia's model that maybe what you are looking at here are US-FB associations that are stronger than CS-US associations, so that potentially the US could be something that is prepared. So the abdomen would be the US and that's why that association may potentially be stronger

Jim Pfaus: Again, when do your gonads come online? When does puberty occur? When do you become aroused by a sexual stimulus? I mean if you're 9 years old and this begins to happen and you're in perhaps a same-sex social group and the abdomen of a little boy who is your best friend becomes part of your love map, well, who is to say that as you grow up into a big adult you're not going to find the abdomens of little boys attractive, and is that abnormal? If you express it as an adult toward a little boy, we say you're going to jail. But can you ever lose that early experience? It is very similar to the effects of drugs of abuse. Yes, you can quit taking drugs, but the fact is the arousal induced by drug paraphernalia or certain circumstances in which drugs were always taken never goes away. So I think, again, what gets there first changes the brain in a profound way. It garners much of the associative strength. Although stimuli that come later can also be conditioned, they will carry less incentive value. The first cut will always be the deepest.

Ray Rosen: It sounds like you're putting more emphasis on primacy versus preparedness.

Jim Pfaus: I would say primacy is an integral part of the cascade that is preparedness, yes.

Jim Geer: Heather, I'd like to ask you a couple of questions about the design. Why did you choose to use a nonpaired CS rather than a random one?

Heather Hoffmann: Because Martin Lalumière advised me that it might not work with a randomized control. Also, it was because I was using video, which is a little harder to make random, although I could have done a better job at that. In the past, when I did animal research, the explicitly unpaired has worked fine for me. Martin suggested that a randomized control might not be the best of situations, that is, I may get some conditioned arousal in the controls. And this is what I did find in the second study. We used a procedure more similar to a random one and we did see some conditioning in the unpaired groups.

Jim Geer: Another question: You talked about baseline presentation of conditioned stimuli. Did you do that with your subjects before they began conditioning?

Heather Hoffmann: Yes, I showed baseline presentations of the five slides I showed you initially; they had two presentations each.

Jim Geer: Aren't there a lot of data that suggest that if you do that, you make it more difficult to condition?

Heather Hoffmann: Again, I think it takes many more trials; there were only two to three presentations of each slide. Latent inhibition would probably not occur in that situation.

Jim Geer: Okay.

Heather Hoffmann: I didn't use the probe trial type of procedure; I compared baseline presentation with test presentation because there was some arousal to those slides prior to conditioning, particularly the slides of the females for the men.

Jim Geer: That always is a problem if you don't have a pure CS. If you get arousal to it to begin with, are you conditioning? I'm sure you understand the issues.

Heather Hoffmann: True, but if you look at the literature, about half the studies do use what I would called more prepared stimuli, photographs of nudes that are paired then with the film.

Tillmann Krüger: I have a question for Don and maybe also for Heather. Yesterday I mentioned these two multiorgasmic males. One of them reported he was not always multiorgasmic, but that he became multiorgasmic at the age of 18. I think he told us that his sexual arousability was always very high and that his ejaculation occurred very soon. Consequently, after the first orgasm he tried to remain sexually aroused and to keep the erection and after a while he succeeded and was able to stay on a high level of sexual arousal. This subject told us something about a learning process. How would you explain this cognitive process? What kind of learning might that be? This may be an interesting issue, because in our studies we have shown that there may be changes in the psychophysiology and the endocrine response pattern in these subjects.

Don Strassberg: In our lab, we've seen a couple of guys like that and I'm not sure if it really reflects something learned or if it in fact relates to the refractory period. We sort of assume that everybody has a measurable refractory period, but people differ in this respect, and certainly teenagers can have such a short refractory period as to essentially make them multiorgasmic; that is, they don't lose their erections enough that they can actually continue to engage in intercourse. Again in our lab, we've seen that on occasion, so I'm not sure if that really is a function of learning. I know that the man you described said he didn't have this capacity and then he did. I don't know how one would learn that, but I certainly believe that there are people who, even well into adulthood, have such short refractory periods that they in effect are multiorgasmic or have the capacity to be multiorgasmic.

Tillmann Krüger: Tantra techniques, for example, also describe a kind of a learning technique for the phenomenon of multiple orgasms.

Don Strassberg: Yeah, I don't know. I've also heard of books or videos that are commercially available that supposedly teach men to have the sustained capacity to have an orgasm for an hour, but I'm not sure why or how this is supposed to work.

I did have a comment I wanted to make about this primacy issue. One of the techniques that has been around for some time in treating sex offenders is some variant of masturbatory reconditioning, where basically you try to get them to start masturbating, usually to their preferred stimulus, and then earlier and earlier in the sequence introduce a difference stimulus and that's the stimulus that they are focusing on when they have an orgasm. There's not a great deal of research data on it, but by and large the data I have seen suggests that it's not a terribly effective technique. That is, men, even those motivated to change the target of their arousal, don't seem able to really change very much as a function of a technique that attempts to associate the new target with orgasm. Perhaps the primacy issue and/or how long the preferred stimulus has been associated with orgasm (e.g., for decades) renders this association very resistant to change, particularly when the change technique is expected to take effect in a matter of only days or weeks. But it's conceivable to me that even if you tried masturbatory reconditioning for years you might not be able to overcome the initial association.

John Bancroft: We found in an earlier study of hypogonadal men that whereas, as I was commenting on yesterday, their erectile response to visual stimuli did not differ according to whether they were on testosterone replacement or not, their erectile response to fantasy was greater on testosterone (Bancroft & Wu, 1983). That was before we had found the rigidity and duration effect I referred to earlier. But Julian Davidson's group (Kwan, Greenleaf, Mann, Crapo, & Davidson, 1983) did not replicate that finding and I just don't think we have enough evidence to answer the question of testosterone and sexual response to fantasy. It needs to be looked at further.

Roy Levin: Did you not say, John, in your paper that in fact it was because you only used one measure of penile arousal?

John Bancroft: Yes.

Roy Levin: And that's why you got your response?

John Bancroft: When we used rigidity and also looked at duration of response, we found a difference between hypogonadal men and eugonadal men in relation to visual stimuli, but this hasn't been replicated in terms of fantasy. It remains an interesting question. In any new studies of hypogonadal men, it would be good to look systematically at what role testosterone has in the response to fantasy.

Roy Levin: Could I just add about learning, just a quick thing? When you ask people about their first coitus in terms of learning, most people say it wasn't very pleasurable, the orgasm wasn't very pleasurable, and you actually learn to associate pleasure with the orgasm so it isn't automatically that orgasm gives you pleasure. If you go back to the literature, you'll find that, in fact, you ask people about their very first one and it wasn't pleasurable at all. So there's a real learning curve on even associating orgasm and pleasure.

Kevin McKenna: I have a question for Walter or Jim Pfaus or maybe Serge. Is sexual conditioning really dependent on the hippocampus or is it the cerebellum?

Jim Pfaus: In our odor conditioning studies, we get activation of the hippocampus to the conditioned odor alone. I will show you this in females, but it's identical in males. So there is hippocampal regulation to some extent, but this is an odor and it's an odor that's in space and time. You get very strong hippocampal activation by place cues that are associated with sexual reward. So there's clearly hippocampal activation, but there's also amygdala activation. And in terms of looking at the cerebellum, the cerebellum is activated anytime the animal moves. So I don't know if it's the movement or the motion with regard to these other structures.

Kevin McKenna: Have there ever been any lesion studies to see what blocks the conditioning?

Jim Pfaus: With the cerebellum?

Kevin McKenna: Yes.

Jim Pfaus: Well, in our studies, not yet. Lesions are among the next experiments we will do. Tod Kippin did a few, but things were not exactly as obvious as we would have liked. I also believe that our CS processing is being done by the piriform cortex. This is the primary olfactory cortex. It is a long structure and impossible to lesion completely.

Serge Stoléru: There are some interesting experiments that have been performed on operant conditioning in monkeys by Rolls (Rolls, 1999), and he's shown that the orbitofrontal cortex is very important in mediating the association between the incentive and the response, and that, for example, if you change a contingency relationship it is the orbitofrontal cortex that will mediate learning the new contingency between a motor response and an outcome that has changed, for example, from a reward to a punishment.

Brian Mustanski: I haven't heard much discussion coming from an individual differences perspective. I know Heather Hoffmann talked a little bit in her paper about individual differences in conditionability. I think that this is a very interesting and important perspective that has clinical implications for the understanding of sexual problems. Following up on what Michael was saying, for example, there is evidence that in some paradigms individuals with obsessive-compulsive disorder condition faster than controls (Tracy, Ghose, Stecher, McFall, & Steinmetz, 1999). It would be interesting to look at differences in conditionability in sexual and nonsexual paradigms between paraphilic and control subject. In other words, are individual differences in conditionability related to paraphilias? I'm wondering if anyone is thinking about doing these sorts of studies.

Also, as a behavioral geneticist, I'm very interested in the sources of individual differences. It would be interesting to consider this for something like what Ellen was talking about in regards to the correlation between subjective arousal and genital arousal. Are there individual differences in the magnitude of this correlation and, if so, what are the sources of those individual differences and what does that mean? One could start out with a relatively simple design by just looking at typical individual differences variables, like personality, and see how they predict the correlation between genital and subjective arousal. But, you could also use a more advanced design, like bringing siblings into the lab; of course, twins would be preferable from a behavioral genetics standpoint. At first you may think it's hard enough to get participants into a lab for sexuality research, there's no way we're going to get twins in the lab. But surprisingly, having worked with twins for a while now, they actually are much more interested in participating in research across a variety of different topics. We've done some sexuality research with twins and we actually get very reasonable participation rates (e.g., Mustanski, Viken, Kaprio, Winter, & Rose, 2003). You may even get higher participation rates if you're working with twins compared to singletons. But, even with nontwin siblings you can partition variance into within-family and between-family variance. This can give you an idea of whether familial factors, either heritable or common environmental, are explaining variance. Using such a within-family design can help to control for other variables that differ between families (such as social class) that are correlated with the variable of interest. This has been done for things like the relationship between personality and substance use (Dick, Johnson, Viken, & Rose, 2000), but it could also be used to understand the source of variability in the genital-subjective arousal correlation. I guess I am interested in if people are interested in individual differences and what they think the sources of these differences might be.

Jim Geer: Part of the difficulty is the way the correlations are done. The correlations that are basically being talked about here are between-subject correlations—they're not within-subject correlations, which I think would more likely reflect those individual differences. The within-subject correlations, and we just did this once, were considerably higher than between-subject correlations. So there's this methodological thing that makes it hard, at this point, to separate out the methodology variance from the variance attributed to the independent variables, although perhaps Ellen could speak more sensibly to that.

Ellen Laan: It is true that most of the research used between-subjects correlations, but not only between-subjects correlations. In one study we calculated within-subject correlations; that study was partly a replication of your Korff and Geer (1983) study. In the study we instructed the women in all four conditions to attend to their genitals but correlations were high in only two of the four conditions. We found that correlations were high only in the conditions where women were exposed to stimulus materials that differed in intensity. Differences in stimulus intensity boost within-subject correlations, which makes sense; there is more variability in the data. I don't think there have been designs like that used in men.

Jim Geer: Very few. When we did it, we had the correlations up into the 80s and 90s when doing within-subject correlations.

Brian Mustanski: If you're finding such big dissociation in within-subject versus between-subject correlations, that's great evidence that there are important individual differences that are not being detected by the between-person correlations. In the alcohol–condom use literature, for example, evidence from within-person correlations revolutionized the way people understood how alcohol consumption influences condom use (e.g., Leigh, Gillmore, & Morrison, 1998). It is even possible to get between-person correlations that are totally unrepresentative of what is found with within-person correlations (Tennen & Affleck, 1996)! The designs where data is collected by continuous monitoring of subjective arousal are a great way to calculate a within-person correlation.

Jim Geer: That's right.

Alessandra Rellini: Actually, we did that (Rellini, McCall, Meston, & Randall, 2003). We continuously measured subjective arousal to erotic video, in combination with vaginal pulse amplitude (VPA), and actually found a strong correlation between VPA and subjective arousal in women that was measured.

Brian Mustanski: You mean within persons?

Alessandra Rellini: Within. Well, we used hierarchical linear modeling (HLM), a measure that gives you both results for within and between subjects. HLM first looks at the correlation and regression of VPA on continuous subjective sexual arousal for each woman and then uses the pool of individual slopes to calculate if there is a difference between participants on any specific variable. And when we did analyses between subjects—the differences between people—we found a significant difference (Rellini et al., 2003). I was talking to Dr. Laan earlier on how these results don't change the fact that there's a very significant difference between men and women, but perhaps what we're seeing is that women vary a great deal on the scale and so when we use analysis like repeated measure ANOVA, we blunt the effect and thus are unable to see the differences within people. So we think that women are accurate at perceiving their engorgement, but there is a very large variability within subjects.

Julia Heiman: I wanted to come back to something we were discussing a little bit before the meeting. It is important not to create a new mythology that women do not know what is going on with their bodies, because I was just looking over several studies before I came and many show good correlations between VPA and subjective on a Likert scale. So I think that what is probably important to study is when there is a lack of correlation and the factors contributing to a positive or negative correlation between the body and subjective experience domains. We do not have all of the answers. That's one point. The second point is, what is being correlated? Is the correlation between a report of sexual arousal and VPA? Or is it between perception of genital response? We need to clarify what we're talking about. Those are two rather different types of subjective experience and information. There are other areas to differentiate. I often get differences, for example, between a report of physical sexual arousal and emotional sexual arousal in response to erotic stimuli.

Alessandra Rellini: Yes, and when we ask this question of women, we ask them to monitor how subjectively they felt aroused, not to monitor the VPA or how they felt engorged, because those studies have been already conducted. Once we found that what women felt subjectively was significantly correlated with their physiological sexual arousal, then we felt we had a method that could really tell us changes through time, and we decided to compare women with the sexual dysfunction female sexual arousal disorder (FSAD), and controls. Those are very preliminary studies that we want to replicate before talking extensively about the results; however, it seems like the relationship between subjective and physiological is weaker in women with FSAD. But again that was a small sample size and we're really unfamiliar with this methodology still, so we'll let you know later.

Don Strassberg: There's some old data that actually comes from Masters and Johnson when they were looking at things that predict which women are most likely to experience orgasm during intercourse. Those who had, as teenagers, masturbated to orgasm were much more likely to be orgasmic with partner stimulation. I'm wondering if anybody who's been looking at the relationship between self-report and genital measures has ever noticed or asked about a difference between those who, in fact, have a long history of having masturbated to orgasm versus those who have not.

Ellen Laan: Two sources of data: In an earlier study back in the 1990s (Laan, Everaerd, van Aanhold, & Rebel, 1993), we found that women who masturbate frequently versus women who do not masturbate at all have higher between-subject correlations, so that might suggest—but we haven't replicated that—that women who do masturbate indeed are better perceivers of their genital response. The thing you said about orgasm consistency is interesting because Stewart Brody, who is an American working in Germany, had this theory that women who have more consistent orgasms during intercourse will be the ones that have higher correlations between genital and subjective, and I thought that that wouldn't be the case. I think the women who have more consistency in orgasm during masturbation will be the ones, you know, that have higher correlations. So he analyzed one of my data sets and actually he was right. We published that but I can't really explain it.

John Bancroft: On this issue of masturbation history—we did a study of students recalling their childhood sexual experiences. Whereas males reported starting masturbating during a relatively short window of time around either side of the onset of puberty, females were much more variable, with quite a lot reporting onset of masturbation several years before menarche and others starting quite a lot later (Bancroft, Herbenick, & Reynolds, 2003). So you've got a big spread in developmental histories, which ought to be looked at as a source of individual variance in adult responsiveness.

Erick Janssen: I have a question for our brain experts. We are talking a lot about the role of awareness or the perception of genital responses. Does it really involve feedback, the perception of what is happening in our genitals, or could it just be the activation in our brain of representations that are relevant to genital response and that might be more easily activated in men than in women, more in some women than in other women, and so on?

Kevin McKenna: That's a good question, but it's actually a testable hypothesis, although not an easily testable hypothesis, using an interventional study where you block the response. I mean, Ellen's model was very interesting with the idea in the male that they are really attending to the genital response. What happens if you block the genital response? What happens in that case? It's not an easily doable experiment, but it is doable. Or perhaps impotent men before and after treatment so that in one case they have a response and in another case they don't. So, I wonder if those kinds of things were to change women's sexual responses, and whether or not it's the perception of the response that's really key. An interventional study could provide the answers.

Ellen Laan: Meredith Chivers's work (see Chivers & Bailey, this volume) is interesting in this respect. In one study she calculated within-subject correlations between genital and subjective sexual arousal in male-to-female transsexuals. Genital responses were captured with VPA. These subjects had genital-subjective correlations comparable to the men in the study, which were much higher than the ones of the women in the study. So apparently these higher correlations in men are not only influenced by having external genitalia that generate more peripheral feedback to the brain than do women's genitals, because male-to-female transsexuals do not have these external genitalia anymore. But they *used* to have them. Perhaps this "peripheral feedback pathway" is still engraved in the brain. But perhaps these data speak against direct peripheral feedback as an explanation for higher genital-subjective correlations in men and for activation in the brain of representations relevant to genital response. Male-to-female transsexuals' brains may still be male in this respect.

Walter Everaerd: I think your question, Erick, touches on a very important subject: that is, the difference between knowing about emotional reactions and having an emotional reaction, and that's always a point in our studies. We ask people what they feel and you're never certain whether they tell you what the representation is of the emotion they had, or whether they're reporting about what they're feeling. So I'm quite sure that we have representations about emotions distinct from what's happening in the sensory pathway, so there must be a contribution from that representation. It's very clear.

Jim Pfaus: Erick, your question also touches on how behaviors get sensitized, or automated, such that they don't require the same sensory input to reproduce the response. Frank Beach published a large paper in 1942 about the sensory stimuli that were required for sexually inexperienced male rats to copulate (Beach, 1942). He blinded them, he restricted olfactory input, and he deafened them, all in an effort to determine what sensory stimuli were important to get naïve male rats to copulate. One of the nuggets in there was denervation of the penis. Denervation of the penis eliminated copulatory behavior. About 20 years later his student Richard Whalen did a study showing that if you allowed male rats to mount and intromit, so they're actually getting penile stimulation, penile feedback, but you never let them ejaculate, they will all show normal copulation to ejaculation when you finally let them do so (Whalen, 1961). This includes normal ejaculation latencies, despite the fact that they have never ejaculated before. In contrast, males that were allowed only to mount—because now instead of deenervating the penis you put lidocaine on it—those males mounted on the final test, but had trouble intromitting and ejaculating. They required serious retraining in order to get them to display normal copulatory behavior. So, clearly penile feedback is very important for copulatory responses. Now it turns out in learning how to copulate and learning what to attend to, male rats clearly know they're about to ejaculate because they emit a 50 kHz call that females respond to. He clearly has some sensory feedback and some anticipation that he knows what is about to happen. Now it turns out when a male rat is sexually experienced, however, you could put lidocaine on his penis and he will copulate to ejaculation without any overt sign of a problem. It is as if sensory feedback from the penis no longer matters. The behavior is so automated that he gets to ejaculation without it. The same phenomenon can be observed following removal of the olfactory bulbs. Bulbectomy severely disrupts copulation in sexually naïve rats but has little or no effect in sexually experienced rats. Experience automates behavior and gives rise to expectancies that can maintain the behavior, even in the absence of sensory stimulation.

Jim Geer: There was some work that Joe Herbert did, I don't know whether it was published or not, in which he reported some results with primates that when he would deenervate the penis and they would bring in a receptive female—these were experienced animals—they would mount several times and then they'd give up on her. If you bring in a new female, they try it all over again and then they quit with that one. It's not my fault, it's hers; something about her was his interpretation.

David Rowland: I'd like to comment on a study that Julia Heiman and I did quite a few years ago in which we looked at measures of subjective arousal in men who were dysfunctional, that is, who were not getting erections; this was probably about 15 years ago. In any case, we had items on the questionnaire about "general sexual arousal," "mental sexual arousal," and "physical sexual arousal." In dysfunctional men, the assessment of general sexual arousal was closer to mental arousal than physical arousal. In other words, they were assessing their arousal to the situation by what was going on in their head and not by what was going on in their genitals, because there wasn't much going on in their genitals. So, this may provide a model for assessing arousal during a genital nonresponse situation. And that makes sense; people can be mentally aroused without being physically aroused. I think this happens in many people throughout the day—they have sexual thoughts going on in their head, but they're not necessarily showing genital responses. So as we look at the assessment of arousal, perhaps we need to think of the kinds of items we're including.

Don Strassberg: It's also the case, I think consistent with that, in men who are post–radical prostatectomy; they are not getting erections. Many of those men still get aroused and have orgasms, but they're not getting any of the more traditional kinds of feedback from their genitals.

Erick Janssen: I'm fascinated by the issue of voluntary control and how it might be relevant to other studies, including yours, Meredith. We will talk more about it tomorrow, I am sure, but in my mind incompatibilities exist between the various models, and it makes me think that we should incorporate the notion of response level in our discussion. What levels of response are we talking about? Low levels of genital response may be less subject to control than later or higher response levels, where attention seems to play a more important role—consistent with our and David Barlow's models (Barlow, 1986; Janssen, Everaerd, Spiering, & Janssen, 2000). How much do we really know about people's ability to modify response levels in the lab, and the strategies they might use? I know studies have found that internally generated distraction can be used to change one's response levels. But I also remember Walter Everaerd saying years ago that a true demonstration of voluntary control of genital response requires that you are truly attending to a stimulus—I'm not talking about just following objects on a monitor or screen; attention is much more complex than that—and that you *still* can modify your response. I've always found that a challenging and interesting notion. We can do a lot when we watch something. An example would be showing subjects sex films from the 1920s or 1930s, where if they would just watch, nothing might happen (other than putting a smile on their faces), but if they would use their imagination, if they would be willing to process the stimulus in a different way, it may work and they might become aroused. There are lots of issues and questions here, related to voluntary control, that I find fascinating. Meredith, when it comes to your study, where you found that men show specificity in their response patterns and women do not, to what degree might that be related to processes of voluntary control? Maybe not even voluntary, maybe men and women are not even aware of what they are doing, or why or how. In other words, it could involve explicit but also implicit cognitive processes. But what if men are programmed or taught and have learned to be more specific because they are not really "supposed" to respond to stimuli that do not match their sexual orientation, and maybe those rules are less strict or simply different for women? I am not necessarily saying that men would just look away from a sexual film clip that does not match their orientation, as attention is much more complex than that, but what are your thoughts on this?

Meredith Chivers: I don't know if I should get into this today or tomorrow, but I've thought a lot about your question with men and whether or not their category specificity of sexual arousal is a function of voluntary inhibition of arousal to a nonpreferred sexual stimulus. I wondered if men would exhibit an initial penile response that is consciously detected then inhibited. So I talked to Ray Blanchard and asked him about his experience with men who were coming through the phallometric laboratory at the Centre for Addiction and Mental Health. I asked him if, using a volumetric apparatus that is very, very sensitive, he has observed an initial increase in penile volume to nonpreferred sexual stimuli that then declines. Dr. Blanchard said he'd never seen anything like that; men typically showed no detectable response to nonpreferred sexual stimuli.

In the data I'll show tomorrow, men do show a small response to nonpreferred film stimuli, which, relative to their response to their preferred sexual category, is not as high. This is different from what Ray Blanchard saw, but the stimuli used by his laboratory are still pictures whereas my stimuli were films of people having sex. Certainly you wonder whether or not there is just something arousing about sex in general, regardless of who is depicted, that triggers a nonspecific and low level of response. According to your model, Erick, this response is suppressed when it comes into conscious awareness.

I addressed the issue of category specificity being the result of nonpreferred response suppression in my paper. Specifically, I examined data where men had the ability to suppress and increase responses to preferred and nonpreferred sexual stimuli. From the paper:

> It is unlikely that men's arousal patterns, reported in the research reviewed, are explained by conscious suppression of arousal to nonpreferred sexual stimuli. Although heterosexual male research participants might be motivated to suppress sexual arousal to the male-male stimuli, because of stigma or concern about being labeled as homosexual, gay men would not be similarly motivated to suppress arousal to female-female stimuli and gay men's sexual arousal is still category specific. Conscious suppression of arousal to nonpreferred sexual stimuli is also unlikely. Neither heterosexual nor homosexual men are able to increase their erections to nonpreferred sexual stimuli, even when motivated to do so (Adams, Motsinger, McAnulty, & Moore, 1992). This suggests that, under typical conditions, men are not suppressing their genital responses

to nonpreferred stimuli; if they were, they would be able to increase genital arousal, when sufficiently motivated to do so, by ceasing their suppression efforts.

References

Adams, H. E., Motsinger, P., McAnulty, R. D., & Moore, A. L. (1992). Voluntary control of penile tumescence among homosexual and heterosexual subjects. *Archives of Sexual Behavior, 21*, 17–31.

Bancroft, J. (2002). Sexual arousal. In L. Nadel (Ed.), *Encyclopedia of cognitive science* (pp. 1165–1168). London: Wiley.

Bancroft, J., Herbenick, D., & Reynolds, M. (2003). Masturbation as a marker of sexual development. In J. Bancroft (Ed.), *Sexual development in childhood* (pp. 156–185). Bloomington: Indiana University Press.

Bancroft, J., & Wu, F. C. W. (1983). Changes in erectile responsiveness during androgen therapy. *Archives of Sexual Behavior, 12*(1), 59–66.

Barlow, D. H. (1986). Causes of sexual dysfunction: The role of anxiety and cognitive interference. *Journal of Consulting and Clinical Psychology, 54*, 140–157.

Beach, F. A. (1942). Analysis of the stimuli adequate to elicit mating behavior in the sexually inexperienced male rat. *Journal of Comparative Psychology, 33*, 163–207.

Dick, D. M., Johnson, J. K., Viken, R. J., & Rose, R. J. (2000). Testing between-family associations in within-family comparisons. *Psychological Science, 11*, 409–413.

Janssen, E., Everaerd, W., Spiering, M., & Janssen, J. (2000). Automatic processes and the appraisal of sexual stimuli: Toward an information processing model of sexual arousal. *Journal of Sex Research, 37*(2), 8–23.

Korff, J., & Geer, J. H. (1983). The relationship between sexual arousal experience and genital response. *Psychophysiology, 20*, 121–127.

Kwan, M., Greenleaf, W. J., Mann J., Crapo, L., & Davidson, J. (1983). The nature of androgen action on male sexuality: A combined laboratory/self-report study on hypogonadal men. *Journal of Clinical Endocrinology and Metabolism, 57*, 557–562.

Laan, E., Everaerd, W., van Aanhold, M., & Rebel, M. (1993). Performance demand and sexual arousal in women. *Behaviour Research and Therapy, 31*, 25–35.

Leigh, B.C., Gillmore, M. R., & Morrison, D. M. (1998). Comparison of diary and retrospective measures for recording alcohol consumption and sexual activity. *Journal of Clinical Epidemiology, 51*, 119–127.

Mustanski, B. S., Viken, R. J., Kaprio, J., Winter, T., & Rose, R. J. (2003). Multivariate behavior genetic analyses of sexual health. *Behavior Genetics, 33*, 713.

Paredes, R. G., & Alonso, A. (1997). Sexual behavior regulated (paced) by the female induces conditioned place preference. *Behavioral Neuroscience, 111*, 123–128.

Paredes, R. G., & Martinez, I. (2001). Naloxone blocks place preference conditioning after paced mating in female rats. *Behavioral Neuroscience, 115*, 1363–1367.

Paredes, R. G., & Vazquez, B. (1999). What do female rats like about sex? Paced mating. *Behavioural Brain Research, 105*, 117–127.

Ramsey, G. V. (1943a). The sex information of younger boys. *American Journal of Orthopsychiatry, 8*(2), 347–352.

Ramsey, G. V. (1943b). The sexual development of boys. *American Journal of Psychology, 56*(2), 217–234.

Rellini, A., McCall, K. M., Meston, C. M., & Randall, P. K. (2003). The relationship between self-reported and physiological measures of female sexual arousal. Manuscript under review.

Rolls, E. T. (1999). *The brain and emotion.* New York: Oxford University Press.

Tennen, H., & Affleck, G. (1996). Daily processes in coping with chronic pain: Methods and analytic strategies. In M. Zeidner & N. S. Endler (Eds.), *Handbook of coping: Theory, research, applications* (pp. 151–177). Oxford, England: John Wiley & Sons.

Tracy, J. A., Ghose, S. S., Stecher, T., McFall, R. M., & Steinmetz, J. E. (1999). Classical conditioning in a nonclinical obsessive-compulsive population. *Psychological Science, 10,* 14–18.

Whalen, R. E. (1961). Effects of mounting without intromission and intromission without ejaculation on sexual behavior and maze learning. *Journal of Comparative and Physiological Psychology, 54,* 409–415.

Part 4.

Sexual Motivation and Arousal

Desire Emerges from Excitement

A Psychophysiological Perspective on Sexual Motivation

STEPHANIE BOTH, WALTER EVERAERD,
AND ELLEN LAAN

In the dominant model of human sexual response, sexual desire, excitement, and orgasm are distinguished as consecutive phases (American Psychiatric Association, *Diagnostic and Statistical Manual of Mental Disorders*, 2000). The model is based on the psychophysiological research of Masters and Johnson (1966) and on the ideas of the psychiatrist and sex therapist Helen Kaplan (1995), who introduced the desire phase as the phase preceding sexual excitement. Kaplan was seeing in her clinic many female patients complaining about a lack of desire for sex. Absence of sexual desire, she reasoned, points to a phase in the normal sexual response cycle that activates the wanting to experience sexual excitement. Kaplan stated:

> By thus examining the current sexual experiences of 2,109 patients and couples with chief complaints of deficient sexual desire I came to the conclusion that *the pathological decrease of these patients' libido is essentially an expression of the normal regulation of sexual motivation gone awry* [italics added]. More specifically, sexual motivation or desire, just like other needs or motives, such as hunger and thirst, is regulated by CNS control mechanisms. (pp. 3–4)

Kaplan conceptualized sexual desire as an expression of a drive, comparable to hunger and thirst, influenced by sensors that signal changes in the internal environment of the body. In her view on sexual desire, psychoanalytic thinking can be heard, thinking that has long dominated ideas about sexual motivation. Even though there is little evidence for a homeostatic mechanism in human sexual motivation, the essence of the concept of sexual drive remains in the dominant model of sexual response and in the *DSM-IV* diagnosis of hyposexual desire that is based on that model.

In this contribution, first the concepts libido, lust, and drive that were introduced by Freud will be discussed. Then modern motivation theory and the close reationship between emotion and motivation mechanisms will be elaborated upon. This relationship will be illustrated by recent experimental studies that we conducted on motor preparation, sexual arousal, and action. Sexual arousal and desire will be considered in the light of current knowledge about neurobiological mechanisms of emotion and motivation. After that, we will talk about the interaction of emotion and motivation circuits in the brain and the role of dopamine in motivation. We will conclude that current knowledge about emotion and motivation mechanisms argues against Helen Kaplan's assumption that desire and excitement are distinctive sexual response phases. Desire results from the conscious awareness of the sexually excited state of the body and the brain. This means that the experience of sexual desire can only come about through sexual excitement.

The Drive Model versus Incentive Motivation Models of Sexual Motivation

The Concepts of Libido, Lust, and Drive

Sexual motivation is a construct, used to explain the generation of sexual action. Sexual desire is the (subjective) experience of being attracted to or pushed toward objects or behaviors with potential rewarding effects. As we noted before, in Freud's days, sexual motivation was seen as a constant force (Everaerd, Laan, Both, & Spiering, 2001). For sexual desire, Freud (1953) preferred the use of the word *libido*. "Everyday language possesses no counterpart to the word 'hunger,' but science makes use of the word 'libido' for that purpose" (p. 135). In a footnote, added by Freud, it is explained that the German language word *Lust* is ambiguous, because it can either mean the experience of need and of a gratification. In a note on page 212, the explanation has been elaborated upon. "The word 'Lust' takes into account the part played by preparatory sexual excitations which simultaneously produce an element of satisfaction and a contribution to sexual tension." *Lust* has two meanings and is used to describe the sensation of sexual tension ("Ich habe Lust" = "I should like to," "I feel impulse to") as well as the feeling of satisfaction. Thus, the word *lust* refers to sexual arousal and the wanting to have more of that, as well as to sexual satisfaction. We will come across these two different meanings later on when we discuss concepts of wanting and liking that are important in recent motivation theories.

Libido, according to Freud (1964), is fuelled by the sexual instincts. An instinct arises from a source within the body:

> Its source is a state of excitation in the body, its aim is the removal of that excitation; on its path from its source to its aim the instinct becomes operative psychically. We picture it as a certain quota of energy which presses in a particular direction. It is from this pressing that it derives its name of "Trieb" (literally "drive"). (p. 96)

Freud made clear that libido does not arise from an external stimulus. "An instinct, then, is distinguished from a stimulus by the fact that it arises from sources of stimulation within the body, that it operates as a constant force and that the subject can not avoid it by flight, as is possible with an external stimulus" (p. 96). Freud conceived of the instinct as energy that pushes toward a certain direction. From that push factor, the German word *Trieb*, drive, is derived. Thus the sexual instinct comes from a source within the body, it operates as a constant force, and the subject cannot escape from it as is possible in the case of an external stimulus. In this view, libido is the result of an internal bodily tension, and there would be a need to neutralize this state. How the drive builds up remains unclear.

In her discussion of the regulation of sexual motivation, Kaplan (1995) used the concepts libido, lust, and drive. She localized the sexual instinct in the hypothalamus, the organ in the brain where physiological deficits and the restoration of homeostasis are signaled. "Once again we can learn from the similarities between eating and sex. More specifically, under normal circumstances, a state of starvation activates the ventromedial hypothalamic 'appetite centers.' This neurophysiologic activity produces a subjective feeling of hunger" (Kaplan, p. 17). Because it is unknown how processes in the hypothalamus contribute to sexual motivation, for the time being she considered it to be a black box that, in interaction with sexual inciters, activates sexual desire and lust. There is, however, no evidence of any adverse effects of sexual abstinence. As Beach (1956) concluded, "No genuine tissue or biological needs are generated by sexual abstinence. . . . What is commonly confused with a primary drive associated with sexual deprivation is in actuality sexual appetite, and this has little or no relation to biological or physiological needs" (p. 4). In the case of sex, there does not seem to be a biological need that demands satisfaction, as is the case in hunger and thirst. More recently, Herbert (2001) proposed that sexual behavior may be thought of as a form of adaptation or response to a perceived deficit. He suggested that the hypothalamus uses the current levels of gonadal steroids to monitor the current levels of sexual interest and behavior. He underlined, however, that sexual behavior is a complex activity that relies upon the receipt and analysis of complex social stimuli. Animals and humans will only be brought into sexual readiness by changes in hormone levels when a sexually attractive stimulus is perceived.

Incentive Motivation

According to the drive model, we have sex because we feel sexual desire; this is an expression of Freud's view that there is a constant force that seeks an outlet. Incentive motivation theories emphasize that sexual motivation is the result of the activation of a sensitive sexual response system by sexually competent stimuli that are present in the environment (Bindra, 1974; Singer & Toates, 1987). Once the sexual system, whose sensitivity is influenced by hormones and neurotransmitters, interacts with the stimulus, the individual is pushed toward sexual activity. In this view, sexual motivation does not emerge through a deficit signaled by the hypothalamus, but through the attractiveness of possible rewards in the environment. Desire is activated, through expectations of reward, by attractive and rewarding stimuli in the environment.

Motivation is strongly related to emotion mechanisms. Emotion and motivation mechanisms interact in such a way that it is sometimes hard to distinguish them; they are two sides of one coin. According to Bindra (1974), motivation emerges in the interaction of the organism and the environment. There is no motivation without a stimulus that predicts reward or danger (Schultz, 1998). Our brains are designed to adequately respond to changes in the environment, to avoid danger, and to approach situations that may be rewarding. Emotions can be looked upon as action mechanisms that help the organism to adapt to aspects of the environment that promote or endanger survival. In this view, emotions serve to satisfy concerns and, therefore, result in motivational states or action tendencies (e.g., Frijda, 1986; Lang, 1993; LeDoux, 2001). The motivational state or action tendency is reflected in the physiological changes that accompany emotions and that prepare the body for action.

Cognitive neuroscience is revealing how emotions, the consequent motivational states or action tendencies, and emotional feelings appear (Craig, 2002; Damasio, 2003; LeDoux, 2001). The actual or imagined presence of an emotionally competent stimulus activates the emotion-triggering sites in the brain. These emotion-triggering sites subsequently activate the emotion-execution sites that activate changes in the internal organs and in the musculoskeletal system. Damasio and LeDoux, and a long time before them William James (1884), stress that the conscious experience of emotion, what we call feelings, is the result of the perception of these changes. Feelings do not precede but follow emotion; feelings are based on the feedback of the emotional bodily and brain responses to the brain. Feelings are the end result of the whole "machinery of emotion."

We propose that the mechanism through which sexual emotional states and feelings of sexual excitement and desire appear will be similar as in other emotions that are coupled with relatively strong bodily reactions. Recently functional imaging studies showed that the subjective experience of different emotions like anger, disgust, anxiety, and sexual arousal is associated with activation of the insula and the orbitofrontal cortex (Craig, 2002; Morris, 2002; Sumich, Kumari, & Sharma, 2003). This indicates that the insula has a generalized role that is not specific to any particular emotion. Its role seems to be the representation of peripheral autonomic, and possibly somatic, arousal that provides input to conscious awareness of emotional states.

We suppose that processing of an actually present or imagined sexual stimulus automatically results in preparation of the organism for sexual action. When we become aware of these bodily changes, through feedback of these bodily responses to the brain, we experience sexual excitement and desire. Thus, sexual desire does not appear out of the blue. Without a stimulus that activates arousal, there will be no desire. In fact, there is no good reason to assume that desire and excitement are two fundamentally different things. Perhaps we can phenomenologically distinguish them such that feelings of excitement represent the subjective experience of genital changes, perhaps combined with a conscious evaluation that the situation is indeed "sexy," and that feelings of desire represent the subjective experience of an action tendency, of a willingness to behave sexually.

Processing of emotionally competent stimuli results in physiological changes that prepare the body for action. In case of threatening stimuli, avoidance behavior will be activated, and in case of attractive (sexual) stimuli, appetitive behavior will be triggered. Appetitive behavior includes locomotor responses to the goal and occurs in parallel with autonomic and endocrine responses that prepare for efficient interaction with the goal (Robbins & Everitt, 1999). The generation of sexual appetitive behavior involves specific genital reactions. However, there will also be changes in the somatic motor system. Signals are sent to the muscles to prepare for action. Eventually, these changes may result in sexual behavior. We will illustrate this process by discussing recent psychophysiological studies on motor preparation, sexual arousal, and action.

Sexual Arousal and Action Tendency

Research in women by Ellen Laan showed that there is an automatic relationship between sexual stimuli and genital response, and that this response may emerge without the person being aware of it (Laan & Everaerd, 1995). Recently, we focused on somatic motor system changes that result from the processing of emotionally competent stimuli. More specifically, we searched for an appropriate measure for motor preparation. One way to do this is to monitor changes in the amplitude of reflexes. Motor preparation involves heightened activity in the spinal cord, and that activity will be expressed as a stronger reflex (Brunia & Boelhouwer, 1988). The reflex we use is the Achilles tendon reflex, for short, the T-reflex. Tendon reflexes are not sensitive to valence of an affective state, but they are augmented in states of preparation for action and are modified by differences in arousal intensity (Bonnet, Bradley, Lang, & Requin, 1995; Brunia & Boelhouwer, 1988; Brunia & van Boxtel, 2000). Therefore, investigation of T-reflex modulation offers a window on the generation of action.

Bonnet et al. (1995) hypothesized that stimuli that elicit emotional arousal will facilitate T-reflex magnitude, relative to neutral, low arousal stimuli. They stated that the T-reflex, which functions when the limb is activated for walking, standing, and other activities, is inherently nondirectional (one can run either toward or away from stimulation). Since the T-reflex is nondirectional, it would be involved both in actions that are appetitively and defensively motivated. They studied the modulation of T-reflexes during the presentation of pictures from "The International Affective Picture System" designed by Lang, Öhman, and Vaitl (1988). These pictures were designed to induce emotions varying in valence (positive to negative) and in intensity (low to high). As expected, T-reflexes were significantly augmented when elicited during processing of highly arousing emotional pictures (either negative or positive) as compared with neutral pictures.

Similar to Bonnet et al., we hypothesized emotional stimuli to automatically generate action tendencies. These action tendencies will result in increased spinal excitability, reflected in facilitated T-reflex magnitude. We studied reflex modulation by appetitive (sexual) and aversive (anxiety and sexual threat) stimuli (Both, Everaerd, & Laan, 2003) and by sexual stimuli varying in intensity (Both, van Boxtel, Stekelenburg, Everaerd, & Laan, 2005). In these studies, T-reflex amplitude, genital response, subjective sexual arousal, and subjective action tendencies were measured.

In the first study, subjects were shown four film clips of 5 minutes each: a sex stimulus depicting consensual sexual activity, an anxiety-provoking film, a sexually threatening film, and a neutral film that was not expected to be emotionally arousing. It was expected that the three emotional stimuli would result in changes in subjective action tendencies, the sexual film in a facilitated approach tendency, and the sexually threatening and the anxiety-provoking film in a facilitated avoidance tendency. It was also expected that the three emotional stimuli would result in stronger T-reflexes than the neutral film, and that T-reflexes during the neutral film would not be higher than during the preceding rest period. Both the positive and the negative emotional stimuli resulted in motor preparation, and the subjects reported that during the threatening stimuli they felt the wish to avoid and during the consensual sexual stimulus the wish to approach. The increase in reflex amplitude in response to the sexual stimulus did not differ from the increase in response to the threatening stimuli.

In the second study, sexual stimuli were used that differed in intensity. The low intensity stimulus depicted erotic kissing, the medium stimulus showed kissing and caressing, and the high intensity stimulus depicted intercourse. From a previous study of Ellen Laan (Laan, Everaerd, van der Velde, & Geer, 1995), we knew that these particular clips evoked distinct and increasing levels of genital arousal in women. As expected, T-reflex amplitude increased with increasing levels of sexual stimulation, and these were significant differences.

These studies demonstrate that in interaction with emotionally competent stimuli, a tendency is generated to avoid or approach. Negative or positive emotional stimuli generate an affective response, and part of this affective response is the generation of an action tendency, which is an expression of motivation. This action tendency increases as the intensity of the emotional state increases. To demonstrate that confrontation with a sexually competent stimulus leads to action tendencies and, eventually, sexual action, we studied sexual activity after laboratory-induced sexual arousal (Both, Spiering, Everaerd, & Laan, 2004). Male and female subjects were randomly assigned to a neutral or sexual condition. In the neutral condition, subjects were exposed to a 15-minute neutral film, and in the sexual condition, to a 15-minute erotic film. We expected that only in the sexual condition genital responses, subjective feelings of sexual arousal, and approach tendencies would be elicited. Subjects completed, 24 hours after the experimental session, a questionnaire about their sexual behavior during these 24 hours. We expected that subjects in the erotic film condition would engage in more sexual activity than the subjects in the neutral film condition. As expected, the subjects that were exposed to the erotic film had genital responses, increased T-reflexes, and reported sexual arousal and approach tendencies. Those exposed to the neutral film did not show these specific reactions. Moreover, the subjects who had seen the erotic film had engaged in more sexual activity than the subjects who did not see the erotic film. In sum, these studies show that confrontation with sexual stimuli results in action tendencies, and these action tendencies increase the likelihood of actual sexual behavior.

Neurobiological Mechanisms

In retrospect, Bindra's view that emotion and motivation mechanisms are closely intertwined is in agreement with current ideas about how the brain may work. Sensory information is converted in the brain to set off motor responses in the autonomic and somatic nervous system. Bindra had no clear idea of the neurobiological mechanism that may explain the inter-action of limbic and motor systems. Mogenson, Jones, and Yim did a proposal in 1980 that still inspires motivation research (Mogenson, Jones, & Yim, 1980; LeDoux, 2001). Recently Holstege (1998) did a similar proposal, the "emotional-motor system." Holstege distinguishes the somatic motor system and the emotional motor system. The somatic motor system is controlled by the motor cortex and the brainstem. Through this system, voluntary movements are controlled. The emotional motor system is controlled by structures that are part of or are connected with the emotional circuit in the brain, the limbic system. Through the emotional motor system, specific emotional behaviors—for example, mating behavior—and more general changes, like increased muscle tension, are initiated.

Mogenson et al. (1980), and more recently LeDoux (2001), present the following sketch of the interaction between the limbic system, the emotion circuit, and the motor system, the motivation circuit. The interface between the amygdala, part of the limbic system, and the motor system is the nucleus accumbens. The nucleus accumbens receives direct input from the amygdala and indirect input from the ventral tegmental area. This area is the source of the dopaminergic connections to the nucleus accumbens. This nucleus accumbens passes the information on to the globus pallidus, which is connected to cortical and brainstem areas that control movement. This interface between the emotional and the motor circuit is necessary because primary (emotional) needs need to be transformed into actions, to satisfy those needs. Dopamine has an important role in the motivational circuit; it seems to be involved in both reward signaling and in the initiation of motor responses (Kalivas & Nakamura, 1999; Phillips, Suber, Heien, Wightman, & Carelli, 2003). Dopamine has long been regarded as the transmitter responsible for the experience of satisfaction. However, studies in rats have shown that dopamine is not involved in the valence or appreciation of a stimulus, but in the tendency to approach a stimulus (Berridge, 1996).

Berridge introduced the concepts of "liking" and "wanting." Liking represents the affective response to a stimulus. Both rats and humans exhibit specific facial expressions with the negative or positive appreciation of food; from these specific facial expressions the affective response can be derived. Wanting represents the tendency to approach a stimulus. This tendency may express itself in the frequency and intensity with which a rat presses a lever to obtain food. Berridge showed that manipulation of the dopamine system affects the instrumental behavior (wanting) and not the facial expressions (liking). The difference between wanting and liking is relevant for understanding disorders related to motivation. It explains why a person who is addicted to some substance can crave for the drug intensely, whereas subsequent intake of the drug may not be very satisfying.

Animal studies have shown facilitating effects of dopamine on sexual motivation (Melis & Argiolas, 1995), and observations in humans also showed a facilitating effect of dopamine on sexual motivation and sexual arousal (Meston & Frohlich, 2000). We reasoned that measuring somatic motor system activity through means of T-reflex modulation may offer a sensitive measure to investigate the effects of a psychomotor stimulant drug like dopamine on sexual arousal and sexual motivation in humans. We wanted to find out whether a dopamine agonist, that increases dopamine levels in the brain, would affect sexual response, particularly action tendencies. We expected dopamine to affect the wanting component of sexual motivation, specifically the instigation of action, and, therefore, to result in stronger T-reflex magnitudes in response to sexual stimulation. Secondly, based on the evidence for dopaminergic influences on penile response in men (e.g., Giuliano & Allard, 2001; Heaton, 2000), we expected levodopa to facilitate genital response. Conscious emotional feelings and subjectively experienced tendencies for approach behavior may also be affected by levodopa. Although Berridge (1996) underlines that awareness of a motivational state may be dissociable from the underlying motivational processes that give rise to the conscious experience, it may be expected that substantial changes in the underlying processes will enter consciousness and will be reflected in subjective report. Both men and women participated to allow for investigation of gender differences in the effects of dopamine on sexual responses.

Subjects (19 men and 28 women) were given a single dose of levodopa (100 mg), which increases dopamine levels in the brain (Both, Everaerd, Laan, & Gooren, 2005). Participants visited the laboratory two times, receiving at one visit a placebo and at the other visit levodopa, following a double-blind crossover protocol. Fifty minutes after placebo/drug administration, when substantial dopamine levels were expected, subjects were asked to engage in a pleasant sexual fantasy and then they were shown an erotic film. T-reflexes, genital responses, subjective action tendencies, and subjective sexual arousal in response to erotic stimulation were measured. We found that levodopa did not affect the subjective and the genital responses. There was, however, a significant effect of levodopa on T-reflexes. In men, T-reflexes were stronger with levodopa, both in the sexual fantasy and in the erotic film condition. In women, there were no effects of levodopa at all. Thus, in accordance with evidence from studies in male rats, an increased level of dopamine resulted in stronger instigation of action in response to sexual incentives in human males. The absence of an effect of levodopa on T-reflex magnitude in women is in line with the conflicting reports about the effects of dopamine on sexual motivation in female rats (Meston & Frohlich, 2000) and warrants further study. The fact that levodopa increased male T-reflex magnitude during sexual stimulation shows that, in line with the expectations, dopamine is involved in the energetic aspects of motivated behavior, and that T-reflex modulation offers a sensitive measure for dopaminergic effects on the generation of sexual appetitive behavior in humans. About the sex difference in the effect of levodopa, we can only speculate. As noted before, studies on dopaminergic effects on sexual motivation in female rats revealed conflicting results. These conflicting results are often attributed to possible interactions of dopamine with the hormonal treatments that are used to induce estrus in female rats. There is evidence for steroid-dopamine interactions (e.g., Balthazart, Baillien, & Ball, 2002; Becker, 1999; Giuliano & Allard, 2001). The gender difference in the effect of levodopa in the present study might be due to differences in sex steroid levels in the brain. Perhaps the effect of dopamine depends on testosterone levels, which are higher in males. It would be informative to include hormonal status as a variable in future studies on dopaminergic effects on sexual responses in women.

Conclusion

The mechanism of sexual motivation can be summarized as follows: Processing of a sexually competent stimulus (actually present or imagined) automatically energizes emotional systems, resulting in bodily changes that prepare for sexual action. The elicited action tendency increases as the intensity of the emotional state increases. Dopamine is important for the transformation of emotion into action. It seems to be involved in both reward signaling and in the initiation of behavioral action. The bodily changes that are elicited by a sexually competent stimulus include motor responses involved in general approach behavior and motor responses involved in sex-specific responses, for example, relaxation of genital smooth muscles. The processing of a sexually competent stimulus is largely involuntary and unconscious. Feelings of sexual excitement and desire emerge when motor responses enter consciousness through the feedback of the bodily and brain responses to the brain.

From this follows that the experience of sexual feelings is a consequence of an incentive energizing the sexual system. Feelings of sexual desire and excitement result from the awareness of the sexually excited state of the body and the brain. Hence, the experience of sexual desire can only come about through sexual excitement. Contrary to Kaplan's proposal, sexual desire does not precede sexual excitement; excitement precedes sexual desire.

Recently other authors have, in accordance with our view, stated that sexual desire may emerge during sexual excitement, and they have proposed modifications of the dominant model of sexual response (Basson, 2000; Levin, 2001). The consequences of the changed view on sexual desire are important for practice. From an incentive motivation model, it should be concluded that hyposexual desire is not a manifestation of a malfunctioning instinct but an indication that the emotion-motivation mechanism is not activated. In some cases, hypoactive sexual desire may be caused by a lack of brain chemicals, but in most cases the cause will be the absence of attractive stimuli. In fact, Kaplan was aware of that, since an important part of her treatment for hyposexual desire consisted of what she called "[l]ibido enhancing sexual homework assignments: fantasy and friction" (Kaplan, 1995, p. 6). That homework could be sexual fantasy, explicit erotic material, masturbation, or other methods of erotic stimulation. Secondly, an incentive motivation view emphasizes the importance of the evaluation of the stimulus, which is determined by individual histories of sexual rewards. When a patient has little or no experience with sexual rewards or a mainly negative sexual or relational history, pharmacological enhancement of the sensitivity of the sexual system (be it with androgens, dopamine, or other prosexual drugs) will not facilitate sexual desire.

We expect that the study of somatic motor system activity through means of T-reflex modulation may offer a sensitive measure to investigate (disorders in) the signaling of sexual reward and the instigation of action tendencies in humans. In conclusion, it's obvious that our knowledge about sexual motivation, about hypoactive as well as hyperactive sexual desire, will only increase by further studies into the behavioral mechanisms through which sexual action is instigated and regulated.

References

American Psychiatric Association. (2000). *Diagnostic and statistical manual of mental disorders* (text revision). Washington, D.C.: Author.

Balthazart, J., Baillien, M., & Ball, G. F. (2002). Interactions between aromatas (estrogen synthase) and dopamine in the control of male sexual behavior in quail. *Comparative Biochemistry and Physiology, 132,* 37–55.

Basson, R. (2000). The female sexual response: A different model. *Journal of Sex & Marital Therapy, 26,* 51–65.

Beach, F. A. (1956). Characteristics of masculine sex drive. In M. R. Jones (Ed.), *Nebraska symposium on motivation* (pp. 1–31). Lincoln, Neb.: University of Nebraska Press.

Becker, J. B. (1999). Gender differences in dopaminergic function in striatum and nucleus accumbens. *Pharmacology Biochemistry and Behavior, 64,* 803–812.

Berridge, K. C. (1996). Food reward: Brain substrates of wanting and liking. *Neuroscience and Biobehavioral Reviews, 20,* 1–25.

Bindra, D. (1974). A motivational view of learning, performance, and behavior modification. *Psychological Review, 81,* 199–213.

Bonnet, M., Bradley, M. M., Lang, P., & Requin, J. (1995). Modulation of spinal reflexes: Arousal, pleasure, action. *Psychophysiology, 32,* 367–372.

Both, S., Everaerd, W., & Laan, E. (2003). Modulation of spinal reflexes by aversive and sexually appetitive stimuli. *Psychophysiology, 40,* 174–183.

Both, S., Everaerd, W., Laan, E., & Gooren, L. (2005). Effect of a single dose of levodopa on sexual response in men and women. *Neuropsychopharmacology, 30,* 173–183.

Both, S., van Boxtel, G., Stekelenburg, J., Everaerd, W., & Laan, E. (2005). Modulation of spinal reflexes by sexual films of increasing intensity. *Psychophysiology, 42,* 726–731.

Both, S., Spiering, M., Everaerd, W., & Laan, E. (2004). Sexual behavior and responsiveness to sexual cues following laboratory-induced sexual arousal. *Journal of Sex Research, 41,* 242–259.

Brunia, C. H. M., & Boelhouwer, A. J. W. (1988). Reflexes as a tool: A window in the central nervous system. *Advances in Psychophysiology, 3,* 1–67.

Brunia, C. H. M., & van Boxtel, G. J. M. (2000). In J. Cacioppo, L. Tassinari, & G. Berntson (Eds.), *Handbook of psychophysiology* (pp. 507–532). New York: Cambridge University Press.

Craig, A.D. (2002). How do you feel? Interoception: The sense of the physiological condition of the body. *Nature Reviews, 3,* 655–666.

Damasio, A. (2003). *Looking for Spinoza: Joy, sorrow, and the feeling brain.* Orlando: Harcourt.

Everaerd, W., Laan, E., Both, S., & Spiering, M. (2001). Sexual motivation and desire. In W. Everaerd, E. Laan, & S. Both (Eds.), *Sexual appetite, desire and motivation: Energetics of the sexual system* (pp. 95–110). Amsterdam: Royal Netherlands Academy of Arts and Sciences.

Freud, S. (1953). *The standard edition of the complete psychological works of Sigmund Freud, Volume VII.* London: Hogarth Press.

Freud, S. (1964). *The standard edition of the complete psychological works of Sigmund Freud, Volume XXII.* London: Hogarth Press.

Frijda, N. H. (1986). *The emotions.* Cambridge University Press, Cambridge.

Giuliano, F., & Allard, J. (2001). Dopamine and sexual function. *International Journal of Impotence Research, 13*(Suppl. 3), S18–S28.

Heaton, J. P. (2000). Central neuropharmacological agents and mechanisms in erectile dysfunction: the role of dopamine. *Neuroscience and Biobehavioral Reviews, 24,* 561–569.

Herbert, J. (2001). Sexual behavior as adaptation: Relating brain, endocrine system and the social environment. In W. Everaerd, E. Laan, & S. Both (Eds.), *Sexual appetite, desire and motivation: Energetics of the sexual system* (pp. 13–32). Amsterdam: Royal Netherlands Academy of Arts and Sciences.

Holstege, G. (1998). The emotional motor system in relation to the supraspinal control of micturation and mating behavior. *Behavioral Brain Research, 92,* 103–109.

James, W. (1884). What is an emotion? *Mind, 9,* 188–205.

Kalivas, P. W., & Nakamura, M. (1999). Neural systems for behavioral activation and reward. *Current Opinion in Neurobiology, 9,* 223–227.

Kaplan, H. S. (1995). *The sexual desire disorders: Dysfunctional regulation of sexual motivation.* New York: Brunner/Mazel.

Laan, E., & Everaerd, W. (1995). Determinants of female sexual arousal: Psychophysiological theory and data. *Annual Review of Sex Research, 6,* 32–76.

Laan, E., Everaerd, W., van der Velde, J., & Geer, J. H. (1995). Determinants of subjective experience of sexual arousal in women: Feedback from genital arousal and erotic stimulus content. *Psychophysiology, 32,* 444–451.

Lang, P. J. (1993). The motivational organization of emotion: AffecT-reflex connections. In S. van Goozen, N. E. van der Poll, & J. A. Sergeant (Eds.), *The emotions: Essays on emotion theory* (pp. 61–96). Hillsdale, N.J.: Erlbaum.

Lang, P. J., Öhman, A., & Vaitl, D. (1988). *The international affective picture system.* Gainesville: Center for Research in Psychophysiology, University of Florida.

LeDoux, J. (2001). *The synaptic self.* New York: Viking Penguin.

Levin, R. J. (2001). Sexual desire and the deconstruction and reconstruction of the human female sexual response model of Masters and Johnson. In W. Everaerd, E. Laan, & S. Both (Eds.), *Sexual appetite, desire and motivation: Energetics of the sexual system* (pp. 63–93). Amsterdam: Royal Netherlands Academy of Arts and Sciences.

Masters, W. H., & Johnson, V. E. (1966). *Human sexual response* Boston: Little, Brown.

Melis, M. R., & Argiolas, A. (1995). Dopamine and sexual behavior. *Neuroscience and Biobehavioral Reviews, 19,* 19–38.

Meston, C. M., & Frohlich, P. F. (2000). The neurobiology of sexual function. *Archives of General Psychiatry, 57,* 1012–1030.

Mogenson, G. J., Jones, D. L., & Yim, C. Y. (1980). From motivation to action: Functional interface between the limbic system and the motor system. *Progress in Neuroscience, 14,* 69–97.

Morris, J. S. (2002). How do you feel? *Trends in Cognitive Sciences, 6*, 317–319.

Phillips, P. E., Stuber, G. D., Heien, M. L. A. V., Wightman, R. M., & Carelli, R. M. (2003). Subsecond dopamine release promotes cocaine seeking. *Nature, 422*, 614–618.

Robbins, T. W., & Everitt, B. J. (1999). Motivation and reward. In M. J. Zigmond, F. E. Bloom, S. C. Landis, J. L. Roberts, & L. R. Squire (Eds.), *Fundamental neuroscience* (pp. 1245–1260). San Diego: Academic Press.

Schultz, W. (1998). Predictive reward signal of dopamine neurons. *Neurophysiology, 80*, 1–27.

Singer, B., & Toates, F. M. (1987). Sexual motivation. *Journal of Sex Research, 23*, 481–501.

Sumich, A. L., Kumari, V., & Sharma, T. (2003). Neuroimaging of sexual arousal: Research and clinical utility. *Hospital Medicine, 64*, 28–33.

Models of Sexual Motivation

JAMES G. PFAUS

> An animal without motivation is not a nonmotivated animal . . . it is
> a corpse!
>
> —J. R. Blackburn (1988)

Sexual motivation is the energizing force that generates our level of sexual interest at any given time. It drives our sexual fantasies; compels us to seek out, attend to, and evaluate sexual incentives; regulates our levels of sexual arousal and desire; and enables us to masturbate, copulate, or engage in other forms of sex play. It seems like a straightforward concept, yet it runs into trouble at several important levels. As a concept of something internal, it is often circular, being inferred from a behavior or content of a fantasy. Thus, high levels of sexual interest or behavior are believed to reflect high levels of sexual motivation, and vice versa. Of course, in human experience this is not always true. It also runs into problems of definition when it is equated with vague and outdated terminology such as *libido,* when it is dismembered into fuzzy dichotomies like *physiological versus subjective arousal,* or when it is used to define a set of internal motivational processes that are somehow distinct from the outward expression of sexual performance (as if any sexual performance is not also motivated). Defining the goal of sexual behavior—a necessity if we are to understand what the motivation is driving the organism to *do*—is often tricky because it ranges from different rewards to reproduction.

The value of a concept like sexual motivation lies in its ability to provide a framework, or *heuristic,* within which sexual behaviors can be more easily understood. As a general framework, it should be able to handle animal and human sexual behaviors at different levels of analysis and despite their outward dissimilarities. General models of sexual behavior are almost always conceptual in nature and try to distill the behavioral components down to core variables that can be applied across species or situations (e.g., Bancroft & Janssen, 2000; Everitt & Bancroft, 1991; Pfaus, 1999). As a specific framework, the concept of sexual motivation should be able to define subcomponents and their interrelationships in testable ways. Such models resemble flow diagrams and specify the trajectory of different behaviors or events in time and space (e.g., Beach, 1956; Toates, 1992). Both general

340

and specific models are becoming more of a necessity as we try to understand the relationship between sexual arousal, desire, reward, and inhibition. As we take our first glimpses of human brain activation by sexual stimulation, having a frame of reference for the complicated interaction of different neural substrates for specific sexual responses makes it easier to keep their "role" in the whole behavior in perspective. Indeed, the study of sexual behavior has begun to incorporate a number of heuristics from other scientific domains, including incentive motivation (Berridge & Robinson, 1998; Stewart, 1995; Toates, 1992), information processing (Everaerd, 1995), comparative neurobiology (Ågmo & Ellingsen, 2003; Everitt & Bancroft, 1991; Pfaus, Kippin, & Coria-Avila, 2003), and evolutionary psychology (Abramson & Pinkerton, 1995; Buss, 1994; Symons, 1979). Although the predictions made by these frameworks are sometimes different, if not incompatible, they are leading the study of animal and human sexual behavior together into realms beyond copulation and the peripheral mechanics of penile erection (e.g., Bancroft & Janssen, 2000; Pfaus, Kippin, & Centeno, 2001). The challenge is to provide both general and specific heuristics that can accommodate data derived from these different domains.

Early Conceptions of Sexual Motivation

To know where such models could take us, it is important to know where they have been. The evolution of sexual motivation as a concept parallels that of more general concepts in motivational theory, navigating between many dichotomies, such as the "push" of internal states or drives versus the "pull" of external stimuli or incentives; the fractionation of behavior into appetitive versus consummatory phases; the determining role of biological versus social factors; the distinction between proximate versus ultimate "causes" of behavior; and the notion of different underlying sexual strategies, such as polygamy versus monogamy. It has also been split into multidimensional layers that reside in specific parts of the body and brain and that come together to elicit a conscious awareness of the body itself. Thus, sexual motivation has autonomic, attentional, and evaluative "parts" that likely reflect separate, but interactive, neural systems.

Ancient texts, from Vatsayana's *Kama Sutra* to the Taoist *Art of the Bedchamber* to Ovid's *Ars Amatoria*, generally divided sexual behavior into precopulatory and copulatory components and contained specific prescriptions for attaining or enhancing sexual pleasure. Sex was viewed as a diverse and interactive process that had an impact on social and personal aspects of a person's life, which, in turn, fed back to alter sexual expectations and specific sexual responses. Sexual motivation was believed to compel individuals to copulate, and pleasure was the driving force behind the motivation. An increasing tendency toward biological determinism grew in

Europe during the Middle Ages, Reformation, and Industrial Age, as the physical body was finally able to come under medical scrutiny. By the 19th century, rudimentary information about the anatomy and physiology of sex organs, gonadal secretions, and pregnancy, had been compiled. The Western world began to view sexual behavior as serving the goal of reproduction, which led to a concept of sex drive in men as a "need" to expel semen and in women as a "need" to get pregnant and give birth. Sexual behavior that deviated from the goal of reproduction, as in the case of masturbation, homosexual contact, fetishism, or bestiality, was viewed as both symptom and cause of various mental disorders (e.g., Morel's [1857] notion of physical and mental degeneration from sexual "misbehavior," as cited in Ellis, 1915). However, although heterosexual activity solely for pleasure, as with prostitutes or mistresses, was frowned upon by polite society as immoral, it was generally not viewed as a sign of mental depravity.

Ancient thinkers emphasized the multivariate nature of sexuality at many levels of analysis. This kept it wondrous and magical and extremely difficult to study scientifically. For sexual behavior to come under scientific scrutiny, it needed an easier model to work from and generate testable hypotheses about. Albert Moll (1897, 1933) was the first modern sexologist to envision a dual system of sexual motivation. He conceived of two separate impulses, *detumescence*—the drive to reduce sexual tension—and *contrectation*—the drive to approach, touch, and otherwise interact with a sexual incentive. These impulses could be directed at any appropriate sexual incentive, and both were imbued with distinctive types of pleasure. This dichotomy was similar to a prevailing dualistic theory in ethology at the time that differentiated preparatory behaviors that bring animals into contact with goal objects from consummatory behaviors that animals display in contact with the goal (e.g., Craig, 1918; Woodworth, 1918). Sigmund Freud (1922, 1927) and Wilhelm Reich (1942/1978) described the experiential, cognitive, and biological nature of sexual tension that impulses like detumescence and contrectation tried to reduce, and wrote specifically about the pleasurable sensations that reinforce sexual approach and tension reduction. The notion that there is a biological "need" for sex (whether it is to assure genetic mutation and fitness or pleasure through tension reduction) remains fraught with controversy. Sex has been regarded by many physiological psychologists as a primary drive, often equated in animals with thirst and hunger (e.g., Milner, 1970; Stellar, 1954). However, this notion was challenged by others, including Ellis (1915, 1933), Krafft-Ebing (1929), and Beach (1956). No tissue damage has been observed with sexual abstinence, nor does engaging in sexual activity necessarily maintain physical well-being. Sexual desire does not necessarily disappear in hypogonadal individuals or following castration. Homosexual copulation does not propagate the species, and heterosexual copulation is often observed at times when reproduction is unlikely or impossible. Neither masturbation nor paraphilic sexual behaviors serve a reproductive end, yet they occur with relatively high frequency in many human societies. The notion of a build-up of "tension" during sexual arousal and desire or its "release" during orgasm has never been demonstrated scientifically, although sympathetic, parasympathetic, and hormonal components of sexual arousal and orgasm have been described. Beach (1956) stated that "no one ever died from the lack of sex" [p. 3], noting that sex was indispensable for a species but not for any one individual. Moreover, he argued that much of what was considered a primary drive for reproduction was actually a reflection of sexual appetitive based on experience with the incentive characteristics of potential mates, partners, or other erotic stimuli. The Kinsey Reports on the sexual behavior of human males (Kinsey, Pomeroy, & Martin, 1948) and females (Kinsey, Pomeroy, Martin, & Gebhard, 1953) reinforced the idea that sexual appetite had a wide range of expression in humans that deviated dramatically from sex for the sake of reproduction. Moreover, ethological studies of primate sexual behavior have revealed nonreproductive roles of sex in social control (e.g., deWaal, 1987). Thus, sexual behavior can serve a variety of social and physiological functions ranging from reproduction to reward. These functions serve as motivational variables that all models of sexual function must take into account.

Modern Models of Sexual Motivation

Motivation occurs in all aspects of sexual behavior. It occurs before we have sex, for example, as a "drive" when we recognize internal hormonal and neurochemical actions that make us feel "horny" and are thereby propelled to think or fantasize about sex, or search for potential sex partners. It occurs when we identify and move toward potential sex partners or other external sexual incentives. It occurs when we overcome obstacles to obtain sexual reward. It occurs during sexual interactions, increasing or decreasing our responsiveness to sexual stimulation. And it occurs after orgasm, when the motivation to engage in sexual activity is temporarily inhibited. Sexual motivation also occurs in relation to other motivational systems. For example, an acute and highly stressful situation can inhibit sexual arousal and desire by activating the sympathetic nervous system and distracting our attention away from sexual incentives, whereas an acute but mildly stressful circumstance may synergize with sexual arousal and desire (e.g., being "naughty" or engaging in risky sex). By definition, sexual arousal, desire, reward, and inhibition are all sexually motivated. For motivational models to provide predictive validity, they must account for the relationship between these variables in a testable way.

Three types of models of sexual motivation have emerged in the modern era. The first type consists of models of sexual function and dysfunction that specify the relationships among different internal physiological processes that underlie sexual arousal or copulation. The second consists of models of sexual responsiveness that specify the relationship between external sexual incentives and the physiological or psychological processes they activate, such as arousal and desire. The third are models that attempt to unite the two. To a large extent, these models overlap such that the real difference between them is the particular focus on internal or external events in the first type, external events in the second type, or some hierarchy of the two in the third type. Orthogonal to this is the theoretical nature of model, being either dichotomous (e.g., arousal vs. performance, appetitive vs. consummatory), or multifactorial. However, with the exception of the model of human sexual response proposed by Masters and Johnson (1966), models of human sexual behavior have been derived largely from clinical case studies, anecdotal reports, and questionnaire-based retrospectives, whereas models of animal sexual behavior have been derived from direct observation of precopulatory and copulatory behaviors in laboratory and field settings. As such, we have more direct knowledge from animals regarding the motivation to obtain a sexual incentive, to initiate copulation, and to avoid or terminate copulation than we have from humans.

Beach (1956) generated one of the first flow-diagram models of copulatory behavior. This model used the intercorrelations among consummatory measures of male rat copulatory behavior to derive a two-factor theory of male sexual motivation. In this conceptualization, copulatory behavior was initiated by a "Sexual Arousal Mechanism" (SAM) that increased the male's physiological and psychological excitement in the presence of a sexual incentive such that a copulatory threshold was reached. Copulation was initiated and maintained by an "Intromission and Ejaculation Mechanism" (IEM) that further modified the male's internal state such that an ejaculatory threshold was reached. Ejaculation, in turn, fed back to inhibit both the SAM and IEM. Subsequently, Sachs (1978), Dewsbury (1979), and Pfaus, Mendelson, and Phillips (1990) used factor analysis of multiple correlations of male rat copulatory behavior to examine the structure of copulation (i.e., during the IEM). Those studies revealed that copulation could be broken down further into conceptually distinct factors that reflect its initiation and rate, along with the amount of genital stimulation received prior to ejaculation. Interestingly, in the factor analysis of Pfaus et al., an appetitive measure (conditioned level changing displayed in anticipation of copulation in bi-level chambers) was not correlated with any of the consummatory measures. Indeed, this measure formed its own factor, accounting for 5% of the intersubject variance for all measures. This suggests that appetitive behaviors are statistically—and perhaps neurologically—distinct from consummatory behaviors.

Beach (1956) noted that the IEM was relatively stereotyped and species-specific in terms of the pattern of behaviors that it elicited (e.g., multiple mounts and vaginal intromissions by male rats compared to continuous intromission in male humans), whereas the SAM was relatively flexible and subject to the influence of learning. Other studies have examined more appetitive aspects of sexual behavior in rats and primates, especially sexual approach behaviors. Operant responses, such as crossing electrified grids, climbing over obstruction boxes, straight-alley running, bar pressing, and maze learning, have been studied in male and female rats using copulation with a sexually receptive or vigorous partner as the positive reinforcer (reviewed in Pfaus, Kippin, & Centeno, 2001). Although these behaviors are not copulatory per se (and indeed could be observed for other reinforcers, like food or water), the use of a sexual reinforcer made them conditionally sexual. Everitt, Fray, Kostarczyk, Taylor, and Stacey (1987) took this a step further by training male rats to bar press for a second-order stimulus (a small light within a testing chamber) that had been paired with access to a sexually receptive female. The males adjusted their responding for this light up or down depending on the schedule of its presentation. This could not be done using a receptive female as the reinforcer, specifically because she cannot be presented in discrete units. Thus, animals can learn a vast array of tasks to obtain primary sexual incentives (e.g., the actual partner), or secondary incentives (objects of learned sexual significance).

Animals can also learn Pavlovian associations between neutral objects and sexual incentives, such that the neutral objects become conditionally sexual and lead to conditioned sexual excitement and arousal. For example, male Japanese quail learn to associate buzzers or lights (the conditioned stimulus or CS) with the presentation of a receptive female (the unconditioned stimulus, or UCS) and will eventually display courtship behaviors in response to the CS alone (Domjan, Lyons, North, & Bruell, 1986; Farris, 1967). The same stimuli previously paired with copulation will also decrease the latency to initiate copulation in male quail (Domjan, et al., 1986; Domjan, O'Vary, & Green, 1988; Köksal, Domjan, & Weisman, 1994). Adult male rats can learn to associate neutral odors (almond, lemon) with copulation and will choose to ejaculate preferentially with receptive females that bear those odors (Kippin & Pfaus, 2001a, 2001b; Kippin, Samaha, Sotiropoulos, & Pfaus, 2001; Kippin, Talianakis, Schattmann, Bartholomew, & Pfaus, 1998). Female rats learn the same association between odors and the ability to pace or control their copulatory contact (Coria-Avila, Ouimet, Pacheco, Manzo, & Pfaus, 2005). A neutral odor (methyl salicylate, or wintergreen) paired with copulation can also increase serum testosterone and luteinizing hormone levels in male rats (Graham & Desjardins, 1980). Rats can also show sexual excitement in anticipation of receiving a sexual incentive. Male rats learn to run from level to level in bi-level chambers in anticipation of receiving access to a sexually receptive female (Mendelson & Pfaus, 1989; Pfaus et al., 1990). This level changing behavior is enhanced by unconditioned olfactory cues present in the chamber, although in some strains of rat (e.g., Wistar rats), the olfactory cues are critical for the expression of appetitive level changing (van Furth & van Ree, 1996). Finally, male rats can learn to associate environments and neutral tactile stimuli with copulation, such that presentation of the stimuli increase sexual arousal and lead to faster ejaculations (Zamble, Hadad, Mitchell, & Cutmore, 1985; Zamble, Mitchell, & Findlay, 1986), or result in conditioned place preferences for the environments associated with copulation (Ågmo & Berenfeld, 1990; Hughes, Everitt, & Herbert. 1990; Mehrara & Baum, 1990; Miller & Baum, 1987; Paredes & Alonso, 1997; Paredes & Vazquez, 1999). Indeed, male rats display more frequent female-directed behavior and initiate copulation faster in environments associated with the (presumably positive) reinforcing effect of opioid agonists, like morphine, compared with environments associated with saline injections (Mitchell & Stewart, 1990).

A decade after Beach, Masters and Johnson (1966) presented one of the first multivariate physiological models of human sexual response. Their "EPOR" model emphasized a cascade of sexual responses that formed around the build-up and release of sexual excitement: a steep increase in sexual excitement (E) during sexual desire and arousal, to a less-steep plateau (P) during actual sexual stimulation, to the abrupt release of sexual excitement or tension during orgasm (O), to a prolonged period of relaxation known as "resolution" (R). This model applied to the sexual responses of both men and women, although individual differences existed in the actual response patterns, especially concerning the ability of women to experience multiple orgasms.

The models proposed by Beach (1956) and Masters and Johnson (1966) were useful because they specified the relationship and direction of different physiological mechanisms that generated both excitatory and inhibitory aspects of consummatory sexual behavior. However, with few exceptions these models did not delineate the relationship between appetitive and consummatory components of sexual behavior. For example, according to Masters and Johnson, "desire" was anything that increased sexual excitement, with erection being its most obvious and unambiguous behavioral manifestation. Although Beach accepted the notion that sexual drive could be inferred from some learned appetitive responses (e.g., the running speed of male rats in an alleyway that leads to a sexually receptive female), he doubted the sexual validity of other appetitive responses (e.g., crossing electrified grids to obtain a sex partner) if they did not correlate with copulatory measures or were not diminished by castration.

Another type of dichotomous model was proposed recently by Bancroft and Janssen (2000). This model emphasized a dual control of male sexual response in which the net expression of sexual behavior is based on the influence of excitatory and inhibitory mechanisms in the brain. As in earlier theories of general neural excitation and inhibition proposed by Gray (1971, 1975), and earlier still by Pavlov (1927), this model stressed the adaptive nature of both mechanisms. For example, the adaptive nature of sexual excitement would drive individuals to seek out sex partners for reproductive or reward purposes. The adaptive nature of sexual inhibition would guard against situations that threaten the individual, including chronically stressful life events. The propensity for sexual excitement, but especially inhibition, was viewed as an individual tendency: "For the majority, the presence of a fairly typical level of inhibition proneness is adaptive, helping to keep the individual out of trouble. Those whose propensity for central inhibition of sexual response is too high have increased vulnerability to sexual (e.g., erectile) dysfunction. For those whose inhibitory propensity is too low, an increased likelihood of engaging in high risk sexual behavior may result" (p. 571). It is useful here to note that inhibition may also result from nonstress pathways that terminate sexual interest after orgasm, or that reduce sexual interest when sexual activity has become habitual or routine. This latter inhibition (induced perhaps by habituation) may be situationally specific. It may be revealed only during certain kinds of sexual activities or with particular partners. It may also lead to a disinhibition of sexual activity under different circumstances or with different partners, as would be predicted from the opponent-process theory of Solomon and Corbit (1974). Finally, it is possible to view the excitation-inhibition dichotomy as orthogonal to the appetitive-consummatory dichotomy. To the extent that appetitive states are neurologically distinct from consummatory states, variable amounts of excitation and inhibition could apply to either phase at the same time, rendering individuals "ready to go" but unable to function, or vice versa.

Taking more than one dichotomous dimension into account increases the complexity of any model. However, if the relationship between different components can be delineated, then multivariate models can account for a greater degree of the variance. Such models typically emphasize a relationship between several variables at different levels of analysis. For example, cognitive models have been proposed to account for acculturation and experience (Geer & O'Donohue, 1987). Margaret Mead (1949) noted the diverse ways that precopulatory and copulatory activity are initiated by men and women across different cultures, and discussed many social endpoints, not only sexual ones, that such behaviors serve in those societies. Hardy (1964) proposed an "appetitional" theory of sexual motivation that deemphasized certain biological mechanisms, especially hormonal determinants, in favor of cognitive-affective experiences. To Hardy, sexual behavior served a "greater goal" of hedonic reward (relative to reproduction), which could be achieved in a variety of culturally determined sexual circumstances, from making a necessary instrumental response to obtain a sexual incentive to genital stimulation and orgasm. Hardy emphasized that sexual motivation is based on learned expectations of affective (hedonic) change. Such expectations were aroused by real external incentives, or imagined internal fantasies, that had been associated by experience with some form of sexual gratification. Sexual motivations were categorized into "approach," "avoidant," and "ambivalent," which reflected positive, negative, or mixed affect concerning a particular sexual fantasy, incentive, or behavior. Hardy also noted that a degree of habituation could occur to sexual stimuli in each category, such that the initial experience was usually more intense than subsequent experiences. Finally, Hardy argued that sexual incentives that are more immediate will be considered more attractive and responded to with greater vigor than those more distant. However, these aspects applied to human sexual behavior, not necessarily animal sexual behavior. Hardy believed strongly that extrapolation from animal studies to humans should be limited in light of interspecies differences in the expression of sexual behavior, and because of the relative independence of human sexual response (as it was conceived of in the early 1960s) on genetic or endocrine status compared to experiential factors.

Whalen (1966) attempted to synthesize elements of Hardy (1964) and Beach (1956). He argued that sexual motivation in animals and humans could be reduced to common components that consisted of both hormonal and experiential factors. Following Winokur (1963), Whalen defined six basic the elements of sexual behavior: (i) Sexual Identification, or the gender role played by an individual; (ii) Object Choice, or the persons or things that an individual directs sexual attention to; (iii) Sexual Gratification, or the reward or pleasure derived from sexual activities; (iv) Sexual Arousal, or the momentary level of sexual excitation; (v) Sexual Arousability, or an individual's characteristic rate of approach to orgasm as a result of sexual stimulation; and (vi) Sexual Activity, as sexual behavior observed directly or inferred from the content of fantasies. Whalen regarded sexual arousal and arousability as being unique indicators of sexual motivation, with arousal as a transient state between nothing and orgasm and arousability as a more solid physiological feature of each individual (similar perhaps to Ovid's notion of "temperament"). For example, as sexual arousal increases along a linear dimension, some individuals may achieve orgasm faster than others. An individual who needs less stimulation to achieve orgasm was said to have more arousability than someone who needs more stimulation to achieve orgasm. Knowledge of the level of arousal required for orgasm was therefore crucial in this analysis, both to provide more accurate estimates of arousability and to keep the entire notion from being circular. Whalen provided some animal and human evidence that arousal and arousability decay at different rates after ejaculation, supporting the contention that these two elements are distinct. Most importantly, the level of arousal was determined by external factors, such as unconditioned or conditioned incentives and expectancies, whereas arousability was determined by internal factors, such as hormonal activity and genitosensory feedback. However, arousability could also be conditioned by experience, especially the pleasure produced by genitosensory stimulation (similar perhaps to the mechanisms by which neutral odors paired with ejaculation come to elicit increases in serum androgen levels, e.g., Graham & Desjardins, 1980, or partner preferences, e.g., Kippin et al., 1998). Whalen did not believe that inferences about sexual motivation could be made on the basis of sexual identification or object choice because these aspects of sexuality were theoretically independent of underlying motivational variables. For example, a person's choice of hair color, body shape, or gender as components of sexual attraction does not allow any inference about level of arousability or frequency of sexual contact. Object choice also varies across cultures or even experiments: simply because dogs that have been masturbated by an experimenter will subsequently focus appetitive sexual behavior toward that experimenter (Beach, 1950) does not mean that their more general motivation to obtain sexual gratification has been altered.

Like the models proposed by Beach, Hardy, and Whalen (all of which are reminiscent of the more general model of affect proposed by William James [1890]), Byrne's "Sexual Behavior Sequence" model (1977) and Barlow's "Working Model of Sexual Dysfunction" (1986) specified an interactive role for both unconditioned sexual stimuli, especially autonomic activation, and conditioned sexual stimuli in the generation of sexual arousal, affect, and cognition. Both authors believed that arousal, affect, and cognition could shape particular sexual responses based on excitatory or inhibitory feedback. For example, in the case of arousal, genital stimulation could enhance, but ejaculation inhibit, genital blood flow. The degree of affective processing of this behavior (e.g., as appetitive or aversive) would feed back to shape the rate of further blood flow. A second dichotomous dimension of "erotophobia-erotophilia" was also proposed by Byrne which attempted to predict the degree of sexual responding to erotic cues. For example, an individual of high erotophilia could have a high degree of subjective sexual arousal that would lead to highly positive reactions to sexual stimulation. Actual sexual stimulation, in turn, could feed forward to increase subjective sexual arousal further. Thus, a complex set of feedback systems in sexual behavior existed to allow arousal, affect, and cognition to interact in generating a net sexual response to any given stimulus.

Barlow (1986) elucidated five factors or dimensions that differentiated sexually functional from dysfunctional men. First, an affective factor existed along a positive to negative dimension in which sexually functional individuals displayed positive affect to sexually arousing stimuli, whereas sexually dysfunctional individuals displayed more negative affect. Second, an arousal factor existed in which sexually functional individuals experience more subjective arousal and control over their arousal than do sexually dysfunctional individuals. Third, the demand characteristics of sexual performance-related stimuli distracted sexually dysfunctional individuals, but enhanced the arousal of sexually functional individuals. Fourth, the demand characteristics of nonsexual performance-related stimuli had the opposite effect of distracting sexually functional individuals but having no effect on sexually dysfunctional individuals. The fifth factor, anxiety, could arouse sexually functional men, but inhibit arousal in sexually dysfunctional men. In Barlow's model, the perception of either internal or external sexual stimulation initiated a process of increased attention on sexually arousing stimuli and evaluation as either rewarding (in the case of functional men) or aversive (in the case of dysfunctional men). These evaluations then fed back to either increase or decrease, respectively, autonomic arousal. Ongoing feedback was critical in this model, as continued attention to sexual cues would increase arousal and initiate sexual approach, whereas continued attention to nonsexual cues would decrease arousal and/or lead to aversive responses.

Factor analytic techniques have allowed researchers to uncover underlying multivariate structures for sexual arousal, desire, and orgasm. A multidimensional model of sexual arousal was proposed by Stoléru et al. (1999) that specified the interrelationship between perceptual-cognitive, emotional, motivational, and physiological components. These were based on positron emission tomography studies of brain activation in response to erotic visual stimuli. Similarly, Toledano and Pfaus (2006) reported a four-factor model of sexual arousal and desire, with orthogonal factors relating to cognitive-emotional, motivational, physiological, and negative-aversive components. Those factors were derived from a principal components analysis conducted on the intercorrelations among 55 adjectives or descriptors associated with sexual arousal and desire (comprising the Sexual Arousal and Desire Inventory). The factors together accounted for over 40% of the intersubject variance for all descriptors. Mah and Binik (2001, 2002) used factor analyses of the intercorrelations among descriptors of the experience of orgasm to reveal a two-tiered model of sensory and cognitive processing. The principal components analysis revealed 10 factors that were subsumed into two overall dimensions, one sensory and the other cognitive-affective. The sensory dimension was linked to factors that reflected overall bodily sensations, including a buildup, flooding, flushing, shooting, throbbing, and spasms. The cognitive dimension was linked to factors that reflected pleasure and satisfaction, relaxation, emotional intimacy, and ecstasy. Gould (1981) cautioned against viewing factor analyses as "real" because factors can change if the descriptors that load onto them change. However, factor analyses are a useful first step in trying to make sense of a large body of data because they help organize and simplify the data into metastructures. These structures may indeed be neurologically valid and may tap into different components of an underlying motivational structure. To the extent that the overall structure remains stable in subsequent replications, or with different descriptors, the factors themselves become components that must be accounted for in any motivational theory.

Bancroft (1989) proposed a "Psychosomatic Circle of Sex." Individual feedback loops were specified and linked together into five dimensions that relay information processing throughout the central and autonomic nervous systems. The first two dimensions involve the brain: (i) cognitive processes in the cortex that influence (ii) emotional processes in limbic and hypothalamic systems. In this case, "cognitions" span a range of conditioned responses, including cultural beliefs and attitudes, attentional mechanisms, learned sexual incentives, and learned inhibition over sexual responding. The affective dimension came from the interaction of cortical structures with limbic/hypothalamic structures. Together, these systems influence the spinal cord and autonomic processes related to the mechanics of sexual response: (iii) sexual reflex centers in the spinal cord; (iv) parasympathetic genital responses such as erection; and (v) other sympathetic autonomic responses consistent with sexual arousal (e.g., increased heart rate). In the models of Byrne, Barlow, and Bancroft, the perception of arousal (genital and peripheral) was sufficient to initiate awareness of a sexually motivated state. The positive or negative outcome of that state was then dependent on interpretation from cognitive feedback. This model was similar to that proposed by Pfaff (1980) to account for quantum neural control of lordosis in female rats by different brain "modules" that compiled and interpreted different types of sensory and hormonal stimulation.

Toates (1992) proposed an interactive system for male sexual behavior based on an incentive systems model (Toates & O'Rourke, 1978). The stimulation of sexual arousal depends on both the value of sensory information coming from the external sexual incentive and the state of arousability of the nervous system, a value that is set by both hormone action on target tissues in the brain and periphery and by any positive feedback from the system that modulates incentive value. In a systems analysis, several "comparators" exist to determine incentive value based on the memory of previous interactions with similar incentives, or to determine the level of sexual arousability. Both comparators can feed back on one another to increase or decrease net arousal. An ejaculatory mechanism for males was also proposed that activates an inhibitory feedback system. In turn, this system reduces arousability two ways, by inhibiting arousal and by devaluing the incentive. Surprisingly, Toates took for granted that sexual motivation serves the goal of fertilization (p. 97) and did not raise the issue of sexual pleasure or nonreproductive sexual behavior in primates or other animals.

An important aspect of systems analysis is information processing from different modalities. Current sensory information (both external and internal) must be compared to previous experience at many levels of analysis, and ongoing changes in experience must register immediately so that the requisite excitatory or inhibitory neural systems can be activated. The processing and evaluation of sexual incentives, fantasies, sex play, and tactile sexual stimulation occur almost simultaneously at cognitive, emotional, endocrine, and spinal levels. Everaerd, Geer, and their colleagues (Dekker & Everaerd, 1988; Everaerd, 1995; Geer & Fuhr, 1976; Geer & Head, 1990; Geer, Lapour, & Jackson, 1993; Geer & McGlone, 1990; Janssen & Everaerd, 1993; Laan, Everaerd, van der Velde, & Geer, 1995) have applied hypotheses from information processing theory, particularly those related to attention, encoding and identification, response selection, and response production, to the study of sexual arousal. As in other systems analyses, these processes are thought to interact throughout a sexual experience. The ability to attend to features of a sexual stimulus requires both innate and conditional mechanisms that can select them from an array of other external or tactile stimuli. Encoding and identifying sexual stimuli are viewed as a second layer of processing. Some stimuli may be perceived at a subconscious level until they reach a critical threshold for the activation of sexual arousal or excitement, after which they are regarded consciously as sexual. Such encoding and identification mechanisms may be innate and preprogrammed, as with a male rat attending to the odors of an estrous female or a sexually functional human male experiencing erection while being stimulated by an attractive partner, whereas cognitive mechanisms must also exist to allow conditioned stimuli, for example, neutral odors associated with copulation, fetish objects, and so forth, to elicit a threshold sexual response. Encoding also requires memory for both Pavlovian and operant associations. This creates an economy of behavior, such that less and less attention is required for a stimulus to be perceived. Some of this may take the form of subliminal priming, which then feeds back to focus the attentional mechanisms more exclusively on sexual stimuli. However, stimuli may be encoded several ways depending on experience. For example, if an individual's social conditioning has been negative or aversive with regard to sexual expressions, a sexual stimulus may evoke feelings of anxiety rather than feelings of arousal. Finally, experience in response selection and production allows sexual responses to be determined more quickly or efficiently in a given situation. Experience with efficient sexual responding then can feed back to facilitate ongoing sexual behavior. Although the incorporation of concepts from information processing to sexual motivation is useful theoretically, specific mechanisms, such as distractors that facilitate or inhibit attention, evaluation, or behavioral reaction to sexual stimulation, have only begun to be tested.

Integration

Multivariate systems can be brought together within the framework of the motivational and behavioral cascades that define phases of sexual arousal, desire, reward, and inhibition. The incentive sequence model was proposed by Pfaus (1996, 1999) to account for specific kinds of information processing required of rats or humans during complex sequences of sexual behavior (Figure 1). For successful copulation to occur, all animals must be able to respond to hormonal and neurochemical changes that signal their own arousal and desire, to identify external stimuli that predict where potential sex partners can be found, to actively seek out or work to obtain sex partners, to distinguish external cues (chemosensory, visual, auditory, tactile) and behavioral patterns of potential sex partners from those that are not sexually receptive, and to pursue desired sex partners once contact has been made or solicited. At each step, animals depend not only on the perception of their own internal state but on an accurate prediction of external events. Such predictions are based on experience, both with the relation between external and internal stimuli and the relation of those stimuli to their sexual consequences. Such experience makes sexual behavior appear "automated" and competent. In this model, the behavioral stream moves from left to right, from appetitive to precopulatory to consummatory behaviors. The appetitive and consummatory phases are viewed as overlapping Venn diagrams, with the precopulatory phase in the middle of the overlap. Hormonal and neurochemical systems that underlie these phases can be specified with knowledge of how they interact with previous or subsequent behaviors (or sensory inputs) in each phase. More importantly, the model is a set of core events that define the motivational sequences for all animals. This allows the behavior of different species to be contrasted with a common set of descriptors, for example, making it possible to specify both homologues and analogues of sexual desire between birds, rats, and humans (e.g., Pfaus, Kippin, & Coria-Avila, 2003). In turn, this helps to identify neural systems in animals that may have been conserved during evolution to subserve similar aspects of sexual behavior in humans. For example, in many species, dopamine may activate certain appetitive responses (such as conditioned excitement) and provide the necessary focusing of attention during copulation (Pfaus & Phillips, 1991). Ejaculation or orgasm may activate endogenous opioid and serotonergic systems that produce concomitant feelings of euphoria, relaxation, and satiety during a sustained period of sexual refractoriness or inhibition that feeds back to inhibit neural systems involved in both appetitive and consummatory motivation.

The forces that drive net behavioral output at any one time are summarized in Figure 2. Experience with sexual reward generates both Pavlovian and operant expectancies (associations between stimuli and between stimuli and responses made on them). These activate both arousability and attention toward the stimuli and integrate them with behavioral responses that have been successful in the past. Steroid and peptide hormones also activate arousability and attention toward sexual incentives, and experiential factors can increase steroid hormone levels in anticipation of sexual activity (Anonymous, 1970; Graham & Desjardins, 1980). These internal mechanisms summate with sensory input from the genitals (e.g., the perception of vaginal or penile blood flow) and sensory input from external incentives (features of potential partners, context, etc.) to elicit the net be-

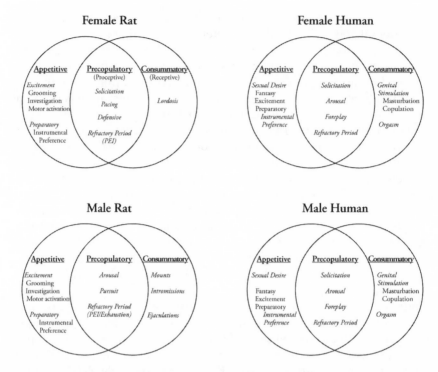

Figure 1. Incentive sequences for human and rat sexual behavior (modified from Pfaus, 1996, 1999). The behavioral stream moves from left to right, through appetitive, precopulatory, and consummatory phases of behavior. This conforms to the movement of animals from distal to proximal to interactive with respect to the sexual incentive. Three types of appetitive responding reflect relative degrees of learning and necessity. "Preparatory" behaviors are learned responses that animals must make in order to acquire the incentive (e.g., operant behaviors, pursuit, etc.). "Anticipatory" behaviors are learned responses that occur in anticipation of an incentive, but are not necessary to obtain it (e.g., conditioned psychomotor stimulation that characterizes behavioral excitement). Unlearned appetitive responses also exist that are instinctual (e.g., unconditioned anogenital investigation). These aspects of behavior also occur once copulatory contact has been made, especially if copulation occurs in bouts (as it does in rats).

havioral output. Excitatory and inhibitory feedback occurs in all domains of this flow diagram. For example, ejaculation or orgasm in males results in a postejaculatory refractory period that presumably feeds inhibition back on the neural substrates of arousability and attention. Of course, sexual motivation can be inferred from the strength of each force that forms the flow diagram.

The neurochemistry of both positive and negative feedback from sexual stimulation has begun to be elucidated. For example, phasic dopamine re-

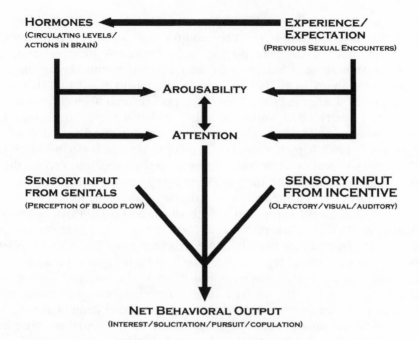

Figure 2. Hypothetical relationship between experience, hormonal activation, arousability, attention, and stimulus processing from genital sensations and external incentives on net sexual responding at any given time. Note that excitatory and inhibitory feedback can occur anywhere in this flowchart to strengthen or reduce responding. Such feedback provides moment-to-moment modulation of sexual motivation.

lease occurs in the nucleus accumbens of male rats in response to incentive cues of sexually receptive females, whereas tonic release of dopamine occurs during copulation (Damsma, Pfaus, Wenkstern, Phillips, & Fibiger, 1992; Everitt, 1990; Mitchell & Gratton, 1992; Pfaus, Damsma, et al., 1990). However, at the point of ejaculation, dopamine release drops precipitously and remains low in this structure throughout the absolute refractory period (Blackburn, Pfaus, & Phillips, 1992; Lorrain, Riolo, Matuszewich, & Hull, 1999). Dopamine antagonists infused into the nucleus accumbens of male rats inhibit conditioned sexual excitation in response to cues that predict the availability of sex partners (Pfaus & Phillips, 1991), thus decreases in mesolimbic dopamine transmission likely reduce both the arousability of the male rat and the attention displayed toward sexual incentives (a common occurrence following ejaculation). Serotonin released in the lateral hypothalamic area during ejaculation is correlated with an inhibition of dopamine release in the nucleus accumbens (Lorrain et al., 1999). If related, then activation of serotonin receptors in the lateral hypothalamus activates a currently unspecified inhibitory pathway. Moreover,

lesion studies have shown that the nucleus accumbens and lateral hypothalamus play opposite roles in the control of male rat sexual behavior,
with the nucleus accumbens playing an excitatory role in sexual arousal
(erection and intromission), and the lateral hypothalamus playing an inhibitory role in sexual arousal but a facilitative role in ejaculation (Kippin,
Sotiropoulos, Badih, & Pfaus, 2004). The nucleus accumbens is also activated by primary odors associated with copulation (e.g., estrous odors),
and conditioned odors (e.g., almond) associated with sexual reward (Blackburn et al., 1992; Kippin, Cain, & Pfaus, 2003; Mitchell & Gratton, 1992).
This makes it ideal as an interface between the hypothalamic centers that
control autonomic outflow, the processing of emotionally relevant information by the limbic system, and motor activation. Indeed, the medial preoptic
area is critical for the expression of both female and male sexual behavior
in the rat (Hoshina, Takeo, Nakano, Sato, & Sakuma, 1994; Paredes &
Baum, 1997), and this hypothalamic structure sends large lateral fiber
bundles to the ventral tegmentum, which in turn houses the mesolimbic dopamine cell bodies that send projections to the nucleus accumbens.
Dopamine actions on D2 and D1 receptors, respectively, in the medial preoptic area also facilitate penile erection and ejaculation (Hull et al., 1989,
1999), whereas opioid actions in this structure inhibit sexual behavior in
males (Band & Hull, 1990; Hughes, Everitt, & Herbert, 1987, 1990). However, administration of opioid antagonists, such as naloxone, block the induction of conditioned place preference by sexual reward in both male and
female rats (Ågmo & Berenfeld, 1990; Paredes & Martinez, 2001), suggesting that opioid actions are critical in linking conditioned cues to sexual reward. Some of this integration may occur at the level of the ventral tegmentum, where opioid receptor activation suppresses inhibitory GABA
interneurons, thereby facilitating dopamine cell firing (Johnson & North,
1992). Indeed, in contrast to the suppression of copulation following infusions of morphine to the medial preoptic area, infusions of morphine to the
ventral tegmental area stimulate sexually sluggish males to mount receptive females (Mitchell & Stewart, 1990). However, sexual reinforcement
can also be blocked by naloxone infusions to the medial preoptic area
(Ågmo & Gomez, 1993). We do not yet know the precise pathways of
sexual arousal, desire, reward, or inhibition, but the current focus on brain
imaging in humans and animals should begin to provide details on them,
in addition to how hormonal states and experience with sexual reward alter their function.

Conclusions

Despite our best efforts, there is not yet a "grand unified theory" of
sexual motivation. Perhaps there can never be one that takes all forms of
sexual behavior into account for all species at every level of analysis. What

there can be, however, is comparative information. Each model of sexual motivation, even the ancient holistic conceptualizations, has a peculiar focus that can inform other models. Moreover, knowing how analogous and homologous behaviors between species serve similar motivational endpoints and utilize the same brain regions and neurotransmitter systems may well allow us to generate useful animal models of human sexual response (Ågmo & Ellingsen, 2003; Pfaus, Kippin, & Coria-Avila, 2003). Becoming aware of these, and more importantly, testing the hypotheses they generate, should be an important focus of animal and clinical studies. Another important focus should be on rectifying what exactly is meant by sexual "arousal," "desire," "reward," and "inhibition." Despite being imbued with motivation, these terms are not rigorously defined or differentiated. Indeed, despite being conceptually distinct, they obviously interact with one another. We need to understand how. Substantial progress has been made defining the consequences of sexual stimulation by manipulating monoamine, amino acid, and peptide transmitters in the brain and by examining how different kinds of stimulation alter neuronal activity. The challenge for the future is to see how this information can be integrated coherently. To that end, it would be wise to utilize models of motivation as the heuristics they were intended to be.

References

Abramson, P. R., & Pinkerton, S. D. (1995). *With pleasure: Thoughts on the nature of human sexuality.* New York: Oxford University Press.

Ågmo, A., & Berenfeld, R. (1990). Reinforcing properties of ejaculation in the male rat: The role of opioids and dopamine. *Behavioral Neuroscience, 104,* 177–182.

Ågmo, A., & Ellingsen, E. (2003). Relevance of nonhuman animal studies to the understanding of human sexuality. *Scandinavian Journal of Psychology, 44,* 293–301.

Ågmo, A., & Gomez, M. (1993). Sexual reinforcement is blocked by infusion of naloxone into the medial preoptic area. *Behavioral Neuroscience, 107,* 812–818.

Anonymous. (1970). Effects of sexual activity on beard growth in man. *Nature, 226,* 869–870.

Bancroft, J. H. (1989). *Human sexuality and its problems.* Edinburgh: Churchill Livingstone.

Bancroft, J. H., & Janssen, E. (2000). The dual control model of male sexual response: A theoretical approach to centrally mediated erectile dysfunction. *Neuroscience and Biobehavioral Reviews, 24,* 571–579.

Band, L. C., & Hull, E. M. (1990). Morphine and dynorphin(1-13) microinjected into the medial preoptic area and nucleus accumbens: Effects on sexual behavior in male rats. *Brain Research, 524,* 77–84.

Barlow, D. H. (1986). Causes of sexual dysfunction. *Journal of Consulting and Clinical Psychology, 54,* 140–157.

Beach, F. A. (1950). Sexual behavior in animals and man. *Harvey Lectures, 43*, 259–279.

Beach, F. A. (1956). Characteristics of masculine "sex drive." *Nebraska Symposium on Motivation, 4*, 1–32.

Berridge, K. C., & Robinson, T. E. (1998). What is the role of dopamine in reward: Hedonic impact, reward learning, or incentive salience? *Brain Research. Brain Research Reviews, 28*, 309–369.

Blackburn, J. R., & Pfaus, J. G. (1988). Is motivation modulation? A comment on Wise. *Psychobiology, 16*, 303–304.

Blackburn, J. R., Pfaus, J. G., & Phillips, A. G. (1992). Dopamine functions in appetitive and defensive behaviours. *Progress in Neurobiology, 39*, 247–279.

Buss, D. M. (1994). *The evolution of desire.* New York: Basic Books.

Byrne, D. (1977). The imagery of sex. In J. Money & H. Muspah (Eds.), *Handbook of sexology* (pp. 327–350). Amsterdam: Elsevier.

Coria-Avila, G. A., Ouimet, A., Pacheco, P., Manzo, J., & Pfaus, J. G. (2005). Olfactory conditioned partner preference in the female rat. *Behavioral Neuroscience, 119*, 716–725.

Craig, W. (1918). Appetites and aversions as constituents of instincts. *Biological Bulletin, 34*, 91–107.

Damsma, G., Pfaus, J. G., Wenkstern, D., Phillips, A. G., & Fibiger, H. C. (1992). Sexual behavior increases dopamine transmission in the nucleus accumbens and striatum of male rats: Comparison with novelty and locomotion. *Behavioral Neuroscience, 106*, 181–191.

Dekker, J., & Everaerd, W. (1988). Attentional effects on sexual arousal. *Psychophysiology, 25*, 45–54.

deWaal, F. B. M. (1987). Tension regulation and nonreproductive functions of sex in captive bonobos (*Pan paniscus*). *Nat. Geog. Res., 3*, 318–335.

Dewsbury, D. A. (1979). Factor analysis of measures of copulatory behavior in three species of muroid rodent. *Journal of Comp. Physiol. Psychol., 93*, 868–878.

Domjan, M., Lyons, R., North, N. C., & Bruell, J. (1986). Sexual Pavlovian conditioned approach behavior in male Japanese quail (*Coturnix japonica*). *Journal of Comparative Psychology, 100*, 413–421.

Domjan, M., O'Vary, D., & Green, P. (1988). Conditioning of appetitive and consummatory sexual behavior in male Japanese quail. *Journal of the Experimental Analysis of Behavior, 50*, 505–519.

Ellis, H. (1915). *Analysis of the sexual impulse: Vol. III. Studies in the psychology of sex.* Philadelphia: F. A. Davis & Co.

Ellis, H. (1933). *The psychology of sex.* New York: Emerson Books.

Everaerd, W. (1995). Information processing approach and the sexual response in human studies. In J. Bancroft, (Ed.), *The pharmacology of sexual function and dysfunction* (pp. 175–184). Amsterdam: Elsevier.

Everitt, B. J. (1990). Sexual motivation: A neural and behavioral analysis of the mechanisms underlying appetitive and copulatory responses of male rats. *Neuroscience & Biobehavioral Reviews, 14*, 217–232.

Everitt, B. J., & Bancroft, J. (1991). Of rats and men: The comparative approach to male sexuality. *Annual Review of Sex Research, 2*, 77–118.

Everitt, B. J., Fray, P., Kostarczyk, E., Taylor, S., & Stacey, P. (1987). Studies of instrumental behavior with sexual reinforcement in male rats (*Rattus norvegicus*):

I. Control by brief visual stimuli paired with a receptive female. *Journal of Comparative Psychology, 101,* 395–406.

Farris, H. E. (1967). Classical conditioning of courting behavior in the Japanese quail, *Coturnix coturnix japonica. Journal of the Experimental Analysis of Behavior, 10,* 213–217.

Freud, S. (1922). *Beyond the pleasure principle.* New York: Albert & Charles.

Freud, S. (1927). *The ego and the id.* London: Hogarth Press.

Geer, J. H., & Fuhr, R. (1976). Cognitive factors in sexual arousal: The role of distraction. *Journal of Consulting and Clinical Psychology, 44,* 238–243.

Geer, J. H., & Head, S. (1990). The sexual response system. In J. T. Cacioppo & L. Tassinary (Eds.), *Principles of psychophysiology* (pp. 599–630). New York: Cambridge University Press.

Geer, J. H., Lapour, K. L., & Jackson, S. R. (1993). The information processing approach to human sexuality. In N. Birbaumer & A. Öhman (Eds.), *The structure of emotion: Psychophysiological, cognitive, and clinical aspects* (pp. 135–155). Toronto: Hogrefe-Huber.

Geer, J. H., & McGlone, M. S. (1990). Sex differences in memory for erotica. *Cognition and Emotion, 4,* 71–78.

Geer, J. H., & O'Donohue, W. T. (1987). *Theories of human sexuality.* New York: Plenum Press.

Gould, S. J. (1981). *The mismeasure of man.* New York: W. W. Norton.

Graham, J. M., & Desjardins, C. (1980). Classical conditioning: Induction of luteinizing hormone and testosterone secretion in anticipation of sexual activity. *Science, 210,* 1039–1041.

Gray, J. A. (1971). *The psychology of fear and stress.* London: Weidenfeld and Nicholson.

Gray, J. A. (1975). *Elements of a two-process theory of learning.* London: Academic Press.

Hardy, K. R. (1964). An appetitional theory of sexual motivation. *Psychological Review, 71,* 1–18.

Hoshina, Y., Takeo, T., Nakano, K., Sato, T., & Sakuma, Y. (1994). Axon-sparing lesions of the preoptic area enhances receptivity and diminishes proceptivity among components of female rat sexual behavior. *Behavioral Brain Research, 61,* 197–204.

Hughes, A. M., Everitt, B. J., & Herbert J. (1987). Selective effects of beta-endorphin infused into the hypothalamus, preoptic area and bed nucleus of the stria terminalis on the sexual and ingestive behaviour of male rats. *Neuroscience, 23,* 1063–1073.

Hughes, A. M., Everitt, B. J., & Herbert J. (1990). Comparative effects of preoptic area infusions of opioid peptides, lesions and castration on sexual behaviour in male rats: Studies of instrumental behaviour, conditioned place preference and partner preference. *Psychopharmacology, 102,* 243–256.

Hull, E. M., Lorrain, D. S., Du, J., Matuszewich, L., Lumley, L. A., Putnam, S. K., et al. (1999). Hormone-neurotransmitter interactions in the control of sexual behavior. *Behavioural Brain Research, 105,* 105–116.

Hull, E. M., Warner, R. K., Bazzett, T. J., Eaton, R. C., Thompson, J. T., & Scaletta, L. L. (1989). D2/D1 ratio in the medial preoptic area affects copulation of male rats. *Journal of Pharmacology and Experimental Therapeutics, 251,* 422–427.

James, W. (1890). *The principles of psychology: Vol. 1 and 2.* New York: Holt.

Janssen, E., & Everaerd, W. (1993). Determinants of male sexual arousal. *Annual Review of Sex Research, 4,* 211–245.

Johnson, S. W., & North, R. A. (1992). Opioids excite dopamine neurons by hyperpolarization of local interneurons. *Journal of Neuroscience, 12,* 483–488.

Kinsey, A. C., Pomeroy, W. B., & Martin, C. E. (1948). *Sexual behavior in the human male.* Philadelphia: W. B. Saunders.

Kinsey, A. C., Pomeroy, W. B., Martin, C. E., & Gebhard, P. H. (1953). *Sexual behavior in the human female.* Philadelphia: W. B. Saunders.

Kippin, T. E., Cain, S. W., & Pfaus, J. G. (2003). Estrous odors and sexually conditioned neutral odors activate separate neural pathways in the male rat. *Neuroscience, 117,* 971–979.

Kippin, T. E., & Pfaus, J. G. (2001a). The development of olfactory conditioned ejaculatory preferences in the male rat: I. Nature of the unconditioned stimulus. *Physiology & Behavior, 73,* 457–469.

Kippin, T. E., & Pfaus, J. G. (2001b). The nature of the conditioned response mediating olfactory conditioned ejaculatory preference in the male rat. *Behavioural Brain Research, 122,* 11–24.

Kippin, T. E., Samaha, A.-N., Sotiropoulos, V., & Pfaus, J. G. (2001). The development of olfactory conditioned ejaculatory preferences in the male rat: II. Parametric manipulation of conditioning session number and duration. *Physiology & Behavior, 73,* 471–485.

Kippin, T. E., Sotiropoulos, V., Badih, J., & Pfaus, J. G. (2004). Opposing roles of the nucleus accumbens and anterior lateral hypothalamic area in the control of sexual behaviour in the male rat. *European Journal of Neuroscience, 19,* 698–704.

Kippin, T. E., Talianakis, S., Schattmann, L., Bartholomew, S., & Pfaus, J. G. (1998). Olfactory conditioning of sexual behavior in the male rat (*Rattus norvegicus*). *Journal of Comparative Psychology, 112,* 389–399.

Köksal, F., Domjan, M., & Weisman, G. (1994). Blocking of the sexual conditioning of differentially effective conditioned stimulus objects. *Animal Learning and Behavior, 22,* 103–111.

Krafft-Ebing, R. V. (1929). *Psychopathia sexualis* (English translation of the 12th German edition by F. J. Rebman). New York: Physicians and Surgeons Book Co.

Laan, E., Everaerd, W., van der Velde, J., & Geer, J. H. (1995). Determinants of subjective experience of sexual arousal in women: Feedback from genital arousal and erotic stimulus content. *Psychophysiology, 32,* 444–451.

Lorrain, D. S., Riolo, J. V., Matuszewich, L., & Hull, E. M. (1999). Lateral hypothalamic serotonin inhibits nucleus accumbens dopamine: Implications for sexual satiety. *Journal of Neuroscience, 19,* 7648–7652.

Mah, K., & Binik, Y. M. (2001). The nature of human orgasm: A critical review of major trends. *Clinical Psychology Review, 21,* 823–856.

Mah, K., & Binik, Y. M. (2002). Do all orgasms feel alike? Evaluating a two-dimensional model of the orgasm experience across gender and sexual context. *Journal of Sex Research, 39,* 104–113.

Masters, W. H., & Johnson, V. E. (1966). *Human sexual response.* Boston: Little, Brown.

Mead, M. (1949). *Male and female.* New York: Morrow.

Mehrara, B. J., & Baum, M. J. (1990). Naloxone disrupts the expression but not the acquisition by male rats of a conditioned place preference response for an oestrous female. *Psychopharmacology, 101,* 118–125.

Mendelson, S. D., & Pfaus, J. G. (1989). Level searching: A new assay of sexual motivation in the male rat. *Physiology & Behavior, 45,* 337–341.

Miller, R. L., & Baum, M. J. (1987). Naloxone inhibits mating and conditioned place preference for an oestrous female in male rats soon after castration. *Pharmacology, Biochemistry, & Behavior, 26,* 781–789.

Milner, P. (1970). *Physiological psychology.* New York: Holt, Reinhart & Winston.

Mitchell, J. B., & Gratton, A. (1992). Mesolimbic dopamine release elicited by activation of the accessory olfactory system: A high speed chronoamperometric study. *Neuroscience Letters, 140,* 81–84.

Mitchell, J. B., & Stewart, J. (1990). Facilitation of sexual behaviors in the male rat in the presence of stimuli previously paired with systemic injections of morphine. *Pharmacology, Biochemistry, and Behavior, 35,* 367–372.

Moll, A. (1897). *Untersuchungen über die libido sexualis* [Analysis of the sexual libido]. Berlin: Fischer's Medicin Buchhandlung.

Moll, A. (1933). *Libido sexualis: Studies in the psychosexual laws of love verified by clinical sexual case histories.* New York: American Ethnological Press.

Paredes, R. G., & Alonso, A. (1997). Sexual behavior regulated (paced) by the female induces conditioned place preference. *Behavioral Neuroscience, 111,* 123–128.

Paredes, R. G., & Baum, M. J. (1997). Role of the medial preoptic area/anterior hypothalamus in the control of masculine sexual behavior. *Annual Review of Sex Research, 8,* 68–101.

Paredes, R. G., & Martinez, I. (2001). Naloxone blocks place preference conditioning after paced mating in female rats. *Behavioral Neuroscience, 115,* 1363–1367.

Paredes, R. G., & Vazquez, B. (1999). What do female rats like about sex? Paced mating. *Behavioural Brain Research, 105,* 117–127.

Pavlov, I. P. (1927). *Conditioned reflexes* (G. V. Anrep, Trans.). Oxford: Oxford University Press.

Pfaff, D. W. (1980). *Estrogens and brain function.* Berlin: Springer-Verlag.

Pfaus, J. G. (1996). Frank A. Beach Award: Homologies of animal and human sexual behaviors. *Hormones and Behavior, 30,* 187–200.

Pfaus, J. G. (1999). Revisiting the concept of sexual motivation. *Annual Review of Sex Research, 10,* 120–157

Pfaus, J. G., Damsma, G., Nomikos, G. G., Wenkstern, D. G., Blaha, C. D., Phillips, A. G., et al. (1990). Sexual behavior enhances central dopamine transmission in the male rat. *Brain Research, 530,* 345–348.

Pfaus, J. G., Kippin, T. E., & Centeno, S. (2001). Conditioning and sexual behavior: A review. *Hormones and Behavior, 40,* 291–321.

Pfaus, J. G., Kippin, T. E., & Coria-Avila, G. (2003). What can animal models tell us about human sexual response? *Annual Review of Sex Research, 14,* 1–63.

Pfaus, J. G., Mendelson, S. D., & Phillips, A. G. (1990). A correlational and factor analysis of anticipatory and consummatory measures of sexual behavior in the male rat. *Psychoneuroendocrinology, 15,* 329–340.

Pfaus, J. G., & Phillips, A. G. (1991). Role of dopamine in anticipatory and consummatory aspects of sexual behavior in the male rat. *Behavioral Neuroscience, 105,* 727–743.

Reich, W. (1942/1978). *The function of the orgasm.* New York: Farrar Straus Giroux.

Sachs, B. D. (1978). Conceptual and neural mechanisms of masculine copulatory behavior. In T. E. McGill, D. A. Dewsbury, & B. D. Sachs (Eds.), *Sex and behavior: Status and prospectus* (pp. 267–295). New York: Plenum Press.

Solomon, R. L., & Corbit, J. D. (1974). An opponent-process theory of motivation: I. Temporal dynamics of affect. *Psychological Review, 81,* 119–145.

Stellar, E. (1954). The physiology of motivation. *Psychological Review, 61,* 5–22.

Stewart, J. (1995). How does incentive motivational theory apply to sexual behavior? In J. Bancroft, (Ed.), *The pharmacology of sexual function and dysfunction* (pp. 3–11). Amsterdam: Elsevier.

Stoléru, S., Gregoire, M. C., Gerard, D., Decety, J., Lafarge, E., Cinotti, L., et al. (1999). Neuroanatomical correlates of visually evoked sexual arousal in human males. *Archives of Sexual Behavior, 28,* 1–21.

Symons, D. (1979). *The evolution of human sexuality.* New York: Oxford University Press.

Toates, F. (1992). *Motivational systems.* Cambridge: Cambridge University Press.

Toates, F., & O'Rourke, C. (1978). Computer simulation of male rat sexual behavior. *Medical and Biological Engineering and Computing, 16,* 98–104.

Toledano, R. R., & Pfaus, J. G. (2006). The Sexual Arousal and Desire Inventory (SADI): A multidimensional scale to assess subjective sexual arousal and desire. *Journal of Sexual Medicine, 3,* 853–877.

van Furth, W. R., & van Ree, J. M. (1996). Appetitive sexual behavior in male rats: I. The role of olfaction in level-changing behavior. *Physiology & Behavior, 60,* 999–1005.

Whalen, R. E. (1966). Sexual motivation. *Psychological Review, 73,* 151–163.

Winokur, G. (1963). Aspects of sexual behavior: A classification. In G. Winokur, (Ed.), *Determinants of human sexual behavior* (pp. vii–viii). Springfield, Ill.: Charles Thomas.

Woodworth, R. S. (1918). *Dynamic psychology.* New York: Columbia University Press.

Zamble, E., Hadad, G. M., Mitchell, J. B., & Cutmore, T. R. H. (1985). Pavlovian conditioning of sexual arousal: First- and second-order effects. *Journal of Experimental Psychology: Animal Behavior Processes, 11,* 598–610.

Zamble, E., Mitchell, J. B., & Findlay, H. (1986). Pavlovian conditioning of sexual arousal: Parametric and background manipulations. *Journal of Experimental Psychology: Animal Behavior Processes, 12,* 403–411.

Discussion Paper

ERICK JANSSEN

Aristotle said that all human actions have one or more of the following seven causes: chance, nature, compulsion, habit, reason, passion, or desire. I think that sums it up quite nicely. And it illustrates the seemingly
all-inclusive nature of this thing we call *motivation*. Most introductory psychology books define the field of motivation as the study of goal-directed
behavior. That, too, makes me wonder. After all, who would devote their
time and energy to the study of pointless behavior? So, what is "it" and
what is "it" not, sexual motivation? During a previous Kinsey Institute
meeting, on the role of theory in sex research, another "it" emerged as
some unyielding source of confusion. That "it" had to do with sexual risk
taking. What *is* sexual risk taking, the experts wondered. What is *sexual*
about risk taking? How do we best define it? I am experiencing something
similar today. Sexual motivation is arguably one of the most important
constructs in sex research, yet it also is one of the most elusive ones.

Aristotle had other things to say about motivation. For example, he
made the distinction between material, formal, efficient, and final causes.
A hormone-related "push" could be seen as a material cause. Safety might
involve a formal one, a sexual film, or other "pull" factor, an efficient one.
And evolutionary psychologists most likely believe they have a claim on
the final one. Although Aristotle's list of seven more specific causes of behavior might sound arbitrary, it was derived from a meticulous conceptual
analysis:

> Now every action of every person either is or is not due to that person
> himself. Of those not due to himself some are due to chance, the others
> to necessity; of these latter, again, some are due to compulsion, the oth-
> ers to nature. Consequently all actions that are not due to a man himself
> are due either to chance or to nature or to compulsion. All actions that
> *are* due to a man himself and caused by himself are due either to habit or
> to rational or irrational craving. Rational craving is a craving for good,
> i.e., a *wish*—nobody wishes for anything unless he thinks it good. Irra-
> tional craving is twofold, viz. anger and appetite (Roberts, 1924).

Thus, Aristotle makes a distinction between what we now call *intrinsic*
and *extrinsic* motivation, and he implies roles for learning, incentives, liking
versus wanting, and even the "control precedence" of emotions. More than

363

anything, Aristotle emphasized the importance of definitions, which he says "must be regarded as adequate, even if they are not exact, provided they are clear." I wonder how much clarity we have gained, centuries later, in our definitions and our approaches to the study of motivation. The two papers for this session, excellent, original, and thought provoking as they are, raised a number of questions for me. Questions about things I think need to be defined and delineated better before progress can be made in this area. The questions involve the relationship between motivation and desire, between "push" and "pull" factors, between desire and arousal, and, more generally, between emotion and motivation.

Let me start with the distinction between motivation and desire. Sexual motivation is, as Stephanie, Walter, and Ellen say, a construct used to explain the generation of sexual action. (Jim goes a—somewhat confusing—step further and states that not just behavior but the experience of desire itself is "sexually motivated.") *Sexual desire* is a phenomenological term, involving the conscious, subjective experience of wanting to do something sexual. What is sexual desire? It is *one* reason to have sex. Sexual desire is motivational, a motive for sex, but other motives for sex exist that do not involve an intrinsic, "true" desire for sex itself. Sexual desire is the experience of action tendencies. It is about wanting, but is it also about liking? I have the impression that when we use the words sexual desire, we tend to think of a state that is positive in valence. Sexual desire is something that feels good. But does it always? How much sexual desire can you experience, or would you be willing to report experiencing, when you are frustrated with or angry at your partner, or when you are viewing sexually explicit materials in which people interact in ways that do not correspond with your values? In other words, I wonder, as I do for sexual arousal, to what degree sexual desire can be experienced in the presence of negative affect. And how clear is it what we want to know when we ask our subjects about this? What *are* people thinking when they say they experience "sexual desire"?

Models of sexual motivation often include the discussion of push and pull factors. And so do Jim's and Stephanie, Ellen, and Walter's papers. While it makes sense to distinguish between factors within us that influence our likelihood to respond and the "intrinsic" potential of certain stimuli to provoke such responses, the two may be not as independent as we might like them to be. And we definitely don't seem to be able to measure one without the involvement of the other. On the pull side we have incentives and sexually competent stimuli. But what exactly are those? Especially the use of the term *sexually competent* makes me think of Masters and Johnson's circular definition of "effective sexual stimulation." How do we know if a stimulus is sexually competent? Because it leads to a sexual response. The distinction between push and pull, or internal factors and incentives, suffers from a similar problem. The push side involves the sensitivities of our sexual response system to stimuli; not a force that can be measured independently from the presence of relevant triggers, I would think—as that would come scaringly close to a Freudian drive (and we do not seem to like push factors that live a life of their own). And how can the effectiveness of an incentive, or pull factor, be established while ignoring the influence of push factors? After all, what is a "sexually competent" stimulus or effective incentive for one person (including sex itself or the orgasms that may or may not follow from it) may, and you do not need to be a clinician to know this, lack any "pull" properties for others.

The fact that you can't really look at the effectiveness of stimuli without taking into account the properties of the receiving system, or the "set point" for the activation of sexual responses (in our dual control model that would include the set point for inhibition, or the prevention or termination of responses), reminds me of discussions of "spontaneous" desire or arousal, but also of proposed gender differences in how sexual desire and arousal come about. In my world, spontaneous desire and arousal do not exist. They refer to states of which we either don't understand the causes or of which the person experiencing them missed the antecedents or triggers. Just because we are not always aware of what starts a sexual response does not mean that no intentional (or "nonspontaneous") processes, even when they take place outside of our consciousness, are involved. In that sense, the use of the word *spontaneous* simply refers to the experience of not being able to pinpoint what it is we are responding to. It also reveals, at least in my view, the importance of understanding that the relevant neurophysiological systems, at a central but also peripheral level, are likely to have different "settings," and that not all relevant processes are under voluntary control or accessible to consciousness. I believe this also is relevant to recent discussions of gender differences in how sexual desire and arousal come about. Women and men may not differ as much in the neurophysiological mechanisms underlying sexual desire and arousal as (on average— after all, we should not forget that within-gender variability is larger than between-gender differences, and that several more recent models were conceived in the minds of clinicians, who are exposed to selected parts, or restricted ranges, of the continuum) in the set points for the activation and inhibition of the mechanisms that underlie sexual desire and arousal. And they may differ in what they want to do with such feelings, once they emerge. That is, we should not confuse the state of sexual desire (and in my mind that state can exist in the presence of other, less positive feelings) with the question of when conditions are met for a man or a woman to want to engage in sex, or to follow up on such feelings. You may experience sexual desire and still not want to act on it. But I am digressing. My main point is that it does not make sense, to me, to assume that women would be more likely than men to start from a "neutral" position. We all start from a neutral position. However, it is possible that (many) men have lower set points for the activation of sexual processes than (many) women—even when involving stimuli that are invisible to their otherwise so perceptive and analytical minds, making them think their response occurred "spontaneously."

What are incentives to have sex, or to be sexual? And do incentives themselves have to be sexual? In the animal literature, if I am not mistaken, sexually "receptive" females are considered an incentive (or an unconditioned stimulus [UCS], in classical conditioning paradigms). How do we translate that notion of female "receptivity" to humans? Complicated, it seems. Also, orgasms are incentives. But are orgasms purely "sexual" or are they feelings that happen to be uniquely associated with and triggered through sexual activity? Also, are all orgasms equal? Do all orgasms fit the definition of an incentive? Like desire, are they really always some pure, unambiguously positive experience? How does this work for someone who experiences orgasms, but sooner than he would like to (e.g., in premature ejaculation), or when they are combined with, or immediately followed by, guilt or other negative feelings? What do we know about this? But even if, in general, orgasms can be an incentive, what about fur coats? Or a trip to another country? Or a desire to please your partner for less selfish reasons? John Bancroft has compiled a long list of why people might want to engage in sex. Having reasons for engaging in sex is not the same thing as experiencing sexual desire. Or is it? Again, our vocabulary and definitions are extremely important, I think. What does it mean when we ask our subjects to indicate using a simple, single item how much "sexual desire" they experience, especially when considering that we ourselves, the so-called experts, are struggling to understand and delineate the concept?

So what about desire versus arousal? And motivation versus emotion? I would like to consider the two together, as I have questions about them that make the most sense to consider in tandem. After all, isn't it true that we, at least traditionally, have tended to approach sexual desire as a motivational and sexual arousal as an emotional state? This is complicated and confusing. After all, emotions are characterized by action tendencies (e.g., approach/avoidance, wanting to do something, as in anger or anxiety, or not, as in depression), but they are clearly motivational. Also, if you can experience sexual desire, there may not be much against calling it an emotion. The distinction, I would not be surprised, reflects our way of looking at desire and arousal, as one being the cause and the other the result of processing sexually relevant stimuli. Yet, it is interesting that Jim discusses, in quite some depth, models of sexual arousal in his review of the literature on sexual motivation. And Stephanie, Walter, and Ellen also teach us that the distinction may not be that straightforward. They propose that sexual desire is a conscious experience that may follow the activation of sexual arousal in the brain (and not the other way around). There are some problems with that, I think. First, I am not sure if, as formulated, that hypothesis is falsifiable. Second, when they talk about sexual arousal, the authors mainly mean "central" sexual arousal, and not necessarily even at a level that involves the conscious experience of "subjective" sexual arousal. So how this all interacts, or does not interact, at higher levels of arousal, where subjective feelings as well as genital responses start becoming stimuli themselves, is another matter. (Also, while sexual arousal, so defined, may not follow sexual desire, I am getting the impression from your paper that we are not talking about sexual arousal preceding desire either, but some type of coactivation.) I think we need to talk about the role of response "intensity," or response levels, in this context as well. Maybe it's just some linguistic issue, maybe I'm just easily confused, but in my mind it all starts with the activation of relevant systems in the brain, no matter what we are talking about. We could call that sexual arousal, yes, but we could call that something else, too. We could call it central sexual arousal, the central activation of arousal, the first step in the cascade of sex, or something else. They are just words. So sexual activation in the brain may lead to, yes or no, the experience of sexual desire and, yes or no, the experience of subjective sexual arousal, and some higher forces know where genital responses come in. I am not sure how much we should look at this in temporal or sequential terms. The same applies to Jim's model. While I think it is very interesting, it reminded me of Masters and Johnson's linear thinking and how they have been criticized for that. What are conditions that need to be met for the assumed "next steps" to occur; are they necessary or sufficient, or in other words, do they always need to occur? And would those processes work the same for animals and humans?

So, back to the emotions, and onward to the T-reflex. It is not easy for me to criticize this work, as I am a student of a school of thought of which Walter is both architect and principal, but I will try. Walter was the first sex researcher to propose that sexual arousal and desire are among the emotions and that we can benefit from the use of emotion theories and paradigms in our study of them. Emotion theorists still seem reluctant to acknowledge or endorse this view. I remember vividly a discussion I had, when I was a graduate student, with a famous, older emotion researcher who told me that he believed sex didn't belong to emotion theories, but to marriage. Walter and others have accumulated quite a bit of evidence to the contrary, I think, and the T-reflex studies are a great example of this. I think it is a beautiful paradigm that allows us to study in a controlled setting the role of "action tendencies" in sexual response and behavior. The paradigm is a window into the processes involved in how our body *prepares* for sexual behavior and motor action, and it allows us to look at that aspect of motivation separately from the experience of sexual desire and, apparently, also from whether or not actual sexual behavior will follow. At the same time, this disconnection between the various components of sexual response and behavior raises several questions. In the study with L-dopa, effects were found on the T-reflex but not on subjective sexual arousal or desire. That indicates that action tendencies or motor preparations as indexed by the T-reflex, indeed, do not need to be translated into the subjective experience of sexual desire or arousal. But you start your paper with the proposition that sexual desire follows sexual arousal. So, is the T-reflex a measure of motivation or desire, or does it reflect the mere initiation, centrally, of sexual arousal? And does it matter? Why would that increase in T-reflex not translate into a stronger experience of sexual desire? So, apparently sexual arousal and desire are related, but not that strongly (or at least not at those response levels), or does it have something to do with the sensitivity of self-report measures and the possible other variables that play into what people report? Do the effects reflect more the wanting component of arousal than the liking component of desire, or am I mixing things up here?

How far should we go in our Aristotelian attempt to define as precisely as possible constructs like sexual arousal, motivation, and desire, or to draw maps with lakes, mountains, and borders to describe and delineate their content and meaning, their commonalities and differences? I would love to hear your views on this. John and I have had many a discussion on this and I think he believes I give too much weight to definitional issues. It is true, I can lie in bed and just wonder about what sexual arousal really "is." What "it" is. Maybe it's just a way of ensuring that I exhaust and confuse myself up to a point where I will fall asleep. At the same time, if we work with constructs whose definitions are up for grabs, more confusion is guaranteed and I am not sure how much progress we will be able to make. So I believe paradigms like the T-reflex may help us structure our thinking and add to this so slowly emerging picture of the relationships among sexual motivation, desire, arousal, and behavior. In conclusion, it's the same old adage: There still is a lot of work to do.

References

Roberts, W. R. (1924). Rhetorica. In W. D. Ross (Ed.), *The works of Aristotle translated into English.* Oxford: Clarendon Press.

General Discussion

Roy Levin: Could I just come in about the distinction between sexual arousal and desire? You can certainly have sexual arousal without desire. There's no question about that. I can give you one instance where you can have sexual arousal, whether you mean on the brain or in the genitals; of course, then you would have to define where the "sexual arousal" is, because a man after ejaculation has "arousal" in his penis, but he has no desire in his brain. So there's sexual arousal without desire there, for example. I wrote some time ago that you could have sexual arousal without desire and desire without arousal and, of course, your model would say that you couldn't have that. I'm not quite sure that there's any real evidence for that statement. I also had a model; in fact, it was at your meeting Ellen that I put forward that there may be two types of desire, so some of what you said I believe in myself. But I find that at the moment—I think John actually wrote an article with somebody, I've forgotten who your co-worker was—but you had trouble with sexual desire, sexual arousal, and sexual stimuli, didn't you? You couldn't really separate those.

John Bancroft: I have a lot of trouble with sexual desire!

Roy Levin: I don't remember that review, but I thought that the patella and the Achilles tendon reflexes, and tell me if I'm wrong, are cord reflexes, they don't go up to the brain. So is dopamine acting on the cord or is it acting on the brain? I remember I used to test reflexes as an undergraduate and what you do: you trigger the patella reflex and then you put your hands together and you pull really hard and you get a much better reflex, and that was, as physiologists said, because you raise the excitation level in the cord, not in the brain, and that's why you got a much bigger reflex. So where are these potentiations taking place?

Stephanie Both: Well, you are right that we cannot state that dopamine is acting only on the brain. It also can act on the spinal cord. However, I think that the fact that we find only an effect of levodopa during sexual stimulation suggests that levodopa affected the processing of the sexual stimulus. We didn't find an effect of dopamine in the resting state, which indicates that there was no general effect of levodopa on excitation level in the cord.

Roy Levin: I think you will find that a lot of people now think that there are things that are happening in the cord, didn't you say that there were things that are happening in the cord, Kevin?

Kevin McKenna: It's definitely a spinal reflex, but the fact that it's potentiated by watching a film indicates that the effect is happening in the brain and it's descending and affecting that spinal reflex.

Roy Levin: Things are coming from the genitals watching the film and then . . .

Kevin McKenna: I don't think so, but the L-dopa could certainly be working in the brain and causing a descending effect.

Marca Sipski: I guess, but I didn't see that you showed that L-dopa caused the reflex. I didn't understand that from what you said and I had a question: is the reflex being facilitated by sympathetic activation? Sympathetic activation increases your blood flow to your muscles and potentially increases reflex responses there. What was going on with your other autonomic nervous system and what was going on with heart rate, and so forth? That's what I'd like to know.

Stephanie Both: Well, we did a couple of studies in which we measured T-reflexes during emotional stimulation. We used sexual films, but also sexual pictures that were showed for a few seconds. We found sexual pictures, in contrast to neutral pictures, to enhance T-reflexes. I think it is unlikely that the effect of exposure to a sexual picture for such a short period of time is due to an increase in blood flow of the muscles. So I think we may be pretty sure that we are measuring increased activity in the motor system.

Marca Sipski: But could the emotional stimulation be causing activation of your sympathetic nervous system and increase heart rate and so on? Were there other—what was going on with the others? Did you measure heart rate?

Stephanie Both: Yes, I did measure heart rate as an indicator of drug bioactivity.

Marca Sipski: What happened with the heart rate?

Stephanie Both: It increased after L-dopa administration, and that was what we expected.

Marca Sipski: And what about without L-dopa?

Stephanie Both: It wasn't the same, but it wasn't raised that much.

Marca Sipski: But it was elevated?

Stephanie Both: Yes, it was, though a facilitatory effect of sexual stimuli on heart rate does not necessarily mean that enhanced T-reflexes are due to increased sympathetic nervous system activity. Brunia and others, who did a lot of work with T reflexes as a tool to study central nervous system changes, state that facilitatory influences on spinal motoneurons stem from the somatic nervous system, whereas increases in heart rate result from changes in the autonomic nervous system (Brunia & Boelhouwer, 1988).

They observed that during a mental task, heart rate decreased while T-reflexes increased, which suggests that the mechanisms that are causing the increases in T-reflexes and in heart rate are different.

Jim Pfaus: Erick, I think your idea about sexual arousal and desire co-occurring is extremely important. This is something that I didn't expect because conceptually the two are separate in my mind. They're obviously intellectually separate in clinical case studies where someone has no desire but is still capable of getting aroused with manual stimulation of the genitals. Conversely, we have people with intact desire but a disrupted ability to become aroused. When my graduate student, Rachel Toledano, was developing the Sexual Arousal and Desire Inventory she had separate adjectives for desire and arousal. Virtually all of our subjects wondered why the same questions were being asked twice. I think the perception may very well be in reality that those two facets of sexual experience co-occur and that it's not really a kind of Cannon/Bard versus James/Lange dichotomy of what comes first. Either one can come first and inform the other. And, in fact, in the cascade from unconscious tendencies to an actual orgasm, all physiological sensations and cognitive appraisals may be informing one another, increasing excitement, arousal, and desire.

John Bancroft: I found the L-dopa experiment very interesting. How you interpret the effect on the T-reflex needs careful thought. I take Marca Sipski's point about possibly being indirectly affected. Maybe Kevin or Jim could help us to get dopamine into perspective here because it has a number of functions in the brain. I'm basing this on Elaine Hull's analysis (e.g., Hull et al., 1998). In the dorsal striatum and the nigro-striatal tract, dopamine (DA) plays a role in preparation for motor activity of a very nonspecific kind. Maybe that's what you're referring to, Stephanie, with the T-reflex. In the ventral striatum, DA has a nonspecific effect on what Elaine calls appetite for a variety of different kinds of appetite, including sexual. Like Jim, I've been struggling with the concept of motivation. I don't quite know what it means. Appetite, does that get us any further? I can think about feeling hungry and I can understand there could be some physiological basis to this. Is there a sexual parallel to this? And there's another dopaminergic system that affects the media preoptic area, at least in the male; I'm not sure about its relevance in the female. But this appears to integrate genital response with appropriate motor behavior, so it's relatively specifically sexual. And then, of course, there is the direct effect of the tubero-infundibular DA system that involves the dopaminergic control of the anterior pituitary, which we were considering yesterday. So what about this dopaminergic effect on appetite? Can Kevin or Jim help us on that?

Jim Pfaus: I think what Elaine Hull means by appetite is appetitive; that is, so that the hunger for sex would be a different H word, horny, for example, or something that would indicate a drive. Imagine that I want sex. There's nothing around me that might be bringing that out, I am just sitting here alone quietly reading a book and suddenly want to have sex. So that's what she means by appetite, and when she talks about the dorsal striatum, her theory is in line with a lot of work done on other motivational systems, for example, on feeding, thirst, and fear. When you have that motivation translated into action, then you're utilizing more and more of the dorsal striatum to get more and more output from the basal ganglia to actually get you into motor preparedness either to run away or to run toward an incentive. If you know you are horny and you go out searching for a potential sex partner, you are moving in a forward-directed, goal-locomotive kind of way. This requires attention and is a phenomenon that mesolimbic dopamine release generally promotes. We can observe hyper-stimulation of forward-directed behavior following treatment with amphetamine or cocaine. Now, if we put an animal with a very low dose of amphetamine in with a potential sex partner, the animal doesn't locomote aimlessly, the animal locomotes right over to the sex partner. If the animal is experienced, it will copulate with the sex partner. So you've got an interplay between these drive states or these appetitive states that are internal, but that are brought out behaviorally depending on the external incentive.

John Bancroft: Then let me ask, where does arousal come in? How does that relate to appetite? Because here we're talking about a norepinephric system that is relatively nonspecific in its effects. How does that fit in with what you've just been saying?

Jim Pfaus: The noradrenergic part of arousal is probably in the periphery, brainstem, and hypothalamus, but the dopaminergic actions occur at the level of the medial preoptic area, anterior hypothalamus, and in limbic terminals of the mesolimbic dopamine system. The arousal provided by sexual stimuli activates these dopamine systems and guide our attention toward them. In the hypothalamus, dopamine likely plays a role in regulating the balance between activation of the parasympathetic nervous system for erection and activation of the sympathetic nervous system for ejaculation. So initially you get activation of parasympathetic outflow and that's controlled at the level of the anterior hypothalamus through a descending circuitry that ends up in the spinal cord and ends up apportioning out what you need and where. As you continue to copulate and dopamine levels continue to go up in this region, you get a shift in activation of neurons in the medial preoptic area that now activate sympathetic outflow and trigger ejaculation through again, a whole cascade of processes in the brain and spinal cord. Noradrenergic mechanisms of sexual arousal have not been studied as extensively in the rat as the dopaminergic mechanisms of attention. That is unfortunate because noradrenaline likely plays a very important role.

Serge Stoléru: I have a question about the dichotomy between the drive model and the incentive model. I understand very well that if there is a stimulus, a competent stimulus, then there may be arousal. I have more difficulty in understanding the other proposition that you said, that is, that when there is no stimulus, then there is no arousal. I would like to know how within this framework the sexual fantasy is conceptualized, because in sexual fantasy the stimulus is not there, so it seems to me that the incentive theory must at least admit that the sexual incentive can be internalized or memorized and recalled.

Stephanie Both: What we think is that sexual motivation will only emerge when there is a sexual stimulus, but the stimulus doesn't have to be external per se, it can also be a thought or a fantasy. About sexual fantasy, it's very hard to say if it's a response to something that you can have perceived without being aware of it. There might have been a sexual stimulus that activated sexual fantasies or memories.

Jim Geer: But you have to ask, where does that come from? What stimulates the sexual fantasy? It gets to be an infinite regress, I understand that . . .

Stephanie Both: I think there can be a lot of things that stimulate fantasy, maybe a smell or something you saw, or a bodily sensation. . . .

Jim Geer: Yes, it's very difficult.

Ray Rosen: I think there are four or five key issues that have been brought up in the discussion and are important to address separately. Before I forget, I'd like to address a short comment to Stephanie. I, like everyone else, found the paradigm and the research very interesting. To me, the critical missing piece is the external validity of the reflex. In other words, I know it's been done in other areas, but we cannot assume that that reflex really will predict sexual approach behavior. And I think that if you can show in any way that the reflex is actually predictive of sexual approach behavior, you'll go a long way in convincing me that it's a valid measure of desire. Action tendency is a concept and I think you need to validate that concept by demonstrating external validity. I'd like to bring up a couple of other issues. One level of confusion is the external stimulus/internal stimulus discussion and the actual nature of the stimulus. Another issue is the neurochemistry and dopamine discussion that the paradigm brings up and there's been a lot of talk about at this meeting. From my perspective, we should not equate increased dopamine with drive. A clear example is the sleep drive. Sleep deprivation is a powerful drive state that can override all other drive states when sleep deprivation is sufficiently great. On the other hand, dopamine is inhibitory of sleep and promotes arousal. So dopamine may be more important in facilitating active behavior than in regulating drive state, per se.

Walter Everaerd: There are lots of data about the relationship between imagery of behavioral events and the factual instigation of those events by external stimuli. A number of studies have shown very clearly that imagery results in the same activation as what an external stimulus does, so that's not such a riddle.

Ray Rosen: Well, I agree, Walter, and I think the understanding of the relationship between fantasy stimuli, external stimuli, visual, tactile in sexual response or sexual behavior is definitely worth pursuing, but I think the attempt to define sexual desire or motivation in regard to external/internal stimuli will end up being impossible or meaningless. I don't feel that's a fruitful direction for us to be going in.

Walter Everaerd: The crucial point may be that Serge has to show that there is a physiological variable that evokes content in the brain that is sexual. And, if that's not possible, it's maybe the other way around; that you first have to produce those contents, cognitive contents, before you get a sexual response.

Erick Janssen: I have the impression that this is about what some call "spontaneous sexual fantasies." The question is not, at least not to me, whether or not imagery could have the same effect as some external stimulus, but what it is that starts the cascade to begin with, what triggers a fantasy in the first place? Is it external—for example, a smell—but could it not be anything? How can we predict when it happens and when it does not, why in this and not in the other person? Those are the more challenging questions, in my view.

Serge Stoléru: I don't think that the incentive versus drive model is a fruitless direction to pursue, really, because there are real questions that must be answered. For example, is there such thing as a hypothalamic tonic activity that would provoke a sexual activity if it is not inhibited? If this exists, I'm ready not to call it a drive, but we must call it a name different from an incentive, because there is something that is pushing, so you can call it any word you want. There is something that is pushing internally and not necessarily needing an incentive to get expressed.

Walter Everaerd: I've recently gone through that literature about hypersexuality and these are results based on temporal lobe operations. They result in disinhibition, not only of sexual behavior but also other kinds of rewarding behaviors.

Serge Stoléru: I do not think that specificity is the issue, here. There is a sexual behavior that is liberated, that is freed when those influences are alleviated, and it's not very important that there are also other behaviors that are freed, you know, because the inhibitory systems can have many effects, but that's not really the issue.

Lori Brotto: I believe that part of the problem in conceptualizing, researching, and discussing sexual desire is that we are constrained by the limits of language. We seem to agree that these constructs exist; however, we may falsely assume that the words we use, and the language we speak when communicating with one another, accurately captures the essence of those constructs. What we unfortunately may end up with is a language describing desire that has different meanings for different women. We have some preliminary data to support the notion that scientists and women themselves might be talking about something very different when discussing sexual desire. In our work in which we both ask women, in an unstructured interview format, to discuss how they conceptualize sexual desire and arousal, and then ask them to complete structured questionnaires that assess sexual desire and arousal problems, we find some very striking differences in these methods of assessment. The women in our study had no difficulty answering questions about sexual desire frequency and intensity, and their sexual desire scores were highly correlated with their sexual arousal scores. However, when asked open endedly about these constructs, they expressed much difficulty in describing them. Some described subtle but important differences between desire and arousal that were not captured in their questionnaires. Others reported these constructs to be the same—again, not picked up in their quantitative data. These differences we found not only in women who experienced sexual difficulties, but also among women without sexual complaints. Now, given that many researchers rely solely upon quantitative questionnaires to measure sexual desire and arousal and changes in them with a given treatment, how can we be sure that these instruments have true construct validity? Again, the language in these instruments limits us from understanding the whole experience of desire. Therefore, as researchers I feel we need to be mindful of the limits of language in describing these very complex constructs and strive to find methods that get closer to capturing women's experiences. Perhaps an integration of quantitative and qualitative data analytic techniques, as has recently been proposed (Tolman & Diamond, 2001), is a step in that direction.

Cynthia Graham: A couple of points: One, following up from what Jim said, we have collected qualitative data suggesting that women really find it very difficult to differentiate arousal and desire; we've got a rich source of data. The other point, regarding Ray's comments, is that clinically great comorbidity exists between desire and arousal, which many of you know about, but I think it's important to keep that in mind. In our clinical experience, we find very few women reporting arousal disorders who do not also report lack of desire. A final quick point is that I found interesting what you said about courtship issues. We also should bear in mind that for many women it may not be that they can't initiate or don't want to, but they may not have the opportunity to do so due to relationship, social, or cultural factors; just something to keep in mind. It may not be a lack of ability or desire to initiate, but lack of opportunity, their partner, relationships, and so on.

Kevin McKenna: I like the idea that, in many cases, sexual desire is produced by sexual stimuli and sexual situations. But I'm a little concerned that it can't exist without external stimuli, or without drives, innate pressures, or whatever you call them. Maybe we do need different terminologies, but in some ways this idea of an innate horniness—maybe that is sexual arousal. Maybe there is a form of sexual arousal that occurs somehow in the brain in response to hormonal levels, but it is a form of arousal in the brain that causes you to go out and seek sexual stimuli. Because I still have a hard time understanding where fantasies come from. Something is driving that. Stephanie, your last sentence was that sexual desire could exist, but that it can only follow a sexual stimulus, and I really have a hard time dealing with that. I don't remember what your last sentence was, but it was something like that.

Stephanie Both: The last sentence was "sexual desire emerges from sexual excitement." What we mean to say is that for sexual desire, for the subjective experience of wanting sex, there must be sexual excitement. When there is no excitement, there may be, as Walter explained, "cold" emotion, but there will be no "hot" emotion. For the experience of "hot" sexual desire, you need emotional responses in the brain and in the body.

Kevin McKenna: But you said "only," and I have difficulty with that.

Serge Stoléru: I think that the issue about vagueness of language is very important, but maybe a good product of the conference would be to arrive at the scientific definition of desire. I have to rephrase that. I mean, what do we, as scientists involved in sexual psychophysiology, refer to when we write or pronounce the phrase *sexual desire*. We should try to reach a consensus regarding the terminology we use, to avoid ambiguous meanings. Another thing is that Cynthia Graham was saying that women have a hard time distinguishing what is sexual arousal and sexual desire. It seems to me that it is perfectly understandable, because it seems to me that sexual desire is just one part of sexual arousal, and that sexual arousal can be thought of as developing within at least a four-dimensional space, and in this space, coordinates may be very small on one or more dimensions. Thus, you arrive at the idea that at every point in time, sexual arousal has a "shape." For some people, at some point in time, one dimension is flattened, and at other times, the shape is different, full-blown (along the cognitive, motivational, emotional, and peripheral dimensions). So, what we have to assess when we assess the state of sexual arousal in a specific individual at a specific point in time is the "shape" of her/his state of sexual arousal. We have to assess the various coordinates, and at some times, there are only the autonomic coordinates; the full-blown would be the four coordinates activated together. I have a proposal about what sexual desire means, just to start with something, just so that it can be criticized. For me, sexual desire means the mental representation of either a sexual state or a sexual action, whose actualization is thought of as a reward. In other words, it is the subject's expectancy that if a certain state—which may be an interpersonal situation—was attained or if certain actions were performed by the subject, then a sexual reward would ensue. That is what I would think of as the meaning of the phrase *sexual desire*.

David Rowland: My recollection of the classic works of Hull and Spence may be incorrect, but I want to go back to some of the original concepts and encourage us to think in those terms rather than to grapple anew with these terms at this conference. Desire is a motivational construct. The whole idea of "motivation" is to explain differences in occurrences and intensities of output or responses, given similar inputs. I think the assumption has always been that this construct is useful as long as we don't know the specific internal and external stimuli that can otherwise account for variation in frequency and intensities of the output or responses. Someone else that went through that classic era of motivation may have a different recollection of these constructs, but desire was considered a motivational state, just as hunger is. What is hunger? It is a motivational construct that explains why we are eating at some times and not at other times, why some times we eat more, and so on. The main idea is that, ultimately, we must at some point identify those internal and external stimuli that underlie the concept of sexual motivation; this was the goal of the early psychologists, to understand the processes underlying the motivational construct so eventually you could discard the construct and the word. I'm sorry if this is Psych 101 for people, I don't mean it to be, but rather as a reference to where some of this terminology actually has come from.

Jim Pfaus: I'm glad you brought up hunger because, in fact, it was Shere Hite who I believe said that "sex can be a five course meal, or a hot dog and a Coke." If we think of desire and drive and arousal and excitement as "static entities" from a motivational standpoint, then we are depriving ourselves of the fact that sex itself is not static: sometimes it's going to be quick, sometimes not so quick; sometimes it's going to be wonderful and sometimes not so wonderful. That's life, that's real experience. Motivational models need to take the effect of feedback from experience into consideration, as they have in the drug addiction literature. We have to build enough plasticity into our models to allow the multivariate expression of behavior in time, and the models also must allow sexual stimuli to tolerate or sensitize in time. Your arousability changes in time, and if it changes, it's okay. Hopefully we all had great sex at 18, although we may appreciate it more at 80. It is not necessarily the case that arousability rises or falls in a linear way, and constructs like "desire" must allow for a degree of randomness and nonlinear change.

References

Brunia, C. H. M., & Boelhouwer, A. J. W. (1988). Reflexes as a tool: A window in the central nervous system. *Advances in Psychophysiology, 3,* 1–67.

Hull, E. M., Lorrain, D. S., Du, J., Matuszewich, L., Bitran, D., Nishita, J. K., & Scaletta, L. L. (1998). Organizational and activational effects of dopamine on male sexual behavior. In L. Ellis & L. Ebertz (Eds.), *Males, females and behavior: Toward biological understanding* (pp. 79–96). Westport, Conn.: Greenwood Press.

Tolman, D. L., & Diamond, L. M. (2001). Desegregating sexuality research: Cultural and biological perspectives on gender and desire. *Annual Review of Sex Research, 12,* 33–74.

Part 5.

Sexual Function and Dysfunction

Sexual Dysfunction, Sexual Psychophysiology, and Psychopharmacology

Laboratory Studies in Men and Women

RAYMOND C. ROSEN, MARKUS WEIGEL, AND NOEL GENDRANO III

Pharmacological treatment of sexual problems, a long-standing topic of interest in sex research and therapy, has increased dramatically in importance since the discovery in the mid-1990s of phosphodiesterase type-5 (PDE5) inhibitors and other potent prosexual drugs (Rosen & McKenna, 2002). Aside from the currently available PDE5 inhibitors (e.g., sildenafil, tadalafil, vardenafil), dopamine agonists (e.g., apomorphine), central and peripheral alpha-blockers (e.g., phentolamine), melanocortin agonists (e.g., PT-141), and a variety of other agents are being actively investigated in both men and women. To date, three specific agents (sildenafil, tadalafil, vardenafil) have been approved in the United States for treatment of male erectile dysfunction (ED) and further approvals are anticipated in the near future. In addition to their use in ED, PDE5 inhibitors have been used experimentally in the treatment of other male and female sexual disorders (see Rosen & McKenna, 2002, for a review). The widespread availability of these new agents has altered significantly the clinical approach to management of sexual problems, which is increasingly in the hands of primary care and nonspecialist physicians. Basic and applied research in sexual dysfunction has also increased markedly in the past decade, driven partly by greater understanding of the underlying physiological mechanisms involved, as well as the considerable influx of funding from the pharmaceutical industry. The potential scientific and societal implications of these developments have been addressed by a number of authors (e.g., Bancroft, 2000; Bass, 2002; Rosen & McKenna, 2002; Tiefer, 1996, 2002).

One area of research that has benefited from these developments has been the use of laboratory psychophysiological methods for the investigation of pharmacological effects on sexual response in men and women. Prior to the advent of sildenafil, a handful of studies had employed laboratory methods to evaluate effects of prosexual drugs in either gender (see Rosen, 1991; Rosen & Ashton, 1993, for reviews of presildenafil studies). Results of these earlier studies had been largely inconclusive, perhaps due to limitations in the study designs or methodology, or possible lack of efficacy of the study drugs being evaluated. Since the advent of sildenafil, however, laboratory psychophysiological studies have played an increasingly pivotal role in the development of new treatment agents and in the investigation of potential mechanisms of action. In this paper, we examine specific ways in which these laboratory methods have been used in recent studies in men and women and the potential advantages and limitations associated with their use.

Laboratory psychophysiological studies have found application in at least three specific areas in the recent development of pharmacological agents for treating male or female sexual dysfunction. First, "proof of concept" studies involving a relatively small number of subjects (e.g., $N = 12$) have been used increasingly to demonstrate initial efficacy of a new drug in either men (Boolel, Gepi-Attee, Gingell, & Allen, 1996; Munoz, Bancroft, & Turner, 1994) or women (Laan, van Lunsen, & Everaerd, 2001; Rosen, Phillips, Gendrano, & Ferguson, 1999). These studies have served to identify initial treatment effects on physiological or subjective indices of arousal, prior to the initiation of large-scale and very costly clinical trials. Second, laboratory psychophysiological studies have been used to establish a dose-response relationship between predetermined doses of the study drug and selected measures of physiological or subjective arousal. Such studies have played an important role in guiding selection of doses for subsequent clinical trials. Third, psychophysiological measures have been used as pharmacodynamic or surrogate endpoints in studies of the mechanism or timing of action of specific agents. For example, recent studies have employed laboratory assessments of penile rigidity and tumescence in response to visual sexual stimulation to establish the onset and duration of action of current PDE5 inhibitors (Eardley, Ellis, Boolell, & Wulff, 2002). These effects have been confirmed with more naturalistic measures in some studies. Examples are provided in each area of application, as well as potential strengths and weakness of specific studies.

Key conceptual and methodological issues need also to be addressed. For example, as noted by Rosen and Beck (1988) and others, sexual psychophysiological studies all suffer from potential limitations in regards to *external validity*. This may be a particular concern when investigating the clinical efficacy of a new treatment agent for male or female sexual dysfunction. Specifically, how predictive are changes in genital blood flow or subjective arousal in the laboratory of actual sexual responses under "real world" conditions? How much change or improvement in laboratory-based measures of response should be judged as "clinically significant," and what external criteria should be used to support this criterion? Will the effects of the drug be comparable when taken under laboratory conditions compared to more naturalistic or "at home" uses of the drug? These and other concerns regarding the ecological or external validity of laboratory-based designs in this area need to be urgently addressed. Another critical issue concerns the need for adequate experimental control and the use of counterbalanced designs. This is particularly relevant in laboratory-based studies with small ns and repeated measures designs, both of which are highly characteristic of psychophysiological studies in this area. The use of double-blind, placebo-controlled designs and counterbalancing for order effects are especially important considerations. Finally, measurement issues and potential sources of recording bias or artifact are ever-present concerns in laboratory psychophysiological research, as is no less the case in the current area of application.

Studies in both men and women are considered in this paper, although special issues and problems pertain to the use of these methods in women. One fundamental issue, which is also addressed by several other presenters at this conference (Laan & Janssen, this volume), is the frequent discordance between subjective and physiological measures of arousal. This is a common and sometimes vexing problem in laboratory psychophysiological studies of sexual arousal in women, which may have particular salience in the use of these methods for evaluating drug effects on sexual response. Assuming differing patterns of subjective and physiological measures of arousal in response to the administration of a drug, what significance should be placed on the various components of response? Rosen and Beck (1988) proposed earlier that subjective arousal be viewed as the final arbiter or "sine qua non" of sexual response in women. Is this concept relevant in assessing pharmacological effects of new treatment agents in women with sexual dysfunction? If the drug is effective at a basic pharmacologic or physiological level, how necessary is a change in subjective arousal? This issue is of less concern in men, since much higher correlations are typically observed between physiological and subjective measures of arousal. Other potential problems in interpreting results of laboratory studies in women concern the relative absence of normative data in sexually functional or dysfunctional women, as well as the relative dearth of studies with proven effective agents. In contrast to the strikingly positive effects of PDE5s on male erectile response, most pharmacological agents evaluated to date in women have shown either weak or inconsistent effects on measures of either genital or subjective arousal. In the absence of clear-cut evidence of efficacy for a specific agent, the relevance of laboratory-based data in women will remain subject to interpretation.

Notwithstanding these concerns, it is evident that psychophysiological methods currently play an important role in the laboratory assessment of psychopharmacological treatment effects in men and women. We consider in this paper recent examples of this trend, as well as potential future directions. This paper will focus primarily on the use of traditional psychophysiological methods, such as genital blood flow measurement via photoplethysmography, mercury strain gauge, or penile rigidity assessment by means of RigiScan monitoring, as well as various other measures of cognitive or subjective arousal. The use of imaging techniques or other more advanced measures of central or peripheral arousal is addressed by other authors at this conference (e.g., Stoléru, Heiman). Moreover, these techniques have not been used to any significant degree to date in the evaluation of psychopharmacological effects of drugs in sexually dysfunctional men or women. This is an important area of potential future investigation.

Psychophysiological Laboratory Studies in Men

Early psychophysiological studies in men investigated the effects of alpha-blockers on waking and sleep erections (Bancroft, Munoz, Beard, & Shapiro, 1995). More recently, much of the attention has been focused on PDE5 inhibitors, dopamine and melanocortin agonists. Bancroft and his colleagues examined the effects of a then new, potent α_2-andrenocepter antagonist, delaquamine, on male erectile response. In a well-designed "proof of concept" study (Bancroft et al., 1995; Munoz, Bancroft, & Beard, 1994; Munoz, Bancroft, & Turner, 1994), the authors examined the drug's effect on penile tumescence in response to visual stimulation, on NPT, and on sleep in men with and without ED. Since delaquamine is thought to produce adrenergic inhibition, it was hypothesized that its main impact would be evidenced in androgen-dependent expressions of sexual arousal, such as NPT and fantasy. The studies are briefly described here, not so much in terms of the results (efficacy of delaquamine), but in terms of the well-designed study and use of psychophysiological methodology for this purpose.

The study participants included 12 healthy men without sexual dysfunction, and 24 men with male ED. Inclusion criteria for men with ED included predominantly psychogenic etiologic factors and an NPT response of at least 25-mm penile circumference increase for at least 5 minutes. Throughout the study, delaquamine was administered via intravenous injection and drug plasma levels were measured (along with blood pressure and heart rate). Target plasma concentrations included a low dose (50 ng/ml) and a high dose (150 ng/ml).

The first phase of the study employed a double-blind, placebo-controlled, between-subjects design to evaluate medication effects on erection in response to series of erotic stimuli (two fantasies and two films) in men without sexual dysfunction (Munoz, Bancroft, & Turner, 1994) and in men with ED (Munoz, Bancroft, & Beard, 1994). Outcome measures included erectile circumferences, as measured by a standard RigiScan device (Dacomed, Inc., Minneapolis, Minnesota), and subjective measures of sexual arousal.

The second phase of the study consisted of a 3-way, double-blind, placebo-controlled crossover design, with intravenous infusion of placebo and the study drug at 2 doses (high, low). The study medication (or placebo) was infused over 9 hours, with rapid infusion during the first 30 minutes to attain the desired plasma concentration (50 ng/ml for low dose and 150 ng/ml for the high dose). Study outcome measures included NPT, assessed via RigiScan device. In addition, sleep polysomnography variables were assessed, such as electroencephalography (EEG), electro-oculography (EOG), and electromyography (EMG). These outcome measures were assessed continuously over three full-night sessions in a sleep laboratory (spaced about a week apart). Sleep variables of interest included total sleep time (minutes), sleep onset latency (minutes from lights out until stage 2), sleep efficacy (% of time asleep), total REM stage minutes, and latency to first REM stage. Erectile response variables that were examined included maximal circumference increase that was sustained at least 10 minutes, maximal duration of erections with > 15-mm penile circumference change, maximal duration of erections with > 30-mm penile circumference change, maximal duration of episode > 60% rigidity, percentage of sleep time above 15-mm circumference change, and sleep time above 60% penile rigidity.

For the data analyses in both study phases, men with ED ($n = 24$) were divided into an older and a younger group based on the age median split (47 years old). The mean sample ages were 32.2 and 53.8 years, for the younger and older sample respectively. The results revealed that the effect of delaquamine on stimulus-induced sexual arousal and NPT was significantly different for sexually functional men, for younger men, and for older men with ED. In sexually functional men the results indicated a significant increase in spontaneous erections and increased reports of subjective sexual arousal, both *before* the presentation of erotic stimuli. In response to the visual erotic stimuli, these men responded with significantly prolonged erections. Furthermore, patients evidenced increased systolic blood pressure and heart rate prior to and during the erotic stimulation. Men with ED showed more modest effects of the medication, as well as an interaction with age. In the older men with ED, there was no significant effect on erection or hemodynamic response. In contrast, a modest yet significant effect was noted in the younger men with ED. Additionally, in the younger sample a blunting of blood pressure and heart rate in response to the erotic stimulus was observed during placebo administration (compared to sexually functional and older men with ED), which was largely eliminated with the higher dose of the drug. Bancroft et al. (1995) speculated that there was a reduction of drug responsiveness in the older sample of men with ED, while younger men with ED evidenced a generalized increase of central alpha$_2$ tone that effected baseline erectile and hemodynamic functioning, which was then normalized by the drug.

Beyond the interesting pattern of results observed, the study represents a prime example of a "proof of concept" evaluation of a pharmacological agent. The methodological strengths of the study include (i) double-blind, placebo-controlled evaluations of the drug; (ii) careful dosing and assessment of plasma concentrations; (iii) different types of erectogenic stimuli—sexual fantasy, erotic films, and NPT; and finally, (iv) a number of secondary outcomes (e.g., blood pressure, sleep assessment, subjective sexual arousal). In addition, the authors analyzed their data in order to determine whether the pharmacological effects of the drug differed in younger and older men. This is a particularly important aspect of the study, since pharmacokinetics and pharmacodynamics of an agent may differ in older individuals. Most of these design features have not been replicated in subsequent studies, despite their potential advantages for studies of this type.

Prostaglandin E1

Injectable alpha-blockers and prostaglandin drugs were among the first efficacious pharmacologic agents used to treat male ED. Exogenous Prostaglandin E1 (PGE_1) induces trabecular helicine and cavernosal arterial smooth muscle relaxation (Hedlund & Andersson, 1986). PGE_1 receptors have been localized in the penile cavernous tissue of men. Prostaglandin E1 is rapidly metabolized in the cavernous tissue. The high correlation between receptor density (and binding affinity) and clinical response suggests that receptor binding may be an important mechanism of action for PGE_1. These erectogenic medications work in the absence of, or requiring only minimal sexual stimulation. However, PGE_1 by itself as a pharmacological agent is an unstable compound. Alprostadil alfadex achieves stability by creating a PGE_1-cyclodextrin clathrate compound.

Psychophysiological methods also have been used to determine dose response and the minimally clinical effective dose. For example, underestimating erectile ability in response in the office may result in the patient increasing the dose at home increasing the risk of unwanted side effects, (e.g., priapism), while overestimation of erectile response may result in unnecessary failures and unwanted anxiety during home use. Therefore, prior to home use of alprostadil, office-based dose titration is recommended.

Goldstein et al. (2000) examined the efficacy and minimum effective dose of alprostadil alfadex in 894 patients (92.3% of the intent to treat sample) with ED of at least 6 months due to vasculogenic, neurogenic, or mixed vasculogenic and neurogenic causes. The study was conducted as three separate open-label trials in 41 different centers. Patients with diabetes were excluded from study 1, but included in studies 2 and 3. All patients received an open-label placebo injection. Thereafter, patients received 5 g (study 1) or 10 g (studies 2 and 3) alprostadil alfadex as the first drug injection. Individual doses were titrated up- or downward over the course of two to four further office visits, with an allowed dose ranges of 1–20 g (study 1) and 1–40 g (studies 2 and 3). The primary efficacy endpoint for the clinical evaluation of erectile rigidity was a positive buckling test. The device used to apply the axial load consisted of a standard weight scale attached to a 2-inch diameter rigid plastic cap with a shallow concavity on its ventral surface (H. Eric Richards, Inc., Canton, Massachusetts). With the patient in a supine position, the plastic cap was applied to the tip of the

Figure 1. Illustration of buckling test (from Goldstein et al., 2000). (Left) Positive test. Application of axial load of 1 kg does not result in penile shaft deformation. (Right) Negative test. Application of axial load of less than 1 kg (in this example 0.5 kg) does result in penile shaft deformation.

penis in a downward direction by the investigator. A force of 1.0 kg was slowly achieved on the weight scale by steadily increasing the downward force. The shaft of the penis was observed for buckling from the resulting load (see Figure 1). If the erect penis was able to support an axial load force of 1 kg without any bending of the penile shaft, the result was considered positive (successful). Penile buckling tests were conducted within 30 minutes after injection, initially at the discretion of the investigator, or at the time of two consecutive circumference measurements that exceeded the flaccid circumference value. Thereafter, the buckling test was performed at 10-minute intervals for up to 60 minutes and at 15-minute intervals beyond that.

The results indicated that no physician reported either difficulty in using the penile buckling device, or adverse events as a result of its use. No patient responded with an erection sufficient for intercourse as a result of the initial placebo injection. Overall, 71% of patients responded with at least one positive (successful) penile buckling test within 60 minutes after alprostadil alfadex injection. At least three consecutive positive buckling tests in the course of a 20-minute period were reported in 58.28% of patients. The cumulative percentage of patients with minimum effective doses varied greatly within the dose range of 0–40 g. At 10 g, 42% of patients in study 1 and 215 and 24% of patients in studies 2 and 3 responded with a positive buckling test; at 20 g, 75% in study 1 and 40% in studies 2 and 3; 30 v and 40 g were associated with 50% and 70% of patients in studies 2 and 3. Penile pain was reported in 30% of patients, while priapism (erection > 4 hrs) occurred in less than 1% ($n = 2$) and local penile bleeding occurred in 3%.

This study raises several designs and methodological issues, especially in contrast to the methodology used by Bancroft et al. (1995). First, the study was not a randomized, double-blind, placebo-controlled trial. This has implications for its internal validity. However, the outcome measure was defined in such a way as to maximize ecological validity (vaginal intercourse for a sample of heterosexual men). In addition, it highlights some issues regarding the use of the RigiScan, which assess circumference change and radial rigidity. Real-time monitoring of radial rigidity with the RigiScan device has been found in some studies to have poor predictive validity of the ability to successfully achieve penile-vaginal intromission (Udelson et al., 1999). In addition, there are significantly greater costs associated with RigiScan assessment. However, the methods used in the Goldstein et al. (2000) study raise concerns regarding standardization. How much buckling is too much? The outcome relied on the subjective judgment of the investigators. This is especially a concern because neither the patient nor the investigators were blinded to the treatment dose. In summary, this study presents evidence that PGE₁ is efficacious in men with ED of organic origin. In addition, it raises interesting questions about the appropriate clinical end-points used to evaluate both the efficacy and effectiveness of pharmacological agents. Unlike the methods used in the earlier study by Bancroft and colleagues, this study was not well controlled; however, its choice of outcomes may have advantages in terms of ecological validity. Lastly, it demonstrates the utility and applicability of psychophysiological techniques in establishing effective treatment doses, both nomothetically as well as idiographically.

PDE5 Inhibitors

As a therapeutic class for the treatment of ED, selective inhibitors of PDE5 enzymes restore and maintain the erectile response to sexual stimulation by selectively blocking cGMP degradation in the corpus cavernosa (Rotella, 2001; Turko, Ballard, Francis, & Corbin, 1999). Unlike prostaglandin drugs, these agents do not initiate or maintain an erection in the absence of sexual stimulation and consequent NO release. Currently, three selective, orally active PDE5 inhibitors comprise the class. Sildenafil (Viagra, Pfizer Inc.) is the prototype PDE5 inhibitor, approved for treatment of male ED in March 1998. Two additional PDE5 inhibitors—tadalafil (IC351, Cialis, Lilly ICOS LLC) and vardenafil (BAY 38-9456, Bayer AG) were approved in 2003.

Sildenafil

To date, sildenafil has been the most extensively studied PDE5 inhibitor. Since its introduction, it has been widely adopted as an effective and well-tolerated treatment for men with ED of various etiologies and degrees of severity. One of the early studies of sildenafil (Boolell et al., 1996) sought to determine the efficacy and safety of the then novel orally active inhibitor of type 5 cGMP on penile erectile activity in men with ED of no established organic cause (Boolell et al., 1996). The study included an objective assessment of efficacy using penile plethysmography, specifically the Rigi-Scan system; and an at-home evaluation of sildenafil where patients self-administered sildenafil once a day for 7 days and recorded their erectile activity and graded their erections. In addition, a subjective global efficacy in response to the question, "Do you feel that the treatment over the past 7 days has improved your erections?"

The first phase of the study was a double-blind, placebo-controlled, 4-

way crossover trial, with a 3-day "washout" period between consecutive study periods. Patients were randomized to receive at each study visit placebo, 10 mg, 25 mg, or 50 mg of sildenafil. Each medication administration was followed by visual sexual stimulation (VSS) begun 30 minutes after dosing. The VSS period lasted 2 hours. Treatment efficacy was examined by means of RigiScan, with the usual measures of tumescence and rigidity (NPTR). The second phase consisted of a placebo-controlled, 2-way crossover study, in which patients received single daily doses of sildenafil (25 mg) of placebo for 7 days. There was a 7-day washout period between each arm of the study.

Results showed a significantly increased duration of rigidity of > 80% at base and tip of the penis during VSS in each treatment group compared to placebo. Of note, onset of penile tumescence was between 10 and 40 minutes post-VSS initiation. This is significantly shorter than the official "labeling" of 60 minutes. Results from the at home phase of the study revealed an average increase in erections in the active drug group (6.1) compared to placebo (1.3, $p < 01$). However, "sequence effects" for total number of erections were higher in patients who received placebo first (10.1), versus those who received sildenafil first (3.6), indicating that order of dosing was a significant factor in the study.

Recent studies have used VSS and RigiScan designs in combination with sildenafil administration to evaluate time to onset, as well as duration of effect (Eardley et al., 2002). A study design similar to the one used by Boolell et al. (1996) was employed and included two phases, both double-blind, 2-way crossover designs. In both phases, the total duration of rigidity during the RigiScan monitoring during the 60 minutes of VSS and patient self-assessment were used as outcome variables.

In phase 1, fasted patients received either a single oral dose of sildenafil (50 mg) or placebo at each treatment visit. VSS began 10 minutes after dosing and continued for 60 consecutive minutes. Patients were given a free choice from a selection of sexually explicit magazines and videos and were instructed to view similar materials on each occasion. Penile rigidity at the base was assessed using continuous RigiScan recording 15 minutes predose to 70 minutes postdose.

In phase 2, patients were administered 100-mg sildenafil or placebo at each treatment period. VSS was administered as above, except that onset of stimulation was delayed until 2 hours postdose in part A and both 2 and 4 hours postdose in the second part of the study. Only patient-rated measures of erectile response were collected in the second phase. Patients rated erectile responses to VSS stimulation on a scale of 1 to 4, where 4 represented a completely firm or hard erection.

A total of 17 and 16 patients were entered into studies 1 and 2, respectively. Mean age for study 1 was 52, while in study 2 the mean age was 57. In study 1, both objective (RigiScan) and subjective (patient reported) measures demonstrated treatment efficacy compared to placebo at the $p = 006$ and $p < 001$ significance levels, respectively. All erections were present within 37 minutes while duration above 60% rigidity was increased roughly 3- to 4-fold compared to placebo. In study 2, significant erectile responses were shown up to 4 hours postmedication administration.

Tadalafil

Tadalafil is a potent, highly selective inhibitor of PDE5 with a longer duration of action, albeit similar mechanism of action to sildenafil. Like sildenafil, the drug was developed initially for use in cardiovascular disease and subsequently adapted for treatment of ED. In an early crossover, "proof of concept" study (Porst, 2002), the efficacy of 100 mg of tadalafil was investigated using a RigiScan-VSS protocol in 44 patients. Randomized patients successfully completed a single-blind, placebo run phase, in which a RigiScan VSS challenge test was used to rule out extreme responders (greater than 80% rigidity for more than 10 minutes) and nonresponders (failure to attain some degree of erection greater than 20% rigidity for at least 2 minutes). This baseline assessment procedure has become commonplace in subsequent trials of this sort.

The major endpoints of the trial were change in duration of penile rigidity of more than 55%, change in area under the curve (AUC) of rigidity over time as measured by rigidity activity units (RAUs), and change in maximum rigidity. Patients were also asked to subjectively rate, on a scale of 1 to 5, the degree of their erections using a Likert-type scale where 1 indicated no erection and 5 indicated a full and rigid erection.

Results indicated significant changes from baseline in 100 mg of tadalafil, compared to placebo across all primary study measures. These differences were highly significant ($p < 001$) for duration of erection > 55% of maximum rigidity, mean change from baseline in AUC rigidity, and change in subjective assessment of rigidity. Mean increase in maximum rigidity was significant at the $p < .01$ level. Headache and back pain were reported as the most common drug-related adverse events (Porst, 2002).

This study provides a well controlled, psychophysiological study with a very novel and interesting new drug (tadalafil). The psychophysiological protocol was valuable in showing both relatively immediate and sustained effects of tadalafil on all of the study dependent variables, both subjective and physiological. The use of a baseline assessment procedure in this study was novel, and the high levels of response achieved were evidence of a robust study design. Overall, this study can be regarded as a prototype for this type of early "proof of concept" study in the future.

Vardenafil

A similar "proof of concept" study has been performed with vardenafil, another PDE5 with potentially increased potency of action (Klotz et al., 2001). The drug has an excellent safety profile and a greater degree of po-

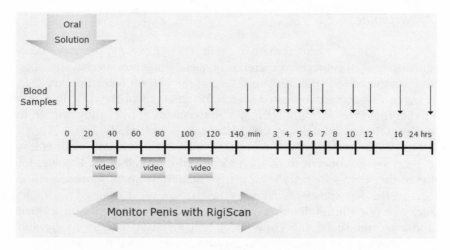

Figure 2. Schematic of experimental design (from Klotz et al., 2001). Twenty minutes after dosing, patients watched an erotic video for three 20-minute periods at the times shown. At time zero, patients took orally placebo, 10-mg, or 20-mg vardenafil. Blood samples were taken to determine the plasma levels of vardenafil (times at which these were taken are indicated by *arrows*).

tency for inhibition of the PDE5 molecule than sildenafil (Rosen & McKenna, 2002). This study employed a 2-center, randomized, double-blind placebo crossover design, which included 42 patients with mild ED. On three separate visits patients received placebo, 10 mg, or 20 mg of vardenafil (study 1) and placebo, 20 mg, or 40 mg of vardenafil (study 2) in a 3-way crossover study design. Subjects were selected as responsive in the baseline assessment condition as well as a past history of sildenafil responsiveness. Blood samples were obtained for pharmacokinetic analysis prior to and following each stimulation period. The primary endpoint of duration of rigidity at the tip and base of the penis of more than 60% and secondary endpoints of rigidity and tumescence at the base and tip were as calculated by conventional RigiScan methodology (see Figure 2).

Results indicated significant, dose-dependent effect of vardenafil on measures of penile tumescence and rigidity. Across both studies, active drug at all dosages (10 mg, 20 mg, 40 mg) demonstrated significantly increased erectile responses compared to placebo on duration of rigidity above 60% and rRAUs, a measurement of rigidity expressed as area under the curve. Increases in penile tumescence corresponded closely with plasma concentrations of the drug at each specific dose. Of note, significant evidence of erectile activity was apparent as early as 20 minutes postdosing in some subjects. The drug was also well tolerated with mild headaches, nasal stuffiness and flushing in about one-third of patients in the study. None of the side effects led to discontinuation.

Apomorphine

This drug has a central mechanism of action, involving primarily dopamine D_1 and D_2 subreceptors, and a completely different mechanism of action compared to PDE5 inhibitors. One of the earliest contemporary studies with this drug investigated several formulations of the drug in 4 pilot studies that used single-blinded, placebo-controlled, increasing dose study designs (Heaton, Morales, Adams, Johnston, & El-Rashidy, 1995). A small group of ED patients (N = 34) were tested on 3 separate days with at least a 3-day washout between doses. VSS procedures used in all 4 studies followed the same scheme: 15 minutes postadministration of apomorphine, barring the occurrence of adverse events, patients were exposed to 10 minutes of erotic stimuli, followed by a 5- to 10-minute neutral film segment and a second 10-minute erotic video. All RigiScan measures were analyzed; however an "Aggregate RigiScan Number" score was derived from these measures of tumescence and rigidity in an attempt to quantify erections. In addition, visual analog scales (VAS) were used to collect information on subjective responses and mood.

Results varied by study. Study 1 assessed the effect of 10-mg and 20-mg liquid apomorphine on erectile response and tolerability in 12 patients (ages from 38 to 60 years). Results indicated that 70% of the patients were considered complete responders, which was operationalized as an "Aggregate RigiScan Number" of at least 16 on a 36-point scale. Significant side effects were reported, including sudden nausea/vomiting, diaphoresis, dizziness, double or blurred vision, decrease in heart rate, and pallor. Side effects lasted up to 40 minutes. Study 2, which evaluated 5-mg sublingual tablets of apomorphine, included 8 patients. Twenty-nine percent of the patients received an "Aggregate RigiScan Number" of at least 16 on a 36 point scale and were considered responders, while the remaining 71% were considered nonresponders. Sublingual administration resulted in a similar side effect profile as in study 1. An intranasal aqueous spray (1.25 mg) per puff (study 3) was tested in only 2 patients because significant bradycardia in addition to the adverse events seen in the previous 2 studies was observed. The study was stopped immediately. Twelve patients participated in a trial of a differently formulated sublingual tablet containing 3, 4, and 5 mg of apomorphine. The study results showed that 67% of patients achieved or exceeded the Aggregate RigiScan Number threshold. Both 3-mg and 4-mg doses produced excellent erections. Erectogenic properties were considered when erectile response was clearly present during the neutral stimuli periods. VAS scores indicated the patients were relaxed during the sessions. With the new formulation of the sublingual tablet, no adverse events were reported.

The results from these 4 studies appear problematic at best. The single-blind design is a major flaw and fails to control for potential expectancy or experimenter bias effects. These might be quite substantial in a study such as this. The scoring technique of converting RigiScan measurements into an aggregate or overall score may have resulted in further problems. Small samples sizes would call into question whether or not there is sufficient statistical power to detect a difference; however, no formal hypothesis testing was done, and only frequencies and response means were generated.

Melanocortin

Wessells, Levine, Hadley, Dorr, and Hruby (2000) investigated the effect of melanocortins on erectile response, as measured by RigiScan. The overall study utilized a double-blind, placebo-controlled crossover design and included patients with ED between the ages of 18 and 75 years of age. Patients were classified as either having no organic etiology or organic etiology and were then enrolled into one of two substudies (psychogenic and organic ED). Melanotan II (0.025–0.157 mg/kg) or a placebo was randomly administered twice by subcutaneous injection for a total of four injections. Each study dose administration was separated by at least 48 hours. Real-time RigiScan monitoring was performed in the home situation. VSS protocols were not utilized. In fact, patients were instructed to avoid erotic stimuli as well as remain awake for the 6-hour session. Patients also were instructed to record erectile events in terms of quantity and duration. The organic subgroup was additionally instructed to record measurements of sexual desire (4-point Likert-type scale using a modification of the IIEF question 12).

A total of 20 patients (10 patients within each subgroup), mean age 51.6 (range: 22–67), were randomized and completed the study. Erectile activity measured by the RigiScan was significantly higher on active drug compared to placebo on all RigiScan measures at the tip of the penis, including duration of rigidity > 80% and tip tumescence activity units TAU. The pattern was echoed when the patients were stratified by ED etiology. Sexual desire, assessed in the organic subgroup only, was significantly higher in the active drug group as compared to placebo at the $p < 001$ level. Nausea and stretching/yawning were significantly more frequent in the active drug group versus placebo. It appears that no primary endpoints were identified a priori. Without defined endpoints, it is difficult to gauge adequate statistical power. In addition, with the design of the trial and the use of subgroups, an ANOVA model may be a more appropriate analysis than the student's t-test that was utilized. A more recent psychophysiological laboratory study with an intranasal formulation of the drug showed a high response rate and mild side effects of treatment (Diamond, Earle, Rosen, Willett, & Molinoff, 2004).

Overall Assessment: RigiScan/VSS Designs

The RigiScan data collection system is a widely utilized tool in the evaluation of ED that has become the gold standard in determining efficacy in pharmacological "proof of concept" clinical trials. The RigiScan system's unique ability to capture measurements of radial rigidity as well as a host of physiologic endpoints at both the base and tip of the penis have set it apart from its predecessors such as the mercury strain gauge and Barlow gauge. Several concerns regarding the RigiScan methodology have been mentioned in the literature (e.g., Goldstein et al., 2000). One common concern is that the tightening of rings in order to assess radial rigidity may be experienced as sexually stimulating and thus influence erectile response. This is more of a concern when assessing NPT, rather than the effects of medication. The second concern is with the measurement of radial rigidity in itself. When the ability to engage in penile-vaginal intercourse is used as an evaluation end-point, axial rigidity rather than radial rigidity may be a more accurate proxy variable. Unfortunately, the studies that have utilized axial rigidity measures to evaluate medication efficacy have not been double-blind, placebo-controlled or used rigorously standardized criteria for evaluating penile buckling (e.g., Goldstein et al., 2000).

RigiScan/VSS design has been used in approximately 10 published studies overall to date. The above studies are cited as recent examples of this. These studies indicate that this design is suitable for use overall in early phase 2, "proof-of-concept" designs. There is generally a high degree of association between the physiological and subjective indices used (e.g., time above 60%; subjective arousal). Dose effects have been established in most studies, and 1 or 2 studies have included a comparison between RigiScan measures and pharmacokinetic testing (Porst, 2002). None of the studies to date have included head-to-head testing of one ED drug against another, although we anticipate these studies will shortly be done. Obviously, the need for careful control and experimental design (e.g., placebo blinding, counterbalanced order) is essential in each of these studies. Fortunately, most studies to date have been moderately or highly attentive to these needs.

Psychophysiological Laboratory Studies in Women

In addition to the above studies in men, approximately 6 studies of this type have been performed in women to date. The studies in women have varied greatly in the type of drug being evaluated (e.g., PDE5, alpha-blocker), study design being used (single-blind, parallel/crossover), and patients or normal controls selected for study. Efficacy results have been much less clear cut than those observed in the male studies above, with much greater discrepancies between subjective and physiological measures of genital response. The topic appears to be growing in importance, however, due in part to the high prevalence of sexual dysfunction problems in women, along with the evident success of pharmacologic interventions in treating male sexual problems. This has led to increased interest in developing effective medications for women. A number of potential pharmacological agents have been identified and are currently being evaluated for this purpose. Studies that include double-blind, laboratory-based assessment of the effects of pharmacological agents on female sexual response in sexually functional and dysfunctional women are reviewed, following a brief discussion of the role of neuromodulators involved in female sexual response.

Neuromodulators of Sexual Response in Women

The presence of a variety of neuromodulators and chemical factors have been demonstrated in vaginal and clitoral tissues; however, the accompanying research into the pharmacological and physiological function of these neurochemical factors in female genital response is, in most cases, still lacking. Giuliano, Rampin, and Allard (2002) note that vaginal sexual arousal is a vasocongestive and neuromuscular event, controlled by facilitatory parasympathetic and inhibitory sympathetic inputs. However, contradictory data have been reported in the literature regarding the role of the sympathetic (SNS) and parasympathetic (PNS) components of female sexual response. Based largely on studies in the rabbit and rat, evidence seems to support the theory that female genital sexual response occurs as a result of a shift in the balance of facilitator parasympathetic and inhibitory sympathetic inputs, as is theorized in men (Giuliano et al., 2002). In contrast, studies in adult women with and without sexual dysfunction have demonstrated facilitatory effects of SNS activation induced by a period of exercise (Meston & Gorzalka, 1995, 1996a, 1996b). Preliminary evidence for the role of adrenergic (sympathetic) and cholinergic (parasympathetic) pathways has been found in animal models and human studies.

Acetylcholine plays a minor role in the regulation of vaginal blood flow, as demonstrated by the inability of intravenous injections of atropine to reduce masturbation induced increases in blood flow (Wagner & Levin, 1980). However, studies of intravenous injections of atropine in rats have demonstrated reductions in vaginal smooth muscle contractions (Giuliano et al., 2001), indicating that acetylcholine may play a role in vaginal contractions. Adrenergic mechanisms have similarly been shown to be important in mediating vaginal smooth muscle tone (Munarriz, Kim, Goldstein, & Traish, 2002).

Various nonadrenergic-noncholinergic (NANC) neurotransmitters have been identified in the female sexual organs, including vasoactive intestinal peptide (VIP). Early findings by Ottesen and colleagues (Ottesen et al., 1983; Ottesen et al., 1987) showed that intravenous injections of VIP resulted in increased vaginal blood flow and increased lubrication in women. Peptide histidine methionine (PHM) has been found in both human vaginal tissue as well as clitoral tissue. Palle, Bredkjaer, Ottesen, and Fahrenkrug (1990) demonstrated increased vaginal blood flow from intravenous or intravaginal injections of PHM. In addition, neuropeptide Y (NPY; Blank et al., 1986; Jorgensen et al., 1989), calcitonin gene related peptide (CGRP;

Hoyle, Stones, Robson, Whitley & Burnstock, 1996), substance P (Hoyle et al.), pituitary adenylate cyclase-activating polypeptides (PACAP; Graf et al., 1995; Steenstrup et al., 1995) have also been identified in human vaginal tissue, but their specific effects have not been studied in vitro or in vivo (Giuliano et al., 2002).

Recent studies have begun to investigate the role of nitric oxide mechanisms in vaginal smooth muscle (Munarriz et al., 2002; Ziessen, Moncada, & Cellek, 2002) and clitoral physiology (Burnett, Calvin, Silver, Peppas, & Docimo, 1997). In vitro studies in several species have shown that nitric oxide synthase (NOS) occurs in vaginal smooth muscle cells, particularly in the proximal area of the vagina (Traish, Kim, Min, Munarriz, & Goldstein, 2002). The PDE5 enzyme has also recently been isolated in tissue samples in the vagina (D'Amati et al., 2002). The specific effects of NO/cGMP in mediating vasodilation or smooth muscle relaxation are unclear. Furthermore, it has been shown that NOS expression is altered significantly by the presence or absence of estrogen or progesterone in the vaginal tissue (Traish et al., 2002). Other investigators have noted that NOS levels are generally low in vaginal tissue in premenopausal women and relatively absent in the postmenopausal vagina (Hoyle et al., 1996). More direct evidence exists for the role of NO/cGMP mechanisms in the clitoris (Burnett et al., 1997; Cellek & Moncada, 1998; Vemulapalli & Kurowski, 2000). In contrast to the vagina, NOS expression in the clitoris is strongly influenced by the presence of androgen (Munarriz et al., 2002).

A number of pharmacologic classes have been studied for their potential role in increasing sexual response in women and/or in the treatment of female sexual dysfunctions. Specific agents include ephedrine, an adrenergic agonist (Meston & Heiman, 1998), combined yohimbine and L-arginine glutamate, an NO precursor (Meston & Worcel, 2002), sildenafil citrate (Basson, McInnes, Smith, Hodgson, & Koppiker, 2002; Laan et al., 2002; Sipski, Rosen, Alexander, & Hamer, 2000), and hormones/hormone precursors, such as tibolone (Laan et al., 2001; Modelska & Cummings, 2003).

Adrenergic Agents

Meston and Heiman (1998) examined the effects of ephedrine sulfate (50 mg), an alpha- and beta-adrenergic agonist, on subjective sexual arousal and vaginal vasocongestion in 20 healthy nonsexually dysfunctional women. Participants (mean age 25.8 years) were screened for the absence of sexual dysfunction with the Derogatis Sexual Function Inventory (DSFI). Individuals with a history of depression or who were taking any medications (except oral contraceptives) were excluded from the study.

This randomized, double-blind crossover design study included 2 sessions scheduled about 1 week apart. In each session participants were administered either ephedrine sulfate (50 mg) or placebo. After a 30-minute absorption period, participants watched a 3-minute neutral film (baseline) followed immediately by a 5-minute erotic film. Vaginal vasocongestion was measured via photoplethysmography (VPA) and subjective sexual arousal was assessed by a series of 7-point Likert rating scales that included physical sexual arousal (6 items), mental sexual arousal (3 items), heart rate (1 item), anxiety (1 item), and positive and negative affect (each 11 items). The 6 items assessing subjective physical sexual arousal included warmth and the genitals, genital wetness or lubrication, genital pulsing or throbbing, any genital feelings, genital tenseness for tightness, and physical sexual arousal.

The study results indicated a significant increase in VPA difference scores with ephedrine administration, as compared to placebo, during erotic film ($p < .01$), but not during the neutral film. In contrast, with the exception of subjective ratings of HR, there were no significant differences on subjective ratings of physical sexual arousal, mental sexual arousal, positive affect, negative affect, or anxiety. Heart rate, but not blood pressure, was significantly increased during the neutral and erotic films for the ephedrine condition. The authors note that interestingly, ephedrine increased vaginal vasocongestion only during erotic film and not during the neutral film. This suggests that ephedrine did not simply facilitate vaginal vasocongestion through an overall increase in peripheral resistance but, rather, acted in some way that selectively "prepared" the body for genital response.

In summary, this study found that administration of 50-mg ephedrine significantly increased vaginal vasocongestion (VPA), as compared to placebo, during the erotic film only. However, the results failed to show significant differences on subjective measures of physiologic or mental sexual arousal. This study stands as an example of good methodological design; for example, participants were scheduled at approximately the same time of the day during both sessions and were asked to abstain from caffeine, alcohol and food prior to the experimental sessions. It presents further evidence of the importance of SNS activation in physiologic female sexual arousal and more specifically for the role of adrenergic-mediated pathways. Other studies by these authors have supported this general conclusion (Meston & Gorzalka, 1995, 1996a, 1996b).

The lack of significant differences in subjective ratings in this study is particularly noteworthy. This finding might support the concept that sexually functional women do not attend to their genital sensations in appraising their level of sexual arousal. A follow-up study that demonstrated the inhibitory effects of clonidine, a selective alpha$_2$-adrenergic agonist, on sexual arousal in women who were in a heightened state of SNS arousal further strongly supports the findings of the present study (Meston, Gorzalka, & Wright, 1997).

In the first study of alpha-adrenergic drugs in sexually dysfunctional women, Rosen et al. (1999) evaluated oral phentolamine (40 mg) on physiological and subjective aspects of sexual arousal in a small sample of postmenopausal women. The purpose of the study was to provide initial data on the safety and tolerability of the drug in women and to evaluate the effects of oral phentolamine on physiological and subjective measures of arousal in response to VSS. Six postmenopausal women with a history of lack of lubrication or subjective arousal during sexual stimulation for at least 6 months were recruited for participation in the study. Subjects ranged in age from 48 to 62 years (mean = 54.5) and were an average of 4.8 years postmenopausal.

Vaginal photoplethysmography recording was used to assess changes in vaginal blood flow following drug administration. Visual sexual stimulation was provided by means of two 20-minute erotic videotapes, showing conventional heterosexual activities. A 10-minute neutral videotape was shown prior to the erotic videotape to facilitate adaptation to the laboratory situation. VPA tracings from several patients in the active drug condition showed marked increases in responding with the erotic stimulation. On the self-report measures of sexual arousal, two of the scales (self-reported lubrication, tingling sensations) showed a significant difference between drug and placebo conditions ($p < .05$), and a third scale (subjective pleasure) approached statistical significance ($p < .10$; see Table 1). Additionally, few adverse drug reactions were noted during the course of the study and the drug was well tolerated overall. These results await replication in a large-scale, controlled clinical trial.

Additional studies have investigated effects of other adrenergic agents, such as yohimbine, as well as precursors to NO. Yohimbine may enhance sexual response by two mechanisms; first, it selectively blocks alpha$_2$-adrenergic receptors pre- and postsynoptically and secondly, blockade of presynaptic alpha$_2$-adrenergic receptors increases NO release from NANC nerves (at least in men; Simonsen, Prieto, Hernandez, de Tejada, & Garcia-Sacristan, 1997). In addition, in men NO donors (such as L-arginine glutamate) have been shown to enhance the effect of yohimbine. Meston and Worcel (2002) evaluated the effect of combined yohimbine (6 mg) and L-arginine glutamate (6 mg), an NO precursor, on subjective sexual arousal and vaginal vasocongestion in 24 postmenopausal women with female sexual arousal disorder (FSAD). The researchers utilized a randomized, double-blind, placebo-controlled, 3-way crossover design to test the effects of placebo, yohimbine alone, and L-arginine plus yohimbine on sexual arousal at 30 minutes, 60 minutes, and 90 minutes postdosing. The procedures included vigorous medical screening and a clinical interview to diagnose FSAD according to strict DSM-IV criteria. Of the 25 women invited into the study, 19 were naturally menopausal and 6 were surgically menopausal, and about 50% ($n = 12$) of the participants were on hormone replacement therapy (HRT). One participant dropped out after visit 2, and the mean age of the 24 participants who completed the study was 53.7 years.

Table 1. *Drug Effects on Self-Report Measures of Arousal Following VSS*[a] *Stimulation*

	Phentolamine (40 mg)	Placebo	t	p
Lubrication ("wetness")	4.2 ± 1.5	3.0 ± 1.4	−2.91	.03*
Stimulation ("tingling")	4.5 ± 1.3	3.1 ± 1.3	−2.70	.04*
Engorgement ("fullness")	4.0 ± 1.6	3.5 ± 1.5	− .59	.58
Subjective pleasure	5.4 ± 1.5	3.4 ± 1.3	−2.11	.10
Subjective arousal	4.2 ± 1.6	3.3 ± 1.2	−1.11	.32

Each item was noted on a scale of 0–10 indicating the degree of subjective arousal.
[a]Visual sexual stimulation *$p < .05$.

Three experimental sessions included assessments of sexual arousal at four time points: once prior to dosing and 30 minutes, 60 minutes, and 90 minutes postdosing. At each time point, participants watched a 3-minute neutral film and 5-minute erotic film, at the end of which they completed subjective ratings of physical and mental sexual arousal, as well as of autonomic arousal, anxiety, positive affect, and negative affect. Experimental sessions were scheduled 5 to 14 days apart. Vaginal pulse amplitude averages for the 3-minute neutral and 5-minute erotic film were calculated for each of the 12 films (4 films per session × 3 sessions).

Results indicated overall significant difference in VPA scores between treatment conditions. Specifically, at 60 minutes postdosing, the VPA difference scores in the L-arginine plus yohimbine condition were significantly higher than those in the placebo condition ($p < .05$). This difference remained significant when conditions were collapsed across the 3 time points (effect size = 0.44). On the other hand, there was no significant difference in VPA change scores (collapsed across assessment time points) between the yohimbine alone and L-arginine plus yohimbine condition, nor was a significant difference between the yohimbine alone and placebo conditions observed. Once again, no differences in the subjective ratings were observed.

In summary, this study showed that L-arginine plus yohimbine significantly increased vaginal vasocongestion, as assessed by VPA, over placebo at 60 minutes after drug administration. However, no effect of treatment was evidenced in the women's subjective ratings of physiologic arousal (e.g., ratings of lubrication), mental sexual arousal, autonomic arousal (e.g., heart rate), nor affective states. Overall this study was well designed and controlled.

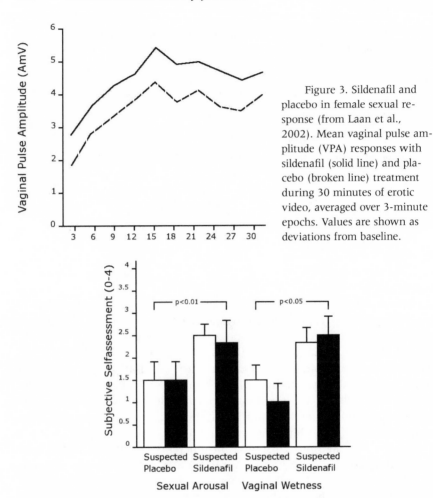

Figure 3. Sildenafil and placebo in female sexual response (from Laan et al., 2002). Mean vaginal pulse amplitude (VPA) responses with sildenafil (solid line) and placebo (broken line) treatment during 30 minutes of erotic video, averaged over 3-minute epochs. Values are shown as deviations from baseline.

Figure 4. Sildenafil placebo response in women (from Laan et al., 2002). Mean (±SEM) sexual arousal and vaginal wetness scores obtained after 30 minutes of erotic video for women who suspected they had received placebo and for women who suspected they had received sildenafil. The open bars represent the women's mean scores when they were actually on sildenafil treatment. $P = 0.01$ for sexual arousal and $p = 0.05$ for vaginal wetness for the treatment suspected to be sildenafil vs. the treatment suspected to be placebo.

PDE5 Inhibitors

PDE5s (sildenafil, vardenafil, tadalafil) have been extensively studied in the context of male ED, but have only recently come to attention in the context of sexual arousal disorders in women. Only two relatively well-controlled, psychophysiological studies of sildenafil's effects in women were available at the time of writing. The design and major findings of these studies is briefly as follows.

In the first study of sildenafil's effects on sexual arousal disorders and anorgasmia in women with spinal cord injury (SCI), Sipski et al. (2000) examined the effects of sildenafil on subjective and physiological measures of sexual arousal, including orgasmic responses, in 19 women with SCI-related sexual dysfunctions. Women received either 50-mg sildenafil or a double-blind placebo in a randomized, placebo-controlled crossover design. Each experimental session entailed two 12-minute periods of VSS and two 12-minute periods of VSS plus manual clitoral stimulation, each separated by a 6-minute baseline period. Vaginal vasocongestion was measured via photoplethysmography (VPA), and the data was averaged over 3-minute epochs. Verbal ratings of subjective sexual arousal (0–10) were also obtained every 3 minutes.

Results showed a borderline significant effect of sildenafil ($p = .07$), with the difference being most pronounced in VSS plus manual stimulation condition. A significant effect for intensity of stimulation was observed, specifically in the VSS plus manual clitoral stimulation condition ($p < .05$). Due to moderate carryover effects and the small sample size, specific mean comparison tests were not performed. The analyses of reports of subjective sexual arousal revealed significant main effects for the drug (sildenafil vs. placebo) and mode of sexual stimulation (VSS vs. VSS + manual stimulation), both $p < .001$, as well as a significant interaction effect ($p < .01$) indicating that like the VPA results, the difference between sildenafil and placebo was significantly increased during the VSS plus manual stimulation.

In summary, this study showed that in women with SCI-related sexual dysfunction, sildenafil significantly increased vaginal vasocongestion and subjective reports of sexual arousal under optimal stimulation conditions (audiovisual plus manual stimulation). The study controlled for menstrual cycle phase, since the effects of NO are effected by estrogen levels. In addition, multiple measures of subjective arousal were taken concurrent with measures of VPA. Due to the small sample size and equivocal drug effect, the findings should be considered preliminary. It is unclear to what degree the carryover effects may have affected the pattern of results. In research using VPA, frequently participants do not return completely to baseline levels between conditions, necessitating other controls. In the present study, the VSS plus manual condition was always performed following the VSS condition.

More recently, Laan et al. (2002) reported results of a double-blind, placebo-controlled crossover design to evaluate the effect of a single does of 50-mg sildenafil in 12 healthy women without sexual dysfunction. Despite the small sample size, the study was well designed and controlled for most potential sources of bias. The 12 study participants (mean age = 23.5) were all menstruating or taking oral contraceptives and nulliparous, except one. After the initial assessment visit, participants attended two experimental sessions that each included 15 minutes of baseline, 50-mg sildenafil or placebo administration, 60 minutes of neutral video (to allow for absorption), 30 minutes of VSS, and 15 minutes of neutral video.

Vaginal vasocongestion was measured via photoplethysmography (VPA), which was recorded during 120 minutes of each recording session. After the last erotic video, participants rated the intensity of their sexual arousal and the amount of vaginal lubrication on 5-point Likert scales. In addition, blood samples used to assess plasma drug concentrations were obtained. Vaginal pulse amplitude (VPA) data was examined in several different manners. The researchers obtained a mean and maximum peak-to-trough difference for the 30-minute VVS period, as well as calculating 3-minute epoch averages for the entire postdosing period. The last 2 minutes before drug administration served as a baseline.

Results showed that sildenafil influenced vaginal blood flow, as physiologic data showed a significant difference in the maximum VPA response during sildenafil administration and placebo conditions. This effect was most pronounced during the first experimental session. There was also a trend toward significance for mean VPA scores. The epoch data also showed that sildenafil's effects were apparent during the first 3-minute epoch of the film presentation, after which the responses for sildenafil and placebo increased at approximately equivalent rates (see Figure 3). While significant differences were observed in vaginal vasocongestion (VPA), there were no treatment-related differences in women's subjective ratings of the intensity of their sexual arousal or the amount of lubrication. Correlations between sildenafil plasma concentrations and VPA were satisfactory (approx. $r = .40$), while low correlations were observed for subjective ratings of sexual arousal ($r = -.11$) and subjective ratings of vaginal lubrication ($r = .09$).

The most interesting findings in this study, perhaps, concern the relationship between the women's ratings of sexual arousal and their subjective estimate of which drug (sildenafil or placebo) they had received. In both sessions, participants rated their sexual arousal and vaginal lubrication significantly higher when they thought they had received sildenafil (attributed drug), regardless of whether or not they had actually received placebo or sildenafil (see Figure 4). Participants were not able to guess beyond chance which treatment they had received.

In summary, this study showed that 50 mg of sildenafil in healthy nonsexually dysfunctional women was well tolerated and significantly increased measures of vaginal vasocongestion (VPA) compared to placebo, but had no effect on subjective ratings of sexual arousal or ratings of lubrication. This, then, is a fairly consistent finding in all of the studies in women reviewed to date.

In addition, a significant placebo effect was noted for the subjective ratings. Subjects were also unable to discern whether they had received an active drug or placebo, although their attribution of this effect was highly significant. The dramatic placebo response and importance of attribution factors in the subjective appraisal of sexual arousal in this study demonstrates that double-blind, placebo-controlled randomized trials are *absolutely essential* for evaluating the effect of sildenafil, and more generally in any laboratory-based, pharmacologic assessment study in female sexual dysfunction.

Although the Laan et al. (2002) study only included 12 women, the finding that sildenafil failed to improve subjective ratings of sexual arousal was replicated in a large clinical trial. Basson et al. (2002) evaluated the efficacy of 12-week sildenafil treatment (10 mg, 50 mg, or 100 mg) in 781 estrogenized and estrogen deficient women, all of whom experienced sexual arousal problems. The study employed a double-blind, placebo-controlled design and included the Sexual Function Questionnaire (SFQ; Quirk et al., 2002), sexual activity logs, Life Satisfaction Checklist (LSC), and two global efficacy questions as outcome measures (no physiological measures of sexual arousal were obtained). Despite the large sample size, the study failed to find significant differences between sildenafil and placebo on any of the outcome measures. The lack of improvement is exemplified by the finding that despite being randomized to 100 mg, about 60% of women stated that lubrication was a problem (about the same number of patients rated lubrication as a problem in the other conditions).

Hormones/Hormone Precursors

Reductions in systemic estrogen and androgens, as occurs after menopause, are frequently implicated in the decline in female sexual functioning. Insufficient androgens have been associated with declines in desire. The effects of HRT have been primarily studied in postmenopausal women. Modelska and Cummings (2003) reviewed the randomized clinical trial (RCT) literature on sexual dysfunction in postmenopausal women. The authors noted only one study on estrogen-progesterone therapy (Sherwin, 1991) and 2 studies that included estrogen-androgen therapy (Sarrel, Dobay, & Wiita, 1998; Shifren et al., 2000) that met criteria to be included in the review (double-blind, placebo-controlled, randomized trial). Sherwin (1991) demonstrated significant increases in sexual desire and arousal as a result of estrogen/progesterone treatment compared to estrogen alone and placebo in health postmenopausal women.

Sarrel et al. (1998) similarly reported significant improvement in sexual desire and intercourse frequency for estrogen plus methyltestosterone, as compared to estrogen alone, or placebo baseline. Orgasm, lubrication, and pain did not significantly differ from baseline with either treatment in this study; however the study was conducted in a very small sample size ($n = 20$). Shifren et al. (2000) found that 300 mg/day of transdermal testosterone resulted in significant improvement in frequency of sexual activity and pleasure orgasm over placebo in oopherectomiezed and hysterectomized women. The study also observed a strong placebo effect on subjective measures of sexual response (Shifren et al.).

In addition to conventional HRT, tibolone, a synthetic steroid with specific estrogenic, progestagenic, and androgenic properties, has been evaluated. In a recent psychophysiological study, Laan et al. (2001) evaluated in a well-controlled crossover design, the effects of 3 months of tibolone treatment (2.5 mg/day) versus 3 months of placebo on measures of vaginal vasocongestion, sexual desire and sexual arousability in 38 postmenopausal women. Participants (mean age 54) had not had menses in at least 12 months (mean 3.8 years), and were physically and psychiatrically healthy, including intact uteri and ovaries. The study procedures included extensive physical and gynecological screening as well as assessment of pelvic floor status and vaginal atrophy level. Participants were assessed at the end of each treatment phase (3 and 6 months). The effects of the treatment were measured with VPA in response to erotic stimulation by fantasy and film, as well as through completion of sexual function diaries during the week prior to the assessment. The diaries included items about frequency of self and partner sexual activity, sexual arousability, frequency of sexual fantasy, desire for sex, and intensity of sexual arousal during sexual activity. In addition, participants recorded climacteric symptoms and adverse events.

Each psychophysiological assessment session included VPA measurement during a 2-minute baseline, 3-minute sexual fantasy, 5-minute erotic film and another 3-minute fantasy and 5-minute film. To facilitate vaso-decongestion, erotic stimulus periods were separated by 6 minutes of a distracter task, the last 2 minutes of which were used as a prestimulus baseline. Since tibolone has both estrogenic and androgenic effects, separate hypotheses were formed for each. The researches hypothesized that the androgenic effects would primarily be seen during the fantasy erotic stimulation, while the estrogenic effects would be manifested by increased VPA at baseline. Research in men indicates that sexual arousal to internal stimuli (such as fantasy) is more testosterone dependent than sexual arousal to external stimuli (Bancroft & Wu, 1983; Carani, Bancroft, Granata, Del Rio, & Marrama, 1992). Similar separate central nervous system pathways may also be present in women.

Results showed that 3-month treatment with 2.5 mg/day of tibolone, as compared with placebo, resulted in significantly more frequent sexual fantasies, higher sexual arousability (i.e., more frequent sexual thoughts, sensitivity to sexual stimuli, and sexual attraction), and marginally more frequent reports of sexual desire as assessed by sexual function diary during the week prior to each outcome assessment. The diary data also indicated that women on tibolone reported greater lubrication during sexual activity. There were no significant differences between the two conditions on measures of sexual initiation/receptivity or frequency of self and partnered sexual activities.

Analysis of the VPA data indicated that tibolone administration was associated with significantly higher VPA amplitudes (peak-to-trough) during the baseline prior to the first erotic stimuli, indicating that tibolone enhanced vaginal blood flow independent of sexual stimulation. Contrasting the two sexual fantasy periods following tibolone treatment with those following placebo indicated a small but significant increase in VPA with tibolone. There were no significant differences on VPA measures between tibolone and placebo during the erotic film presentations. The differences between tibolone and placebo in the fantasy condition but not in the erotic film condition could be taken as tentative evidence for androgen dependent versus less androgen-dependent central nervous system pathways mediating sexual arousal. However, as the authors pointed out, differences between tibolone and placebo could have been overpowered by the erotic stimulus, since films tend to be more powerful stimuli than fantasy. Tibolone was well tolerated and significantly reduced vasomotor climacteric symptoms and the frequency of hot flushes.

Conclusions

In this review paper, we considered the effects of drug and laboratory interaction protocols (e.g., VSS) with psychophysiological parameters (e.g., subjective arousal, physiological response) in various patient groups or controls and using different pharmacological agents or dosages. The major conclusions of this brief review are as follows:

1. A high degree of discordance was evident in most of the studies in women. This could be influenced partly by the lack of very effective pharmacologic agents in these studies, or could be viewed as confirming strongly the discordance observed in other experimental situations. Perhaps the methodology or design of some of these studies may in fact have accentuated the degree of discordance. On the other hand, the male studies reviewed above show a remarkably high degree of concordance—perhaps even more so than in nontreatment studies.
2. Psychopharmacology studies, particularly in men, provide a potentially efficient and cost-effective means of early phase 2 testing of the erectogenic properties of a drug. They can also be used to evaluate pharmacodynamic characteristics, such as the latency or duration of erection. Thus far, these studies have not been successfully performed in women.
3. Given the high degree of placebo responding observed in several recent studies, psychophysiological studies in women must include adequate double-blinding and control for order effects in the study.

Overall, studies in this area have provided useful information in guiding methodology and model development in sexual psychophysiology generally.

References

Bancroft, J. (2000). The medicalization of female sexual dysfunction: The need for caution. *Archives of Sexual Behavior, 31,* 451–455.

Bancroft, J., Munoz, M., Beard, M., & Shapiro, C. (1995). The effects of a new alpha andreocepter antagonist on sleep and nocturnal penile tumescence in normal volunteers and men with erectile dysfunction. *Psychosomatic Medicine, 57,* 345–356.

Bancroft, J., & Wu, F. C. W. (1983). Changes in erectile responsiveness during androgen replacement therapy. *Archives of Sexual Behavior, 12,* 59–66.

Bass, B. A. (2002). Behavior therapy and the medicalization of male sexuality. *Behavior Therapist, 25,* 167–168.

Basson, R., McInnes, R., Smith, M. D., Hodgson, G., & Koppiker, N. (2002). Efficacy and safety of sildenafil citrate in women with sexual dysfunction associated with female sexual arousal disorder. *Journal of Women's Health and Gender-Based Medicine, 11,* 367–377.

Blank, M. A., Gu, J., Allen, J. M., Huang, W. M., Yiangous, Y., Ch'ng, J., et al. (1986). The regional distribution of NPY-, PHM-, and VIP-containing nerves in the human female genital tract. *International Journal of Fertility, 31,* 218–222.

Boolell, M., Gepi-Attee, S., Gingell, J. C., & Allen, M. J. (1996). Sildenafil, a novel effective oral therapy for male dysfunction. *British Journal of Urology, 78,* 257–261.

Burnett, A. L., Calvin, D. C., Silver, R. I., Peppas, D. S., & Docimo, S. G. (1997). Immunohistochemical description of nitric oxide synthase isoforms in human clitoris. *Journal of Urology, 158,* 75–78.

Carani, C., Bancroft, J., Granata, A., Del Rio, G., & Marrama, P. (1992). Testosterone and erectile function, nocturnal penile tumescence and rigidity, and erectile response to visual erotic stimuli in hypogonadal and eugonadal men. *Psychoneuroendocrinology, 17*(6), 647–654.

Cellek, S., & Moncada, S. (1998). Nitrergic neurotransmission mediates the non-adrenergic non-cholinergic responses in the clitoral corpus cavernosum of the rabbit. *British Journal of Pharmacology, 125,* 1627–1629.

D'Amati, G., diGioia, C. R., Bologna, M., Giordano, D., Giorgi, M., Dolci, S., et al. (2002). Type 5 phosphodiesterase expression in the human vagina. *Urology, 60,* 191–195.

Diamond, L. E., Earle, D. C., Rosen, R. C., Willett, M. S., & Molinoff, P. B. (2004). Double-blind, placebo-controlled evaluation of the safety, pharmacokinetic properties and pharmacodynamic effects of intranasal PT-141, a melanocortin receptor agonist, in healthy males and patients with mild-to-moderate erectile dysfunction. *International Journal of Impotence Research, 16,* 51–59.

Eardley, I., Ellis, P., Boolell, M., & Wulff, M. (2002). Onset and duration of action of sildenafil citrate for the treatment of erectile dysfunction. *British Journal of Clinical Pharmacology, 53,* 61S–65S.

Giuliano, F., Allard, J., Compagnie, S., Alexandre, L., Droupy, S., & Bernabe, J. (2001). Vaginal physiological changes in a model of sexual arousal in anesthetized rats. *American Journal of Physiology—Regulatory Integrative & Comparative Physiology, 281,* R140–149.

Giuliano, F., Rampin, O., & Allard, J. (2002). Neurophysiology and pharmacology of female genital sexual response. *Journal of Sex & Marital Therapy, 28*(Supp.), 101–121.

Goldstein, I., Auerbach, S., Padma-Nathan, H., Rajfer, J., Fitch, W., & Schmitt, L. (2000). Axial penile rigidity as primary efficacy outcome during multi-institutional in-office dose titration clinical trials with alprostadil alfadex in patients with erectile dysfunction. Alprostadil Alfadex Study Group. *International Journal of Impotence Research, 12,* 205–211.

Graf, A. H., Schiechl, A., Hacker, G. W., Hauser-Kronberger, C., Steiner, H., Arimura, A., et al. (1995). Helospectin and pituitary adenylate cyclase activating polypeptide in the human vagina. *Regulatory Peptides, 55*(3), 277–286.

Heaton, J. P., Morales, A., Adams, M. A., Johnston, B., & El-Rashidy, R. (1995). Recovery of erectile function by the oral administration of apomorphine. *Urology, 45,* 200–206.

Hedlund, H., & Andersson, K. E. (1986). Comparison of the response to drugs acting on adrenoceptors and muscarinic receptors in human isolated corpus cavernosum and cavernous artery. *Journal of Autonomic Pharmacology, 5,* 81–88.

Hoyle, C. H., Stones, R. W., Robson, T., Whitley, K., & Burnstock, G. (1996). Innervation of vasculature and microvasculature of the human vagina by NOS and neuropeptide-containing nerves. *Journal of Anatomy, 188,* 633–644.

Jorgensen, J. C., Sheikh, S. P., Forman, A., Norgard, M., Schwartz, T. W., & Ottesen, B. (1989). Neuropeptide Y in the human female genital tract: Localization and biological action. *American Journal of Physiology, 257,* E220–E227.

Klotz, T., Sachse, R., Heidrich, A., Jockenhovel, F., Rohde, G., Wensing, G., et al. (2001). Vardenafil increases penile rigidity and tumescence in erectile dysfunction patients: A RigiScan and pharmacokinetic study. *World Journal of Urology, 19,* 32–39.

Laan, E., van Lunsen, R. H., & Everaerd, W. (2001). The effects of tibolone on vaginal blood flow, sexual desire and arousability in postmenopausal women. *Climacteric, 4*(1), 28–41.

Laan, E., van Lunsen, R. H., Everaerd, W., Riley, A., Scott, E., & Boolel, M. (2002). The enhancement of vaginal vasocongestion by sildenafil in healthy premenopausal women. *Journal of Women's Health and Gender-Based Medicine, 11,* 357–365.

Meston, C. M., & Gorzalka, B. B. (1995). The effects of sympathetic activation on physiological and subjective sexual arousal in women. *Behaviour Research and Therapy, 33,* 651–664.

Meston, C. M., & Gorzalka, B. B. (1996a). Differential effects of sympathetic activation on sexual arousal in sexually dysfunctional and functional women. *Journal of Abnormal Psychology, 105,* 582–591.

Meston, C. M., & Gorzalka, B. B. (1996b). The effects of immediate, delayed, and residual sympathetic activation on sexual arousal in women. *Behaviour Research and Therapy, 34,* 143–148.

Meston, C., Gorzalka, B. B., & Wright, J. M. (1997). Inhibition of subjective and physiological sexual arousal in women by clonidine. *Psychosomatic Medicine, 59,* 399–407.

Meston, C., & Heiman, J. R. (1998). Ephedrine-activated physiological sexual arousal in women. *Archives of General Psychiatry, 55,* 652–656.

Meston, C., & Worcel, M. (2002). The effects of Yohimbine plus L-arginine gluta-mate on sexual arousal in postmenopausal women with sexual arousal disor-der. *Archives of Sexual Behavior, 31,* 323–332.

Modelska, K., & Cummings, S. (2003). Female sexual dysfunction in postmeno-pausal women: Systematic review of placebo-controlled trials. *American Journal of Obstetrics and Gynecology, 188,* 286–293.

Munarriz, R., Kim, N. N., Goldstein, I., & Traish, A. M. (2002). Biology of female sexual function. *Urologic Clinics of North America, 29,* 685–693.

Munoz, M., Bancroft, J., & Beard, M. (1994). Evaluating the effects of an alpha$_2$-adrenoceptor antagonist on erectile function in the human male: II. The erec-tile response to erotic stimuli in men with erectile dysfunction, in relation to age and in comparison with normal volunteers. *Psychopharmacology, 115,* 471–477.

Munoz, M., Bancroft, J., & Turner, M. (1994). Evaluating the effects of an alpha$_2$-adrenoceptor antagonist on erectile function in the human male: I. The erec-tile response to erotic stimuli in volunteers. *Psychopharmacology, 115,* 463–470.

Ottesen, B., Gerstenberg, T., Ulrichsen, H., Manthorpe, T., Fahrenkrug, J., & Wag-ner, G. (1983). Vasoacative intestinal polypeptide (VIP) increased vaginal blood flow and inhibits uterine smooth muscle activity in women. *European Journal of Clinical Investigation, 13,* 321–324.

Ottesen, B., Pedersen, B., Nielsen, J., Dalgaard, D., Wagner, G., & Fahrenkrug, J. (1987). Vasoactive intestinal polypeptide (VIP) provokes vaginal lubrication in normal women. *Peptides, 8,* 797–800.

Palle, C., Bredkjaer, H. E., Ottesen, B., & Fahrenkrug, J. (1990). Peptide histidine methionine (PHM) increases vaginal blood flow in normal women. *Peptides, 11,* 401–404.

Porst, H. (2002). IC 351 (tadalafil, Cialis): Update on clinical experience. *Inter-national Journal of Impotence Research, 14*(Suppl. 1), S57–S64.

Quirk, F. H., Heiman, J. R., Rosen, R. C., Laan, E., Smith, M. D., & Boolell, M. (2002). Development of a sexual function questionnaire for clinical trials of female sexual dysfunction. *Journal of Women's Health and Gender-Based Medicine, 11,* 277.

Rosen, R. C. (1991). Alcohol and drug effects on sexual function: Human experi-mental and clinical studies. *Annual Review of Sex Research, 2,* 119–179.

Rosen, R. C., & Ashton, A. K. (1993). Prosexual drugs: Empirical status of the "new aphrodisiacs." *Archives of Sexual Behavior, 22,* 521–543.

Rosen, R. C., & Beck, J. G. (1988). *Patterns of sexual arousal: Psychophysiological proc-esses and clinical applications.* New York: Guilford Press.

Rosen, R. C., & McKenna, K. E. (2002). PDE-5 inhibition and sexual response: Pharmacological mechanisms and clinical outcomes. *Annual Review of Sex Re-search, 13,* 36–88.

Rosen, R. C., Phillips, N. A., Gendrano, N. C., III, & Ferguson, D. M. (1999). Oral phentolamine and female sexual arousal disorder: A pilot study. *Journal of Sex & Marital Therapy, 25,* 137–144.

Rotella, D. P. (2001). Phosphodiesterase type 5 inhibitors: Discovery and therapeu-tic utility. *Drugs of the Future, 26,* 153–162.

Sarrel, P., Dobay, B., & Wiita, B. (1998). Estrogen and estrogen-androgen replace-ment in postmenopausal women dissatisfied with estrogen-only therapy. Sexual behavior and neuroendocrine responses. *Journal of Reproductive Medicine, 43,* 847–856.

Sherwin, B. B. (1991). The impact of different doses of estrogen and progesterone on mood and sexual behavior in postmenopausal women. *Journal of Clinical Endocrinology and Metabolism, 72,* 336–343.

Shifren, J. L., Braunstein, G. D., Simon, J. A., Casson, P. R., Buster, J. E., Redmond, G. P., et al. (2000). Transdermal testosterone treatment in women with impaired sexual function after oophorectomy. *New England Journal of Medicine, 343,* 682–688.

Simonsen, U., Prieto, D., Hernandez, M., de Tejada, I. S., & Garcia-Sacristan, A. (1997). Prejunctional alpha$_2$-adrenoceptors inhibit nitrergic neurotransmission in horse penile resistance arteries. *Journal of Urology, 157,* 2356–2360.

Sipski, M. L., Rosen, R. C., Alexander, C. J., & Hamer, R. M. (2000). Sildenafil effects on sexual and cardiovascular responses in women with spinal cord injury. *Urology, 55,* 812–815.

Steenstrup, B. R., Alm, P., Hannibal, J., Jorgensen, J. C., Palle, C., Junge, J., et al. (1995). Pituitary adenylate cyclase-activating polypeptide: Occurrence and relaxant effect in female genital tract. *American Journal of Physiology, 269,* E108–E117.

Tiefer, L. (1996). The medicalization of sexuality: Conceptual, normative, and professional issues. *Annual Review of Sex Research, 7,* 252–282.

Tiefer, L. (2002). Beyond the medical model of women's sexual problems: A campaign to resist the promotion of "female sexual dysfunction." *Sexual & Relationship Therapy, 17*(2), 127–135.

Traish, A. M., Kim, N. N., Min, K., Munarriz, R., & Goldstein, I. (2002). Role of androgens in female genital arousal: Receptor expression, structure and function. *Fertility and Sterility, 77*(Suppl. 4), 11–18.

Turko, I. V., Ballard, S. A., Francis, S. H., & Corbin, J. D. (1999). Inhibition of cyclic GMP-binding cyclic GMP-specific phosphodiesterase (Type 5) by sildenafil and related compounds. *Molecular Pharmacology, 56,* 124–130.

Udelson, D., Park, K., Sadeghi-Nejad, H., Salimpour, P., Krane, R. J., & Goldstein, I. (1999). Axial penile buckling forces versus RigiScan radial rigidity as a function of intercavernosal pressure: Why RigiScan does not predict functional erections in individual patients. *International Journal of Impotence Research, 11,* 327–337.

Vemulapalli, S., & Kurowski, S. (2000). Sildenafil relaxes rabbit clitoral corpus cavernosum. *Life Science, 67,* 23–29.

Wagner, G., & Levin, R. J. (1980). Effect of atrophine and methylatropine on human vaginal blood flow, sexual arousal and climax. *Acta pharmacologica et toxicological. 46,* 321–325.

Wessells, H., Levine, N., Hadley, M. E., Dorr, R., & Hruby, V. (2000). Melanocortin receptor agonists, penile erection, and sexual motivation: Human studies with Melanotan II. *International Journal of Impotence Research, 12*(Suppl. 4), S74–S79.

Ziessen, T., Moncada, S., & Cellek, S. (2002). Characterization of the non-nitrergic NANC relaxation responses in the rabbit vaginal wall. *British Journal of Pharmacology, 135,* 546–554.

Disabilities, Psychophysiology, and Sexual Functioning

MARCA L. SIPSKI

The study of sexual function is a complicated process. In most research involving human illness, the use of animal models is considered paramount in developing an understanding of physiologic responses. However, when we study sexual responses, the use of animal models does not allow us to communicate and truly assess the animal's responses to sexual stimulation. Thus, by studying persons with scientifically quantifiable specific physiologic dysfunctions with psychophysiologic techniques, we are able to provide a greater understanding about how sexual processes occur in nondisabled persons.

The term *disability* describes the effect of a wide range of disorders on human functional potential and includes both physical and psychological disabilities. This paper will focus on physical disabilities. These disabilities can result from musculoskeletal disorders, neurologic disorders, and cardiovascular and pulmonary dysfunction. Each of these categories of dysfunction may affect sexual functioning; however, their physiologic effects will be based upon the nature of the pathology. Examples of specific diseases under each disorder category are shown in Table 1.

With regard to the impact of disability on sexual function, one must consider the generic effects of disability and how these impact on sexual functioning, for example, depression about disability, partner effects, and fatigue associated with disability. Additionally, one must consider the specific effects of that particular disability on sexual functioning, for example, paralysis, loss of limb, loss of mobility or pain, and changes in sexual functioning as a result of the disability. On top of these considerations, one must also consider the individuals as sexual beings in the absence of their disability and their sexual function in this context. These relationships are pictorially shown in Figure 1.

Psychophysiologic techniques have not commonly been used to study individuals with disabilities. Moreover, there may not be a specific reason to study individuals with certain types of disabilities using psychophysiologic techniques as their disabilities (e.g., arthritis at the hip) would not be expected to result in a change in sexual physiology. However, for individuals with other disabilities affecting the neurologic control of sexual response or the vascular events associated with sexual response, the use of

410

Table 1. *Disorders That Impact Sexual Function*

Musculoskeletal Disorders
       Rheumatoid arthritis
       Osteoarthritis
       Hip replacement
       Amputations
Neurologic Disorders
       Spinal cord injury
       Multiple sclerosis
       Spina bifida
       Stroke
       Traumatic brain injury
       Cerebral palsy
       Dementia
       Neuropathies
Cardiovascular and Pulmonary Disorders
       Cardiac disease
       Vascular disorders
       Emphysema
       Chronic obstructive pulmonary disease
Psychiatric Disabilities
       Chronic schizophrenia
       Depression
       Bipolar disorders
       Other disorders

---

psychophysiologic techniques to study the impact of disability on sexual response would be appropriate.

If we consider the anticipated physiologic effects of various disabilities, specific disorders where psychophysiologic techniques would be useful to study sexual responses include rheumatologic disorders, disorders affecting the vasculature and disorders affecting neurologic functioning. With regards to rheumatologic disorders, progressive systemic sclerosis, rheumatoid arthritis and systemic lupus erythematosus are all disorders where an effect of illness on sexual functioning could be anticipated. In a recent questionnaire study (Bhadauria et al., 1995), 60 women with systemic sclerosis and 23 age and disease duration-matched women with rheumatoid arthritis or systemic lupus were surveyed. 71% of women with systemic sclerosis complained of vaginal dryness, 23% of genital ulcerations

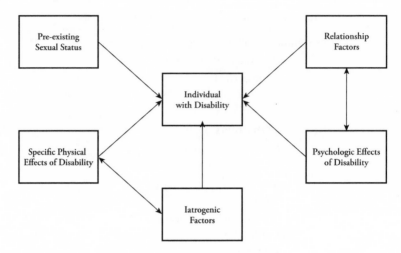

Figure 1. Issues affecting sexual function in an individual with disability.

and 56% of dyspareunia. Although frequency was not specified, these findings were less common in women with rheumatoid arthritis and systemic lupus. Furthermore, 53% of women with systemic sclerosis complained of decreased frequency and intensity of orgasms at present as compared to one year prior to their illness. This compares with 10% of controls who reported decreased intensity of orgasm and 17% who reported decreased number of orgasms. Because the nature of these illnesses could result in a predictable change in sexual response (e.g., decreased vaginal lubrication to psychogenic and/or reflexive stimulation), the performance of research studies using psychophysiologic techniques to document the true nature of these illnesses on sexual responses would be beneficial. Moreover, there are many iatrogenic features of these illnesses and there are many clouding psychosocial and personal issues that could potentially be controlled if subjects were studied in a laboratory-based environment.

Another group of disorders where psychophysiologic techniques would be appropriate to document the effects of disability is in the area of vasculogenic disorders. Although this area has not been well studied in humans, a recent basic science study in a rabbit model (Park et al., 2000) demonstrated that clitoral cavernosal fibrosis could occur because of atherosclerotic-induced chronic arterial insufficiency. This interesting work raises the possibility that atherosclerosis could cause vasculogenic sexual dysfunction in women. Study of women with atherosclerosis via a laboratory-based approach would be an excellent way to document the specific effects of this disorder on sexual arousal.

Neurologic disorders are another area where the use of psychophysiologic techniques may be beneficial in allowing us to delineate the exact effects of disability or illness on sexual response. The impact of stroke on sexual function has recently been documented via a prospective and retrospective standpoint (Korpelainen, Kauhanen, Kemola, Malinen, & Myllylä, 1998; Korpelainen, Nieminen, & Myllylä, 1999). Subjects in the prospective study aged from 32–65 and were free from other neurologic dysfunctions, severe aphasia, psychiatric or other medical disorders. Those in the retrospective study ranged from ages 32–79. Results for the retrospective study are shown in Table 2. In both males and females, a tendency toward worsening of sexual function is noted (e.g., decreased ability for erections, lubrication, and orgasm). A recent study also studied the sexual experiences of 193 men and 129 women living in the community with traumatic brain injury (TBI; Hibbard, Gordon, Flanagan, Haddad, & Labinsky, 2000). As compared to controls, persons with TBIs reported greater physiological difficulties influencing their energy for sex, sex drive, ability to initiate sexual activities and achieve orgasm, physical difficulties influencing body positioning, body movement and sensation, and body image difficulties. While these studies were fairly well designed and tried to eliminate as many confounding factors as possible, they still suffer from being questionnaire studies. Ideally, to augment our understanding of the impact of brain dysfunction on sexual arousal, we should study a population with well-defined disease, for example, using magnetic resonance imaging (MRI), functional MRI (fMRI), or positron emission tomography (PET), and perform single-subject laboratory-based research to determine if there are specific effects from specific injuries on sexual response.

Another neurologic disorder that affects sexual functioning is multiple sclerosis (MS). Multiple sclerosis causes both brain and spinal dysfunction and its effects are variable at different points in time. In light of this fact, it is extremely important to specifically document the neurologic dysfunction of a patient when describing their sexual dysfunctions. Lubrication difficulties are reported in 36% of women with MS (Hulter & Lundberg, 1995) while 58–74% (Hulter & Lundberg; Valleroy & Kraft, 1984) report orgasmic dysfunction; however, the neurological status of these women is unknown, so these findings are uninterpretable.

Two recent studies have provided more specific information about the effects of multiple sclerosis on sexual response. One study of 32 women and 9 men with MS found a significant correlation between brain stem and pyramidal abnormalities and total area of plaques on the brain observed via MRI and the presence of anorgasmia (Barak et al., 1996). Most recently, an electrodiagnostic study of 14 women with MS associated orgasmic difficulties with statistically significant abnormalities or absence of one or both pudendal and cortical evoked potentials (Yang, Bowen, Kraft, Uchio, & Kromm, 2000). One would expect that the specific effects of neurologic dysfunction on sexual responses would be similar with specific neurologic lesions. Thus, it would be useful to study the sexual responses of persons

Table 2. *Erectile Ability in Male Patients (n = 117) and Vaginal Lubrication and Orgasmic Ability in Female Patients (n = 75) Before and After Stroke*

	Erection		Lubrication		Orgasm	
	Before	After	Before	After	Before	After
Normal	73 (62%)	26 (22%)	35 (47%)	18 (24%)	36 (48%)	12 (16%)
Slightly diminished	28 (24%)	29 (25%)	15 (20%)	13 (17%)	14 (19%)	11 (15%)
Markedly diminished	11 (9%)	43 (37%)	7 (9%)	13 (17%)	3 (4%)	17 (23%)
None	3 (3%)	15 (13%)	3 (4%)	9 (12%)	6 (8%)	13 (17%)
Cannot say	2 (2%)	4 (3%)	15 (20%)	22 (29%)	16 (21%)	22 (29%)

with MS and similar neurologic dysfunctions using psychophysiologic techniques to determine if they are similar to the effects of other neurologic dysfunctions on sexual responses. We have recently obtained funding and are actively involved in study of this population.

The study of women with spinal cord injuries using psychophysiologic techniques is probably the most advanced of all areas. We have developed a 78-minute protocol in which 6-minute baseline periods alternate with four 12-minute stimulus periods in order to assess the effects of psychogenic and psychogenic combined with manual sexual stimulation (Sipski, Alexander, & Rosen, 1995). We used vaginal photoplethysmography and measurement of vaginal pulse amplitude (VPA) to measure vaginal blood flow and also monitored heart rate, blood pressure, respiratory rate, and subjective level of arousal. We also looked at varying patterns of injury to determine the impact of specific neurologic dysfunctions on various aspects of sexual response. (Sipski et al., 1995, 1997, 2001). To document the level and degree of spinal cord injury, we used the *International Standards for Neurologic Classification of Spinal Cord Injury* (SCI; American Spinal Injury Association, 2000). These standards allow us to assign a neurologic injury level and also document the degree of preserved sensory function in specific levels of spinal cord injury (see Figure 2). Using this technique, we assign a score of 0, 1 or 2 to the sensory function in each dermatome. For this research, we hypothesized that the degree of preservation of sensory function in the T11-L2 dermatomes, the area where the sympathetic innervation to the genitals arises from, would correlate to the degree of preserved psychogenic responsiveness. Results are shown in Figure 3. As can be seen, there was a highly significant relationship between the degree of preserved sensory function in the T11-L2 dermatomes and the degree of vaginal responsiveness. Grouping according to the T11-L2 sensory score revealed highly significant between-group differences in VPA change scores ($F[3, 83] = 9.40$, $p < .001$). In order to assess whether this might be solely related to the degree of incompleteness of SCI, we also evaluated the relationship between preservation of sensory function and preservation of psychogenic genital vasocongestion in the T6–T9 and S3–S5 dermatomes. There was not a significant relationship in these other dermatomes. Thus, we have demonstrated that the degree of preservation of sensory function in T11-L2 is predictive of psychogenic genital responsiveness in women with SCIs. Additionally, we believe this is further evidence to support the belief that the sympathetic nervous system has regulatory control of psychogenic genital vasocongestion in able-bodied women. We recently completed a similar study in males with SCIs and found a similar relationship between psychogenic erection and the degree of preservation of sensory function in the T11-L2 dermatomes (Sipski, Alexander, & Gomez-Marin, in press).

Orgasm has also been recently studied in women with SCIs (Sipski et

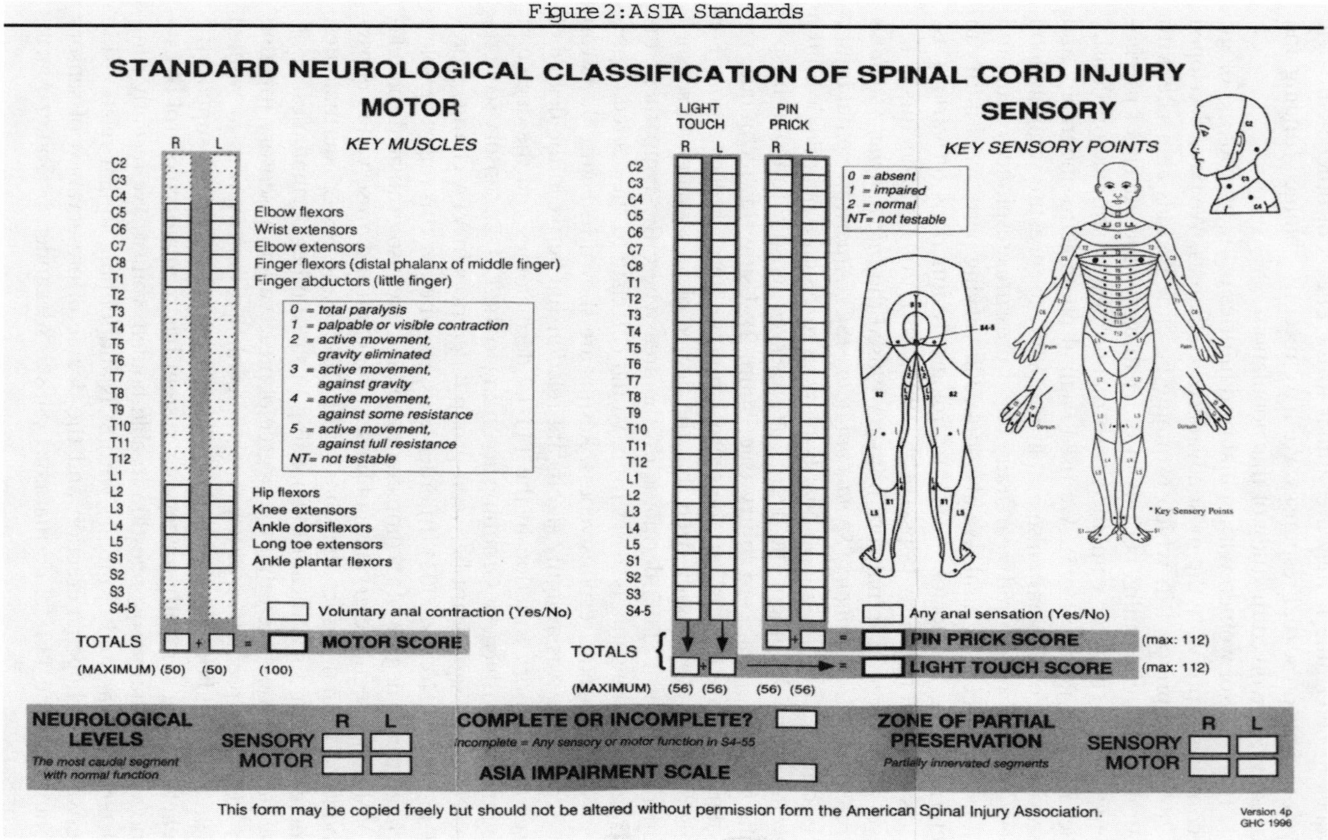

Figure 2: ASIA Standards

STANDARD NEUROLOGICAL CLASSIFICATION OF SPINAL CORD INJURY

MOTOR

KEY MUSCLES

	R	L	
C2			
C3			
C4			
C5			Elbow flexors
C6			Wrist extensors
C7			Elbow extensors
C8			Finger flexors (distal phalanx of middle finger)
T1			Finger abductors (little finger)
T2			
T3			
T4			
T5			
T6			
T7			
T8			
T9			
T10			
T11			
T12			
L1			
L2			Hip flexors
L3			Knee extensors
L4			Ankle dorsiflexors
L5			Long toe extensors
S1			Ankle plantar flexors
S2			
S3			
S4-5			

0 = total paralysis
1 = palpable or visible contraction
2 = active movement, gravity eliminated
3 = active movement, against gravity
4 = active movement, against some resistance
5 = active movement, against full resistance
NT= not testable

☐ Voluntary anal contraction (Yes/No)

TOTALS ☐ + ☐ = ☐ **MOTOR SCORE**

(MAXIMUM) (50) (50) (100)

SENSORY

KEY SENSORY POINTS

	LIGHT TOUCH R	LIGHT TOUCH L	PIN PRICK R	PIN PRICK L
C2				
C3				
C4				
C5				
C6				
C7				
C8				
T1				
T2				
T3				
T4				
T5				
T6				
T7				
T8				
T9				
T10				
T11				
T12				
L1				
L2				
L3				
L4				
L5				
S1				
S2				
S3				
S4-5				

0 = absent
1 = impaired
2 = normal
NT= not testable

☐ Any anal sensation (Yes/No)

TOTALS ☐ + ☐ = ☐ **PIN PRICK SCORE** (max: 112)

☐ + ☐ = ☐ **LIGHT TOUCH SCORE** (max: 112)

(MAXIMUM) (56) (56) (56) (56)

* Key Sensory Points

NEUROLOGICAL LEVELS — *The most caudal segment with normal function* — SENSORY R ☐ L ☐ MOTOR R ☐ L ☐

COMPLETE OR INCOMPLETE? ☐ — *Incomplete = Any sensory or motor function in S4-55*

ASIA IMPAIRMENT SCALE ☐

ZONE OF PARTIAL PRESERVATION — *Partially innervated segments* — SENSORY R ☐ L ☐ MOTOR R ☐ L ☐

This form may be copied freely but should not be altered without permission form the American Spinal Injury Association.

Version 4p
GHC 1996

Figure 2. ASIA standards.

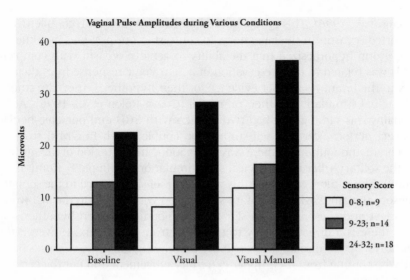

Figure 3. Vaginal pulse amplitude during various conditions in women with spinal cord injuries.

al., 2001). We studied 69 women with varying patterns of SCIs and 21 able-bodied controls subjects during self-stimulation to orgasm. Subjects had up to 75 minutes to stimulate themselves to orgasm using any means they chose. Results revealed that less than 50% of women with SCIs were able to achieve orgasm, compared with 100% of able-bodied women ($p = .001$). Those women with complete lower motor neuron dysfunction affecting the S2–S5 spinal segments were significantly less likely to achieve orgasm (17%) than women with all other levels and degrees of SCIs (59%) ($p = .048$). Time to orgasm was significantly increased in women with SCIs as compared to able-bodied controls ($p = .049$). Subjective descriptions of orgasm were indistinguishable between those women with and without SCIs. While this data should be useful for counseling women with SCIs about their sexual potentials, it may also shed some light into the neurologic pathways that control orgasm in the able-bodied. These results emphasize the need for an intact sacral reflex arc as part of the requirements for orgasmic capability. These findings are also similar to those findings noted during the observance of the urethrogenital reflex in the anesthetized and spinalized rat. We recently completed a similar study in males with SCIs and found a similar though not statistically different decrease in orgasmic potential in men with complete lower motor neuron sacral dysfunction (Sipski, Alexander, & Gomez-Marin, 2006).

Another group has also studied the responses of women with complete SCIs at and below the level of T6 to vaginal self-stimulation, cervical self-stimulation and hypersensitive area stimulation (Whipple, Gerdes, &

Komisaruk, 1996). This group found that three women with complete SCIs reported orgasms in the laboratory. In contrast to our previous hypotheses, this group hypothesized that the ability to achieve orgasm with complete SCIs was related to the preservation of a neurologic response from the cervix to the brain. As further evidence for their hypothesis, they cite studies of vaginal stimulation in their rat model (Cueva-Rolon et al., 1996). Additionally, this same group had two women with SCIs and one able-bodied subject perform cervical self-stimulation coupled with PET-MRI scans of the brain and found that there was "activation" in the region of the nucleus of the solitary tract with cervical self-stimulation (Whipple & Komisaruk, 2002). The authors contrasted this with a lack of signal noted in the somatosensory thalamus when vibratory stimulation was applied to the SCI women's feet and the presence of signal in able-bodied women hypothesizing that there is a direct pathway to the brain from the cervix. However, the authors failed to discuss the possibility that the signal in the women's brain may be coming from their upper extremity movement and not the cervical stimulation.

We have also performed a number of studies using psychophysiologic techniques to assess the effects of treating sexual concerns in the female SCI population. The effects of providing feedback about sexual responses to able-bodied sexually functional and dysfunctional individuals have been studied. Through the use of false feedback in able-bodied subjects, sexual arousal has been shown to increase. Based upon this research we studied how false positive feedback impacted upon sexual arousal in women with SCIs (Sipski, Rosen, Alexander, & Hamer, 2000a). A 42-minute protocol was developed in which four 6-minute baseline periods alternated with three 6-minute periods of audiovisual erotic stimulation. During the first baseline period the subjects rested. After this followed a period of audiovisual stimulation, then either a baseline period with false neutral or false positive feedback. This was followed by another 6-minute period of audiovisual erotic stimulation, another baseline period using the alternate form of feedback, an additional 6-minute period of audiovisual erotic stimulation and then a final 6-minute baseline period. During the baseline periods to provide the feedback, the research assistant went into the testing room with a polygraph tracing and said, congratulations, you are doing really well, keep up the good work, or else there is no change in your responses, please see if you can try harder. To assess subjects' responses they were grouped based upon their T11 to L2 sensory scores in a similar fashion to previous studies and additionally based upon whether they were able-bodied or had SCI. Subjects with very high sensory scores in T11 to L2 (24–32) were also grouped with the able-bodied subjects. For all the subjects as a whole, subjective arousal increased markedly following the presentation of positive feedback. Positive feedback clearly influenced them cognitively and caused them to report greater subsequent levels of arousal. There was no difference in results between the groups for able-bodied and SCI versus the SCI subjects alone. However, the VPA responses only went up in the SCI subjects with the highest T11 to L2 sensory scores and the able-bodied subjects, not in the SCI subjects with the lower sensory scores. We interpret this data as further evidence of the role of the sympathetic nervous system in psychogenic genital arousal. Practically speaking, these results document the need to promote the use of psychogenic means to increase genital sexual arousal in women with preservation of sensory function at T-11 to L-2 and to focus on reflex means of promoting arousal in other women.

The use of sympathetic stimulation as a means to improve sexual responsiveness has been studied in able-bodied women through the use of exercise and medications (Meston & Gorzalka, 1995, 1996a, 1996b; Meston & Heiman, 1998). There has also been work looking at sympathetic stimulation using anxiety provoking videos (Palace & Gorzalka, 1990). We conducted a similar study of women with SCIs in order to assess whether viewing anxiety-provoking videos would result in increased sexual arousal. Subjects were set up in the laboratory and observed erotic videos presented under three different conditions: no previewing of videos, viewing a travelogue sequence prior to an erotic film and viewing an anxiety provoking film prior to an erotic film. The presentation of video sequences was counterbalanced in order to control for possible order effects. Results were assessed based upon the amount of preserved sensation in the T11-L2 dermatomes, similar to our other studies. Additionally subjects with 0–23 scores were assessed in comparison to the subjects with scores of 24–32 plus the able-bodied subjects. Subjective arousal levels were similar between the two groups; however, with regards to the VPA results there was only a significant response to the audiovisual erotic stimulation, both post-neutral and post-anxiety-provoking stimulation, in the groups with greater preservation of sensation in T11-L2. In the group with preservation of less sensation in the T11-L2 dermatomes, there was only a statistically significant change in VPA with audiovisual stimulation post anxiety eliciting stimulation. Thus, the anxiety provoking stimulation seemed useful to increase genital responsiveness in those subjects with minimal preservation of sensation in the T11-L2 dermatomes, providing evidence of the positive regulatory effects of sympathetic stimulation.

On the other hand, in those subjects with greater levels of sensory preservation in the T11-L2 dermatomes, we had anticipated that the anxiety provoking simulation would increase genital arousal, but, in fact, these subjects became less aroused. In addition, during those baseline periods in which anxiety stimulation was presented in this same group of subjects, there was a significant decrease in VPA that did not occur with baselines in which only neutral stimulation was presented. We believe these findings to be evidence for the sympathetic nervous system's role in inhibition of sexual arousal.

In addition to demonstrating the usefulness of studying populations of persons with specific neurologic deficits, our findings emphasize the regulatory nature—both positive and negative—of the sympathetic nervous system in the control of sexual arousal. One can also consider the fact that sympathetic stimulation may be of different varieties. Perhaps we should consider the issue of cognitively positive sympathetic stimulation, cognitively negative and cognitively neutral. In the studies of Meston, sympathetic stimulation was provided through drugs and exercise, activities that are cognitively neutral. In our study, the video's content may have negatively impact on our subject's sexual arousal while in another context there could be cognitively positive sympathetic stimulation, for example, the excitement of forbidden sexual activity.

In another study of women with SCIs, the effects of sildenafil on women with SCI were assessed (Sipski, Rosen, Alexander, & Hamer, 2000b). Subjects received either sildenafil 50 mg or placebo 1 hour prior to the study. The identical protocol was used to assess the effects of sildenafil as was used to assess capacity for psychogenic arousal. Six-minute baseline periods alternated with four 12-minute periods: two with audiovisual erotic and two with audiovisual plus manual stimulation. Subjects included 19 women with both complete injuries and incomplete injuries. VPA and subjective arousal levels during various treatment conditions are shown in Table 3. Although VPA with sildenafil was generally greater than placebo throughout the study, differences were not statistically significant ($p = .07$). However, subjective arousal was significantly increased with sildenafil as compared to placebo ($p = .01$). Blood pressure was mildly decreased and the heart rate was mildly elevated with use of sildenafil.

Despite all of the above works, there is still a major issue that needs to be addressed in persons with disabilities and SCIs with regards to sexual function. This issue becomes even more important when we consider the issue of the effects of neurologic dysfunction on sexual response versus whether the persons report sexual dysfunction. Because the definition of sexual dysfunction requires a person to exhibit personal distress in order to report sexual dysfunction, many of those persons with neurologic disabilities may have alterations in their sexual response, but these may not be causing sexual dysfunction (Sipski, 2001). In order to acknowledge this issue, a new classification system for sexual dysfunction has been proposed for women with spinal cord dysfunctions that takes into account the anticipated effects of neurologic dysfunction on sexual response (see Table 4; Sipski & Alexander, 2002). This instrument still requires validation.

We are currently in the process of conducting another group of new studies. Laboratory-based studies are in process to assess the use of various

Table 3. *Sexual Function Effects of Sildenafil in Women*

Drug	Vaginal Pulse Amplitude*					Subjective Arousal†		
	Visual Stimulation	Visual + Manual Stimulation	F	P	Visual Stimulation	Visual + Manual	F	P
Sildenafil	21.49 ± 2.6	30.69 ± 3.9	2.3	0.07	3.76 ± 0.4	4.68 ± 0.4	6.41	0.01
Placebo	20.29 ± 2.8	25.31 ± 3.84			3.50 ± 0.3	4.08 ± 0.4		

Values presented as mean ± SEM. *Measured as millimeters of deflection. †Score ranged from 0 to 10.

Table 4. *Female Spinal Sexual Function Classification*

Function	Response	Criteria
A: Sexual dysfunction	Present	Desire disorders
		Arousal disorders
		Orgasm disorders
		Pain disorders
	Absent	
B: Psychogenic genital arousal	Intact/normal	SS = 32 T11-L2
	Likely	SS = 16-31 T11-L2
	Unlikely	SS = 1-15 T11-L2
	Not possible	SS = 0 T11-L2
C: Reflex genital arousal	Intact	Normal or hyperactive BC and anal wink reflexes
	Possible	Hypoactive or partially intact BC and/or anal wink reflexes
	Not possible	Absent BC and anal wink reflexes
D: Orgasm	Not possible	No S2-S5 sensation; absent BC and anal wink reflexes
	Possible	All other neurologic lesions

sympathomimetic and sympatholytic drugs on sexual response in women with SCIs. Moreover, we are studying women with predominantly spinal MS to determine whether there are similar sexual effects of neurologic lesions in this population as in women with SCIs. We are also in the process of conducting a study of the use of reflex sacral stimulation to decrease orgasmic dysfunction in women with neurogenic sexual dysfunction.

Overall, the use of psychophysiologic techniques to study persons with other neurologic and physical disabilities is in its infancy. However, with the wide range of issues that impact upon sexual function, the use of laboratory-based studies coupled with detailed anatomic assessments gives us the greatest opportunities to understand the intricacies of sexual responses.

Moreover, as can be seen from experiences assessing the sexual responses with women with SCIs, through the study of persons with specific neurologic or other disabilities we can gain a better understanding of the mechanisms involved in sexual responses in the able-bodied population.

Note

This paper was supported in part by RO1 HD30149 from the National Institutes of Health.

References

American Spinal Injury Association. (2000). *International standards for neurological classification of spinal cord injury.*

Barak, Y., Achiron, A., Elizur, A., Gabbay, U., Noy, S., & Sarova-Pinhas, I. (1996). Sexual dysfunction in relapsing-remitting multiple sclerosis: Magnetic resonance imaging, clinical and psychological correlates. *Journal of Psychiatry and Neuroscience, 21,* 255–258.

Bhadauria, S., Moser, D. K., Clements, P. J., Singh, R. R., Lachenbruch, P. A., Pitkin, R. M., et al. (1995). Genital tract abnormalities and female sexual function impairment in systemic sclerosis. *American Journal of Obstetrics and Gynecology, 172*(2), 580–587.

Cueva-Rolon, R., Sansone, G., Bianca, R., Gomez, L. E., Beyer, C., Whipple, B., et al. (1996). Vagotomy blocks responses to vaginocervical stimulation in genito-spinal-neurectomized rats. *Physiology and Behavior, 60,* 19–24.

Hibbard, M. R., Gordon, W. A., Flanagan, S., Haddad, L., & Labinsky, E. (2000). Sexual dysfunction after traumatic brain injury. *Neurological Rehabilitation, 15*(2), 107–120.

Hulter, B. M., & Lundberg, P. O. (1995). Sexual function in women with advanced multiple sclerosis. *Journal of Neurology, Neurosurgery, and Psychiatry, 58,* 83–86.

Korpelainen, J. T., Kauhanen, M-L., Kemola, H., Malinen, U., & Myllylä, V. V. (1998). Sexual dysfunction I stroke patients. *Acta Neurologica Scandinavica, 98,* 400–405.

Korpelainen, J. T., Nieminen, P., & Myllylä, V. V. (1999). Sexual functioning among stroke patients and their spouses. *Stroke, 30,* 715–719.

Meston, C. M., & Gorzalka, B. B. (1995). The effects of sympathetic activation following acute exercise on physiological and subjective sexual arousal in women. *Behavior Research and Therapy, 33,* 651–664.

Meston, C. M., & Gorzalka, B. B. (1996a). The differential effects of sympathetic activation on sexual arousal in sexually functional and dysfunctional women. *Journal of Abnormal Psychology, 105,* 582–591.

Meston, C. M., & Gorzalka, B. B. (1996b). The effects of immediate, delayed, and residual sympathetic activation on physiological and subjective sexual arousal in women. *Behavior Research and Therapy, 34,* 143–148.

Meston, C. M., & Heiman, J. R. (1998). Ephedrine-activated sexual arousal in women. *Archives of General Psychiatry, 55,* 652–656.

Palace, E., & Gorzalka, B. B. (1990). The enhancing effects of anxiety on arousal in sexual dysfunctional and functional women. *Journal of Abnormal Psychology, 99,* 403–411.

Park, K., Tarcan, T., Goldstein, I., Siroky, M. B., Krane, R. J., & Azadzoi, K. M. (2000). Atherosclerosis-induced chronic arterial insufficiency causes clitoral cavernosal fibrosis in the rabbit. *International Journal of Impotence Research, 12*(2), 111–116.

Sipski, M. L. (2001). A physiatrist's view regarding the report of the International Consensus Conference on Female Sexual Dysfunction: Potential concerns regarding women with disabilities. *Journal of Sex & Marital Therapy, 27,* 215–216.

Sipski, M. L., & Alexander, C. J. (2002). Documentation of the impact of spinal cord injury on female sexual function: The female spinal sexual function classification. *Topics in Spinal Cord Injury Rehabilitation, 8,* 63–73.

Sipski, M. L., Alexander, C. J., & Gomez-Marin, O. (2006). Effects of level and degree of spinal cord injury on male orgasm. Spinal Cord—advance online publication, 27 June 2006; doi: 10, 1038/sj.sc.3101954.

Sipski, M. L., Alexander, C. J., & Gomez-Marin, O. (in press). The effects of spinal cord injury on psychogenic sexual arousal in males. *Journal of Urology.*

Sipski, M. L., Alexander, C. J., & Rosen, R. C. (1995). Physiological parameters associated with psychogenic sexual arousal in women with complete spinal cord injuries. *Archives of Physical Medicine and Rehabilitation, 76,* 811–818.

Sipski, M. L., Alexander, C. J., & Rosen, R. C. (1997). Physiological parameters associated with sexual arousal in women with incomplete spinal cord injuries. *Archives of Physical Medicine and Rehabilitation, 78,* 305–313.

Sipski, M. L., Alexander, C. J., & Rosen, R. C. (2001). Sexual arousal and orgasm in women: Effects of spinal cord injury. *Annals of Neurology, 35,* 35–44.

Sipski, M. L., Rosen, R. C., Alexander, C. J., & Hamer, R. (2000a). A controlled trial of positive feedback to increase sexual arousal in women with spinal cord injuries. *Neurological Rehabilitation, 15,* 145–153.

Sipski, M. L., Rosen, R. C., Alexander, C. J., & Hamer, R. (2000b). Sildenafil effects on sexual and cardiovascular responses in women with spinal cord injury. *Journal of Urology, 55,* 812–815.

Valleroy, M. L., & Kraft, G. H. (1984). Sexual dysfunction in multiple sclerosis. *Archives of Physical Medicine and Rehabilitation, 65,* 125–128.

Whipple, B., Gerdes, C., & Komisaruk, B. R. (1996). Sexual response to self-stimulation in women with complete spinal cord injury. *Journal of Sex Research, 33,* 231–240.

Whipple, B., & Komisaruk, B. R. (2002). Brain (PET) responses to vaginal-cervical self-stimulation in women with complete spinal cord injury: Preliminary findings. *Journal of Sex and Marital Therapy, 28,* 79–86.

Yang, C. C., Bowen, J. R., Kraft, G. H., Uchio, E. M., & Kromm, B. G. (2000). Cortical evoked potentials of the dorsal nerve of the clitoris and female sexual dysfunction in multiple sclerosis. *Journal of Urology, 164,* 2010–2013.

Discussion Paper

JULIA R. HEIMAN

This morning focuses on clinical populations and clinical problems. Several issues are highlighted. One is measurement, a continuing theme of this meeting, which increases in importance when describing clinical populations and treatment effects. A second issue involves the definition of change. It is no longer adequate to have simply a significant change statistically; a clinically meaningful change is increasingly the desired endpoint. A third issue involves the sample selection. How that gets defined varies. For those of us who conduct pharmacological trials, the degree to which one works with not only a self-selected sample but also a highly screened sample deserves comment. Recent trials in investigating sildenafil in women excluded 80% of screened women, even though they had the diagnosis in question. The consequences of this intensity of screening are worth discussing. A fourth issue is the current social environment; using sexually explicit materials is socially sensitive, as is the testing of experimental drugs. For example, on the latter point, revelations about the safety problems of pharmaceutical products not only have important human consequences but also impact potential subjects' willingness to volunteer for studies involving experimental agents.

Let me first talk about Ray Rosen's very thorough summary of outcome assessment, particularly in the area of psychopharmacology. Ray started out with an example, actually an example from 1994, which was a study by Munoz, Bancroft, and Beard. This is a well-designed study on men. That study had a complicated procedure. They included a number of measures of penile response. I think we need to get beyond simply measuring a mean and/or maximum response, particularly for clinical efficaciousness. Can we measure latency, and how confident would we be to measure latency to a certain criterion response? What is interesting about that Munoz et al. study is that subjective measures were seen as secondary outcomes. Penile measures were seen as primary outcomes. That is true, I have the impression, for most of the research in men. The primary measure has been the genital outcome, the secondary measure has been subjective.

Ray's paper also mentions the Goldstein et al. (2000) article where erectile rigidity was measured by a buckling procedure. What happened to that measure? Was it not useful or just too cumbersome? When have you seen a sildenafil or vardenafil study using the buckling force procedure to measure outcome? It was heavily used for a while. We do not hear of its relative value for clinical studies.

In general, what I felt Ray's paper is really capturing, and in some detail, is the issue of what would be desirable in study design and methods used for testing men. What you see, I think, across time, is that less money is being spent on these studies, so there is a contraction of the number of measures used. Now that may be good, but it may not necessarily further the science.

In studies with women, sexually dysfunctional women are increasingly being studied, whereas 3 years ago, we had the greatest amount of data on healthy young volunteers. So, we're a bit more weighted on the healthy side than on women with sexual dysfunction. As for women with sexual dysfunction, the focus is almost exclusively on women with sexual arousal disorder, in large part due to the success of sildenafil in men. Now it turns out that female sexual arousal disorder is very difficult to define. It's defined in the *DSM*, but it clearly overlaps with desire disorders. How often is genital arousal disorder present without subjective arousal problems, which is what the *DSM* implies in the focus on genital symptoms? This distinction may have substantial consequences for how we measure arousal and change in arousal in the lab. In addition, hormonal status has become increasingly important in the study of women. So, for example, in the sildenafil studies that have been done, it has become clear that inadequately androgenized and inadequately estrogenized women do not respond to sildenafil. One wonders how many other types of compounds are being developed for which this might be important. So I would encourage the inclusion of repeated measurement of hormonal status, whether women are on hormonal treatments or not.

I can't resist talking about self-reported arousal–vaginal response differences. What women say about how aroused they are is obviously important. If we only have a vaginal change in a group of women (who have an intact nervous system), and they do not notice a subjective change in arousal after a given treatment, what really are we treating? The importance of having women report how aroused they are is central and clinically more important than using, for example, a continuous measure of arousal. A significant response on a continuous measure of subjective arousal is good for science, but not very clinically meaningful if it is not reflected in a summary statement of some kind about the woman's self-reported arousal. In clinical work, we have to partly rely on what people say. So it looks like we would do well to improve our subjective measures. In addition, multiple sampling of subjective measures, rather than just once or twice, would help with the statistical problem of too few observations to get reliable within-subject correlations.

One of Ray's last slides showed the lack of concordance between subjective and physiological measures, and he asked whether this was a drug or a methodological effect. A third alternative is that it is a real effect. For example, in some of our studies, like in our DHEA studies, we found a significant increase in subjective sexual arousal, but no difference in vaginal pulse amplitude (VPA). However, there was a significant correlation between subjective and physiological measures of arousal. So in other words, you could have people who do not respond subjectively physiologically and still show a good correlation between their subjective and physiological response, even though you have a disentanglement of the two response systems.

With respect to Marca's work, it reminds us that external validity is really important and we are not focusing enough on it. Before pharmacological studies were conducted, few studies had been published that addressed external validity. We need to come back to that issue and see what we can find out about how well correlated laboratory and at-home sexual responses actually are. One of the interesting things I thought about Stephanie Both's study that she presented yesterday was that they tracked immediate sexual response. You can't do this with every drug you might give, but immediate sexual effects in the 24 hours after leaving the lab is, I think, a great idea that should be used more often, particularly with hormonal or dopaminergic agents that might have a more lasting effect.

I want to make a couple of other comments about Marca's paper. First I want to underscore how difficult these studies are to do, and Marca is one of the few people working in this area and producing interesting results. So, in terms of fighting political battles and in terms of what's worth studying, I think it is important for us to pay attention to these difficult samples and how they can benefit from pharmacological and other interventions. Marca points out that sympathetic nervous system (SNS) activity has regulatory functions that are both positive and negative. In one of her studies, she presented anxiety stimuli before sexually arousing stimuli, and as you know from other work in this area, anxiety stimuli or anxiety material presented concurrently typically enhances sexual response. However, in her spinal cord–injured individuals she found decreased response. Thus SNS activation has the potential for both positive and negative regulatory effects on sexual response. I think that's important in terms of conceptualizing some of the apparently contradictory findings in the literature on intact spinal cord individuals.

References

Goldstein, I., Auerbach, S., Padma-Nathan, H., Rajfer, J., Fitch, W., & Schmitt, L. (2000). Axial penile rigidity as primary efficacy outcome during multi-institutional in-office dose titration clinical trials with alprostadil alfadex in patients with erectile dysfunction. Alprostadil Alfadex Study Group. *International Journal of Impotence Research, 12,* 205–211.

Munoz, M., Bancroft, J., & Beard, M. (1994). Evaluating the effects of an alpha$_2$-adrenoceptor antagonist on erectile function in the human male: II. The erectile response to erotic stimuli in men with erectile dysfunction, in relation to age and in comparison with normal volunteers. *Psychopharmacology, 115,* 471–477.

General Discussion

Marca Sipski: We are planning to do a number of clinical trials. Right now, we're doing a clinical trial in which we're starting to use vibratory stimulation in men, to see if vibratory stimulation, which has been traditionally used for fertility purposes, would actually decrease spasticity, which is totally out of this area, but it's been anecdotally reported by many people that, after vibratory stimulation, they will have a decrease in their spasticity. So, we're looking at whether it would decrease spasticity and whether it would improve their orgasmic capability with time. That is in the male population. Then we're actually planning to do a clinical trial looking at the difference between vibratory stimulation and use of clitoral vacuum suction to improve orgasmic function in women with spinal cord injury and multiple sclerosis (MS). One of the issues that came up with this population in the research that we originally did was really just looking at a baseline population. When you get into the clinical trials arena, the issue of female sexual arousal disorder (FSAD) or female sexual dysfunction (FSD) comes in, so then you really have to break out the subset of people who actually complain of sexual dysfunction in addition to their physiological changes. So, we are trying to do some more of the take-home studies, but in the absence of time, I couldn't talk about them.

Kevin McKenna: Marca, that was a really interesting study and I am really interested in you going on in MS. In a lot of the previous studies, there were just some very vague descriptions of the spinal lesion. I like the fact that you characterized it much better than previously. But one of the problems of these studies is that it is such a heterogeneous group, with regard to the degree of the lesion. Are you going to try to use magnetic resonance imaging (MRI) of spinal cord to really characterize exactly the lesion? It is just going to be so hard with such a complex disease.

Marca Sipski: We have looked at our data in a stepwise fashion. Originally we studied women with only injuries above T-6, and then we studied women with injuries only below T-6, although I am reporting on everyone now. However, regardless of how I looked at the data, I came up with the same conclusion. I did think about doing MRIs in spinal cord–injured women, but MRI of the spinal cord is really in its infancy and I think you are actually going to get—and this is what the radiologists have told me—

you are going to get less data from that than from the American Spinal Injury Association (ASIA) exam, which is actually more sophisticated than other things at this point. One of the criticisms I would make is that the ability to test the sensation with the ASIA is not incredible. Actually, with the MS population, we are planning to test, using quantitative sensory testing, to see if that would be better able to differentiate people's sensory differences in that area. We looked at the women in terms of motor changes, too. I didn't report all the negatives we found, but we also looked at their motor function, how that affected sexual response. I think the issue of the MRI, though, is amazingly important when you start thinking about studying people with brain damage and brain injuries, and I would hope that in 5–10 years from now, I would be ready to get into that population, but it's a big leap.

Don Strassberg: Ray, I have a couple of questions. One is sort of a follow-up on a comment that Julia just made, and that is who gets excluded and what is the impact of that process on the generalizability of the findings? In particular, when we've been talking about a third of men, for example, in typical laboratory studies using penile plethysmography (PPG) are nonresponders. But I'm not sure what it means when a man with an erectile dysfunction is a nonresponder. So if you could, talk a little bit about who those guys are that are being excluded. Then, the second question, can you talk some about what the data shows about the impact of sildenafil on women with apparently selective serotonin reuptake inhibitor (SSRI)-induced arousal disorder?

Ray Rosen: Those are both good questions. Regarding the nonresponder issue, personally, I think is a much bigger issue on the women's side, as Julia indicated. On the men's side, it's an issue, but I don't think it's a very big issue. I think what you are seeing in these studies, and I tried to indicate it briefly in my slide about inclusion/exclusion criteria, is that we are selecting the mild to moderate end of the spectrum of erectile dysfunction (ED), and we are excluding men with major organic etiologies, such as diabetics, postprostatectomies, and so forth. In addition, we're selecting men who show at least a minimal level of sexual responsivity to visual stimulation in the laboratory context. That is clearly a limitation of these studies. I don't think you can generalize these findings to more severe ED. There is also a subgroup of men who are unresponsive to visual sexual stimulation or overly inhibited in the laboratory environment. This may be related to satiation with visual sexual stimulation in the media. A few years ago we excluded very few men for this reason; now we are excluding more of these men. Interestingly enough, you would think age would be a big factor, but we don't find it's a big factor. I think the important aspect of the tadalafil study, despite those limitations, it that it had good external validity. The men in the at-home study were not the same men as the lab study; they were a relatively nonselected ED group. However, we replicated the time to onset, duration of action, and the important findings from the lab study in this independent group.

Regarding Don's second question you asked about, women with SSRI-related sexual dysfunction, the answer is affirmative. George Nurnberg and other investigators have shown that PDE5s, including sildenafil, are effective in reversing aspects of the SSRI-related dysfunction that is common in women. It is not clear exactly how this effect is achieved. The hypothesis that I'm most comfortable with is that SSRIs affect nitrergic innervation and that there's some depletion of nitric oxide (NO) as a result. This might be reversed or counteracted by the use of PDE5 inhibitors.

John Bancroft: I just want to describe an interesting example of a "flatliner" (i.e., no erectile response to erotic stimuli in the laboratory). I had a patient in the clinic whose problem was compulsive use of the Internet. He was spending hours on the Internet searching, masturbating with what he found. When he came into the lab, he was a complete "flatliner" and commenting on the erotic stimuli presented to him, "this stuff is of no interest to me." So, to what extent are people getting into habits of searching for particular types of erotic stimuli, which doesn't fit with what is happening in the lab?

Roy Levin: These so-called flatliners, do they respond to vibration?

John Bancroft: We haven't tried that.

Roy Levin: So, they're only flatliners to visual sexual stimuli (VSS)?

John Bancroft: Yes.

Roy Levin: So, it's just because it's a highly specific sort of thing, but it would be a worthwhile thing, just to test them on vibration.

John Bancroft: Yes.

Jim Pfaus: There is some evidence in the literature that female-initiated sexual activity changes over the ovulatory cycle, reaching a peak around ovulation, and dropping down precipitously thereafter. I'm wondering, when we look at women who are on hormone replacement therapy and we are characterizing them with regard to their hormonal status, are attempts being made to characterize them across the cycle? I can imagine how difficult it is to characterize them by just hormone status, but across the cycle would probably be an exceptionally difficult thing to do. But it may also be very instructive because you may find effects during ovulation that you don't find at other points in the cycle. That is my first question. My second question has to do with any potential tolerance that may accrue to PDE5s. It is the case that men are overusing drugs like Viagra. In fact, men without erectile difficulty are taking it "just in case." Of course, the advertising for the drug features men coming out of their houses dancing, and we would all like to be happy in the morning. Given this, it seems appropriate to ask whether tolerance is occurring, and whether we will soon see "new and improved" versions of these drugs.

Kevin McKenna: No tolerance has been found, not in any study.

Jim Pfaus: No tolerance? Okay.

Marca Sipski: I would mention, though, that I actually had a patient that took it—I didn't prescribe it for him—and this is a spinal cord–injured individual, went to a bar, had a lap dance, and had a fractured penis with it. This is somebody that I wouldn't necessarily say needed it, so I think you have to be careful with this. I just want to make a comment on the flatliners. I think, Ray, your idea is a fabulous one in terms of that, because, you know, when I ask people about their arousal level, which I do every 3 minutes, we ask for subjective level of arousal, emotionally and physically. But some people, if they go zero throughout the whole thing, and I have seen this happen in men and in women, if they are going zero in terms of arousal level, and you're looking at it cognitively—not just their penis or their vagina, I mean—they are not going to respond to anything. They come in and then you ask, well, why are they here? Why did they volunteer for this research? They haven't had sex in 10 years, and they are coming in and are going to be zero. So, I think it's great to get those people out, because clearly I think there's something going on psychologically that is not what you really want to be testing in a lab.

Don Strassberg: But the reason I raised the question is, when you're dealing with a group that is known to have ED, does it mean the same thing to eliminate the flatliners as it does in a study with people you have no reason to suspect have ED?

Roy Levin: Can I just answer the point about the menstrual cycle? There are two areas where women seem to suggest that they have increased sexual desire or want sexual activities to occur—so-called ovulation, but also peri-menstrually. A lot of women find that their increased sexiness happens during and after menstruation. So, there are two particular times there in midcycle.

Ellen Laan: Can I say something about that, too? There is not much evidence to date that, for instance, vaginal pulse amplitude (VPA), which is the main measure in all the drug studies in women, is influenced by the menstrual cycle.

Julia Heiman: Just to expand a bit on that. In a couple of studies we have tried to take women in a certain menstrual phase, just to reduce the variability, even though they are on oral contraceptives. The problem is then, what do we say about—can we generalize to—women in other phases?

Ray Rosen: Well, I'm not sure what I can add to what I said before. Again I think this is an increasing phenomenon. I think John's recent case example is an interesting one and I think there are multiple factors involved. I do think that there is a societal habituation to visual stimuli that's also occurring.

Erick Janssen: But why do you exclude them?

Ray Rosen: If someone is unable to respond under any conditions, they're only adding noise to the study. If you have someone who is incapable of responding to laboratory stimulation, then what are you evaluating? In fact, in one early study with Viagra, we didn't exclude flatliners and had high nonresponder rates throughout the study. This markedly affected our power estimates in the study.

Erick Janssen: Was that before the men received any form of treatment?

Ray Rosen: Yes. In this early study that we did, we didn't exclude these patients and they remained nonresponders throughout the study. Again, I want to come back to the main point I was trying to make, that I don't believe excluding nonresponders is affecting the external validity of our findings.

David Rowland: Just a reference back to other kinds of stimulation and how they might affect the flatliners. We have looked at quite a few men under these conditions and basically find that the stimuli provoke about a 5- to 8-millimeter increase in erectile response from zero, but you certainly do not see anything that resembles a typical response. I think this is a level or a kind of inhibition that is laboratory induced for the most part, and the vibrotactile stimulation does not make a lot of difference. The little bit of the difference that you do see under vibrotactile stimulation may result more from anal sphincter contractions than from direct penile engorgement.

Marca Sipski: Back to the other topic, which I wanted to get back to Julia and Ellen on, is there consensus then that you don't have to control for the time of the menstrual cycle when you're measuring VPA repeatedly in different individuals? Because I have done it and it's difficult to get women between day 16 and 21. I've had to do it for grant proposals, although I felt that in the literature there was enough of a case that you didn't need to do it. So I'd like your opinion.

Ellen Laan: In drug studies we only have premenopausal women that are on oral contraceptives because our medical ethics committee won't approve studies in which subjects run the risk of becoming pregnant while participating in an experimental drug study. But even oral contraceptive users are measured in a very strict period within the pill cycle and it is a pain, but we still do it, just to be sure. My reading of the available literature is that there is not much evidence for a menstrual cycle effect in VPA. Menstrual cycle phase might be important in heat measures; for instance, the thermister that Koos Slob uses. He found higher labial temperature during the luteal phase, with several complex order effects. I am not convinced that these higher temperatures in the luteal phase should be construed as a facilitation of sexual arousal. Body temperature is higher in that part of the cycle regardless of sexual or other emotional states.

Julia Heiman: We're controlling for menstrual cycle particularly in pharmacological studies. We actually do not know which hormones are key especially for a given drug. If we can reduce variability, we do, and this is one method that we think helps. How much is unknown.

Marca Sipski: That may be something we want to study collectively though, because it seems as if we're all doing it, even though we don't necessarily feel like we need to be doing it.

Roy Levin: Can I just come back to one comment on the VPA? I mean, in theory you can't compare a woman on day 6 with her VPA with VPA on day 22 because they are different VPAs that you're measuring; they are not continuous. So, say if you get 4 millimeters VPA increase on day 6 and 4 millimeters on day 22, you don't know whether those 4 millimeters are the same or whether they represent a totally different flow, so in you actually can't compare the two. You can only compare the changes that occur on day 1. So, it is not valid to do the comparison.

Ellen Laan: You may be right, you're probably right theoretically, but empirically we at least see pretty high correlations between baseline measures in drug studies where we have two sessions on separate days, often exactly one menstrual cycle apart. You are right, we should also look at repeatability of VPA response rather than VPA baseline. Actually, I do have data from a study that can be used to look at repeatability, so I will calculate test-retest correlations and let you know.

Erick Janssen: I would like to come back to the topic of exclusion. You started your talk, Ray, with an example of a "typical ED sample," but you excluded both high and low responders, and I miss the rationale for that. Are you saying that you think this approach increases external validity, as this is a "typical" sample?

My other point, or question, involves buckling force. I have some issues with endpoints, especially erectile endpoints. Before we had the RigiScan, we measured penile circumference. I remember this study we conducted years ago and that we very much liked to see published in a urological journal. We got into an argument with the reviewers of this urological journal about the fact that we had not measured rigidity, which, in their view, was a much more important endpoint than circumference. We managed to get the manuscript accepted for publication, but only after a long and drawn-out debate. I argued with either type of measure, so also with rigidity, we needed to talk about predictive validity. When it comes to rigidity as an "endpoint," we do not know "how hard is hard enough." It is interesting to note that when the RigiScan was first used, 100% rigidity as measured by the device represented a "full" erection. If I am not mistaken, time has helped us adjust the rules, and we now are down to 60%. So nowadays 60%, in RigiScan land, is hard enough. It indicates that we are not talking about absolute truths, but predictions. And it has always amazed me how long it took, 5 or 6 years or so, before the first publication came out reporting correlations between rigidity and circumference, which, by the way, turned out to be exceedingly high, well above .80. So you can predict penile rigidity pretty well with penile circumference. RigiScan devices are pretty expensive (and not even well validated), so if we could predict rigidity with simpler measures, why would we not? But buckling force, apparently, is another step up, where radial rigidity, as measured by the RigiScan, is in itself not good enough. No, it has to be *axial* rigidity. But relevant data are lacking, and it again raises questions about how hard the penis needs to be for it to go where a man wants it to go. May the force be with you. It makes me think of a graph that I believe Gorm Wagner published, and that Walter Everaerd brought to my attention years ago. The graph shows how with increasing age, the ability to obtain a rigid erection declines, whereas the amount of force needed to enter the vagina increases, and when those two lines cross, "erectile" problems may become manifest. So, in the end, it is not about erection as some absolute endpoint, but about predictions and about the predictive validity of our measures.

Brian Mustanski: The issue of responders and nonresponders reminds me of research on substance abuse. The issue of what to do with nonresponders in a sexual psychophysiology study is similar to the question of what do you do with someone who doesn't drink alcohol when you're studying the frequency of alcohol consumption? Do you throw them out? Well, if you throw them out, you really have a problem because ignoring them is probably not justified. Do you assign them a zero? If you assign them a zero, you probably have some problems in your model as well because the factors that cause someone to start drinking are different than the ones that influence their frequency of consumption. So people who study substance abuse have developed models, like multifactorial threshold models (e.g., Koopmans, Slutske, Heath, Neale, & Boomsma, 1999) and such, which allow you to include these people and explicitly state your assumptions. People may want to investigate those sorts of models in thinking about what to do with nonresponders as well.

References

Koopmans, J. R., Slutske, W. S., Heath, A. C., Neale, M. C., & Boomsma, D. I. (1999). The genetics of smoking initiation and quantity smoked in Dutch adolescent and young adult twins. *Behavior Genetics, 29,* 383–393.

Part 6.

Gender, Sexual Orientation, and Paraphilic Sexual Interests

Cognitive Processes and Gender Differences in Sexuality

JAMES H. GEER AND JASON L. HICKS

A momentary digression to insert a historical note concerning how the senior author became enmeshed in cognitive research: I (Geer) had to be hit on the head several times before it became obvious that cognitive factors influenced genital responding. In the context of the times (prior to 1975), *cognitive* was still a dirty word to many and the study of cognitive variables was just starting to become scientifically acceptable. The senior author was one of those who ignored cognitive variables as being not available to empirical study. Two critical events forced me to recognize that cognitive variables played a role in genital responding.

The first was an anecdotal report by Ray Rosen, who was conducting his dissertation on feedback and genital responding in men. Ray noted that a few participants were showing genital responding in the absence of external sexual stimuli. That is, participants were told that after some music stopped there would be a brief silence and then they would be seeing erotic stimuli. During the silence, some males started to get an erection—to no external stimuli of any kind. Perhaps more persuasive was the simple observation that when male participants were told to imagine themselves in an sexual situation while in a lab setting that was totally new to them they showed an increase in penile diameter. In the complete absence of external or self-stimulation of their genitals, most produced genital changes. The finding that fantasy-based genital changes occur in the absence of external sexual stimuli has been reported more formally in the research literature (e.g., Heiman & Hatch, 1980; Smith & Over, 1987). It seemed that there was no reasonable explanation for these findings other than that the genital changes were the result of cognitive processes that we labeled fantasy. There was no conditioning or S-R learning model that could explain these simple yet powerful observations. It then became obvious that examination of cognitive factors was a research area that warranted serious study.

Studies That Examined Genital Responding and Cognitive Variables

To return to the question of the role of cognitive variables in genital responding, we would note that there are a relatively limited number of studies that have directly investigated cognitive variables and genital responding. Among the earliest was a study that we conceptualized as not only a demonstration of cognitive variables at work in genital processes but also as a clear demonstration that a specific cognitive process influences genital responding. Clinical reports suggested that distraction from erotic stimuli and subsequent attending to nonerotic stimuli when in a sexual situation played a central role in failure to respond adequately. I spoke to my colleague Roger Schvaneveldt, asking him how experimental cognitive psychologists studied distraction. He recommended that I look at a paradigm that Posner and Rossman (1965) had developed. In that paradigm, participants are exposed to identical external stimuli but are asked to process those stimuli in cognitive tasks that differ in the amount of attention required. The crucial point is that all participants experienced the same stimulus inputs, while only the difficulty of processing those stimuli was systematically varied. In males, we found (Geer & Fuhr, 1976) a direct relationship between the amount of distraction from erotic stimuli and the amount of genital change elicited by erotic stimuli. Subsequently Adams, Haynes, and Brayer (1985) and Elliot and O'Donohue (1997) replicated in women that distraction reduced genital responding. These studies clearly demonstrated that not only were cognitive variables able to influence genital responding but that it was possible to empirically demonstrate meaningful relationships between such cognitive variables as distraction and genital responding.

As reported by Barlow (1986), the distraction effect has been usefully applied to help our understanding of clinical phenomena. Further work from Barlow's lab has yielded results suggesting that the cause the individual attributed to producing problems with erectile responding affected future sexual functioning (Weisberg, Brown, Wincze, & Barlow 2002). Further, in the work by Barlow and colleagues, it has been shown that expectancies based on false feedback (Bach, Brown, & Barlow, 1999) effect genital responding. We look forward to hearing the paper by Barlow and colleagues in this meeting that will update and expand upon their work on cognition and sexual functioning.

There have been surprisingly few additional studies reported that have examined directly the effect of cognitive factors on genital responding. The work by Eric Koukounas and colleagues stands out as an exception to that generalization. In that work, they examined attentional variables and emotional variables and their effect upon genital responding. They reported that, similar to the previous studies, distraction reduces genital responding while attention to erotic stimuli increases responding. In that work, they manipulated "absorption" of the individual in the erotic stimuli that genital responding increases when the individual is attending to the erotic stimulus (Koukounas & McCabe, 1997, 2001; Koukounas & Over, 1999).

Walter Everaerd and colleagues also have reported a set of studies that directly address cognitive variables in genital responding. In that research, they have found that training participants to differentially process sexual information influenced the level of genital responding (Dekker & Everaerd, 1989.) In a separate study, Janssen, Everaerd, Spiering, and Janssen (2000) reported a study of the effect of priming on automatic processing. The somewhat surprising results showed an effect of priming on genital responding in which genital responses were lower during sexual as compared to neutral trials. However, on a behavioral measure the expected facilitation of responding via priming was found. The findings reflect complex relationships to be found between and among cognitive and genital functioning.

Several studies have examined the role of attention upon genital responding. While it is tempting to conceptualize attention as the other side of the distraction coin, we are reluctant to do so. Attention is not the simple absence of distraction. The variables that effect attention do not necessarily have the reverse effect upon distraction. Koukounas and colleagues (Koukounas & Over, 2001) have reported that genital responding is greater when participants employ participant rather than spectator attentional focus when viewing erotic stimuli. Dekker and Everaerd (1988) reported that genital responses were greater when participants attended to sexual stimuli plus response as contrasted to sexual stimuli alone. Sakheim, Barlow, Beck, and Abrahamson (1984) reported that focusing upon genital cues during low sexual arousal decreased genital responding but increased it during high levels of arousal. These studies, while differing somewhat in outcome, all point to the finding that the level and focus of attention on erotic stimuli influences genital responding. These findings point to the importance, albeit complex, of cognitive factors upon genital responding.

We would note several other studies to reinforce our point that cognitive variables influence genital functioning. Wilson, Niaura, and Adler (1985) reported a study on the role of alcohol on genital responding. They manipulated distraction as had been done in the Geer and Fuhr (1976) study and found a replication particularly under high distraction and high alcohol levels. Alcohol consumption decreased arousal under the high attention demanding condition. They suggest that alcohol has differential effects under different conditions of attentional demand. Beck and Baldwin (1994), studying genital responding in women, found that given instructions to suppress genital responses women were able to do so using a variety of cognitive strategies. I believe our point is well established: cognitive variables do strongly influence genital responding. While many questions still remain, that simple fact to us appears undeniable. Let us now turn our attention to some demonstrations of the role of cognition in sexuality in general.

Some Representative Studies on Cognition in Sexuality That Do Not Include Genital Measures

The success that we had enjoyed borrowing the distraction paradigm from cognitive psychology encouraged us to look further at cognitive psychology for ideas as to where and how to usefully apply concepts and paradigms to help understand sexuality. Others (e.g., Janssen et al., 2000; Treat, McFall, Viken, & Kruschke, 2001) also have suggested the value of studying cognitive processing in sexuality. Rather than bore you with an enumeration of a rather extensive list of projects, we will select a few that illustrate how this enterprise has developed in both our own research and in a few related studies by others. In order to add some order to this enterprise, we will break the list of studies into several general categories. These categories are studies on (i) memory, (ii) the organization of knowledge, and (iii) information processing.

Memory

We begin with memory studies. Memory has always been a central topic in cognitive research. The general information-processing model suggests that information stored in memory is used to guide and direct behavior. It is typically assumed that the memory for events or material is affected by previous memory stores and thus memory data is not only influenced by what is encoded but also by the context within which it is stored. It also is known that retrieval may be biased by different effects, thus also influencing the output from memory stores. We examined the suggestion that in the domain of sexuality what is recalled from memory is influenced by factors in addition to that which is encoded. To explore that argument, Castille and Geer (1989) developed an ambiguous scenario that was presented to participants. The simple experimental manipulation was to vary the title that was presented along with the scenario. In once instance, the title was "Making Love," while in another it was "Horseback Riding." There were, of course, in the scenario no materials directly relevant to either sexual behavior or to horseback riding. The recall protocols reflected the titles presented with the scenarios. In the making love condition, participants recalled, in error, materials reflecting sexual activity. Similarly, under the horseback riding title, participants recalled, again in error, materials relevant to horseback riding. We subtitled the study "Sex is in the eye of the beholder," as our data clearly showed that by biasing the meaning of ambiguous material, participants placed sexual meaning on material that had no sexual content.

In another study, we examined whether or not the sexes differed in their memory for an erotic story. In that study (Geer & McGlone, 1990), we presented the same erotic story to all participants. The story contained sentences that could be identified as having either sexual content, romantic content or neutral content. After a brief delay, we then presented to the participants sentences, some of which had been in the story and some of which had not been in the story. Participants were asked to tell us whether or not the sentence had been in the story. We found clear gender differences. Men more accurately and quickly recognized sentences with sexual content while women more accurately and quickly recognized the romantic sentences. There were no gender differences for neutral sentences. These data made it clear that while hearing the same content, the genders remember different aspects of the story; that is, somehow they process the material differently. It is not yet clear where in the processing sequence the genders differ. Do the genders encode differently, do they have differing previously stored material or do they show a retrieval bias? The answer is not yet clear. We turn our attention next to a series of studies on the organization of knowledge.

Knowledge Organization

One of the central issues in cognitive psychology is how to best represent the organization of information in the cognitive system. How is it that when we are asked, "What is your mother's maiden name?" most of us can answer correctly within a second? How can we so quickly and accurately scan the thousands of words in our lexicon and accurately report the answer? One widely used model of knowledge representation is the network model proposed by Collins and Loftus (1975). In that model of semantic organization, words are conceptualized as being nodes in a network with the links in the net being the representation of the associations between and among words. When a word is presented, say "cat," in a priming paradigm, word cat is activated and all associated (linked) words are in turn activated. When a second word is presented after a prime, say "dog," and if that word had been activated by the priming word, as would be the case in our example, any search for that second word is more quickly resolved than had the second word not been activated by the prime. There are literally hundreds of studies in which priming has been demonstrated. It is important to note that from the network model the meaning of a word is determined by its associative links.

The representation of semantic networks has been a serious problem. A solution proposed by Schvaneveldt and colleagues (Schvaneveldt, 1990) is the use of "Pathfinder." Pathfinder is a program that asks participants to rate the similarity of pairs of words from any domain of interest. From those similarity data, Pathfinder computes, using graph mathematics, the individual's semantic network for the set of presented words. Schvaneveldt presents data that establish the usefulness of Pathfinder in several different contexts. We have applied Pathfinder to the domain of sexuality in several studies. We will briefly describe two of those studies. In the first, we asked the simple question, do the genders differ in their semantic organization of words from the domain of sexuality? From the network perspective, this is asking whether the meaning of sexual words differ between the genders. We presented for similarity ratings four categories of words. They were: sexual words, romantic words, positive words, and negative words. We found that the gender's semantic networks for sexual words differed in several ways. First, using a measure of similarity of networks we found that women's networks were more similar to each other than to men's. Likewise men networks were more similar to each other than to women's. If we accept that the pattern of associates reflects the meaning of words, the same word has somewhat different meanings to the genders. It follows that communication within the genders would be more accurate than communication between the genders. These views are consistent with the suggestions of many, but these data provided the first empirical demonstration of the suggestion.

In addition to the similarity data, other interesting findings emerged. Men had more links between sexual words and positive words than did women. On the other hand, women had more links between romantic words and positive words than did men. In general, the linkage analyses supported the view that explicit sexual material was viewed more positively by men while relationship words are viewed more positively by women. In a follow-up study (Manguno & Geer, 1998), we examined networks yielded by men and women in which the variable of sexual orientation was examined. We found, in disagreement with the stereotypical view that gays are similar to the opposite gender, that both male and female homosexual's networks were more similar to their own gender than they are to the opposite gender. The difference was that the gay male linked more positive words to male genitals than did their heterosexual male peers and the gay female linked more positive words to female genitals that did the contrasting heterosexual females. Our point is that the cognitive model provided the necessary research protocol to examine the question of how the genders differ in their store of sexual knowledge. Without these methodologies we would be saddled with, at best, sheer speculation.

Information Processing

The network findings naturally lead to the question, do the genders differ in the processing of sexual information? The data reported above argue that there are gender differences in the knowledge store. Are there gender differences in cognitive processing that may account for the storage effects? We began this research focus with what we thought was a very simple cognitive paradigm: the lexical decision task. In that task, participants are shown a letter string and their task is to indicate whether or not the string is a word in English. The dependent variable in this task is the decision time, as errors are quite infrequent. In our first study on the lexical decision task (Geer & Bellard, 1996), we identified a phenomena we called SCID: sexual content induced delay. That is, sexual words were identified more slowly by women than men. Further, women were faster in identifying relationship words than sexual words. The genders did not differ in decision time for neutral words. Further work (Geer, 1991a) revealed that when sexual words were grouped into socially acceptable versus unacceptable, the SCID effect was accentuated. Everaerd and colleagues have been exploring the SCID phenomena and have added to our understanding of the limitations and variables that influence it. They have reported (Spiering, Everaerd, & Elzinga, 2002) that SCID seems to function early in the processing sequence in the elicitation emotional response. They report that later on, after the sexual system has been activated, priming by sexual stimuli act to facilitate decisions, functioning as the typical priming stimuli. In as-yet-unpublished work, Spiering, Everaerd, and Laan (personal communication) conclude that men and women cognitively process sexual material similarly, but that they differ in the affective processing of sexual information. Their work examining the SCID phenomena in detail fits well the view noted by Massaro and Cowan (1993), that the information-processing model continues to progress by parsing phenomena into increasingly smaller detailed subprocesses.

With your indulgence, we will use one more example of cognitive research in sexuality that illustrates the increasingly detailed analyses of processes. Cognitive studies have broken attitudes down into the categories Explicit and Implicit (Greenwald, McGhee, & Schwartz, 1998.) We hasten to point out that the distinction between implicit and explicit has been applied to a range of domains in cognitive psychology. As argued by Kihlstrom (1987), "Contemporary research in cognitive psychology reveals the impact of nonconscious mental structures and processes on the individual's conscious experience, thought, and action" (p. 1445). Among these are memory (Schacter & Buckner, 1998; Squire, 1992) and learning (Kihlstrom, Mulvaney, Tobias, & Tobis, 2000). There also is a research literature that argues that attitudes can be placed in this two-dimension system. Explicit attitudes are a phenomena that may be seen as resulting from controlled or conscious processes. On the other hand, "Implicit attitudes are manifest as actions or judgments that are under control of automatically activated evaluation, without the performer's awareness of that causation" (Greenwald, McGhee, & Schwartz, p.1464). Implicit attitudes reflect automatic attitudes and/or emotions that the individual may be unwilling to admit.

Greenwald, McGhee, and Schwartz have developed the Implicit Attitude Test (IAT) to investigate implicit attitudes. They provide convincing data that indicate the effectiveness of the IAT in identifying implicit attitudes. We have borrowed that paradigm to study whether or not the genders differ in implicit attitudes toward sexual material. In a paper to be presented at the IASR convention next week, we will show the well-documented finding (Oliver & Hyde, 1993) that women have more negative explicit attitudes but also that women show automatic or implicit negative attitudes toward sexually implicit stimuli. This work extends the study of explicit and implicit phenomena in sexuality conducted by Everaerd and colleagues using a priming paradigm to investigate implicit effects (Spiering et al., 2002). Our point is that the use of concepts from cognitive psychology has resulted in useful empirical findings that add substantively to our understanding of sexuality.

Some Suggestions for Further Use of Cognitive Psychology

In this section of the paper, we discuss further how cognitive theories and paradigms might enhance the study of gender differences in sexual arousal. Although the benefits of the classic information-processing approach to the study of sexual arousal have been documented (e.g., Geer & Manguno-Mire, 1996), continuing efforts in mainstream contemporary cognitive psychology may provide more benefits. We will present examples of concepts from cognitive psychology that we believe can usefully inform sex research. We do not suggest that this list is exhaustive nor even the most important. It represents only our considerations at this point in time. We identify and discuss five general areas in cognition that may be fruitfully applied: the distinction between controlled and automatic processing, the roles of cognitive distraction and inhibition, monitoring the source of one's processing to appraise and control behavior, the role of schemas and scripts, and the burgeoning field of cognitive neuroscience. We stress that, in some instances, work has already been done in these areas but also that more can be done as newer models and paradigms add even more value. Additionally, many principles and concepts in these separate areas overlap, making the distinction between each fuzzy as opposed to definite.

Controlled versus Automatic Processing

Many have recognized the utility of the proposed dichotomy between controlled and automatic processing introduced in classic cognitive research (e.g., Posner & Snyder, 1975; Schneider & Shiffrin, 1977). Importantly, automatic processes are assumed to operate without awareness, to operate obligatorily upon initiation, and to interfere less with other activities (i.e., to take less processing resources). Controlled processes, in contrast, are generally assumed to operate in conscious awareness, to be under control and therefore modifiable, and to require a finite amount of processing resources.

Two important theoretical issues concerning the relationship between automatic and controlled processing are how the processes interact and how they should be measured. Jacoby (1991, 1998) proposes in his process dissociation model that automaticity and control are independent processes. As such, they sometimes operate in concert and other times in opposition. One can consciously attend to environmental cues that also elicit a congruent automatic response, placing both processes in concert. Or one can consciously divert attentional resources away from the very same environmental cues, pitting control and automaticity against one another (e.g., Geer & Fuhr, 1976). More importantly, Jacoby (1991) argues strongly that no task or behavior is process-pure. In other words, any behavioral response is the product of a mixture of automatic and controlled processes. Therefore, in order to properly estimate the relative contribution of automaticity and control to a given task or behavior, people must be placed in situations that place both processes in concert and in other situations that place both processes in opposition. One cannot devise a single task that purportedly measures "automatic" or "controlled" processing, according to this logic. Rather, one must set up a condition in which restrictions are placed on either type of process, through instructions or other methods, and compare it to a nonrestricted condition to properly estimate the contribution of automaticity and control. We point to this issue to note that investigators who study automatic and/or controlled processing in the belief that these processes do not interact are prematurely pruning the search tree of possibilities.

Consider interference produced in the Stroop (1935) task, in which the speed of naming of the printed color of a word is slowed when the word names a different color (e.g., the word "red" is printed in blue and the subject must quickly produce "blue" as the response). The relatively unpracticed, controlled process of color naming is disrupted by the relatively more practiced, and automatic, task of word reading. Lindsay and Jacoby (1994) argued that these two processes of color naming and word reading are independent processes, which is not a controversial claim, but they also argue that simple reaction time measures of either task are not process pure. Baseline measures of color naming are often indexed by reaction times to control items, which might be color patches, or neutral words printed in various colors. But those stimuli themselves may interfere with color naming. Thus, there is no way to directly map performance on a given task to a unique process. One must, therefore, create a condition in which each process operates in concert and a condition in which each operates in opposition, in addition to manipulating aspects of the environment or instructions to theoretically alter the balance of these relative automatic and controlled contributions to performance. Estimating the relative contribution of each process is done by solving a set of simple algebraic equations.

The distinction between automatic and controlled processing is exemplified in the sexual arousal literature by the finding of response discordance, a dissociation between self-reported ratings and objective physiological response to sexual films (Laan, Everaerd, van Bellen, & Hanewald,

1994). Laan et al. (1994) showed that although genital measures of arousal in women were similar to "man-made" and "woman-made" films, subjective ratings of arousal were substantially higher in response to the "woman-made" films. Spiering, Everaerd, and Laan (personal communication) argued that the perception of sexual stimuli activates implicit memory, leading to the automatic physiological response, whereas the subjective ratings are affected by multiple sources of information available to explicit memory.

According to Jacoby's (1991) process dissociation logic, what is required in this example is a comparison of at least two different conditions to estimate the separate contributions of automatic and controlled processes to either subjective experience or to physiological arousal—one in which the automatic response (i.e., arousal) is congruent with controlled processes and one in which the automatic response is incongruent. For example, one could create a congruent situation by asking participants to focus on their physiological response in making subjective ratings. An incongruent condition might involve asking people to ignore the physiological response when making subjective ratings, or perhaps to think of non-arousal related physiological information. The combination of these conditions, theoretically, could be used to estimate the relative contribution of both automatic and controlled processes in the measurement of either subjective or physiological response. Rather than arguing, for example, that subjective responses are determined by controlled processes, one could estimate the extent to which both automatic and controlled processes each contribute to subjective response.

Distraction and Suppression as Control

The notion of cognitive control highlights the role of attentional distraction and cognitive inhibition and also the subtle difference between them. Distraction, or divided attention, involves the direction of cognitive resources away from some cues and toward others, for example, listening to a conversation while trying to read a book. However, thought suppression, a paradigm used to study inhibition, involves consciously thinking about a concept or cue so as to suppress its influence on behavior (e.g., Wegner, 1994). In practice, thought suppression is achieved simply by asking people not to think about various topics (e.g., sleep or sex) but to report verbally or nonverbally when such thoughts do occur. Under certain conditions, the very act of suppressing a concept makes it ironically more accessible and more likely to affect behavior. Such ironic effects are more likely to occur under conditions of stress or high mental load. Wegner (1994) proposed a model that implicates two processes—an operating process that seeks out mental contents and stimuli consistent with one's goals and a monitoring process that seeks out mental contents and stimuli inconsistent with one's goals. The monitoring process essentially serves as a warning system to indicate that one is about to fail with regard to the desired goal.

According to theory, the operating process demands attentional resources, whereas the monitoring process operates without awareness. Therefore, under conditions of high mental load or stress, the monitoring process can "win out" and produce behaviors inconsistent with one's goals.

For example, Wegner (1994) reported that under certain conditions the goal of falling asleep is easier in the face of considerable distraction. Some people were asked to listen to an audiotape that strongly encouraged them to fall asleep as fast as possible. Others received no such encouragement in the audiotape. Additionally, some subjects also heard restful, New Age music on the audiotape whereas others heard more complex music (a medley of John Philip Sousa marches). The restful music was intended to produce a low mental load and the complex music a high mental load. Under the instruction to fall asleep faster, those receiving the restful music did indeed fall asleep faster than those receiving no such instruction. The operating process was able to do its job and seek out stimuli consistent with the goal of falling asleep. However, those who heard complex music actually fell asleep *slower* when they received the instruction to fall asleep fast, as compared to the condition not receiving the instruction. Presumably, under the high mental load produced by complex music, the operating process was taxed and the monitoring process had a greater impact on behavior by bringing to mind stimuli that distracted one from falling asleep. The operating process was less able to detect these impending distractions and less able to exert control over behavior.

In fact, Wegner and colleagues (Wegner, Shortt, Blake, & Page, 1990) have applied the thought suppression technique to thoughts of sex. Subjects were asked to report whatever came to mind during 3- or 4-minute time periods. In one set of time periods, subjects were told to express thoughts about sex (period 1) and then to suppress thoughts about sex (period 2). In another set of time periods, subjects did the same for the target concept of dancing (do, and then do not, think about dancing). Although they did not measure genital responses, Wegner et al. (1990) did measure skin conductance levels as a general indication of physiological arousal. They found that under both expression periods and suppression periods of thoughts about sex, skin conductance levels deviated from baseline and, most importantly, were no different on average across these periods. However, reported thoughts about sex were fewer and the time spent talking about sex was longer in the suppression condition. Although skin conductance levels did return to baseline toward the end of the suppression period, they began at the same level as compared to the expression condition and remained statistically similar, although nominally lower, throughout the period. The same patterns of behavior resulted even when subjects thought they were reporting their thoughts about sex privately (i.e., not recorded or measured). Moreover, even when the average level of intrusive thoughts dropped near baseline in 30-minute periods (experiment 3), skin conductance levels still spiked when such intrusive thoughts did periodically occur, but only for the exciting thoughts. That is, reports of thoughts about dancing or about the weather did not show the same spikes in skin conductance levels under suppression conditions.

What are the implications of the Wegner et al. (1990) study and of Wegner's (1994) theory of thought control for measures of genital arousal? First, both expressing and suppressing thoughts about sex may be generally arousing, at least in the first few minutes. Second, because of the operation of separate operating and monitoring processes in the theory, perhaps purposefully trying to increase or maintain sexual arousal may backfire under high-load or high-stress conditions, thereby decreasing arousal. Correspondingly, trying to suppress concepts related to sexual arousal may have the unintended consequence of increasing arousal under high-stress conditions. Measurement of genital response under such conditions would be interesting indeed. The work by Bancroft and Janssen (2000) on the role of inhibition in sexuality raises the interesting question as to whether or not inhibition to the sex researcher overlaps with inhibition as studied by the cognitive researcher.

Monitoring the Source of Current Processing

An important issue in current memory research is the role that awareness plays in behavior. Specifically, ongoing behavior is affected by past behavior and experiences, and an awareness of possible sources of influence on behavior promotes interpretation and control over responding. For example, it is well known that processing a stimulus is facilitated if that stimulus has been processed once before, a phenomenon known as priming (e.g., Schacter, 1987). However, people often attribute facilitated processing to sources other than memory; for example, to the clarity of the stimulus (e.g., "that word looks clearer or brighter to me"). The opposite can also occur—unusually fluent processing of a novel stimulus can be attributed to memory instead of to the current processing conditions (Whittlesea, Jacoby, & Girard, 1990). The point here is that one's performance on a task, especially fluent performance, is often attributed to whatever source of influence on behavior is most salient or apparent.

One context in which this might be relevant to studies of sexual arousal is cases when people experience both positive and negative emotions in the same encounter or experience. In other words, to what source do people attribute these subjective feelings? The most obvious alternatives are to either oneself or to a sexual partner (or some other external source), including one's own thoughts or performance, or to physiological feedback. In addition, both physical and subjective reactions can be attributed to these multiple possible sources. These attributional processes might affect subjective experience and/or genital response and perhaps the sometimes reported dissociation between the two. Sex researchers concerned with the source of sexual arousal would be well advised to examine work on source monitoring (Johnson, Hashtroudi, & Lindsay, 1993) as a potential source of both paradigms to study the phenomena and as a source of useful theoretical models to generate testable hypotheses.

The Role of Semantic Memory, Schemas, and Scripts

Semantic memory generally refers to the representation of conceptual knowledge. This includes both associations between concepts (e.g., PALM-TREE or LOVE-JEALOUSY) and more molar knowledge units such as schemas and scripts (Bower, Black, & Turner, 1979; Schank & Abelson, 1977). As mentioned earlier, the ability to measure and compare associative networks has helped us understand many interesting gender differences in the representation of concepts related to sexual arousal and romance. Regarding schemas and scripts, Gagnon and Simon (1973) have noted the importance of scripts related to sexual behaviors and encounters. Geer and coworkers have gone so far as to compare males and females in their representation of a heterosexual encounter (Geer & Broussard, 1990).

What is less clear, however, is how such scripted knowledge is activated and used in the process of a true sexual encounter, or in the processing of a visually or verbally depicted encounter. Deviations from the expectations generated by scripts could certainly have an effect on sexual arousal. A heterosexual encounter may be going well from a male's perspective but not well from the female's perspective, and vice versa. But how such "expectation violations" relate to psychophysiological measures of arousal is unknown. Scripted actions could be developed to be consistent with, or deviate from, the scripts measured in research subjects to determine how deviations affect both subjective and physiological arousal.

Cognitive Neuroscience

The American Psychological Association called the 1990s the "decade of the brain." Although psychophysiological research in sexuality is now decades old, only recently have the newest neuroimaging methods been applied to this area. Positron emission tomography (PET), magnetic resonance imaging (MRI), functional MRI, and recordings of electroencephalographic event-related potentials (ERPs) comprise the techniques of choice in contemporary research. These methods have been applied across many different areas in psychological inquiry, including the study of cognitive, social and clinical psychology. These methods offer the opportunity to measure the brain structures and processes related to both physiological response and subjective experience in sexual arousal. That a section of this conference was given to this very issue is a testament to the fact that the area of cognitive neuroscience may provide insights into the association, or lack of association, between subjective and physiological measures of arousal. The first papers in this conference should make it clear that neuroscience has much to offer sex researchers and cognitive psychologists alike.

Summary

In an overall summary we would like to emphasize several points. First, there can be no serious doubt that cognitive variables influence genital responding and in some aspects the genders differ in this processing. However, we wish to emphasize that we are not saying that only cognitive variables influence genital responding. To ignore biological and experiential variables as important would be foolish. To ignore conditioning and reinforcement in sexuality would be a serious error.

Our second point is that, in general, sex researchers have been guilty of not paying enough attention to cognitive science. We deliberately use the words *cognitive science* as the disciplines of computer science, philosophy, neuroscience, and others have become increasingly linked in multidisciplinary approaches to cognitive psychology's phenomena, theory, and paradigms. Sex research must join in that effort or be left behind in the study of behavior. Geer (1991b) once subtitled a paper "Bringing Sex in from the Cold." In that presentation, it was argued that ignoring the dramatic advances made in cognitive science was leaving sex research behind. That concern is still important more than 15 years later.

One last point relates to what has just been presented concerning cognitive neuroscience. Sex research has always had as an important component an interest in biological variables and events. From hormonal influences to genital responding, sex researchers have been interested in biological variables. As noted above, there has been a beginning of examining sexual phenomena with the new methodologies available from neuroscience. We must expand that research in the domain of sexuality. To ignore the exploding domain of neuroscience in sex research is to invite obsolescence. Interest in biological variables leads rather naturally into consideration of the question, from where did these arise? One cannot ignore genetic factors as the substrate for building physiological structures. Once one admits that we inherit much that determines our physiology, one cannot ignore the role of evolution in that process. The natural alliance between evolution theory with its focus upon reproductive success and sexual behavior warrants our pointing to the confluence of these perspectives. While there are many legitimate concerns over speculations based on evolutionary considerations, the recent trends to generate and successfully test evolutionary hypotheses (e.g., Buss, 1999) demand our research attention and theoretical consideration. Our point is that if we ignore or downplay both cognitive science and the role of genetic variables in sex research, be it genital responding or any other aspect of sexuality, we do so at great risk.

References

Adams, A. E., Haynes, S. N., & Brayer, M. A. (1985). Cognitive distraction in female sexual arousal. *Psychophysiology, 22,* 689–696.

Bach, A. K., Brown, T. A., & Barlow, D. H. (1999). The effects of false negative feedback on efficacy expectancies and sexual arousal in sexually functional males. *Behavior Therapy, 30,* 79–95.

Bancroft, J. & Janssen, E. (2000). The dual control model of male sexual arousal: A theoretical approach to centrally mediated erectile dysfunction. *Neuroscience and Biobehavioral Reviews, 24,* 571–579.

Barlow, D. H. (1986). Causes of sexual dysfunction: The role of anxiety and cognitive interference. *Journal of Consulting and Clinical Psychology, 54,* 140–148.

Beck, J. G., & Baldwin, L. E. (1994). Instructional control of female sexual responding. *Archives of Sexual Behavior, 23,* 665–684.

Bower, G. H., Black, J. B., & Turner, T. (1979). Scripts in memory for text. *Cognitive Psychology, 11,* 177–220.

Buss, D. M. (1999). *Evolutionary psychology: The new science of the mind.* Boston: Allyn and Bacon.

Castille, C. O., & Geer, J. H. (1989). Ambiguous stimuli: Sex is in the eye of the beholder. *Archives of Sexual Behavior, 22,* 131–143.

Collins, A. M., & Loftus, E. F. (1975). A spreading activation theory of semantic processing. *Psychological Review, 82,* 407–428.

Dekker, J., & Everaerd, W. (1988). Attentional effects on sexual arousal. *Psychophysiology, 25,* 45–54.

Dekker, J., & Everaerd, W. (1989). A study suggesting two kinds of information processing of the sexual response. *Archives of Sexual Behavior. 18,* 435–447.

Elliot, A. N., & O'Donohue, W. T. (1997). The effects of anxiety and distraction on sexual arousal in a nonclinical sample of heterosexual women. *Archives of Sexual Behavior, 26,* 607–624.

Gagnon, J. H., & Simon, W. (1973). *Sexual conduct: The social sources of human sexuality.* Chicago: Aldine.

Geer, J. H. (1991a, August). *Erotic, romantic, and neutral words used as primes and targets in a lexical decision task.* Poster presented at International Academy of Sex Research meetings, Barre, Ontario, Canada.

Geer, J. H. (1991b, July). *The information processing approach in helping understand sexuality and its disorders.* Invited paper presented at International Congress: Stress, Anxiety and Emotional Disorders, Braga, Portugal.

Geer, J. H., & Bellard, H. (1996). Sexual content induced delays in unprimed lexical decisions: Gender and context effects. *Archives of Sexual Behavior, 25,* 379–395.

Geer, J. H., & Broussard, D. B. (1990). Scaling heterosexual behavior and arousal: Consistency and sex differences. *Journal of Personality and Social Psychology, 58,* 664–671.

Geer, J. H., & Fuhr, R. (1976). Cognitive factors in sexual arousal: The role of distraction. *Journal of Consulting and Clinical Psychology, 44,* 238–243.

Geer, J. H., & Manguno-Mire, G. (1996). Gender differences in cognitive processes in sexuality. *Annual Review of Sex Research, 7,* 211–245.

Geer, J. H., & McGlone, M. S. (1990). Sex differences in memory for erotica. *Cognition and Emotion, 4,* 71–78.

Greenwald, A. G., McGhee, D. E., & Schwartz, J. L. K. (1998). Measuring individual differences in implicit cognition: The implicit association test. *Journal of Personality and Social Psychology, 74,* 1464, 1480.

Heiman, J. R., & Hatch, J. P. (1980). Affective and physiological dimensions of male sexual response to erotica and fantasy. *Basic and Applied Social Psychology, 1,* 315–327.

Jacoby, L. L. (1991). A process dissociation framework: Separating automatic from intentional uses of memory. *Journal of Memory and Language, 30,* 513–541.

Jacoby, L. L. (1998). Invariance in automatic influences of memory: Toward a user's guide for the process-dissociation procedure. *Journal of Experimental Psychology: Learning, Memory, and Cognition, 24,* 3–26.

Janssen, E., Everaerd, W., Spiering, M., & Janssen, J. (2000). Automatic processes and the appraisal of sexual stimuli: Toward an information processing model of sexual arousal. *Journal of Sex Research, 37,* 8–23.

Johnson, M. K., Hashtroudi, S., & Lindsay, D. S. (1993). Source monitoring. *Psychological Bulletin, 114,* 3–28.

Kihlstrom, J. F. (1987). The cognitive unconscious. *Science, 4821,* 1445–1452.

Kihlstrom, J. F., Mulvaney, S., Tobias, B. A., & Tobis, I. P. (2000). The emotional unconscious. In G. H. Bower, J. P. Forgas, J. F. Kihlstrom, & P. M. Niedenthal (Eds.), *Counterpoint: Cognition and emotion.* New York: Oxford University Press.

Koukounas, E., & McCabe, M. (1997). Sexual and emotional variables influencing sexual response to erotica. *Behaviour Research and Therapy, 35,* 221–230.

Koukounas, E., & McCabe, M. (2001). Sexual and emotional variables influencing sexual response to erotica: A psychophysiological investigation. *Archives of Sexual Behavior, 30,* 393–408.

Koukounas, E., & Over, R. (1999). Allocation of attentional resources during habituation and dishabituation of male sexual arousal. *Archives of Sexual Behavior, 28,* 539–552.

Koukounas, E., & Over, R. (2001). Habituation of male sexual arousal: Effects of attentional focus. *Biological Psychology, 58,* 49–64.

Laan, E., Everaerd, W., van Bellen, G., & Hanewald, G. (1994). Women's sexual and emotional responses to male- and female-produced erotica. *Archives of Sexual Behavior, 23,* 153–169.

Lindsay, D. S., & Jacoby, L. L. (1994). Stroop process dissociations: The relationship between facilitation and interference. *Journal of Experimental Psychology: Human Perception and Performance, 20,* 219–234.

Manguno, G. M., & Geer, J. H. (1998). Network knowledge organization: Do knowledge structures of sexual and emotional information reflect gender or sexual orientation? *Sex Roles, 39,* 705–729.

Massaro, D. W., & Cowan, N. (1993). Information processing models: Microscopes of the mind. *Annual Review of Psychology, 44,* 383–425.

Oliver, M. B., & Hyde, J. S. (1993). Gender differences in sexuality: A meta-analysis. *Psychological Bulletin, 114,* 29–51.

Posner, M. I., & Rossman, E. (1965). Effect of size and location of informational transforms upon short-term retention. *Journal of Experimental Psychology, 70,* 496–505.

Posner, M. I., & Snyder, C. R. R. (1975). Facilitation and inhibition in the processing of signals. In P. M. A. Rabitt & S. Dormec (Eds.), *Attention and performance: Vol. 5.* New York: Academic Press.

Sakheim, D., Barlow, D. H., Beck, J. G., & Abrahamson, D. J. (1984). The effect of an increased awareness of erectile cues on sexual arousal. *Behaviour Research and Therapy, 22,* 151–158.

Schacter, D. L. (1987). Implicit memory: History and current status. *Journal of Experimental Psychology: Learning, Memory, and Cognition, 13,* 501–518.

Schacter, D. L., & Buckner, R. L. (1998). On the relations among priming, conscious recollection, and intentional retrieval: Evidence from neuroimaging research. *Neurobiology of Learning and Memory, 70,* 284–303.

Schank, R. C., & Abelson, R. (1977). *Scripts, plans, goals, and understanding.* Hillsdale, N.J.: Erlbaum.

Schneider, W., & Shiffrin, R. M. (1977). Controlled and automatic human information processes: I. Detection, search, and attention. *Psychological Review, 84,* 1–66.

Schvaneveldt, R. W. (1990). *Pathfinder associative networks: Studies in knowledge organization.* Norwood, N.J.: Ablex.

Smith, D., & Over, R. (1987). Does fantasy-induced sexual arousal habituate? *Behaviour Research and Therapy, 25,* 477–485.

Spiering, M., Everaerd, W., & Elzinga, E. (2002). Conscious processing of sexual information: Interference caused by sexual primes. *Archives of Sexual Behavior, 31,* 159–164.

Squire, L. R. (1992). Memory and the hippocampus: A synthesis from findings with rats, monkeys, and humans. *Psychological Review, 99,* 195–231.

Stroop, J. R. (1935). Studies of interference in serial verbal reactions. *Journal of Experimental Psychology, 18,* 643–662.

Treat, T. A., McFall, R. M., Viken, R. J., & Kruschke, J. K. (2001). Using cognitive science methods to assess the role of social information processing in sexually coercive behavior. *Psychological Assessment, 13,* 549–565.

Wegner, D. M. (1994). Ironic processes of mental control. *Psychological Review, 101,* 34–52.

Wegner, D. M., Shortt, J. W., Blake, A. W., & Page, M. S. (1990). The suppression of exciting thoughts. *Journal of Personality and Social Psychology, 58,* 409–418.

Weisberg, R. B., Brown, T. A., Wincze, J. P., & Barlow, D. H. (2002). Causal attributions and male sexual arousal: The impact of attributions for a bogus erectile difficulty on sexual arousal, cognitions, and affect. *Journal of Abnormal Psychology, 110,* 324–334.

Whittlesea, B. W. A., Jacoby, L. L., & Girard, K. (1990). Illusions of immediate memory: Evidence for an attributional bias for feelings of familiarity and perceptual quality. *Journal of Memory and Language, 29,* 716–732.

Wilson, G. T., Niaura, R., & Adler, J. L. (1985). Alcohol, selective attention and sexual arousal in men. *Journal of Studies on Alcohol, 46,* 107–115.

Discussion Paper

RAYMOND C. ROSEN

It's an honor to be serving as discussant on this paper for many reasons, not the least of which is the mentorship that I received from Jim throughout my career. Jim and Walter have developed this area of research into one of the most intriguing and challenging aspects of sexual psychophysiology. And I think Jim's work, also, is paradigmatic, in the sense of keeping sexual psychophysiology in line with advances in cognitive neuroscience generally and maintaining the flow from cognitive neuroscience into sexual psychophysiology. A general comment that I raised earlier in the meeting and would like to return to is how general processes of cognitive science or cognitive psychology can be applied to specific phenomena within sexuality or sexual arousal. The challenge for me is to explain how sexual responses are different, as well as similar, to other phenomena in cognitive psychology. Can you say there's anything that's different about the way sexual stimuli are handled or how memory or attentional processes for sexual stimuli might in any way be different? If indeed there are no differences, then I think that's an interesting conclusion and worth thinking further about. On the other hand, we need to consider possible differences as well as similarities.

The studies of network linkages that Jim began to discuss at the end of his presentation are intriguing. These studies are particularly interesting since there's a rich literature in cognitive neuroscience using that type of methodology and Jim has picked up one particularly interesting aspect. Two simple questions I would like to raise: Firstly, can we make any inferences or speculate about the underlying mechanisms involved? For example, are there any hints in the data that this might be a biological phenomenon; are male and female brains in any sense "prewired" for this difference? Do we have information that these network linkage differences might be due to underlying biological differences in male/female brains, or is it more likely due to cultural factors or social learning differences? A second point I would like to bring up is whether men and women are responding differently to sexual stimuli, versus other kinds of "gender-linked" activities or behaviors? For example, have these studies been replicated with activities such as sports or child rearing? Another general comment, and it's been a thread throughout the meeting, is the need for more studies of external validity. I am concerned in regard to both Walter's and Jim's work that these may be artificial or contrived paradigms that may be lacking in "real-world" application. They may be ideal approaches for isolating some of these phenomena and examining them in a laboratory setting. But, if we're to make generalizations to "real-world behavior," we need to know more about the predictive or external validity of these paradigms to actual behavior. Is there any work, Jim, from your group or other work, that allows us to make statements about how predictive these effects will be of behavior outside the laboratory? This is a key issue that needs further exploration.

The Sexual Psychophysiology of Sexual Orientation

MEREDITH L. CHIVERS AND J. MICHAEL BAILEY

Psychophysiological assessment of sexual orientation was initially developed in the 1950s for the purpose of objectively detecting atypical sexual interests. The Czechoslovakian army, wishing to prevent gay men from enlisting, hired Dr. Kurt Freund to develop an objective method to assess the sexual orientation of new male recruits. His research showed that men's sexual preferences could be assessed by examining relative penile volume-increases to stimuli from preferred and nonpreferred sexual categories; in the case of sexual orientation the categories varied by gender. Freund expanded his research program from assessing gender preferences in adult men (1963–1975) to include assessing age preferences in adult men (1967–1996). He showed that both gender (sexual orientation) and age (pedophilia) preferences could be objectively assessed by examining patterns of penile erection to categories of relevant stimuli.

The relationship between sexual arousal patterns and sexual orientation in women could be investigated with the invention of the vaginal photoplethysmograph in the 1970s (Geer, Morokoff, & Greenwood, 1974; Sintchak & Geer, 1975). It was not until the 1980s, however, that two studies (Steinman, Wincze, Sakheim, Barlow, & Mavissakalian, 1981; Wincze & Qualls, 1984) directly examined this relationship and concluded that women also showed arousal patterns congruent with their stated sexual orientation. More recent research, however, has reported a sex difference in the specificity of sexual response, with respect to sexual orientation, suggesting that models of sexual orientation that assume strong relationships between sexual attractions, sexual response, and sexual orientation, as had been observed in males, may not be applicable to females (Chivers, 2005).

In this paper, we review the research examining the sexual psychophysiology of sexual orientation in men, women, and postoperative male-to-female transsexuals (transsexual women, hereafter), and briefly review other psychophysiological studies that relate to the assessment of sexual orientation. We then discuss how this research complements and extends our understanding of sex differences in sexual orientation and extends our

458

knowledge of sex differences in sexual response, with an emphasis on female sexuality.

A Note on the Assessment of Sexual Orientation

How sexual orientation is assessed is influenced by how the researcher defines the construct of sexual orientation and by the nature of the research question regarding the relationship between sexual response and sexual interests. The common definition of sexual orientation seems straightforward —relative sexual interest in males and in females; however, reliable assessment of sexual orientation requires an understanding of how manifestations of sexual orientation—that is, sexual behavior, sexual fantasies, sexual attractions, and sexual identity—are related, and issues surrounding the measurement of each, particularly for women (for a discussion see Mustanski, Chivers, & Bailey, 2002).

The most commonly used self-report items for assessing sexual orientation are the Kinsey Scales. These are unidimensional 7-point scales assessing relative direction of sexual attractions, fantasies, and behaviors to same- and opposite-sexed individuals; higher scores indicate greater same-sex interest and lower scores greater opposite-sex interest (Kinsey, Pomeroy, & Martin, 1948). In general, there is a strong relationship between the direction of sexual attractions, sexual fantasies, and sexual behaviors in men (Diamond, 1993); thus, using any of these variables to determine a man's sexual orientation is usually not problematic. This is not the case for women, who have shown less agreement between sexual fantasy and sexual attraction (Bailey, Dunne, & Martin, 2000) and between sexual behavior, sexual attraction, and sexual fantasy (Laumann, Gagnon, Michael, & Michaels, 1994). This suggests that, among women, there is greater discordance among these indices of sexual orientation than among men.

Similarly, self-reported sexual identity may not accurately represent sexual orientation in women, such that a woman who defines her sexuality as lesbian is assumed to only have sexual contact with other women, or a heterosexual woman is assumed to never fantasize sexually about other women. Defining sexual orientation using self-identity is problematic in women because of the lower concordance among indices of sexual orientation—sexual fantasy, behaviors, and attractions—and self-identification as heterosexual, bisexual, or lesbian (Kinsey, Pomeroy, Martin, & Gebhard, 1953; Laumann et al., 1994; Rust, 1992). In men, this is generally not problematic, as the agreement between attraction, fantasy, behavior, and sexual identity is typically strong (Chivers, 2003). Researchers are therefore encouraged to measure multiple indices of sexual orientation, in addition to reporting of sexual identity, especially when conducting research on females.

Assessment of Sexual Orientation Using Sexual Psychophysiology

Sexual arousal is believed to be another manifestation of sexual orientation, in that a person is expected to show significantly greater sexual response to stimuli that depict that person's preferred category of sexual targets or sexual activities. *Category specificity* refers to sexual arousal that is highly dependent on characteristics that are prototypical of a preferred category of sexual targets or activities. With respect to sexual orientation, category specificity describes a pattern of sexual arousal that is highly dependent upon gender features of a sexual stimulus. A category-specific pattern of sexual response would manifest as little to no sexual response to stimuli depicting the nonpreferred gender and greatest sexual response to stimuli depicting the preferred gender. This model for understanding the relationship between sexual arousal and sexual orientation does not, however, accurately describe female sexual response and sexual orientation, as will be discussed later.

Men

As discussed earlier, Freund (1963) developed phallometric assessment to objectively assess sexual preferences in men. Based on their erectile responses to slides of nude males or females, Freund (1963) correctly classified all 65 heterosexual men and 48 of 58 gay men. He replicated his results (Freund, Langevin, Cibiri, & Zajac, 1973, 1974) and concluded that gay and heterosexual men could be discriminated based on their penile responses to male or female stimuli. Other researchers have also replicated these results (Barr & McConaghy, 1971; Langevin, Stanford, & Block, 1983; Sakheim, Barlow, Beck, & Abrahamson, 1985), demonstrating that the relationship between sexual orientation and genital sexual arousal is strong, that men exhibit a category-specific pattern of sexual arousal, and that sexual orientation can be objectively assessed in men using genital responses as an indicator of relative sexual attractions.

Freund's studies used slide stimuli depicting males and females accompanied by audio recordings describing sexual interactions with the depicted individuals. Male sexual orientation can also be reliably discriminated using sexual responses to films of female-female (lesbian) and male-male (gay) copulation (Chivers, Rieger, Latty, & Bailey, 2004; Chivers & Bailey, 2005; Chivers & Blanchard, 2006; Mavissakalian, Blanchard, Abel, & Barlow, 1975; Sakheim et al., 1985). Male-male and female-female copulation films are homogeneous with respect to the gender of depicted persons, whereas female-male copulation films (heterosexual films) present both male and female targets, and genital responses to heterosexual films do not discriminate between gay and heterosexual men (Chivers et al., 2004; Mavissakalian et al., 1975; Sakheim et al., 1985). Men's self-reported sexual arousal also demonstrates category-specificity: Men typically do not report sexual arousal to nonpreferred sexual stimuli (Chivers et al., 2004; Mavissakalian et al., 1975; Sakheim et al., 1985; Steinman et al., 1981).

A few researchers have examined the question of whether bisexual men show a "bisexual" pattern of sexual arousal, that is, genital and subjective arousal to both male and female categories of sexual stimuli. McConaghy and Blaszczynski (1991) measured genital sexual arousal to slides of nude men and women in 20 men with atypical sexual preferences (e.g., pedophilia, exhibitionism, bondage, and fetishism), and the men who identified as bisexual showed arousal to both female and male sexual stimuli. It is unclear, however, whether these results would generalize to bisexual men who did not also have atypical sexual preferences. Tollison, Adams, and Tollison (1979) examined genital and self-reported sexual arousal in heterosexual, bisexual, and homosexual men to slides of nude males and females and to films of male-male and female-male copulation. Bisexual-identified men were indistinguishable from homosexual-identified men in their genital arousal patterns, which were specific to male stimuli, but they did report a pattern of subjective sexual response consistent with their sexual identity. Heterosexual men showed category-specific genital and self-reported arousal responses. Finally, Rieger, Chivers, and Bailey (2005) investigated genital and subjective sexual arousal to films of male-male versus female-female copulation in heterosexual, bisexual, and homosexual men. Bisexual men, as a group, did not show a "bisexual" genital sexual arousal pattern. Most bisexual men responded with significantly greater genital response to one gender category or another, though they reported subjective sexual arousal to both male and female stimuli. Heterosexual and homosexual men showed category-specific self-reported and genital sexual responses. We interpreted these results to mean that male bisexuality is not associated with a distinct pattern of genital sexual arousal, and that male genital sexual arousal tends to be, on average, specific to male or to female sexual stimuli, but not to both.

One concern regarding the interpretation of male sexual psychophysiological research is men's ability to consciously manipulate their sexual responses. Some men can control their genital arousal when they are motivated to do so (Adams, Motsinger, McAnulty, & Moore, 1992; Freund, 1963). It is unlikely, however, that category-specific sexual response in males is explained by conscious suppression of arousal to nonpreferred sexual stimuli because there is evidence that men cannot consciously augment their responses to nonpreferred stimuli: Neither heterosexual nor homosexual men are able to increase their erections to nonpreferred sexual stimuli, even when motivated to do so (Adams et al.). This suggests that men are not suppressing their genital responses to nonpreferred stimuli because they would cease to inhibit their responses when sufficiently motivated to do so, as in the Adams et al. study. Although conscious inhibition of response to nonpreferred sexual stimuli is unlikely to explain category-specific responding, it is still possible that inhibition occurs at earlier levels of stimulus processing, such as during automatic or unconscious appraisal of preferred and nonpreferred sexual stimuli (e.g., Janssen, Everaerd, Spiering, & Janssen, 2000).

Women

Do women also exhibit a category-specific pattern of sexual arousal? Research examining the sexual psychophysiology of female sexual orientation first conducted in the 1980s proposed that women's self-reported and genital arousal was category specific; however, a close examination of those results suggests otherwise. More recent research contradicts these early conclusions and suggests that female genital response is nonspecific and self-reported sexual arousal is category specific.

Schmidt (1975) examined women's self-reported arousal ratings to same- and opposite-sex sexual stimuli in the laboratory and their self-reported frequency of masturbation, orgasm, and sexual activity the day after viewing these stimuli. Women's responses were not significantly different between types of sexual stimuli viewed. All women reported high arousal in the lab, and similar levels of sexual activity and orgasm after the experiment, regardless of whether the film was same- or opposite-sex. Schmidt stated, "these data. . . . probably result from greater inhibitions in adult men against same-sex stimulation and/or a greater 'bisexual' capacity in women" (p. 361). Wilson and Lawson (1978) measured heterosexual women's arousal to female sexual stimuli in the context of an alcohol expectancy study. Although they did not directly compare arousal to female-male and female-female stimuli, examination of the reported means reveals comparable levels of genital response to both types of stimuli. Blackford, Doty, and Pollack (1996) investigated subjective sexual arousal in heterosexual, bisexual, and lesbian women to film stimuli depicting female-male penile-vaginal intercourse and female-female oral sex. Women reported patterns of sexual arousal that reflected their sexual identity. Chivers and Bailey (2000) reported that bisexual women, similar to heterosexual and lesbian women, demonstrated nonspecific self-reported and genital arousal responses to films of male-male, female-male, and female-female couples copulating, suggesting that bisexual women show a nonspecific pattern of sexual arousal.

Two studies conducted in the 1980s directly addressed the relationship between arousal patterns and sexual orientation in women. Steinman et al. (1981) examined subjective and genital arousal in 8 heterosexual women and 8 heterosexual men in response to films of male-male, female-female, and female-male copulation. The authors reported that women were most sexually aroused (genitally and subjectively) to the female-male stimuli, but this conclusion is not supported by analyses showing a significant difference between categories of sexual stimuli. The authors did not report means or standard deviations for genital or subjective responses, so effect sizes could not be calculated. Examining the figures, however, it appears as if women's subjective and genital responses to female-male films were not substantially higher than genital or subjective responses to female-female films or genital response to male-male films. The results for men suggest that their genital and subjective sexual responses exhibited category specificity.

A second study conducted by Wincze and Qualls (1984) investigated the sexual arousal patterns of 8 lesbian women and 8 gay men. The authors reported that women showed higher subjective arousal and experienced higher genital arousal when viewing films depicting female-female sex compared to female-male and male-male copulation and stated, "both groups showed the greatest genital and subjective responding to the films of their stated sexual preference" (p. 368). By examining the effect sizes for the difference between lesbian women's preferred and nonpreferred sexual stimuli, we conclude that only women's self-reported sexual arousal is category specific. Comparing effect sizes for genital and subjective sexual responses to female-female versus female-male films (Cohen's $d = .01$ and $d = .41$, respectively), and effect sizes for arousal to female-female versus male-male films (Cohen's $d = .18$ and $d = 1.04$, respectively), women's genital arousal patterns were not category specific because the effect sizes for the difference between preferred and nonpreferred sexual stimuli were small. Women's subjective arousal patterns did show category specificity but were still smaller than gay men's sexual responses (subjective arousal to female-female vs. female-male stimuli, $d = 1.21$). The genital effect for women is much smaller than for gay men in the same study; the effect size for the difference between arousal to male-male and to female-female films was large, at 1.44 in men. Also, the data presented in the paper showed that lesbians experienced their highest genital sexual arousal to films depicting group sex (content and gender of people unspecified), rather than female-female sex, a finding that was not discussed by the researchers.

More recently, Laan, Sonderman, and Janssen (1995) measured subjective and genital arousal in 23 self-identified lesbian and heterosexual women to erotic film clips depicting lesbian and heterosexual sex. No effect of sexual orientation was observed for either subjective or genital arousal: Both lesbians and heterosexual women, whether self-identified or based on their Kinsey scores, experienced highest subjective and genital arousal to female-male films, suggesting again that women do not show a category-specific pattern of sexual response.

We have conducted a series of studies (Chivers et al., 2004) designed to further elucidate the relationship between women's sexual interests and sexual arousal patterns and to rule out alternative explanations for the findings we obtained. We assessed genital and self-reported sexual arousal to films of male-male, female-female, and female-male couples engaging in sexual activity in a sample of 20 lesbian and 23 heterosexual women (determined using relative Kinsey sexual attraction scores) recruited from the community. Similar to Laan et al. (1995), we observed nonspecific sexual responses; heterosexual and lesbian women showed genital responses to all sexual stimuli and these responses were not significantly different from each other, but they did report a somewhat category-specific pattern of sexual arousal. The male sexual arousal literature suggests discrimination by sexual orientation is better using arousal to a sexually explicit, purely female stimulus (typically a film of female-female copulation) and arousal to a sexually explicit, purely male stimulus (typically a film of male-male copulation; Mavissakalian et al., 1975; Sakheim et al., 1985), therefore we examined this association in women. By calculating the difference score obtained by subtracting responses to the male-male copulation from the female-female copulation stimuli and correlating this with Kinsey sexual attraction score, we obtained a small sexual orientation effect for genital response, $r = .26$, and a somewhat larger effect for self-reported arousal, $r = .42$. These correlations translate into relatively small effect sizes: Less than 7% of the variability in genital response and 18% of the variability in self-reported arousal could be accounted for by relative sexual attractions. We concluded that women demonstrated a nonspecific pattern of sexual response.

After obtaining these results, we wished to rule out competing explanations for the pattern of nonspecific sexual response in women. As ascertainment biases are commonly observed in female sexual psychophysiology research (e.g., Morokoff, 1986), we wanted to replicate the nonspecificity observed in the community sample in a sample of undergraduate women recruited in a manner to reduce volunteer biases. We examined the sexual arousal patterns of younger and less sexually experienced heterosexual women ($n = 29$) and detected the same nonspecific pattern of genital arousal we found in the sample of community volunteers. Moreover, the variables that differentiated women who chose to participate in the study from those who declined to participate (number of male sexual partners, masturbation frequency, frequency of orgasm during masturbation, preferred frequency of sex, and frequency of erotica use) were not significantly related to category-specific responding. We surmised that our results generalized to other women.

Another possible explanation for the nonspecific sexual response we had observed in women was the nature of our sexual stimuli. It is possible that films of couples copulating were not effective at generating a differential pattern of sexual response: By examining genital and self-reported arousal responses in a sample of 46 men using the same stimuli, we could compare male and female arousal patterns and determine whether our sexual stimuli were capable of eliciting a category-specific pattern of sexual arousal in men. As expected, men showed category-specific patterns of genital and subjective arousal, ruling out the possibility that the stimuli used with women were not capable of eliciting a specific sexual arousal pattern. Correlations between sexual arousal to male-male versus female-female stimuli and Kinsey sexual attraction scores were very high: for genital arousal, $r = .88$, and for self-reported arousal, $r = .92$. Seventy-seven percent of the variability in genital response and 85% of the variability in self-reported response was explained by sexual orientation in our male sample, a stark contrast to the values obtained for the female sample. Our stimuli were therefore capable of eliciting category-specific sexual responses in males, suggesting nonspecific responding in women is not explained by stimulus problems.

Last, although women's genital sexual arousal can be reliably measured (e.g., Janssen, 2002; Laan & Everaerd, 1995), research supporting its construct validity is less abundant than for male phallometric measures (Janssen, 2002). Before concluding that women do not have a category-specific sexual arousal pattern, it would be desirable to demonstrate that the vaginal photoplethysmograph can detect such a pattern. Lawrence, Latty, Chivers, and Bailey (2005) studied the patterns of sexual arousal in 11 transsexual women (5 preferring men and 6 preferring women) following sex reassignment surgery and in 72 natal women. All transsexual participants displayed category-specific genital and self-reported sexual arousal. Five transsexual women preferring men showed greater genital and subjective responses to male than to female stimuli, while 6 transsexual women preferring women showed the opposite pattern. We concluded that transsexual women display category-specific genital arousal even after undergoing sex reassignment surgery.

The sex difference[1] in the specificity of sexual arousal reported in this series of studies is remarkable for two reasons. First, natal women's sexual responses were not congruent with their self-reported sexual attractions, unlike what is usually observed in men. Second, all women showed significant increases in genital response to all films of couples copulating, consistent with Laan and Everaerd's (1995) speculation that female genital response is automatic. We had shown that cues other than gender influenced women's sexual responses. Some other feature of the films of couples copulating was sexually arousing to women and initiated an automatic genital response that may not correspond with a woman's self-reported sexual arousal, or with her relative sexual attractions to women and to men.

We speculated that the common aspect of our films was sexual activity. To test this hypothesis, we presented heterosexual women and men with film stimuli depicting sexual activity without a plausible sexual partner (a film of female and male bonobo chimpanzees engaging in repeated penile-vaginal intercourse; Chivers & Bailey, 2005). Women, but not men, experienced genital responses to the nonhuman sexual stimuli. We also replicated the results reported in Chivers et al. (2004) by finding category-specific sexual arousal in 18 heterosexual men and nonspecific sexual arousal in 18 heterosexual women, using the same human sexual stimuli as Chivers et al. At this point, we had observed nonspecific sexual responses in three samples of natal women and category-specific responses in two samples of biological males. We concluded that, collectively, our results illustrated a sex difference in the specificity of sexual response, with respect to sexual orientation.

There was a concern that lingered, however, regarding the nature of the stimuli to which women responded nonspecifically; all studies that showed this effect used film clips depicting sexual interactions between couples (e.g., Chivers et al., 2004; Chivers & Bailey, 2005; Laan et al., 1995; Steinman et al., 1981; Wilson & Lawson, 1978; Wincze & Qualls, 1984). In each of these studies, the gender of the people depicted was confounded with sexual activity. We could not yet reasonably conclude from these studies that the female sexual response system does not differentially respond to the preferred gender, because specificity of arousal responses to gender features only, and not to gender features presented within the context of sexual activity, had not yet been systematically examined in women.

Since the Kinsey Sexual Psychophysiology meeting in July 2003, the first author has continued this program of research and recently reported results of a study that disentangled the effects of gender cues and sexual activity cues on women's sexual responses (Chivers & Blanchard, 2006). By using stimuli that depict solitary, nude females and males engaging in nonsexual (exercise) or solitary sexual activity (masturbation), and the same copulation stimuli used by Chivers et al. (2004), we examined the effects of stimulus gender (male or female) and sexual activity (none/exercise, masturbation, or couples copulating) on self-reported and genital sexual arousal of 20 homosexual and 27 heterosexual women, and 17 homosexual and 27 heterosexual men.

Heterosexual women demonstrated nonspecific genital responses to the copulation films, replicating previous research using these stimuli, and also showed nonspecific self-reported and genital responses to the films of males and females exercising and masturbating. Males showed category-specific genital and self-reported responses to all types of sexual activity. Homosexual women, in contrast, showed a very different pattern of responses. Nonspecific genital responses to the copulation films were found for homosexual women, replicating Chivers et al. (2004) and Laan et al. (1995). In response to films of solitary males and females, however, homosexual women demonstrated category-specific genital response; that is, they showed significantly greater response to the female than male stimuli. Homosexual women's genital responses to the solitary male films were not significantly greater than their responses to a control stimulus.

Two important insights follow from this latest study. First, nonspecificity of genital responses was found in heterosexual but not homosexual women; women with predominantly same-sex attractions did show category-specific genital and self-reported sexual responses to films of solitary women and men, while women with predominantly opposite-sex attractions did not. Second, the nonspecificity observed by Laan et al. (1995) and Chivers et al. (2004) in homosexual women was probably related to an effect of sexual activity that obscured category-specific response patterns. Explicit depictions of sexual activity may produce an automatic genital response (Chivers, 2005) that overrides category-specific response in women, whereas preferred gender cues are necessary for strong genital responses to manifest in men, even when they are presented in the context of explicit sexual acts. We interpreted these data to suggest that a difference in the relative potency of visual gender and sexual activity features to generate sexual arousal responses exists for women and men.

Psychophysiological Assessment of Sexual Orientation Using Other Methodologies

The sex difference in the specificity of sexual arousal observed using sexual psychophysiology converges with research examining the neural correlates of sexual response in women and men to preferred and nonpreferred sexual stimuli. Brain imaging studies have reported category-specific activation patterns for heterosexual and gay men, in response to still images of male and female nudes (Bailey, Safron, & Reber, 2006; Wallen, 2006), whereas nonspecific responses have been observed in heterosexual women (Wallen, 2006).

Cognitive paradigms for studying sexual interests, such as viewing time and choice reaction time (see Seto, this volume, for a description of these methodologies) have also demonstrated sex differences in response specificity. Wright and Adams (1999) reported the exact same pattern of results as Chivers and Blanchard (2006), with respect to solitary male and female stimuli: Gay and heterosexual men's and lesbian women's responses discriminated between images of nude males and females, whereas heterosexual women's did not. Gaither (2004), too, found a similar pattern: Heterosexual men's viewing time and choice reaction time responses discriminated between female and male sexual stimuli, whereas heterosexual women's did not.

Studies examining electroencephalography (EEG) responses to sexual stimuli also suggest that men's responses discriminate between preferred and nonpreferred genders, whereas women show a nonspecific response. Contingent negative variation (CNV), an EEG response thought to reflect anticipation of pleasurable stimuli, is specific to preferred gender in men and nonspecific in women (Costa, Braun, & Birbaumer, 2003; Costell,

Lunde, Kopell, & Wittner, 1972). Costa et al. reported that heterosexual women showed increases in CNV to both preferred (male) and nonpreferred (female) sexual stimuli, whereas heterosexual men showed increased CNV to preferred stimuli only.

Discussion

Category-specific sexual response is a phenomenon that is more characteristic of males. In this review, we have presented data suggesting a strong association between sexual orientation and sexual responses in men who are sexually attracted to sexually mature women or men. We note that category-specific sexual responding is also observed among other groups of males with less typical sexual orientations, such as those with pedophilic sexual interests (for a review, see Seto, in press), or fetishism (Freund, Seto, & Kuban, 1997).

The female sexual response system, however, is differently organized. The nonspecificity of female sexual response suggests sexual arousal is not a strong determinant of sexual interests among women, because women respond to both preferred and nonpreferred sexual stimuli but report significantly greater sexual interest in one gender or another. Recent models of female sexual interests describe female sexual orientation as a more variable phenomenon relative to males' more categorical expression of sexual interests (Peplau & Garnets, 2000). Greater variability among the psychological and behavioral aspects of female sexual orientation, compared to males, supports this model: Men report greater exclusivity of same- or opposite-sex sexual experiences (Kinsey et al., 1948; Kinsey et al., 1953; Laumann et al., 1994; Rust, 1992); the correlation between self-reported sexual attractions and actual sexual behaviors is much higher and positive in men (Bailey et al., 2000); men show greater temporal stability of their sexual identity than women (Diamond, 2000a, 2000b, 2003; Kinnish, Strassberg, & Turner, 2005; Savin-Williams & Diamond, 2000); and the distribution of sexual attractions is bimodal for men—that is, almost exclusively toward the opposite or same-sex—and unimodal for women, implying less exclusivity of relative sexual attractions in women (Bailey et al., 2000). Diamond (2000a, 2000b) reported that women's first awareness of same-sex sexual attractions more often emerged from an emotionally intense attachment to another woman, whereas men report that sexual arousal to same- or opposite-sex persons was a more important source of information about their sexual attractions (Bell, Weinberg, & Hammer-smith, 1981; Savin-Williams & Diamond, 2000). The specificity of sexual responses, with respect to sexual orientation, is one of several aspects of sexual psychology that demonstrate a similar pattern, wherein females demonstrate less specificity. Intraindividual flexibility among female sexual attractions, identity, attitudes, behavior, and the specificity of sexual arousal may be an emergent property of a generally more plastic female mating psychology, compared to that of males (Baumeister, 2000; Chivers, 2005).

Baumeister, Catanese, and Vohs (2001) have proposed that the flexibility observed in female sexuality is likely related to a weaker female sex drive. Baumeister and colleagues argued that a weaker female sex drive allows for greater influence of external factors on determining the direction and expression of female sexuality. Male sexuality may not be so easily controlled by external factors, likely because the male sex drive is more persistent. Category-specific sexual attractions and sexual responses may be related to a higher sex drive. Higher sex drives may mean greater awareness of sexual response and responsivity to sexual stimuli, greater interest in seeking sexual gratification, and therefore more directing of mating effort toward particular categories of sexual stimuli and, in theory, greater number of sexual contacts. In men, category-specific arousal may be important to the formation of sexual preferences by directing sexual interests toward reinforcing sexual experiences. For women, whose sex drive is, on average, lower, who experience relatively lower awareness of genital responding (Laan & Janssen, this volume), and for whom sexual responses are not category specific, mating effort would not be similarly directed and reinforced. Women's sexual choices may not be motivated by sexual responses to external sexual stimuli but other variables such as cultural expectations (Baumeister & Twenge, 2002) or romantic attachments (Diamond, 2000a, 2000b).

If women's sex drive were as high as men's, would a category-specific pattern of arousal emerge? Indirect evidence suggests not. Lippa (2006, in press) reported that lesbian women and both gay and heterosexual men described greater sexual interest in their preferred gender as their self-reported sex drive increased; heterosexual women, however, reported greater sexual interest in both women and men as their sex drive increased. The implication of these data is that sex drive is not directly related to specificity of response. Instead, sex drive may activate, in women, a predisposition that is otherwise unexpressed (sexual responsiveness to other women) rather than directing sexual attractions toward one gender or another.

Nonspecificity of sexual response may be more characteristic of heterosexual than homosexual women because initial results suggest that women with predominantly same-sex attractions do show a category-specific pattern of response to films of solitary women and men (Chivers & Blanchard, 2006). If this result is replicated, we might propose that similarities between lesbian women's and gay and heterosexual men's sexual response patterns indicate a common developmental factor, such as prenatal androgens (for a review, see Mustanski et al., 2002).

Nonspecificity also implies that the gender features depicted in a visual sexual stimulus are not strong determinants of sexual response in women. This raises the question of what is "sexual" about sexual stimuli? Some have posited that sexual meanings emerge from processing of sexual cues, and this in turn activates physical and psychological sexual responses (Van Lunsen & Laan, 2004); however, *what* sexual cues or features generate this response has not been described. The sex and sexual orientation differences in sexual psychophysiology discussed in this paper provide clues as to the types of features capable of inducing a sexual response and suggest these features may differ for women and for men. For example, Chivers and Blanchard (2006) have proposed that sexual activities are more salient to female sexual response, whereas males respond differentially to preferred gender features. Using an experimental paradigm similar to those employed in studies of sexual orientation, sexual psychophysiologists could gain more insight into the features of sexual stimuli that make them "sexual" and how individual differences, such as sexual orientation, influence what is considered sexual by whom.

Conclusions

Female and male sexuality differ in many important ways, and the specificity of sexual response is among these sex differences. On average, males demonstrate category-specific sexual responses, whereas, on average, females do not. If the results of Chivers and Blanchard (2006) showing category-specific responding among homosexual women are replicated, objective assessment of female sexual interests using sexual psychophysiology is theoretically possible, provided researchers use sexual stimuli that contain fewer sexual activity cues than films of couples copulating.

The research on specificity of sexual arousal also suggests that the features that elicit sexual responses are also sexually dimorphic, such that males are more responsive to gender features, whereas females are more responsive to sexual activity features, at least with respect to genital responses to visual sexual stimuli. Considering this evidence, Chivers and Blanchard (2006) propose that the female sexual response system, at least among heterosexual women, is not oriented to respond differentially to one gender or another. That alternate methodologies, such as brain imaging, EEG, and behavioral studies of sexual orientation have obtained similar patterns of results supports the conclusion that the male and female sexual response and attraction systems are differently organized.

Note

1. We use the term *sex difference* instead of *gender difference* because category-specific arousal patterns were observed in biological males, regardless of chosen gender (e.g., transsexual women).

References

Adams, H. E., Motsinger, P., McAnulty, R. D., & Moore, A. L. (1992). Voluntary control of penile tumescence among homosexual and heterosexual subjects. *Archives of Sexual Behavior, 21*, 17–31.

Bailey, J. M., Dunne, M. P., & Martin, N. G. (2000). Genetic and environmental influences on sexual orientation and its correlates in an Australian twin sample. *Journal of Personality & Social Psychology, 78*, 524–536.

Bailey, J. M., Safron, A., & Reber, P. J. (2006, July). *Neural correlates of sexual arousal in heterosexual and homosexual men.* Invited presentation for the 32nd meeting of the International Academy of Sex Research (IASR), Amsterdam, the Netherlands.

Barr, R. F., & McConaghy, N. (1971). Penile volume changes to appetitive and aversive stimuli in relation to sexual orientation and conditioning performance. *British Journal of Psychiatry, 119*, 377–383.

Baumeister, R. F. (2000). Gender differences in erotic plasticity: The female sex-drive as socially flexible and responsive. *Psychological Bulletin, 126*, 347–374.

Baumeister, R. F., Catanese, K. R., & Vohs, K. D. (2001). Is there a gender difference in strength of sex drive? Theoretical views, conceptual distinctions, and a review of relevant evidence. *Personality and Social Psychology Review, 5*, 242–273.

Baumeister, R. F., & Twenge, J. M. (2002). Cultural suppression of female sexuality. *Review of General Psychology, 6*, 166–203.

Bell, A. P., Weinberg, M. S., & Hammersmith, S. K. (1981). *Sexual preference: Its development in men and women.* Bloomington, Ind.: Alfred C. Kinsey Institute of Sex Research.

Blackford, L., Doty, S., & Pollack, R. (1996). Differences in subjective arousal in heterosexual, bisexual, and lesbian women. *Canadian Journal of Human Sexuality, 5*, 157–167.

Chivers, M. L. (2003). *A sex difference in the specificity of sexual arousal.* Unpublished doctoral dissertation. Northwestern University, Evanston, Illinois.

Chivers, M. L. (2005). Leading comment: A brief review and discussion of sex differences in the specificity of sexual arousal. *Sexual and Relationship Therapy, 4*, 377–390.

Chivers, M. L., & Bailey, J. M. (2000). *Genital and subjective sexual arousal in heterosexual, bisexual and lesbian women.* Poster presented at the 26th annual meeting of the International Academy of Sex Research (IASR), Paris, France.

Chivers, M. L., & Bailey, J. M. (2005). A sex difference in features that elicit genital response. *Biological Psychology, 70*, 115–120.

Chivers, M. L., & Blanchard, R. (2006). *Do women have a "sexual" orientation? Insights from sexual psychophysiology.* Invited paper for the 32rd meeting of the International Academy of Sex Research (IASR), Amsterdam, the Netherlands.

Chivers, M. L., Rieger, G., Latty, E., & Bailey, J. M. (2004). A sex difference in the specificity of sexual arousal. *Psychological Science, 15*, 736–744.

Costa, M., Braun, C., & Birbaumer, N. (2003). Gender differences in response to pictures of nudes: A magnetoencephalographic study. *Biological Psychology, 63*, 129–147.

Costell, R. M., Lunde, D. T., Kopell, B. S., & Wittner, W. K. (1972). Contingent negative variation as an indicator of sexual object preference. *Science, 177,* 718–720.

Diamond, L. M. (2000a). Passionate friendships among adolescent, sexual-minority women. *Journal of Research on Adolescence, 10,* 191–209.

Diamond, L. M. (2000b). Sexual identity, attractions, and behavior among young sexual-minority women over a 2-year period. *Developmental Psychology, 36,* 241–250.

Diamond, L. M. (2003). What does sexual orientation orient? A biobehavioral model distinguishing romantic love and sexual desire. *Psychological Review, 110,* 173–192.

Diamond, M. (1993). Homosexuality and bisexuality in different populations. *Archives of Sexual Behavior, 22,* 291–310.

Freund, K. (1963). A laboratory method for diagnosing predominance of homo- or hetero-erotic interest in the male. *Behaviour Research and Therapy, 1,* 85–93.

Freund, K., Langevin, R., Cibiri, S., & Zajac, Y. (1973). Heterosexual aversion in homosexual males. *British Journal of Psychiatry, 122,* 163–169.

Freund, K., Langevin, R., Cibiri, S., & Zajac, Y. (1974). Heterosexual aversion in homosexual males: A second experiment. *British Journal of Psychiatry, 125,* 177–180.

Freund, K., Seto, M. C., & Kuban, M. (1997). Frotteurism and the theory of courtship disorder. In D. R. Laws & W. O'Donohue (Eds.), *Sexual deviance: Theory, assessment, and treatment* (pp. 111–130). New York: Guilford Press.

Gaither, G. A. (2004, November). *Test-retest reliability and discriminant validity of Choice Reaction Time and Viewing Time as measures of sexual interest.* Paper presented at the 46th annual meeting of the Society for the Scientific Study of Sexuality (SSSS), Orlando.

Geer, J. H., Morokoff, P., & Greenwood, P. (1974). Sexual arousal in women: The development of a measurement device for vaginal blood volume. *Archives of Sexual Behavior, 3,* 559–564.

Janssen, E. (2002). Psychophysiological measures of sexual response. In M. W. Wiederman & B. E. Whitley (Eds.), *Handbook for conducting research on human sexuality* (pp. 139–171). Mahwah, N.J.: Erlbaum.

Janssen, E., Everaerd, W., Spiering, M., & Janssen, J. (2000). Automatic processes and the appraisal of sexual stimuli: Toward an information processing model of sexual arousal. *Journal of Sex Research, 37,* 8–23.

Kinnish, K. K., Strassberg, D. S., & Turner, C. W. (2005). Sex differences in the flexibility of sexual orientation: A multidimensional retrospective assessment. *Archives of Sexual Behavior, 34,* 173–184.

Kinsey, A. C., Pomeroy, W. B., & Martin, C. E. (1948). *Sexual behavior in the human male.* Bloomington: Indiana University Press.

Kinsey, A. C., Pomeroy, W. B., Martin, C. E., & Gebhard, P. H. (1953). *Sexual behavior in the human female.* Philadelphia: Saunders.

Laan, E., & Everaerd, W. (1995). Determinants of female sexual arousal: Psychophysiological theory and data. *Annual Review of Sex Research, 6,* 32–76.

Laan, E., Sonderman, J., & Janssen, E. (1995). *Straight and lesbian women's sexual responses to straight and lesbian erotica: No sexual orientation effects.* Poster presented at 21st annual meeting of the International Academy of Sex Research (IASR), Provincetown, Massachusetts.

Langevin, R., Stanford, A., & Block, R. (1983). The effect of relaxation instructions on erotic arousal in homosexual and heterosexual males. *Behavior Therapy, 6,* 453–458.

Laumann, E. O., Gagnon, J. H., Michael, R. T., & Michaels, S. (1994). *The social organization of sexuality: Sexual practices in the United States.* Chicago: University of Chicago Press.

Lawrence, A., Latty, E., Chivers, M. L., & Bailey, J. M. (2005). Measuring sexual arousal in postoperative male-to-female transsexuals using vaginal photoplethysmography. *Archives of Sexual Behavior, 34,* 135–145.

Lippa, R. A. (2006). Is high sex drive associated with increased sexual attraction to both sexes? It depends on whether you are male or female. *Psychological Science, 17,* 46–52.

Lippa, R. A. (in press). The relation between sex drive and sexual attraction to men and women: Cross-cultural findings for heterosexual, bisexual, and homosexual men and women. *Archives of Sexual Behavior.*

Mavissakalian, M., Blanchard, E. B., Abel, G. C., & Barlow, D. H. (1975). Responses to complex erotic stimuli in homosexual and heterosexual males. *British Journal of Psychiatry, 126,* 252–257.

McConaghy, N., & Blaszczynski, A. (1991). Initial stages of validation by penile volume assessment that sexual orientation is distributed dimensionally. *Comprehensive Psychiatry, 32,* 52–58.

Morokoff, P. J. (1986). Volunteer bias in the psychophysiological study of female sexuality. *Journal of Sex Research, 22,* 35–51.

Mustanski, B., Chivers, M. L., & Bailey, J. M. (2002). A review and critique of the evidence for a biological basis of human sexual orientation. *Annual Review of Sex Research, 13,* 89–140.

Peplau, L. A., & Garnets, L. D. (2000). A new paradigm for understanding women's sexuality and sexual orientation. *Journal of Social Issues, 56,* 329–350.

Rieger, G., Chivers, M. L., & Bailey, J. M. (2005). Sexual arousal patterns of bisexual men. *Psychological Science, 16,* 579–584.

Rust, P. C. (1992). The politics of sexual identity: Sexual attraction and behavior among lesbian and bisexual women. *Social Problems, 39,* 366–386.

Sakheim, D. K., Barlow, D. H., Beck, J. G., & Abrahamson, D. J. (1985). A comparison of male heterosexual and male homosexual patterns of sexual arousal. *Journal of Sex Research, 21,* 183–198.

Savin-Williams, R. C., & Diamond, L. M. (2000). Sexual identity trajectories among sexual-minority youths: Gender comparisons. *Archives of Sexual Behavior, 29,* 607–627.

Schmidt, G. (1975). Male-female difference in sexual arousal and behavior during and after exposure to sexual explicit stimuli. *Archives of Sexual Behavior, 4,* 353–365.

Seto, M. C. (in press). *Understanding pedophilia and sexual offending against children: Theory, assessment, and intervention.* Washington, D.C.: American Psychological Association.

Sintchak, G., & Geer, J. H. (1975). A vaginal plethysmograph system. *Psychophysiology, 12,* 113–115.

Steinman, D. L., Wincze, J. P., Sakheim, D. K., Barlow, D. H., & Mavissakalian, M. (1981). A comparison of male and female patterns of sexual arousal. *Archives of Sexual Behavior, 10,* 529–547.

Tollison, C. D., Adams, H. E., & Tollison, J. W. (1979). Cognitive and physiological indices of sexual arousal in homosexual, bisexual, and heterosexual males. *Journal of Behavioral Assessment, 1,* 305–314.

Van Lunsen, R., & Laan, E. (2004). Genital vascular responsiveness and sexual feelings in midlife women: Psychophysiologic, brain, and genital imaging studies. *Menopause, 11,* 741–748.

Wallen, K. (2006). *Functional imaging evidence of sex differences in response to opposite and same-sexed nudes.* Invited paper for the 32nd meeting of the International Academy of Sex Research (IASR), Amsterdam, the Netherlands.

Wilson, G. T., & Lawson, D. M. (1978). Expectancies, alcohol, and sexual arousal in women. *Journal of Abnormal Psychology, 87*(3), 358–367.

Wincze, J. P., & Qualls, C. B. (1984). A comparison of structural patterns of sexual arousal in male and female homosexuals. *Archives of Sexual Behavior, 13*(4), 361–370.

Wright, L. W., & Adams, H. E. (1999). The effects of stimuli that vary in erotic content on cognitive process. *Journal of Sex Research, 36,* 145–151.

Psychophysiological Assessment of Paraphilic Sexual Interests

MICHAEL C. SETO

Introduction

The paraphilias, from the Greek words for love (*philia*) beyond the usual (*para*), are atypical sexual interests. Atypical sexual interests, by definition, are rare in the general population. Conceptually, they can be divided into two categories, atypical target interests and atypical activity interests (see Freund, Seto, & Kuban, 1996). In the former category, the focus of sexual thoughts, fantasies, and urges are targets other than sexually mature humans; in the latter category, the activities are highly unusual for individuals who prefer sexually mature humans. A target or activity is considered to be a preference when it is critical for sexual gratification.

According to the most recent edition of the *Diagnostic and Statistical Manual of Mental Disorders* (*DSM-IV-TR*), the primary nosological system used by mental health professionals in Canada and the United States, the diagnostic criteria for paraphilias are (i) recurrent and intense sexually arousing fantasies, urges, or behavior directed toward body parts or non-human objects, suffering or humiliation of either partner in the sex act, or sexual activity with a nonconsenting person; and (ii) these fantasies, urges, or behavior cause clinically significant distress or impairment in functioning (American Psychiatric Association, 2000). The *DSM-IV-TR* specifically mentions a number of the more common paraphilias: fetishism (nonliving object), frotteurism (touching or rubbing against nonconsenting person), pedophilia (prepubescent child), masochism (being humiliated, bound, or otherwise made to suffer), sadism (psychological or physical suffering of others), and transvestic fetishism (cross-dressing). Outside of Canada and the United States, the disorders of sexual preference listed in the 10th revision of the *International Classification of Mental and Behavioural Disorders* are quite similar in content to the disorders described by *DSM-IV-TR* (ICD-10; World Health Organization, 1997). Neither the *DSM-IV-TR* nor ICD-10 specifically list biastophilia, defined as a paraphilic interest in nonconsenting, coercive sex that may be conceptually different than sadism, which can involve a consenting partner (Lalumière, Quinsey, Harris, Rice, & Trautrimas, 2003). Atypical sexual interests can be viewed as psychopathological to the extent that they interfere with reproductively viable sexual behavior (see Seto, 2002; Spitzer & Wakefield, 2002).

Paraphilias and Sexual Offending

Paraphilic sexual interests have an important role in many contemporary theories of sexual offending (e.g., Lalumière & Quinsey, 1996; Quinsey & Lalumière, 2001; Seto & Barbaree, 1997). Many sex offenders with child victims are thought to be motivated by a sexual preference for prepubescent children and many rapists are thought to be motivated by a sexual preference for nonconsenting, forced sex. Some sex offenders may be motivated by both pedophilic and biastophilic interests, because they show substantial sexual arousal to depictions of nonconsenting, coercive sexual activity involving children (Chaplin, Rice, & Harris, 1995). Similarly, many, if not most, men charged with indecent exposure (or an equivalent criminal offense) are thought to be motivated by peodeiktophilia (exhibitionism).

In this paper, I will briefly review common assessment methods that are available for paraphilic sexual interests and then focus in much greater detail on phallometry, the psychophysiological assessment of erectile response. I will then discuss the implications of phallometric research findings for theory and clinical practice with sex offenders and suggest future directions for research in this area.

Assessment Methods

Self-Report

CLINICAL INTERVIEWS

Sexual histories are typically obtained through clinical interviews. Questions pertain to age of onset of sexual thoughts, fantasies, and behavior, initiation of sexual intercourse, number and type of sexual partners and relationships, and use of pornography or other sexually arousing stimuli. More specific questions pertain to thoughts, feelings, fantasies, urges or behavior regarding paraphilic targets or activities, and sexual offenses. For example, individuals who acknowledge having frequent, detailed fantasies about having sex with children, collect and masturbate to media depicting children, or engage in repeated sexual acts involving children are likely to be pedophilic. Clinical interviews also include questions that can help clinicians rule out other explanations for thoughts, urges, fantasies, or behavior involving children; for example, ego-dystonic thoughts about molesting a child are sometimes reported by individuals with obsessive-compulsive disorder.

Although self-report is informative, there are potential problems with recall biases and other cognitive effects in gathering data on sexual behavior in this way (see Wiederman, 2002, for a review). In forensic contexts, offender self-report is very vulnerable to dissimulation because of the obvious nature of the questions and the legal or social sanctions that offenders may face in acknowledging illegal sexual behavior. Whether it is a result of self-deception or an effort to present oneself in a socially desirable manner, many sex offenders minimize or rationalize their sexual interests and behavior (e.g., Kennedy & Grubin, 1992).

QUESTIONNAIRES

A number of published questionnaires have been used to assess paraphilic sexual interests, including the Clarke Sexual History Questionnaire–Revised (Langevin & Paitche, 2001) and Multiphasic Sex Inventory II (Nichols & Molinder, 1984). The Clarke Sex History Questionnaire–Revised is intended for adult respondents and contains items tapping different aspects of conventional and paraphilic sexuality, including early childhood experiences, sexual dysfunction, fantasies, exposure to pornography, and behavior. The Multiphasic Sex Inventory II has versions for adult men, women, and adolescent boys and girls, and also contains items tapping different aspects of conventional and paraphilic sexuality. In addition, the Multiphasic Sex Inventory contains scales tapping antisocial behavior and personal history.

There are a few published studies regarding the psychometric properties of the Clarke Sexual History Questionnaire (Curnoe & Langevin, 2002; Langevin, Lang, & Curnoe, 2000) and Multiphasic Sex Inventory (Kalichman, Henderson, Shealy, & Dwyer, 1992; Simkins, Ward, Bowman, & Rinck, 1989), but there are few published data on the discriminative and predictive validity of these questionnaires among sex offenders. Like interviews, these questionnaires are potentially vulnerable to self-report biases. Both the Clarke Sexual History Questionnaire and the Multiphasic Sex Inventory contain validity scales, but the ability of these scales to detect lying has not been established and suspected lying means only that the results of the questionnaire cannot be interpreted.

Behavioral Measures

SEXUAL OFFENSE CHARACTERISTICS

Sexual victim characteristics that are empirically related to paraphilic sexual interests. For adult sex offenders with child victims, these characteristics include having more sexual victims, having very young victims, having male victims, and having unrelated victims. Adult offenders with many of these characteristics are much more likely to be pedophilic in their sexual arousal to depictions of children than individuals with few of these characteristics (Seto & Lalumière, 2001). Recent studies have demonstrated that the same sexual victim characteristics have validity for adolescent sex offenders with child victims (L. Ennis, personal communication, February 26, 2003; Madrigano, Curry, Fedoroff, & Bradford, 2003; Seto, Murphy, Page, & Ennis, 2003) and that scores on this behavioral proxy scale predict recidivism among adult sex offenders with child victims (Seto, Harris, Rice, & Barbaree, 2004).

The relevant correlates of biastophilic sexual interests among rapists are less clear. Possible candidates include number of sexual victims, the presence of other paraphilic interests such as exhibitionism, excessive use of force during the commission of the sexual assault, humiliation of the victim, and a relatively indiscriminate selection of victims (e.g., having very young and very old victims, having both related and unrelated victims).

A potential problem with using proxy variables such as victim characteristics is that first-time offenders may not yet have a history that reflects their level of paraphilic sexual interests. However, a recent study found that the proxy scale developed by Seto and Lalumière (2001) correlated with recidivism among first-time offenders as well as it did for repeat offenders, in two different samples (Seto et al., 2004).

Psychophysiological Measures

POLYGRAPHY

Polygraphy is a psychophysiological method for assessing changes in heart rate, blood pressure, skin conductance, and respiration while subjects are asked specific questions about their behavior. Polygraphy is not a method for directly assessing sexual interests; instead, it is a method for assessing the veracity of self-reported sexual interests. There are two main types of polygraph test: the control question test and the guilty knowledge test. In the control question test, subjects are asked relevant questions about their behavior (such as their sexual offense history or their involvement in potentially risky activities such as spending time alone with children) and control questions about neutral topics. It is assumed in this test that deceptive individuals will react more strongly to relevant questions than control questions. In the guilty knowledge test, subjects are asked questions about the specific details of a crime that are thought to be known only to investigators and the person who committed the crime. It is assumed in this test that subjects will respond more strongly to questions containing relevant information about the crime than to control questions.

The control question test is more commonly used than the guilty knowledge test in the polygraphic assessment of sex offenders. More than half of the probation and parole agencies responding to a nationwide American survey reported regularly using polygraph tests to monitor the treatment and supervision compliance of sex offenders living in the community (English, Jones, Pasini-Hill, Patrick, & Cooley-Towell, 2000). In different versions of the control question test, offenders are questioned about their past offenses, officially unknown victims, sexual thoughts and fantasies, and current behavior.

Some research suggests that offenders who undergo polygraph testing report more victims and offenses than are officially known (Ahlmeyer, English, McKee, & English, 2000; Emerick & Dutton, 1993; Hindman & Peters, 2001). Unfortunately, there is little methodologically strong research on polygraph testing, and there is a great deal of controversy over the accuracy of polygraph testing (see National Research Council, 2003, for a recent review). There is some empirical support for the validity of the guilty knowledge test, but this test is unlikely to be of much assistance in monitoring treatment and supervision compliance. The accuracy of polygraph testing as it is commonly practiced is not well established.

It is likely that polygraph testing can increase disclosure through its function as a bogus pipeline technique (see Roese & Jamieson, 1993, for a review). Subjects may reveal more information because they believe testing can detect deception, whether or not it actually can do so. There is a risk, however, that some subjects may make "false confessions" or be identified as deceptive because of their generally high levels of anxiety about the testing. This is a professional and ethical concern because important decisions, including reincarceration, are based in part on the outcomes of polygraph tests.

VIEWING TIME

A promising psychophysiological measure for use with sex offenders is unobtrusively measured viewing time, sometimes referred to as visual reaction time, which correlates well with self-reported sexual interest and phallometric responding in samples of nonoffending volunteers recruited from the community. The basic viewing time procedure involves showing a series of pictures depicting children and adults of both sexes; these pictures can depict clothed, semi-clothed, or nude figures. Subjects are either asked to examine the pictures to answer later questions, or they are asked to rate each picture as they proceed on a number of attributes. Subjects are instructed to proceed to the next picture at their own pace and are presumed to be unaware that the key dependent measure is the amount of time they spend looking at each picture.

A number of studies have demonstrated that unobtrusively recorded viewing time is correlated with self-reported sexual interests among community volunteers (Quinsey, Ketsetzis, Earls, & Karamanoukian, 1996; Quinsey, Rice, Harris, & Reid, 1993; but not Gaither, 2001). Viewing time can distinguish sex offenders with male child victims from those who do not have any male victims (Abel, Huffman, Warberg, & Holland, 1998), and several studies have shown that adult sex offenders with child victims can be distinguished from other men by the amount of time they spend looking at pictures of children relative to pictures of adults (Harris, Rice, Quinsey, & Chaplin, 1996), or in combination with questionnaire responses (Abel, Jordan, Hand, Holland, & Phipps, 2001; Abel, Lawry, Karlstrom, Osborn, & Gillespie, 1994). However, Smith and Fischer (1999) were not able to replicate this result in a study of adolescent sex offenders and nonoffenders with viewing time but without the questionnaire component, and Barboza-Whitehead (2001) found that a viewing time measure did not discriminate adolescent sex offenders who denied committing their sexual offenses from those who admitted to their offenses. No published studies have yet demonstrated that scores on viewing time measures, whether alone or in combination with self-report, predict recidivism among sex offenders.

A potential problem for viewing time measures is that they may become vulnerable to faking once it is widely known that viewing time is the key variable of interest. Also, it is not clear how nonexplicit visual stimuli can be used to assess sexual interests in coercive sex or other illegal sexual activities. One test developer has claimed that a measure based on a combination of viewing time and offender self-report can assess sexual interests in biastophilia and sadism (URL page retrieved on March 21, 2003: www.abelscreen.com/Product_Information.html), but there are no peer-reviewed studies as yet demonstrating the discriminative or criterion-related validity of viewing time measures for these paraphilias.

PHALLOMETRY

Phallometry involves the measurement of penile responses to stimuli that systematically vary on the dimensions of interest, such as the age and sex of the figures in a set of slides depicting female children, male children, female adults, and male adults. Phallometry was developed by Kurt Freund, who showed that it could reliably discriminate between homosexual and heterosexual men (Freund, 1963). Responses are recorded as increases in either penile circumference or penile volume; bigger increases in circumference or volume are interpreted as evidence of greater sexual arousal to the presented stimulus. Circumferential devices, typically a mercury-in-rubber strain gauge placed over the mid-shaft of the penis, are the most commonly used phallometric device. Changes in the conductance of the mercury reflect changes in penile circumference and can be calibrated to give a precise measure of penile erection. Penile response is considered to be specifically sexual, unlike other psychophysiological responses such as pupillary dilation, heart rate, and skin conductance (Zuckerman, 1971). Phallometric assessment of penile responses correlate significantly with a combination of viewing time and self-report described in the previous section (Letourneau, 2002).

Sexual interests are optimally reported in terms of relative responding to the category of interest; for example, the response to pictures of prepubescent children minus the response to pictures of adults—more positive scores indicate greater sexual interest in children. Relative responses are more informative than absolute responses because relative responses take individual responsivity into account. Responsivity can vary for a variety of reasons, including the man's age, health, and the amount of time since he last ejaculated. For example, the observation that an individual exhibits a 10 mm increase in penile circumference in response to pictures of children is more meaningful when we know whether he exhibits a 5 mm or 20 mm increase in response to pictures of adults. The first pattern of responses are from someone who is generally less responsive in the laboratory but is nonetheless twice as aroused by pictures of children compared to pictures of adults, indicating a sexual preference for children; the second pattern of responses are from someone who is generally more responsive in the laboratory but who is twice as aroused by pictures of adults compared to pictures of children, indicating a sexual preference for adults. Empirical studies comparing known groups of sex offenders with men who have not committed sexual offenses find that indices of relative responding are better at discriminating groups than levels of absolute responding. Similarly, empirical studies find that indices of relative responding are better at predicting sexual recidivism than levels of absolute responding (see below). Recommendations for stimulus content, test procedure, and data analysis can be found in Lalumière and Harris (1998) and Quinsey and Lalumière (2001).

Phallometry has been used for a variety of purposes, including research on sexual orientation, sexual dysfunctions, and the cognitive processes underlying sexual arousal (see other papers in this volume). Phallometry has also been used extensively to study paraphilic sexual interests.

Discriminative validity. Phallometry can reliably distinguish between groups of sex offenders against children and men who have not committed sexual offenses against children (e.g., Barbaree & Marshall, 1989; Freund & Blanchard, 1989) and between groups of rapists and nonrapists (see Lalumière & Quinsey, 1994, for a quantitative review; see Lalumière et al., 2003, for a recent update). Other investigators have shown that phallometry can distinguish men who admit to sadistic fantasies, cross-dress, or expose their genitals in public from men who do not (Freund et al., 1996; Marshall, Payne, Barbaree, & Eccles, 1991; Seto & Kuban, 1996). Reviewers of the scientific literature conclude that phallometrically measured sexual interests are the most consistently identified distinguishing characteristics of sex offenders, in contrast to other variables that have been studied, such as empathy, social skills, and general psychopathology (see Quinsey & Lalumière, 2001).

As with other psychological or psychophysiological tests, group discrimination using phallometry is not perfect; the distributions of phallometric scores for sex offenders and men who have not committed sexual offenses overlap (for exceptions, see Chaplin et al., 1995; Rice, Chaplin,

Harris, & Coutts, 1994). At the level of individual diagnosis, the sensitivity of phallometric tests, defined as the proportion of sex offenders identified as paraphilic on the basis of their phallometric responses, can be calculated after setting a suitable cut-off score (there is no "gold standard" for identifying a pattern of sexual arousal as paraphilic). This is a very conservative approach because not all sex offenders would be expected to be paraphilic. Given the highly negative consequences of being identified as paraphilic, conservative cut-off scores associated with high specificities should be used; specificity is the percentage of nonoffenders who would be identified as having nonparaphilic sexual interests.

Using a cut-off score of greater sexual arousal to rape than to consenting sex, the specificity of phallometry is approximately 90% and the sensitivity is 60% across studies of rapists using stimuli depicting consenting and nonconsenting sex (Lalumière et al., 2003). In a sample of 147 sex offenders with unrelated child victims, using a cut-off score with 97.5% specificity, sensitivity was 50% using stimuli depicting children and adults (Freund & Watson, 1991). Because sensitivity values are lower than the specificity values, the presence of paraphilic responding is more informative than its absence.

The discriminative validity of phallometry could be increased in several ways. In their meta-analysis, Lalumière and Quinsey (1993) found that stimulus sets that included more exemplars of brutal and graphic sexual violence produced greater discrimination, and therefore higher sensitivity values around 70%. Using standardized scores to calculate indices of relative responding and using indices based on differences in the responses to different stimulus categories also increase discrimination (Harris, Rice, Quinsey, Chaplin, & Earls, 1992). The addition of a semantic tracking task that requires offenders to push buttons when they see violent or sexual content reduces faking and subsequently increases discriminative validity for both sex offenders with child victims and rapists (Harris, Rice, Chaplin, & Quinsey, 1999; Proulx, Côté, & Achille, 1993; Quinsey & Chaplin, 1988). Regardless of the level of accuracy in individual diagnosis, relative responding can be used to rank sex offenders, and relative responding rather than diagnosis is predictive of sexual reoffending.

Predictive validity. A recent meta-analysis of seven studies, with a combined sample size of almost 5,000 sex offenders, found that phallometrically measured sexual interest in children was the single best predictor of sexual recidivism by sex offenders among the variables that were studied; its correlation with sexual recidivism ($r = .32$) was higher than risk variables such as offender age, number of prior offenses, and antisocial personality (see Hanson & Bussière, 1998, for a quantitative review). There is also some evidence that relative sexual interest in violent stimuli predicts sexual recidivism among rapists in studies that have used well-validated stimulus sets (Quinsey, Lalumière, Rice, & Harris, 1995; Rice, Harris, & Quinsey, 1990).

Reliability. A curious aspect of the research on phallometry is an apparent contradiction in the findings regarding its reliability and validity. Traditional internal consistency and test-retest analyses suggest the reliability of phallometric testing is moderate (Barbaree, Baxter, & Marshall, 1989; Davidson & Malcolm, 1985; Fernandez, 2002; but see Gaither, 2001). The validity of a test is constrained by its reliability, yet the discriminative and predictive validity of phallometric testing is quite good. This apparent contradiction suggests two nonexclusive possibilities: (i) the discriminative and predictive effect sizes that have been obtained are conservative estimates of validity and would be higher if reliability could be increased; and (ii) phallometric testing is different from traditional paper-and-pencil tests and different indices of reliability are required for evaluations of phallometric test properties.

Professional and Ethical Issues in the Use of Phallometry

Despite the consistent evidence supporting the clinical and research use of phallometry, there is debate over the interpretation of these findings. Part of this is explained by the limitations of the more common narrative (as opposed to meta-analytic) approach to reviewing a set of findings, but some of it can also be attributed to the different emphasis given to paraphilic sexual interests in opposing theories of sexual aggression. In addition, practical and ethical objections have also been raised regarding phallometry (see Launay, 1999, and Marshall & Fernandez, 2000, for recent critiques; see Seto, 2001, for a counterpoint).

One of the main criticisms of phallometric testing is its lack of standardization in stimuli, procedures, and data analysis. Howes (1995) identified a great deal of heterogeneity in methodologies in a survey of 48 phallometric laboratories operating in Canada and the United States. Laboratories vary on the number and nature of stimuli they present, duration of stimulus presentations, and the minimal arousal level considered acceptable for clinical interpretation of individual response profiles.

Unfortunately, most laboratories do not use optimal procedures and scoring methods. Standardization is clearly needed in phallometric testing, because some testing procedures have been validated while others have not. Standardization would also facilitate the production of normative data and thereby aid in the interpretation and reporting of phallometric test results. Fortunately, there is empirical evidence to guide decisions about these methodological issues, such as the number and kinds of stimuli to present, the use of circumferential or volumetric devices, and the optimal transformations of data for interpretation (see Lalumière & Harris, 1998;

Quinsey & Lalumière, 2001). Guidelines on phallometric testing procedures have been developed by a large international organization of clinicians and researchers who work with sex offenders (Association for the Treatment of Sexual Abusers, 1993, 2001).

Phallometry has been criticized because it is an intrusive procedure, requiring men to partially undress, place a device around their penis, and have their erectile responses recorded while a laboratory technician monitors the session. Sessions are often conducted with a camera trained on the upper body of the subject, in order to minimize attempts to fake the test such as looking away or tampering with the phallometric device. The procedure is obviously more intrusive than interviewing or administering a paper-and-pencil questionnaire, but it provides valuable information that cannot otherwise be obtained. Phallometry can identify paraphilic sexual interests among men who deny any such interest. Moreover, it is not redundant in the assessment of men who admit having paraphilic sexual interests because it is the relative strength of those interests that predicts sexual recidivism. For example, two men may admit to having a pedophilic interest in children, but one of them may respond substantially more to stimuli depicting children than to pictures of adults, suggesting that his risk for sexual recidivism is higher.

Two additional objections that have been raised about phallometry are that (i) presenting visual stimuli depicting children is unethical because the children could not provide informed consent when the pictures were made (some laboratories use child pornography seized by police); and (ii) presenting stimuli depicting illegal content such as sex with children or nonconsenting sex is unethical because it could have deleterious effects, particularly for adolescents or first-time offenders.

Regarding the first objection, audiotaped stimuli can be used to gauge relative interest in sexual interactions with imaginary children, and the emergence of digital image manipulation software will allow users to create realistic human figures that do not depict real individuals. Regarding the second objection, phallometry is clinically appropriate only for individuals who are known to have committed sexual offenses, not those who are only suspected of doing so (e.g., in custodial disputes when an allegation is made against the father; there is no evidence that phallometry could have sufficient probative value in court proceedings of this kind; see Barbaree & Peacock, 1995). Offenders who are clinically assessed using phallometry have already engaged in illegal sexual behavior and are likely to be exposed to other accounts of sexual offenses in group therapy, reading materials, and video presentations. Although comparable research has not been done with sex offenders, Malamuth and Check (1984) showed that research volunteers exposed to depictions of rape were less accepting of rape myths than volunteers exposed to depictions of consenting sex after a short debriefing procedure. Sex offenders would receive much more than a short debriefing in any treatment or supervision that takes place after their phallometric assessment; in fact, a common target of sex offender treatment programs are antisocial attitudes about sex with children or rape. Finally, I argue that the value of the information that is thus obtained outweighs the potential cost of exposure to unconventional and explicit sexual content.

Although it has been suggested that phallometry is not useful for some groups of sex offenders such as adolescent sex offenders or first-time incest offenders, this assumption is not supported by existing evidence. Seto, Lalumière, and Blanchard (2000) evaluated the use of phallometric testing for adolescent sex offenders with child victims. Because an age-matched comparison group was not available, these adolescents were compared to young adults who had not committed sexual offenses involving children. As a group, adolescents with male victims had relatively higher responses to pictures of children than the young adult comparison subjects. Adolescents with both male and female children as victims responded more to pictures of children than to pictures of adults. In another study testing a hypothesis about incest avoidance, Seto, Lalumière, and Kuban (1999) distinguished incest offenders with female child victims according to their degree of genetic relatedness to their victims: biological fathers, extended family members such as uncles or grandfathers, and stepfathers. A majority of the incest offenders were convicted for the first time of a sexual offense. Nonetheless, all three groups had higher average indices of relative responding to children than the comparison groups of rapists and nonoffenders. These findings suggest that phallometry can be useful for both adolescent sex offenders and first-time incest offenders.

Conclusion

Paraphilic sexual interests are important to consider in the assessment of sex offenders. Although paraphilic sexual interests can most easily be assessed using self-report, either through interviews or questionnaires, sex offenders may minimize or deny their sexual interest in children or nonconsenting sex because of social or legal consequences. Self-disclosure might be increased through the use of polygraphy, which may reflect only a bogus pipeline effect, but the validity of polygraph results has been questioned and the scientific evidence is limited. In contrast, studies have reliably demonstrated that phallometric responses can reliably distinguish groups of sex offenders from groups of men who have not committed sexual offenses, and can predict sexual recidivism. Some of the criticisms made regarding the clinical use of phallometry have merit, but they can be at least partially addressed through standardization of stimuli and procedures and the use of new technologies such as digital image manipulation software.

The use of phallometry is hampered in the United States because possession of visual stimuli depicting children in sexually suggestive or explicit situations is prohibited under current legislation (Child Pornography Prevention Act of 1996). The use of digital image manipulation software to create images of "virtual children" is currently permitted following an April 2002 decision by the U.S. Supreme Court in *Ashcroft v. Free Speech Coalition,* but legislators are reportedly developing a new statute that can survive a Supreme Court challenge. Until the legal landscape is settled, evaluators in the United States can continue to validly use audiotapes describing sex with children compared to sex with adults (e.g., Chaplin et al., 1995; Murphy, Haynes, Stalgaitis, & Flanagan, 1986). In Canada, the Criminal Code provides an exemption under the child pornography statute for the possession of visual sexual stimuli depicting children for scientific and clinical purposes (Criminal Code of Canada, R.S.C. 1985, Chap. C-46).

Alternatives to phallometry such as measures based on viewing time and behavioral proxy scales have shown promise, but more research is needed on these measures. Ideally, alternative measures will be less intrusive and less vulnerable to faking. In this context, an interesting choice reaction time procedure has been reported by Wright and Adams (1994, 1999). In this procedure, subjects are instructed to locate a dot that appears on slides of nude men and women as quickly as possible. In both studies, heterosexual and homosexual male and female volunteers took longer to react to the appearance of the dot when examining a picture of someone of their preferred sex (females for heterosexual men and homosexual women and males for heterosexual women and homosexual men). I am not aware of any study that has attempted to use a choice reaction time procedure to examine pedophilic or other paraphilic target preferences.

A potentially intriguing new research method is suggested by the use of neurological recordings to assess sexual interests. Several recent studies have examined brain area activation in response to sexual versus neutral stimuli among volunteers (Karama et al., 2002; Park et al., 2001; Redouté et al., 2000; Stoléru et al., 1999). One case study demonstrated that functional magnetic resonance imaging detected differential activation of the anterior gyrus and right orbitofrontal cortex of an androphilic (male-preferring) pedophile compared to two gynephilic (female-preferring) controls (Dreßing, Obergriesser, Tost, Kaumeier, & Ruf, 2001). The development of neuroimaging methods to assess sexual interests is intriguing because it could reveal the brain structures involved in processing of sexual stimuli and, at the same time, could provide an assessment of sexual interest that is more difficult to fake than phallometry, viewing time, and sexual offense history. Neuroimaging methods are not practical for routine clinical practice, however, with currently available technologies.

Future research on the psychophysiological assessment of paraphilias should examine paraphilias other than pedophilia and biastophilia. Development of procedures for assessing sexual interests in exhibitionism, voyeurism, and other paraphilias identified in *DSM-IV-TR* and ICD-10 could contribute a great deal to further scientific work on the etiology and development of sexual preferences.

References

Abel, G. G., Huffman, J., Warberg, B., & Holland, C. L. (1998). Visual reaction time and plethysmography as measures of sexual interest in child molesters. *Sexual Abuse: A Journal of Research and Treatment, 10,* 81–95.

Abel, G. G., Jordan, A., Hand, C. G., Holland, L. A., & Phipps, A. (2001). Classification models of child molesters utilizing the Abel Assessment for child sexual abuse interest. *Child Abuse & Neglect, 25,* 703–718.

Abel, G. G., Lawry, S. S., Karlstrom, E., Osborn, C. A., & Gillespie, C. F. (1994). Screening tests for pedophiles. *Criminal Justice and Behavior, 21,* 115–131.

Ahlmeyer, S., Heil, P., McKee, B., & English, K. (2000). The impact of polygraphy on admissions of victims and offenses in adult sexual offenders. *Sexual Abuse: A Journal of Research and Treatment, 12,* 123–138.

American Psychiatric Association. (2000). *Diagnostic and statistical manual of mental disorders* (text revision). Washington, D.C.: Author.

Ashcroft v. Free Speech Coalition, 122 S. Ct. 1389, 1406 (2002).

Association for the Treatment of Sexual Abusers. (1993). *The ATSA practitioner's handbook.* Beaverton, Ore.: Author.

Association for the Treatment of Sexual Abusers—Professional Issues Committee. (2001). *Practice standards and guidelines for members of the Association for the Treatment of Sexual Abusers* (3rd ed.). Beaverton, Ore.: Author.

Barbaree, H. E., Baxter, D. J., & Marshall, W. L. (1989). The reliability of the rape index in a sample of rapists and nonrapists. *Violence and Victims, 4,* 299–306.

Barbaree, H. E., & Marshall, W. L. (1989). Erectile responses among heterosexual child molesters, father-daughter incest offenders, and matched non-offenders: Five distinct age preference profiles. *Canadian Journal of Behavioural Science, 21,* 70–82.

Barbaree, H. E., & Peacock, E. J. (1995). Assessment of sexual preferences in cases of alleged child sexual abuse. In T. Ney (Ed.), *True and false allegations in child sexual abuse.* (pp. 242–259). New York: Brunner/Mazel.

Barboza-Whitehead, S. E. (2001). Discriminant validity of the Abel Assessment for Sexual Interest with juveniles who admit versus deny their sexual offenses. *Dissertation Abstracts International: Section B: The Sciences & Engineering, 61*(12-B), 6697.

Chaplin, T. C., Rice, M. E., & Harris, G. T. (1995). Salient victim suffering and the sexual responses of child molesters. *Journal of Consulting and Clinical Psychology, 63,* 249–255.

Child Pornography Prevention Act of 1996, 18 U.S.C. § 2256 (2000).

Criminal Code of Canada, R.S.C. 1985, Chap. C-46.

Curnoe, S., & Langevin, R. (2002). Personality and deviant sexual fantasies: An examination of the MMPIs. *Journal of Clinical Psychology, 58,* 803–815.

Davidson, P. R., & Malcolm, P. B. (1985). The reliability of the Rape Index: A rapist sample. *Behavioral Assessment, 7,* 283–292.

Dreßing, H., Obergriesser, T., Tost, H., Kaumeier, S., & Ruf, M. (2001). Homosexual pedophilia and functional networks—a fMRI case report and literature review. *Fortschritte der Neurologie, Psychiatrie, 69,* 539–544.

Emerick, R. L., & Dutton, W. A. (1993). The effect of polygraphy on the self-report of adolescent sex offenders: Implications for risk assessment. *Annals of Sex Research, 6,* 83–103.

English, K., Jones, L., Pasini-Hill, D., Patrick, D., & Cooley-Towell, S. (2000). *The value of polygraph testing in sex offender treatment.* Washington, D.C.: National Institute of Justice.

Fernandez, Y. M. (2002). Phallometric testing with sexual offenders against female victims: An examination of reliability and validity issues. *Dissertation Abstracts International: Section B: The Sciences & Engineering, 62*(12-B), 6017.

Freund, K. (1963). A laboratory method of diagnosing predominance of homo- and hetero-erotic interest in the male. *Behaviour Research and Therapy, 1,* 85–93.

Freund, K., & Blanchard, R. (1989). Phallometric diagnosis of pedophilia. *Journal of Consulting and Clinical Psychology, 57,* 100–105.

Freund, K., Seto, M. C., & Kuban, M. (1996). Two types of fetishism. *Behaviour Research and Therapy, 34,* 687–694.

Freund, K., & Watson, R. J. (1991). Assessment of the sensitivity and specificity of a phallometric test: An update of phallometric diagnosis of pedophilia. *Psychological Assessment, 3,* 254–260.

Gaither, G. K. (2001). The reliability and validity of three new measures of male sexual preferences. *Dissertation Abstracts International: Section B: The Sciences & Engineering, 61*(9-B), 4981.

Hanson, R. K., & Bussière, M. T. (1998). Predicting relapse: A meta-analysis of sexual offender recidivism studies. *Journal of Consulting and Clinical Psychology, 66,* 348–362.

Harris, G. T., Rice, M. E., Chaplin, T. C., & Quinsey, V. L. (1999). Dissimulation in phallometric testing of rapists' sexual preferences. *Archives of Sexual Behavior, 28,* 223–232.

Harris, G. T., Rice, M. E., Quinsey, V. L., & Chaplin, T. C. (1996). Viewing time as a measure of sexual interest among child molesters and normal heterosexual men. *Behaviour Research and Therapy, 34,* 389–394.

Harris, G. T., Rice, M. E., Quinsey, V. L., Chaplin, T. C., & Earls, C. (1992). Maximizing the discriminant validity of phallometric assessment data. *Psychological Assessment, 4,* 502–511.

Hindman, J., & Peters, J. (2001). Polygraph testing leads to better understanding adult and juvenile sex offenders. *Federal Probation, 65,* 8–15.

Howes, R. J. (1995). A survey of plethysmographic assessment in North America. *Sexual Abuse: A Journal of Research and Treatment, 7,* 9–24.

Kalichman, S. C., Henderson, M. C., Shealy, L. S., & Dwyer, S. M. (1992). Psychometric properties of the Multiphasic Sex Inventory in assessing sex offenders. *Criminal Justice & Behavior, 19,* 384–396.

Karama, S., Lecours, A. R., Leroux, J.-M., Bourgouin, P., Beaudoin, G., Joubert, S., et al. (2002). Areas of brain activation in males and females during viewing of erotic film excerpts. *Human Brain Mapping, 16,* 1–13.

Kennedy, H., & Grubin, D. (1992). Patterns of denial in sex offenders. *Psychological Medicine, 22,* 191–196.

Lalumière, M. L., & Harris, G. T. (1998). Common questions regarding the use of phallometric testing with sexual offenders. *Sexual Abuse: A Journal of Research and Treatment, 10,* 227–237.

Lalumière, M. L., & Quinsey, V. L. (1993). The sensitivity of phallometric measures with rapists. *Annals of Sex Research, 6,* 123–138.

Lalumière, M. L., & Quinsey, V. L. (1994). The discriminability of rapists from non-sex offenders using phallometric measures: A meta-analysis. *Criminal Justice and Behavior, 21,* 150–175.

Lalumière, M. L., & Quinsey, V. L. (1996). Sexual deviance, antisociality, mating effort, and the use of sexually coercive behaviors. *Personality and Individual Differences, 21,* 33–48.

Lalumière, M. L., Quinsey, V. L., Harris, G. T., Rice, M. E., & Trautrimas, C. (2003). Are rapists differentially aroused by coercive sex in phallometric assessments? *Annals of the New York Academy of Sciences, 989,* 211–224.

Langevin, R., Lang, R. A., & Curnoe, S. (2000). The prevalence of sex offenders with deviant fantasies. *Journal of Interpersonal Violence, 13,* 315–327.

Langevin, R., & Paitche, D. (2001). *Clarke Sex History Questionnaire for Males-Revised (SHQ-R).* Toronto: Multi-Health Systems.

Launay, G. (1999). The phallometric assessment of sex offenders: An update. *Criminal Behaviour and Mental Health, 9,* 254–274.

Letourneau, E. J. (2002). A comparison of objective measures of sexual arousal and interest: Visual reaction time and penile plethysmography. *Sexual Abuse: A Journal of Research and Treatment, 14,* 207–223.

Madrigano, G., Curry, S., Fedoroff, P., & Bradford, J. (2003, May). *Sexual arousal of juvenile sex offenders: How do they compare to adult sex offenders?* Paper presented at the 3rd Annual Canadian Conference on Specialized Services for Sexually Abusive Youth, Toronto, Canada.

Malamuth, N. M., & Check, J. V. P. (1984). Debriefing effectiveness following exposure to pornographic rape depictions. *Journal of Sex Research, 20,* 1–13.

Marshall, W. L., & Fernandez, Y. M. (2000). Phallometric testing with sexual offenders: Limits to its value. *Clinical Psychology Review, 20,* 807–822.

Marshall, W. L., Payne, K., Barbaree, H. E., & Eccles, A. (1991). Exhibitionists: Sexual preferences for exposing. *Behaviour Research and Therapy, 29,* 37–40.

Murphy, W. D., Haynes, M. R., Stalgaitis, S. J., & Flanagan, B. (1986). Differential sexual responding among four groups of sexual offenders against children. *Journal of Psychopathology and Behavioral Assessment, 8,* 339–353.

National Research Council, Committee to Review the Scientific Evidence on the Polygraph. (2003). *The polygraph and lie detection.* Washington, D.C.: National Academy Press.

Nichols, H. R., & Molinder, I. (1984). *Multiphasic Sex Inventories.* [Available from the authors at 437 Bowes Drive, Tacoma, Wash., 98466-7047].

Park, K., Seo, J. J., Kang, H. K., Ryu, S. B., Kim, H. J., & Jeong, G. W. (2001). A new potential of blood oxygenation level dependent (BOLD) functional MRI for evaluating cerebral centers of penile erection. *International Journal of Impotence Research, 13,* 73–81.

Proulx, J., Côté, G., & Achille, P. A. (1993). Prevention of voluntary control of penile response in homosexual pedophiles during phallometric testing. *Journal of Sex Research, 30,* 140–147.

Quinsey, V. L., & Chaplin, T. C. (1988). Preventing faking in phallometric assessments of sexual preference. *Annals of the New York Academy of Sciences, 528*, 49–58.

Quinsey, V. L., Ketsetzis, M., Earls, C., & Karamanoukian, A. (1996). Viewing time as a measure of sexual interest. *Ethology and Sociobiology, 17,* 341–354.

Quinsey, V. L., & Lalumière, M. L. (2001). *Assessment of sexual offenders against children* (2nd ed.). Newbury Park, Calif.: Sage.

Quinsey, V. L., Lalumière, M. L., Rice, M. E., & Harris, G. T. (1995). Predicting sexual offenses. In J. C. Campbell (Ed.), *Assessing dangerousness: Violence by sexual offenders, batterers, and child abusers* (pp. 114–137). Newbury Park, Calif.: Sage.

Quinsey, V. L., Rice, M. E., Harris, G. T., & Reid, K. S. (1993). The phylogenetic and ontogenetic development of sexual age preferences in males: Conceptual and measurement issues. In H. E. Barbaree, W. L. Marshall, & S. M. Hudson (Eds.), *The juvenile sex offender* (pp. 143–163). New York: Guilford Press.

Redouté, J., Stoléru, S., Grégoire, M.-C., Costes, N., Cinotti, L., Lavenne, F., et al. (2000). Brain processing of visual sexual stimuli in human males. *Human Brain Mapping, 11,* 162–177.

Rice, M. E., Chaplin, T. C., Harris, G. T., & Coutts, J. (1994). Empathy for the victim and sexual arousal among rapists and nonrapists. *Journal of Interpersonal Violence, 9,* 435–449.

Rice, M. E., Harris, G. T., & Quinsey, V. L. (1990). A follow-up of rapists assessed in a maximum-security psychiatric facility. *Journal of Interpersonal Violence, 5,* 435–448.

Roese, N.J., & Jamieson, D. W. (1993). Twenty years of bogus pipeline research: A critical review and meta-analysis. *Psychological Bulletin, 114,* 363–375.

Seto, M. C. (2001). The value of phallometry in the assessment of male sex offenders. *Journal of Forensic Psychology Practice, 1,* 65–75.

Seto, M. C. (2002). Precisely defining pedophilia. *Archives of Sexual Behavior, 31,* 498–499.

Seto, M. C., & Barbaree, H. E. (1997). Sexual aggression as antisocial behavior: A developmental model. In D. Stoff, J. Breiling, & J. D. Maser (Eds.), *Handbook of antisocial behavior* (pp. 524–533). New York: Wiley.

Seto, M. C., Harris, G. T., Rice, M. E., & Barbaree, H. E. (2004). The Screening Scale for Pedophilic Interests and recidivism among adult sex offenders with child victims. *Archives of Sexual Behavior, 33,* 455–466.

Seto, M. C., & Kuban, M. (1996). Criterion-related validity of a phallometric test for paraphilic rape and sadism. *Behaviour Research and Therapy, 34,* 175–183.

Seto, M. C., & Lalumière, M. L. (2001). A brief screening scale to identify pedophilic interests among child molesters. *Sexual Abuse: A Journal of Research and Treatment, 13,* 15–25.

Seto, M. C., Lalumière, M. L., & Blanchard, R. (2000). The discriminative validity of a phallometric test for pedophilic interests among adolescent sex offenders against children. *Psychological Assessment, 12,* 319–327.

Seto, M. C., Lalumière, M. L., & Kuban, M. (1999). The sexual preferences of incest offenders. *Journal of Abnormal Psychology, 108,* 267–272.

Seto, M. C., Murphy, W. D., Page, J., & Ennis, L. (2003). Detecting anomalous sexual interests among juvenile sex offenders. *Annals of the New York Academy of Sciences, 989,* 118–130.

Simkins, L., Ward, W., Bowman, S., & Rinck, C. M. (1989). The Multiphasic Sex Inventory: Diagnosis and prediction of treatment response in child sexual abusers. *Annals of Sex Research, 2,* 205–226.

Smith, G., & Fischer, L. (1999). Assessment of juvenile sexual offenders: Reliability and validity of the Abel Assessment for Interest in Paraphilias. *Sexual Abuse: A Journal of Research and Treatment, 11,* 207–216.

Spitzer, R. C., & Wakefield, J. L. (2002). Why pedophilia is a disorder of sexual attraction—at least sometimes. *Archives of Sexual Behavior, 31,* 499–500.

Stoléru, S., Grégoire, M.-C., Gérard, D., Decety, J., Lafarge, E., Cinotti, L., et al. (1999). Neuroanatomical correlates of visually evoked sexual arousal in human files. *Archives of Sexual Behavior, 28,* 1–21.

Wiederman, M. W. (2002). Reliability and validity of measurement. In M. W. Wiederman & B. E. Whitley, Jr., (Eds.), *Handbook for conducting research on human sexuality* (pp. 25–50). Mahwah, N.J.: Erlbaum.

Wright, L. W., & Adams, H. E. (1994). Assessment of sexual preference using a choice reaction time task. *Journal of Psychopathology & Behavioral Assessment, 16,* 221–231.

Wright, L. W., & Adams, H. E. (1999). The effects of stimuli that vary in erotic content on cognitive processes. *Journal of Sex Research, 36,* 145–151.

World Health Organization. (1997). *The ICD-10 classification of mental and behavioural disorders: Clinical descriptions and diagnostic guidelines.* Geneva: Author.

Zuckerman, M. (1971). Physiological measures of sexual arousal in the human. *Psychological Bulletin, 75,* 297–329.

Discussion Paper

DAVID L. ROWLAND

I want to preface my response with three points: First, a note of appreciation to the authors who provided very interesting and thought-provoking papers. Second, this is not my area of expertise and therefore my comments are those of an outsider, so I hope I do justice to these papers and other participants will add to my comments. Third, these areas of research make me a bit nervous because there's an evaluative and, in some instances, even judgmental interpretation that is drawn from the psychophysiological data. Such judgments carry legal and social consequences for the individual. Although I don't deal with this issue directly in my comments, it is important to note that, for good reason, the use of phallometric data for verification of paraphilias is controversial within some circles.

I would like to begin by discussing Drs. Chivers and Bailey's "The Sexual Psychophysiology of Sexual Orientation" and more specifically, their conceptualization and measurement of "sexual orientation." A problem endemic to research on sexual orientation is that a very complex and dynamic bio-psycho-social developmental process is reduced to a simple dichotomous categorization of either "heterosexual" or "homosexual." Sexual orientation has multiple dimensions, including sexual attraction, sexual arousal, actual behavior, homo- and heteroeroticism, self-identity, and so on. It's unclear how all of these various elements can adequately be represented in a simple label, particularly when there are gradations in each of these dimensions and when they are known to change over the lifespan. But by necessity (or at least by tradition), research on sexual orientation has relied on this simple dichotomy that, in my view, fails to capture the multiple dimensions of this state we call "sexual orientation." Chivers and Bailey have acknowledged this problem in their paper, pointing out the many possible ways to assess sexual orientation and some of the problems surrounding each of them.

The question then is which of these dimensions—attraction, arousal, behavior, self-identity, and so forth—provides the best measure for determining sexual orientation; how does one deal with inconsistencies among these dimensions (e.g., an individual who reports homoerotic fantasies but engages only in heterosexual behavior); or how does one generate a composite that captures all these dimensions? Take the example of a bisexual person who chooses a life partner of the same sex. Based on a behavioral criterion, this individual is homosexual; however, based on a scale measuring attraction, this individual might be bisexual. How should this individual be categorized in terms of sexual orientation, and/or what composite variable is used to capture these seemingly discordant components of sexual orientation?

The issue of determining sexual orientation is further compounded by the social desirability of one orientation over the other. Consider the example of a woman who, on a homo-heteroeroticism scale, indicates greater attraction toward women than men. Due to various social pressures, however, she has a sexual relationship with an opposite sex partner whom she finds arousing. In this situation, social norms lead to inconsistency between behavior and attraction, and once again, the obvious dichotomous categorization of heterosexual and homosexual appears inadequate.

My second comment pertains to the general reliance upon genital response in favor of self-report measures as a means for assessing sexual arousal. A number of studies have identified subsets of men and women who show physiological, genital response in the absence of comparable levels of subjective sexual arousal. In other words, there is a disconnection between their genital response, which suggests strong sexual arousal, and their subjective evaluation of their state of arousal, which suggests low or absent sexual arousal. Because such discordance can and does occur, I am concerned about giving greater credibility to "psychophysiologically assessed" genital response than to self-reported assessments. There are, of course, good reasons to question self-report assessments in studies on paraphilics and perhaps also in studies dealing with socially sensitive issues such as sexual orientation, but let me pose the question this way. If we assume that a person is not being deceitful about his or her level of self-reported arousal, which measure should we accept as being the more valid index of sexual arousal—his or her self-reported arousal or his or her genital response? I don't have an answer to that question, but it is certainly one that is relevant to the issues discussed here, where the focus appears to be on interpretation of genital measures as a means of assessing sexual orientation.

My third comment regarding Chivers and Bailey's paper is related to the "category-specific arousal" seen in men. Specifically, heterosexual men are aroused by heterosexual stimuli; homosexual men are aroused by homosexual stimuli. In contrast, women, whether heterosexual or lesbian, tend to show arousal responses to both male and female sexual stimuli. This finding suggests that male and female homosexuality may not be similar or even parallel phenomena. Although this difference in arousal cues adds to the growing list of ways that differentiate male from female homosexuality, I find the explanation offered by the authors to account for these differences not fully convincing. If, in fact, women are more likely to become aroused to nonspecific sexual stimuli—male or female—wouldn't we expect *higher* rates of same-sex pairings in women than we currently see, or at least higher rates than we see in men? That is, if women's arousal responses are less likely to differentiate between male and female stimuli, and women are more likely to find same-sex stimuli to be arousing, then why doesn't the rate of lesbianism in the population (relative to male homosexuality) reflect this?

Regarding Dr. Seto's paper, given my general concerns about the use of psychophysiological assessments to verify paraphilic sexual interests, I nevertheless found this to be a very balanced presentation. The logic behind these studies seems inherently sound, the idea of the S-R (stimulus-response) paradigm being extended to the study of sexual paraphilias. Thus, the pedophile should show arousal to scenes depicting children, the rapist to scenes depicting force, and so on. Despite this tight logic, however, there appears to be no methodological gold standard for reliably assessing paraphilic tendencies. Each of the various methodologies—questionnaires, polygraphy, viewing times, and so on—has its problems, and this has led Dr. Seto to place reasonable confidence in the use of phallometric measures. However, in reviewing some of the correlational data—which are not strong—and the information on predictability with respect to recidivism, even the phallometric approach does not seem particularly adequate. One of the dangers is that in the absence of really good assessment measures, we are forced to use the less than adequate measures that are available. And as these measures are used with increasing frequency, they gain wider acceptance as "credible" and "objective" measures. Of course, it is better to rely on a poor measure than no measure at all. On the other hand, given the magnitude of the consequences of making a classification error (particularly false positives), this issue needs to be carefully considered. In my view, even though better than chance, the probability of misclassification remains unacceptably high because even small rates of error have large consequences for the individual—although I would be interested in hearing Dr. Seto's thoughts on this point. As Seto points out in his chapter, using conservative cut-off scores and high specificities minimizes misclassification errors. On the other hand, what should we view as an acceptable rate of error here? Would three false positives out of a hundred trials be acceptable? Let me place it in a slightly different context. If you or I were the ones being tested, three errors out of a hundred would probably be unacceptable, even more so if you or I ended up being one of those errors or false positives.

Two other comments are relevant to this presentation. First, I would be interested in hearing about arousal patterns to unusual sexual stimuli in groups of nonparaphilic men. Such data probably already exist, but their inclusion might assist the readership in understanding the relationships between attraction, arousal, and actual behavior. I raise this point because the rich (and often deviant) sexual fantasy lives of nonparaphilic men and women may well include socially forbidden situations and partners, yet these fantasies typically remain, for the large majority of people, just that—fantasies that are never acted upon through real-life behaviors. Chivers and Bailey cite a study by Wincze and Qualls that reports that lesbians experienced the highest levels of arousal to scenes depicting group sex. Does that mean that lesbians, in fact, are more likely than other groups to engage in group sex? Should we assume concordance between what turns them on and how they then behave? I doubt that many people would make such an assumption. Yet we as researchers often assume concordance among attraction, arousal, and behavior in paraphilics. I would pose this question: To what extent do we see consistency among attraction, arousal, and behavior in nonparaphilics? And to what extent should we expect such consistency among these processes in paraphilics?

Finally—and this point was raised at the end of your talk—I wonder about female paraphilias (or the lack thereof). Your point about its being a measurement issue is interesting. I wonder if you might elaborate on this. Do you think the absence of studies on female paraphilias is because the incidence is so low? Or are the paraphilias nongenital in nature and therefore not amenable to psychophysiological evaluation? Is it that women don't lie about the paraphilias they do have? Or is it that we just are not able to identify the right tools to assess them? One theme that has run through much of this symposium, as well as through both the Chivers and Bailey and Seto papers, is the similarity between men and women regarding some issues of sexuality. At the same time these papers also point out fundamental differences between men's and women's sexuality. The challenge is to know when to apply sex-specific models to explain sexual response and behaviors, and when to apply cross-sex models.

General Discussion

Kevin McKenna: I have a general comment for both Meredith and Michael, especially since both of them were interested in the idea of the specificity of what is arousing about the images. It seems like there is another psychophysiological measure that would be really helpful and that's eye movement. It is really pretty easy now to measure eye movements, and you can measure exactly what somebody is looking at and for how long. I think you might be able to detect deliberate distraction strategies from it. There's a large amount of literature about eye movement control operating on a largely subconscious, or nonconscious, level, and this might be a very useful thing in addition to subjective reports and genital measures. You can find out what people are really interested in by how much time they spend looking at genitals versus looking at something else. I think it would be really useful and it's not that hard anymore and not ridiculously expensive either.

Jim Geer: I want to respond just briefly to some of Ray's comments. He asked whether we have looked at other aspects of gender differences, like sports, and so on. The answer to that is, not to my knowledge. We use as control words in our research another domain, the kitchen domain, which involves kitchen appliances, and I really don't think that there's a gender difference there, but it's an interesting and reasonable question. What do I think, you asked, about the difference of biological versus cultural influences on networks? Well, language is cultural, in the sense that we learn English or French or German or Spanish. But if we were to look at some of the literature, many people think basic language mechanisms are wired in. I don't know that we can say anything about looking at that level. It would be very nice if we could, but I'm not optimistic that we have the methodology at this point. And you wondered about generality of this stuff. The only thing I can speak to is the fact that these networks do make predictions concerning the sexual orientation of the individual as well as the gender of the individual, which suggests to me some external validity, although it's not been looked at in clinical populations, which would be interesting.

Walter Everaerd: This is related to the question about sex differences.

In a priming study where we measured recognition times for men and women in reaction to sexual stimuli, we found, preovulatory, a greater sensitivity to these stimuli in women, while postovulatory, reaction times to reproduction-relevant stimuli were longer. In men you don't find that. So there are gender differences that are dependent on hormonal and endocrine factors.

Heather Hoffmann: I think the obvious question for me is the etiology of target specificity. Are we talking about a predisposition? Perhaps not exclusively, but potentially also some learning mechanisms could be involved, and why would they or how would they be different between men and women?

Meredith Chivers: It's a fascinating question and in the paper that Mike and I wrote, I started speculating about this a little bit. Roy Baumeister recently published an article looking at sex differences and sex drive, or the concept of sex drive, and concluded that there were reasonable data to show that men do have a higher sex drive than women. If this is true, perhaps awareness of sexual arousal is linked to a higher sex drive. Therefore in women, who typically aren't as aware of their physical arousal as men, physical sexual arousal may not be an important factor in any learning process because the perceived levels of arousal are not substantially different between different sexual stimuli. My data show that, indeed, the levels of genital arousal women experience are not substantially different, suggesting again that any learning process involved in the development of sexual preferences is likely not dependent on a relatively static factor like genital arousal. And as to the etiology, who knows? We really don't know what's going on. Certainly what I'm proposing is that, for women, there is little differentiation in genital arousal between types of sexual stimuli and that a nonspecific response pattern is an adaptive mechanism. (The byproduct of nonspecific and automatic genital arousal is lubrication, which protects the genital tract during intercourse.) But I don't know how a learning model would apply to women based on a physiological response to sexual stimuli because this factor doesn't vary as much in women as it does in men. I can certainly see how a learning model might apply to subjective or cognitive sexual arousal or experiences, but not to physiological responses. It is also possible that genital response potentiates a positive appraisal of a sexual stimulus, much in the way sympathetic nervous system arousal can enhance appraisals of attractiveness. This research has yet to be conducted, however.

Heather Hoffman: Yes, and, again, I think this might be another reason we have more difficulty seeing conditioned arousal in women; we may be looking at just weaker responses. They can learn, but it's not going to be that functional for them so it's more easily extinguished.

Meredith Chivers: The other thing I've been thinking about is the influence of individual differences in sex drive and in a woman's ability to detect her sexual arousal on how conditionable a woman might be—and if so, whether those women show category-specific responses. I've been curious about looking at women with higher than average serum testosterone levels, such as very masculine lesbian women or female-to-male transsexuals. Higher serum testosterone has been associated with higher sex drive, and I wonder if those high testosterone women would show a more category-specific response, perhaps through mechanisms of learning, in that they have a higher level of sexual arousal in general, which becomes conditioned to the stimuli they prefer.

Heather Hoffmann: Yes, and on the learning end, too, it might go back to differences in masturbatory practices. John talked about an undifferentiated arousal response becoming more differentiated through masturbation in boys at puberty. In girls, not having that masturbatory experience may fit in somehow.

Michael Seto: It's a really interesting question. The short answer to the question about etiology of category-specificity or etiology of paraphilias in men is, who knows? But there is this puzzle or maybe even a paradox that really strikes me, which is, on the one hand, there are data suggesting that female genital response is less specific. It's more, I don't know if you want to call it fluid, more plastic, whatever word you like, yet men are much more likely to develop paraphilias by any count, whether you look at surveys, clinical samples, correctional situations, men are more likely to develop these atypical sexual interests. So to me, trying to reconcile those two lines would be really interesting in studying the development of sexual preferences.

John Bancroft: I was very interested in Meredith's paper. I think there is general agreement in this room that there are some fundamental questions about what vaginal pulse amplitude (VPA) actually means in women. You reported on the study where, if I've understood you correctly, you were measuring VPA in male-to-female transgendered individuals, who presumably had had gender reassignment surgery. Presumably you put the photometer in their surgically created vaginas. What are the implications of this? What was the type of surgery used? Where was the tissue from that created the vagina? What would we expect from a relatively recently created surgical vagina in this respect?

Meredith Chivers: I'm not a physiologist so I can't comment specifically on what the structures might be, but the sex reassignment surgery that's typical these days for male-to-female transsexuals is one where the penis is stripped of it's corpus cavernosa and inverted into the body to create a neo-vagina, and likely what the vaginal photoplethysmograph is picking up on is either vasocongestion in the penile skin and or just general pelvic vasocongestion. We really don't know what it is that we're picking up in that respect, but I think probably the best answer would be just general pelvic vasocongestion.

John Bancroft: But you were getting a reasonably clear pulse amplitude signal?

Meredith Chivers: One thing to note: the study that specifically looks at the data with the male-to-female transsexuals, Anne Lawrence was the lead author on that. And one thing that we noticed is that the actual raw signal from the male-to-female transsexuals was significantly lower than it was in natal females.

Roy Levin: I reviewed a paper about 2 years ago about male-to-female transsexual women who inserted a photoplethysmograph, and there were hundreds of artifacts from the pelvic muscles, the strong pelvic muscles of the person squeezing it, and I rejected the paper because I couldn't believe half of what was going on. Did you find that you got a lot of interference from the pelvic muscles contracting? Because the male muscles are very strong.

Meredith Chivers: I have to admit that I wasn't the one who actually ran that study and actually looked at the raw data itself; however, I do have some of that data on my laptop. We can take a look at it later if you'd like.

John Bancroft: There are some of the newer surgical procedures where part of the erectile tissue is used, to create a sort of a clitoral shaft, but that's presumably not relevant to what you would expect with a VPA measure.

Lori Brotto: We also attempted to measure physiological sexual arousal in postsurgical male-to-female transsexual women a few years ago. Fifteen such women, who did not have any complications with surgery, inserted a vaginal photoplethysmograph and underwent testing. When we finally got to analyzing the data, there were numerous artifacts scattered throughout 14 of the 15 data outputs, leaving the data largely uninterpretable. Even despite our efforts at removing the artifacts and using more sophisticated methods of spectral analysis, the data were really too messy to come to any reasonable conclusions. Therefore Roy's point about pelvic muscle interference in the physiological signals of transsexual women is a very important one, and any study able to detect such signals clearly requires replication if the findings are to be considered valid.

Roy Levin: No, that's absolutely what I found.

Kim Payne: I wanted to respond to Michael Seto's comment, quite some time ago, about this issue of women's plasticity and paraphilias in men. Baumeister and Tice (2000) actually address this issue in a chapter on female sexual plasticity and they posit a critical period in male childhood development where sexuality is strongly influence by environmental factors. After this critical period in development is over, male sexuality remains solidified throughout adulthood.

Marca Sipski: I have a question that comes to my mind in terms of this, and it is kind of related to both sets of studies, Jim Geer's and Meredith's. I wonder how similar VPA really is to penile size. We have done a study where we used the Stroop test, and we used the Stroop test in both men and women, and men did the Stroop test and then did the Stroop test plus masturbation. In men, the Stroop test prevented able-bodied men from having erections during masturbation. In contrast, in women, doing the Stroop test alone then doing the Stroop test plus masturbation did not impact their VPA. Their VPA increased during masturbation and there was a significant change in VPA. So I'm wondering, when we're looking at erections versus VPA, is VPA so much more sensitive that if we're going to compare males and females, we really have to look at something like penile plethysmography, just in terms of measuring blood flow as opposed to actually measuring erection size? I guess another way to put it is, is it that much easier for a woman's vagina to become aroused than it is for a man to have an erection? Just because VPA goes up doesn't mean you're lubricated. And you know, penile blood flow is going to go up a lot quicker than that the male's actually going to have an erection, so in the women we're measuring the beginning of the cycle and the men we're measuring the end of the cycle. And so I guess I would say in Meredith's study, maybe men *would* have an increase in that blood flow; we're just not seeing it because they're not at the point of getting hard.

John Bancroft: May I refer to my comments on the first morning about our measurement of penile pulse amplitude. I don't think that measurement tells you anything about what is going on inside the corpus cavernosum. Roy Levin is of the opinion that we were measuring pulse amplitude in the skin. He may well be right. I do think it would be helpful to get some new research done on penile pulse amplitude, in such a way to allow direct comparison of the sexual responses of men and women.

Markus Wiegel: Just to what Dr. Bancroft was saying, we might not be able to use pulse amplitude, but we can measure blood flow in the penis using Doppler ultrasound and actually then get a measure of blood flow for the dorsal artery.

Marca Sipski: And you can do the same in women, too.

Roy Levin: That's right. It's never actually blood flow, it's velocity that people measure and so you have to be a little bit careful with that measure because you really need the diameter of the vessel and to multiply it by the velocity to get blood flow. Velocities can change with diameters, so you have to be a little bit careful.

Michael Seto: Just one point of clarification: I didn't get into methodology because of time constraints, but in the studies that we have done on pedophilia we are using the volumetric apparatus to measure penile response, that's measuring any change in penile volume. It's not the case that we're looking at situations where subjects are achieving very large responses approaching full erection to these different stimulus categories. In fact, oftentimes the changes we're talking about could be as small as 1 cc, which is a discernible change, but certainly not anything approaching rigidity in terms of erection.

Julia Heiman: I would like to comment on Meredith's interesting study. Before we just accept the finding of women being nonspecific in their response, given that there are measurement issues, it really begs going after more in-depth at a qualitative level and trying to get at what is it that women are attending to. Let me give you an example of my own research. When we started out, the data found that comparing romantic, erotic romantic, and erotic stimuli, the romantic material did not result in any enhanced genital or subjective arousal effects. When we presented just romantic material, it was equivalent to control material. The romantic material didn't make any difference. A number of years after that, after Jim Geer started to use cognitive measures, and when his team asked women to listen to erotic material, they found romantic elements in it, more so than the men did. In other words, though we were presenting material that we had arranged to have this certain content, the women listened to it with different filters. So I think the finding of women's plasticity, and for that matter "specificity," deserves more critical exploration. Given that the latter fits into Michael's work on paraphilia, we also might ask, if this gender difference in fact holds up over studies, what might be the value and the cost of sexual specificity in men versus women.

Ray Rosen: In thinking about Marca's comments, the fact that VPA may be more sensitive than erectile measures should argue against, not for, the hypothesis. In other words, they see target specificity in men and lack of specificity in the women. If the VPA were the more sensitive measure it would lead to greater specificity in the women.

Erick Janssen: That depends on the response levels we are talking about. Are we talking about initial, early responses, or later and higher response levels?

Kevin McKenna: If you had really, really sensitive measure of penile erection, you might see a response to other stimuli.

Ray Rosen: However, their design is looking at differential responsiveness to stimulus A versus stimulus B. The more sensitive your measure, in principle, the larger the differences between responses to stimulus A versus stimulus B.

Kevin McKenna: It's a threshold and a saturation effect.

Ray Rosen: I'm having a hard time seeing how a less sensitive measure would give greater differential responding to two stimuli.

Kevin McKenna: Because we don't know where VPA saturates. So if you have a very sensitive but basically almost an all-or-none response, they respond and you see the VPA response, right? In the penis you only see it when it gets above a big threshold. It takes a lot of blood to make an erection. So if you were looking at only the very bottom part of penile erection and the very bottom part of VPA, you'd see them both go up.

John Bancroft: I think they're measuring different things. When you're measuring erection, you're measuring a cumulative process, which to some extent is relatively slow in its reversal, whereas VPA seems to be something that can change very quickly. We reported a very interesting single-case study of a man with erectile dysfunction. We first induced a full erection with intracavernosal papavarine and proceeded to measuring penile pulse amplitude. We periodically switched on a sexual stimulus during this prolonged full erection and each time the sexual stimulus came on the pulse amplitude went right down. Then, when the sexual stimulus was switched off, the pulse amplitude would come right back again. Switch it on again and it would go right down again repeatedly (Bancroft, 1989, p. 443). I was thinking of this when Kevin asked whether there was some way in which we could block erections from occurring and study these other effects. It's difficult to do that, but what you can do is create a full erection pharmacologically and then see what else is happening. I think VPA has a different relationship to stimulus onset and offset than erection and we have to keep that in mind. I don't think it's a sensitivity issue. We're looking at different physiological patterns.

Tuuli Kukkonen: In listening to this discussion about VPA, it seems that there is very little agreement on many different aspects of it. I really feel that we should be looking for alternative ways of measuring sexual arousal and not leaving out, as Roy mentioned, ultrasonography and the assessment of blood velocity in men and women. I just completed a study using ultrasonography with women and blood velocity does increase during sexual arousal and to me that seems to be a more useful measure, something we can compare between men and women as opposed to VPA and erection. I believe it is important to keep an open mind to other methods of measurement.

Also, I wanted to ask Meredith, if sexual arousal is nonspecific for women, then it doesn't matter what kind of visual stimuli we use to elicit a genital response—as long as it has some erotic material? So basically we just have to show some kind of erotic flick and they will respond.

Meredith Chivers: Well, I think, yes. I think that is safe to say; however, I would definitely want to be sensitive to who those women are and what you're showing them and certainly not wanting to offend them. But yes, I'll bet you can show any stimulus depicting sexual activity and you'll get an increase of VPA.

I just want to take a couple of seconds to respond to several questions that have been tossed my way. I agree that directly comparing VPA and penile erection is problematic and we just don't know what VPA really means, but with this research program at least, what I'm interested in is relative patterns of arousal. Directly comparing the two is just too problematic at this point and I certainly echo other's concerns about finding something that we can compare between the two.

When I was talking about future directions in research, I wanted to mention that I'm going to be doing a postdoc at the Centre for Addiction and Mental Health with Ray Blanchard. One of the things I've been considering doing is using a labial thermistor in addition to VPA, and I'd be curious to hear from folks who have used a thermistor whether or not you think this is a good idea.

Erick Janssen: I have my ideas about it, although I have not used the device myself. We have used a labial clip to measure pulse amplitude in the labia, but I have not used the thermistor. I am very much in favor of multimethod approaches—using multiple measures of genital response in women—and the thermistor, I think, is next in line to VPA.

Roy Levin: I've spent all my life trying to measure fluid in the vagina, and Ray, it's really very difficult, I can tell you that, much more complicated than you think. The wicking quality of the tampon sucks the fluid out from between spaces between the epithelia; it is not an easy thing to do. You can only measure over a fixed time period and I've actually tried to sort of actually show that there's an increase in fluid when women get sexually aroused and you look through the literature and you show me the data—what quantitative data—it does not exist.

Jim Geer: We worked with a labial thermistor briefly and gave up on it. The reason we did was its time course. It was very slow in terms of onset, and it lasted after stimuli were turned off. And that was the major problem with it, so we did not use it. Not that we have anything a lot better but the thermistor was very slow reacting.

Markus Wiegel: A response to Tuuli's comment. I think if VPA doesn't distinguish or discriminate between stimuli, then we need to be even more careful about what stimuli we choose for women. When we show men a stimulus that isn't arousing, we know about it. With women, based on Meredith's research, we wouldn't necessarily see a difference in genital arousal, which may explain some of the discrepancies between subjective responses and VPA measures. As a result, I think it actually argues for the opposite, that we need to be much more careful about what stimuli we're going to choose for women, and maybe let women choose from a range of stimuli. A quick comment to Meredith: I think it would be interesting if you also looked at clitoral blood flow to see if that was more stimulus-specific than vaginal vascongestion.

Meredith Chivers: I wanted to come back to the question of the sensitivity of the vaginal photoplethysmograph and whether it is possible that the sensitivity can obscure a category-specific response in women. The film stimuli that I used were 2 minutes in length and I wondered whether what we were seeing was an initial level of arousal. If we lengthened that stimulus to say maybe 10–15 minutes, would VPA remain stable, drop, or increase?

Dong Woo Kang: I'm afraid it is too late to comment about VPA, but I think about the difference between male and female sexual response. For male erectile response, the first most important thing is arterial blood flow and then cavernosal engorgement, but the second thing necessary for erectile function is venous blockage. Without this, even if we have a partial erection, we can't get enough rigidity. So, I think VPA is a very good instrument, but only for the measurement of vasocongestion, not for the whole response of female sexual arousal.

Erick Janssen: If I understand it correctly, you are making a point similar to one Serge made earlier, about the relevance of distinguishing between tumescence and rigidity, that the two may be under control of different processes and that women and men may have tumescence mechanisms in common?

Dong Woo Kang: Indeed.

Serge Stoléru: I'd like to come back to the relation between cognitive processes and sexual arousal. In the slide that was presented by Dr. Geer, the dependent measure was sexual arousal and you manipulated sexual arousal with cognitive tasks, and you showed very impressively that cognitive tasks were decreasing sexual arousal. I was wondering whether it would not be interesting to do the reverse experiment. I mean, that the dependent measure would be a cognitive operation and that the distracter would be sexual and the measure would be the cognitive operation, which would or would not be influenced by the sexual distracter. It seems to me that this would have some ecological validity, because in usual circumstances this process of sexual distracters interfering with cognitive tasks is, I think, operating. And another thing is that, from a neuroimaging perspective, I have always wondered what the deactivation of the temporal areas meant. Such an experiment could show that it reflects the decrease of cognitive functioning in response to visual sexual stimulation, and also I think it could be very interesting to compare women and men on such a paradigm.

Jim Geer: I understand the question. I think it is indeed an interesting thing to do and there are tasks out there in the cognitive literature that indeed look at exactly that; that is, give them continuous tasks, reaction time tasks, and then distract them and see how the reaction time gets influenced by that, and you could easily do that with sexual stimuli. To my knowledge it's not been done in sexuality.

Kevin McKenna: I believe there was actually a report that I heard recently that, in fact, people did not attend to commercials during sexually explicit TV shows. On TV shows that had a lot of sexual content to them, they didn't watch the commercials.

Jason Hicks: I think that would be interesting as well. I know Walter and Ellen talk a lot about automatic physiological arousal and I wonder if you can actually look at the stages of genital response, and even subjective sexual arousal, and see at various stages early on versus later how much that takes away from attention from some other secondary task. So you can imagine that maintaining arousal is much more attention demanding than initiating arousal and you might actually be able to sort of parametrically see that kind of response.

References

Bancroft, J. (1989). *Human sexuality and its problems.* Edinburgh: Churchill Living-stone.

Baumeister, R. F., & Tice, D. M. (2000). *The social dimension of sex* (pp. 127–150). New York: Pearson Allyn & Bacon.

Appendix

Ten critical questions about vaginal pulse amplitude (VPA) obtained from free-standing photoplethysmographs in the vaginal lumen: answers needed for the perplexed!

Roy J. Levin

Is VPA . . .

1. . . . linear or even curvilinear with respect to increasing vasocongestion?
2. . . . a signal that increases with increasing vasocongestion or blood flow as measured simultaneously by any other method?
3. . . . in absolute output levels (or percentage change) any indication of the increase in real or actual vaginal blood flow or is it merely an index of vasocongestion?
4. . . . measured on day 1 (say of the menstrual cycle) comparable with the amplitude measured on day 14 in the same subject or, especially, in different subjects?
5. . . . a signal that allows us to amalgamate amplitudes from different subjects and come up with a meaningful mean amplitude?
6. . . . the kind of signal for which an amplitude of (say) 4 units on day 1 means the same as an amplitude of 4 units on day 14?
7. . . . a signal that allows us to tell what an increase in amplitude of (say) 20% means? Has it any bearing on the percentage increase in real blood flow?
8. . . . a signal that reflects the total volume of blood in the peripheral circulation viz small arteries, arterioles, venules, or small veins? Is this the same as an index of *flow* (volume change against time)?
9. . . . a signal that increases if venules/veins contract? The total blood volume may increase (arterial inflow but no or reduced outflow), yet the flow could actually decrease, or would the amplitude decrease because a large percentage (80%) of the blood in the peripheral circulation is on the venous side?
10. . . . a signal where a 10% amplitude increase for subject A could be a much larger increment in actual blood flow than an increase in amplitude of 20% for subject B?

Contributors

Michael Bailey is Professor of Psychology at Northwestern University in Evanston, Illinois. Bailey's primary interests have been in the causes and development of sexual orientation. It has recently become clear to him, however, that sexual orientation researchers have not paid sufficient attention to the meaning and phenomenology of sexual orientation. His work with Meredith Chivers is an attempt to do so, and he believes they have shown that sexual orientation means something very different to women than it does to men. He has published a book, *The Man Who Would Be Queen*, that is as controversial as it is true.

John Bancroft is a Senior Research Fellow at the Kinsey Institute. He was a Clinical Reader in Psychiatry at Oxford University from 1969 to 1976, after which he joined the Medical Research Council's Reproductive Biology Unit in Edinburgh, Scotland, where he remained, as leader of the Behavior Research Group, until becoming Director of the Kinsey Institute from 1995 to 2004. He is the author of *Human Sexuality and Its Problems* (1989); was founding editor, from 1990 to 1995, of the *Annual Review of Sex Research;* and has been involved in various aspects of sex research for the past 40 years. His principal research interests have been the relationship between reproductive hormones and sexual behavior, fertility control and its relevance to sexual behavior, psychophysiological aspects of male sexual response, the impact of the menstrual cycle on the sexuality and well-being of women, sexual dysfunction in men and women, and high risk sexual behavior.

David H. Barlow is Professor of Psychology and Psychiatry at Boston University. He received his Ph.D. from the University of Vermont in 1969. Dr. Barlow has published over 500 articles, chapters, and books, mostly in the area of the nature and treatment of emotional disorders. He is the recipient of numerous awards, including the distinguished Scientific Award for Applications of Psychology from the American Psychological Association.

Stephanie Both is a clinical psychologist and works as a researcher and sexologist at the Leiden University Medical Center in the Department of Psychosomatic Gynecology and Sexology. She obtained her Ph.D. in clinical psychology from the University of Amsterdam in 2004. She has several years of clinical experience in sex therapy, previously at the Amsterdam Center of Sexual Health and currently at Leiden University. Her research work focuses on the psychophysiological study of sexual motivation and sexual arousal in women and men. Recently her work is focused on appetitive and aversive conditioning of sexual response in women.

Andrea Bradford is a doctoral student in clinical psychology at the University of Texas at Austin, where she received her master's degree in 2004. Andrea is an active member of the International Society for the Study of Women's Sexual Health and is also affiliated with the Society for Sex Therapy and Research, the American Psychological Association, and the American Medical Writers Association. Her research interests include women's health psychology and psychophysiology.

Lori Brotto has a Ph.D. in clinical psychology from the University of British Columbia and completed a Fellowship in Reproductive and Sexual Medicine from the University of Washington. She is currently an Assistant Professor in the UBC Department of Obstetrics and Gynaecology as well as a registered psychologist. She is the Director of the UBC Sexual Health Laboratory, where research primarily focuses on developing and testing psychological and pharmacological interventions for women with sexual difficulties following cancer treatment. Her clinical work includes individuals and couples with sexual dysfunction. Dr. Brotto trains gynecology residents and medical students at UBC and teaches an undergraduate course in Human Sexuality. She is the recipient of a Scholar Career Award from the Michael Smith Foundation for Health Research as well as a New Investigator Award from the Canadian Institutes of Health Research.

Klynt H. Brummett is a 2001 graduate of Indiana University, Bloomington. He received his master's degree in clinical mental health counseling in 2003 from Valparaiso University. He has worked as a child and family therapist for a hospital in Indianapolis.

Meredith L. Chivers received her doctorate in clinical psychology from Northwestern University, Evanston, Illinois, in 2003. Dr. Chivers is a licensed psychologist and is currently an Ontario Women's Health Scholar postdoctoral research fellow at the Centre for Addiction and Mental Health, Toronto, Ontario. Dr. Chivers is also an adjunct professor in the Department of Psychology at the University of Western Ontario, London, Ontario, and a member of the Coalition for Research in Women's Health at the University of Toronto. She is an editorial board member for the *Archives of Sexual Behavior,* a member of the International Academy of Sex Research, and a board member for the Sex Information and Education Council of Canada (SIECCAN). Dr. Chivers's research examines the determinants of female sexual response, female sexual interests, and sex differences in sexual psychophysiology.

Walter Everaerd is Professor Emeritus at the Department of Psychology, University of Amsterdam, and adviser to Emotional Brain Inc., Almere, the Netherlands. His research interests include sex and emotion, and emotion and memory.

Michael Exton is a Six Sigma Blackbelt at Eli Lilly Australia and Associate Professor at the Department of Clinical Pharmacology, University of New South Wales, Sydney, Australia.

James H. Geer is a visiting scholar at Franklin and Marshall College in Lancaster, Pennsylvania. Following retirement from Louisiana State University, Dr. Geer moved to the Lancaster area and has established a relationship with the Department of Psychology at F&M. He will continue research in sexuality, working with students and colleagues at F&M. In addition to LSU, Dr. Geer has held faculty positions at the State University of New York at Buffalo, the University of Pennsylvania, and SUNY at Stony Brook. During his over 30 years of research in sexuality, Dr. Geer has made contributions in the areas of the psychophysiology of sexual arousal and the role of cognitive variables in sexuality. He plans on continuing research on cognitive variables with a developing interest in examining the evolutionary perspective.

Isaias Noel Gendrano III is a Ph.D. student at the UMDNJ-School of Public Health, focusing on epidemiology with a concentration in biostatistics. He is currently a medical program coordinator at Merck & Co., Inc., in the department of clinical pharmacology. His current academic research areas of interest include epidemiological perspectives on obesity, exercise, and sexual health. Previously, he contributed to research on the pharmacological treatment of sexual dysfunction, research on depression and erectile dysfunction, and research on sexual health in obese diabetics at the UMDNJ-Robert Wood Johnson Medical School, Department of Psychiatry.

Cynthia Graham is Research Tutor on the Oxford Doctoral Course in Clinical Psychology. She is also an Associate Research Fellow at the Kinsey Institute and a Visiting Research Fellow in the Rural Center for AIDS/STD Prevention at Indiana University. Dr. Graham's research interests are in the area of sexual behavior and reproductive biology of women and in gender differences in sexual behavior. She has carried out research on psychophysiological sexual response patterns in men and women; the effects of steroidal contraceptives on mood and sexuality in women; the relationship between the menstrual cycle and changes in mood, physical state, and sexuality; menstrual synchrony; condom errors and problems reported by men and women; and methodological issues involved in recall data on sexual behavior.

Julia R. Heiman is Director of the Kinsey Institute and Professor of Psychological and Brain Sciences and Clinical Psychiatry at Indiana University. Dr. Heiman's career has focused on understanding patterns of sexuality from an integrated psychosocial-biomedical perspective. She first worked at the Long Island Research Institute and the State University of New York at Stony Brook helping to develop and test couples' treatments for sexual problems. In 1981, she became a faculty member at the University of Washington School of Medicine, where, in1987, she cofounded and directed the UW Reproductive and Sexual Medicine Clinic to address sexual problems in men, women and couples. Dr. Heiman continues to publish broadly in the area of sex research on male and female sexual function and dysfunction, with her primary interests being psychophysiological components of sexual arousal patterns, sexual dysfunction treatment, sexuality and health, and sexual and relationship correlates of histories of childhood sexual and physical abuse. She has served as president of the International Academy of Sex Research and editor in chief of the *Annual Review of Sex Research* (2000–2004). She has earned the Distinguished Scientific Achievement Award from the Society of the Scientific Study of Sex (2001), the Richard J. Cross Award (2006), and the SSTAR Masters & Johnson Award (2006).

Jason L. Hicks is Associate Professor of Psychology at Louisiana State University. He received his Ph.D. in cognitive/experimental psychology from the University of Georgia in 1993. His research revolves around the topic of human memory, primarily false memory, source memory, and prospective memory (memory for delayed intentions).

Heather Hoffmann is Professor of Psychology at Knox College in Galesburg, Illinois. She received her Ph.D. in experimental psychology from the State University of New York at Binghamton and was recently a visiting scholar at the Kinsey Institute at Indiana University. She is currently examining the role of learning in sexual arousal in women and men.

Erick Janssen is Associate Scientist and Director of Education & Research Training at the Kinsey Institute, and Adjunct Associate Professor in the Department of Psychological & Brain Sciences and the Program in Cognitive Science at Indiana University, Bloomington. He received his Ph.D. in 1995 at the University of Amsterdam, the Netherlands. His research, supported by federal and other grants, focuses on the psychophysiology of sex, sexual excitation and inhibition, mood and sexuality, risky sexual behavior, sexual dysfunction, sex and the Internet, and sexuality in close relationships. He is a member of the editorial boards of the *Archives of Sexual Behavior, Journal of Psychology and Human Sexuality,* and the *Dutch Journal of Sexology,* and a reviewer for various other journals. He is the first person to have received the Hugo G. Beigel Research Award, for best article published in the *Journal of Sex Research,* twice, in 2001 and 2003.

Tillmann Krüger is a medical doctor and works as a clinician and researcher in neurology at the University of Zurich, Switzerland, and at the Institute of Behavioral Sciences at the Swiss Federal Institute of Technology Zurich. His research covers the field of neuroendocrinology of human sexual behavior and the imaging of brain morphology and function in normal and deviant sexual behavior.

Tuuli Kukkonen is completing her Ph.D. in clinical psychology at McGill University. Her research involves the psychophysiological assessment of sexual arousal through thermography, including an exploration of its potential clinical applications and as an instrument to directly compare sexual arousal in men and women.

Ellen T. M. Laan is Associate Professor in the Department of Sexology and Psychosomatic Obstetrics and Gynaecology of the Academic Medical Center, University of Amsterdam. After receiving her Ph.D. in 1994 she became a postdoctoral fellow of the Royal Netherlands Academy of Arts and Sciences in 1995. She is a member of several professional societies and has served on panels concerning the classification and treatment of female sexual dysfunction. Dr. Laan is a member of the editorial board of a number of professional sexology journals. Her research concerns the underlying central and peripheral mechanisms of female sexual response; gender differences in sexual motivation and experience of sexual arousal; psychophysiological assessment of sexual function in women with gynecological cancers, with dyspareunia, intersex women, and in somatically healthy women; and efficacy of sex therapy. Her work has been supported by grants from the Royal Netherlands Academy of Arts and Sciences and Netherlands Organisation for Scientific Research.

Roy Levin was formerly Reader in Physiology in the Department of Biomedical Science at the University of Sheffield, Sheffield, Yorkshire, from 1977 until his retirement in 2000. His research was in gastroenterology and reproductive physiology. He is currently an Honorary Research Associate at the Sexual Physiology Laboratory, Porterbrook Clinic (Sexual and Relationship Therapy), Sheffield. He became a full elected member of the Physiological Society (1964–2000) and of the International Academy of Sex Research in 1982. He has served on the editorial boards of the *International Journal of Impotence Research: The Journal of Sexual Medicine,* the European Society for Sexual and Impotence Research (ESSIR) newsletter, he *Menopause Review,* and the recently published *Journal of Sexual Medicine.* He is the science editor of the journal *Sexual and Relationship Therapy* and currently writes their "Science Update" reviews. He was voted onto the board of directors of the International Society for the Study of Women's Sexual Health (ISSWSH) as a Director-at-Large (2001–2003). He has published numerous articles, reviews, and book chapters on the physiology of human sexual responses in males but especially in relation to the female. He is a regular speaker at national and international conferences. The World Association of Sexology (Sexual Health) awarded him their Gold Medal for lifetime achievement in sexology and sexual health at their conference at Montreal in the summer of 2005.

Kenneth R. Maravilla is Professor in the Departments of Radiology and Neurological Surgery at the University of Washington School of Medicine in Seattle, Washington. He serves as Director of the MR Research Laboratory and as Director of the neuroscience core for the Center on Human Development and Disability. Dr. Maravilla is a former deputy editor of the *American Journal of Neuroradiology* (AJNR) and has served on the editorial boards of the AJNR, the *Journal of Magnetic Resonance Imaging (JMRI)*, and the *Korean Journal of Radiology*. He has authored or coauthored over 140 peer-reviewed publications, one book, more than 15 book chapters, and over 100 abstracts. Dr. Maravilla's research interests include the innovation and development of new techniques and new clinical applications for MR imaging, the assessment of new MRI contrast agents for CNS applications, the study of functional MR brain imaging, and the use of high-resolution MR imaging for study of the peripheral nervous system. Most recently, Dr Maravilla has pioneered new MRI methods for dynamic assessment of the sexual arousal response in women and fMRI (functional MRI) techniques for evaluating brain activation correlated with the sexual arousal response in women.

Kevin McKenna received his undergraduate degree from the University of Toronto. He received a Ph.D. in biomedical engineering from Johns Hopkins University School of Medicine. After a postdoctoral fellowship at the VA Medical Center/ University of Pittsburgh, he joined the faculty at Northwestern University School of Medicine (now Feinberg School of Medicine). He is now Professor of Physiology and Urology. His research focuses on the neural control of sexual function, with an emphasis on the central neural pathways, and on translational studies of sexual dysfunction in disease models, such as diabetes.

Cindy Meston is Associate Professor of Clinical Psychology at the University of Texas at Austin. She received her Ph.D. in clinical psychology from the University of British Columbia in 1995 and completed a postdoctoral fellowship in Sexual and Reproductive Medicine at the University of Washington, School of Medicine, in 1996. She is the past president of the International Society for the Study of Women's Sexual Health, a full member of the International Academy of Sex Research, a member of the Society for the Scientific Study of Sex, and a member of the American Psychological Association and the Canadian Psychological Association. She currently serves as associate editor for the *Journal of Sexual Medicine* and is on the editorial board of *Archives of Sexual Behavior* and the *Journal of Sex and Marital Therapy*. She is currently funded by the NICHD to examine the relation between early childhood sexual abuse and adult sexual function.

Harold Mouras received his Ph.D. in cognitive neuroscience at the Université Pierre et Marie Curie in 2004. For his dissertation he used functional magnetic resonance imaging to investigate the neural correlates of human male sexual motivation. He developed an MRI-compatible volumetric penile plethysmography device to allow him to study the correlation between brain and physiological responses. Dr. Mouras is currently a researcher at the University of Geneva, where he explores brain correlates of emotional regulation across the life span.

Brian Mustanski is Assistant Professor of Psychology in the Psychiatry Department at the University of Illinois at Chicago. He received his doctorate in psychology, with a minor in behavior genetics, from Indiana University. While there, he trained extensively at the Kinsey Institute. He has been the recipient of both National Institutes of Health and National Science Foundation research and training awards and has published over 25 academic articles and book chapters. Dr. Mustanski's research focuses on understanding human sexuality and its problems (i.e., sexual dysfunction, HIV) from a bioecological perspective. His past research has focused on the genetics of sexual orientation and the role of affect and sexual risk taking. He is currently leading an interdisciplinary, longitudinal study of sexual minority youth. In addition, Dr. Mustanski conducts applied research on HIV prevention among youth with psychiatric illness and sexual minority youth. In his clinical work, Dr. Mustanski specializes in the treatment of sexual dysfunction and obsessive-compulsive disorder.

Kimberley Payne received her Ph.D. in clinical psychology at McGill University in 2006. She currently works in supervised practice in Ontario, Canada, where she does a combination of sex therapy and neuropsychology and offers specialized services for women suffering from dyspareunia.

James G. Pfaus is Professor of Psychology at Concordia University, Montréal. He received his Ph.D. in biopsychology in 1990 from the University of British Columbia. He received the Frank A. Beach Award in Behavioral Endocrinology, Society for Neuroscience, in 1995. Dr. Pfaus's research is generally concerned with the neurochemical and molecular events that subserve sexual behavior and neuroendocrine functions. He is interested in the role of brain monoamine and neuropeptide systems in sexual arousal, desire, reward, and inhibition in laboratory animals and the role played by steroid hormones and cell-signaling mechanisms in the neuronal and behavioral responses to primary and conditioned sexual stimuli, especially those that induce sexual partner preferences. His research in human sexual function currently is focused on subjective and objective measures of sexual desire in women and men and exploring the sexual functioning of individuals under stress or with anxiety disorders. His research is funded by grants from CIHR, FRSQ (Québec), NSERC (Canada), and several pharmaceutical and biotech companies.

Nicole Prause is currently a psychology intern at the Boston Consortium in Clinical Psychology, including appointments as a clinical fellow at the Harvard Medical School Department of Psychiatry and as a teaching fellow for Boston University. She received her Ph.D. in psychology from the Department of Psychological and Brain Sciences at Indiana University, Bloomington, in 2006, where she also worked with the Kinsey Institute. Her research interests include the role of attention and emotional cognitive processes in sexual arousal (including sexual desire) and the development of psychophysiological methods of assessing sexual and emotional responses.

Alessandra Rellini received her training in clinical psychology at the University of Texas at Austin while working in Dr. Cindy Meston's female sexual psychophysiology laboratory. She is the recipient of a number of scholarships and grants including the prestigious NRSA grant sponsored from the National Institute of Mental Health. Her area of interest is the sexual function of women with a history of childhood sexual abuse. Currently, Alessandra is a predoctoral fellow at Yale University, where she is receiving training in dialectical behavioral therapy and in brain imaging research. Alessandra is expecting to receive her Ph.D. in the summer of 2007, upon completion of her internship.

Raymond C. Rosen is Professor of Medicine and Psychiatry at Robert Wood Johnson Medical School and Chief Scientist at New England Research Institutes. He has served as principal investigator for a large number of NIH- and industry-funded studies in male and female sexuality and has authored or coauthored 8 books and more than 200 peer-reviewed articles and book chapters on various aspects of male and female sexuality. He is the author (with Gayle Beck) of *Patterns of Sexual Arousal: Psychophysiological Processes and Clinical Applications* (Guilford Press, 1988). Dr. Rosen is a past president of the *International Academy of Sex Research* and vice-chair of the *2nd International Consultation on Sexual Dysfunction* (2004). He received the Lifetime Scientific Contribution award from the American Association of Sex Educators, Counselors and Therapists, and the *Masters and Johnson Award* for distinguished contributions to sex research and therapy. Dr. Rosen has served as a senior consultant and advisor for the NIH, FDA, and pharmaceutical industry and has received more than 50 grants and awards for research in sexual dysfunction. He is a member of several professional organizations and serves on the editorial boards of the *Archives of Sexual Behavior, Journal of Sexual Medicine, Menopause,* and the *Annual Review of Sex Research.* His is also past editor of the *Annual Review of Sex Research.*

David L. Rowland is Professor of Psychology and Dean of Graduate Studies at Valparaiso University. He also has an appointment as Senior Associate, the Johns Hopkins University Bloomberg School of Public Health. He has authored over 100 published research and review articles on reproductive processes, health, and methodology. He serves as editor of the *Annual Review of Sex Research* and on the editorial boards of *Archives of Sexual Behavior,* the *Journal of Sex Research,* and the *International Journal of Impotence Research.* Over the past several years, he has participated on the national advisory boards in the development of standards for assessment and treatment of male sexual dysfunction.

Stephanie A. Sanders is the Associate Director of the Kinsey Institute, a Professor of Gender Studies, and a Research Fellow of the Rural Center for AIDS/STD Prevention at Indiana University in Bloomington. A biopsychologist by training, she has conducted research on sex/gender differences in behavior; sexual behavior patterns related to risk for sexually transmitted infections; sexual orientation and sexual behavior; sexual arousal in women; sex hormones and behavior; the effects of prenatal exposures to drugs and hormones on behavioral, cognitive, and social development; and women's menstrual cycling. She has been active in various leadership positions, including president of the Society for the Scientific Study of Sexuality (SSSS).

Lisa Scepkowski is a doctoral candidate in clinical psychology at Boston University, where she received her master's degree in 2001. She is currently a psychology intern in the Sexual Behaviours Clinic at the Centre for Addiction and Mental Health in Toronto, Ontario. Lisa is a 2004 recipient of a Sexuality Research Fellowship from the Social Science Research Council, with support provided by the Ford Foundation. She is a member of the International Society for the Study of Women's Sexual Health and a student member of the Association for Behavioral and Cognitive Therapies. Her research interests include cognitive and emotional processes in sexual arousal, psychophysiology, and neuroendocrine influences on sexual motivation.

Rebecca Schacht has an M.S. in clinical psychology and is nearing completion of her Ph.D. in clinical psychology from the University of Washington, under the mentorship of William H. George, Ph.D. Her research is focused on the influence of sexual assault on women's perception and experience of subsequent sexual contexts.

Manfred Schedlowski has been Professor of Psychology and Behavioral Immunobiology at the ETH Zürich since April 2004. Born in Hannover in 1957, he studied psychology at the University of Bielefeld and the University of Braunschweig. After gaining his Ph.D. at the Department of Medical Psychology of Hannover Medical School and following postdoctoral research stays at the University of Newcastle and the Brain-Behaviour Research Institute, La Trobe University in Melbourne, Australia, he worked at the Department of Clinical Immunology and the Department of Clinical Psychiatry of Hannover Medical School. He obtained his habilitation at Hannover Medical School in 1993. In October 1997, Professor Schedlowski became Director and Head of the Department of Medical Psychology at the Medical Faculty of the University Essen–Duisburg. In his research he analyzes the mechanisms of the communication processes among the brain, the neuroendocrine system, and the immune system. In particular, he is interested in the effects of behavior on immune functions and focuses on the psychological and biochemical mechanisms responsible for these effects, as well as on the clinical relevance of this biochemical network for the maintenance of health and the pathophysiology of disease.

Michael Seto is a psychologist with the Law and Mental Health Program at the Centre for Addiction and Mental Health in Toronto and is cross-appointed as an Associate Professor in the Department of Psychiatry and the Centre of Criminology at the University of Toronto. He is also a consultant to the Behavioural Sciences Section of the Ontario Provincial Police and the Niagara Child Development Centre. Dr. Seto has published extensively on paraphilias and sexual offending and regularly presents at scientific meetings and professional workshops on these topics. His main research interests are pedophilia, sexual offending against children, child pornography offending, risk assessment, psychopathy, and program evaluation.

Marcalee Sipski Alexander is Professor of Physical Medicine and Rehabilitation at the University of Alabama's School of Medicine in Birmingham and holder of the Spain Endowed Chair in Neuroscience Research. Dr. Sipski produced the video *Sexuality Reborn* with Dr. Craig Alexander. She has been funded by NIH with coin-vestigators C. Alexander and R. Rosen to research the neurologic control of sexual response in women with SCIs and has also studied the control of sexual response in males with SCIs. Most recently she teamed up with Dr. Lesley Marson to study sexual responses in women with multiple sclerosis; they will also incorporate animal models to confirm findings in women with SCI and test the use of new treatment methods for sexual dysfunction in women with spinal cord disease. Dr. Sipski is also the president of the American Spinal Injury Association.

Mark Spiering works at the clinical psychology program of the University of Amsterdam. In 2004 he finished his dissertation, "Central Activation of the Sexual System." His current main research interests are in fundamental aspects of sexuality, for example, cognitive processing of sexual information, sexual motivation, gender differences, and sexuality and religion.

Serge Stoléru is a researcher at Inserm and at the Université Pierre et Marie Curie in Paris, France. He received his M. D. from University Claude-Bernard (Lyon, France) and his Ph.D. in clinical psychology from University René Descartes (Paris). He was first a child psychiatrist and later became a full-time researcher at the Institut National de la Santé et de la Recherche Médicale (Inserm). His research work has focused for the last 10 years on the cerebral correlates of sexual desire and arousal in humans.

Donald S. Strassberg is a Professor and the Director of Clinical Training in the Department of Psychology, University of Utah, where he has been a faculty member for 31 years. His primary areas of research are human sexual function, dysfunction, and deviation. He currently serves on the editorial boards of *Archives of Sexual Behavior,* the *Journal of Sex and Marital Therapy, Sexual Abuse: A Journal of Research and Treatment,* and the *Journal of Sexual Offender Civil Commitment: Science and the Law.* He maintains a part-time private practice as a clinical psychologist specializing in sexual and other relationship problems and is a Diplomate in Clinical Psychology (American Board of Professional Psychology) and a Fellow of the Albert Ellis Institute.

Wendi L. Tai is a graduate student at Indiana University, Bloomington, working toward a Ph.D. in counseling psychology. Her current research and professional interests include career and identity development, multicultural issues, and college student mental health. She completed a master's degree in clinical mental health counseling at Valparaiso University in 2003.

Markus Wiegel is a Ph.D. candidate at Boston University whose dissertation focuses on the characteristics of female sexual abusers of children. He currently is a research associate at Abel Screening, Inc. Previously, he contributed to research on the pharmacological treatment of sexual dysfunction at the UMDNJ Robert Wood Johnson Medical School, Department of Psychiatry. Mr. Wiegel was the Assistant Director of the Sexuality Research and Treatment Program at the Center for Anxiety and Related Disorders at Boston University. He has conducted research and published in the areas of child sexual abusers, sexual dysfunction, and anxiety disorders.

Index

DATE DUE

Demco, Inc. 38-293